PERCEPTION OF FACES, OBJECTS, AND SCENES

ADVANCES IN VISUAL COGNITION

Series Editors
Gillian Rhodes
Mary A. Peterson

Perception of Faces, Objects, and Scenes: Analytic and Holistic Processes
Edited by Mary A. Peterson and Gillian Rhodes

Perception of Faces, Objects, and Scenes

Analytic and Holistic Processes

EDITED BY

Mary A. Peterson and Gillian Rhodes

OXFORD
UNIVERSITY PRESS

OXFORD
UNIVERSITY PRESS

Oxford University Press, Inc., publishes works that further
Oxford University's objective of excellence
in research, scholarship, and education.

Oxford   New York
Auckland   Cape Town   Dar es Salaam   Hong Kong   Karachi
Kuala Lumpur   Madrid   Melbourne   Mexico City   Nairobi
New Delhi   Shanghai   Taipei   Toronto

With offices in
Argentina   Austria   Brazil   Chile   Czech Republic   France   Greece
Guatemala   Hungary   Italy   Japan   Poland   Portugal   Singapore
South Korea   Switzerland   Thailand   Turkey   Ukraine   Vietnam

Copyright © 2003 by Oxford University Press, Inc.

First issued as an Oxford University Press paperback 2006
Published by Oxford University Press, Inc.
198 Madison Avenue, New York, New York 10016

www.oup.com

Oxford is a registered trademark of Oxford University Press

Library of Congress Cataloging-in-Publication Data
Perception of faces, objects, and scenes : analytic and holistic
processes / edited by Mary A. Peterson and Gillian Rhodes.
        p. cm.—(Advances in visual cognition)
Includes bibliographical references and index.
   ISBN-13   978–0–19–516538–8; 978–0–19–531365–9 (pbk.)
   ISBN   0–19–516538–1; 0–19–531365–8 (pbk.)
   1. Visual perception.   2. Whole and parts (Psychology)   I. Peterson,
Mary A., 1950–   II. Rhodes, Gillian.   III. Series.
   BF241 .P434 2003
   152.14—dc21   2003004246

9 8 7 6 5 4 3 2 1

Printed in the United States of America
on acid-free paper

Contents

Contributors

Hervé Abdi, Program in Human Development and Communication Sciences, The University of Texas at Dallas, USA. Herve@utdallas.edu

James C. Bartlett, Program in Human Development and Communication Sciences, The University of Texas at Dallas, USA. jbartlet@utdallas.edu

Marlene Behrmann, Department of Psychology, Carnegie-Mellon University, USA. behrmann@CNBC.cmu.edu

Heinrich H. Bülthoff, Max-Planck-Institute for Biological Cybernetics, Germany. heinrich.buelthoff@tuebingen.mpg.de

Isabelle Bülthoff, Max-Planck-Institute for Biological Cybernetics, Germany. isabelle.buelthoff@tuebingen.mpg.de

Martha J. Farah, Department of Psychology, University of Pennsylvania, USA. mfarah@cattell.psych.upenn.edu

Steven L. Franconeri, Department of Psychology, Harvard University, USA. francon@wjh.harvard.edu

Frédéric Gosselin, Départemente de psychologie, Université de Montréal, Canada. frederic.gosselin@umontreal.ca

John M. Henderson, Department of Psychology, Michigan State University, USA. john@eyelab.psy.msu.edu

Andrew Hollingworth, Department of Psychology, University of Iowa, USA. andrew-hollingworth@uiowa.edu

John E. Hummel, Department of Psychology, University of California Los Angles, USA. jhummel@psych.ucla.edu

Ruth Kimchi, Department of Psychology, University of Haifa, Israel. rkimchi@research.haifa.ac.il

Paolo Martini, Department of Psychology, University of Chicago, USA. pmartini@wjh.harvard.edu

Elinor McKone, School of Psychology, Australian National University, Australia. Elinor.McKone@anu.edu.au

Stephen R. Mitroff, Department of Psychology, Yale University, USA. stephen.mitroff@yale.edu

Janice E. Murray, Department of Psychology, University of Otago, New Zealand. jmur@psy.otago.ac.nz

Ken Nakayama, Department of Psychology, Harvard University, USA. ken@wjh.harvard.edu

Mary A. Peterson, Department of Psychology, University of Arizona, USA. mapeters@u.arizona.edu

Gillian Rhodes, Department of Psychology, University of Western Australia, Australia. gill@psy.uwa.edu.au

Maria Schuchinsky, Department of Psychology, University of Otago, New Zealand.

Philippe G. Schyns, Department of Psychology, Glasgow University, Scotland. philippe@psy.gla.ac.uk

Jean H. Searcy, Program in Human Development and Communication Sciences, The University of Texas, USA. jeansearcy@mindspring.com

Daniel J. Simons, Department of Psychology, University of Illinois, USA. dsimons@uiuc.edu

James W. Tanaka, Department of Psychology, Oberlin College, USA. tanaka@cs.oberlin.edu

Michael J. Tarr, Department of Cognitive & Linguistic Sciences, Brown University, USA. michael.tarr@brown.edu

PERCEPTION OF FACES, OBJECTS, AND SCENES

Introduction

Analytic and Holistic Processing— The View Through Different Lenses

MARY A. PETERSON AND GILLIAN RHODES

We readily recognize the faces of our friends and the objects around us. We do so effortlessly, but these cannot be simple tasks for our visual systems. Faces are all extremely similar as visual patterns. We see objects from different viewpoints and in different arrangements. How does the visual system solve these problems? The contributors to this volume attempt to answer this question by considering how analytic and holistic processes contribute to the perception of faces, objects, and scenes. The role of parts and wholes in perception has been studied for a century, beginning with the debate between structuralists who championed the role of elements and Gestalt psychologists who emphasized the role of wholes. In this volume we bring together 21st-century views. The contributors to this volume ask whether analytic and holistic processes contribute differently to the perception of faces and objects. They also consider whether different mechanisms code holistic and analytic information or whether a single universal system can suffice. The contributors to this collection offer some intriguing answers to these questions.

The reader will quickly discover that there is no single definition of the terms "analytic" and "holistic." Some, but not all, authors use terms such as "global," "configural," and "coarse" as synonyms for "holistic." Similarly, some, but not all authors, use terms such as "piecemeal," "local," "part-based," "componential," "fine-grained," and "analytic" inter-

3

changeably. Different authors working within the same domain sometimes use these terms in subtly different ways, and authors working within distinct domains can use them very differently. Our hope is that including chapters summarizing research in these different areas in one collection will highlight what the important distinctions are and promote a consensus on what terms should be used to characterize them, which may facilitate communication among researchers and encourage greater theoretical integration of these areas.

The reader will also discover that no single technique or set of techniques can be used to distinguish between holistic and analytical processes. Nevertheless, the ensemble of techniques summarized in this volume provides critical information regarding how analytical and holistic processes are involved in face, object, and scene perception. In what follows, we provide an overview of the different issues as they are discussed within the domains of face, object, and scene perception.

Faces

Configural/Holistic Processing

In the face perception literature, the term "configural" refers to spatial-relational information. The term rarely denotes a spatial feature alone; rather, it refers to conjoint information regarding components such as the eyes, nose, mouth, and chin and the spatial relations between them. Of course, the "components" of a face may be configurations in their own right. For instance, an eye is a particular configuration of curved edges. Hence, as used in the face perception literature, the term "configural" applies to higher level configurations composed from component parts or features.

The span of configural information can be small (e.g., specifying the relationship between two adjacent components) or it might be large (e.g., specifying the relationship between nonadjacent components separated by large distances, or specifying the relationship among all of the components in the face). Bartlett, Searcy, and Abdi (chapter 1) investigated the span of configural information by asking observers to classify upright or inverted face stimuli on the basis of internal or external features. Adapting the Garner interference task, they found that for many (but not all) observers, internal and external features in upright faces were not coded independently. Thus, in their task, the span of configural information *could* be quite large, encompassing both internal and external facial components (although the span of configural information could also be smaller). For Bartlett and colleagues, configural information spanning the entire face would be "holistic" information.

Tanaka and Farah (chapter 2) take an explicitly holistic approach, arguing that faces are recognized as undifferentiated wholes, rather than in terms of their constituent parts. They use a part-whole task to test their hypothesis, reasoning as follows: If some portion of a stimulus is represented as an independent part, then it should be easy to recognize that portion as part of the stimulus regardless of whether it is shown in isolation or within the context of the whole stimulus. Alternatively, if a stimulus is represented as an undifferentiated whole, then it should be much easier to recognize any portion as a part of the stimulus when it is viewed within the context of the whole stimulus rather than in isolation. In this view, it should be extremely difficult to recognize a part as being a component of a stimulus when it is isolated from the whole stimulus. Consistent with the holistic view, Tanaka and Farah describe research indicating that face components (e.g., the eyes, nose, and mouth) were better recognized as belonging to a certain face when they were shown within the context of the whole (upright) face than when they were shown alone. This pattern of results was not found with parts of houses, scrambled faces, or inverted faces. Based on a series of studies producing similar results, Tanaka and Farah argue that recognition of upright faces relies almost exclusively on holistic representations whereas recognition of other kinds of objects, including inverted faces, relies on part-based as well as holistic representations (see also Davidoff & Donnelly, 1990; Donnelly & Davidoff, 1999).

Dual Routes to Recognition

If configural/holistic and componential/part-based processing are conceived of as distinct computational systems, we can ask how they contribute to the processing of faces and other objects. Several authors in the current collection hold the view that configural/holistic coding and componential/part-based processing constitute dual routes to face recognition, but that it is configural coding that is the hallmark of face processing. (Bartlett et al., chapter 1; McKone, Martini, & Nakayama, chapter 4; Murray, Rhodes, & Schuchinsky, chapter 3), a position that others have taken before (e.g., Carey & Diamond, 1977; Rhodes, 1985; Rhodes, Brake, & Atkinson, 1993; Sergent, 1984). Evidence that these two routes are distinct often arises from orientation effects.

Yin's (1969) classic article showed that stimulus inversion interferes with face recognition more than with object recognition. This difference is typically ascribed to differences in the relative importance of configural and componential memory for the perception of faces and objects. It is often argued that rotating a stimulus 180° from upright so that it is inverted interferes with the extraction of configural information, which is more critical for face recognition than for object recognition. Consistent with this view, Moscovitch, Winocur, and Behrmann (1997) reported the case of a brain-damaged patient, CK, whose ability to recognize upright faces was intact, but whose ability to recognize inverted faces and both upright and inverted objects was impaired. This pattern of preserved and impaired abilities suggested that CK's brain damage interfered with analytical/part-based coding, but not with configural coding (necessary for the identification of upright faces). It also suggested that inverted faces do not activate the same configural codes as upright faces (but see Murray, 2002, who found that inverted faces retain some configural information that can interfere with component processing). CK's pattern of impaired and preserved abilities is consistent with the dual-route hypothesis.

But do large inversion effects for face recognition obtained with non-brain-damaged participants require a dual route explanation? Murray et al. (chapter 3) point out that impaired performance in an inverted condition compared to the upright condition could reflect either a quantitative or a qualitative change in perception. A quantitative change in perception could arise if stimulus inversion simply increased the noise in a single recognition mechanism (Valentine, 1991), whereas a qualitative change in perception would be consistent with the dual-route hypothesis, with configural coding no longer available for misoriented faces. One cannot distinguish between these two accounts without testing stimuli at orientations between upright and inverted. According to Murray et al., the single-route view would predict a smooth change in perception, with performance becoming increasingly worse as the noise increased with increasing disorientation from upright. On the other hand, the dual-route view would predict that a discontinuity in the function relating orientation to perception would be visible at the point where configural information drops out.

Murray et al. (chapter 3) asked observers to rate the bizarreness of distorted faces that were rotated from the upright by 15° increments. Faces were distorted by either adding white to the eyes and blackening the teeth (a part of component change) or by moving the eyes and mouth up or down in an otherwise normal face (a configural change). Consistent with the dual-route account, Murray et al. found a clear discontinuity near 90° in the function relating orientation to bizarreness rating. This discontinuity was evident for the faces that were distorted by a configural change but not for the faces that were distorted by a part change. Note that, unlike most investigators, Murray et al. did not have to infer the use of configural information from identification accuracy. Rather, they directly measured the degree to which either componential or configural distortions rendered the face more bizarre. Thus, their results show that configural information drops below some critical threshold when face stimuli are disoriented from their upright by 90°. (See also McKone et al., chapter 4.)

McKone et al. (chapter 4) summarize a series of techniques they have designed to isolate configural/holistic processes. Their approach is built on the assumption that configural processes are holistic in that they sum information from across the whole face area. Part-based processes necessarily sum information over a smaller area, an area encompassing a subset of the whole. McKone et al. suppose that spatial summation should render holistic processes more *sensitive* than part-based processes (just as spatial summation renders rod function more sensitive than cone function).

Accordingly, they hypothesize that holistic processes should continue to operate even when part-based processes cannot support above-chance performance.

The techniques summarized by McKone et al. (chapter 4) include tasks requiring (1) discrimination between identical twins, (2) categorical perception of the identity of faces presented in noise, (3) identification of peripherally presented faces, (4) perception of Mooney faces, and (5) salience matching of superimposed faces. In all cases, they were able to obtain excellent performance with upright faces under conditions where performance with inverted faces was poor. In many cases, they showed that performance with inverted faces remained poor even after many training trials. Thus, to the extent that these techniques succeed in isolating holistic processes in non-brain-damaged individuals, they provide strong evidence that the perception of upright faces relies more heavily on holistic processes than the perception of inverted faces (see also Murray et al., chapter 3; Tanaka & Farah, chapter 2).

McKone et al. point out that these five techniques can be used to assess possible holistic processes in the perception of objects as well. Their initial investigations suggest that tasks involving object identification cannot access holistic processing mechanisms. Faces may be unique in their reliance on configural processes that span large areas or that prevent part decomposition—that is, on holistic processes. The possibility remains open that objects may engage other sorts of configural coding. By design, McKone et al.'s techniques may assess only holistic configural processes.

Neuroanatomical Evidence for Dual Routes

Bartlett, Devous, and Abdi (2000, described in chapter 1) investigated whether configural/holistic and componential/analytic routes to face recognition had different neural substrates. Their observers learned a set of faces and later viewed the learned faces among completely new faces and "conjunction faces" composed of new conjunctions of learned components (e.g., eyes, nose, and mouth drawn from different learned faces). Learned faces produced more activation than new faces or conjunction faces in right occipital and right medial temporal brain regions (regions that have previously been shown to be critical for face identification). In addition, learned faces (that were recognized as such) produced more activation than new faces or conjunction faces in left-parietal and right-anterior brain regions (regions that are thought to be involved in conscious recollection and working memory processes). Conjunction faces differed from new faces in producing more activation in posterior left regions and left-temporal regions (regions that have previously been implicated in component memory). Frontal and parietal brain regions involved in conscious recognition did not respond to the conjunction stimuli. Indeed, although conjunction faces elicit feelings of familiarity, they are not often identified as learned faces. Bartlett et al. took these imaging results as evidence that the two routes to face recognition (i.e., analytic and holistic) are neuroanatomically distinct.

Spatial Scales: Coarse to Fine

Schyns and Gosselin (chapter 5) investigate how information at different spatial scales—coarse versus fine—in a single system is used for various judgments regarding faces (e.g., discriminating between two different identities, genders, or emotional expressions). In the hands of these authors, the coarse versus fine distinction cuts across the analytic and holistic distinction, although it need not (see Sergent, 1984). Schyns and Gosselin discuss a method, called Bubbles, which determines which diagnostic features (in terms of both location and scale information) are used for different tasks. Observers are asked to categorize sparse samples of coarse or fine facial information according to identity, gender, or expression. Bubbles keeps track of which samples reliably support correct categorization performance and uses them to determine the *effective stimulus* for the task. Bubbles identifies diagnostic components, but these components can be conjunctions (e.g., one eye and the mouth).

Schyns and Gosselin define conjunctions of components as "holistic information." For instance, according to Schyns and Gosselin, the diagnostic conjunctions for identity judgments are "holistic" in that they involve the two eyes and the mouth. However, for Schyns and Gosselin, the term "holistic" does not imply that the conjunctions span the whole face or object, as it does for Bartlett et al. Nor does the term "holistic" imply that faces are recognized as undifferentiated wholes, rather than in terms of their components, as it does for Tanaka and Farah. For Schyns and Gosselin, holistic information need not be composed of contiguous regions of a face. For them, the term "holistic" simply means that information from several separate locations (contiguous or not) is diagnostic for accurate categorization. Schyns and Gosselin did not manipulate the orientation of their stimuli, so unlike the other authors in this section, they could not investigate whether stimulus inversion differentially affected analytic versus holistic information. Their methods could be adapted easily to investigate whether or not different diagnostic features support accurate performance with upright and inverted stimuli.

What Causes Differential Coding of Faces and Objects?

Why are faces typically coded holistically/configurally whereas objects are typically coded analytically/componentially? An answer commonly given to that question is that people must be experts at individuating a vast number of different faces, all of which are highly similar in that they are constructed from a small set of components. Therefore, faces cannot be distinguished by a listing of their components alone or even a detailed description of those components; the spatial relationships among the components are necessary for individuation. It follows from this line of rea-soning that holistic/configural codes might be used whenever perceivers must become experts at discriminating among highly similar exemplars. Both Tarr (chapter 7) and Tanaka and Farah (chapter 2) discuss evidence consistent with this claim. On this view, holistic processing is not reserved for faces alone. Other objects are likely to be coded holistically if there are a sufficient number of them, if they are constructed from a small number of parts, and if they must be individuated at the subordinate level. However, note that task demands alone may not be sufficient for the de-velopment of configural processing. The work of LeGrand, Mondloch, Maurer, and Brent (2001) indicates that the ability to code faces confi-gurally may be critically dependent upon the first few months of an infant's visual experience.

Task demands are different for experts versus novices, which almost certainly leads them to rely on different types of stimulus information. As Tarr and colleagues point out, novices need only identify objects at the basic level, whereas experts must identify objects at the subordinate level. The diagnostic features for subordinate-level recognition are certainly dif-ferent from those for basic-level recognition, just as the diagnostic features for discrimination of gender are different from those for identification (Schyns & Gosselin, chapter 5). Both configural/holistic coding and com-ponential/analytic coding might reflect the extraction of those statistical regularities in the stimulus that reliably support accurate performance for tasks of different types. That is, the visual system may extract the partic-ular diagnostic features, components, or configurations that permit accu-rate task performance, much as Bubbles does. For some tasks and some stimulus sets, components or small-span configurations may suffice, but for other tasks and stimulus sets, large-span or holistic configural infor-mation may be required. (See also Tarr, chapter 7.) Schyns and Gosselin point out that perceivers can use information at different scales flexibly for different tasks; the same may be true of componential versus configural coding, although perceptual learning or expertise may be required in some cases.

Recent work conducted in the domain of artificial language learning illustrates the flexible use of different types of configural information. Gomez (2002) has begun to explore the conditions under which partici-pants depend on nonadjacent versus adjacent dependencies in learning artificial languages. Both adjacent and nonadjacent dependencies can be considered configural information, but nonadjacent dependencies have a larger span than adjacent dependencies. Gomez investigated only condi-tions in which nonadjacent dependencies rather than adjacent dependen-cies were used to categorize three-component exemplars of an artificial grammar. (She did not investigate conditions in which componential in-formation might be used.) Gomez (2002) found that the relative domi-nance of adjacent versus nonadjacent information was a function of the variability of the middle component in the learned language. These results are consistent with the view that the stimulus set itself may influence whether observers rely predominantly on large-span configurations (coding nonadjacent dependencies), short-span configurations (coding adjacent dependencies) or, by inference, isolated parts. The importance of choosing the appropriate set of objects for comparison with faces has been stressed by Gauthier and Tarr (1997; see Tarr, chapter 7), who have pointed out that many comparisons between object perception and face perception failed to equate the stimulus characteristics of faces and objects.

The artificial grammar research can also be taken to suggest that a continuum of configural codes might exist, ranging from small-span through mid-span to large-span configural codes. Different types of configural codes (or combinations thereof) may be differentially capable of supporting accurate performance on different types of tasks with different types of stimuli. On this view, large-span configural codes are not necessarily holistic, although they do have a long range. (See also Schyns and Gosselin, chapter 5.) Consistent with this view, Tarr (chapter 7) argues that a wide range of features at a number of different scales code objects of all types (including faces). Like Schyns and Gosselin (chapter 5), Tarr considers a (single) recognition system to be sufficiently flexible to adapt to the wide range of situations we encounter daily.

At first glance, it might seem difficult for a single recognition system to account for the discontinuity in recognition performance as stimuli are increasingly disoriented from their typical upright (see Murray et al., chapter 3). However, a discontinuity would be consistent with a single recognition system dedicated to coding configurations ranging from small to large spans, including as few as two features, or as many components as there are in a face. In a "single" system such as this a discontinuity might reflect a switch from dominance of large-span (holistic) to small-span codes for a particular task, or vice versa.

Objects

One versus Two Systems for Holistic
and Analytic Processing

The dependence of recognition on orientation has been an important issue within the field of object recognition, as well as within the field of face recognition. Here, the debate has centered on whether or not there is a single orientation-independent representation (an "object-centered representation," in the terminology of Marr, 1982) or multiple viewpoint-specific representations of an object, rather than on whether configural/holistic versus componential/analytic information is employed. Despite the difference in emphasis, however, viewpoint independence has generally been associated with part-based/analytic approaches to object recognition whereas viewpoint dependence has often been assumed to require holistic,

template-like representations (e.g., see Biederman, 1987; Bülthoff & Bülthoff, chapter 6; Hummel, chapter 8; Poggio & Edelman, 1990).

Bülthoff and Bülthoff (chapter 6) summarize evidence favoring the use
of viewpoint-specific representations in the perception of moving objects
(point-light walkers), moving faces, and moving scenes (i.e., scenes presented to viewers as if they were moving through them). Bülthoff and
Bülthoff assume that viewpoint-dependent representations are holistic, and
that view-independent representations are analytic. They do not test these
particular assumptions, however. Instead, they test other predictions arising
from the viewpoint-dependent account.

One prediction is that performance with stimuli shown in learned views
should be better than performance with stimuli shown in novel views.
Bülthoff and Bülthoff (chapter 6) review evidence that recognition of both
moving point-light walkers and moving scenes is better for learned views
than for novel views. Another prediction arising from the viewpoint-
dependent account concerns the extent to which the representation codes
two-dimensional (2-D) versus three-dimensional (3-D) information.
Viewpoint-dependent representations are considered 2-D in nature because
they capture image features, whereas viewpoint-independent representations are assumed to have 3-D properties so that they can represent objects
in all of their views. Consistent with the viewpoint-dependent approach,
Bülthoff and Bülthoff show that recognition of moving point-light walkers
is neither improved by the addition of 3-D information nor disrupted by
the addition of distorted 3-D information.

Given that different image-based views of a single object can have very
different features, viewpoint-dependent theories of recognition must specify how two different views become linked as representing a single object.
Bülthoff and Bülthoff (chapter 6) point out that observers seldom see
objects from only one viewpoint. Instead, they often see objects from
different angles either because they move relative to the object or because
the object moves relative to them. The relative movement provides a sequence of images gradually changing from the initial view to a very different one. Critically, these different views are seen within a short period
of time; hence, they occur in temporal contiguity. Bülthoff and Bülthoff
review experiments testing whether temporal contiguity can be used to
link disparate views of faces into a single representation. The experiments
showed that participants confused two different faces as different views
of one face when the different faces had been presented in a coherent
temporal sequence. The different faces were not confused when they were
not viewed in temporal contiguity. This means that both the degree of
similarity between views and the temporal proximity of the views are
important for linking different views in an object representation. These
results suggest a means by which holistic viewpoint-dependent representations can accomplish generalization to different exemplars/instances of
a class.

In chapter 7, Tarr summarizes the evidence he and his colleagues have obtained for viewpoint-dependent recognition. Tarr does not conceive of viewpoint-dependent representations as holistic templates, however. Indeed, it is known that template-like object representations are not capable of generalizing to different exemplars/instances of a class (Neisser, 1967). Yet Tarr has shown that view-dependent object representations can support such generalization. As an alternative to holistic templates, Tarr favors models in which objects are described in terms of configurations of local features (see Perrett & Oram, 1998; Peterson, 1995, 1998, chapter 10; Reisenhuber & Poggio, 1999; Ullman & Sali, 2000). On these models, object recognition is accomplished via multiple local comparisons. Depending upon the object, the set of similar objects, and the task, these comparisons can be accomplished using either a single distinctive feature or configural information in which features are precisely spatially located relative to one another. Tarr argues that one does not need different systems (or routes) for recognizing objects and faces or for viewpoint-dependent and viewpoint-independent recognition (as some have argued; e.g., Hummel, chapter 8; Jolicœur, 1990). Rather, a single flexible visual recognition system can suffice (see also Schyns & Gosselin, chapter 5).

Taking a computational perspective, Hummel (chapter 8) argues the opposite, namely that holistic and analytical processes are served by different systems because they have different computational requirements. According to Hummel, holistic object representations are generated and used "all of a piece." Conjunction codes in which features are statically bound by virtue of their retinotopic spatial locations underlie holistic processes. Hummel considers holistic processes to be computationally costly in terms of the number of storage units they require (although they are not costly in terms of computation time). He also considers conjunction codes to be of limited usefulness for tasks requiring the flexible recombination of features because the features bound within a (holistic) conjunction code cannot be assessed independently. For Hummel an analytic representation of an object is one in which the parts are represented independently of each other *and of their spatial relationships*. An analytic representation of an object is created by dynamically binding together the contents of the current focus of attention. Dynamic binding is computationally costly in that it takes time, but it is flexible because the features are bound together temporarily rather than permanently and, therefore, can be considered together or separately under different situations.

Because analytic and holistic object representations have complementary strengths and weaknesses, Hummel (chapter 8) argues that a well-designed visual system would employ both types of representation for object recognition. In his view, static conjunctive codes are generated quickly for all objects, regardless of whether or not they are attended. These conjunction codes form the substrate for dynamic analytic codes that are generated over time only for attended objects. It is interesting to consider whether this theory can be extended to face recognition where attention does not seem to transform holistic face representations into analytic representations but rather appears to be needed to create the holistic representations (Palermo & Rhodes, 2002). Accordingly, it may be difficult to square the two routes to object recognition in Hummel's model with the face-recognition literature indicating that a holistic/configural route is used primarily for upright faces, whereas a componential/analytic route is used primarily for inverted faces and objects. Note also that the static/holistic and dynamic/analytic codes discussed by Hummel are used to represent objects that have already been segregated from their surrounds. Yet there is evidence that small-span configural memories of objects (called "partial configurations") are accessed in the course of figure as-signment (Peterson, chapter 10). The relationship between these partial configurations and the holistic versus analytic representations discussed by Hummel remain to be specified.

Analytic and Holistic Processes in Perceptual Organization

Chapters 9 to 11 are concerned primarily with those processes of percep-tual organization that group together features into candidate parts of ob-jects and segregate objects from one another. Debates concerning analytic and holistic processing can be found here as well. For instance, in studying perceptual organization, a recurrent question concerns the relative tem-poral ordering of holistic and analytic processes. Is a holistic analysis conducted first and a local analysis later, or is the order reversed such that local features are first available (e.g., lines and edges) and whole are later constructed from these features? In this literature, the terms "configural," "holistic," and "featural" have different connotations than they do in the face-perception literature.

Kimchi (chapter 9) defines properties that depend upon the interrela-tions among component parts as "holistic." (Thus, for Kimchi as for Hum-mel, configural/conjunctive properties are considered holistic properties, regardless of their span.) The component parts to which Kimchi refers are often simple oriented lines. Thus, Kimchi's components are smaller than the "components" (or parts, or features) of the face perception literature. For her, the facial features (e.g., eyes, nose, and lips) in the face-perception literature are themselves holistic configurations.

Kimchi points out that the "local first, holistic later" view is based on a logical analysis of how complex features are constructed from simple features. She argues that the logical structure of the stimulus does not necessarily predict the processing sequence. Kimchi summarizes evidence that configural/holistic properties like closure can be available early in the course of visual processing. In the experiments she reviews, she uses hi-erarchical stimuli in which task-specific patterns are present at both the local and the global levels; for instance, many small squares (or diamonds) may make up either a large square or a large diamond. The argument has often been made that these stimuli are processed faster at the holistic, global level, than at the local, analytic level. Kimchi's experiments show that the time course of the availability of local and global attributes of a stimulus differs for patterns depending on whether they are composed of a few relatively large components or many relatively small components. In the former case, both local and global attributes are available early (although the representation of global attributes is weaker than the representation of local attributes). In the latter case, the global configuration is represented initially and the components are represented later. Thus, Kimchi's work shows that neither the local nor the global level is necessarily processed before the other, supporting the view that the visual system is highly interactive.

Figure and ground perception is a central constituent of perceptual organization. Most theorists have accepted a global first assumption for figure-ground perception, in that it has been assumed that whole, bounded regions of uniform luminance are first segregated into figures and grounds, after which whole figures serve as substrates for access to object memories. Peterson (chapter 10) summarizes her research showing that object memories can exert an influence on figure assignment. She supposes that these object-memory effects arise from matches between partial configurations in object memory and portions of borders rather than whole continuous borders (or whole regions). The proposed partial configurations code boundary features and their spatial relationships; hence they code configural information conjunctively. These local configurations are larger than a single feature (or a single part) but substantially smaller than the whole object; hence, in the terminology of Bartlett et al. (chapter 1), they are small-span configurations. Peterson does not use the term "holistic" to refer to small-span configurations; she reserves the term "holistic" for region-wide processes. However, the small-span configurations are larger than a single part or feature; hence, they are not completely analytic.

Peterson (chapter 10) supposes that known objects are represented by a number of overlapping partial configurations within posterior regions of the ventral pathway (Peterson, 1995, 1998, chapter 10). Both physiological and computational evidence supports the idea of overlapping local configurations. (See Mozer, 1991; Perrett et al., 1998; Tanaka, 1996; Tarr, chapter 7; Ullman & Sali, 2000.) Peterson presents behavioral evidence consistent with her proposal; her evidence suggests that different portions of the continuous border of a region of uniform texture, color, and luminance can be matched to different object memories before figure assignment is completed. In this view, small-span conjunctive (configural) codes play a role in a fundamental process of perceptual organization—the segregation of objects from their backgrounds.

Behrmann (chapter 11) takes a neuropsychological perspective on questions concerning analytic and holistic processing. She examines the behavior of seven brain-damaged patients who have problems with perceptual organization. These "integrative agnosic" patients seem to be disproportionately impaired on tasks tapping holistic configural processes compared to part-based processes. For instance, integrative agnosics seem to be unable to group contours into whole shapes and to accomplish contour assignment, although they can perceive the contours. Integrative agnostics are impaired at identifying the shapes of familiar letters (*X*s and *O*s) when they are embedded in small amounts of noise. Furthermore, almost all such "integrative agnosic" patients are impaired at face recognition; hence, configural coding seems to be impaired. Further tests of these patients employing object and face identification tasks similar to those used in the various chapters in this collection are likely to provide critical information regarding analytic versus holistic processing. One question is whether integrative agnosics are equally impaired on all types of configural coding, or whether they can accomplish some small span configural coding.

Scenes

Because we seem to perceive individual objects and the scene in which they are embedded as wholes, it is tempting to assume that the world—and the objects in it—are represented in a holistic fashion. However, Hochberg and his colleagues showed that the perceived organization of an object is not necessarily based on object-wide information (Hochberg, 1968; Hochberg & Peterson, 1987; Peterson & Gibson, 1991; Peterson & Hochberg, 1983; 1989. Peterson and Hochberg (1983; Hochberg & Peterson, 1987) altered small (less than 1° of visual angle) 2-D and 3-D Necker cubes by adding local depth cues (occlusion and shading) at an upper intersection. Observers fixating at that "biased" intersection perceived the depth organization consistent with the local cues. Observers fixating at a lower, ambiguous intersection were free to see an alternative depth organization, however. Thus, Hochberg and Peterson showed that the whole configuration is not the effective stimulus for perception. Hochberg (1968) argued that, contrary to the assumption that our representations of objects are complete and densely detailed, the perception of an object is "not everywhere dense."

More recently, investigators have shown that our memories of scenes are relatively incomplete and imprecise as well: scene memories seem to preserve only partial information from one glance at a scene to the next (Irwin, 1991; Rensink, 2000; Simons, Mitroff, & Franconeri, chapter 12). Thus, scene memories are not holistic in nature. But how much partial information is preserved, and what are the best methods to use to assess the amount of preserved information? Simons et al. (chapter 12) and Henderson and Hollingworth (chapter 13) discuss recent research relevant to these questions.

Much of the work discussed in chapters 12 and 13 uses the change detection paradigm in which observers are shown two views of a scene separated by a blank screen or a mask, and are asked to report any changes that occur between successive views. Observers do not perform very well when they are asked to explicitly report whether or not a change has occurred. They either take an inordinately long time to detect a change made between successive views, or they fail to detect it unless they were attending to the change item when the first view disappeared and the second view appeared. These results suggest that, except for recently attended items, observers do not have explicit access to the contents of a previous view of a scene. Indeed, explicit tests in which observers are asked to report the item that changed suggest that observers are "blind" to many aspects of a scene. Such results could be taken to suggest that only minimal, local scene information (i.e., information regarding the attended items) is perceived and preserved in memory. Our holistic impression of the scene may arise from having the world as a memory to which one can return whenever one wants to answer any specific question (O'Regan, 1992).

Both Simons et al. (chapter 12) and Henderson and Hollingworth (chapter 13) review the evidence obtained when change-detection abilities are measures via both explicit and implicit measures. The explicit measures consistently show that only partial information is retained. Both Simons et al. and Henderson and Hollingworth conclude that visual memory retains representations that are abstracted away from the sensory properties of an image. For Henderson and Hollingworth, abstract visual properties of an object including shape and position are joined into a "relatively detailed" scene representation. Thus, for them, visual scene memory is not minimal and localist to the extreme, nor is it complete and precise (see also, Irwin, 1991).[1] Exactly where scene perception and memory lie along this continuum is not yet known, however. One investigator's "relatively detailed" representation may be another investigator's "relatively sparse" representation.

There is still some debate regarding how to interpret the results obtained with implicit measures of change detection. Simons et al. (chapter 12) point out flaws in the studies they review and conclude that none of the evidence supports the view that changes can be detected implicitly when they cannot be detected explicitly. However, Henderson and Hollingworth (chapter 13) review their own recent evidence indicating that gaze duration can implicitly index change detection, even when direct report cannot. Thus, it seems that at least some implicit measures are more sensitive than explicit measures. (Simons et al. agree that eye movements may differ from other implicit measures.) Nevertheless, implicit measures have not yet provided information regarding exactly what type of abstract partial information is preserved across views.

As used in the scene-perception literature, the term "holistic" denotes scene-wide information; it does not refer to configural information per se. Nevertheless, configural coding seems critical to the perception of a real-world scene. Simons (1996) showed that memory for the spatial arrangement of unrelated objects is excellent under conditions in which memory for the identity of the individual objects is impaired. In addition, Bülthoff and Bülthoff (chapter 6) review evidence that memory for scenes is viewpoint-dependent (see also Diwadkar & McNamara, 1997), a characteristic of configural coding. Note that the components within a scene configuration are themselves objects, and objects are configurations of components, and the components in objects are often composed of lower level features themselves. Questions concerning the role played by configurations at these various levels remain to be addressed.

Concluding Remarks

The Gestalt psychologists argued that the whole is different from the sun of the parts. The chapters in this collection provide a snapshot of current thinking on how the processing of wholes and parts contributes to our remarkable ability to recognize faces, objects, and scenes. They illustrate the diverse conceptions of analytic and holistic processing that currently coexist within one research area (e.g., face perception) and across research areas (e.g., face and object perception, object and scene perception). They also illustrate the variety of approaches brought to bear on the issues (experimental studies of normal processing, neuropsychological investigations of impaired processing in people with integrative agnosia, functional imaging of normal brains at work, and computational modeling). Our hope is that the Gestalt coda will apply to books—that this collection of chapters on face, object, and scene perception will inspire new and different approaches to these issues, approaches that integrate conceptions from the various research areas, perhaps. At the very least, we hope that this volume will inspire continued efforts to understand how we transform a barrage of photons into the faces of our friends and the familiar objects we see in the scenes around us.

In closing, we would like to thank Catharine Carlin of Oxford University Press for her enthusiastic and energetic support of this project.

Notes

1. Peterson and Gibson, 1991, reached a similar conclusion for representations of perceived objects.

References

Biederman, I. (1987). Recognition-by-components: A theory of human image understanding. *Psychological Review, 94*, 115–117.
Carey, S., & Diamond, R. (1977). From piecemeal to configural representation of faces. *Science*, 195, 312–314.

Davidoff, J., & Donnelly, N. (1990). Object superiority: A comparison of complete and part probes. *Acta Psychological 73*, 225–243.

Diwadkar, V. A., & McNamara, T. P. (1997). Viewpoint dependence in scene recognition. *Psychological Science, 8*, 302–307.

Donnelly, N., & Davidoff, J. (1999). The mental representations of faces and houses: Issues concerning parts and wholes. *Visual Cognition, 6*, 319–343.

Gauthier, I., & Tarr, M. J. (1997). Becoming a "Greeble" expert: Exploring the face recognition mechanism. *Vision Research, 37*, 1673–1682.

Gomez, R. L. (2002). Variability and detection of invariant structure. *Psychological Science, 13*, 431–436.

Hochberg, J. (1968). In the mind's eye. In R. N. Haber (Ed.), *Contemporary theory and research in visual perception* (pp. 309–331). New York: Holt, Rinehart, Winston.

Hochberg, J., and Peterson, M. A. (1987). Piecemeal organization and cognitive components in object perception: Perceptually coupled responses to moving objects. *Journal of Experimental Psychology: General, 116*, 370–380.

Irwin, D. E. (1991). Information integration across saccadic eye movements. *Cognitive Psychology, 23*, 420–456.

Jolicoeur, P. (1990). Identification of disoriented objects: A dual-systems theory. *Mind & Language, 5*, 387–410.

Le Grand, R., Mondloch, C. J., Maurer, D., & Brent, H. P. (2001). Early visual experience and face processing. *Nature, 410*, 890.

Marr, D. (1982). *Vision.* New York: W. H. Freeman.

Moscovitch, M., Winocur, G., & Behrmann, M. (1997). What is special about face recognition? Nineteen experiments on a person with visual object agnosia and dyslexia but normal face recognition. *Journal of Cognitive Neuroscience, 9*(5), 555–604.

Mozer, M. C. (1991). *The perception of multiple objects.* Cambridge, MA: MIT Press.

Murray, J. (2002). Evidence from visual search for holistic processing of inverted faces. Poster presented at the Vision Sciences Society Meeting, Sarasota, FL, May 14, 2002.

Neisser, U. (1967). *Cognitive psychology.* New York: Appleton-Century-Crofts.

O'Regan, J. K. (1992). Solving the 'real' mysteries of visual perception: The world as an outside memory. *Canadian Journal of Psychology, 46*(3), 461–488.

Palermo, R., & Rhodes, G. (2002). The influence of divided attention on holistic face perception. *Cognition, 82*, 225–257.

Perrett, D. I., Oram, M. W., & Ashbridge, E. (1998). Evidence accumulation in cell populations responsive to faces: An account of generalization of recognition without mental transformations. *Cognition, 67*, 111–145.

Peterson, M. A. (1995). *The relationship between depth segregation and object recognition: Old assumptions, new findings, and a new approach to object recognition.* Unpublished manuscript.

Peterson, M. A. (1998). Figure-ground illuminates object recognition. Talk given in the Object and Face Recognition Symposium at the International Neuropsychological Symposium, Jerusalem, Israel, June.

Peterson, M. A., & Gibson, B. S. (1991). Directing spatial attention within an object: Altering the functional equivalence of shape descriptions. *Journal of Experimental Psychology: Human Perception and Performance, 17*, 170–182.

Peterson, M. A., & Hochberg, J. (1983). Opposed-set measurement procedure; A quantitative analysis of the role of local cues and intention in form perception. *Journal of Experimental Psychology: Human Perception and Performance, 9*, 183–193.

Peterson, M. A., & Hochberg, J. (1989). Necessary considerations for a theory of form perception: A theoretical and empirical reply to Boselle and Leeuwenberg, *Perception, 18*, 105–119.

Poggio, T., & Edelman, S. (1990). A network that learns to recognize three-dimensional objects. *Nature, 343*, 263–266.

Rensink, R. A. (2000). The dynamic representation of scenes. *Visual Cognition, 7*, 17–42.

Rhodes, G. (1985). Lateralized processes in face recognition. *British Journal of Psychology, 76*, 249–271.

Rhodes, G., Brake, S., & Atkinson, A. (1993). What's lost in inverted faces? *Cognition, 47*, 25–57.

Riesenhuber, M., & Poggio, T. (1999). Hierarchical models of object recognition in cortex. *Nature Neuroscience, 2*(11), 1019–1025.

Sergent, J. (1984). An investigation into component and configural processes underlying face perception. *The British Journal of Psychology, 75*, 221–242.

Simons, D. J. (1996). In sight, out of mind: When object representations fall. *Psychological Science, 7*, 301–305.

Tanaka, K. (1996). Inferotemporal cortex and object vision. *Annual Review of Neuroscience, 19*, 109–139.

Ullman, S., & Sali, E. (2000). Object classification using fragment-based representation. In S.-W. Lee, H. H. Bülthoff, & T. Poggio (Eds.), *Biologically motivated computer vision, 1811* (pp. 73–87). Berlin: Springer-Verlag.

Valentine, T. (1991). A unified account of the effects of distinctiveness, inversion and race in face recognition. *Quarterly Journal of Experimental Psychology, 43A*, 161–204.

Yin, R. K. (1969). Looking at upside-down faces. *Journal of Experimental Psychology, 81*, 141–145.

1

What Are the Routes to Face Recognition?

JAMES C. BARTLETT, JEAN H. SEARCY,
AND HERVÉ ABDI

What is holistic processing of faces? We view it as processing in which parts or piecemeal features (mouths, eyes, noses, etc.) (1) are not explicitly represented in memory codes (Tanaka & Farah, 1993), (2) are explicitly represented, but relatively inaccessible to conscious analysis or verbal report (Carey & Diamond, 1994), or (3) are consciously accessible, but internally encoded or described in a way that is influenced by other features (Bruce & Humphreys, 1994). These characterizations vary, but all are derived from a key observation: piecemeal features of upright faces are not encoded independently of each other. As Bruce and Humpreys (1994) state: "it seems to be difficult or impossible to encode a particular part or 'feature' of an upright face without some influence from other, more distant features" (p. 152).

In an early study supporting this observation, Young, Hellawell, and Hay (1987) created facial composites (i.e., new synthetic faces) by aligning the top and bottom portions of two different famous faces. They also created noncomposites with the top and bottom portions misaligned (i.e., shifted laterally with respect to each other). Participants were asked to identify either the top or bottom portion of each face. Their responses were slower with composites than noncomposites, but this effect disappeared when the faces were inverted. The pattern indicated that the upright composites were processed holistically while the inverted composites were not. Later studies reinforced the conclusion that well-formed, upright faces evoke holistic processing, while inverted or fragmented faces, along with a variety of nonfacial stimuli, generally do not (Carey & Diamond, 1994; Endo, 1986; Endo, Masame & Maruyama, 1989, 1990; Farah, Tanaka, & Drain, 1995; Farah, Wilson, Drain, & Tanaka, 1998; Hole, 1994; Tanaka & Sengco, 1997).

Converging with this evidence that well-formed, upright faces evoke holistic processing is a second line of work showing that spatial-relational or "configural" information is more readily encoded from upright faces than from inverted faces (Bartlett & Searcy, 1993; Friere, Lee & Symons, 2000; Kemp, McManus & Pigott, 1990; Leder & Bruce, 2000; Rhodes, 1988; Rhodes, Brake & Atkinson, 1993). For example, Searcy and Bartlett (1996) showed that an ordinary face can be made grotesque by (1) moving selected features (i.e., moving the mouth up and moving the eyes farther apart), or (2) altering these features (blackening some teeth and discoloring the eyes). However, while the first effect is reduced when the face is upside-down, the second one is not (see also Murray, Young & Rhodes, 2000; Murray, Rhodes & Schuchinsky, chapter 3 this volume).

The concepts of holistic and configural encoding are tightly interwoven. However, the latter seems broader because configural processing need not be holistic. For example, the processing of relations between adjacent facial features (e.g., the distance separating mouth and tip of nose) is configural but not holistic (Leder & Bruce, 2000). Actually, truly holistic processing implies not only the encoding of interfeatural relations but also interactive, nonindependent encoding across broad regions of a face. At the same time, findings supportive of holistic processing are generally supportive of configural encoding as well. This point is illustrated by the Young et al. (1987) study discussed above: while the findings stand as evidence for holistic face processing, the authors themselves couched their major conclusions in terms of configural processing.

Configural processing—holistic or not—is generally contrasted with piecemeal featural processing. A number of studies dating from the 1960s have suggested that piecemeal features play a role in face recognition (Leder & Bruce, 2000; Macho & Leder, 1998; Rakover & Teucher, 1997; Sergent, 1984; Tversky & Krantz, 1969; Valentin, Abdi, & Edelman, 1999). Such evidence that features are also important (Cabeza & Kato, 2000) has been amassed with little knowledge of what piecemeal features *are* (but see Rhodes et al., 1993). However, it is implicit in the literature that piecemeal features refer to aspects of faces that (1) can be measured or described independently of each other, (2) are local in their spatial extent, and (3) are marked by discontinuities in the surface of a face. Nose shape and eye color are typical examples of piecemeal-feature information.

Here we focus on four basic questions that pertain to the nature of configural face-processing and its interrelations with piecemeal-feature processing, as well as holistic processing. First, do configural processing and piecemeal-feature processing differ qualitatively in the sense that they are governed by different rules of operation? Although the effects of face inversion support a qualitative difference, the question is complex because inversion affects processing of piecemeal-feature information as well as configural information (Rakover & Teucher, 1997). Second, is configural processing holistic in the sense that it encompasses the entire extent of the face, or at least the internal facial region (Moscovitch, Winocur, & Behrmann, 1997)? Or, is such processing merely local in the sense that it is restricted to encoding relations between adjacent facial features (Leder & Bruce, 2000)? Third, what are the roles of configural and featural information in the learning and retention of faces? While configural information has been considered to be critical for distinguishing among faces in long-term memory, a new face composed of previously viewed features 2is often recognized as old. This "conjunction effect" has been interpreted as evidence that long-term memory for piecemeal features is better than that for configural information (Reinitz, Lammers & Cochran, 1992; Reinitz, Morrissey & Demb, 1994). Finally, are configural processing and piecemeal-featural processing anatomically distinct, perhaps showing different patterns of hemispheric asymmetries (Rhodes, 1985, 1993)?

In the remainder of this chapter, we review recent studies motivated by these questions and offer answers to them. Specifically, we marshal evidence that (1) while inversion affects the processing of features, it affects the processing of configural information in a very different way; (2) configural processing can be holistic in the sense of spanning large facial regions, though it appears to reflect an optional strategy not used by all observers, (3) while novel conjunctions of previously viewed features are perceived as familiar, the sense of conscious recollection that a face was seen before involves configural processing; and (4) a distributed network for configural face-processing appears to be separable from one or more networks used in featural face-processing. Taken together, the evidence favors a dual-route hypothesis (cf. Sergent, 1984) holding that featural and configural processing play distinct but complementary roles in perception and recognition of faces.

Do Featural and Configural Processing Differ Qualitatively?

Facial inversion has been the principal tool used to address this question. Searcy and Bartlett (1996) examined the perceptual grotesqueness of faces that were distorted by altering either their features (e.g., blackening out some teeth) or the spatial relations among features (i.e., moving eyes and mouths). They found that inversion reduced the perceived grotesqueness of spatially altered faces, but not of featurally altered faces. Murray et al. (2000) extended this finding, showing discontinuities in the function relating perceived grotesqueness to facial orientation with spatially altered faces but not featurally altered faces or normal faces (see also Bartlett & Searcy, 1993, and Murray et al., chapter 3 this volume). Another relevant finding from face-matching studies is that while inversion slows detection of differences among faces, the effect is smaller with featural differences than with spatial-relational differences (inversion-upright difference = 78 msec vs. 274 msec, respectively, in Searcy & Bartlett, 1996). Accuracy measures reveal a similar pattern: Freire et al. (2000) found that accuracy in detecting spatial differences among faces fell from 81% with upright presentation to 55% with inverted presentation. By contrast, accuracy in detecting featural differences was unaffected by inversion (91% vs. 90%, respectively). Leder and Bruce (2000, Experiments 1–3) extended this finding from perception to long-term memory. They had observers learn names for faces that were distinguishable from each other in terms of either spatial relations (mouth-nose distance) or feature values (e.g., mouth shape, eye shape). Inversion of the stimuli at test impaired performance in the relational condition, but not in the featural ("local") condition.

These findings suggest a qualitative difference in the effects of inversion on configural versus featural processing. However, recognition tasks that are focused on features sometimes show inversion effects. Using a recognition task with different types of foils, Rhodes et al. (1993) found that inversion impaired the detection of feature-swap foils in which one facial feature had been replaced with another. Importantly, the effects of inversion were reduced (or reversed) when the features were studied and tested in isolation, devoid of face context. Tanaka and Farah (1993, Experiment 2) made a similar observation: participants were trained to name several faces and then were tested on their ability to distinguish features of these faces from subtly different features. The test features were presented either by themselves (isolated part condition) or in the context of study faces (whole face condition). Orientation of the stimuli also was varied, and, as shown in figure 1.1 (panel A), inversion reduced performance in the whole face condition, but not in the isolated part condition.

Why should inversion impair processing of features shown within facial context but not processing of features shown by themselves? A plausible answer draws on the classic distinction between *nominal* and *functional* stimulus information. If two faces are identical except for nose shape, the nominal difference between the two faces is featural in nature. Yet, if nose shape affects the Gestalt of the face, this featural difference might be perceived as a difference in configuration. What is nominally a featural difference might be, functionally, a configural difference. In light of this distinction between nominal and functional facial information, the studies by Rhodes et al. (1993) and Tanaka and Farah (1993) can be interpreted as follows: Distinguishing between a previously viewed feature and a subtly different feature shown outside of face context must be based on featural information. However, distinguishing between a previously viewed face and a similar face with one altered feature might be based on what is *functionally* configural information. Since inversion impairs configural encoding, it impairs performance only in the latter of these cases.

Yet recognition of features outside of face context is sometimes affected by inversion. Rakover and Teucher (1997) had their participants view study lists of features (e.g., 10 drawings of noses) followed by tests con-

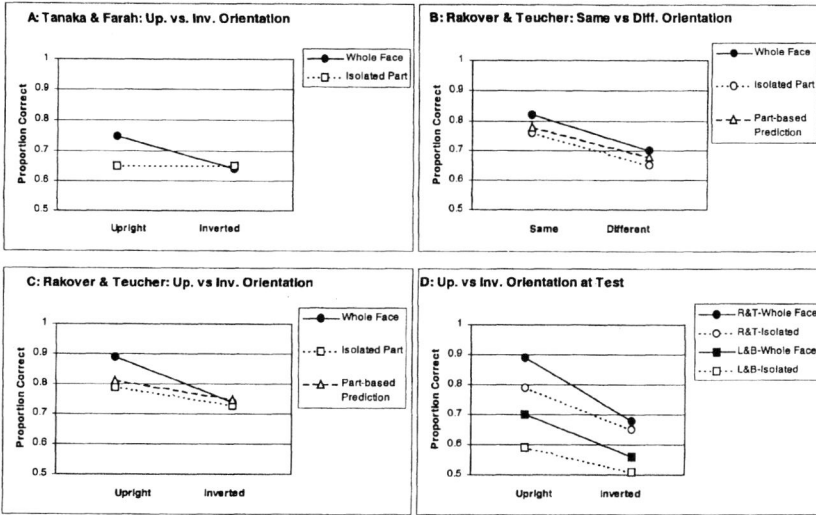

FIGURE 1.1 Effects of orientation manipulations in the whole-face and isolated conditions of Tanaka and Farah (panel A), Rakover and Teucher (panels B, C, & D), and Leder and Bruce (panel D). Panels A and C show effects of upright versus inverted orientation at study *and* test. Panel B shows effects of a *change* in orientation between study and test. Panel D shows effects of orientation *at test*, given upright presentation at study. Predictions of Rakover and Teucher's mathematical model for whole-face recognition based on part recognition are included in panels B and C.

taining old and new features. The orientation of the stimuli at study and test was manipulated factorially across four experimental groups. Recognition was higher in the upright-upright condition ($M = .79$) than in the inverted-inverted condition ($M = .73$), but the difference was small and statistically reliable for only one feature (foreheads) out of five. A greater reduction in performance appeared in the upright-inverted and inverted-upright conditions ($M = .65$ in both cases). In fact, both of these *changed-orientation* conditions fell reliably below the upright-upright condition with each of the five features.

In interpreting their findings, Rakover and Teucher (1997) argue that inversion impairs processing of isolated facial features, and that this is why upside-down faces are difficult to recognize. However, even in the absence of processing *impairments*, a change in orientation between study and test can reduce recognition of a facial feature owing to Rock's (1973) assignment-of-directions principle. By this principle, the orientation of a form can affect which part is perceived as being top (and bottom and sides) and this, in turn, can affect interpretation (an inverted smile might be interpreted as a scowl), as well as recognition (a scowl seen at test might be a poor retrieval cue for a smile seen at study). Apart from this effect of assignment of directions, Rakover and Teucher's data do not stand as evidence that inversion *impairs* processing of isolated features (save, perhaps, foreheads).

What about recognition of whole faces? Rakover and Teucher's Experiment 2 examined whole-face recognition in the same set of orientation conditions of Experiment 1. The results are summarized in figure 1.1, which also includes: (1) the feature-recognition data from Experiment 1, and (2) quantitative predictions for whole-face recognition derived from a model that assumes that only feature-based processing supports whole-face recognition (see Rakover & Teucher, 1997). Panel B of the figure displays (1) the average of the upright-upright and inverted-inverted conditions, and (2) the average of the upright-inverted and inverted-upright conditions, and reveals the effects of a *change* in orientation between study and test (i.e., the assignment-of-directions factor): whole-face recognition and piecemeal-feature recognition are equally affected. Panel C displays performance in the upright-upright and inverted-inverted conditions, and reveals the effects of facial inversion apart from study-test changes in orientation: inversion impaired whole-face recognition more than isolated-feature recognition, and more than the feature-based model predicted. The effects of inversion in Panel C resembled those of Tanaka and Farah (1993) shown in Panel A. Thus, the accumulated data support the conclusion that, apart from the assignment-of-directions factor, inversion impairs recognition of faces more than recognition of their isolated parts. Configural processing appears to differ qualitatively from piecemeal-feature processing.

What Is the Span of Configural Face Processing?
(Is it Holistic?)

Three possible answers to this difficult question have been stated or implied in the literature to date. First, configural processing involves template-like structures (Bartlett & Searcy, 1993; Farah et al., 1998; Yuille, 1991) that cover a very large span, perhaps encompassing the entire face including chin line and hair. Second, data from a patient with object agnosia (without prosopagnosia) have led Moscovitch et al. (1997) to conclude that configural processing pertains primarily to the internal facial region. Third, the configural component of face processing encodes relations between spatially adjacent features such as the distance between the eyes or between the mouth and tip of nose (making it local as opposed to holistic, see Leder and Bruce, 2000). What does the experimental evidence say?

Well, there is precious little of it. In a pioneering application of multidimensional scaling techniques to similarity ratings of faces, Rhodes (1988) identified 16 configural dimensions (along with 11 featural dimensions) that appeared to contribute to her participants' judgments. However, the spatial extent of these dimensions was not determined in the study.

Noting that many configural dimensions might be encoded by observers in a local way (e.g., eye position might be encoded as eye-to-nose distance), Leder and Bruce (2000) attempted to determine whether inversion impairs processing of *local* spatial relations in addition to, or instead of, more *global* (i.e., holistic) information. Their Experiment 4 employed the task of learning names for eight schematic, upright, faces that differed from each other only with respect to locations of their features (eyes, noses, mouths, chins, and hairlines). For example, one face had its eyes closer together than did any other face, while another had its mouth moved down and closer to its chin than did any other face. The subsequent test required participants to identify upright and inverted faces that were masked to reveal (1) only the proximal interfeatural relations that distinguished them from each other (the isolated-relational condition), (2) the proximal interfeatural relations along with the outer contour of the face (the context-relational condition), or (3) only one feature involved in a proximal interfeatural relation along with the outer contour (the context-part condition). They also included a whole face (unmasked) condition. Collapsing over orientation, performance in the isolated-relational condition was only slightly lower than performance in the context-relational and whole-face conditions, while performance in the context-part condition was considerably impaired. Importantly, inversion at test disrupted performance in all of these conditions (there was no interaction).

Leder and Bruce concluded that "the critical information that is used in face recognition and that is disrupted by inversion consists of relations between single features" (p. 534), and that "relational information is processed in a local and possibly independent way" (p. 535). We view these data differently based on two considerations. First, the inversion effect in Leder and Bruce remained robust in the (admittedly difficult) context-part condition. Because the test stimuli in the context-part condition were lacking in local interfeatural relations, this finding suggests that (1) the locations of parts were encoded with respect to more distal facial features (i.e., those of the outer contour), and (2) inversion disrupted this type of encoding. Second, because the study faces were always upright, the inverted condition of Leder and Bruce was, in fact, a learn-upright/test-inverted condition. As we saw previously, such a condition could confound an assignment-of-directions effect with an inversion-related impairment in configural processing. In fact, the data from Leder and Bruce (2000) resemble those of Rakover and Teucher (1997; see figure 1.1, panel D). In both cases, a comparison of an upright-upright condition with an upright-inverted condition suggests inversion hurt performance in the whole face condition more than in the isolated condition (i.e., the isolated-relational condition of Leder and Bruce and isolated-part condition of Rakover and Teucher). The interactive pattern is weak, but for Rakover and Teucher, it becomes more convincing if the upright-inverted condition is replaced by an inverted-inverted condition (panel C). If the same result were found in the Leder and Bruce paradigm it would show that, apart from the assignment of directions factor, inversion impairs encoding of global configuration more than relations between adjacent parts.

In sum, recognition of upright faces involves a global type of configural processing that is disrupted by inversion. This type of configural processing appears to co-exist with the localized processing of piecemeal features that is considerably less vulnerable to disruption by inversion. A local form of configural processing appears also to exist, but whether such processing is impaired by inversion, or simply is subject to effects of orientation on the assignment of directions, has not been determined.

Are Internal Regions of Faces Special?

The internal and external regions of faces can differ in their salience and effectiveness as cues in face recognition memory (Ellis, Shepherd, & Davies, 1979). However, that these regions might be processed *in differing ways* has been suggested only recently by Moscovitch et al. (1997) from their studies of CK, a victim of closed-head injury. While CK is impaired at both reading and object recognition, he performs normally in recognizing faces, *as long as the faces are presented upright.* Yet he suffers much more than normal participants when faces are inverted. In a clever extension of this basic observation, Moscovitch et al. (Experiment 12) compared CK and controls in recognizing faces of well-known persons when (1) the external face region had been inverted and the internal face region remained upright, and (2) the internal face region had been inverted and the external face region remained upright. While recognition performance was unimpaired in case 1, it was significantly disrupted in case 2, especially with CK. Based on this and other findings, Moscovitch and Moscovitch (2000) suggested that CK has an intact "face system" that "forms holistic representations of faces based on orientation-specific global configurations primarily of internal features" (p. 201).

While an internal-only view of configural face processing fits some of the data, it has a problem with one finding reported by Moscovitch and Moscovitch (2000). In their Experiment 1, they assessed recognition of famous faces that had been masked to reveal *only* their internal features or *only* their external features. Regardless of mask condition, recognition was *drastically* impaired if the test faces were inverted. A "super" face-inversion effect with external facial features seems to contradict an internal-only view of configural face processing, as the authors acknowledged. They chose nonetheless to retain their internal-only hypothesis, arguing that the effects of inversion are not restricted to holistic information. Like Rakover and Teucher (1997), they suggested that recognition of features can be orientation-specific.

Indeed, feature-recognition *can* be orientation-specific, particularly when orientation changes between study and test (as occurs in famous-face recognition when the test items are inverted). But it is nonetheless surprising, by the internal-only view, that the effects of inversion were not appreciably larger with internal-only faces (where both configural and featural encoding should have been affected) than with external-only faces (where only featural encoding should have been affected). As usual, more research is needed.

An Analysis of Configural Face-Processing Based on Garner Interference

To test the internal-only view of configural face-processing against the whole-face view, we turned to Garner's (1974) selective attention paradigm. The basic task is to classify stimuli on one dimension while values on a second, task-irrelevant, dimension (1) remain constant (control condition), (2) vary orthogonally to the relevant dimension, or (3) vary redundantly with the relevant condition (correlated condition). A slowing of decision in the orthogonal condition as compared to the control implies that the two dimensions are integral (not kept separate) at some stage of processing, or that unique configurations emerge from different combinations of levels of each dimension (Pomerantz, Pristach & Carson, 1989). Integrality and configurality both qualify as subtypes of holistic processing that differ from separability. The clearest case of separability is simply no difference among conditions.

In a first test of the whole-face hypothesis, Bartlett, Helm, and Jerger (2001) had 12 undergraduates perform the Garner selective attention task using the four stimuli shown in figure 1.2. On each of 24 trials, a sequence of 32 faces was shown. The task was to classify each face in the sequence by its internal features (12 trials) or its external features (12 trials). On half (6) of the trials of each type, all faces were inverted. On the remaining 6 trials, all faces were upright. Finally, within each subset of 6 trials, there were 2 trials for each of 3 Garner conditions: control, orthogonal, and correlated.

On control-condition trials, only the task-relevant features—internal or external—were allowed to vary. Thus, when classification was by internal features, the control sequence included only faces A and B, or only faces C and D (see figure 1.2). Similarly, when classification was by external features, the control sequence included only faces A and C, or only faces B and D. On the orthogonal condition trials, internal and external features varied independently of each other. Thus, the sequence included all four faces, and participants were required to focus their attention on one facial region (internal or external), and to ignore the other. On the correlated-condition trials, the internal and external features were redundant in the sense that they varied together. In this case, the sequence included only faces A and D or only faces B and C. A slowing of responses in the orthogonal condition compared to both others reflects a breakdown in selective attention that suggests holistic processing.

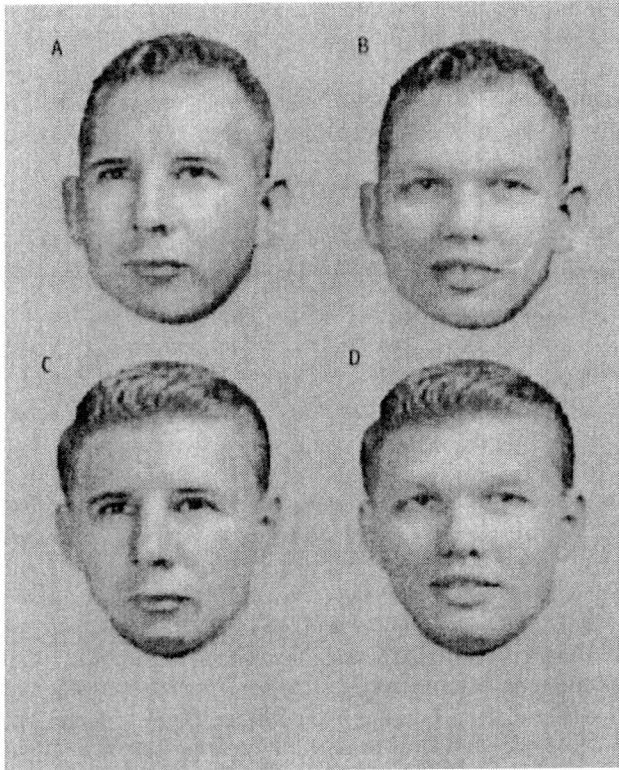

FIGURE 1.2. The four face-stimuli used by Bartlett, Helm, and Jerger (2001). Faces A and B share the same external features as do faces C and D. Faces A and C share the same internal features as do faces B and D. Faces A and D are copies of original photographs from a college yearbook. Faces B and C were created using image-graphics programs by "pasting" the internal region of face A onto the external region of face D and vice versa.

As shown in figure 1.3 (top panel), the reaction times followed an interactive pattern consistent with the notion that upright faces were processed as wholes. Responses were slower in the orthogonal condition than in the other two, but this was true only when the faces were upright. The condition effect and the condition-by-orientation interaction were both reliable by ANOVA (F's (2,22) = 7.34 and 3.72, respectively, with MSe's = 2216 and 3371, and p's < .01 and .05), and follow-up analyses supported the condition effect with upright faces only (F (2,22) = 7.90, MSe = 3626, p < .01). The pattern of the upright condition corresponds to configurality, as the orthogonal condition differed from the control and correlated conditions (p's < .01 by Tukey's HSD test) which did not differ from each other. We also found an overall advantage of external-feature

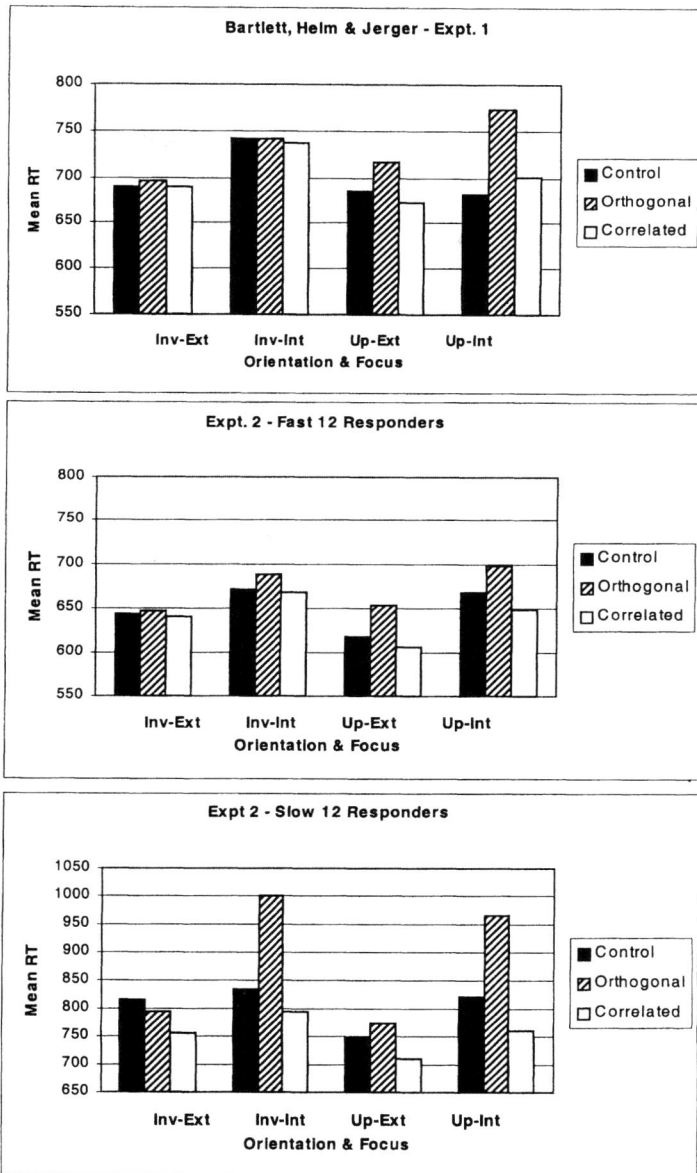

FIGURE 1.3. Mean reaction-time (RT) in the control, orthogonal, and correlated conditions with upright (up) and inverted (inv) faces and an internal (int) or external (ext) attentional focus in Bartlett, Helm, and Jerger (2001). The top panel shows RTs from Experiment 1; the middle and lower panels show RTs for fast and slow responders in Experiment 2.

focus over internal-feature focus (F (1,11) = 10.32, MSe = 5174, $p <$ .01).

A second experiment using the same procedures produced a more complex result. However, the outcome was clarified when we divided the participants into fast and slow responders based on the overall median RT. The 12 fast responders had an average RT of 654 msec, which is comparable to the first investigation (711 msec). The pattern of their RTs was similar as well, suggesting Garner interference with upright faces (F (2,22) = 3.60, MSe = 4201, $p <$ .05), but not inverted faces ($p >$ .10, see figure 1.3, middle panel). In contrast, the 12 slow responders (M = 815 msec) showed Garner interference when attention was focused on internal features, but not when it was focused on external features, regardless of orientation (the focus-by-condition interaction was reliable, F (2,22) = 6.44, MSe = 14,672, $p <$ .05). This pattern corresponds to asymmetric interference, which has been reported to hold between the facial dimensions of expression (conveyed by internal features) and identity (possibly cued by external features; LeGal, 1999; Schweinberger & Soutkup, 1998; but see Etcoff, 1984). The asymmetric pattern does *not* stand as evidence for holistic processing. Instead, such asymmetries are commonly attributed to one dimension being processed faster than or prior to the other.

The differing patterns shown by fast and slow responders suggest the existence of two separate routes in face processing. In one route (the slow route), facial features are processed separately from each other, with external features enjoying an advantage in speed. In the other route (the fast route), internal features and external features are not encoded independently (unless the faces are inverted). Rather, the encoding is configural and is spatially extended across the whole of an upright face (i.e., not just across the internal face-region). We view such spatially extended configural processing as essentially holistic.

How Important Is Configural Processing in Long-Term Memory?

While configural processing might be important in perceptual classification tasks, research on the *conjunction effect* suggests it might be less useful in long-term memory tasks. In a typical experiment, participants view a list of items such as words or faces, and then perform a recognition test in which some of the lures are recombinations of the parts of study items. These conjunction lures evoke many false alarms, several times as many as entirely new items. The conjunction/new difference in false-alarm rates is known as the conjunction effect (Jones & Jacoby, 2001; Kroll, Knight, Metcalfe, Wolf, & Tulving, 1996; Reinitz, et al., 1992, 1994; Searcy, Bartlett, & Memon, 1999).

A Feature-Based View of the Conjunction Effect

In interpreting their findings, Reinitz et al. (1994) argued that holistic representations are not directly stored in long-term memory, but are reconstructed at retrieval based on memory for features and relations between features. Features are encoded and retained rather well, but relational information is effortful to encode (Reinitz et al., 1994), subject to inaccurate encoding (Reinitz & Hannigan, 2001), and rapidly forgotten (Hannigan & Reinitz, 1999). Hence, reconstructions formed at retrieval often miscombine features seen previously at study, and, in some cases, these reconstructions match conjunction foils (see also Kroll et al., 1996).

Although the feature-based hypothesis fits several results, an alternative view is suggested by data from Searcy et al.'s (1999) Experiment 2. In that experiment, 76 young adults and 75 seniors viewed a study list containing 16 faces each presented two times, and then took a test containing 8 old faces, 8 conjunctions, and 8 new items. The conjunctions were constructed by recombining the internal and external regions of photographs of faces, using image-graphics software to make seamless conjunctions similar to those in figure 1.2. We computed rates of old judgments in response to old faces (hit rates), as well as conjunctions and new faces (false-alarm rates). As shown in figure 1.4 (top panel), hit rates for old items exceeded false-alarm rates for conjunctions, which in turn were much higher than false-alarm rates for new faces. The new finding was that there were age-related differences, and these differences varied with the seniors' performance on a perceptual face-matching test used to assess posterior brain damage, the Benton Face Recognition Test (BFRT; Benton & Van Allen, 1968).

First, compare the young adults with the majority (77%) of the seniors who scored normally on the BFRT (see white and striped bars in figure 1.4). The two groups did not differ in false-alarm rates for conjunctions or in hit rates for old faces. Nor did they differ in discrimination (A') between old faces and conjunctions (figure 1.4, lower panel). By contrast, the seniors exceeded the young adults in false alarms with new faces (a frequent finding; see Bartlett & Fulton, 1991). Because of this effect, discrimination between conjunctions and new faces—a criterion-free measure of the conjunction effect—was smaller with seniors than with young adults.

Next, consider seniors who scored poorly on the BFRT (see black bars in figure 1.4). As compared to other seniors, these low-BFRT participants showed increased false-alarm rates for new items *and* conjunctions, and reduced hit rates for old faces. As a result, old/conjunction discrimination by the low-BFRT seniors was reduced as compared to normal-BFRT seniors, as well as young adults. And yet conjunction/new discrimination was the same among low- and normal-BFRT seniors (i.e., it was reduced as compared to young adults).

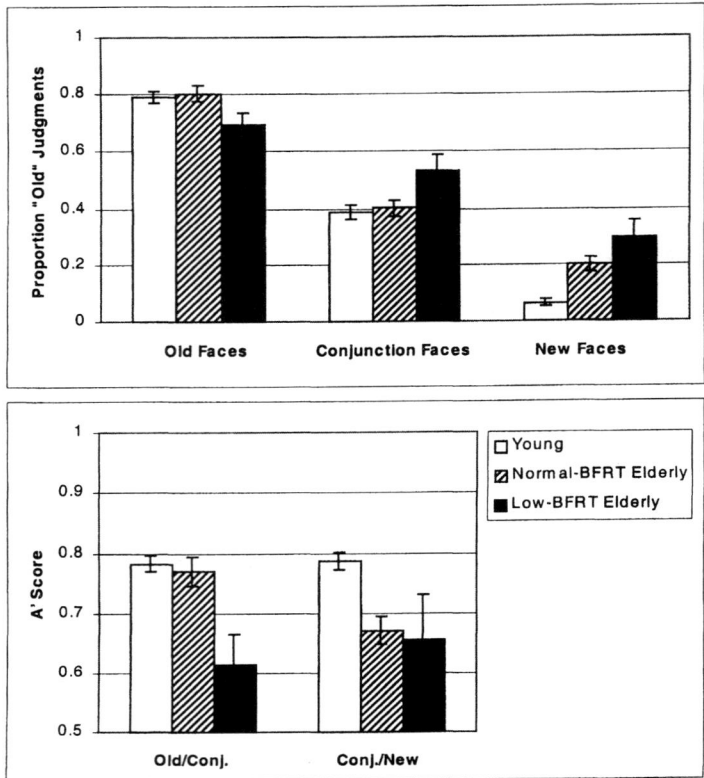

FIGURE 1.4. Upper panel: Proportions of "old" judgments in response to old faces, conjunctions, and new faces by young participants and elderly adults with normal or low scores on the Benton Face Recognition test (BFRT). Lower panel: A' scores for old/conjunction discrimination and conjunction/new discrimination in each participant-group.

The A' data might be explained by the feature-based view if (1) conjunction/new discrimination reflects the accuracy or efficiency of featural encoding while old/conjunction discrimination reflects the accuracy or efficiency of relational encoding, and (2) seniors as a group are generally impaired in encoding facial features while only those seniors with face-matching problems are impaired at encoding relations between features. This feature-based account has a degree of plausibility, but it is dogged by two problems. First, seniors as a group are *generally* deficient in encoding relations or bindings between features (see, e.g., Chalfonte & Johnson, 1996). Thus, it is puzzling that seniors with normal-BFRT scores distinguished conjunctions from old faces as well as young adults. Second, the feature-based view does not explain the observation that young adults and normal-BFRT seniors differed *only* with respect to false-alarm rates for new faces. If there are age-related deficits in featural encoding, hits to old faces and false-alarms to conjunctions should have been affected as well.

A Dual-Route View of the Conjunction Effect

In light of these problems with the feature-based interpretation, we suggest an alternative view that extends the dual-route hypothesis sketched earlier in this chapter. By this extended dual-route view, a holistic route to face recognition involves specialized mechanisms in posterior brain regions that perform holistic processing of upright faces. These holistic processing mechanisms are largely immune from the effects of normal aging, except for a subset of elderly persons with subtle lesions or processing inefficiencies in posterior brain regions (i.e., our low-BFRT seniors). Thus, the age-invariance and BFRT-related deficit in old/conjunction discrimination can be explained by assuming that holistic processing is the primary basis of distinguishing conjunctions from truly old items.

The pattern of conjunction/new discrimination can be interpreted based on much prior evidence that (1) false-alarm rates for new faces are *consistently* increased in old age across a number of conditions (see Searcy et al., 1999, for a review), and that (2) age-related deficits in *context recollection* are a cause of this effect (Bartlett, 1993; Bartlett & Fulton, 1991; Bartlett, Strater & Fulton, 1991). Specifically, several findings suggest that, because the set of human faces is homogenous in nature, entirely new faces can often feel familiar. Conscious recollection of contextual information can aid in the rejection of these faces as new (e.g., a participant might reject a familiar-looking face if she recollects that it resembles someone at the office as opposed to a face from a prior study list). However, since seniors have impairments in recollective processes (e.g., Jennings & Jacoby, 1997), they are more prone than are young adults to call new faces old. A modest extension of this line of theory is that while recollective processes aid rejection of new faces, they do not aid rejection of conjunction faces (not even in young adults). Thus, young adults' superiority in conscious recollection helps them (compared to older adults) to avoid false alarms with entirely new faces. However, it does not help them with conjunction faces as such faces generally cannot be rejected based on conscious recollection.

SUPPORT FOR THE DUAL-ROUTE VIEW: FAMILIARITY WITHOUT RECOLLECTION

In support of the recollection account, there is evidence suggesting that conjunction false alarms are frequently the result of perceived familiarity in the absence of recollection (see Jones & Jacoby, 2001). In the full attention condition of their Experiment 4, Reinitz et al. (1994) employed the standard procedure of presenting their participants with a study list of faces, followed by a test including old, conjunction, and new faces. However, instead of asking their participants just for old-new responses, they instructed them to judge whether each test item was (1) remembered (i.e., consciously recollected) as having been seen in prior study list, (2) known to have been present in the prior study list despite not evoking an explicit recollection, or (3) new (see Gardiner & Richardson-Klavehn, 2000). The rate of remember (i.e., recollection) judgments was higher for old items than conjunctions, and was lowest for new items (M s = .64, .35, and .02, respectively). In contrast, the rate of know judgments was approximately the same for old items and conjunctions, though again it was lower for new items (M s = .23, .28, and .05, respectively). While Reinitz et al. used schematic face drawings, we replicated this pattern in a classroom project using the more naturalistic faces of our prior studies. The 21 students viewed a study list including 16 faces each presented two times. There followed a test in which participants judged items as remembered, known or guessed to be old, or else as new. Rates of remember judgments averaged .52, .11, and .04 for old, conjunction, and new items, respectively, while rates of know judgments averaged .19, .17, and .02 for the three item-types, respectively (guess judgments were rare). Both studies suggest that recollection experiences are considerably more frequent for old faces than conjunctions. They also suggest there are two different bases for conjunction false alarms: (1) erroneous recollection experiences (reflected in remember responses), and (2) familiarity without recollection (reflected in know responses).

Another relevant finding comes from Bartlett, Searcy and Truxillo (1996), who had their young-adult participants view a study list in which 8 faces appeared one time, and 8 additional faces appeared 8 times. The subsequent test included 4 old faces that had appeared once, 4 old faces that had appeared 8 times, 4 conjunctions of *parts that had appeared once*, and 4 conjunctions of *parts that had appeared 8 times*. The test also included 8 entirely new faces. Half of the 112 participants saw all faces upright at both study and test, while the remainder saw all faces inverted.

As shown in figure 1.5 (top panel), hit rates were higher with eight study presentations than with only one. False-alarm rates were higher with inverted faces than with upright faces. For both upright and inverted faces, false-alarm rates rose from (1) entirely new faces to (2) conjunctions whose parts were seen one time at study, to (3) conjunctions whose parts were seen eight times at study. Thus, repetition at study increased conjunction false alarms. Area-under-ROC scores (see middle panel) confirmed that old/conjunction discrimination was decreased by inversion and increased by repetition. Conjunction/new discrimination was unaffected by inversion, but was increased by repetition.

Bartlett et al. (1996) replicated these findings in two similar experiments, and Neville-Smith, Abdi, and Bartlett (2002) extended the effects of repetition at study to (1) a between-participants manipulation of repetition, and (2) a one-day test delay. A study list of 32 upright faces was followed by a test containing 16 old faces, 16 conjunctions, and 16 new

Bartlett et al. (1996)

Proportion "Old" Judg.

1
0.8
0.6
0.4
0.2
0

Legend:
···O··· HRs-Upright
···□··· HRs-Inverted
—●— FARs-Upright
—■— FARs-Inverted

0   1X   8X
Presentation Frequency

Bartlett et al. (1996)

Area-under-ROC Scores

1
0.9
0.8
0.7
0.6
0.5

Legend:
□ 1X-Upright
■ 1X-Inverted
▦ 8X-Upright
■ 8X-Inverted

Old/Conj.   Conj./New

Neville-Smith et al. (unpublished)

Area-under-ROC Scores

1
0.9
0.8
0.7
0.6
0.5

Legend:
□ 1X-Imm.
▦ 1X-Delay
▦ 3X-Imm.
■ 3X-Delay

Old/Conj.   Conj./New

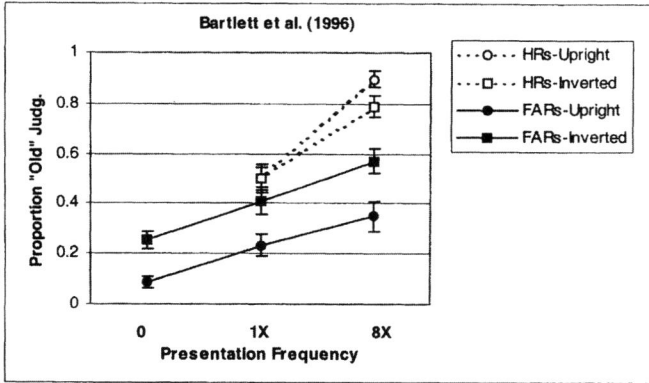

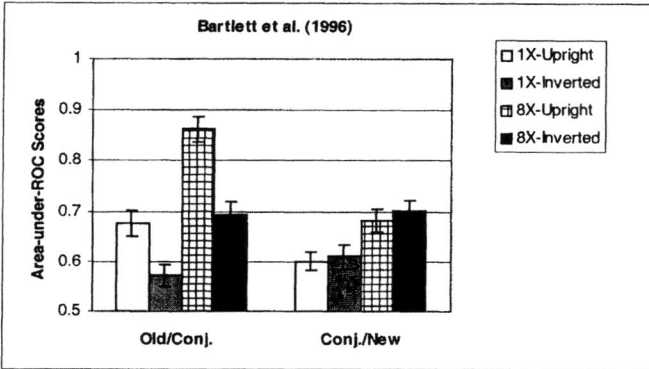

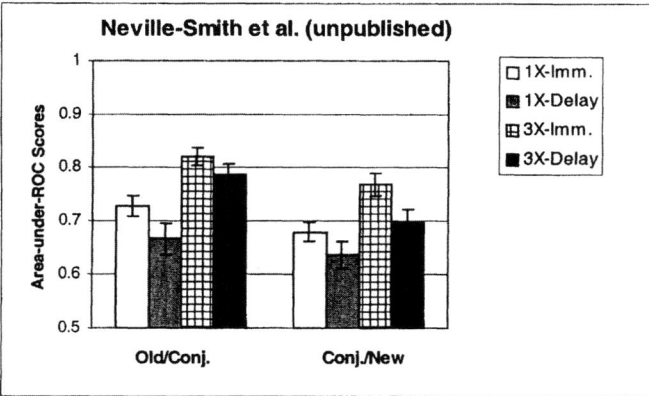

FIGURE 1.5. Upper panel: Hit rates (HRs) for old faces presented once or eight times (1× and 8×), and false-alarm rates (FARs) for entirely new faces (0), and for conjunctions whose parts had been presented once or eight times (1× and 8×) in Bartlett et al. (1996). Half of the participants saw all faces upright (circles), while the rest saw all faces inverted (squares). Middle panel: Area-under-ROC scores for old/conjunction and conjunction/new discrimination by study-frequency and orientation in Bartlett et al. Lower panel: Area scores for old/conjunction and conjunction/new discrimination by study frequency (1 vs. 3 presentations), with the test following immediately (Imm.), or after a one-day delay, in Neville-Smith et al. (2002).

items. Repetition at study (1 vs. 3 presentations) and retention interval (1 vs. 3 days) were manipulated factorially across four groups of participants ($n = 24$ per group). Both old/conjunction scores and conjunction/new scores rose with repetition (figure 1.5, bottom panel), a pattern that held at both test delays.

That inversion impaired old/conjunction discrimination supports other evidence that it impairs holistic processing. That repetition at study improved old/conjunction discrimination is an intuitively obvious learning effect any theory can explain. However, that repetition increased conjunction/new discrimination is a counterintuitive, "ironic" effect specifically supportive of memory theories that distinguish familiarity from recollective processes (Kelley & Jacoby, 2000; Jones & Jacoby, 2001). Such theories hold that repetition at study will increase false alarms when it causes certain lures in a recognition test to be perceived as more familiar than otherwise would be the case, and when *conscious recollection is unlikely to be helpful in combating the effect*. Viewed in this light, the findings from Bartlett et al. (1996) and Neville-Smith et al. (2002) converge with the findings from our remember/know studies: The data suggest that conjunctions are frequently perceived as familiar in the absence of recollection (see Jones & Jacoby, 2001, for further evidence on this point).

In summary, our findings suggest that old faces and conjunctions are reliably distinguished because holistic processing supports recollective experiences in response to the former more than the latter. Conjunction-new differences in false recognition occur for two reasons. First, since features contribute to face recognition, and since conjunction faces are composed of old features, conjunctions might sometimes produce a false sense of conscious recollection. Second, when conjunctions do *not* produce a sense of recollection, they nonetheless can be perceived as familiar and judged old for that reason.

A new question arises at this point in our story: What kind of face processing supports perceived familiarity? One possibility is that perceived familiarity is based on piecemeal-feature processing. However, we have simulated the conjunction effect with an autoassociative network model that learns and remembers faces using a familiarity-like process and *no* explicit coding of standard facial features. We turn to this model next.

A PCA MODEL OF THE CONJUNCTION EFFECT

A well-developed model of face recognition is the principal component analysis (PCA) model of Abdi, O'Toole and colleagues (Abdi, 1988; O'Toole, Deffenbacher, Valentin, & Abdi, 1994; Valentin, Abdi, & O'Toole, 1994; and see Abdi, Valentin, & Edelman, 1999, for a technical presentation). Though the PCA model is often presented in statistical terms, it is formally equivalent to an *autoassociative memory* that learns pictures of faces using a pixel-based code. Viewed in this way, the PCA model is a set of completely interconnected linear units, each representing a face-image pixel. The connections between units are used to store faces and, as in all connectionist models, the connection values represent the knowledge of the system. These values can be modified with different learning rules, including Hebbian and Widrow-Hoff.

At any given level of learning, a face is recognized as follows: When the face image is given as an input to the memory, the activation of each unit is initially set to the activation value corresponding to the gray-level value of the pixel associated to this unit. Then, each unit propagates its activation to all the other units through their interconnections. Each unit will settle on a new level of activation that determines its response (the response is proportional to the activation). The pattern of response across the set of units is also an image (i.e., the output image) that can be compared to the original input image. The comparison can be made by visual inspection or, quantitatively, by using a correlation coefficient or a cosine (here we use the cosine) computed from the pixel values between the input and output images. The cosine is an estimate of perceived familiarity: The larger the cosine between input and output, the more familiar the face is to the model. When a set of learned (old) faces is compared to a set of new faces, the overlapping distributions of cosine values can be used to derive a discrimination index such as d'. The value of d' varies with degree of learning, and by varying the number of learning trials in the Widrow-Hoff mode, it is possible to match the d' of the model to the d' derived from the human data for a given set of stimuli in any given test condition (see Abdi, Valentin, Edelman & O'Toole, 1995, or Edelman, 1998, for examples).

We followed this procedure for the stimuli and conditions of the study by Neville-Smith et al. (2002; figure 1.5, lower panel). For each combination of repetition and test-delay condition, we matched the model to the human participants with respect to old/new d'. Then, holding the degree of learning constant, we used the model to *predict* d's for old/conjunction discrimination and conjunction/new discrimination shown by human participants. The model showed high levels of conjunction/new discrimination, and such discrimination was increased by repetition, just as in the human-participant data (figure 1.6). Hence, the conjunction effect, and its ironic increase with repetition, can be produced by a PCA model using a pixel-based code and a familiarity-like process for making recognition judgments. Explicit encoding of standard facial features (e.g., nose shape, eye color) is not a prerequisite for the effect to occur.

ENHANCING THE PCA MODEL WITH HOLISTIC PROCESSING AND CONSCIOUS RECOLLECTION

Despite its success, the PCA (autoassociative) model does not fit the data perfectly: As shown in figure 1.6, at any given level of old/new d', the model overestimates conjunction/new d' and underestimates old/conjunction d'. By the dual-route hypothesis, this failure is attributable to the lack

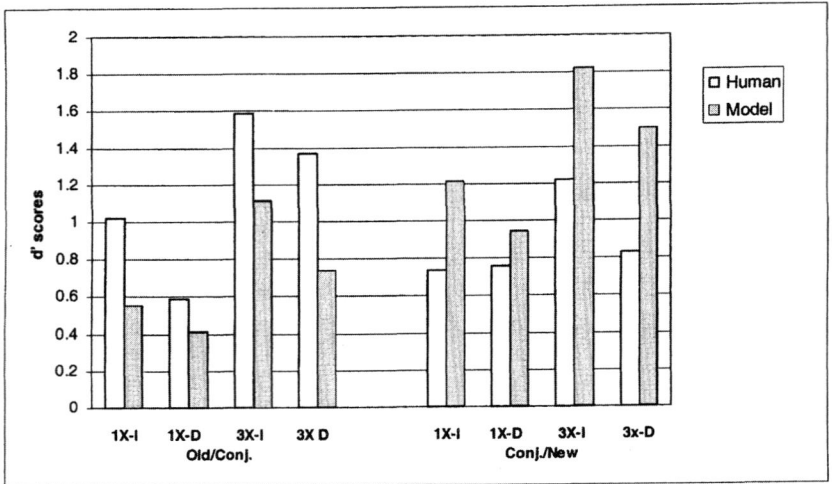

FIGURE 1.6. The white bars show old/conjunction and conjunction/new d's by study frequency (1 vs. 3 presentations), with the test following immediately (I) or after a one-day delay (D) in Neville-Smith et al. (2002). The gray bars show performance of a computer-implemented autoassociative model presented with the same faces. Learning-parameters were adjusted so that the model matched the human participants in old/new d's (not shown).

of any mechanism for holistic processing. Indeed, the pixel-based code might be viewed as a culprit based on the assumption that such codes are *non*-holistic.[1] However, before rejecting the pixel-based code, it is important to consider the *pattern completion* property of autoassociative models, including those using a pixel-based code: when presented with a new (nonstudied) stimulus, an autoassociative network provides an output image that tends to reproduce a previously learned stimulus. To illustrate this point, we show examples of study items, test items, and outputs of the model at two levels of learning in figure 1.7. Note that the outputs in response to old items resemble the old items themselves. By contrast, the outputs in response to conjunctions differed from the conjunctions themselves, often showing a striking resemblance to one of a conjunction's parents (particularly at the higher level of learning).

   In light of the pattern-completion power of autoassociative memories, we believe that our model's imperfect fit with our data reflects its retrieval and decision-making processes rather than constraints of the pixel-based code. The PCA model makes a recognition judgment based solely on the cosine of a face's pixel values with the output of the network. This familiarity-like process is apparently insensitive to configural differences that are readily apparent when a test face and the output of the model are examined by eye. Hence, one way of improving the PCA model is to

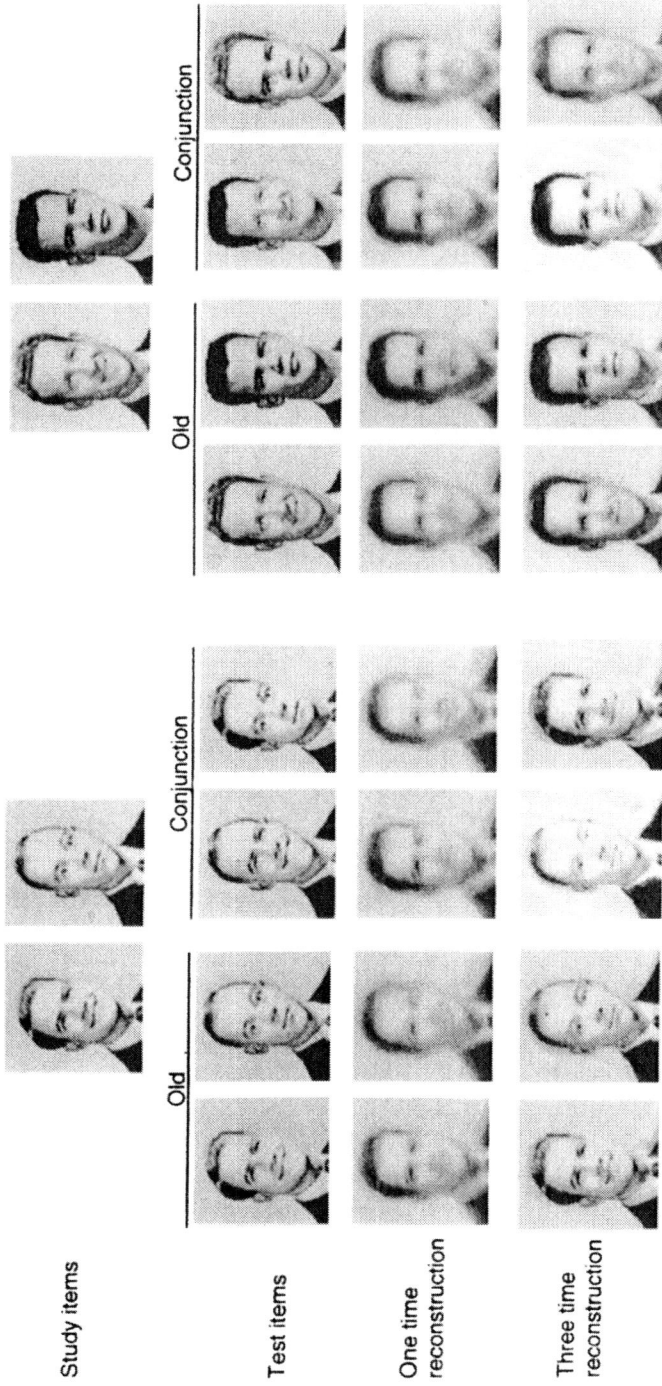

FIGURE 1.7. Row 1 displays four examples of study items learned by the autoassociative network model in Neville-Smith, et al. (2002). Row 2 displays examples of old and conjunction items presented in the test. Rows 3 and 4 display the model's reconstructions of each of the test items at the low (one time) and high (three times) level of learning. Note that the model's reconstructions of old items are highly similar to the old items themselves, particularly at the high level of learning. In contrast, the model's reconstructions of conjunctions are obviously different from the conjunctions themselves, particularly at the high level of learning. In fact, the model's reconstruction of a conjunction tends to resemble one of the study faces more than the conjunction itself.

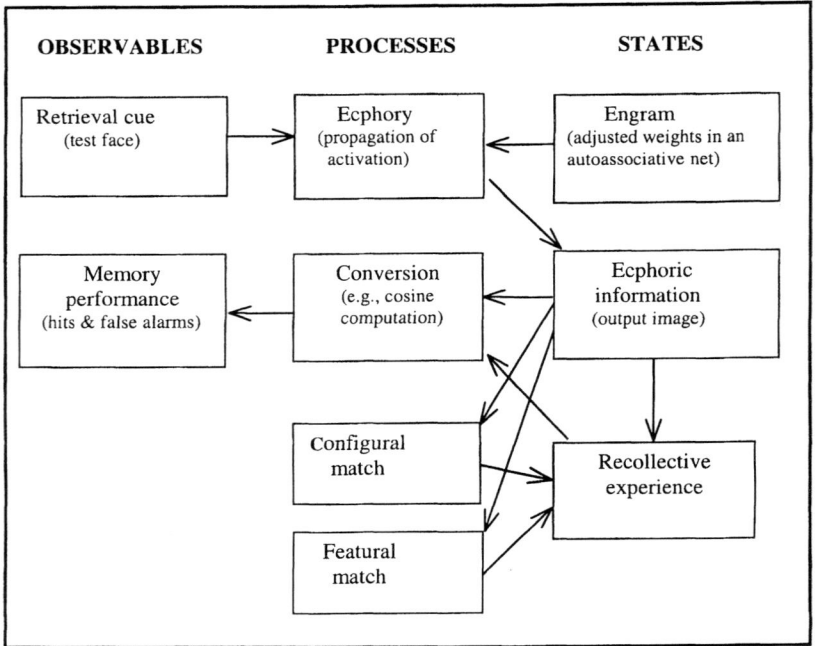

FIGURE 1.8. An elaboration of the autoassociative model of face recognition placed in the framework of Tulving's (1983) General Abstract Processing System (GAPS). A test face (retrieval cue) interacts with the weight-adjusted autoassociative network (engram) to propagate activation in the network (ecphory), producing an output image (ecphoric information). The output image can elicit a recognition judgment (hit or false alarm) through computation of the cosine between the image and the cue (conversion). It can also elicit recollective experience either directly (as in GAPS) or through the detection of configural matches and featural matches between output image and test cue (additions to GAPS). As in GAPS, both ecphoric information and recollective experience affect recognition judgments through conversion processes.

propose retrieval and decision-making processes that are more sensitive to configural information than is a pixel-based cosine.

In future research, we plan to extend the PCA model along the lines of figure 1.8: the architecture of the model comes from Tulving's (1983) General Abstract Processing System (GAPS), a conceptual framework for retrieval from episodic memory. We have inserted those terms from the PCA model that correspond to Tulving's concepts of retrieval cue (test face), engram (autoassociative memory), ecphory (propagation of activation), ecphoric information (output image), conversion (cosine computation), and memory performance (*old/new judgments*). Viewed from the perspective of GAPS, our PCA model is deficient in two key respects. First, the conversion process (cosine computation) is primitive. Second, recollection experiences have not been considered. To correct both deficiencies, we propose a *holistic* process that treats the output image as a template that is tested for its configural match with a recognition cue. A configural match between image and cue: (1) is more likely for old faces than for conjunctions and new items, and (2) is key to the experience of recollecting a face.

A *featural* conversion process should also be considered. Just as the output image might be treated as a template, it also might be subject to analysis by features, allowing assessment of featural match between the output image and the recognition cue. Featural matches should be more frequent for conjunctions than new faces, and these might, in some cases, evoke erroneous recollection that a face was seen before. Indeed, the use of feature-matches for recollecting faces has been dramatically supported by Rapcsak, Polster, Comer, & Rubens (1994), who found that two victims of right-hemisphere stroke were prone to false recollection of faces based on matches with single features (e.g., seeing a stranger, one patient exclaimed "There's my father! I'd recognize that hooked nose anywhere!" Rapcsak et al., p. 569). Impairments in configural processing (owing to right-temporo-parietal damage), and decision-making deficits (owing to right-frontal damage) appear to account for this strange disorder. Following Rapcsak et al., we believe such false recollection usually (though not always) is inhibited through configural processes involving right-posterior brain regions and executive processes involving right-frontal regions.

In summary, we propose a holistic route to face recognition that supports discrimination between old faces and conjunctions. Such discrimination entails configural processing of the output produced by an autoassociative memory in interaction with a cue. However, we suggest that a featural route is operative as well, and that conjunction false-alarms are partially due to feature-based processing along this second route. In addition, our behavioral studies and simulations suggest that conjunction false-alarms are also the result of perceived familiarity in the absence of recollection. Familiarity is based on a low-level code (pixels, in our simulation) in which neither features nor configural properties are explicitly represented. A brain-imaging study, reported below, appears generally in line with these speculations.

Are the Routes to Face Recognition Anatomically Separable?

A final source of evidence for the dual-route conception comes from a recent neuroimaging study (Bartlett, et al., 2000) in which we measured regional cerebral blood flow (rCBF) using Single-Photon Emission Computed Tomography (SPECT) during viewing of previously studied (old) faces, conjunctions of such faces, and new faces. Six right-handed young-adult participants (50% female) viewed three sequences of 42 faces (from the same set used in our prior experiments) across three sessions spaced two to four days apart. Each sequence began with 29 unfamiliar faces followed without interruption by 12 critical faces that were (in different sessions): (1) repeats of faces from positions 2 through 13, (2) conjunctions of faces from positions 2 through 13, or (3) entirely new faces not seen previously in the study. Faces were shown for 6.3 sec each so that the 12 critical faces spanned 76 sec in which rCBF was measured. Counterbalancing ensured that each condition was administered in each of the three sessions, and each test face served in all three conditions, across the six participants. Participants responded to each face in each sequence with an old/new judgment. The rate of old judgments for the 12 critical faces averaged .54, .38, and .07 in the old, conjunction, and new conditions, respectively. Thus, a robust conjunction effect was supported by the data.

20mCi of ^{99m}Tc HMPAO was administered for each scan, with injection timed so that tracer uptake in brain began during presentation of the first critical face, continuing for 60 to 90 sec. SPECT images were acquired 90 minutes postinjection on a PRISM 3000S 3-headed SPECT camera (Picker International, Cleveland, OH) using ultra high-resolution fan-beam collimators with a reconstructed resolution of 6.5mm (Devous, 1995). Data were automatically resliced to 2 mm³ voxels, normalized and co-registered, reformatted into Talairach space (Talairach & Tournoux, 1988), and smoothed to 14 mm FWHM.

Eigenanalysis from SPM 96 (Friston et al., 1995) supported two orthogonal patterns of rCBF that accounted for virtually all of the between-condition variance (64.9% and 35.1%, respectively). The first eigencomponent distinguished old faces (component score = −.80) from conjunction and new faces (component scores = +.35 and +.45), showing little hint of the conjunction effect. The second eigencomponent distinguished conjunctions (component score = −.75) from new items (component score = +.70), with old items showing a near-zero score (+.05), a pattern that fits the conjunction effect.

To explore the brain structures involved in the first eigencomponent, we used the conjunction routine in SPM 96 to identify clusters of increased rCBF in the old condition as compared to both others (i.e., O > C&N clusters).[2] Panel A of figure 1.9 shows that two O > C&N clusters appeared in the left-superior parietal lobule (Brodmann 7), a region implicated in spatial attention, and successful retrieval from episodic memory (Cabeza & Nyberg, 2000). Another O > C&N cluster appeared in the left-superior-temporal gyrus (Brodmann 13), and proximal insula, an area activated during face recognition in a working memory task (Jiang, Haxby, Martin, Ungerleider, & Parasuraman, 2000). A medial-frontal O > C&N effect appeared in and near the rectal gyrus (Brodmann 25 & 11), previously implicated in object- and famous-face classification, facial encoding, and visual memory (Cabeza & Nyberg, 2000; Haxby et al., 1996; Sergent, Ohta, & MacDonald, 1992). Finally, several right-frontal and right-anterior-temporal O > C&N clusters included (1) the "episodic retrieval"

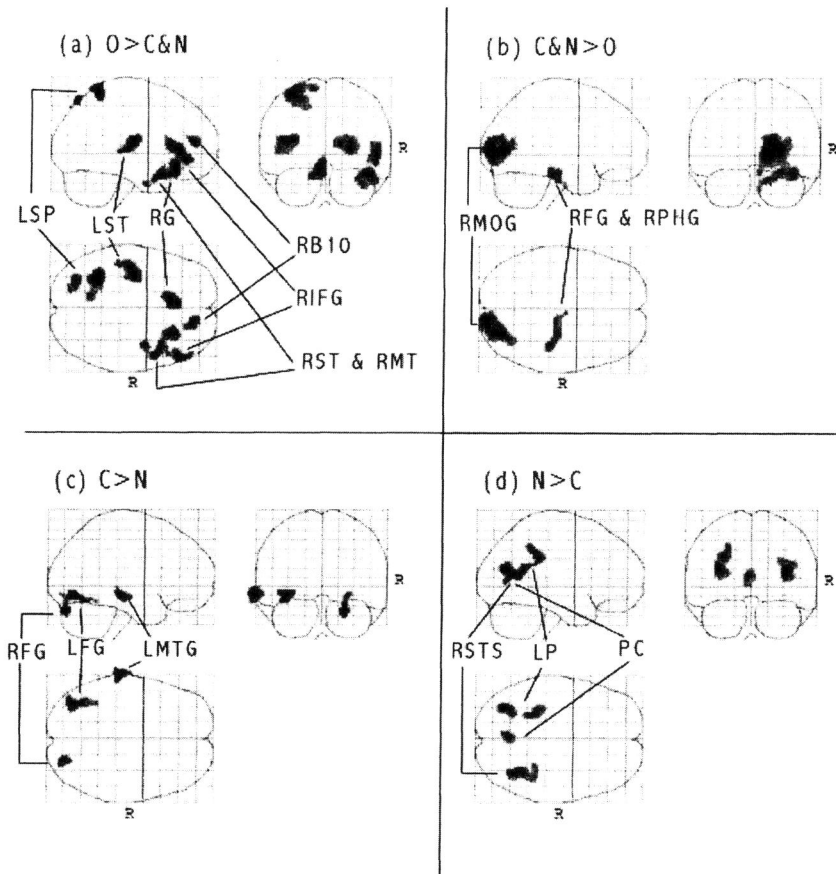

(a) O > C&N

LSP
LST   RG
         RB10
         RIFG
         RST & RMT
R

(b) C&N > O

RMOG   RFG & RPHG
R

(c) C > N

RFG   LFG   LMTG
R

(d) N > C

RSTS   LP   PC
R

FIGURE 1.9. Each panel displays transverse (lower left), sagittal (upper left) and coronal (upper right) views of voxel-clusters showing reliably greater rCBF for (a) old faces than conjunction and new faces (O > C&N clusters), (b) conjunction and new faces than old faces (C&N > O clusters), (c) conjunction faces than new faces (C > N clusters), and (d) new faces than conjunction faces (N > C clusters) in Bartlett, Devous, and Abdi (2000). Each display shows clusters in two dimensions, collapsing the third as if the brain were transparent and only reliable clusters were opaque. Panel a shows reliable O > CN clusters in primarily left-posterior and right-anterior brain regions including the left-superior parietal lobule (LSP), left-superior-temporal gyrus (LST), rectal gyrus (RG), right-prefrontal Brodmann's area 10 (RB10), right-inferior frontal gyrus (RIFG), and the right-superior and right-middle temporal gyri (RST and RMT). Panel b shows reliable C&N > O clusters in two right-posterior areas, the right-middle occipital gryus (RMOG), and the right-fusiform and right-parahippocampal gyri (RFG and RPHG). Panel c shows reliable C > N clusters in the right- and left-fusiform gyri (RFG and LFG), and in the left-middle temporal gyrus (LMTG). Panel d shows reliable N > C clusters in the right-superior temporal sulcus (RSTS), the posterior cingulate (PC), and two nearby left-parietal (LP) areas.

area of medial frontal gyrus (Brodmann 10; see Buckner, 1996; Cabeza & Nyberg, 2000), (2) an insular area near Brodmann 13, (3) the inferior frontal gyrus (Brodmann areas 45, 46, and 47), implicated in working-memory for faces and other stimuli (Buckner, 1996; Courtney, Ungerleider, Keil, & Haxby, 1996; Petrides, 1994; Smith & Jonides, 1999), and (4) the superior and medial temporal gyri (Brodmann areas 21 and 38), implicated in object and face classification (Sergent et al., 1992), and autobiographical memory (Markowitsch, 2000).

Since right-posterior brain regions are known to be critical in face processing (Rhodes, 1985), it might appear puzzling that O > C&N clusters were absent from these areas. There were, however, two right-posterior clusters showing *reduced* rCBF in the old condition as compared to both others (figure 1.9, Panel B). One of these C&N > O clusters was in the right occipital lobe in the region of the cuneus and middle occipital gyrus (Brodmann 17 and 18), overlapping with areas (1) showing reduced activation to repeated faces in a working memory task (Jiang et al., 2000), and (2) increased activation in famous-face classification (Sergent et al., 1992), and visual imagery (Kosslyn, Thompson, Kim, & Alpert, 1995). A second C&N > O cluster extended from the right-anterior fusiform gyrus (Brodmann 20) to the right parahippocampal cortex, previously implicated in famous-face identification (Sergent et al., 1992), as well as in novelty detection (Habib & Lepage, 2000). These C&N > O clusters are in line with observations that facial repetition and familiarity are linked to decreases as well as increases in neural activation (George et al., 1999; Henson, Shallice, & Dolan, 2000; Jiang et al., 2000). Taken together with the O > C&N clusters, they support the existence of a holistic route to face recognition in which old faces differ from conjunctions and new items in (1) producing better configural matches in right-occipital brain regions, (2) being processed as are *non*-novel stimuli in right-medial-temporal regions, and (3) evoking conscious recollection and working-memory processes in left-parietal and right-anterior brain regions.

To explore the brain structures involved in our second eigencomponent, we examined those clusters showing greater activation with conjunctions than new items (C > N clusters) as well as vice versa (N > C clusters). Figure 1.9 (Panel C) shows two C > N clusters in the ventral left and right occipital areas (Brodmann 18, 19, & 37) both of which included the fusiform gyrus and surrounding structures. Although the fusiform activation was bilateral, it subsumed a larger area in the left hemisphere, extending more anteriorly to include the "fusiform face area" (FFA, see George et al., 1999; Henson et al., 2000; Kanwisher, McDermott, & Chun, 1997; Sergent et al., 1992). The leftward asymmetry is in line with recent evidence for greater activation in the left FFA than in the right FFA when matching faces based on features (Rossion et al., 2000). Additionally, the C > N contrast identified an area of the left middle-temporal gyrus (Brodmann 21) that has been linked to word recognition and object classification. The pattern suggests that conjunctions differed from entirely new faces in producing more activation of featural representations in the pos-terior left hemisphere (cf. Rhodes, 1985), along with verbal and/or se-mantic encoding of these representations in the left-temporal lobe. What perhaps is most striking is the lack of any evidence that frontal and parietal brain mechanisms responded more strongly to conjunctions than to new items. As these areas have been linked to conscious recollection, the data support our prior conclusion that feature-matches are seldom the basis for recollection of a face.

The N > C contrast was also of interest. A right-lateralized N > C cluster (Brodmann 22 & 39) spanned the superior temporal sulcus, a pro-posed site of processing changeable features of faces including eye gaze, expression, and lip movement (Haxby, Hoffman & Gobbini, 2000). Other N > C clusters appeared in the posterior cingulate (Brodman 31) and two nearby left-posterior areas that have been linked to successful retrieval from episodic memory (Cabeza & Nyberg, 2000). We view the N > C clusters in light of the hypothesis developed earlier in this paper when discussing age differences (figure 1.4); perhaps new faces are more likely than conjunctions to evoke recollection of information—including both featural and episodic information—that can aid in their rejection as new.

Summary and Conclusions

Starting from the premise that configural processing and featural process-ing both play roles in face recognition, we marshaled evidence that the two types of processing differ qualitatively in the way they are affected by facial inversion: configural processing is more disrupted by inversion, though the qualitative way in which features are interpreted depends on the assignment of directions, and, hence, orientation. We next asked if configural processing is holistic in the sense of extending across large regions of a face, as opposed to encompassing only the internal facial region or immediately adjacent features. Two studies using the Garner-interference paradigm suggested that truly holistic processing is performed by some participants in at least some task conditions. We then turned to a phenomenon of face recognition memory: a new face composed of pre-viously viewed features is often recognized as old. Although this con-junction effect has been attributed to feature-based processing, several be-havioral findings, a computer simulation, and a neuroimaging study all converge on the conclusions that (1) one's sense of consciously recollect-ing a face depends on holistic processing, and (2) perceived familiarity *in the absence of recollection* is often the basis for conjunction false alarms. Taken together, the findings suggest that holistic processing and featural processing represent two routes to face recognition, and that perceived familiarity in the absence of recollection plays a critical role in face-recognition errors.

Notes

Completion of this chapter was aided by National Science Foundation Grant SBR 9515231 to the first and second authors. We thank Michael D. Devous, Sr., of the Nuclear Medicine Center at the University of Texas Southwestern Medical Center, for his support and active collaboration on the neuroimaging study, Susan Jerger for many valuable discussions of attention in face processing, and Marsha Neville-Smith for her contributions to the research on the conjunction effect. We also thank Gillian Rhodes and Mary Peterson for their comments on an earlier version of this chapter.

1. On the other hand, if holistic representations are defined as unparsed with respect to piecemeal features (Tanaka & Farah, 1993), a pixel-based code qualifies as holistic.

2. Contrasts were tested at the .01 level, and were restricted to voxels significant at the .05 level in an omnibus F test.

References

Abdi, H. (1988). A generalized approach for connectionist auto-associative memories: Interpretation, implication and illustration for face processing. In J. Demongeot, T. Hervé, V. Rialle, & C. Roche (Eds.), *Artificial intelligence and cognitive sciences* (pp. 149–166) Manchester: Manchester University Press.

Abdi, H., Valentin, D., & Edelman, B. E. (1999). *Neural networks.* Thousand Oaks, CA: Sage.

Abdi, H., Valentin, D., Edelman, B. E., & O'Toole A. J. (1995). More about the difference between men and women: Evidence from linear neural networks and the principal-component approach. *Perception, 24*, 539–562.

Bartlett, J. C. (1993). Limits on losses in face recognition. In J. Cerella, W. Hoyer, J. Rybash, & M. Commons (Eds.), *Adult information processing: Limits on loss.* (pp. 351–379). New York: Academic Press.

Bartlett, J. C., Devous, M. D., Sr., & Abdi, H. (2000, November). *Regional cerebral blood flow (rCBF) imaging of the facial conjunction effect.* Paper presented at the 41st meeting of the Psychonomic Society, New Orleans.

Bartlett, J. C., & Fulton, A. (1991). Familiarity and recognition of faces in old age. *Memory & Cognition, 19*, 229–238.

Bartlett, J. C., Helm, A., & Jerger, S. (2001). *Selective attention to inner and outer parts of faces: Evidence for holistic and featural processing.* University of Texas at Dallas.

Bartlett, J. C., & Searcy, J. (1993). Inversion and configuration of faces. *Cognitive Psychology, 25*, 281–316.

Bartlett, J. C., Searcy, J. H., & Truxillo, C. (1996, November). *Both parts and wholes affect face recognition.* Paper presented at the 37th annual meeting of the Psychonomic Society, Chicago.

Bartlett, J. C., Strater, L., & Fulton, A. (1991). False recency and false fame of faces in young adulthood and old age. *Memory & Cognition, 19*, 177–188.

Benton, A. L., & Van Allen, M. W. (1968). Impairment in facial recognition in patients with cerebral disease. *Cortex, 4*, 344–358.

Bruce, V., & Humphreys, G. W. (1994). Recognizing objects and faces. *Visual Cognition, 1* (2/3), 141–180.

Buckner, R. L. (1996). Beyond HERA: Contributions of specific prefrontal brain areas to long-term memory retrieval. *Psychological Bulletin and Review, 3*, 149–158.

Cabeza, R., & Kato, T. (2000). Features are also important: Contributions of features tural and configural processing to face recognition. *Psychological Science, 11*, 429–433.

Cabeza, R., & Nyberg, L. (2000). Imaging cognition II: An empirical review of 275 PET and fMRI studies. *Journal of Cognitive Neuroscience, 12*, 1–47.

Carey, S., & Diamond, R. (1994). Are faces perceived as configurations more by adults than by children? *Visual Cognition, 1* (2/3), 253–274.

Chalfonte, B. L., & Johnson, M. K. (1996). Feature memory and binding in young and older adults. *Memory & Cognition, 24*, 403–416.

Courtney, S. M., Ungerleider, L. G., Keil, K., & Jaxby, J. V. (1996). Object and spatial visual-working memory activate separate neural systems in human cortex. *Cerebral Cortex, 6*(1), 39–49.

Devous M. D., Sr. (1995). SPECT functional brain imaging: Technical considerations. *Journal of Neuroimaging, 5*, S2–S13.

Edelman, B. E. (1998). *Placing faces.* Ph.D. Dissertation, University of Texas at Dallas.

Ellis, H. D., Shepherd, J. W., & Davies, G. M. (1979). Identification of familiar and unfamiliar faces from internal and external features: Some implications for theories of face recognition. *Perception, 8*, 431–439.

Endo, M. (1986). Perception of upside-down faces: An analysis from the viewpoint of cue saliency. In H. D. Ellis, M. A. Jeeves, F. Newcombe, & A. Young (Eds.), *Aspects of face processing* (pp. 53–58). Dordrecht: Nijhoff.

Endo, M., Masame, K., & Maruyama, K. (1989). Interference from configuration of a schematic face onto the recognition of its constituent parts. *Tohoku Psychologica Folia, 48*, 97–106.

Endo, M., Masame, K., & Maruyama, K. (1990). A limited use of configural information in the perception of inverted faces. *Tohoku Psychologica Folia, 49*, 114–125.

Etcoff, N. L. (1984). Selective attention to facial identity and facial emotion. *Neuropsychologia, 22*, 281–295.

Farah, M. J., Tanaka, J. W., & Drain, H. M. (1995). What causes the face inversion effect? *Journal of Experimental Psychology: Human Perception and Performance, 21*, 628–634.

Farah, M. J., Wilson, K. D., Drain, H. M., & Tanaka, J. R. (1998). What is "special" about face perception? *Psychological Review, 105*, 482–498.

Freire, A., Lee, K., & Symons, L. A. (2000). The face-inversion effect as a deficit in the encoding of configural information: Direct evidence. *Perception, 29*, 159–170.

Friston, K. J., Holmes, A. P., Worsley, K. J., Poline, J. P., Fritch, C. D., & Frackowiak, R. S. J. (1995). Statistical parametric maps in functional imaging: A general linear approach. *Human Brain Mapping, 2*, 189–210.

Gardiner, J. M., & Richardson-Klavehn (2000). Remembering and knowing. In E. Tulving & F. I. M. Craik (Eds.), *The Oxford handbook of memory* (pp. 229–244). New York: Oxford University Press.

Garner, W. R. (1974). *The processing of information and structure.* New York: Wiley.

George, N., Dolan, R. J., Fink, G., Baylis, G. C., Russell, C., & Driver, J. (1999).

Contrast polarity and face recognition in the human fusiform gyrus. *Nature Neuroscience, 2*, 574–579.

Habib, R., & Lepage, M. (2000). Novelty assessment in the brain. In E. Tulving (Ed.), *Memory, consciousness, and the brain: The Tallinn Conference* (pp. 265–277). Philadelphia: Psychology Press.

Hannigan, S. L., & Reinitz, M. T. (2000). Influences of temporal factors on memory conjunction errors. *Applied Cognitive Psychology, 14*, 309–321.

Haxby, J. V., Hoffman, E. A., & Gobbini, M. I. (2000). The distributed human neural system for face perception. *Trends in Cognitive Sciences, 4*, 223–233.

Haxby, J. V., Ungerdeider, L. G., Horwitz, B., Maisog, J. M., Rapoport, S. L., & Grady, C. L. (1996). Face encoding and recognition in the human brain. *Proceedings of the National Academy of Sciences, USA, 93*, 922–927.

Henson, R., Shallice, T., & Dolan, R. (2000). Neuroimaging evidence for dissociable forms of repetition priming. *Science, 287*, 1269–1272.

Hole, J. (1994). Configural factors in the perception of unfamiliar faces. *Perception, 23*, 65–74.

Jennings, J.M. & Jacoby, L.L. (1997). An opposition procedure for detecting age related deficits in reptition: The telling effects of repetition. *Psychology and Aging, 12*, 352–361.

Jiang, Y., Haxby, J. V., Martin, A., Ungerleider, L. G., & Parasuraman, R. (2000). Complementary neural mechanisms for tracking items in human working memory. *Science, 287*, 643–644.

Jones, T. C., & Jacoby, L. L. (2001). Feature and conjunction errors in recognition memory: Evidence for dual-process theory. *Journal of Memory and Language, 45*, 82–102.

Kanwisher, N., McDermott, J., & Chun, M. M. (1997). The fusiform face area: A module in human extrastriate cortex specialized for face perception. *Journal of Neuroscience, 17*(11) 4302–4311.

Kelley, C. M., & Jacoby, L. J. (2000). Recollection and familiarity: Process-dissociation. In E. Tulving & F. I. M. Craik (Eds.), *The Oxford handbook of memory* (pp. 215–228). New York: Oxford University Press.

Kemp, R., McManus, C., & Piggot, T. (1990). Sensitivity of displacement of facial features in negative and inverted images. *Perception, 19*, 531–543.

Kosslyn, S. M., Thompson, W. L., Kim, I. J., & Alpert, N. M. (1995). Topographical representations of mental images in primary visual cortex. *Nature, 378*, 496–498.

Kroll, N. E. A., Knight, R. T., Metcalfe, J., Wolf, E. S., & Tulving, E. (1996). Cohesion failure as a source of memory illusions. *Journal of Memory and Language, 35*, 176–196.

Leder, H., & Bruce, V. (2000). When inverted faces are recognized: The role of configural information in face recognition. *Quarterly Journal of Experimental Psychology, 53A* (2), 513–536.

LeGal, P. M. (1999). *Cognitive aspects of emotional expression processing.* Ph.D. dissertation, University of Sterling.

Macho, S., & Leder, H. (1998). Your eyes only? A test of interactive influence in the processing of facial features. *Journal of Experimental Psychology: Human Perception and Performance, 24*, 1486–1500.

Markowitsch, H. J. (2000). Neuroanatomy of memory. In E. Tulving & F. I. M. Craik (Eds.), *The Oxford handbook of memory* (pp. 465–484). New York: Oxford University Press.

Moscovitch, M., & Moscovitch, D. A. (2000). Super face-inversion effects for isolated internal or external features, and for fractured faces. *Cognitive Neuroscience, 17* (1/2/3), 201–219.

Moscovitch, M., Winocur, G., & Behrmann, M. (1997). What is special about face recognition? Nineteen experiments on a person with visual object agnosia and dyslexia but normal face recognition. *Journal of Cognitive Neuroscience, 9,* 555–604.

Murray, J. E., Yong, E., & Rhodes, G. (2000). Revisiting the perception of upside-down faces. *Psychological Science, 11,* 492–496.

Neville-Smith, M. Abdi, H., & Bartlett, J. C. (2002). [Simulating the facial conjunction effect]. The University of Texas at Dallas. (Unpublished observations).

O'Toole, A.J., Deffenbacher, K., Valentin, D., & Abdi, H. (1994). Structural aspects of face recognition and the other-race effect. *Memory & Cognition, 22,* 208–224.

Petrides, M. (1994). Frontal lobes and working memory: Evidence from investigations of the effects of cortical excisions in nonhuman primates. In F. Boller & J. Grafman (Eds.), *Handbook of neuropsychology* (vol. 9, pp. 59–82). Amsterdam: Elsevier.

Pomerantz, J. R., Pristach, E. A., & Carson, C. E. (1989). Attention and object perception. In B. E. Shepp & S. Ballesteros (Eds.), *Object perception: Structure and process* (pp. 53–89). Hillsdale, NJ: Erlbaum.

Rakover, S. S., & Teucher, B. (1997). Facial inversion effects: Parts and whole relationship. *Perception & Psychophysics, 1997, 59,* 752–761.

Rapcsak, S. Z., Polster, M. R., Comer, J. F., & Rubens, A. B. (1994). False recognition and misidentification of faces following right hemisphere damage. *Cortex, 30,* 565–583.

Reinitz, M. T., & Hannigan, S. L. (2001). Effects of simultaneous stimulus presentation and attention switching on memory conjunction errors. *Journal of Memory and Language, 44,* 206–219.

Reinitz, M., Lammers, W., & Cochran, B. (1992). Memory conjunction errors: miscombination of stored stimulus features can produce illusions of memory. *Memory & Cognition, 20,* 1–11.

Reinitz, M. T., Morissey, J., & Demb, J. (1994). Role of attention in face encoding. *Journal of Experimental Psychology: Learning, Memory and Cognition, 20,* 161–168.

Rhodes, G. (1985). Lateralized processes in face recognition. *British Journal of Psychology, 76,* 249–271.

Rhodes, G. (1988). Looking at faces: First-order and second-order features as determinants of facial appearance. *Perception, 17,* 43–63.

Rhodes, G. (1993). Configural coding, expertise, and the right-hemisphere advantage for face recognition. *Brain and Cognition, 22,* 19–41.

Rhodes, G., Brake, K., & Atkinson, A. (1993). What's lost in inverted faces? *Cognition, 47,* 25–57.

Rock, I. (1973). *Orientation and form.* New York: Academic Press.

Rossion, B., Dricot, L., Devolder, A., Bodart, J. M., de Gelder, B., & Zoontjes, R. (2000). Hemispheric asymmetries for whole-based and part-based processing in the human fusiform gyrus. *Journal of Cognitive Neuroscience, 12* (5), 793–802.

Schweinberger, S. R., & Soukup, G. R. (1998). Asymmetric relationships among perceptions of facial identity, emotion, and facial speech. *Journal of Experimental Psychology, Human Perception and Performance, 24*, 1748–1765.

Searcy, J. H., & Bartlett, J. C. (1996). Inversion and processing of component and spatial-relational information in faces. *Journal of Experimental Psychology: Human Perception and Performance, 22*, 904–915.

Searcy, J. H., Bartlett, J. C., & Memon, A. (1999). Age differences in accuracy and choosing rates on face recognition and eyewitness identification tasks. *Memory & Cognition, 27*, 538–553.

Sergent, J. (1984). An investigation into component and configural processes underlying face perception. *British Journal of Psychology, 75*, 221–242.

Sergent, J., Ohta, S., & MacDonald, B. (1992). Functional neuroanatomy of face and object processing. *Brain, 115*, 15–36.

Smith, E. E., & Jonides, J. (1999). Storage and executive processes in the frontal lobes. *Science, 283*, 1657–1661.

Talairach, J., & Tournoux, P. R. M. (1998). *Co-planar stereotactic atlas of the human brain*. New York: Thieme Medical Publishers.

Tanaka, J. W., & Farah, M. J. (1993). Parts and wholes in face recognition. *Quarterly Journal of Experimental Psychology, 45* (A3), 34–79.

Tanaka, J. R., & Sengco, J. A. (1997). Parts and their configuration in face recognition. *Memory & Cognition, 25*, 583–592.

Tulving, E. (1983). *Elements of episodic memory*. New York: Oxford University Press.

Tversky, B., & Krantz, D. H. (1969). Similarity of schematic faces: A test of interdimensional additivity. *Perception & Psychophysics, 5*, 124–128.

Valentin, D., Abdi, H., & Edelman, B. (1999). From rotation to disfiguration: Testing a dual-strategy model for recognition of faces across view angles. *Perception, 28*, 817–824.

Valentin, D., Abdi, H., & O'Toole, A. J. (1994). Categorization and identification of human face images by neural networks: A review of the linear autoassociator and principal component approaches. *Journal of Biological Systems, 2*, 413–429.

Valentine, T. (1988). Upside-down faces: A review of the effect of inversion upon face recognition. *British Journal of Psychology, 79*, 471–491.

Young, A. W., Hellawell, D., & Hay, D. C. (1987). Configural information in face perception. *Perception, 16*, 747–759.

Yuille, A. L. (1991). Deformable templates for face recognition. *Journal of Cognitive Neuroscience, 3*, 59–70.

2

The Holistic Representation of Faces

JAMES W. TANAKA AND MARTHA J. FARAH

When we see the face of a familiar friend or colleague, there is a flash of recognition that occurs instantaneously and without conscious effort. Introspectively, speeded recognition of a familiar face appears *not* to depend on the identification of a particular facial feature, such as a distinctive nose or pair of eyes, as much as on the recognition of the whole face that emerges from the features. Nearly a century ago, psychologists characterized this type of visual apprehension as a perceptual *gestalt* where the perception of the whole stimulus takes precedence over the sum of its individual parts. While face recognition provides the prime example of gestalt perception, this concept has proved to be elusive and difficult to operationalize in the laboratory. In our work, gestalt or *holistic* recognition is formalized in an experimental paradigm where recognition of a face part or object part is measured when presented in the context of the whole stimulus relative to when presented in isolation (see Kimchi, chapter 9, this volume, for other experimental approaches to holistic processing). We argue that holistic recognition is indexed by the extent to which part recognition is facilitated by the presence of the whole face or object context.

While in principle, holistic recognition can be employed for the recognition of virtually any class of object, the central focus of this chapter is whether face recognition can be distinguished from other types of object recognition according to its holistic processes. In this chapter, we will use the term "object recognition" in reference to the recognition of nonface objects only and review experiments that address the holistic recognition of face and nonface objects. We begin the chapter by comparing the holistic perception of faces to the more analytic perception of misoriented face and nonface objects (section 1). We then examine the role that holistic and part-based representations play in the recognition of faces and objects (section 2) and describe how configural information is encoded in holistic representations and part-based representations (section 3). The question of how learning and experience influence holistic face recognition is examined by studying the holistic face recognition processes of young children who have considerably less experience recognizing faces than older children and adults (section 4). The effects of experience on holistic recognition are further explored by investigating the holistic recognition of experts who specialize in the recognition of particular classes of objects (i.e., cells, cars, dogs, artificial stimuli; section 5). At the neuroantomical level, there is evidence to suggest that specific brain areas support the holistic processing of faces and perhaps, that these areas can be recruited for other forms of expert recognition (section 6). Finally, these findings are summarized in the context of a model of visual object recognition based on a continuum of holistic to part-based representations for faces, objects, and words (section 7).

By reviewing the evidence from studies of normal participants, children, and brain-damaged patients, we propose that as objects of recognition, faces can be distinguished from nonface objects (e.g., cars, houses) in the degree to which they are represented holistically. That is, whereas normal object recognition depends on the decomposition of the object into its constituent parts, the holistic face hypothesis maintains that faces are represented and recognized as undifferentiated wholes.

1. Perception of the Parts and Wholes of Faces

Given that all human faces share the same basic features (i.e., eyes, nose, mouth) arranged in the same general configuration, the capacity to distinguish one face from another must depend on the fine-grained analysis of a face's featural and configural information. Despite the formidable demands placed on the face-processing system, humans are able to quickly and accurately identify a familiar face in a single glance, seemingly without much conscious effort. What are the perceptual processes underlying our ability to abstract information from a face stimulus? Psychologists have employed visual matching and masking paradigms in an attempt to understand the perceptual processes of face perception. Here, we discuss evidence drawn from these studies and their implications concerning the special properties of face perception in contrast to other forms of object perception.

A fundamental question in face perception is whether the features of a face are processed in a parallel or a serial manner (Sternberg, 1969). That is, when we look at a face, do we inspect each feature individually or do we process the features simultaneously in a parallel? This question has been investigated using a sequential matching paradigm where participants are asked to judge whether two consecutively presented faces are identical or different. Using this paradigm, Bradshaw and Wallace (1971) found that when the number of mismatching features is increased in the different trials, reaction time decreased. Based on these findings, they argued that the face features were scanned in a serial, self-terminating search; otherwise, if features were processed simultaneously in parallel, a single feature mismatch should be as readily detected as multiple feature mismatches.

However, findings from other face matching studies were not consistent with Bradshaw and Wallace's (1971) serial account of face perception. In their experiments, Smith and Nielsen (1970) varied the number of features in the same trials (e.g., faces with eyes and nose versus faces with an eyes, nose, mouth). They found that the number of same features did not influence reaction times, suggesting that participants were not performing a feature-by-feature comparison, but perceiving the face as an unified whole. Following a similar logic, Sergent (1984) reasoned that if facial features are perceived independently, the time to make a different response when faces varied by two features should never be faster than the time to make a different response when faces varied by the most salient of the two features. She found the reaction time to differences in chin contours was faster than differences in internal spacing between the nose and mouth. Contrary to the featural position, differences in chin contour and internal spacing produced even faster reaction times than differences in chin contour alone. Moreover, this effect was found for upright, but not inverted faces. Based on these data, Sergent concluded that whereas some features may be processed independently of each other, information from other features are combined into a more integral or holistic representation (Garner, 1974).

While the foregoing studies suggest that the features of a face are processed in parallel, they do not address whether this perception is different from the perception of features from nonface objects. This issue is of interest because much of the research on face recognition (to be discussed in the next section) has focused on the question of whether faces are recognized via a different process than other kinds of objects. Farah, Wilson, Drain, and Tanaka (1998) investigated the perceptual basis of face, object, and word recognition. In this study, participants performed a same-different matching task in which an upright face, an inverted face, a house, or a word stimulus was presented briefly, followed by a mask and a second stimulus of the same type. In a previous word perception study, Johnston and McClelland (1980) showed that words were equally masked by whole word patterns and nonword letter patterns, suggesting that word representations are decomposed into letter parts prior to recognition. Following this logic, Farah et al. (1998) reasoned that if faces are perceived as wholes rather than as parts, a whole-face mask should be more disruptive to whole-face matching performance than a mask consisting of face parts. In contrast, whole or fragmented masks of inverted faces, houses, and words should have little effect on the matching performance of these nonholistic stimuli. These predictions were borne out by their results in which whole face masks selectively disrupted the perception of normal faces whereas whole and part masks equally impaired the perception of inverted faces, houses, and words. These results suggest that whereas objects such as inverted faces, houses, and words are perceived analytically with respect to their parts, upright faces are perceived holistically—in terms of the whole face.

Are different attentional systems employed for the holistic processing of faces versus the analytic processing used for inverted faces and nonface objects? Using a divided attention task, Palermo and Rhodes (2002) asked participants to match two flanker faces while encoding a centrally presented, upright target face. When the flanking faces were presented in their upright orientation, they found that the matching task interfered with performance on the encoding task. However, when the flanking faces were inverted, the matching task no longer interfered with the encoding task. According to Palermo and Rhodes, when two tasks compete for the same holistic attentional resource, dual-task performance suffers. However, in the situation where the tasks tap into separate holistic and analytic attentional resources, dual-task performance is relatively unaffected. From these results, they argue that the resources of holistic and analytic attention can be independently recruited depending on the perceptual task or tasks at hand.

2. Holistic Representations in Face Recognition

If faces are perceived holistically, are they also recognized holistically? Upon closer analysis, the holistic approach seems to be at odds with conventional models of object recognition that emphasize the decomposition of an object into parts prior to recognition (Biederman, 1987; Hoffman & Richards, 1985; Marr & Nishihara, 1978). (For the alternative view-based approach, see chapters in this volume by Tarr [7] and Bülthoff & Bülthoff [6]). In Biederman's Recognition-by-Components (RBC) model (Biederman, 1987), a chair, for example, would be decomposed into its constituent parts of legs, back, and seat at a relatively early stage of processing. Following the decomposition stage in Biederman's model, the spatial configuration of parts are specified relative to one another so that the chair parts are described as the leg parts are below the seat part, which are positioned above the back part and so on. The description of an object's parts and their relative positions is said to be "viewpoint-independent" in the sense that this description is not influenced by the viewpoint of the observer. According to the RBC model, object recognition occurs by matching the parts (e.g., GEONS) and their spatial arrangement to the appropriate structural description in object memory.

In contrast, the holistic hypothesis maintains that face recognition differs from other types of object recognition in that it involves relatively little part decomposition. Obviously, faces *do* contain identifiable parts or features, such as the eyes, nose, and mouth. However, unlike the parts, such as GEONS, used to recognize most objects, the holistic approach maintains that the features of a face are not independently specified in the face representation. According to the holistic hypothesis, the primary representation in face recognition is at the level of the whole face. Hence, faces are recognized in terms of their undifferentiated wholes, not in terms of their constituent parts.

While the claim that a face is recognized more in terms of its whole rather than its parts is not new or even controversial, empirical methods for testing the holistic hypothesis were difficult to operationalize in the laboratory. Borrowing from previous experimental methods, we (Tanaka & Farah, 1991) developed a test of the part/whole distinction based on the following assumption: if some portion of a stimulus is represented as a part of a stimulus, then when viewed in isolation, that portion should be easier to recognize as part of the stimulus than other portions that are not explicitly represented as parts. The psychological reality of good part information in recognition was demonstrated in several experiments. Bower and Glass (1976) found that when participants were asked to draw a pattern from memory, some portions of a stimulus provided better retrieval cues than others. In other work, Palmer (1977) asked participants to independently rate the goodness of fragments from geometric patterns and found that the fragments rated high in part goodness served as better cues in recognition than fragments that were rated low. Not unexpectedly, parts that were rated high in goodness conformed to Gestalt principles of perceptual organization, such as closure and good continuation.

In face recognition, the holistic hypothesis predicts that the recognizability of the part is significantly enhanced when it is embedded in the whole face than when shown in isolation. To test this prediction, Tanaka and Farah (1993) instructed participants to memorize a set of normal faces and comparison stimuli (i.e., scrambled faces, inverted faces, houses; see figure 2.1). After learning, participants identified the face parts (eyes, nose, mouth) or house parts in a two-forced choice recognition task where the part was presented in isolation and in the context of the whole face. Note that in the whole-face test condition, the target, and the foil faces were identical with the exception of the critical part under test. For example, if participants were asked to identify Joe's nose, recognition of the nose was tested in the isolated-part condition (figure 2.2a) and in the whole-face condition, where the face outline and nontarget features (e.g., face outline, hair, eyes, mouth) were held constant (figure 2.2b). Hence, in the whole-face condition, the nontarget parts by themselves provided no additional

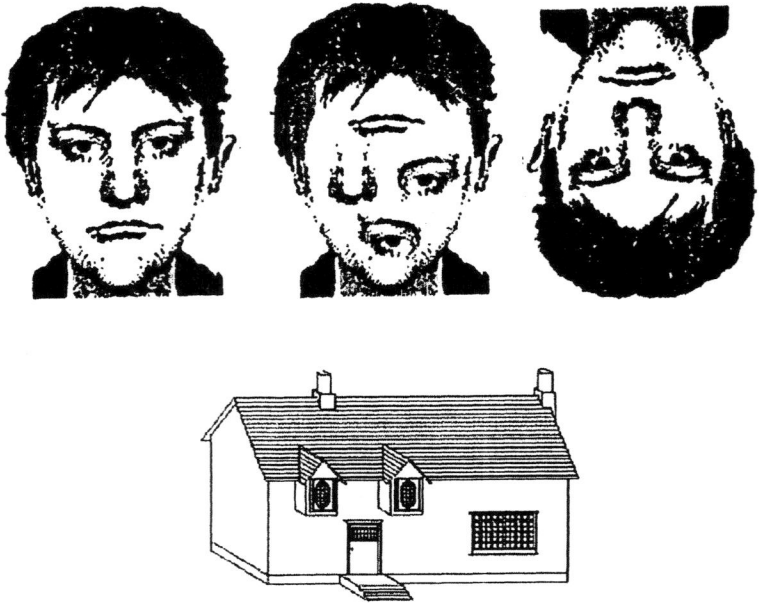

FIGURE 2.1. Sample of whole face, scrambled face, inverted face, and house stimuli used in Tanaka and Farah (1993).

diagnostic information, but served as a context for the target part. In this paradigm, holistic encoding was measured by how much better participants were able to recognize the part when it was tested in the context of the whole face versus when tested alone.

The critical finding was that participants recognized parts from normal faces better when presented in the whole face than when shown in isolation, as shown in figure 2.3. In contrast, recognition of the parts from scrambled faces, inverted faces, and houses was essentially the same when tested in isolation or in the whole-object context. Assuming that the relative magnitude of the part/whole recognition difference provides a measure of holistic processing, these results suggest that intact, upright faces are recognized more holistically than scrambled faces, inverted faces, or houses (see Donnelly & Davidoff, 1999, for an alternative account).

A robust finding in the face-recognition literature is that inversion disproportionately impairs the recognition of faces relative to nonface objects (Valentine & Bruce, 1986; Yarmey, 1971; Yin, 1969; also Murray, Rhodes, & Schuchinsky (chapter 3, this volume) for a review of the face-inversion literature). Tanaka and Farah's (1993) findings suggest a plausible explanation for the face-inversion effect: if face recognition relies more heavily on holistic representations than other kinds of object recognition, and if inversion is especially disruptive to holistic encoding, then inversion

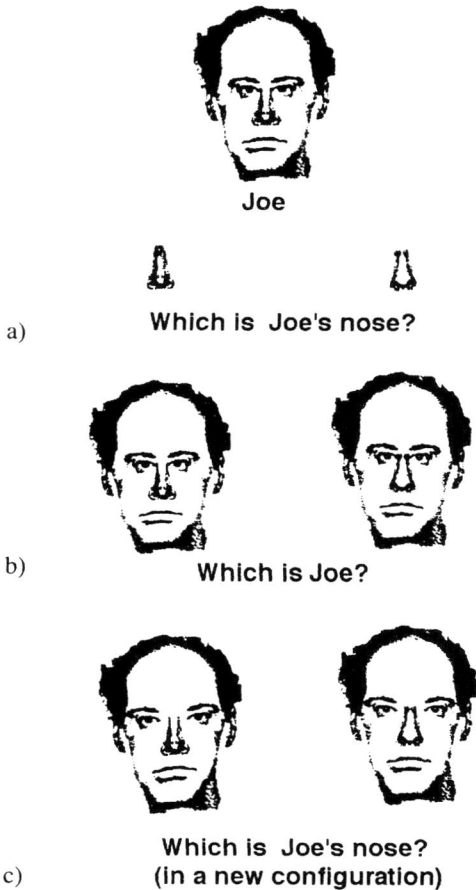

FIGURE 2.2. Example of holistic recognition paradigm. Joe's nose feature is tested in (a) isolation (b) in the whole face and (c) in a new configuration. Reprinted, with permission, from Tanaka and Sengco (1997).

should be more detrimental to face recognition than other kinds of object recognition. As a test of this account, Farah, Drain, and Tanaka (1995) attempted to undo the effects of face inversion by inducing participants to encode faces more analytically—that is, more in terms of their features than in terms of the whole face. This was accomplished by asking participants to learn a piecemeal version in which the face outline, eyes, nose, and mouth features were shown in separate boxes. After learning either a piecemeal face or a normal whole-face control, participants identified the intact version shown in either its upright or its inverted orientation. For faces learned as whole faces, the expected face-inversion result was obtained where whole faces were much better recognized in their upright

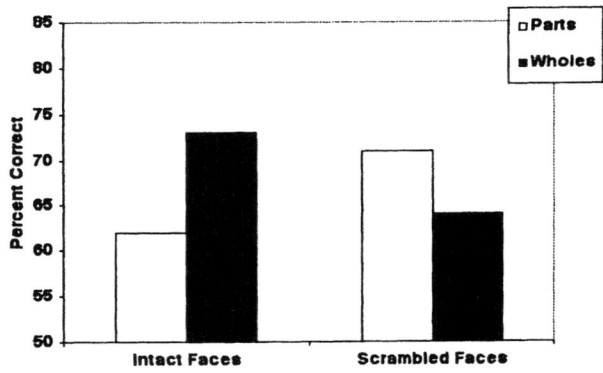

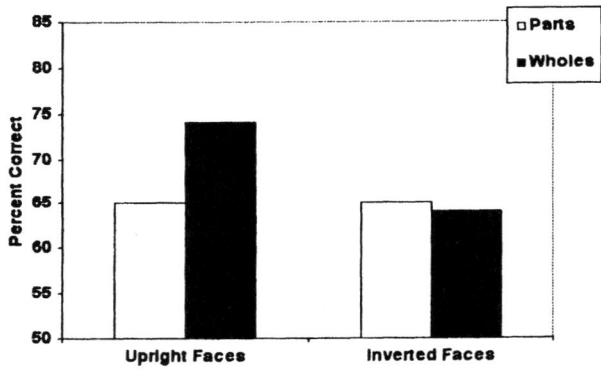

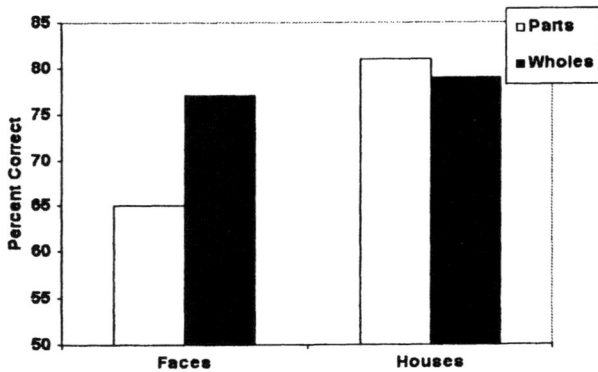

FIGURE 2.3. Results from the parts/wholes test with normal faces, scrambled faces, inverted faces, and houses.

orientation than in their inverted orientation. However, for the faces learned as piecemeal features, recognition was the same whether the whole faces were tested in their upright or their inverted orientation. Thus, if the holistic face encoding can be inhibited, the effects of face inversion are significantly reduced.

3. Configural Information and Holistic Representations in Face Recognition

In a holistic face representation, there is an intimate relation between the features of a face and their spatial configuration. As shown in figure 2.4, changes in configural information can dramatically alter our impressions of a highly familiar face, such as Bill Clinton. Consistent with this observation, Hosie, Ellis, and Haig (1988) found that recognition of a well-known celebrity was significantly disrupted by configural changes to the eyes, nose, and mouth features. In addition, they found that changes in the spatial arrangement of these features were more detrimental to recognition than changes to external features, such as the hairline. These results suggest that the face-recognition system is acutely tuned to information about the configuration of the internal features of a familiar face. Indeed, Haig (1984) found that after a brief familiarization period, participants were able to detect slight changes in the distances among the eyes, nose, and mouth features of a face; in some instances, sensitivity approached the limits of visual acuity!

Perhaps the most striking demonstration of configural influences in the recognition of familiar faces was carried out by Young and colleagues (Young, Hellawell, & Hay, 1987). They developed an ingenious technique in which the top half of a well-known person was fused with the bottom half of another well-known person. The configural cues in the composite face created the impression of a completely novel face such that participants in their study had difficulty recognizing the identities of the separate face halves. However, if Young et al. disrupted configural cues by misaligning the top and bottom halves or by inverting the composite face, participants improved in their ability to recognize the face halves. Young et al.'s results suggest that the features of a face are not perceived independently of one another, but are integrated in a configural representation.

The notion that the configuration of features can play as large a role in face recognition as the features themselves was addressed in a multidimensional scaling study by Rhodes (1988). Rhodes drew a distinction between two types of facial information: first-order featural information and second-order featural information. First-order features referred to the separable parts of a face identified by common labels such as eye, nose, and mouth. Second-order features or feature configuration, on the other hand, refer to the specific shape of a feature as well as the spatial relation between features. In Rhodes' analysis, both first-order features (i.e., eyes,

FIGURE 2.4. Changing configural information in the face of former U.S. President Bill Clinton. The photograph at the far left is the original. In the middle photograph, the distance between the eyes has been increased. In the photograph on the right, the distance between the eyes and the distance between nose and the mouth features have been increased.

eyebrows, and mouth) and the second-order features (i.e., spatial relations between the eyes and eyebrows, between the eyes and nose, and between the mouth and chin shape) emerged as significant predictors of face similarity. These findings suggest that faces are perceived in terms of both their individual features and the configuration of those features.

How is configural information computed in a face representation? Using a different terminology than Rhodes (1988), Diamond and Carey (1986) distinguished between what they called first-order relational information and second-order relational information. First-order relational properties refer to the discrete, categorical relations that describe the configuration of object features. For example, a first-order description of a face would include such statements as "the eyes are above the nose" and "the mouth is below the nose." Second-order relational properties, on the other hand, specify the spatial configuration of a stimulus in reference to the prototypical object. Second-order relational properties assume that object is a member of an object class that has a well-defined prototypical configuration, such as automobiles, dogs, and faces. A further assumption of Diamond and Carey's hypothesis is that the observer must be equipped with the knowledge or expertise of the configural prototype to detect the second-order relational information of a stimulus. Diamond and Carey suggested that of the stimuli whose spatial structures would allow for the encoding of second-order relational properties, faces are the only class of stimuli for which most people have sufficient expertise to have access to second-order relational properties.

Diamond and Carey employed the inversion paradigm to test their second-order relational hypothesis. Consistent with the prediction that inversion disrupts sensitivity to second-order relational properties, Diamond and Carey found that dog judges demonstrated an inversion effect for dog breeds in their area of expertise that was equal to the inversion effect they showed for faces. Tanaka and Farah (1991) tested Diamond and Carey's explanation of the inversion effect by comparing the size of the inversion effect obtained when participants recognized dot patterns that were distinguishable with respect to either their first-order or second-order relational properties. Contrary to Diamond and Carey's claims, it was found that inversion had comparable effects on the recognition of the two types of dot patterns even when participants were sensitive to the second-order relational properties of the stimuli. These findings indicate that second-order relational properties were no more vulnerable than first-order relational properties to manipulations of inversion. One caveat to the research was that although the participants were proficient enough to distinguish the dot patterns according to their second-order relational properties, they were not dot experts to the same degree as most people are face experts or dog experts as the participants used in the Diamond and Carey study. Thus, our results are informative about the role of second-order relational information in the face inversion effect, but not about the interaction between second-order relational information and expertise.

While the face-recognition processes are finely tuned to the configural properties of a face, it is not clear how configural information is represented in memory. On one hand, it has been suggested that the spatial configuration may be encoded as a kind of local feature in the face representation (Bruce, 1988; Rhodes, Brake, & Atkinson, 1993). For example, the distance between the eyes could be encoded as a spatial value, independent from a description of the eyes themselves. According to this approach, featural and configural information contribute two separate sources of input to a face-recognition system. Disruption of either type of information should produce decrements in recognition. One limitation of the featural versus configural distinction is that these two types of information are interdependent to the extent that any changes in a facial feature (e.g., shape of the nose) will produce concomitant changes in the configural relations it shares with other features (e.g., spatial distances among nose, eyes, and mouth).

In contrast to the relational view, the holistic view maintains that featural information and configural information are not distinguishable in the face representation. Hence, according to the holistic hypothesis, changes in one type of information (configuration) should affect memory for the other type of information (feature). As a test of this prediction, Tanaka and Sengco (1997) asked participants to learn faces in one configuration and then tested their recognition for a part when presented in isolation, in a new configuration or in an old configuration. For example, as shown in figure 2.2, participants may have learned to recognize a version of Joe with his eyes spaced close together. They were then asked to recognize Joe's nose when the target and foil noses were presented in isolation (figure 2.2a), in the previously learned whole face with the eyes spaced close together (figure 2.2b) and in a new configuration with eyes spaced far apart (figure 2.2c). They found that recognition of a part was best when tested in the old configuration, followed by performance in the new configuration, and was poorest when tested in isolation. Importantly, they found that modifying the distance between the eyes impaired recognition of other nose and mouth features—features whose spatial locations were not directly changed.

These findings support the integration of featural and configural information in a unitary holistic representation. These results do not seem consistent with the idea that configural information is encoded independently from featural information for several reasons. First, if participants in the Tanaka and Sengco (1997) experiment encoded the spatial distance between the eyes independent from the information about the eye part itself, it is not clear why recognition of the eye feature should be disrupted when its configural properties are changed. Second, an independent spatial coding scheme could not account for the impaired recognition of nose and mouth features—features whose spatial properties were not directly changed in the new configuration. Of course, it is possible that a large number of spatial distances (e.g., the distance between the eyes and nose, the distance between the eyes and mouth, etc.) could be simultaneously and independently encoded, but such an encoding process would be computationally cumbersome and functionally equivalent to a holistic representation.

4. Face Recognition in Children

Although experiments with very young infants indicate that humans are born with an innate preference for facelike stimuli (Johnson & Morton, 1991), other research has shown that normal face-processing abilities are not fully developed until about the age of 12. The development of face-processing abilities is shown in studies where older children (12-year-olds) perform better than younger children (6-year-olds) on tasks involving face perception (Ellis, 1992; Saltz & Siegel, 1967) and face recognition (Carey, Diamond, & Woods, 1980). However, an important question is whether these age-related differences in face processing reflect the gradual enhancement of an existing face mechanism or whether there is a discontinuous shift in processing from one face mechanism to another.

The initial behavioral evidence supported the latter viewpoint, specifically that young children perceive faces in a fundamentally different manner from adults. Carey and Diamond (1977) found that 8- and 10-year-old children, like adults, demonstrated the normal face inversion effect such that faces were better recognized in their upright orientation than in the inverted orientation. Unexpectedly, 6-year-olds showed no face inversion effect such that they recognized inverted faces equally as well as upright faces. Carey and Diamond speculated that 6-year-olds were using a featural encoding strategy for processing upright and inverted faces. They hypothesized that around 8 years of age, children switched from a feature-based strategy to a configural approach to face recognition. Some evidence to support this claim was reported in a follow-up experiment where they found that 6-year-olds were more easily misled by featural changes in faces, such as changes in paraphernalia and facial expressions, than 8- and 10-year-olds.

Other researchers have challenged Carey and Diamond's encoding switch claims (Flin, 1985; Valentine, 1988). Flin (1985) argued that the absence of a face inversion effect in the 6-year-old might be the result of floor effects if the recognition task used by Carey and Diamond was too difficult. In her experiment, Flin modified the task so that it was more appropriate for the abilities of the younger children. She found that while overall face recognition performance improved with age, d' values between upright and inverted face conditions remained essentially constant for the 6-, 8-, and 10-year-old participants. Flin claimed that when age-related performance differences are taken into account, there is little evidence to support the encoding switch hypothesis.

Consistent with this interpretation, Carey and Diamond (1994) found in a more recent study that young children are sensitive to configural properties of a face. Using Young et al.'s (1987) composite face recognition paradigm described in section 3, Carey and Diamond found that 6-year-old children, like the 10-year-olds and the adults, were slower to recognize composite faces of the schoolmates when they were properly aligned than when they were misaligned. However, composite interference was found only when the faces were presented in their upright orientation; when the faces were inverted, young children, like the older children, recognized the inverted composite faces as quickly as their noncomposite versions. Once again, these findings suggest that any differences in the face-recognition abilities of young children versus those of older children and adults reflect differences in degree, not kind.

While the above findings indicate that young children, like adults, are influenced by configural information in face recognition, it is a separate issue as to whether they encode faces holistically. The parts/wholes paradigm described above provides a good test of the holistic hypothesis. Tanaka, Kay, Grinnell, Stansfield, and Szechter (1998) administered the parts and wholes test in their upright and inverted orientations to groups of 6-, 8-, and 10-year-old children. The main finding of their study was that when presented with upright faces, overall performance of the children improved with age, but the magnitude of the holistic effect (i.e., the difference between recognition of the part in isolation and in the whole face) remained constant across the three age groups. For inverted faces, there was no overall improvement with age nor was there any evidence of holistic representation. Thus, by 6 years, it appears that young children, similar to their older counterparts, encode faces as holistic representations.

Is there a critical period for developing the ability to process configural information in faces? Recently, LeGrand, Mondloch, Maurer, and Brent (2001) found that children deprived of patterned visual input at a very young age were impaired in their ability to process configural, but not featural, aspects of a face. In their study, the target population was a group of children who underwent corrective surgery to remove dense central cataracts shortly after birth (1 month to 6 months). Nine years after surgery, these children were tested for their recognition of featural and configural face information. The children with cataract surgery performed comparably to age-matched control participants on a face-matching task requiring the detection of a featural change. However, these children were selectively impaired in their ability to detect changes in face configuration (e.g., moving the position of eyes and mouth) relative to control participants. According to the researchers, the impoverished visual input brought out by the dense cataracts impeded the development of normal face-processing abilities in the children. However, this was not a global impairment in configural perception because these children performed normally on a task requiring the discrimination of geometric patterns that differed in their internal features. Le Grand et al. speculated that the selectivity of this deficit indicates a separate system for processing configural information in faces that is different from the system used for processing configural information in nonface objects.

5. Object Expertise and Holistic Representations

While much of the developmental evidence suggests that face recognition is somehow distinct from other forms of object recognition, there is an alternative account to the faces are special claim. Among the thousands of objects that humans are able to recognize, faces are arguably the most ubiquitous and the most ecologically important—so much so that in order to be a competent member of any social group, all people must become face experts (Carey, 1992). Like other kinds of perceptual experts (e.g., birdwatchers, dog judges; Tanaka & Taylor, 1991), face experts must individuate familiar faces quickly, accurately, and at specific levels of abstraction (Tanaka, 2001). That is, like a bird expert who can effortlessly identify a bird at the subordinate level of yellow-rumped warbler or a dog expert who recognizes a dog as a border collie, experts in face recognition can easily individuate a familiar face in terms of its specific identity, such as "Tom Cruise" or "Woody Allen." Given that holistic representations facilitate expert face recognition, it is conceivable that holistic representations might also facilitate other forms of expert object recognition. In this sense, holistic representations may not be uniquely face-specific, but are employed to subserve other types of perceptual expertise.

As a test of the expert holistic hypothesis, the holistic strategies of real-world experts who specialized in the recognition of particular classes of objects were examined (Tanaka et al., 1996, as described in Tanaka & Gauthier, 1997). If holistic recognition results from general expertise rather than face-specific processes, it follows that individuals who have significant experience in other object domains should demonstrate holistic representation for the recognition of objects in the domain of expertise. To test this prediction, expert participants who had extensive experience in the recognition of biological cells, automobiles, or Rottweiler dogs were recruited. Cells, cars, and Rottweiler dogs were selected as the appropriate comparison stimuli for faces because, like faces, these objects had local identifiable features that were organized in a prototypical configuration. Using the parts/wholes paradigm, the experts were asked to identify parts of objects from their domain of expertise as well as parts from faces tested in isolation or in the whole object (face) context (as shown in figure 2.5). Contrary to the expertise hypothesis, experts did not demonstrate greater holistic effects for recognition of objects in their knowledge domain than novices. Do these results argue against the expertise explanation of holistic recognition? Not necessarily. The fact that cell, car, and dog expertise does not rely on the generation of holistic representations for those objects does not necessarily mean that some other, untested form of expertise does not require holistic representation.

In laboratory studies of expertise, Gauthier and Tarr and associates (Gauthier & Tarr, 1997; Gauthier, Williams, Tarr, & Tanaka, 1998) trained participants to recognize artificial Greeble objects. Greebles were designed to be structurally similar to faces in that all Greebles had the same basic features arranged in a canonical configuration. After training, it was found that Greeble experts recognized parts reliably faster than Greeble novices when those same parts were shown in an original configuration but not when viewed in a new configuration. Moreover, for experts, changing the spatial position of one Greeble part disrupted the recognition of the other parts whose spatial positions were unchanged. These findings are consistent with Tanaka and Sengco's (1997) evidence that changing the inter-eye distance in a face disrupted recognition of the nose and mouth features. Thus, for people who are expert in the recognition of faces or Greebles, the distinction between featural and configural information is blurred in the sense that changing one type of information (i.e., configural) affects recognition of the other type (i.e., featural). The Greeble findings indicate that, like faces, other nonface objects can be represented holistically if the special conditions of face recognition can be reproduced. That is, holistic recognition is most likely to be in evidence when the following conditions are met: (1) exemplars of the object category share the same degree of visual complexity and structural similarity as faces and (2) fast,

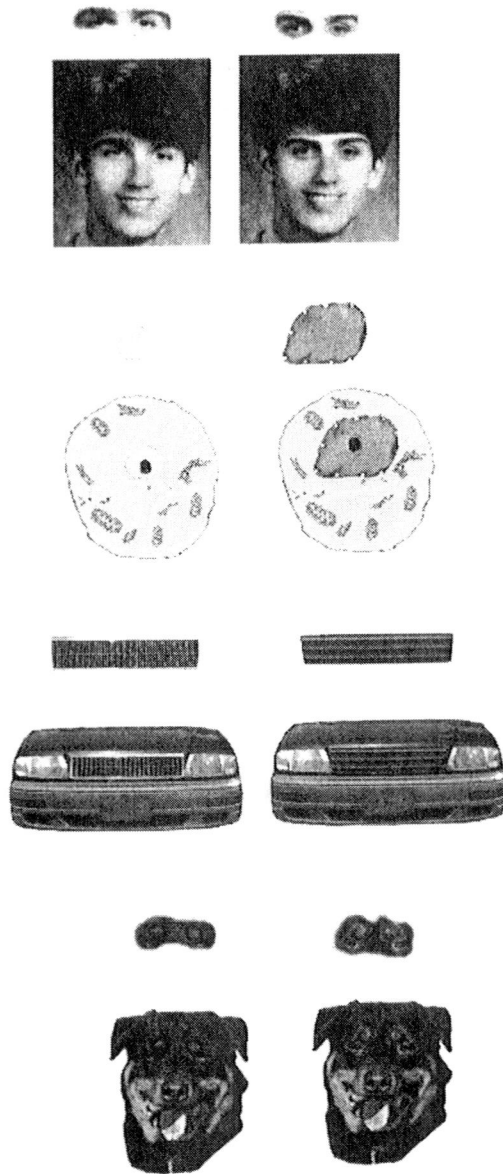

FIGURE 2.5. Examples of the parts and wholes stimuli used to test face, cell, car, and dog expertise. After Tanaka and Gauthier (1997).

accurate, and specific (i.e., expert) recognition of these objects is required. While the Greeble work demonstrates that holistic representation is not exclusive to faces, the work done with real-world experts indicates that faces are privileged in the sense that they are the best example of holistic recognition in the real world.

6. Holistic Face Representations and the Brain

An important question in vision research is whether the cognitive processes and neural mechanisms recruited for the recognition of faces are somehow distinct from the processes used for the recognition of other kinds of objects. On the behavioral side, we have argued that face recognition involves holistic processing whereas normal object recognition relies on part processing. On the neurological side, brain imaging experiments by several researchers (Kanwisher, McDermott, & Chun, 1997; Puce, Allison, Gore, & McCarthy, 1995; Sergent, Ohta, & MacDonald, 1992) have revealed that the extrastriate area of the temporal cortex, a region referred to as the fusiform face area (FFA), is differentially activated when people view faces relative to other objects. Although it is tempting to conclude that the FFA is responsible for holistic analysis, such a conclusion is unwarranted given that face recognition differs from other kinds of object recognition in a variety of ways (e.g., faces are recognized at a more subordinate level, are perceptually more complex, are more familiar, are socially more important, and carry more affective information than nonface objects). However, compelling evidence linking FFA activation to holistic analysis has been provided by Gauthier, Tarr, Anderson, Skudlarksi, and Gore (1999), where they found that an increase in FAA activation was correlated with holistic recognition of Greebles. While faces differ from Greebles in many other ways (as mentioned above), these results suggest that both types of recognition might recruit the FFA for purposes of holistic recognition.

A more direct connection between holistic representation and brain function is shown by neuropsychological studies of brain-damaged individuals with prosopagnosia. Prosopagnosia is the selective impairment of face-recognition ability due to brain injury (Farah, 1990, 2000). What is striking about prosopagnosia is that although these patients experience modest difficulty recognizing common objects, they are far more impaired in their recognition of faces, failing to recognize the faces of close friends, associates, family members, and even their own face. Do prosopagnosic patients fail to process faces holistically? As discussed in previous sections, holistic processes are inhibited when a face is turned upside down, as evidenced by the face inversion effect. To examine the effects of prosopagnosia on the face inversion effect, Farah, Wilson, Drain, and Tanaka (1995) tested patient LH for his recognition of upright and inverted faces.

Surprisingly, LH demonstrated an inverted inversion effect where his recognition of upside down faces was superior to his recognition of upright faces. They interpreted this finding in terms of a face-specific processing module that is mandatorially engaged by upright faces in both normal adults and prosopagnosic patients. However, in the case of prosopagnosic patients, such as LH, the face-processing module is damaged to the point where holistic recognition of upright faces is inferior to the featural processes used for recognizing inverted faces. Similarly, it has been shown that disrupting the spatial configuration of a face has little effect on LH's face-recognition abilities—that is, he performed poorly whether the spatial configuration of the face was intact or scrambled (Farah, 1995). Thus, while LH's featural processing of inverted faces was fully functional, his compromised face processor could not take advantage of configural information provided by upright faces.

7. Words, Objects, and Faces: The Parts-to-Wholes Continuum

In this chapter, we have contrasted the characteristics of holistic representations with the characteristics of part-based or featural representations. However, by drawing distinctions between these two types of representations, we do not mean to imply that their differences are categorical. Instead, it is more plausible to assume that the representation of any visual pattern lies along a holistic-to-featural continuum where some objects are weighted more toward a holistic representation and others are biased toward a featural representation. In our work, we have focused on the holistic aspects of face recognition and hypothesized that among the many objects that humans are able to recognize, faces lie on the extreme end of the holistic continuum. Other evidence indicates that visual patterns, such as words, lie on the opposite, parts-based end of the continuum as shown by Johnston and McClelland (1980).

An analysis of the breakdowns that occur in face, object, and word recognition owing to brain damage lends further support for the proposal of two types of visual representation. Whereas all pairwise combinations of face, object, and word recognition deficits are logically dissociable due to brain injury, only certain combinations of impairments seem to occur together. Specifically, in a review of 99 published cases, Farah (1991, 1997) found no unambiguous cases of intact object recognition with impaired face and word recognition or cases of impaired object recognition with intact face and word recognition. This pattern of deficits suggests the presence of two types of visual representations: one representational form essential for face recognition, useful for object recognition and not used for word recognition, and the other representation form essential for word recognition, useful for object recognition and not used for face recognition. Whereas studies of prosopagnosic patients indicate an impairment of holistic representations, studies of alexic patients indicate that their impairment in visual word recognition is caused by a deficit in part-based representation (Farah & Wallace, 1991). According to this view, the co-occurrence of breakdowns can be interpreted as impairments in holistic and part-based representations. Face recognition requires the ability to represent complex visual patterns as an integrated whole and this ability is useful to a lesser degree for object recognition, but not needed for word recognition. On the other hand, the ability to represent a pattern as multiple parts is essential to word recognition, useful to a lesser degree for object recognition, but not needed for face recognition. Note that the holistic position allows for a combination of representational types, some of which are holistic and some of which feature explicitly represented parts. According to this view, face recognition is not distinctive because it relies exclusively on holistic representations, it is only distinguished because the representation of faces is disproportionately more holistic than the representation of other types of objects.

Concluding Remarks

In this chapter, we have experimentally defined holistic processing as the improved ability to recognize a part stimulus when presented in the context of the whole stimulus than when presented in isolation. Using this criterion, it has been shown that faces are recognized more holistically than other kinds of objects (e.g., houses, inverted faces, scrambled faces). Moreover, configural and featural information is bound together in a holistic face representation such that changes in a face's configuration influences recognition of its features. While the ability to recognize faces holistically occurs at a relatively early age and is the consequence of normal human development, the holistic recognition of nonface objects is only achieved through focused training and extensive experience. At the neurological level, face recognition and holistic processing are intimately associated to the degree that damage to the putative face area of the brain (i.e., FAA) produces a functional breakdown in holistic face recognition. In summary, the holistic view with its emphasis on the recognition at the level of the whole face stands in stark contrast to conventional theories of object recognition that emphasize recognition at the level of parts. Echoing the previous claims of the Gestalt psychologists, we believe that when it comes to face recognition, the whole is indeed different from the sum of its parts.

References

Biederman, I. (1987). Recognition-by-components: A theory of human image understanding. *Psychological Review, 94,* 115–147.

Bower, G. H., & Glass, A. L. (1976). Structural units and the redintegrative power of picture fragments. *Journal of Experimental Psychology: Human Learning and Memory, 2,* 456–466.

Bradshaw, J., & Wallace, G. (1971). Models for the processing and identification of faces. *Perception and Psychophysics, 9,* 443–448.

Bruce, V. (1988). *Recognizing faces.* London: Erlbaum.

Carey S. (1992). Becoming a face expert. *Philosophical Transactions Royal Society of London, B335,* 95–103.

Carey, S., & Diamond, R. (1977). From piecemeal to configurational representation of faces. *Science, 195,* 312–314.

Carey, S., & Diamond, R. (1994). Are faces perceived as configurations more by adults than by children? *Visual Cognition, 1,* 253–274.

Carey, S., Diamond, R., & Woods, B. (1980). The development of face recognition—a maturational component? *Developmental Psychology, 16,* 257–269.

Diamond, R., & Carey, S. (1986). Why faces are and are not special: An effect of expertise. *Journal of Experimental Psychology: General, 115,* 107–117.

Donnelly, D., & Davidoff, J. (1999). The mental representations of faces and houses: Issues concerning parts and wholes. *Visual Cognition, 6,* 319–343.

Farah, M. J. (1990). *Visual agnosia: Disorders of object recognition and what they tell us about normal vision.* Cambridge, MA: The MIT Press.

Farah, M. J. (1991). Patterns of co-occurrence among the associative agnosias: Implications for visual object representation. *Cognitive Neuropsychology, 8,* 1–19.

Farah, M. (1995). Is face recognition "special"? Evidence from neuropsychology. *Behavioral Brain Research, 76,* 181–189.

Farah, M. J. (1997). Distinguishing perceptual and semantic impairments affecting visual object recognition. *Visual Cognition, 4,* 199–206.

Farah, M. J. (2000). *The cognitive neuroscience of vision.* Malden, MA: Blackwell.

Farah, M., Drain, H., & Tanaka, J. (1995). What causes the face inversion effect? *Journal of Experimental Psychology: Human Perception and Performance, 21,* 628–634.

Farah, M. J., & Wallace, M. A. (1991). Pure alexia as a visual impairment: A reconsideration. *Cognitive Neuropsychology, 8,* 313–334.

Farah, M. J., Wilson, K. D., Drain, H. M., & Tanaka, J. W. (1995). The inverted face inversion effect in prosopagnosia: Evidence for mandatory, face-specific perceptual mechanisms. *Vision Research, 35,* 2089–2093.

Farah, M. J., Wilson, K. D., Drain, M., & Tanaka, J. W. (1998). What is "special" about face perception? *Psychological Review, 105,* 482–498.

Flin, R. H. (1985). Development of face recognition: An encoding switch? *British Journal of Psychology, 76,* 122–134.

Garner, W. R. (1974). *The processing of information and structure.* Potomac, MD: Erlbaum.

Gauthier, I., & Tarr, M. J. (1997). Becoming a "Greeble" expert: exploring the face recognition mechanism. *Vision Research, 37,* 1673–1682.

Gauthier, I., Tarr, M. J., Anderson, A. W., Skudlarksi, P., & Gore, J. C. (1999). Activation of the middle fusiform "face area" increases with expertise in recognizing novel objects. *Nature Neuroscience, 2,* 568–573.

Gauthier, I., Williams, P., Tarr, M. J., & Tanaka, J. W. (1998). Training "Greeble" experts: A framework for studying expert object recognition processes. *Vision Research, 38*, 2401–2428.

Haig, N. (1984). The effect of feature displacement on face recognition. *Perception, 13*, 104–109.

Hoffman, D., & Richards, D. (1985). Parts in recognition. *Cognition, 18*, 65–96.

Hosie, J., Ellis, H. D., & Haig, N. D. (1988). The effect of feature displacement on the perception of well-known faces. *Perception, 17*, 461–474.

Johnson, M. H., & Morton, J. (1991). *Biology and cognitive development: The case of face recognition*. Oxford: Blackwell.

Johnston, J. C., & McClelland, J. L. (1980). Experimental tests of a hierarchical model of word identification. *Journal of Verbal Learning and Verbal Behavior, 19*, 503–524.

Kanwisher, N., McDermott, J., & Chun, M. M. (1997). The fusiform face area: A module in human extrastriate cortex specialized for face perception. *Journal of Neuroscience, 17*, 4302–4311.

LeGrand, R., Mondloch, C. J., Maurer, D., & Brent, H. P. (2001). Early visual experience and face processing. *Nature, 410*, 890.

Marr, D., & Nishihara, H. (1978). Representation and recognition of the spatial organization of three-dimensional shapes. *Proceedings of the Royal Society of London, B 200*, 269–294.

Palermo, R., & Rhodes, G. (2002). The influence of divided attention on holistic face perception. *Cognition, 82*, 225–257.

Palmer, S. E. (1977). Hierarchical structure in perceptual representation. *Cognitive Psychology, 9*, 441–474.

Puce, A, Allison, T., Gore, J. C., & McCarthy, G. (1995). Face-sensitive regions in human extrastriate cortex studied by functional MRI. *Journal of Neurophysiology, 74*, 3, 1192–1199.

Rhodes, G. (1988). Looking at faces: First-order and second-order features as determinants of facial appearance. *Perception, 17*, 43–63.

Rhodes, G., Brake, S., & Atkinson, A. (1993). What's lost in inverted faces? *Cognition, 17*, 25–57.

Sergent, J. (1984). An investigation into component and configural processes underlying face perception. *The British Journal of Psychology, 75*, 221–242.

Sergent, J., Ohta, S., & MacDonald, B. (1992). Functional neuroanatomy of face and object processing. *Brain, 115*, 15–36.

Smith, E., & Nielsen, G. (1970). Representations and retrieval processes in short-term memory: Recognition and recall of faces. *Journal of Experimental Psychology, 85*, 397–405.

Sternberg, S. (1969). The discovery of processing stages: Extensions of Donder's method. *Acta Psychologica, 30*, 276–315.

Tanaka, J. W. (2001). The entry point of face recognition: Evidence for face expertise. *Journal of Experimental Psychology: General, 130*, 534–543.

Tanaka, J. W., & Farah, M. J. (1991). Second-order relational properties and the inversion effect: Testing a theory of face perception. *Perception and Psychophysics, 50*, 367–372.

Tanaka, J. W., & Farah, M. J. (1993). Parts and wholes in face recognition. *Quarterly Journal of Experimental Psychology, 46A*, 225–245.

Tanaka, J. W., & Gauthier, I. (1997). Expertise in object and face recognition. In R. L. Goldstone, P. G. Schyns, & D. L. Medin (Eds.), *Psychology of learning and motivation* (vol. 36, pp. 83–125). San Diego: Academic Press.

Tanaka, J. W., Giles, M., Szechter, L., Lantz, J. A., Stone, A., Franks L., & Vastine, K. (1996). *Measuring parts and wholes recognition of cell, car and dog experts: A test of the expertise hypothesis.* Unpublished manuscript, Oberlin College, Oberlin, OH.

Tanaka, J. W., Kay, J. B., Grinnell, E., Stansfield, B., & Szechter, L. (1998). Face recognition in young children: When the whole is greater than the sum of its parts. *Visual Cognition, 5,* 479–496.

Tanaka, J. W., & Sengco, J. (1997). Features and their configuration in face recognition. *Memory and Cognition, 25,* 583–592.

Tanaka, J. W., & Taylor, M. (1991). Object categories and expertise: Is the basic level in the eye of the beholder? *Cognitive Psychology, 23,* 457–482.

Valentine, T. (1988). Upside-down faces: A review of the effect of inversion upon face recognition. *British Journal of Psychology, 79,* 471–491.

Valentine, T., & Bruce, V. (1986). The effect of race inversion and encoding activity upon face recognition. *Acta Psychologica, 61,* 259–273.

Yarmey, A. D. (1971). Recognition memory for familiar "public" faces: Effects of orientation and delay. *Psychonomic Science, 24,* 286–288.

Yin, R. (1969). Looking at upside-down faces. *Journal of Experimental Psychology, 81,* 141–145.

Young, A. W., Hellawell, D., & Hay, D. C. (1987). Configural information in face perception. *Perception, 10,* 747–759.

3

When Is a Face Not a Face?

The Effects of Misorientation on Mechanisims of Face Perception

JANICE E. MURRAY, GILLIAN RHODES,
AND MARIA SCHUCHINSKY

From birth, the face plays an important role in human social interactions. As a mother studies the face of her newborn infant, so too does the infant explore the face of its mother. The newborn rapidly learns to discriminate its mother's face from that of a stranger (Bushnell, Sai, & Mullen, 1989; Field, Cohen, Garcia & Greenberg, 1984; Pascalis, de Schonen, Morton, Deruelle, & Rabre-Grenet, 1995) and by adulthood, will be able to discriminate and recognize hundreds (Bharick, Bharick, & Wittlinger, 1975), or even thousands of faces. This ability is particularly impressive given that all faces share the same parts in a common arrangement.

What mechanisms underlie the successful discrimination of so many faces? As with other classes of visual stimuli, the individual components or features of a face can serve as one source of information (e.g., the size of the nose, color of the eyes). However, component information may be of limited use given the common configuration and similarity of features across faces. There is considerable evidence that the spatial relations among the components of a face (e.g., the relative position of the nose and mouth), and/or its global configuration or gestalt, play the more important role in face recognition (for recent reviews, see Bartlett, Searcy & Abdi, chapter 1 this volume; Searcy & Bartlett, 1996; Farah, Wilson, Drain & Tanaka, 1998; Tanaka & Farah, chapter 2 this volume). We will refer to these attributes as configural information, although a variety of terms can be found in the literature, often with slightly different meanings (relational, holistic, interactive, etc.).

Configural Processing and Face Inversion

A signature phenomenon associated with face perception is the inversion effect. In marked contrast to the ease with which we recognize other inverted objects, even ones normally seen in an upright orientation, we are notoriously bad at recognizing upside-down faces (e.g., Carey & Diamond, 1977; Diamond & Carey, 1986; Yin, 1969). Considerable evidence suggests that what is impaired by inversion of faces is the encoding of configural information (Bartlett & Searcy, 1993; Leder & Bruce, 1998, 2000; Rhodes, Brake, & Atkinson, 1993; Searcy & Bartlett, 1996; Tanaka & Farah, 1993; Tanaka & Sengco, 1997; Young, Hellawell, & Hay, 1987). The inversion effect suggests that configural coding plays an important role in recognizing upright faces, but that it is difficult to use with inverted faces. In suggesting a diminished role for configural coding mechanisms in processing inverted faces, this view indicates a qualitative difference in the processing of upright and inverted faces, with a shift from reliance on configural information in the upright face to reliance on component information in the inverted face.

Valentine (1988, 1991), however, challenges the view that there is a qualitative difference between the processing of upright and of inverted faces. He has argued that faces are represented in a multidimensional space that includes both component and configural dimensions, and that inversion impairs face perception by adding noise to the encoding process. Both configural and component coding mechanisms are subject to the increased error in encoding that occurs as a result of viewing the face in the non-upright position. In this view, the effect of inversion on face processing is purely quantitative in nature. Encoding simply becomes more difficult and error prone, and the relative contribution of configural or component information is unaffected by inversion.

Previous efforts to determine the degree of impairment for either type of face information have involved manipulating either configural or component information, and observing the effects of inversion on perception or recognition of the altered faces (e.g., Bartlett & Searcy, 1993; Leder & Bruce, 1998, 2000; Rhodes, Brake, & Atkinson, 1993; Searcy & Bartlett, 1996). These studies have demonstrated that the effects of inversion are pronounced when changes to configural information must be detected, with smaller or nonexistent inversion effects observed following changes to component information. Searcy and Bartlett (1996), for example, had participants make perceptual judgments about faces that were made to look grotesque by adding white to the eyes and blackening the teeth (a component change) or by moving the eyes and mouth up or down in an otherwise normal face (a configural change). The results showed that inversion reduced the perceived grotesqueness of faces distorted through changes to configural information, with perception of grotesqueness relatively unaffected by inversion when faces were distorted by changes to component information. These results supported the dual-mode view (Carey & Diamond, 1977) that upside-down faces do not engage the configural coding mechanisms that are the hallmark of face perception, but rather engage the component processing mechanisms that characterize object perception. Evidence that inversion reduces perceived distinctiveness more dramatically when the distinctive features are configural (distances between internal features) than when they are local components (lip or eyebrow thickness) supports the same conclusion (Leder & Bruce, 1998). These results are also important in showing that the effects of inversion occur at the level of perceptual encoding, and not necessarily at the level of memory retention or retrieval.

While consistent with the view that upright and inverted faces are processed by different mechanisms, the studies described above do not directly test for a qualitative shift in processing strategy at some intermediate orientation between 0° and 180°. Such a shift can be revealed only in an assessment of changes in face processing across a full range of orientations from upright to upside down. Evidence of a discontinuity in the function relating departure from upright and some measure of face processing would provide strong support for the dual-mode view. Alternatively, a continuous function would support the noise account (Valentine, 1988) because on that view, encoding of configural information is not disproportionately disrupted when the face is inverted.

In previous work, Valentine and Bruce (1988) examined sequential face matching and recognition across a limited range of orientations (0°, 45°, 90°, 135°, 180°), and did not observe any discontinuity in their response-time functions. However, their procedures may not have been sufficiently sensitive to detect the suggested shift in processing strategy. It may be difficult to detect a discontinuity when a small number of orientations are tested. Moreover, in both tasks participants saw a small number of faces repeatedly. Under these conditions, it might well be possible to respond successfully using component features, in which case no discontinuity would be expected (although there may well be some orientation effect—see Rhodes et al., 1993).

In recent work, we further pursued the question of a qualitative shift in processing strategy (Murray, Yong, & Rhodes, 2000). In our studies, we focused on perceptual coding of faces, and manipulated both component and configural information to determine the effects of orientation on the encoding of each type of information. Following Searcy and Bartlett (1996; Bartlett & Searcy, 1993) we asked participants to judge the bizarreness of faces that were made to look bizarre by changing either component information or configural information. In the latter condition we employed the Thatcher illusion (Thompson, 1980), in which the result of inverting the eyes and mouth in an otherwise normal upright face is a face that is perceived as highly grotesque or bizarre looking when viewed upright (see figure 3.1B). Critically, the perception of bizarreness is all but lost when the face is inverted. To achieve a bizarre face derived from changes to component information, we whitened the eyes and blackened some of the teeth in the faces (see figure 3.1C). Searcy and Bartlett (1996) found that inversion produced no reliable change in perceived grotesqueness for this type of distortion. Both types of distorted faces, as well as unaltered faces, were shown at 24 orientations. These included 0° and 180°, with the intermediate orientations created by rotating the faces in 15° steps of clockwise or counterclockwise rotation in the image plane.

The key condition was that involving the Thatcherized faces, with the component distortion and unaltered face conditions serving as controls. For Thatcherized faces, perception of bizarreness relies on the ability to encode distortions of configural information (Bartlett & Searcy, 1993). Inverting the eyes and mouth in a face alters the spatial configuration formed by the relative position of the components of the face. This second-order relational change (Diamond & Carey, 1986) is one in which the first-order relations, the more categorical relations among the components (e.g., the mouth is below the nose, the eyes above the nose), are maintained. In this sense, what is changed is the global configuration of the face, with the spatial distortion compared to some prototype face (Rhodes, Brennan, & Carey, 1987) or to some more holistic representation in which individual components are not explicitly coded (Tanaka, & Farah, 1993). By tracking changes in the perception of bizarreness as the Thatcherized face is rotated from the upright, we were able to test the dual-mode assertion that there is a switch from processing configural information to processing predominantly component information with increasing departures from upright. Such a qualitative difference in encoding would predict a discontinuity in the function relating orientation and perceived bizarreness at the point where the configural coding mechanisms can no longer be engaged. Alternatively, a continuous and gradual reduction in bizarreness ratings would be expected for Thatcherized faces if the inversion effect is derived from an increase in difficulty in encoding any face information, rather than a switch from one mode of processing to another. As can be seen in figure 3.2A, the results supported the dual-mode hypothesis. For both component-distortion and unaltered faces, perception of bizarreness increased linearly, with no deviations from linearity present in the functions relating orientation and bizarreness. Critically, the function for Thatcherized faces showed a discontinuity that was not present in the functions for the other two types of faces. This discontinuity, which occurred between 90° and 120°, is consistent with a qualitative shift in processing strategy.

In a second experiment, we altered configural information by changing the internal spacing between the eyes, as well as moving the eyes and mouth up or down (the spatial-distortion condition; see figure 3.1D). We again observed a discontinuity in the function relating orientation and

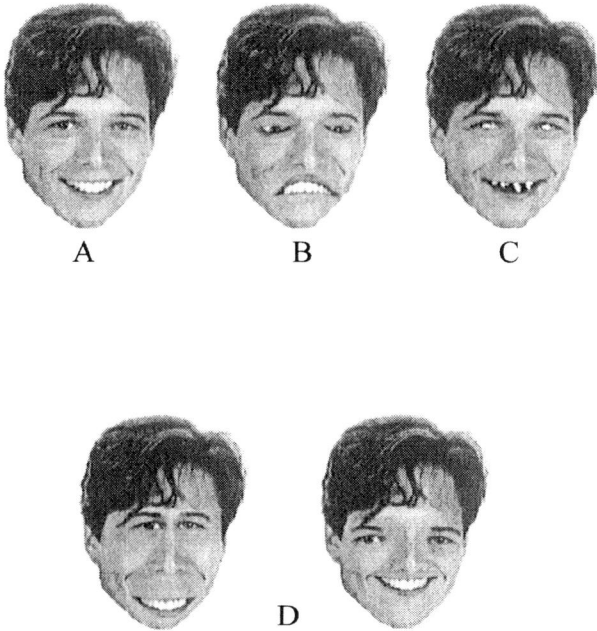

FIGURE 3.1. Different types of face stimuli used in bizarreness rating experiments. In the top row, an unaltered face (A), a Thatcherized face (B), and a component-distortion face (C) are shown. In the bottom row, two spatial-distortion faces are presented (D). In the face on the left, the eyes were moved upward and closer together and the mouth downward, whereas in the face on the right, the eyes and mouth were moved in the opposite direction. Reprinted, with permission, from Murray, Yong, and Rhodes (2000).

perceived bizarreness of configurally distorted faces but not in the functions for component-distortion faces and unaltered faces (see figure 3.2B).

For both types of configural distortion, the shift in processing mode from configural to predominantly component took place between 90° and 120°. Three other recent sources of data converge on this estimate of the range of sensitivity of a configural coding mechanism. Moscovitch, Winocur, and Behrmann (1997) reported the results of an in-depth assessment of CK, who had significant deficits in object recognition. Their testing showed an individual with an impoverished component-based object-recognition system but an intact face-recognition system. Although not formally tested across a range of orientations, Moscovitch et al. noted that CK could not recognize famous faces at deviations beyond 90° from upright. A second body of consistent evidence is found in recent work of McKone, Martini, and Nakayama (2001). They demonstrated a technique for isolating configural processing in face perception through the addition of visual noise. Using categorical perception of faces as their index of

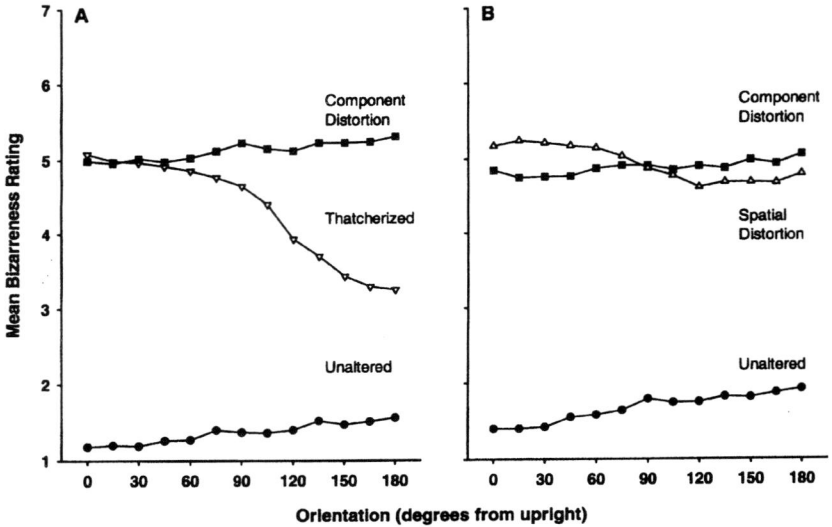

FIGURE 3.2. Effects of orientation on bizarreness ratings from 0° to 180°. Ratings for clockwise and counterclockwise rotations of equal magnitude were averaged. The figure in panel A shows the mean bizarreness ratings for unaltered, Thatcherized, and component-distortion faces. In panel B, mean bizarreness ratings are shown for unaltered, spatial-distortion, and component-distortion faces. Reprinted, with permission, from Murray, Yong, and Rhodes (2000).

configural processing, they found that categorical perception could be observed in upright but not inverted faces when feature information was disrupted through the addition of noise. In further testing, they found the limits of categorical perception for faces in noise to be between 45° and 90° for one observer, and between 90° and 112° for two others. Finally, Stürzel and Spillman (2000) have shown that Thatcherized faces lose their grotesque appearance at around 100°. Considered together, the results of these diverse studies are striking in their convergence on an estimated limit for configural processing. The studies seem to point to the conclusion that there is a qualitative shift from configural to component processing, and that it occurs around 90°. This may be the point at which faces fail to engage configural coding mechanisms.

   The discussion thus far has focused primarily on the processing of configural information in the pre-shift portion of the rating function. If we accept that faces rotated beyond approximately 90° no longer engage the configural coding mechanisms that are the hallmark of face perception, then the question of what encoding mechanisms are engaged remains. The results of our experiments provide some indication as to the nature of this postshift processing. Two points are of significance. First, the effects of orientation continued to be observed in the postdiscontinuity portion of the function for both types of configural distortion, although whether or not postdiscontinuity ratings increased or decreased linearly with changes in orientation depended on the type of configural distortion. For Thatcherized faces, in which the eyes and mouth were inverted, the ratings continued to decrease, indicating less perceived bizarreness for the postdiscontinuity orientations at 120° and beyond. When the configural distortion was created by changing the internal spacing of the eyes, and moving the eyes and mouth up or down, the pattern of decreasing ratings for prediscontinuity orientations reversed direction at the point of the discontinuity, and postdiscontinuity ratings increased linearly over the last five orientations.

We have argued that these results for postdiscontinuity ratings reflect the effects of orientation on encoding component properties (Murray et al., 2000). Perception of bizarreness derived from individual components may also be orientation sensitive, with nonupright components perceived as unusual or unpleasant (Parks, Coss, & Coss, 1985; Rakover & Teucher, 1997). Orientation-specific perception of components would account for the direction of the postdiscontinuity orientation effect for both types of configural distortion used in our experiments. In the spatial-distortion condition, the eyes, nose, and mouth remained in their normal orientation with respect to the rest of the face. As the face was rotated beyond the point where configural information was no longer available, the increasing departure from upright would lead to increasing bizarreness ratings if perception of bizarreness was based on component properties. In the case of the Thatcherized faces, the eyes and mouth are inverted in the upright face, and when the Thatcherized face is inverted, those parts of the face become upright. Therefore, once configural information was no longer available, the eyes and mouth would appear increasingly normal as the face was rotated further from upright. Accordingly, based on the information provided by the eyes and mouth, bizarreness ratings could be expected to decrease for postdiscontinuity orientations, as was found, although inverted faces might never appear entirely normal owing to the presence of the inverted nose and external facial features. In addition to explaining the direction of the postdiscontinuity orientation effect, orientation-specific encoding of component properties would account for the linear effect of orientation on bizarreness ratings found for unaltered and component-distortion faces across the full range of orientations from upright to inverted.

A second aspect of the postdiscontinuity results is significant. Perceived bizarreness for spatial-distortion faces remained relatively high following the loss of configural information. Bizarreness ratings in the postdiscontinuity portion of the curve were comparable to those obtained for component-distortion faces and clearly different from the ratings for unaltered faces. This suggests that changing the spatial relations among components by altering their internal spacing impacts on more than configural coding mechanisms. One possibility is that changes to internal spacing of components also affect encoding of component properties. Moving the mouth up or down might be expected to alter the perception of the component property "chin." In addition to being encoded in terms of configural properties, the distance between the eyes might also be encoded as a component property. Inverting the eyes and mouth in an otherwise normally oriented face might also impact on encoding of component properties in similar ways.

In summary, we propose that upright faces engage configural coding mechanisms that are critical for successful face perception. These configural coding mechanisms are sensitive to orientation, and are no longer engaged when the face is rotated beyond about 90°. At greater orientations, faces are processed in a qualitatively different manner, engaging primarily component processing mechanisms that encode orientation-specific information about individual components.

Recent work by Moscovitch and Moscovitch (2000) has led to a similar proposal. They investigated the recognition of fractured faces (whose internal features were moved apart and separated by gaps) and found evidence that inversion interferes with component information as well as configural information. Fracturing faces altered the spatial relations within a face and its global structure while leaving information about the individual components intact. Moscovitch and Moscovitch found that recognition of inverted fractured faces was far worse than recognition of upright fractured faces. This, they argued, supported the proposal that representation of components is orientation specific. They also observed that recognition performance for inverted fractured faces was much worse than that for inverted intact faces, and interpreted this as evidence that some information about the spatial relations between features (e.g., categorical relations like above, below and beside) is used for recognition of inverted faces.

In light of these findings, coupled with their work with patient CK (Moscovitch et al., 1997; Moscovitch & Moscovitch, 2000), and other existing evidence, Moscovitch and Moscovitch proposed a modified version of their earlier characterization of upright and inverted face recognition. They argued that recognition of upright faces relies on a face-recognition system that operates on orientation-specific, global configural information and that inversion renders this system largely unavailable. This leaves face recognition reliant on the object system. The object system integrates orientation-specific information about the individual components with information about categorical spatial relations (left–right, up–down) and the piecemeal alignment of components to produce an object-system counterpart to the face representation. The spatial-relational information used by the object system is considered distinct from that used by the face system, in that the latter type of information is global and configurational, supporting gestalt properties of the face, whereas the former is restricted to more local areas of the face and/or codes categorical relations.

The data and proposals from both Murray et al. (2000) and Moscovitch and Moscovitch (2000) point to a critical role for configural information in the processing of upright faces that is distinct from other forms of relational information (e.g., categorical relations) that underlie object processing and the processing of nonupright faces. The results suggest that the ability to encode configural information in faces is fundamental to our expertise with faces, a view first proposed by Diamond and Carey (1986). Another way to test this claim is through an examination of the cross-race effect. We discuss this effect in the next section.

Expertise-Based Configural Coding

It is well documented that faces from an unfamiliar racial group are more difficult to recognize than faces from one's own race (for reviews see Anthony, Cooper, & Mullen, 1992; Bothwell, Brigham, & Malpass, 1989; Brigham, 1986; Brigham & Malpass, 1985; Chiroro & Valentine, 1995; Ferguson, Rhodes, Lee, & Sriram, 2001). It is logical, therefore, to consider the possibility that this decrement in recognition performance is the result of a reduced ability to code configural information in faces with which we have less experience, and hence less expertise. Although some evidence supports this view, other evidence does not. In what follows, we will review the contradictory lines of evidence and then discuss recent research relevant to this issue.

Rhodes, Tan, Brake, and Taylor (1989) examined the differences in recognizing own-race and other-race faces using the inversion paradigm. The rationale was simple. If a reduced ability to encode configural information in other-race faces underlies poorer cross-race recognition, then the disruptive effect of inversion should be smaller in other-race faces relative to own-race faces. This is the pattern of effect that Rhodes et al. found, results consistent with the view that encoding of configural information is critical for expert face recognition.

In contrast to Rhodes et al. (1989), Valentine and Bruce (1986) found a larger inversion effect for other-race faces using somewhat different procedures and different measures. A larger other-race inversion effect would be expected within a multidimensional space framework if, as argued by Valentine (1991), other-race faces are encoded inappropriately on dimensions typical of own-race faces. While wholly appropriate for discriminating among own-race faces, the same dimensions are likely to be unsuitable for discriminating among other-race faces (e.g., hair color is a less salient feature for Asian faces than for Caucasian faces). Other-race faces would be more densely clustered in some face space owing to the resulting high proportion of shared feature values among other-race faces. As a consequence, discrimination difficulty among other-race faces would be greater than among own-race faces, and inversion, by increasing the error in encoding the face, would have a more detrimental effect on recognition of other-race faces, as was found.

Potentially important differences between the two studies (Rhodes at al., 1989; Valentine & Bruce, 1986) suggest that more weight be given to the Rhodes et al. study. Other-race faces were shown for longer than own-race faces in Valentine and Bruce (1986), rather than for equal amounts of time as in Rhodes et al. (1989). Also, Rhodes et al. tested participants from both races whereas Valentine and Bruce tested only Caucasians. In testing participants from both of the races represented in the stimuli, Rhodes et al. ensured that any own-race, other-race differences were a function of the racial match between stimuli and participants, and not simply a function of possible differences in the stimuli themselves.

Further evidence suggestive of a configural coding account of the cross-race effect is found in the work of Fallshore and Schooler (1995). They exploited the finding that verbally describing a previously seen face produces poorer recognition of the same face in a subsequent forced-choice recognition task (Schooler & Engstler-Schooler, 1990). Fallshore and Schooler considered this *verbal overshadowing* effect to be the result of an overemphasis of featural information at the expense of configural information when a verbal description of the face is required. To assess this, they turned to the cross-race effect and reasoned that if configural information is made less available through verbalization, and further, if configural information differentiates own- and other-race face recognition, then the verbal overshadowing effect should be observed for own-race faces only. This is precisely what they found. Fallshore and Schooler then went on to test whether the verbal overshadowing effect is lost when the own-race face is inverted. If indeed configural information is already disrupted in the inverted own-race face, then verbalization would be expected to have no further impact. This prediction was also borne out in the results, and taken together, Fallshore and Schooler's results are consistent with the view that it is the perceptual encoding of configural information that is disrupted by inversion and underlies our expertise with faces.

Levin (1996, 2000) has recently posed a different argument. He suggests that the cross-race recognition deficit is not due to expertise differences, but instead results from the coding of race-specifying information as a feature in other-race faces. This other-race feature is absent in own-race faces, allowing for successful identification of faces. However, the cost of such a feature selection is a reduction in the available individuating information, and it is this that leads to the poorer recognition performance for other-race faces. To support this view, Levin reported the results of visual search experiments in which the target was an own-race face among other-race faces, or the reverse. As would be predicted by the feature-selection hypothesis, he found a "feature present" search asymmetry for other-race faces; participants who showed a cross-race deficit in a subsequent recognition task revealed faster search for other-race faces among own-race faces than for own-race faces among other-race faces. He also found that the search asymmetry favoring other-race faces was maintained with inversion, from which he concluded that the effect did not depend on differential coding of configural information in own- and other-race faces.

The results described above exploring the relationship between coding of configural information and expertise are not conclusive. Different inversion studies have yielded opposing results (Rhodes et al., 1989; Valentine & Bruce, 1986), whereas the work of Fallshore and Schooler (1995) provides support for the notion of expertise-based coding of configural information. Levin argues that an expertise account of the cross-race effect is not needed, and cites his work in support of this view (1996, 2000). However, Levin's findings are not necessarily at odds with the configural coding account. If configural information is reduced in other-race faces, then the encoding of features, including nonconfigural race-specifying information, would be the only available alternative. And a race-specifying feature would seem particularly appropriate where the task requires a simple classification such as determination of the race of a face, as in Levin's studies.

Our bizarreness rating task, in which changes in encoding of the face can be tracked as the face is rotated away from upright, seems well suited to investigating whether or not the encoding of configural information is differentially disrupted in other-race faces. Of particular interest is the function relating changes in perception of orientation and bizarreness where perception of bizarreness is derived from changes to configural information. If lack of expertise in other-race faces does arise from a reduced ability to encode configural information, then we might expect this to be reflected in performance on our task in a number of ways. First, other-race faces may not appear as bizarre as own-race faces when the perception of bizarreness is based on distortions of configural information (e.g., Thatcherized faces). This cross-race difference would be most evident for upright faces where configural information in own-race faces, but not other-race faces, can be fully encoded. Second, if the ability to encode configural information is already reduced in other-race faces, then any additional effect of changes in orientation should be relatively small in other-race faces over the range of orientations where configural information is potentially available (i.e., from 0° to 90 °). This leads to the second prediction. As the face is rotated from 0° to 90°, the magnitude of the orientation effect should be greater for own-race faces than for other-race faces. Third, differences in ratings for other-race and own-race faces would not be expected for postshift orientations where, we argue, predominantly component information is processed. Taken together, these considerations also lead to a predicted larger inversion effect for own-race versus other-race faces, owing to the differences in ability to encode configural information at (or near) upright. Finally, because any perception of bizarreness in unaltered faces or component-distortions faces would not be derived from configural information (Murray et al., 2000), we would predict no differences in ratings between own-race and other-race faces for these two types of faces.

To test these ideas, we again carried out the bizarreness judgment task. Subjects rated the bizarreness of 16 female and 16 male faces on a scale from 1 to 7 where 1 represented the most normal-looking face and 7 represented the most bizarre. Half the faces to be judged were Caucasian (New Zealanders) and half were Asian (Malaysian Chinese). The faces in both sets were without any distinguishing features (e.g., facial hair, glasses) and all had short hair. Our subjects were all Caucasians who rated the Caucasian (own-race) and Asian (other-race) faces in separate sessions. In each session, the faces were shown once at each of the 24 orientations in each Thatcherized, component distortion and unaltered version for a total of 576 trials per session.

Our preliminary results from 24 subjects are shown in figure 3.3. As is evident, subjects did not differ in their rating of own- and other-race faces for either component distortion or unaltered faces. This was confirmed in separate analyses of variance for each type of face in which there were no significant effects of race, nor any interaction between race and orientation ($F < 1$ for all effects). Consistent with our previous findings, there was a linear increase in perception of bizarreness as the face was rotated further from the upright for both unaltered faces, $F (1,23) = 28.90, p < .001$ and component-distortion faces, $F (1,23) = 4.79, p < .05$, and there was no significant deviation from linearity for either type of face ($F < 1$ in each case). As predicted, these results indicate that sensitivity to changes in component information does not vary as a function of expertise.

The functions for Thatcherized faces reveal cross-race differences. Prior to looking at the overall functions, we first assessed the inversion effect in an analysis with orientation (0° and 180°) and race (own-race and other-race) as factors. There was a significant effect of orientation, $F (1,23) = 59.83, p < .001$, as well as a significant interaction between the two variables, $F (1,23) = 6.16, p < .05$. The inversion effect was significant for both own-race (mean difference between upright and inverted ratings = 1.9), $t (23) = 8.03, p < .001$ and other-race faces (mean difference between upright and inverted = 1.4), $t(23) = 6.01, p < .001$. However, as further analysis of the difference scores revealed, the magnitude of the effect was significantly smaller for other-race faces, $t(23) = 2.48, p <.025$. This result is consistent with the previous findings of Rhodes et al. (1989), who found a smaller effect of inversion in other-race faces using a recognition paradigm. Importantly, what is readily apparent from figure 3.3, is that the difference in the cross-race inversion effect arises at 0° and not at 180°. Consistent with our first prediction, there was a significant difference between the ratings of own-race (M = 5.5) and other-race (M = 5.0) faces at 0°, $t(23) = 2.52, p < .025$. In contrast, at 180°, there was no significant difference between own-race (M = 3.5) and other-race (M = 3.5) faces, $t < 1$.

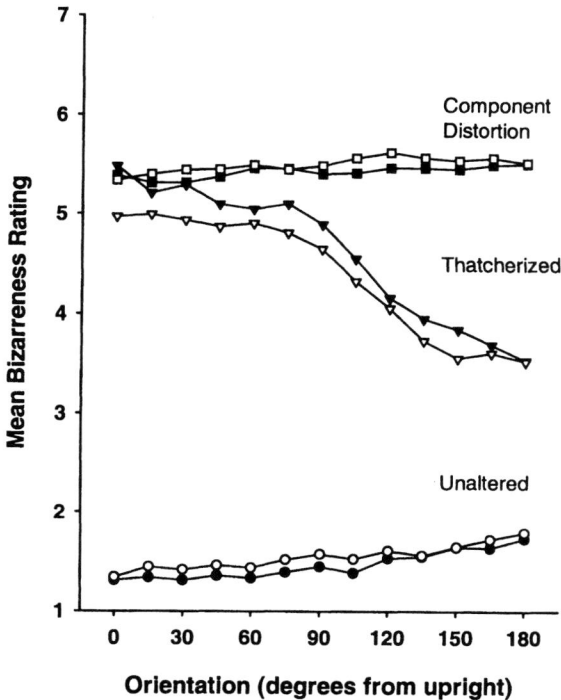

FIGURE 3.3. Effects of orientation on bizarreness ratings from 0° to 180° for own-race (filled symbols) and other-race faces (unfilled symbols). Ratings for clockwise and counterclockwise rotations of equal magnitude were averaged. Mean bizarreness ratings are shown for unaltered, Thatcherized, and component-distortion faces.

An analysis of Thatcherized faces across all orientations revealed the expected linear effect of orientation, $F (1,23) = 59.88, p < .001$, as well as a significant deviation from linearity, $F (11, 253) = 12.95, p < .001$. As can be seen in figure 3.3, the discontinuity in the function relating orientation and rated perception of bizarreness occurred between 90° and 120° for both own-race and other-race faces. These results are in accord with the view that a qualitative shift from configural to component processing occurs at around 90°. They also suggest that the point at which the shift occurs does not depend on expertise. Differential use of configural information in processing other-race and own-race faces apparently does not entail a cross-race difference in the range of orientations over which configural coding mechanisms can operate.

We next analyzed for cross-race differences in ratings for the pre- and post-shift portions of the curve. A significant interaction between race and the linear component of the orientation effect was found for ratings in the pre-shift portion of the curve, $F(6, 138) = 2.81, p < .025$. In support of our second prediction, the effect of orientation from 0° to 90° was less marked for other-race faces in contrast to own-race faces. For both types of faces, ratings decreased in a linear fashion with increasing deviation from upright, but, as indicated by a significant orientation$_{linear}$ by race interaction, $F(1, 23) = 4.29, p < .05$, the magnitude of the linear effect of orientation was less for other-race faces. This is precisely what would be predicted by an expertise-based coding of configural information account. Since the perception of bizarreness in the Thatcherized face is created through a distortion of configural information, it follows that other-race faces will be perceived as less bizarre than own-race faces, and be less affected by changes in orientation across the range of orientations where this information is normally available.

Finally, our third prediction that any cross-race differences in perceived bizarreness would not be apparent for postshift orientations where perception arguably relies on component information was confirmed in our experiment through an analysis of the ratings for the last five orientations from 120° onward. There was no significant effect of race, $F < 1$, nor did the significant linear effect of orientation, $F(1,23) = 26.24, p < .001$ vary as a function of race, $F(4,92) = 1.78$, *ns*. The results of our experiment lend strong support to the contention that a difference in the ability to encode configural information underlies the relative deficit in cross-race face recognition. Clear differences in encoding configural information in own-race and other-race faces were observed across orientations from upright to approximately 90°. It is over this range of orientations, we argue, that faces engage configural coding mechanisms. Notably, these differences in perception were not observed for configurally distorted faces rotated beyond 90°, or for faces distorted through changes to component information, further implicating difficulty in encoding configural information as the source of the cross-race face processing deficit. Not surprisingly, the ability to process configural information in other-race faces is not entirely lacking. As would be expected, bizarreness created in Thatcherized other-race faces was perceived, though, as detailed above, not to the same extent as in own-race faces. We can conclude that our ability to encode configural information in faces from races other than our own is relatively impaired.

Conclusions

It is well established that upright faces engage configural coding mechanisms (for reviews see Diamond & Carey, 1986; Searcy & Bartlett, 1996). Our results demonstrate that these configural face-coding mechanisms are no longer engaged when a face is oriented more than about 90° from upright, suggesting that the visual system no longer processes such an image as a face. Beyond this point, coding must rely on component coding mechanisms typically used in object recognition that encode orientation-specific information about individual components, and may be sensitive to nonconfigural information about the spatial relations among components. Converging evidence for a coding shift at around 90° comes from a neuropsychological patient with intact face-processing and impaired object-processing mechanisms (Moscovitch et al., 1997). Initial observations suggest that faces oriented more than 90° no longer engaged this intact face-processing mechanism, although formal testing remains to be completed. Psychophysical data also suggest that faces misoriented by more than about 90° fail to engage face-specific configural coding mechanisms (McKone et al., 2001). When configural face-processing mechanisms were isolated by presenting faces in visual noise, categorical perception of faces occurred, but was limited to faces misoriented less than 90° from upright.

The ability to use configural coding mechanisms appears to require expertise with a class of stimuli (e.g., Diamond & Carey, 1986; Rhodes et al., 1989; Tarr, chapter 7 this volume), and the relatively poor recognition of faces from an unfamiliar race may well be the result of limited encoding of configural information for other-race faces (Rhodes et al., 1989; Fallshore & Schooler, 1995). Our results support this view. We found that an own-race advantage in encoding was limited to orientations at which configural coding could be used. Interestingly, there was a discontinuity in the coding function at around 90°, for both own-race (Caucasian) and other-race (Chinese) faces. This result indicates that configural coding could be used to some degree for these other-race faces, which is not surprising given that the participants had some experience with Chinese faces.

We have focused on whether inverted faces engage the configural coding mechanisms that distinguish normal face processing from object processing generally. We note, however, that configural coding may not be restricted solely to face processing. Several studies suggest that experts with other homogeneous classes (i.e., whose members share a common configuration) may also use configural coding to discriminate those stimuli (dogs—Diamond & Carey, 1986; Greebles—Gauthier & Tarr, 1997; Tarr, chapter 7 this volume). In these cases we would predict that, like faces, these stimuli would fail to engage configural coding mechanisms when rotated beyond about 90°.

References

Anthony, T., Cooper, C., & Mullen, B. (1992). Cross-race identification: A social cognitive integration. *Personality & Social Psychology Bulletin, 18*, 296–301.

Bartlett, J. C., & Searcy, J. (1993). Inversion and configuration of faces. *Cognitive Psychology, 25*(3), 281–316.

Bharick, H. P., Bharick, P. O., & Wittlinger, R. P. (1975). Fifty years of memory for names and faces: A cross-sectional approach. *Journal of Experimental Psychology: General, 104*, 54–75.

Bothwell, R. K., Brigham, J. C., & Malpass, R. S. (1989). Cross-racial identification. *Personality & Social Psychology Bulletin, 15*, 19–25.

Brigham, J. C. (1986). The influence of race on face recognition. In H. D. Ellis, M. A. Jeeves, F. Newcombe, & A. W. Young (Eds.), *Aspects of face processing* (pp. 170–177). Dordrecht: Martinus Nijhoff Publishers.

Brigham, J. C., & Malpass, R. S. (1985). The role of experience and contact in the recognition of faces of own-and other-race persons. *Journal of Social Issues, 41*, 139–155.

Carey, S., & Diamond, R. (1977). From piecemeal to configural representation of faces. *Science, 195*, 312–314.

Chiroro, P., & Valentine, T. (1995). An investigation of the contact hypothesis of the own-race bias in face recognition. *Quarterly Journal of Experimental Psychology, 48A*, 879–894.

Diamond, R., & Carey, S. (1986). Why faces are and are not special: An effect of expertise. *Journal of Experimental Psychology: General, 115*, 107–117.

Fallshore, M. F., & Schooler, J. W. (1995). The verbal vulnerability of perceptual expertise. *Journal of Experimental Psychology: Learning Memory and Cognition, 21*, 1608–1623.

Farah, M. J., Wilson, K. D., Drain, M., & Tanaka, J. N. (1998). What is "special" about face perception? *Psychological Review, 105*, 482–498.

Ferguson, D., Rhodes, G., Lee, K., & Sriram, N. (2001). "They all look alike to me": Prejudice and cross-race face recognition. *British Journal of Psychology, 92*, 567–577.

Field, T. M., Cohen, D., Garcia, R., & Greenberg, R. (1984). Mother-stranger face discrimination by the newborn. *Infant Behavior & Development, 7*, 19–25.

Gauthier, I., & Tarr, M. (1997). Becoming a "Greeble" expert: Exploring the face recognition mechanism. *Vision Research, 37*, 1673–1682.

Leder, H., & Bruce, V. (1998). Local and relational aspects of face distinctiveness. *Quarterly Journal of Experimental Psychology, 51A*, 449–473.

Leder, H., & Bruce, V. (2000). When inverted faces are recognised: The role of configural information in face recognition. *Quarterly Journal of Experimental Psychology, 53*, 513–536.

Levin, D. T. (1996). Classifying faces by race: The structure of face categories. *Journal of Experimental Psychology: Learning Memory and Cognition, 22*(6), 1364–1382.

Levin, D. T. (2000). Race as a visual feature: Using visual search and perceptual discrimination tasks to understand face categories and the cross race recognition deficit. *Journal of Experimental Psychology: General, 129*, 559–574.

McKone, E., Martini, P., & Nakayama K., (2001). Categorical perception of face identity in noise isolates configural processing. *Journal of Experimental Psychology: Human Perception & Performance, 27*, 573–599.

Moscovitch, M., & Moscovitch, D. A. (2000). Super face-inversion effects for isolated internal or external features, and for fractured faces. *Cognitive Neuropsychology, 17*, 201–219.

Moscovitch, M., Winocur, G., & Behrmann, M. (1997). What is special about face recognition? Nineteen experiments on a person with visual object agnosia and dyslexia but normal face recognition. *Journal of Cognitive Neuroscience, 9*, 555–604.

Murray, J. E., Yong, E., & Rhodes, G. (2000). Revisiting the perception of upside-down faces. *Psychological Science, 11*, 498–502.

Parks, T. E., Coss, R. C., & Coss, C. S. (1985). Thatcher and the Cheshire cat: Context and the processing of facial features. *Perception, 14(6)*, 747–754.

Pascalis, O., de Schonen, S., Morton, J., Deruelle, C., & Rabre-Grenet, M. (1995). Mother's face recognition by neonates: A replication and an extension. *Infant Behavior & Development, 18*, 79–85.

Rakover, S. S., & Teucher, B. (1997). Facial inversion effects: Parts and whole relationship. *Perception & Psychophysics, 59(5)*, 752–761.

Rhodes, G., Brake, S., & Atkinson, A. P. (1993). What's lost in inverted faces? *Cognition, 47*, 25–57.

Rhodes, G., Brennan, S., & Carey, S. (1987). Identification and rating of caricatures: Implications for mental representations of faces. *Cognitive psychology, 19*, 473–497.

Rhodes, G., Tan, S., Brake, S., & Taylor, K. (1989). Expertise and configural coding in face recognition. *British Journal of Psychology, 80*, 313–331.

Searcy, J. H., & Bartlett, J. C. (1996). Inversion and processing of component and spatial-relational information in faces. *Journal of Experimental Psychology: Human Perception & Performance, 22*, 904–915.

Schooler, J. W., & Engstler-Schooler, T. Y. (1990). Verbal overshadowing of visual memories: Some things are better left unsaid. *Cognitive Psychology, 22*, 36–71.

Stürzel, F., & Spillman, L. (2000). Thatcher illusion: Dependence on angle of rotation. *Perception, 29*, 937–942.

Tanaka, J. W., & Farah, M. J. (1993). Parts and wholes in face recognition. *Quarterly Journal of Experimental Psychology, 46A*, 225–245.

Tanaka, J. W., & Sengco, J. A. (1997). Faces and their configuration in face recognition. *Memory & Cognition, 25*, 583–592.

Thompson, P. (1980). Margaret Thatcher: A new illusion. *Perception, 9*, 483–484.

Valentine, T. (1988). Upside-down faces: A review of the effect of inversion upon face recognition. *British Journal of Psychology, 79*, 471–491.

Valentine, T. (1991). A unified account of the effects of distinctiveness, inversion, and race in face recognition. *Quarterly Journal of Experimental Psychology, 43A*, 161–204.

Valentine, T., & Bruce, V. (1986). The effect of race, inversion and encoding activity upon face recognition. *Acta Psychologica, 61*, 259–273.

Valentine, T., & Bruce, V. (1988). Mental rotation of faces. *Memory and Cognition, 16(6)*, 556–566.

Yin, R. K. (1969). Looking at upside-down faces. *Journal of Experimental Psychology, 81*, 141–145.

Young, A. W., Hellawell, D., & Hay, D. C. (1987). Configural information in face perception. *Perception, 16*, 747–759.

4

Isolating Holistic Processing in Faces (And Perhaps Objects)

ELINOR MCKONE, PAOLO MARTINI,
AND KEN NAKAYAMA

It is well established that faces, at least, are processed "holistically." Many theoretical issues regarding holistic processing, however, are rather poorly understood. It remains a matter of debate whether holistic processing is possible for other types of objects, in ordinary subjects as well as for experts in the object domain; this is relevant to theories of the role and origin of holistic processing. Moreover, even for faces, there is much debate about exactly what holistic processing is, and little is known of its specific properties (e.g., its sensitivity to image plane rotation, depth rotation, etc.) as might be necessary to construct viable theories of face recognition. In this chapter, we suggest that progress in understanding these issues has been constrained by methodological difficulties. In particular, many previous methods of studying face (and object) recognition confound holistic processing with contributions from part-based processing. We then give an overview of five experimental techniques that *isolate* the holistic component of processing. We demonstrate the use of our techniques in exploring the exact properties of holistic processing for faces, and describe their potential value in investigating whether holistic processing occurs for other objects.

Faces as Special Objects

Face recognition is, perhaps, the most interesting of all classes of visual recognition, for the simple reason that humans identify other people almost entirely by their faces, rather than, for example, by their hands or their smell. Correspondingly, much empirical evidence suggests that—in ordinary adult subjects at least—faces form a "special" class of object. In neuroimaging research, faces produce specific activation of a region of the right fusiform gyrus (e.g., Kanwisher, McDermott, & Chun, 1997), in comparison to other objects requiring within-class discrimination (individual hands, individual houses). In neuropsychology, both pure prosopagnosia (poor face recognition with intact within-class object discrimination; McNeil & Warrington, 1993) and pure object agnosia (poor object recognition with intact face recognition; Moscovitch, Winocur, & Behrmann, 1997) have been reported.

Behaviorally, faces and objects are dissociated most clearly by their sensitivity to orientation. In recognition memory, for example, all stimuli are remembered more poorly when studied (and tested) upside down, as compared to upright, but this inversion effect is only small for objects and much larger for faces (e.g., Yin, 1969).

The usual explanation of the disproportionate inversion effect for faces is that it reflects a special type of cognitive processing for upright faces, variously referred to as *holistic, relational,* or *configural.* There is little agreement on exactly what this type of processing actually is (of which more later), but the general idea is that either there is no decomposition into parts (Tanaka & Sengco, 1997), beyond perhaps simple lines and edges of early vision (Moscovitch et al., 1997), or that there are interactions between multiple parts over a broad region of the face (cf. Rhodes, 1988). It is also assumed that holistic processing includes detailed coding of distance information (e.g., Cooper & Wojan, 2000; Rhodes, 1988), such as how far it is between the eyes, or between the top of the eyelid and the eyebrow. In contrast to the holistic processing received by upright faces, it is argued that inverted faces and scrambled faces (and objects, regardless of orientation) are processed in a "part-based" manner. Again, it is not entirely clear what this means, but presumably part-based processing involves some sort of "structural description" coding (cf. Biederman, 1987)—that is, decomposition into abstract geonlike parts— plus some coding of basic relationships among these parts, but only in a only discrete fashion (the nose is *above* the mouth; the handle is *to the side of* the cup) rather than full-distance information (Cooper & Wojan, 2000).

With respect to faces as stimuli, several paradigms have been used to confirm that upright faces are processed holistically, while inverted faces are not. Many of these results are reviewed at length by other authors in the present volume. Briefly, major paradigms include the *composite effect* (Young, Hellawell, & Hay, 1987), in which two different half-faces fuse, slowing naming of the top half. This composite effect occurs for upright faces, but is absent (Young et al. 1987) or weaker (Carey & Diamond, 1994) for inverted faces. Similarly, in the *part-whole paradigm* (Tanaka & Farah, 1993) a face part is remembered better in the context of the whole face than in isolation; this occurs for upright faces but not inverted faces (and for intact faces but not scrambled faces). In *configural versus local alteration* paradigms (Bartlett & Searcy, 1993; Leder & Bruce, 1998; Rhodes, Brake & Atkinson 1993), perceived bizarreness and distinctiveness are affected by relational/configural changes (eyes shifted closer together, mouth shifted down, eyes and mouth flipped to produce the grotesque "Thatcher" illusion); this occurs for upright faces, but relational effects are weaker or absent for inverted faces. Local feature changes (bushier eyebrows, thickened lower lip, blackened teeth), in contrast, affect perception similarly in both orientations.

Surprisingly, there have been relatively few direct comparisons of holistic processing between faces and objects. Of the techniques developed above for faces, the part whole paradigm is the only one to have been used to any extent with objects. In nonexperts—that is, people who do not have specific expertise in the relevant object domain—the general finding is of no advantage of wholes over parts. This has been obtained for houses, dog faces, car fronts, and the artificial "Greebles" (Tanaka & Gauthier, 1997; Tanaka & Farah, 1993, chapter 2 this volume; Tanaka & Sengco, 1997), although Tanaka and Gauthier (1997) did find a wholes advantage for biological cells. (In experts, there is some evidence of holistic processing from the part whole paradigm—e.g., in dog experts looking at dog faces, Tanaka & Gauthier, 1997; also see Tarr, chapter 7 this volume.) Thus, Tanaka and colleagues, along with most other face-recognition researchers, have accepted that nonexperts do *not* process objects holistically, even in the upright orientation.

In the more general perceptual literature, however, there are many references to ordinary subjects showing "holistic" or "configural" processing of stimuli other than faces. For example, Kimchi (1994) demonstrated a relative processing dominance of "configural" (gestalt-like) properties such as closure and intersection rather than local properties such as line orientation and direction of line curvature. The word superiority effect (Reicher, 1969; Wheeler, 1970) is also sometimes taken as an example of "holistic" processing; here, perception of a degraded letter is more accurate when that letter is presented in a whole word than alone. Finally, Cave and Kosslyn (1993) argued that objects are recognized "holistically," based on a finding of little difference in naming times between line drawings of common objects broken at natural boundaries (i.e., into geonlike parts) and the same objects broken at arbitrary locations. This literature on objects, however, has generally made no reference to the specific paradigms used to show "holistic" processing of faces.

Overall, it is clear from studies that have contrasted faces and objects that faces do receive some sort of special processing. The studies of face recognition per se also make it clear that upright faces are processed holistically while inverted faces are not. The situation regarding holistic processing of objects, however, is less clear. There is evidence suggesting at least some sort of "processing of the whole" for objects, even in nonexperts; it remains unclear, however, whether this represents the same sort of holistic processing carried out for faces or whether, perhaps, it might be attributed to the simpler "discrete" relationships among parts included in a part-based structural description.

The Origin and Role of Holistic Processing

Within the face-recognition literature, the generally accepted position is that in ordinary adults holistic processing occurs only for faces and not for other object classes. This has led to a conceptualization of the subsystems of visual cognition something like that illustrated in figure 4.1. In this model, there is a specialized system for faces; this utilizes holistic processing and is accessed by upright faces only. Inverted faces, scrambled faces, single face parts, and objects regardless of orientation are then processed by a generic "object recognition" system, that utilizes part-based processing.

Within the face-recognition literature, debate has been centred on the *origin* of holistic processing for faces. In one view, the ability to recognize other people by their faces is so essential to social survival that, as with language, evolution has produced innate knowledge of basic facial structure (e.g., Farah, Rabinowitz, Quinn, & Liu, 2000). Morton and Johnson (1991), for example, propose that there is an innate system that orients newborns to faces; this can then support rapid development of a full-face processor through learning. Moreover, the holistic processing necessary to support discrimination among highly similar individuals (especially given great changes in the facial image with view, lighting direction, expression, makeup, facial movement, and so on) is so resource intensive that it must be saved only for faces, even in adults. Thus, this first version of the role of holistic processing is straightforwardly compatible with the model in figure 4.1: holistic processing is specific to the face-recognition system and, as indicated, occurs for *no* other objects.

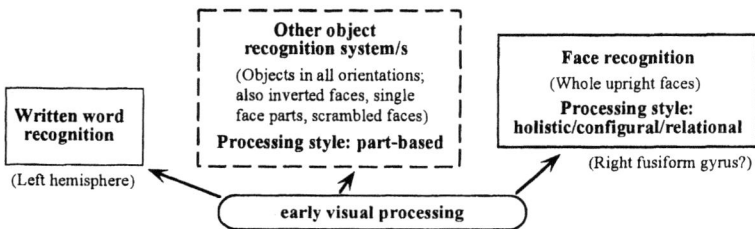

FIGURE 4.1. Proposed functional architecture of visual pattern recognition. The "other object recognition system/s" box is shown with a dotted outline to indicate that it may comprise multiple specific systems and/or cortical areas for different types of stimuli (which share a part-based processing style).

In a second view, holistic processing is a general property of expertise in making within-class discriminations (Diamond & Carey, 1986; Gauthier & Tarr, 1997), rather than being tailored specifically for faces. Face recognition demands discrimination of individual exemplars (*Bill* vs. *John*), which differ only in minor ("second-order") deviations from a shared "first-order" configuration (the same parts in the same fixed layout: two eyes, chin, nose, etc., with eyes always *above* the nose). Most object recognition, in contrast, requires only *between-class* discrimination (*dog* vs. *bird*), where the parts (and their first-order configurations) differ substantially between different objects. According to the expertise hypothesis, then, face recognition behaves as special simply because, by adulthood, humans have had 20 or more years of discriminating individual faces, but almost no practice at making similar within-class discriminations about objects. Thus, this second version of the role of holistic processing argues that the "face recognition system" in figure 4.1 should actually be thought of as an "expert within-class discrimination system": while most people use this system only for faces, experts in other object domains (e.g., dog-show judges who are capable of discriminating one Scotch Terrier from another) will also use it to achieve holistic processing for their objects of expertise.

There is also a third possible interpretation of the "holistic processing" system shown in figure 4.1: It can operate even for *objects* by *nonexperts*. From the perspective of the face-recognition literature, this proposal seems rather odd and perhaps even something of a "straw man"—after all, it fails to explain why there is anything special about faces. From outside the face-recognition literature, however, it would seem quite a reasonable proposal. In addition to the empirical evidence of some sort of "processing of the whole" for objects described earlier, there exists an entire class of theories in which objects (even by nonexperts) are *not* recognized via decomposition into parts, but instead by a form of template matching to a particular stored view of the object (e.g., Bulthoff, Edelman, & Tarr, 1994; Tarr, chapter 7 this volume; Tarr & Bulthoff, 1995; Ullman, 1989). Given that this stored view includes full distance information, and that recognition is achieved via some measure of total overlap between the image (after appropriate transformations) and the stored representation, it is difficult to see how "view-based" representations of objects would differ from "holistic" representations of faces (indeed, researchers in this area often list faces as simply one example of objects). In this third view, then, the "face recognition system" in figure 4.1 is not a face-recognition system at all; instead, it is a holistic processor, which can potentially operate for any stimulus, object or face, regardless of expertise. To explain the finding that holistic processing is stronger for faces than for objects, and perhaps stronger for objects of expertise than for other objects, some other mechanism would then be needed; for example, if parallel part-based and holistic systems were available for *any* visual stimulus (as suggested by several theorists, e.g., Kosslyn et al., 1989), then particular tasks might bias processing toward using one system or the other (e.g., Cooper & Wojan, 2000).

Thus, we have at least three very different ideas about holistic processing in faces and objects. These range from a theory in which only faces receive holistic processing, to a theory in which faces and objects of expertise receive holistic processing, to a theory in which all objects can be processed holistically (perhaps depending on task requirements).

The Exact Nature of Holistic Processing for Faces

One point on which all three theories agree is that *faces*, at least, are processed holistically. Even for faces, however, the exact nature of this processing is not well understood. For example, different researchers use different terminology to describe what is "special" about faces. Some have suggested a coding of the exact spatial relations between face features (distances between eyes, etc.), perhaps relative to the prototypical config-uration (e.g., Rhodes, 1988; Diamond & Carey, 1986); correspondingly, the terms "relational" and "configural" suggest interactions between mul-tiple features across broad regions of the face. Others have suggested a coding in which there are no component parts (Tanaka & Farah, 1993), perhaps instead working via a principal components analysis of face im-ages in which an individual face becomes a point in multidimensional "face-space" (O'Toole, Deffenbacher, Valetin, & Abdi, 1994; Valentine, 1991); in these cases, the term "holistic" is more commonly used. In general, though, researchers have not made strong claims about exact forms of representation; rather, many agree that it is genuinely unclear which is the most appropriate way of thinking about the special processing for faces.

There is also little empirical knowledge of the specific properties of holistic processing for faces. It is clear that any complete theory of face recognition—and certainly a viable computational model—would need to explain the properties of holistic processing for faces in some detail. At present, however, there is very little information regarding what these properties actually are. Ideally, we would like to know the operational range of holistic processing with many factors, such as image plane ro-tation, depth rotation, degree of structural deviation from a normal face, and so on. Is a face lying on its side (90° rotation) processed holistically? Is a profile? What about a face with one eye hidden? At present, the literature contains suprisingly little information relevant to such basic questions.

Isolating Holistic Processing

The preceding discussion indicates much confusion about the role of ho-listic processing in face and object recognition, as well as a limited understanding of its exact nature even for faces. We suggest that a primary factor constraining progress in this area is that, in many standard tasks, it is difficult to disentangle the contributions of holistic processing from the contributions of part-based processing (also see Moscovitch et al., 1997). This arises, according to the model in figure 4.1, because the "holistic" and "part-based" systems operate simultaneously on the information provided from early vision; thus, overall performance will be based on some (poorly understood) combination of these two systems. To investigate holistic processing directly, it is necessary to be able to study the holistic system *in isolation*—that is, independent of the part-based system.

We illustrate this with faces. There is general agreement that faces are processed by the holistic system. Even an upright face, however, could also be processed in parallel as a part-based object. Thus, in most simple tasks, experimental performance with an upright face stimulus will reflect a combination of contributions from both the "face/holistic" and "object/part-based" systems (Bartlett & Searcy, 1993; Moscovitch et al., 1997; Rhodes et al., 1993). In recognition memory, for example, the ability to discriminate studied from new faces will not necessarily reflect face/holistic information: recognizing "the guy with the spiked green hair," or "the girl with the blue eyes," or even (in a poorly designed experiment) "the photograph that was unusually dim" might be sufficient for accurate memory performance. Attempting to determine the properties of the face/holistic recognition system from such an experiment is then impossible, since performance is based on some combination of whole-face processing, part-based processing from the object-recognition system (hairstyle, eye color), and perhaps even early vision (brightness of photograph).

Given these sorts of confounds, previous approaches to face recognition have tried to examine holistic face processing by *disrupting* it in some way—for example, by inverting or scrambling the face with normal subjects, or by focusing on prosopagnosia, the inability to recognize faces, in brain-injured subjects. This approach, however, relies on interpreting what *cannot* be done *without* the holistic system for faces, rather than directly studying what *is* done *by* this system.

To investigate the face/holistic system directly, we would like to be able to study it where part-based processing has been switched off altogether. Can it be taken for granted, however, that this would even be possible? According to the theoretical model shown in figure 4.1 it *should* be possible because holistic and part-based processing operate in parallel on the outputs of early visual processing—that is, part-based processing is not a stage on the way to holistic processing. Alternatively, serial theories of pattern recognition in which small parts are put together to construct bigger parts, which are eventually used to construct wholes (e.g., Perrett & Oram, 1998), would suggest that holistic processing could *not* operate without part-based processing if successful identification of parts must precede successful identification of the whole. Given these very different ideas, it can be seen that even demonstrating the *ability* for holistic processing to operate without part-based processing would be an important finding theoretically.

The first indication that holistic processing can operate without part-based processing (for faces) came from a neuropsychological patient reported by Moscovitch et al. (1997). Patient CK demonstrates perfect recognition of upright whole faces, regardless of low-level visual format; this includes real people, photographs, cartoons, "Mooney" faces, hidden faces, and so on. However, CK's pattern recognition is extremely poor (several standard deviations below controls) with all other visual stimuli, including objects, words, inverted faces, and faces presented as separated parts. In terms of the model in figure 4.1, then, CK appears to have a straightforward deficit: he has an intact holistic processing system for faces, but a severely damaged part-based processing system for all other object types. Thus, CK demonstrates an organic isolation of holistic processing for faces.

Experimental Isolation of Holistic Processing for Faces

Patient CK's responses to different types of face stimuli (e.g., rotated faces, half-faces) can potentially tell us much about the properties of an isolated holistic face-processing system (e.g., see Moscovitch et al., 1997; Moscovitch & Moscovitch, 2000). However, patients such as CK are exceedingly rare. There are only a few other reported cases of object agnosia without prosopagnosia (e.g., Humphreys & Rumiati, 1998; McMullen, Fisk, Phillips, & Maloney, 2000; Rumiati, Humphreys, Riddoch, & Bateman, 1994), and the patients were not tested in nearly so much detail as CK. Inspired by the existence of such patients, however, our own work in this area has concentrated on finding ways to isolate holistic processing for faces via experimental means in normal subjects.

We have now developed several techniques that achieve this aim. Each relies on a comparison between upright faces, processed as *holistic plus parts*, and inverted faces, processed as *parts only*. In order to *isolate* holistic processing, the idea is then to discover some signature phenomenon that exists for upright whole faces, *but does not occur at all for inverted faces* (or for a single face part, or for scrambled faces). Under these circumstances, the signature phenomenon can be attributed purely to the holistic system in figure 4.1, with no contribution from the part-based system.

The techniques we have developed are all, at first glance, very different. All, however, are implementations of a single theoretical idea. This idea is that (1) the holistic processing mechanism should have *greater sensitivity* (i.e., be able to respond on the basis of less information in the stimulus) than the part-based mechanism because it sums information from across the whole face area; and (2) holistic processing therefore should continue to operate even when the smaller parts that make up that face are not sufficient to support above-chance performance. Thus, it should be possible for holistic processing to remain "above threshold" when identification of parts falls "below threshold." This idea predicts that holistic processing can then be isolated by making the task difficult in some way: it should be possible to "push" processing until a point is reached at which the signature phenomenon of interest disappears entirely for inverted faces, but remains present for upright faces.

Once a signature phenomenon has been discovered that isolates holistic processing for upright faces in this manner, this phenomenon can then be used to index holistic processing with various less-than-ideal face stimuli (rotated faces, half-faces, faces with various parts covered, etc.). For example, if the signature phenomenon in question were still to be obtained with 45° of rotation in the image plane, then this would indicate that holistic processing survives this degree of misorientation from upright. The indexing of holistic processing in this manner allows a closer investigation of its exact properties than has been possible in the literature to date.

We now give an overview of our various techniques for isolating holistic processing for faces. To reiterate, each technique produces a signature phenomenon that exists *only* for upright faces. Inverted faces provide the primary control stimulus, given that inverted faces (1) do not access the holistic face recognition system, but (2) are matched to upright faces, in low-level visual properties (spatial frequency components, etc.) and also in the amount of local feature information available to the part-based/object-recognition system (eye color, nose contour, etc). Other control stimuli include a *single isolated feature* (e.g., nose alone) and/or a *scrambled face* (all features retain their orientation, but are switched in position). Again, these control stimuli are not expected to access the holistic face recognition system; unlike inverted faces, however, they are matched to upright faces in terms of amount of pre-experimental exposure to the upright orientation of each feature (i.e., people have seen upright noses exactly as often as upright whole faces), and also in terms of lighting direction (which becomes important in some of the techniques).

Technique 1. Categorical Perception of Identity in Noise

McKone, Martini, and Nakayama (2001) isolated holistic face processing via categorical perception of face identity in noise. "Categorical perception" refers to the distortion of a physical continuum (e.g., wavelength of visible light) into perceptual categories (color bands of the rainbow). Experimentally, it is demonstrated by showing better pair discrimination of stimuli that cross a category boundary than of a physically equidistant pair that falls within the same perceptual category.

With faces, the physical continuum is created by morphing the face of one individual into that of another. Previous studies (e.g., Beale & Keil,

1995) had already demonstrated that categorical perception occurred between two individuals; for example, if a forced-choice between John F. Kennedy (face 1) and Bill Clinton (face 2) predicted a category boundary at the morph containing 52% Clinton, then a 40%–60% morph pair was seen as more dissimilar (one seen as Kennedy, the other as Clinton) than a 20%–40% morph pair (both seen as Kennedy). Levin and Beale (2000), however, had demonstrated that this effect occurred for inverted faces as well as for upright faces (although it was weaker inverted). Thus, we argued that, with the types of face stimuli used in previous studies, categorical perception for upright faces relied on a *combination* of part-based and holistic processing.

In our experiments, we attempted to make face identification more difficult, to the point where no single part alone would be sufficient to support·categorical perception. To do so, we removed the hair, chose two similar endpoint individuals, and added heavy noise to the stimuli (see figure 4.2). Under these circumstances, we found that categorical perception for upright faces was still possible. This was done using several measures, with results from a pair-similarity rating task shown in figure 4.2. Despite the categorical perception for upright whole faces, however, there was no such effect for inverted faces, nor for a single feature presented alone (the nose, shown upright). Moreover, there was no learning of categorical perception for these control stimuli even with 10,000–30,000 trials over six months of practice. Thus, we argued that the presence of categorical perception in noise provides a signature phenomenon that *isolates* holistic processing, in the sense that the phenomenon depends purely on this component of processing. The presence or absence of categorical perception in noise can then be used to index the presence or absence of holistic processing, for various types of face stimuli.

Technique 2. Learning Identical Twins

The rationale for adding noise in Technique 1 was partly to mimic the real-world unreliability of an individual's face from one view to the next, thus encouraging integration over the whole. In Robbins and McKone (in press), we included this unreliability directly in the stimulus set by using multiple different photographs (in different poses) of a set of identical twins. Our rationale was then that, if the twins were sufficiently difficult to tell apart, discrimination ability would rely solely on holistic processing (i.e., no purely local cues would be sufficient to distinguish between them).

By choosing twins whose faces were sufficiently similar, we were indeed able to isolate whole-face processing: learning of identity was possible when the stimuli were trained upright (6/6 subjects learned the twins with excellent generalization to new photographs and tasks), but not inverted (0/9 subjects showed generalizable learning, even given eight hours of training with feedback). Thus, the ability to discriminate between these

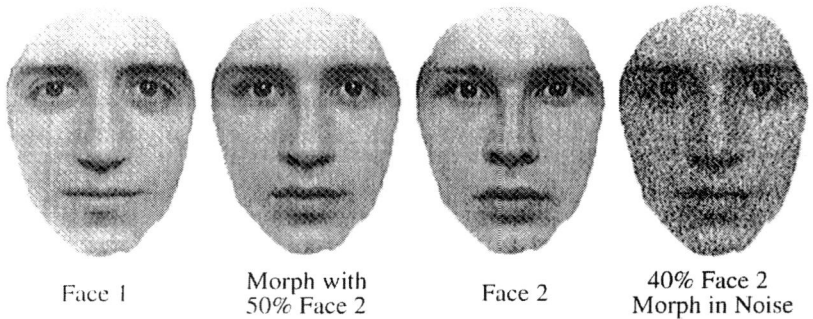

| Face 1 | Morph with 50% Face 2 | Face 2 | 40% Face 2 Morph in Noise |

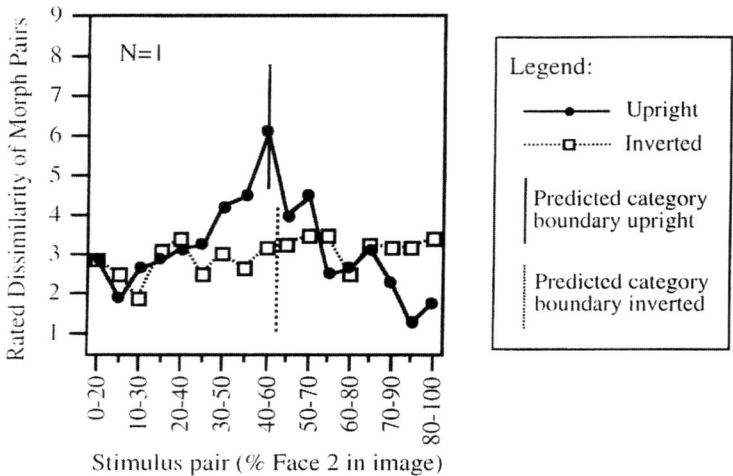

FIGURE 4.2. Isolating holistic processing via categorical perception of face identity in noise. Sample stimuli are shown at top, then data for one subject from a similarity rating task. Note that categorical perception corresponds to a peak in pair discriminability (i.e., higher scores) across the category boundary predicted from a binary Face 1–Face 2 decision task for single morphs. After McKone, Martini, & Nakayama (2001).

particular identical twins relies solely on holistic processing, and discrimination accuracy can be taken as an index of the strength of holistic processing.

Technique 3. Peripheral Identification

A third way of making face identification difficult is to present the faces in peripheral vision, since this degrades the input to early visual processing. McKone (in press) described an isolation technique that relied on this fact. Pre-experimental training was used to ensure that subjects knew the

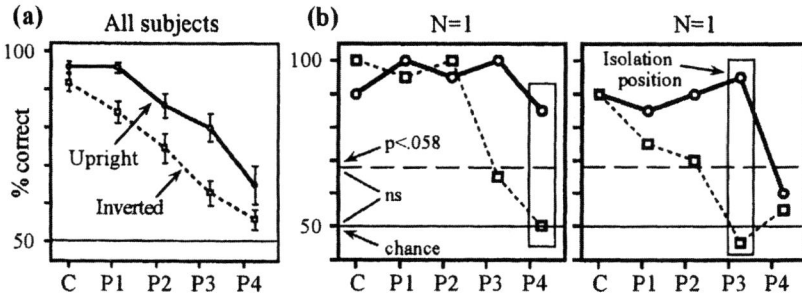

FIGURE 4.3. Isolating holistic processing via peripheral identification. (a) Identification accuracy (Face 1 vs. Face 2) averaged across all subjects, with central (C) and increasingly peripheral (P1–P4) presentation. (b) Sample data for two individual subjects showing selection of the position which isolates holistic processing. After McKone (in press).

identity of two male faces (Face 1 and Face 2 in figure 4.2) when they were presented in central vision; this was was done in both upright and inverted orientations. In the experiment itself, stimuli were then presented either centrally or in one of four positions to the left or right of fixation (maximum eccentricity = 21°), for 150 ms (to prevent eye movements to the stimulus). The task was to report the identity of the face.

The obvious expectation was that identification accuracy would fall with increasing eccentricity of presentation. Critically, however, the prediction was that accuracy should fall off more slowly for upright faces than for inverted faces. In the upright orientation, a holistic representation should be available in memory, in addition to any part-based representations available to both upright and inverted faces. This representation of the whole should then assist in "seeing through" the degradation of visual processing introduced by peripheral presentation, allowing identification ability to survive further into the periphery with upright faces. Results showed that accuracy did indeed fall off more slowly for upright faces than for inverted faces (see figure 4.3).

To *isolate* holistic processing, the idea was then that, at a certain distance from fixation, performance with inverted faces would have reached chance (50% in this 2AFC task), while performance with upright faces remained good. Again, this pattern was observed: for the sample subject shown in figure 4.3, identification accuracy at Position 4 (21° from fixation) was 50% for inverted faces, but 85% for upright faces. It was possible to choose a position that isolated holistic processing in this manner for 17 of the 21 subjects tested. To index the strength of holistic processing, identification accuracy can then be assessed at each subject's individual "isolation position."

In addition to the inverted face control, McKone (in press) also tested a nose-alone stimulus in the same paradigm. In contrast to the whole-face results, there was no separation in the periphery between upright noses and inverted noses. This disposed of two alternative explanations of the whole-face results. Like faces, noses have a strong canonical upright; thus, the mere existence of a pre-experimentally familiar orientation is not sufficient to produce the peripheral separation. Also like the faces, the noses were lit (weakly) from above; a property of early visual processing is a preference to see surfaces as lit from above, but the nose control indicated that this was not the origin of the peripheral separation. Instead, the signature separation obtained with the whole-face stimulus could be attributed only to holistic processing of upright faces.

Technique 4. Mooney Face

In a fourth technique, McKone (in press) also described a method for isolating holistic processing based on "Mooney" faces. Mooney (1957) developed a set of high-contrast photographs in which the face is formed of white (lit) surfaces and black (unlit) shadows. In general, it is harder to see the face in a Mooney stimulus when it is shown inverted than when it is shown upright. To *isolate* holistic processing, however, the aim was to select a Mooney face that was difficult enough that it could be seen when upright, but *not at all* when inverted.

Not just any Mooney face will do for this purpose: the "easy" one in figure 4.4 can be seen even inverted, presumably reflecting strong local information about the outline of eyes, eyebrows, etc. Figure 4.4 shows the

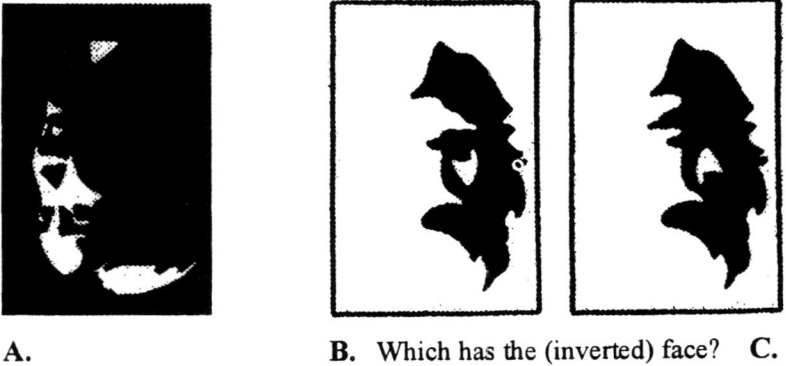

A.   **B.** Which has the (inverted) face?   **C.**

FIGURE 4.4. Isolating holistic processing via a difficult Mooney face. (A) An "easy" Mooney stimulus, in which the face can be seen even inverted. (B & C) The experimental stimuli, comprising one "difficult" Mooney face and one distractor. In the inverted form (as drawn), an upside-down face is not seen in either member of the pair. Rotate the page 180° to view the same stimuli upright; the 3-dimensional face should become visible, along with its sex, race and age. Answer: C (female, white, young adult, looking toward camera and lit from top right). After McKone (in press); A and C are taken from Mooney (1957).

actual stimulus selected for testing, along with a distractor nonface stimulus formed from a rearrangement of the original contours. Both the real face and the distractor are printed in the inverted orientation. Of 72 subjects shown this pair and instructed to choose the upside-down face, only 64% (chance = 50%) picked the correct stimulus, and only 17% could correctly report its sex, race, and age group. When the stimuli were shown upright, in contrast, 93% chose the real face and 80% correctly reported all three attributes. Thus, for most people (although not all), this particular Mooney face isolates holistic processing: it can be seen upright, but not inverted. Note also that a percept of an inverted face does not seem to develop with additional exposure. Viewing time makes no difference (indeed, unrestricted viewing was used in the present experiment), and there appears to be no learning with practice—if a subject does not see the inverted face within the first showing or two it seems they never do (with up to two years of exposure for several lab group members).

To index holistic processing, a rating of the strength of the face percept can then be used; it is necessary only to select those subjects who clearly see the face upright, but do not see it at all inverted. McKone (in press) used this method to ensure that the perception of the upright Mooney face could not be attributed to lighting direction: the strength of the face percept fell off symmetrically with rotation away from upright (clockwise or anticlockwise), despite the fact the face is lit from top right, rather than directly from above.

Technique 5. Salience Matching of Superimposed Faces

The results of the isolation techniques described above are consistent with our initial idea that holistic processing for upright faces is more perceptually sensitive than part-based processing for inverted faces. The final isolation technique, developed by Martini, McKone, and Nakayama (2002) relies on a slightly different implementation of this idea: rather than find a phenomenon that exists for upright faces but not for inverted faces, Martini et al. put an upright and an inverted face *in conflict* with one another. This was done by superimposing two copies of the same face in overlapping spatial locations, with the expectation that the upright face would be perceived as stronger than the inverted face when the stimuli were in fact physically identical.

This is demonstrated in figure 4.5. Here, the contrast of the upright face image is the same as that of the superimposed inverted face image (i.e., this is a 50:50 stimulus), but the upright face is perceived more strongly. Martini et al. allowed subjects to adjust the relative contrast of the two face images until they were seen as being equally strong; at this point, the percept is of rivalry between the two (i.e., as in the Necker cube, the upright face interpretation is seen for a while, followed by the inverted face interpretation, followed by the upright face, etc.). The percentage of upright:inverted in the image required to equate perceptual

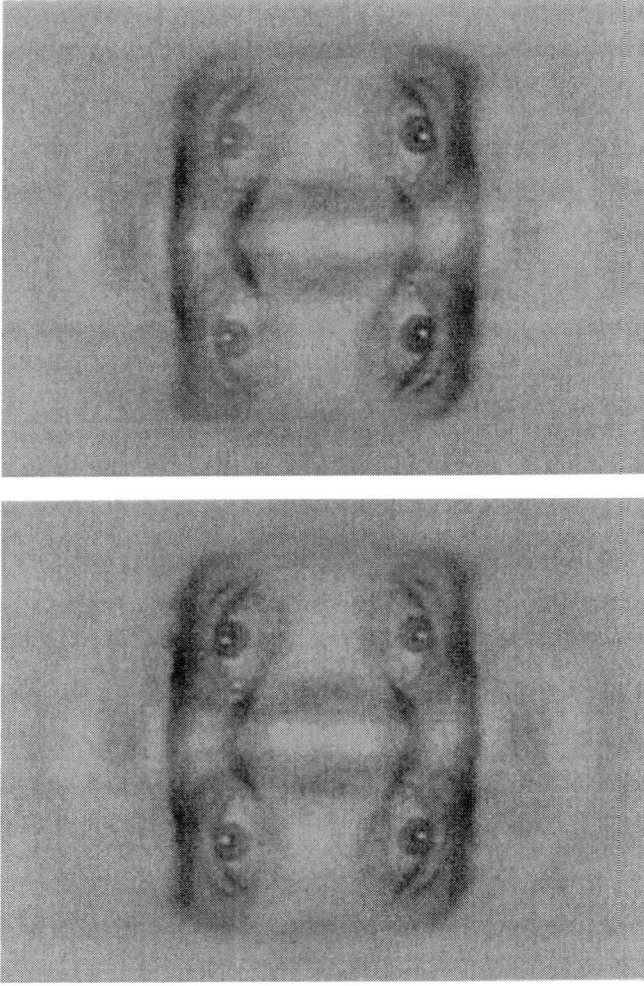

A. 50:50 stimulus (U:I) **B. 40:60 stimulus (U:I)**

FIGURE 4.5. Isolating holistic processing via salience matching of superimposed faces. Each image shows two copies of the same face (Face 1 of Figure 2) superimposed in the upright and inverted orientation. In (A), the 50:50 stimulus has equal contrast for each orientation: here, the percept is that the upright face is stronger than the inverted face (rotate page 90 to confirm the physical equality of the two orientations; rotate page 180 to confirm that upright is always perceived as stronger). In (B) the upright component has lower contrast than the inverted component; a contrast ratio of 40:60 produces the approximate point of matched perceptual salience. After Martini, McKone, & Nakayama (2002).

salience was $M = 40:60$ ($SD = 6$, $N = 12$), indicating a clear perceptual bias toward the upright face.

As a control, we tested a scrambled face stimulus via superposition of an upright scrambled face and the same image inverted. When the facial configuration was broken in this manner, there was no bias toward upright. Further conditions tested indicated that the strength of the bias was not related to exactly where the two faces were superimposed (i.e., which features overlapped), and was also independent of lighting direction (i.e., the same bias was obtained for weakly bottom-lit as for weakly top-lit faces).

Given that the perceptual bias toward upright cannot be attributed to low-level or part-based information, this phenomenon provides a fifth method for isolating holistic processing for faces. The strength of the perceptual bias toward upright, determined from the contrast ratio required to match perceptual salience, can then be used to index the strength of holistic processing.

Converging Evidence from Five Techniques

The results described above confirm that, for faces at least, it is possible to isolate holistic processing from part-based processing—that is, it is possible to find a series of phenomena that exist for upright whole faces, but do not exist *at all* for inverted faces, single features, or scrambled faces, even with large amounts of practice and/or unrestricted viewing time. One advantage of grouping all five techniques together here is that it emphasizes the converging results from different specific methods. With any single technique it might (perhaps) be possible to come up with an alternative explanation of our "isolation" findings. This becomes increasingly implausible, however, as multiple methods all confirm the same result. We thus conclude that our isolation techniques do, indeed, provide access to high-level representations in the "face/holistic" system in figure 4.1, rather than reflecting the peculiarities of any one task or any one stimulus manipulation.

The Exact Properties of Holistic Processing for Faces

Having isolated holistic processing, we can then use our various techniques to explore the exact properties of holistic face representations. As noted earlier in this chapter, many properties are of theoretical interest, but very few have received any experimental investigation in the literature. We now describe what *is* known from studies of holistic processing in isolation—that is, unconfounded from part-based influences. Two of the results come from our own investigations, and a third comes from Moscovitch et al.'s (1997) results with patient CK, who has an organic isolation of holistic processing.

Orientation Tuning of Holistic Processing for Faces

We have investigated one property of holistic face processing in some detail, namely its orientation tuning with rotation in the image plane. We know that holistic processing occurs for upright faces, and that it does not occur for inverted faces; the question is, what happens at intermediate rotations? At what orientation does holistic processing drop out, and what is the shape of the function relating orientation and strength of holistic processing?

Using a simple measure of face recognition—reaction time in famous nonfamous decisions—Valentine and Bruce (1988) claimed that face identification ability falls off *linearly* with rotation between upright (0°) and inverted (180°). Indeed, they used this finding to argue that there was nothing qualitatively different about the processing of upright and inverted faces (the evidence for differences reviewed in the first section of this chapter had not yet been produced at that time). As with all the simple measures of face recognition, however, we suggest that Valentine and Bruce's method is likely to have confounded holistic processing with part-based processing—that is, reaction time at any given orientation probably reflected some poorly understood combination of holistic and part-based contributions to identification.

Figure 4.6 indicates that, when holistic processing is studied in isolation, a very different pattern emerges. We have investigated orientation tuning using four of our five isolation techniques (categorical perception in noise, peripheral identification, Mooney face, and superimposed faces). The same result was obtained in every case: when the whole-face component of processing is isolated, falloff with rotation was clearly curvilinear, with slow falloff close to 0°, followed by sharp decay between approximately 30° and 120°. In general, whole-face processing was still reasonably strong at 45° from upright, but had largely disappeared by somewhere around 90°, corresponding to a face lying on its side. There was also substantial variation in the breadth of tuning across individuals, with the drop-out point ranging from 60° to 120° for different subjects.

Our results are consistent with data from a number of other sources. Patient CK shows a similar breadth of orientation tuning (approx. 45°–90° from upright) in informal tests of rotating an inverted face toward upright until he can identify it (Moscovitch et al., 1997). Data from Murray, Yong, and Rhodes (2000; also see Murray, Rhodes, & Schuchinsky, chapter 3 this volume) also suggest that holistic processing drops off most steeply between 60° and 135°; the technique used by these authors did not isolate holistic processing per se, but instead used Thatcher faces to pit the orientation of holistic information against the orientation of part-based information (i.e., as a Thatcher face is rotated, the orientation of the eyes and mouth varies in the opposite direction to the orientation of the overall facial structure). Finally, in single-cell recording from face-specific or face-body specific cells in monkeys, Ashbridge, Perrett, Jellema, and Oram

1 subject (10 hrs) — 0°, 22.5°, 45°, 67.5°, 90°, 180°

predicted category boundary

Rated dissimilarity of morph pairs differing by 20% of continuum

0-20   40-60   80-100
% Face 2 in morph

1. Categorical perception of identity in noise
(Note peak across predicted category boundary at 0°-45° but no peak at 67.5°-180°)

Mean 17 Ss (1 hr each)   linear
% correct (Face 1/Face 2)
80
50
0   45   90   135   180
Orientation (°)

3. Peripheral identification

Mean 11 Ss (1 hr each)
Rated strength of Mooney face
9
2
-180   0   +180

N=1
9
1
2 individual Ss

N=1
9
1
0   90   180
Orientation (°)

4. Mooney face

Proportion of inverted required to match perceived salience

6 individual subjects (1 hr each)
.7
.5
0   90   180

1 subject (3 hrs)
.7
.5
-180   0   +180
Orientation contrasted with inverted

5. Superimposed faces

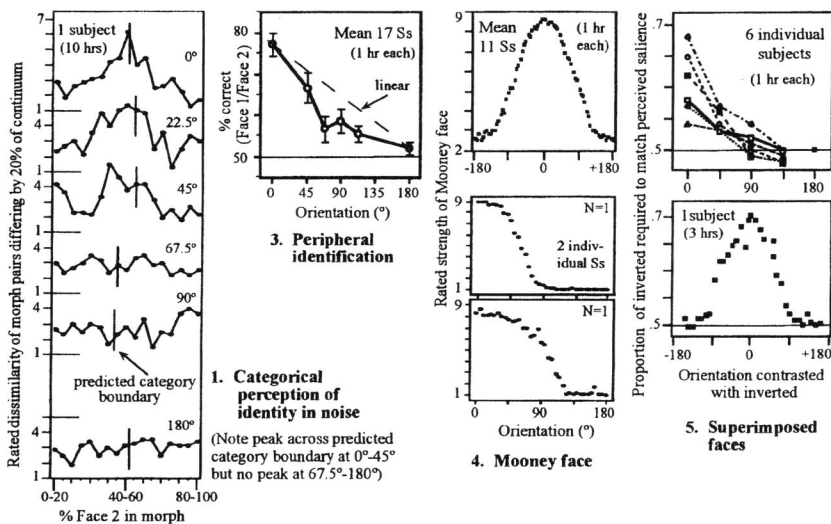

FIGURE 4.6. Effect of image plane rotation on holistic processing, as determined using four of the isolation techniques. Technique numbers are as referred to in the text. 1. After McKone et al. (2001). 3 & 4. After McKone (in press). 5. After Martini et al. (2002).

(2000) found the same broad yet constrained orientation tuning as observed here in humans: responses were reduced by half when the stimulus was rotated 45° or 90° away from the cell's preferred orientation, and responses reached their minimum value at 135°. (Also note that most of the cells had their preferred orientation at upright.)

The observed orientation tuning of holistic processing for faces contradicts the major computational model of face recognition in the literature, namely the principal-component analysis (PCA) approach (e.g., Hancock, Burton, & Bruce, 1996; O'Toole et al., 1994). The PCA approach is holistic, in the sense that each individual's face is expressed in terms of component eigenfaces, and each eigenface includes information from across the spatial extent of the face. However, it is assumed (1) that all face images have been aligned to upright prior to entry to the PCA identification, and (2) the PCA stage operates on pixel-by-pixel intensity information. Neither of these stages would predict anything like the observed orientation tuning of holistic face processing. The pre-alignment stage (e.g., rotation to upright) should operate for *any* orientation, while the pixel-based PCA stage can tolerate only tiny deviations from true upright (i.e., the correlation between the image and the internal representation would be very small even by 2° of misorientation). Thus, current PCA approaches can provide no explantion of why the orientation tuning of holistic processing should be broad (enduring until approximately 90°), yet still constrained (not possible beyond 90°–135°, however many times the subject has seen the stimuli).

In general, our orientation tuning results would appear to be incompatible with any theoretical models of face recognition in which faces are presumed to be rotated to upright prior to recognition. This includes all current "face-space" approaches (e.g., Valentine, 1991), not just the specific PCA model.

Size Tuning of Holistic Processing for Faces

We have conducted preliminary investigations of how holistic face processing varies with the size of the face image. We know of no previous studies of this issue. Figure 4.7 shows the size-tuning curve determined from the Mooney face technique; the superimposed-faces method also produced a similar pattern. As can be seen, holistic processing operates over a broad range of visual angles and remains strong from approximately 1° vertical extent to 11°. This corresponds to a very broad range of equivalent viewing distances from a real face (between 11 m and 60 cm, respectively). Holistic processing drops off rapidly outside this range (approaching zero at 12 m and 10 cm). Within the plateau region of strong holistic processing, there is a maximum at approximately 2°.

Again, we know of no specific theories of face recognition that would predict or explain this particular pattern of size tuning. We speculate that the broad operational range indicates a role for holistic processing, both in identifying individuals during approach in the environment and also in

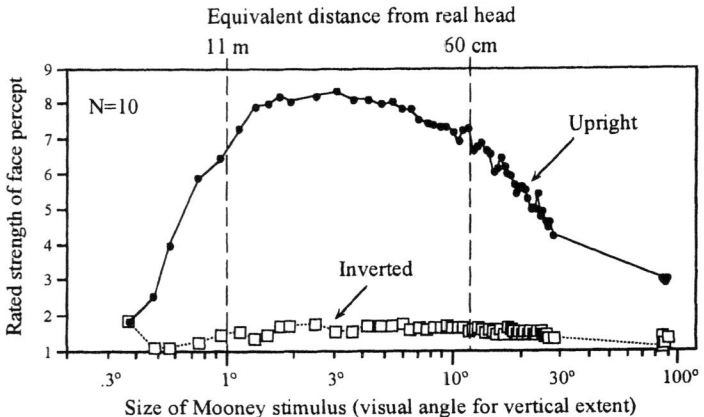

FIGURE 4.7. Size tuning of holistic face processing, determined from the Mooney face technique. Note log scale on x-axis. Vertical extent covers the entire stimulus including hair and neck; the face region itself is approximately 65% of this size. Equivalent viewing distances from a real head (assuming 20 cm forehead to chin) are approx. 1° = 11m, 11° = 60cm.

perceiving facial expressions at closer conversational distances. Regarding the maximum at 2°, we note that this visual angle corresponds to a real face seen at 5 m. Interestingly, this does *not* seem to be simply the most common viewing distance for faces (which we would assume is more like 1–2 m). The 2° does, however, correspond approximately to the size of the central region of the fovea; perhaps the fact that this region provides the highest-acuity information for pattern processing has led to a holistic face representation that operates particularly efficiently at this size of stimulus. We also speculate that the peak at 2° might have some social significance, such as corresponding to a distance at which people normally first identify a stranger, or expect a social response (nod, smile, etc), during approach. All of these possibilities remain to be explored.

How Much of the Face Is Required to Activate Holistic Processing?

Also of strong interest is the effect of increased deviation from normal facial configuration on holistic processing. Results from the previous literature demonstrate that face-stimuli with extreme violations of normal structure are not processed holistically: a single face feature is not treated as a face, nor is a scrambled face, nor is an "exploded" face that has been cut into sections and moved apart (e.g., Moscovitch et al., 1997; Tanaka & Farah, 1993). A major theoretical reason for the existence of holistic processing for faces, however, must surely be to allow reliable recognition in the absence of information about every face part (see McKone et al., 2001). The appearance of any given local feature varies substantially with lighting conditions and facial expression; moreover, in depth-rotated views, one eye or even a half-face is not visible. Thus, the face-recognition system would be expected to operate with at least some face stimuli that are less than structurally perfect. It is then of interest to know exactly *how* similar (and in what way) a stimulus has to be to a normal whole face in order to activate the holistic processing system.

Where the holistic system has been isolated, the only data available on this issue come from patient CK (Bartlett, Searcy & Abdi, chapter 1 this volume, discuss a few nonisolation studies). Moscovitch et al. (1997) reported that CK could identify famous people from a vertical half-face stimulus, but not from a horizontal half-face; this suggests that a vertical half-face is sufficient to activate holistic processing (perhaps owing to the similarity of a vertical half-face to a profile?). Patient CK can also reliably identify famous faces with one feature cut out from the image (i.e., the eyes, or the nose, or the mouth); he can then choose the correct feature (e.g., the correct nose, of two alternatives) to match the rest of the face, but *only* if he has identified the person. These results indicate that no single particular feature of the face is necessary to activate holistic processing, and moreover that the representation of the whole, once activated, can fill in quite a large missing section of the face.

Thus, CK shows that—as we might expect—holistic processing can survive quite a substantial deviation from a whole, normal face. The exact degree of deviation that can be tolerated has not yet been explored, however, either in CK or in normal subjects. For example, we do not know what happens if successively more parts of the face, beyond one single feature, are missing or covered. Moreover, the severity of structural violation that can be tolerated might be dependent on the *type* of violation; for example, holistic processing might be more sensitive to alterations that break first-order rules (the nose must be *centered* in the face; eyes must be *equal* in height) than equivalent alterations that do not (e.g., changing the specific distance between the eyes; cf. Cooper & Wojan, 2000).

Investigating Other Properties of Holistic Processing for Faces

There are many other properties of holistic processing for faces that we would like to know about, particularly if the eventual aim is to construct computational models of face recognition that accurately reflect human behavior. (One obvious question, for example, is how holistic processing varies with depth rotation.) Our "isolation" techniques provide a straightforward method for investigating these properties. The peripheral presentation technique, for example, could be used; once the "isolation" eccentricity has been determined for each subject using whole front-view faces, it is a simple matter to test identification accuracy at that eccentricity for, say, different depth-rotated views or faces with successively greater proportions of the face missing.

Of course, not all techniques are suitable for all questions (e.g., peripheral presentation cannot be used with size variations; the Mooney face could not be used to examine depth rotation), but in general, it should be possible to assess any given question via at least two or three of our different techniques. Moreover, it should be possible to do this with reasonable efficiency. With the peripheral presentation technique, we were able to get good data at six orientation conditions, plus determining the isolation point, using only 1 hour per subject and 21 subjects. With the overlaid faces technique, we were able to test 21 size conditions, using only 1 hour per subject and 12 subjects. With the Mooney face, we tested 72 orientation conditions in 1 hour per subject; this produced data that were stable enough to analyze even on a single-subject basis. This relative efficiency of our methods allows for a much more detailed investigation of holistic face processing than has been possible in the previous literature.[1]

Faces, Objects, Expertise

Another use of our isolation techniques could be in assessing possible holistic processing in *objects*. As described at the beginning of this chapter, there are at least three competing views about the role and origin of holistic processing. In one view, holistic processing arises from an innate face representation and remains unique to (upright) faces even in adulthood. In the second view, holistic processing can develop for any object as long as the object class has a shared first-order configuration and the subject has sufficient expertise at making within-class discriminations; moreover, presuming that the expertise has been obtained with the objects in one orientation only (e.g., dogs and birds, like faces, have a strong canonical upright), then only upright objects of expertise will be processed holistically, while the same objects inverted will continue to receive only part-based processing. In the third view, holistic processing can potentially occur for any stimuli (objects, faces, words), at least as long as the task requires this type of processing. (Recall that these theories correspond to different interpretations of the role of the "face/holistic" and "object/part-based" systems in figure 4.1.)

To evaluate the different theories of holistic processing, it is necessary to make direct comparisons between faces and objects, experts and non-experts, using strictly equivalent procedures in each case. Our isolation techniques are well suited to this task. In the peripheral identification technique, for example, the face stimuli could simply be changed from face 1 vs. face 2, to dog 1 vs. dog 2; after a pre-training phase to learn the dogs' identity with central presentation, the question would then be whether dogs show the same separation between upright and inverted in the periphery as do faces. Similarly, in the "superimposed" technique, the stimulus could be a dog (upright and inverted) instead of a face; the question would then be whether the dog shows the facelike bias toward the upright in perceptual salience matching. Implementations of our other techniques for objects are also possible.

Let us consider the expected outcome from our "isolation" techniques if holistic processing did *not* occur for a certain stimulus class. Under these circumstances, none of the signature phenomena we have obtained for faces (a peripheral advantage for upright stimuli, a bias toward the upright in superimposed stimuli, etc.) would be expected because there is *nothing to isolate*. For faces, the logic behind our isolation techniques was as follows: if processing is "pushed" by making the face-recognition task difficult in some way, then information from any single local region of the face will become insufficient to support reliable performance on the task, and face recognition will then rely purely on the holistic component of processing (since this integrates information from across the entire face region, and so is more sensitive than part-based processing). If, however, there was no holistic processing for a certain class of stimuli, both the upright and the inverted orientation will receive only part-based processing; thus, as processing is "pushed" by making the task more difficult, performance should degrade equally for the two orientations (i.e., there is no "whole" to take over when parts become insufficient to support performance). This will make it impossible to find a signature phenomenon that exists for the upright orientation but not for the inverted orientation—that is, if there is no holistic processing, it will not be possible for the whole to remain "above threshold" when all the parts have been pushed "below threshold."

We can now consider the various predictions for objects in our techniques, arising from different theories of the role and origin of holistic processing. According to the "faces only" theory, the signature phenomena of holistic processing that we have identified for faces should never exist for objects, neither in ordinary subjects nor in experts. For example, there should be no separation between upright and inverted in the periphery, no bias toward upright in superimposed objects, and it should be impossible to find a "Mooney object" equivalent of the Mooney face (i.e., one that can be seen upright but never upside down), even in experts.

The "expertise" theory makes different predictions. In ordinary (nonexpert) subjects, our signature phenomena will still be obtained for faces but no other objects. However, in experts (e.g., dog-show judges of many years experience tested on their own breed of expertise; Diamond & Carey, 1986), the "isolation" techniques will produce exactly the same pattern of results for objects of expertise as for faces; this will be true as long as the objects have a strong canonical upright since, as with faces, subjects will have had the opportunity to learn holistic processing in the upright orientation but not the inverted orientation. (The expertise hypothesis also predicts that, in young children, our signature phenomena would not be obtained even for faces, since the development of holistic processing for upright faces would require many years of expertise.)

Finally, the "anything can be holistic" theory makes different predictions again. Here, the only explanation of bigger inversion effects for faces than for objects is that a view-based (and thus orientation-specific) representation is being preferred for faces, while a more view-independent representation is being preferred for objects. However, since this theory presumes that view-based "holistic" representations do *exist* for all objects, then it should be possible to force processing to rely on this representation by carefully matching the task demands for objects to those usually required for faces. Since this is the case in our isolation techniques, then the prediction of this third view of holistic processing is that *all* objects should show the same pattern of results as for faces in our techniques, *even by nonexperts.*

To date, we have made only one preliminary investigation of whether holistic processing can operate in isolation from part-based processing for objects, limited to ordinary nonexpert subjects. Using the peripheral identification technique, McKone and MacPherson (2002) tested dog stimuli, requiring within-class discrimination among Dachshund 1, Dachshund 2, and Dachshund 3. Subjects were given initial identification training with feedback, which ensured excellent identification with central presentation (both upright and inverted). When the stimuli were then flashed at various positions in the periphery, no inversion effect emerged at any eccentricity.

A face control experiment (Face 1 vs. Face 2 vs. Face 3), revealed the usual peripheral inversion effect for faces.

Thus, our results so far argue against the "any object can be processed holistically" theory; it seems that faces *are* genuinely different from objects, even when the task is the same and involves within-class discrimination in both cases. This conclusion is consistent with results from Tanaka and Farah's (1993) part-whole paradigm, which usually shows no whole-over-part advantage for objects by nonexperts. It suggests, however, that researchers in the general pattern-recognition literature advocating "holistic" or "configural" processing of nonface objects will need to reconsider exactly what they might mean by these terms. In the word-superiority effect, for example, the whole is clearly important in identifying the parts, but we suggest that this cannot reflect the same holistic processing as occurs for faces.

Having rejected (on the basis of our preliminary data at least) the third theory of the origin and role of holistic processing, this leaves us with either the "faces only" approach or the "expertise" hypothesis. As yet, we have not discriminated between these possibilities by using any of our isolation techniques with expert subjects. The expertise hypothesis, however, makes straightforward predictions. For example, in our dogs experiment, dachshund experts should show a facelike separation between upright and inverted in peripheral identification. Moreover, as for faces, it should then be possible to select an eccentricity for each subject that *isolates* holistic processing for dachshunds (i.e., identification accuracy has reached chance for inverted dogs, but remains good for upright dogs).

If holistic processing were to be obtained for objects of expertise, our isolation techniques would provide an efficient means for comparing the particular properties of this holistic processing with those for faces; these properties could include the orientation tuning of holistic processing, its size tuning, the proportion of the object required to activate it, and so on. Exploration of several such properties could be used to provide a very strong test of whether experts develop genuinely facelike special processing for objects.

A Word of Warning on Using the Techniques

A primary aim of this chapter has been to summarize our techniques for isolating holistic processing, with the hope of encouraging other researchers to use them. Anyone intending to do so, however, should keep in mind that there are some important technical requirements for getting the methods to work. Most important, it is essential to avoid any gross local cues in the stimuli that could still support performance when the task is made "difficult." Even for faces, one could imagine stimuli for which local cues would always outweigh holistic information. For example, we would not expect peripheral identification to isolate holistic processing if Face 1 had spiked hair while Face 2 was bald, or Face 1 was wearing spectacles while Face 2 was not, or the Face 1 photograph was dim while the Face 2 photograph was bright. For other objects, this is potentially quite a problem; parrots, for example, have strong local color boundaries that might remain the primary cue to identification however degraded the stimulus became. There are also some specific requirements of each technique (e.g., superimposed faces only works with gray-scale pictures and not line drawings; the type of noise in categorical perception must be matched to the type of local information in the stimulus, etc.). These requirements are described more fully in the original papers on each isolation method.

Conclusions

We have described five different techniques that isolate holistic processing for faces in normal subjects. The simple ability to isolate holistic processing makes it clear that, for faces, not only is the whole "more than the sum of its parts," but the whole can actually operate *without* the parts. We have then demonstrated how our techniques can be used to study the properties of holistic face representations—unconfounded with contributions of part-based processing—in some detail.

Our research to date has focused on faces because it is well established that faces, at least, receive holistic processing. Whether holistic processing occurs in isolation only for faces or can do so for other objects under certain circumstances remains largely to be investigated. Given the theoretical debates about the role and origin of holistic processing, the properties of holistic "face" processing revealed in our various techniques (e.g., the orientation tuning, etc.) may turn out to be the unique properties of face recognition—that is, what makes faces different from other objects. Alternatively, it may turn out that our data reflect properties of holistic processing in general, as used for expert recognition of any objects (or even for objects in nonexperts).

Notes

Preparation of this chapter was aided by Australian Research Council grant F01027 to the first author. We thank Gillian Rhodes, Mary Peterson, and Brad Duchaine for comments on an earlier version of this chapter.
   1. The best of the previous methods that have been used to demonstrate holistic processing for faces—for example, the composite paradigm (Young, Hellawell, & Hay, 1987), or the part-whole paradigm (Tanaka & Farah, 1993)—could, technically, be used to explore its properties. These methods, however, mostly require a full experiment just to test the basic upright and inverted face conditions. Plotting, say, the orientation tuning of holistic processing with these paradigms would be extremely time-consuming and unwieldy.

References

Ashbridge, E., Perrett, D. I., Jellema, T., & Oram, M. W. (2000). Effect of image orientation and size on object recognition: Responses of single units in the macaque monkey temporal cortex. *Cognitive Neuropsychology, T*, 13–34.

Bartlett, J. C., & Searcy, J. (1993). Inversion and configuration of faces. *Cognitive Psychology, 25*(3), 281–316.

Beale, J. M., & Keil, F. C. (1995). Categorical effects in the perception of faces. *Cognition, 57*, 217–239.

Biederman, I. (1987). Recognition-by-components: A theory of human image understanding. *Psychological Review, 94*, 115–147.

Bulthoff, H. H., Edelman, S. Y., & Tarr, M. J. (1994). How are three-dimensional objects represented in the brain? *CogSci Memo No 5.*

Carey, S., & Diamond, R. (1994). Are faces perceived as configurations more by adults than by children? *Visual Cognition, 1*(2/3), 253–274.

Cave, C. B., & Kosslyn, S. M. (1993). The role of parts and spatial relations in object identification. *Perception, 22*(2), 229–248.

Cooper, E. E., & Wojan, T. J. (2000). Differences in the coding of spatial relations in face identification and basic-level object recognition. *Journal of Experimental Psychology: Learning Memory and Cognition, 26*(2), 470–488.

Diamond, R., & Carey, S. (1986). Why faces are and are not special: an effect of expertise. *Journal of Experimental Psychology: General, 115*(2), 107–117.

Farah, M. J., Rabinowitz, C., Quinn, G. E., & Liu, G. T. (2000). Early commitment of neural substrates for face recognition. *Cognitive Neuropsychology, 17*(1–3), 117–123.

Gauthier, I., & Tarr, M. J. (1997). Becoming a "greeble" expert: Exploring mechanisms for face recognition. *Vision Research, 37*(12), 1673–1682.

Hancock, P. J. B., Burton, A. M., & Bruce, V. (1996). Face processing: Human perception and principle components analysis. *Memory & Cognition, 24*, 26–40.

Humphreys, G. W., & Rumiati, R. I. (1998). Agnosia without prosopagnosia or alexia: Evidence for stored visual memories specific to objects. *Cognitive Neuropsychology, 15*(3), 243–277.

Kanwisher, N., McDermott, J., & Chun, M. M. (1997). The fusiform face area: A module in human extrastriate cortex specialized for face perception. *Journal of Neuroscience, 17*(11), 4302–4311.

Kimchi, R. (1994). The role of wholistic/configural properties versus global properties in visual form perception. *Perception, 23*(5), 489–504.

Kosslyn, S. M., Koenig, O., Barrett, A., Cave, C. B., Tang, J., & Gabrieli, J. D. (1989). Evidence for two types of spatial representations: Hemispheric specialization for categorical and coordinate relations. *Journal of Experimental Psychology: Human Perception and Performance, 15*(4), 723–735.

Leder, H., & Bruce, V. (1998). Local and relational aspects of face distinctiveness. *Quarterly Journal of Experimental Psychology, 51A*, 449–473.

Levin, D. T., & Beale, J. M. (2000). Categorical perception occurs in newly learned faces, cross-race faces, and inverted faces. *Perception & Psychophysics, 62*, 386–401.

Martini, P., McKone, E., & Nakayama, K. (2002). *Orientation tuning of human face processing estimated by contrast matching in transparency displays.* Manuscript in preparation.

McKone, E. (in press). Isolating the special component of face recognition: Peripheral identification, and a Mooney face. *Journal of Experimental Psychology: Learning Memory, & Cognition.*

McKone, E., & MacPherson, S. (2002). *Are faces unique? The origin of inversion effects in face and object recognition.* Manuscript in preparation.

McKone, E., Martini, P., & Nakayama, K. (2001). Categorical perception of face identity in noise: A method for isolating configural processing. *Journal of Experimental Psychology: Human Perception and Performance, 27*, 573–599.

McMullen, P. A., Fisk, J. D., Phillips, S. J., & Maloney, W. J. (2000). Apperceptive agnosia and face recognition. *Neurocase, 6*(5), 403–414.

McNeil, J. E., & Warrington, E. K. (1993). Prosopagnosia: a face-specific disorder. *Quarterly Journal of Experimental Psychology: A, 46*(1), 1–10.

Mooney, C. M. (1957). Age in the development of closure ability in children. *Journal of Psychology, 11*, 219–226.

Morton, J., & Johnson, M. H. (1991). CONSPEC and CONLEARN: A two-process theory of infant face recognition. *Psychological Review, 98*, 164–181.

Moscovitch, M., & Moscovitch, D. A. (2000). Super face-inversion effects for isolated internal or external features, and for fractured faces. *Cognitive Neuropsychology, 17*(1–3), 201–219.

Moscovitch, M., Winocur, G., & Behrmann, M. (1997). What is special about face recognition? Nineteen experiments on a person with visual object agnosia and dyslexia but normal face recognition. *Journal of Cognitive Psychology, 9*(5), 555–604.

Murray, J. E., Yong, E., & Rhodes, G. (2000). Revisiting the perception of upside-down faces. *Psychological Science, 11*(6), 492–496.

O'Toole, A. J., Deffenbacher, K. A., Valetin, D., & Abdi, H. (1994). Structural aspects of face recognition and the other race effect. *Memory and Cognition, 22*, 208–224.

Perrett, D. I., & Oram, M. W. (1998). Visual recognition based on temporal cortex cells: Viewer-centred processing of pattern configuration. *Zeitschrift fur Naturforschung, 53c*, 518–541.

Reicher, G. M. (1969). Perceptual recognition as a function of meaningfulness of stimulus material. *Journal of Experimental Psychology: General, 81*, 275–280.

Rhodes, G. (1988). Looking at faces: First-order and second-order features as determinants of facial appearance. *Perception, 17*(1), 43–63.

Rhodes, G., Brake, S., & Atkinson, A. P. (1993). What's lost in inverted faces? *Cognition, 47*, 25–57.

Robbins, R. A., & McKone, E. (in press). Can holistic processing be learned for inverted faces? *Cognition.*

Rumiati, R. I., Humphreys, G. W., Riddoch, J. M., & Bateman, A. (1994). Visual object agnosia without prospagnoisa or alexia: Evidence for hierarchical theories of visual recognition. *Visual Cognition, 2/3*, 181–225.

Tanaka, J. W., & Farah, M. J. (1993). Parts and wholes in face recognition. *Quarterly Journal of Experimental Psychology: A, 46*(2), 225–245.

Tanaka, J., & Gauthier, I. (1997). Expertise in object and face recognition. *The Psychology of Learning and Motivation, 36*, 83–125.

Tanaka, J. W., & Sengco, J. A. (1997). Features and their configuration in face recognition. *Memory and Cognition, 25*(5), 583–592.

Tarr, M. J., & Bulthoff, H. H. (1995). Is human object recognition better described by geon structural descriptions or by multiple views? Comment on Biederman and Gerhardstein (1993). *Journal of Experimental Psychology: Human Perception and Performance, 21*, 1494–1505.

Ullman, S. (1989). Aligning pictorial descriptions: An approach to object recognition. *Cognition, 32*, 193–254.

Valentine, T. (1991). A unified account of the effects of distinctiveness, inversion, and race in face recognition. *Quarterly Journal of Experimental Psychology: A, 43*(2), 161–204.

Valentine, T., & Bruce, V. (1988). Mental rotation of faces. *Memory and Cognition, 16*(6), 556–566.

Wheeler, D. D. (1970). Processes in word recognition. *Cognitive Psychology, 1*, 59–85.

Yin, R. K. (1969). Looking at upside-down faces. *Journal of Experimental Psychology, 81*(1), 141–145.

Young, A. W., Hellawell, D., & Hay, D. C. (1987). Configurational information in face perception. *Perception, 16*(6), 747–759.

5

Diagnostic Use of Scale Information for Componential and Holistic Recognition

PHILIPPE G. SCHYNS AND FRÉDÉRIC GOSSELIN

People can often place an identical visual stimulus into a number of different categories. For example, the top picture of figure 5.1 is a woman, with a neutral expression, called "Mary," if this were her identity. In contrast, the bottom picture is a male, with an angry expression, called John. In a similar vein, the top scene in figure 5.2 is an outdoor scene, a city, or New York at increasingly specific levels of categorization. The bottom picture is an outdoor scene, a highway, and only specialists would know that it is I-95. These different judgments of similar images reveal the impressive versatility of categorization, but also its considerable resilience to failure. For example, if you did not know the identity of the faces (or scenes), you could nevertheless categorize them as male or female (or city or highway). Categorization is this fundamental process that progressively reduces highly variable perceptual inputs into a small number of classes of equivalence (called "categories"—e.g., face, neutral expression, female, outdoor scene, city, New York) whose memory representations mediate thinking and adaptive action.

One fundamental task for recognition theorists is to understand which visual information is used to access categories in memory. Here, we will examine how variations of luminance (the gray levels of an image) are used at different scales to recognize and perceive complex visual events such as faces and scenes. Research in psychophysics and neurophysiology indicates that vision breaks down incoming stimuli into a number of spatial

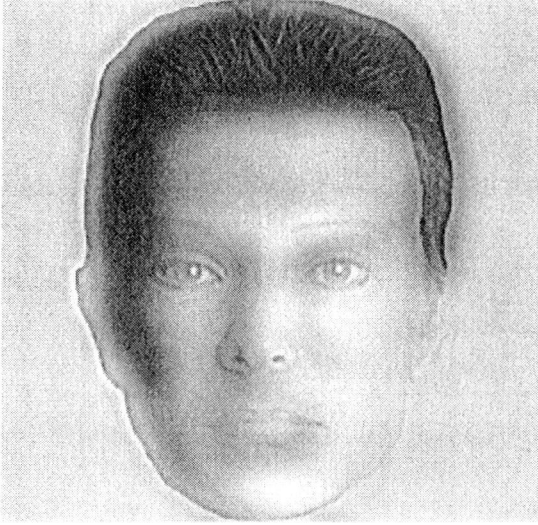

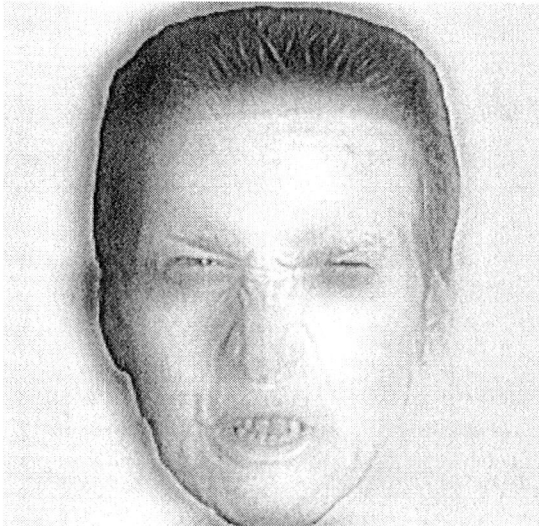

FIGURE 5.1. Two hybrid faces (from Schyns & Oliva, 1999). The fine spatial scale (high spatial frequencies, or HSF) represents a nonexpressive woman in the top picture and an angry man in the bottom picture. The coarse spatial scale (low spatial frequencies, or LSF) represents the angry man in the top picture and the neutral woman in the bottom picture. To see the LSF faces, squint, blink, or step back from the picture until your perception changes.

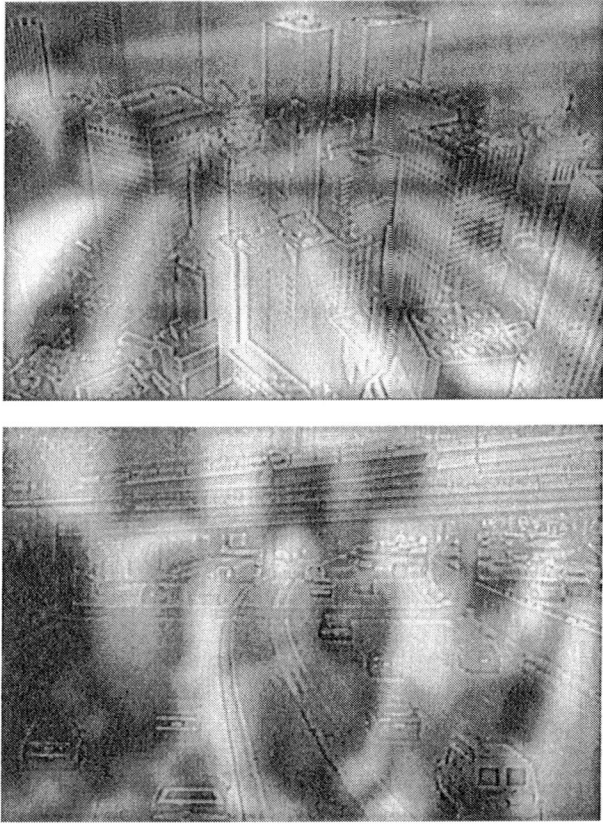

FIGURE 5.2. Two examples of hybrid scenes (adapted from Schyns & Oliva, 1994). The top picture mixes the fine information of a city with the coarse information of a highway. The bottom picture mixes the opposite information.

scales (or spatial frequencies). Spatial filtering is usually construed as an early stage of visual processing, the outputs of which form a basis for the higher level operations of face, object, and scene recognition. A complete account of recognition will therefore require a good understanding of spatial filtering and the constraints they impose.

Spatial filters encode luminance variability (i.e., contrast) in the visual field. For example, spatial filters operating at a fine spatial resolution (i.e., high spatial frequencies) encode the detailed edges portraying the contours of a nose, eyelashes, the precise shape of the mouth and eyes, and so forth. In contrast, coarser spatial filters (i.e., low spatial frequencies) could encode pigmentation and shape from shading from the face. That is, spatial filters encode a wide range of useful information. How we use information at these scales might therefore have implications for how we categorize everyday face, object, and scene categorization from the outputs of spatial filters.

Research on spatial filtering is an established tradition of psychophysics. We will see that the study of scale usage is an excellent medium to examine the interactions between perception and cognition. To illustrate, if the visual cues used for different categorizations of an identical input (face, object, or scene) reside at different spatial frequencies, the low-level processing of spatial frequencies could constrain categorization. On the other hand, the categorization task could itself modify the output of early perceptual processes. At a more general level, the cognitive impenetrability of vision can be addressed (Fodor, 1983; Pylyshyn, 1999; Schyns, Goldstone, & Thibaut, 1998).

The chapter is organized as follows. To begin, we introduce the key concepts of spatial scales and spatial frequency channels. Theories of scale usage are then reviewed in light of recent empirical findings. New methods that can reveal the features underlying different categorizations are finally described.

Spatial Scales

Natural images provide the viewer with a wide spectrum of spatial information, ranging from coarse to very fine. Fine spatial information tends to be associated with image details, whereas coarse spatial information corresponds to larger, less detailed aspects. We can describe this spectrum of spatial information with Fourier analysis (Campbell & Green, 1965; Davidson, 1968). The coarse spatial information in the image becomes the low spatial frequencies (LSFs) and the fine spatial information the high spatial frequencies (HSFs). Examples of low and high spatial frequencies derived from natural images are shown in figures 5.1 and 5.2. HSFs reveal a neutral woman and an angry man in figure 5.1 top and 5.1 bottom, respectively, and a city and highway in figures 5.2 top and 5.2 bottom, respectively. HSFs preserve fine details such as the eyelashes of the faces, the details of their wrinkles, or the windows of the city buildings.

If you squint, blink, defocus, or step back from figures 5.1 and 5.2, their interpretations turn into an angry man in figure 5.1 top, and a neutral woman in figure 5.1 bottom; a highway in figure 5.2 top, and a city in figure 5.2 bottom. LSFs can be seen to correspond to the coarse, less detailed parts of the pictures: properties such as the color and luminance of blobs are carried in the LSFs, whereas fine details, such as the eyelashes, are discarded. Luminance blobs provide a skeleton of information from which fine details can be fleshed out.

A spatial frequency channel is a filter that outputs a restricted range of the information it receives in input. Three channel types are often distinguished. A low-pass channel passes all frequencies below a given cut-off while discarding the frequencies above this cut-off. Conversely, a high-pass channel retains the frequencies above a cut-off while discarding those below it. Finally, a band-pass channel only passes the frequencies between two cut-offs, discarding those at each end.

Psychophysical studies have demonstrated that early vision filters natural stimuli into a number of separate channels, each tuned to a specific bandwidth of spatial frequencies. (See DeValois & DeValois, 1990, for an excellent review of spatial vision.) In their seminal paper on contrast detection, Campbell and Robson (1968) reported that the detection (and the discrimination) of simple sine-wave patterns was predicted by the contrast of their frequency components. This could occur only if early vision was analyzing the patterns with groups of quasi-linear band-pass filters, each tuned to a specific frequency band (see also Graham, 1980; Pantle & Sekuler, 1968; Thomas, 1970; Webster & DeValois, 1985). Frequency-specific adaptation studies demonstrated that the channels were selectively impaired in their sensitivity to contrast, suggesting they are independent (e.g., Blakemore & Campbell, 1969).

The visual input appears to be independently processed by four to six spatial frequency channels (Ginsburg, 1986; Wilson & Bergen, 1979). Further developments indicated that the channels interacted (e.g., Henning, Hertz, & Broadbent, 1975) and were nonlinear (e.g., Snowden & Hammett, 1992). In spite of this, the consensual view is that spatial filtering occurs prior to many other early visual tasks such as motion perception (e.g., Morgan, 1992), stereopsis (Legge & Gu, 1989), edge detection (e.g., Marr, 1982; Watt & Morgan, 1985) and saccade programming (Findlay, Brogan & Wenban-Smith, 1993). Spatial filters therefore provide a plausible candidate for the building blocks of visual perception from which flexible categorizations of faces, objects, and scenes might arise.

Scale Usage for Categorization

If vision filters the input at multiple spatial scales, the question arises as to how information from these channels is used to categorize complex stimuli. Two scenarios of scale usage are possible. Early constraints on the availability and extraction of coarse-and fine-scale information may impose a fixed order on their usage in categorization. More recently, however, it has been suggested that such a fixed view of scale usage may be misguided, and that we should instead consider scale usage as flexible and dependent on the demands of the categorization task at hand.

Fixed Usage: Coarse-to-Fine Hypothesis

A commonly held view is that there is a fixed bias to process scale information from coarse to fine, both in early vision and in its usage for face, object, and scene recognition (e.g., Breitmeyer, 1984; Fiorentini,

Maffei, & Sandini, 1983; Parker & Costen, 1999; Parker, Lishman, & Hughes, 1992, 1997; Schyns & Oliva, 1994). This idea originates in a classical physiology research in which Enroth-Cugell and Robson (1966) determined the spatio-temporal characteristics of X and Y retinal ganglion cells. They observed a sustained response to high-resolution stimuli in X cells, but a transient response to low-resolution stimuli in Y cells. Hubel and Wiesel (1959, 1962) found that this dichotomy was preserved at the lateral geniculate nucleus: Y cells dealing with a transient, gross analysis of the stimulus project to the magnocellular layers of the lateral geniculate nucleus, whereas X cells concerned with a sustained and detailed analysis project to both parvo- and magnocellular layers. Computational vision theorists picked up on this temporal and anatomical distinction to derive models of early visual processes, including edge extraction, stereopsis, and motion (see Marr, 1982, for discussions and examples).

In recognition, researchers soon realized that algorithms could not operate on raw pixel values from a digitized picture. A multiscale representation of the image was required to organize and simplify the description of events (e.g., Marr, 1982; Marr & Hildreth, 1980; Marr & Poggio, 1979; Watt, 1987; Witkin, 1987). For example, edges at a fine spatial resolution are notoriously noisy and represent confusing details that would be absent from a coarser representation. Fine-scale details, however, are often required when the objects to be distinguished are similar or, more generally, when the task requires detailed information. An efficient strategy may initially produce a stable, but coarse description of the image before the noisier, but finer information is extracted for successful categorization. In other words, the LSFs may be extracted and used before the HSFs. This is the *coarse-to-fine hypothesis*.

The notion of a coarse-to-fine recognition strategy is more often assumed than explicitly stated. Parker and Costen (1999) eloquently summarize the general view: "the lower spatial frequencies in an image are processed relatively quickly while progressively finer spatial information is processed more slowly" (p. 18). The status of the coarse-to-fine hypothesis remains to be clarified. Is there a physiological bias in the temporal availability of coarse- and fine-scale information, with LSFs being extracted before HSFs? Would such a bias be so constraining as to result in a coarse-to-fine strategy of using scale information for categorization (i.e., a perceptually driven coarse-to-fine categorization scheme)? Or is there a coarse-to-fine categorization strategy for another reason, namely that an efficient strategy for recognizing complex images first produces a coarse skeleton of the input that is then fleshed out with fine-scale details (i.e., a strategically driven categorization scheme)?

The view that there is a coarse-to-fine bias in the usage of spatial scales for recognition has permeated this research area (e.g., Breitmeyer, 1984; Fiorentini, Maffei, & Sandini, 1983; Parker & Costen, 1999; Parker, Lishman, & Hughes, 1992, 1997; Schyns & Oliva, 1994). Accordingly, the

first theory of scale usage proposes that the most effective route to recognition would be via coarse-scale information that is subsequently fleshed
out with higher spatial frequencies (e.g., Schyns & Oliva, 1994; Sergent,
1982, 1986). The perceptual versus strategical status of this fixed coarse-
to-fine scheme was not addressed until recently (see Morrison & Schyns,
in press).

Schyns and Oliva (1994) used hybrid stimuli similar to those of figure
5.2 to provide evidence of a coarse-to-fine bias in scene processing. Hybrids depict the LSFs from one image and the HSFs from another. This
is achieved by superimposing a low-passed image with a high-passed stimulus.

For their first experiment, Schyns and Oliva (1994) used a matching
task whereby a sample was presented for either 30 ms or 150 ms followed
immediately by a mask and then a target. Participants indicated whether
or not the sample matched the target. Samples were either full-spectrum,
low-passed, high-passed, or hybrid images, and targets were always full-
spectrum scenes. For LSF-hybrids, the low frequencies matched the target
(i.e., the LSFs of the hybrid represent the same scene as the full-spectrum
target), and for HSF-hybrids the high frequencies matched the target. Thus,
a single hybrid could be matched with two different scenes, the one depicted in LSFs and the one in HSFs. The two scenes represented by one
hybrid could both be matched with their respective target at 30 and 150
ms durations. Nevertheless, exposure duration changed the interpretation
of the hybrids: short exposures elicited more accurate matchings of LSF
hybrids compared to the long exposures ($d' = 2.08$ vs. 1.4), whereas the
converse was true of HSF-hybrids ($d' = 1.06$ vs. 3.0). This finding in a
scene-matching task is consistent with a coarse-to-fine mode of processing.
Matching tasks, however, are very different from typical situations of categorization and they tap into different processes (e.g., Biederman & Cooper, 1991). In a second experiment Schyns and Oliva (1994) obtained
evidence for a coarse-to-fine recognition (as opposed to matching) strategy.
Each trial was an animation created by the sequential presentation of two
hybrids for 45 ms each with no ISI. An animation contained two distinct
sequences, one coarse-to-fine and the other fine-to-coarse—that is, observers saw two different scene sequences simultaneously. For example,
if the top hybrid from figure 5.2 is immediately followed by that on the
bottom, the coarse-to-fine sequence would represent a motorway while the
fine-to-coarse animation would depict a city. It is important to stress that
each trial consisted of a single presentation of each of the two hybrids.
When asked to name the animated scene in the sequence, observers chose
the coarse-to-fine interpretation more frequently than the fine-to-course
scenario (67% vs. 29%, respectively). This is evidence in support of a
coarse-to-fine categorization strategy (see also Breitmeyer, 1984; Fiorentini, Maffei, & Sandini, 1983; Parker & Costen, 1999; Parker, Lishman,
& Hughes, 1992, 1997).

Flexible Usage Hypothesis

An alternative to the fixed coarse-to-fine hypothesis was put forward by Oliva and Schyns (1997; Schyns & Oliva, 1999). The images in figures 5.1 and 5.2 can be categorized in a number of ways depending on the use of LSF vs. HSF perceptual cues. In general, the cues subtending different categorizations might themselves be associated with different regions of the spatial spectrum. For example, Schyns and Oliva (1999) showed that the perceptual cues most useful for judging the identity, gender, and expression of a face were associated with different spatial scales (see also Sergent, 1986). Thus, the observer who categorizes an image might be biased to the spatial scales with which task-relevant perceptual cues are associated. Schyns and Oliva (1999) suggested that rather than being fixed in a coarse-to-fine sequence, the scale usage for categorization could be flexible and determined by the usefulness (or diagnosticity) of cues at different scales. We call this the *flexible usage hypothesis*. In contrast, the coarse-to-fine hypothesis neglects the nature of the categorization task and its information requirements. In the flexible-scale usage, the perceptual processing of an identical visual input may be influenced by the nature of the categorization task (Schyns, 1998). There is indeed evidence that categorization can influence the construction of the image percept (e.g., Schyns, Goldstone, & Thibaut, 1998).

In a recognition task, Oliva and Schyns (1997, Experiment 1) demonstrated that the LSF and HSF components of a hybrid scene presented for 30 ms both primed subsequent recognition of a full-spectrum scene. This indicates that the coarse- and fine-scale cues are both available early, arguing against a mandatory, perceptually driven coarse-to-fine scheme. In the related domain of global-to-local processing, researchers have shown that the effect of global precedence was itself modulated by task constraints. For example, Grice, Graham, and Boroughs (1983) illustrated that an advantage for the global interpretations of larger letters made of smaller letters could be overcome when subjects could attend to and fixate the local constituent letters (see also Sergent, 1982; and Kimchi, 1992, for a review).

The flexible-usage hypothesis suggests that categorization mechanisms tune into the scales that represent information relevant to the task at hand. Two factors need to be considered: (1) the categorization task that specifies the visual information required to resolve this categorization, and (2) the multiple levels of representation of this visual information across the different spatial scales. Flexible use might result from a selective use of only a few of these levels for the task at hand. Oliva and Schyns (1997) and Schyns and Oliva's (1999) reported data consistent with the flexible stance. In Oliva and Schyns's (1997), second experiment observers saw scenes, each presented for 135 ms, to identify (city, highway, living room or bedroom). They first saw images meaningful at LSFs or HSFs only—e.g., a fine-scale highway combined with coarse-scale noise. Without discontinuity in presentation, the following images were hybrids—e.g., HSFs depicted a city and LSFs a motorway. Observers identified the hybrids according to the scale at which diagnostic information was initially presented. That is, observers sensitized to fine scales perceived the HSF component from a hybrid, whereas those sensitized to coarse scales perceived the LSF scene from the identical hybrid. Interestingly, observers claimed to be unaware that two different scenes were present in any one hybrid image, arguing against the possibility that observers first perceived two scenes in hybrids and then decided to report the scene consistent with the sensitization phase. This finding suggests that scale usage is flexible and tunes into the scale at which diagnostic information is represented.

The idea that different categorizations of identical visual inputs (e.g., identity, gender, expressive or not) rely on distinct regions of the spatial spectrum is central to the flexible-usage hypothesis. If this is the case (we return to this topic later), then the hypothesis of flexible usage predicts that the perception of identical hybrids should depend on the categorization performed. This question was addressed in Schyns and Oliva (1999) using hybrids derived from the faces of unfamiliar people. For example, a neutral female at HSFs may be superimposed with an angry male at LSFs (see figure 5.1 top). In Experiment 1, stimuli were presented for 50 ms, and the nature of the categorization was found to moderate stimulus perception. To illustrate, when asked whether the face was expressive or not, observers had a tendency to perceive and to report the fine-scale face. However, there was no bias for a gender decision and there was a coarse-scale bias when asked to specify the face expression as happy, angry, or neutral. Again, observers remained unaware of the presence of two faces in any one image. In sum, perception of identical hybrids was determined by the categorization task, suggesting that categorization processes tune into diagnostic information at specific scales.

In their Experiment 2, Schyns and Oliva (1999) isolated the perceptual by-products of a categorization task. In phase one, two subject groups applied a different categorization task (expressive or not, vs. which expression) to an identical set of hybrid faces, to induce two orthogonal scale biases (to HSF and LSF, respectively). In phase two, all subjects had to judge the gender of the same set of hybrid faces. The results established a perceptual transfer of the bias acquired in a first categorization to the subsequent gender task. For example, when one group preferentially categorized the hybrid of figure 5.1a as a female on the basis of its HSF, the other group categorized the same picture as a male on the basis of its LSF. Note that groups only differed on the frequency bandwidth bias acquired in the first phase of the experiment. It is important to stress that in the second phase, all aspects of the experimental task (i.e., the gender categorization, the hybrid stimuli, and their conditions of presentation) were strictly identical across subjects, who nevertheless perceived the same hybrid faces markedly differently. From this perceptual transfer we can conclude that categorization can modify the perception of scale information. Note, however, that we established this flexible-scale usage at very brief (30 ms) exposures. For longer exposures, and this can be experienced by looking at the hybrids of figure 5.1, saccadic eye movements take place and the fine scale seems to dominate perception.

To summarize, it is often assumed, but rarely tested, that spatial scales are processed in a coarse-to-fine manner (e.g., Marr & Hildreth, 1980; Watt, 1987). It would seem that LSFs are extracted before HSFs from simple sine-wave stimuli (e.g., Parker & Dutch, 1987) and that scale information may be integrated more efficiently in a coarse-to-fine sequence (Parker et al., 1992, 1997). However, this does not imply the existence of a mandatory recognition strategy using information from coarse to fine. In fact, the evidence (Oliva & Schyns, 1997; Schyns & Oliva, 1999) conflicts with the view that scale usage for categorization is fixed, and rather suggests it is flexible and driven by the presence of diagnostic information at different scales. Furthermore, converging evidence suggest that the diagnostic use of coarse- and fine-scale cues in categorization tasks does change the perceptual appearance of the incoming stimulus.

Searching for Diagnostic Scale Information

The work reviewed so far demonstrates a flexible attentional control on scale information when this scale is diagnostic (e.g., Oliva & Schyns, 1997). There is also evidence that different categorization tasks tap into different scales of the same stimulus (Schyns & Oliva, 1999). The attentional control of scale use could, therefore, arise from the information demands of different categorization tasks. This section will explore this hypothesis in detail.

Hybrids can be used to ascertain preferred scale usage (e.g., LSF vs. HSF) from the categorization responses of subjects. They can also reveal the scale that is perceived, and inform on the processing of the neglected scale (e.g., Oliva & Schyns, 1997). However, as a general method to search for the information diagnostic of categorization tasks, hybrids are inherently limited. First, it is difficult to create a hybrid composed of more than two different bandwidths of spatial information while preserving the independent perception of each bandwidth. Consequently, hybrids are restricted to dichotomous searches in scale space (e.g., LSF vs. HSF, or midfrequencies vs. HSF, and so forth). A second shortcoming is that the method does not locate in the image plane the cues that are diagnostic at a specific scale. To illustrate, suppose you recognized the faces of figure 5.1 on the basis of HSF cues (e.g., using their eyelashes and the corner of the mouth). From your categorizations, we would know that you preferred to use the HSF plane, but not which cues you used in this plane. To summarize, the search space for diagnostic cues is three-dimensional (the two-dimensional image × multiple spatial scales). Of this space, the hybrid methodology can only search one dimension (the spatial scales), using a dichotomy (e.g., LSF vs. HSF).

We now turn to a method, called Bubbles (Gosselin & Schyns, 2001a), that addresses these two shortcomings and therefore generalizes the search for diagnostic cues to the entire three-dimensional space.

The Diagnostic Information of Identity, Gender, Expressive or Not

In a nutshell, Bubbles can determine the use of information specific to a categorization task. Bubbles samples an input space (here, the 3D space discussed above) to present sparse versions of the stimuli (here, faces). Observers categorize the sparse stimuli (here, into their identity, gender, and expressive or not) and Bubbles keeps track of the information samples that lead to correct and incorrect categorizations. From this information, Bubbles determines how each region of the input space is selectively used in each categorization task, and depicts the selective use with an *effective stimulus*. The following sections discuss in detail the results of Schyns, Bonnar and Gosselin (2002; see also Gosselin & Schyns, 2001a, 2002).

In this application, the image-generation space comprised the two dimensions of the image plane and the third dimension of spatial scales. To compute an experimental stimulus, we decomposed a face picture (see figure 5.3a) into six bands of nonoverlapping spatial frequencies of one octave each—with cutoffs at 90, 45, 22.5, 11.25, 5.62, and 2.81 cycles per face, from fine to coarse, respectively; see figure 5.3b. The coarsest (i.e., sixth) band served as a constant background because it does not contain useful face information, and so only five bandwidths are represented in figure 5.3b. We sampled this image space with *bubbles* of information (hence the name of the technique). The bubbles were a number of Gaussian windows applied to each of the five spatial frequency bands (the size of each bubble was adjusted so that three cycles per face were revealed at each scale—i.e., standard deviations of bubbles were .13, .27, .54, 1.08, and 2.15 deg of visual angle, from fine to coarse scales; see figure 5.3c). Across trials, the locations of all bubbles changed randomly. Thus, after many trials, bubbles sample the entire image space and the search for diagnostic cues is exhaustive.

In a trial, we added the information samples produced by multiplying the scale-specific face information (figure 5.3b) with its respective bubbles (figure 5.3c) to produce a sparse stimulus (figure 5.3e). The subspace revealed by the bubbles was adjusted to maintain categorization of the sparse faces at a set criterion (here, 75% correct). To respond, observers pressed the appropriate keyboard key (i.e., male vs. female; expressive vs. nonexpressive; or, e.g., "John").

On any given trial, we can hypothesize that a correct response means that the samples revealed enough information to categorize the stimulus.

a.

b.
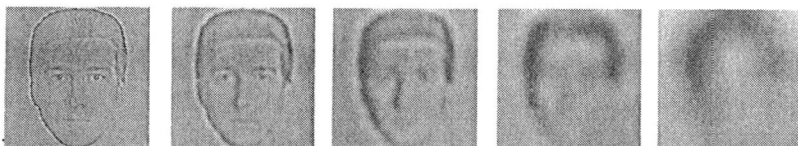

c.
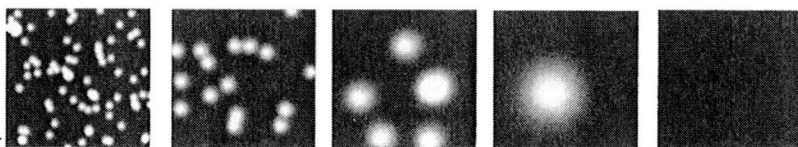

d.

e.
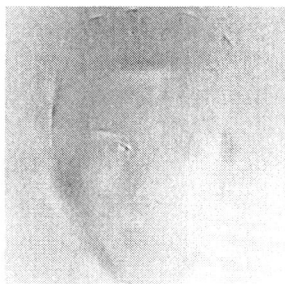

FIGURE 5.3 The application of Bubbles to the 3D space composed of a 2D face (adapted from Gosselin & Schyns, 2001a). Pictures in (b) represent five different scales of (a); (c) illustrate the bubbles applied to each scale; (d) depict the information of the scales of (b) sampled by the bubbles of (c). Note that on this trial there is no revealed information at the fifth scale. By integrating the pictures in (d) we obtain (e), a stimulus subjects actually saw.

An incorrect response means that there was not enough face information in the samples. Across trials, the interaction between the random bubbles and the observer is, therefore, a random search for diagnostic task information, using the observer to tease apart the information samples into diagnostic and nondiagnostic.

Specifically, we keep track of the locations of the bubbles that lead to correct categorizations in a different CorrectPlane for each scale (henceforth, CorrectPlane(scale), for scale = 1 to 5, from fine to coarse). In each of these planes, we literally added the masks of bubbles (see figure 5.3c, for examples of masks) leading to correct responses. In contrast, TotalPlane(scale) is the sum of all masks leading to correct *and* incorrect categorizations.

From CorrectPlane(scale) and TotalPlane(scale), we derive ProportionPlane(scale) = CorrectPlane(scale) / TotalPlane(scale) per observer. ProportionPlane(scale) is the ratio of the number of times a specific region of the input space has led to a successful categorization over the number of times this region has been presented in the experiment. Across subjects, the averaged ProportionPlane(scale) weighs the importance of the regions of each scale for the categorization task at hand (Gosselin & Schyns, 2001a). If all regions were equally important, ProportionPlane(scale) would be uniform. In other words, the probability that any randomly chosen bubble led to a correct categorization of the input would be equal to the expected performance criterion—here, .75. By the same reasoning, regions above (vs. below) the criterion are more (vs. less) diagnostic for these tasks.

We construct a confidence interval around the mean of the ProportionPlane(scale), for each proportion ($p < .01$). Significance is summarized in a DiagnosticPlane(scale) that represents with a 1 a diagnostic proportion and with a 0 a nondiagnostic proportion. The DiagnosticPlane(scale) is a mask that can filter out the nondiagnostic information at each scale of the face image. We can use them to depict the selective use of information in each task. The resulting *effective stimulus* is simply obtained by multiplying the face information at each scale in figure 5.3b with the corresponding DiagnosticPlane(scale).

Figure 5.4 compares the relative use of scale information in the identity (top), gender (middle), and expressive or not (bottom) tasks. The figure reveals a differential use of information across tasks and scales. Whereas the mouth is represented at all scales in identity and expressive, it does not appear at the finest scales in gender. Similarly, the eyes are both represented at all scales in identity, but only one of them figures in the effective face of gender, and both are neglected in the effective face of expressive. The chin is only well defined in identity. Compared to the mouth and the eyes, the nose is much less represented in all tasks.

We can quantify the use of each spatial scale across tasks. To this end, we divided the diagnostic areas revealed at each scale by the total area covered by the face in the image plane. In figure 5.4, the histograms

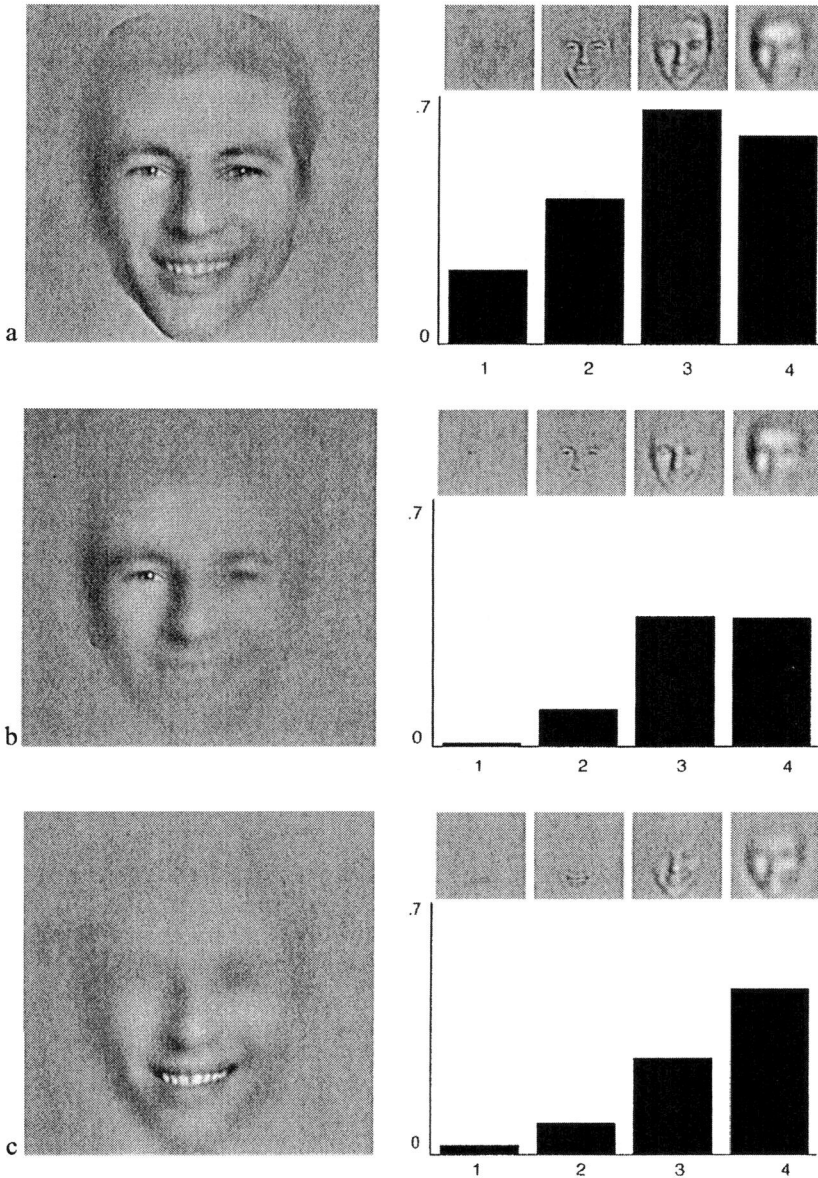

FIGURE 5.4. (a) The larger face depicts the effective face stimulus for the identity task (adapted from Schyns, Bonnar, & Gosselin, in press). The smaller pictures illustrate the diagnostic information used to resolve the identity task at each independent scale from fine to coarse, respectively. The coarsest scale is not depicted as it contains no meaningful information. The bar chart provides a quantitative illustration of the proportion of the face area used to resolve the task at each scale. Figures (b) and (c) follow the same format as figure (a) illustrating the potent face for the gender task and expressive or not task respectively, the diagnostic information for each task at each scale and a quantitative account of the use of information in the bar charts.

represent the use of diagnostic information at different spatial scales—1 means finest, and 4 coarsest scale. The small face pictures illustrate which cues are used. The use of fine-scale information (labeled 1 in the histograms, and depicted in the leftmost small picture) differs considerably across tasks. It depicts the eyes, the mouth, and the chin in identity, whereas in gender the finest scale is only used for the left side eye, and in expressive for the mouth. In contrast, the coarsest scale (i.e., the fourth scale) is much less differentiated. It forms a skeleton that is progressively fleshed out with increasing spatial resolution (see the progression of face information from coarse to fine in the small pictures of figure 5.4, from right to left.)

In sum, Bubbles can search for the information relevant for different categorizations of the same stimuli. It extends the hybrid method presented earlier because it can pinpoint the exact location of the diagnostic features in a complex image space.

Second-Order Holistic Features

It is widely accepted that face processing may rely on both componential cues (i.e., local features such as the mouth, nose, eyes, a mole) and noncomponential information (the spatial relations between these features), though how these cues are integrated remains unclear (e.g., Bartlett & Searcy, 1993; Calder, Young, Keane, & Dean, 1999; Farah, Wilson, Drain, & Tanaka, 1998; Macho & Leder, 1998; see also chapters in this volume of Bartlett, Searcy, & Abdi; Farah & Tanaka; Murray, Rhodes, & Schuchinsky, for discussions of configural vs. featural information). We use the term "relational" to refer to a mode of processing that encodes the spatial relations of the face without making further claims about the nature of this encoding. Relational and component cues are different sorts of information as, for example, turning a face upside down has a greater detrimental effect on encoding of the former (e.g., Bartlett & Searcy, 1993; Leder & Bruce, 1998). They may be associated with different spatial scales. Indeed, Sergent (1986, pp. 23–24) argued, "A face has both component and configurational properties that coexist, the latter emerging from the interrelationships among the former. These properties are not contained in the same spatial-frequency spectrum." More precisely, Sergent (1986) suggested that component and relational properties may be associated with fine and coarse scales, respectively.

Our analysis with Bubbles has focused on information of a strictly componential nature (i.e., each proportion of the ProportionPlanes). When several proportions form a continuous region (as was the case for the diagnostic masks, see figure 5.3b), it is tempting to assume that the face features within the regions are themselves used holistically (configurally). However, this is not necessarily the case. For example, an observer could use holistically two nonadjacent areas of the face (e.g., the two eyes, or one eye and the mouth). Conversely, two adjacent components could be used independently, but assigned to the same diagnostic region.

We define a holistic use of information as a conjunctive use of information. Operationally, a holistic use of information implies that the presentation of information from several separate bubbles (a conjunction of information) does drive recognition performance. Here, we limited the conjunction to two distinct bubbles of information, a second-order analysis. Thus, in this section, we perform a second-order search for the better conjunctions of features in the gender and the identity tasks of Schyns et al. (in press). We restrict our analysis to five main areas of the faces, known from our experiments to be particularly diagnostic: the left eye, the right eye, the nose, the left portion of the mouth, and the right portion of the mouth. We derive the proportion of correct categorizations associated with all possible conjunctions of the five areas of interest. This is summarized in a 5×5 matrix per scale, where each cell represents a feature conjunction. In this cell, we increment a counter each time the stimulus comprised at least one bubble in each of two regions concerned and the categorization was correct. We increment a separate counter every time the conjunction was presented, irrespective of response. We perform this simple analysis for all stimuli, subjects, and responses,[1] and the resulting proportion correct is the division of the two counters. We then compute the significant proportions. Figure 5.5 depicts the Diagnostic-Plane(scale) for feature conjunctions (the plane is now a 5×5 symmetrical matrix).

A white square in figure 5.5 indicates a significant feature conjunction at one of the scales. The DiagnosticPlane(scale) are symmetrical, but to facilitate reading, we have only kept upper triangle of the symmetrical matrices. These results are best interpreted with the potent information depicted in figure 5.4. Remember that the first-order analysis revealed the importance of the eyes and the mouth to identify faces. Note that the diagnostic conjunctions for "Identity" involve mostly relationships between the two eyes and the mouth. In "Gender," these relationships involve mostly the left eye (see figure 5.4) and both corners of the mouth (in the first and second scales), and a recurrent relationship between the left corner of the mouth and the nose across all scales. Thus, the second-order analysis confirms a differentiated use of information across tasks, adopting the form of diagnostic feature conjunctions.

In sum, Bubbles is a search for diagnostic information in any n-dimensional image generation space, even if the space is abstract. Bubbles is therefore *not* restricted to the 2D image plane, but eye scans are. Because bubbles of information are independent samples in the input space, we can compute how second-order relationships between the samples (but also relationship between more than two distinct bubbles of information) contribute to recognition, and thereby ascertain the amount of holistic processing at different *scales*.

Identity

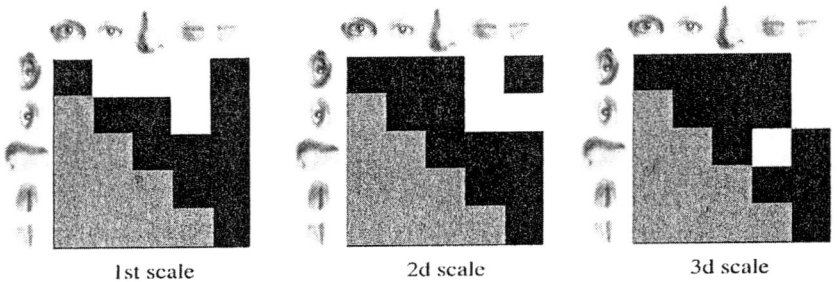

| 1st scale | 2d scale | 3d scale |

Gender

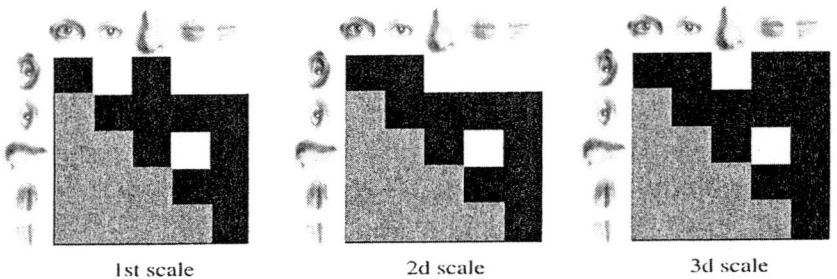

| 1st scale | 2d scale | 3d scale |

FIGURE 5.5. The diagnostic feature conjunctions resulting from the second-order analysis of Bubbles for the Identity and Gender tasks (adapted from Schyns, Bonnar, & Gosselin, 2002). At each scale, a white square reveals a significant conjunction of features that drove recognition performance. Note that the symmetry of the DiagnosticPlane(scale) has been eliminated to improve the readability of the matrices.

In the reported data, the DiagnosticPlanes were averaged across subjects, but we could have performed the analysis on a subject-per-subject basis (opening promising research avenues in visual development, the acquisition of perceptual expertise, and visual agnosia). The analysis can also be performed by item (i.e., stimulus) to enable a finer understanding of the recognition of each stimulus in well-specified task contexts. Succinctly stated, Bubbles is a reverse projection of the memory representation of an object onto the input information. Suitably applied, it could predict, from use of diagnostic information, how early visual filters at different spatial scales would become tuned to optimize the intake of low-level visual information (e.g, contrast and orientation) in different recognition tasks.

FIGURE 6.1 This image of a complex scene illustrates some of the problems encountered in visual processing.

FIGURE 6.7. Interior view of the virtual attic of Wirtshaus Lichtenstein. From H. H Bülthoff and H.A.H.C. van Veen, in M. Jenkin & L. Harris (Eds), *Vision and Action in Virtual Environments: Modern Psychophysics in Spatial Cognition Research, Vision and Attention*, p. 245 (Figure 12.5). New York: Springer. Reproduced with permission from Springer-Verlag.

FIGURE 6.14. Sculpture by Markus Raetz (1994). Picture copyright © Pro Litteris, Zürich, Switzerland. Reproduced with permission of the artist. For an animated computer graphic visualization of a similar object see http://www.kyb.tuebingen.mpg.de/links/metamorphosis.html.

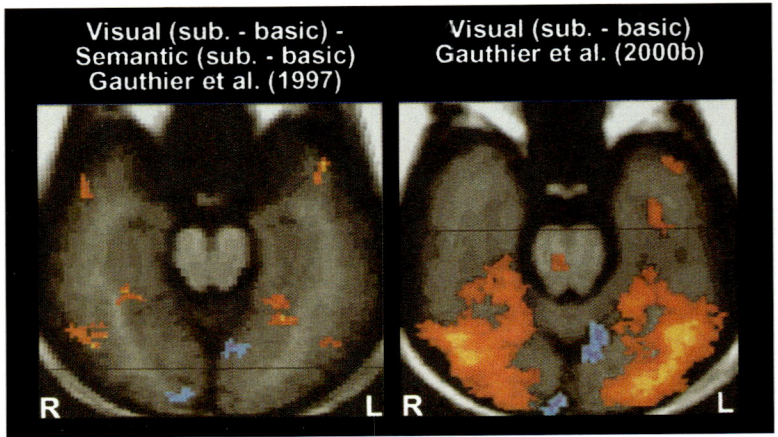

FIGURE 7.7. The regions traced by the ovoids approximate those brain regions typically associated with face recognition based on earlier neuroimaging studies (Kanwisher et al., 1997; Puce et al., 1995). The fMRI maps show the activation we obtained for the subordinate-level recognition of common objects over and above basic-level recognition. The darker "splotches" represent positive activation for this comparison overlaid on structural maps of the human brain. Progressively greater positive activation is depicted by progressively brighter areas within the dark regions. See Gauthier et al. (2000b) for a discussion of how these activation maps correspond to the putatively face-selective regions of visual cortex and an interpretation of the additional regions of activation seen in the right panel.

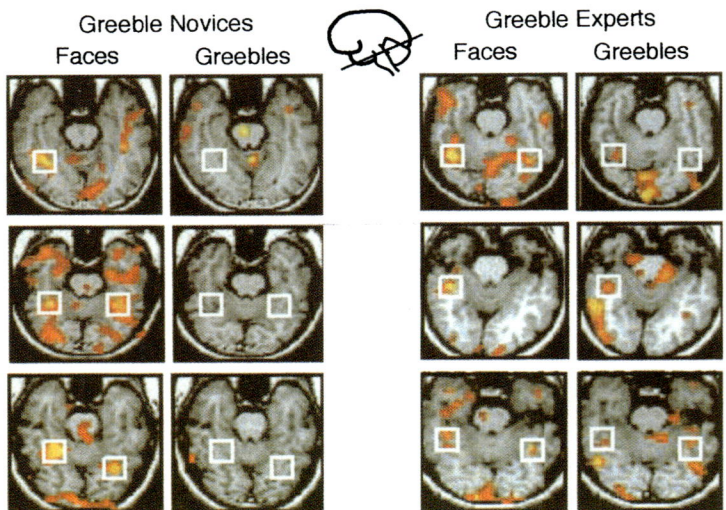

FIGURE 7.8. Brain activation in response to faces and Greebles for three Greeble novices and three Greeble experts. The left panels show the brain activation we obtained using fMRI for three novices when the passive viewing of common objects was subtracted from the passive viewing of faces or Greebles. The right panels show the activation for three experts in the same tasks. Only the voxels showing more activation for faces or Greebles than objects are shown (darker regions with higher activation depicted as brighter areas within these regions). The dashed-line squares denote the middle fusiform gyrus bilaterally (functionally defined) and the lateral occipital gyrus foci for one expert (bottom right). Adapted from Gauthier et al. (1999b).

General Discussion

Researchers in face, object, and scene recognition are often concerned with questions of object representations. For example, they ask key questions such as, Are face, object, and scene representations viewpoint-dependent (Bülthoff & Edelman, 1992; Hill, Schyns & Akamatsu, 1997; Simons & Wang, 1998; Tarr & Pinker, 1989; Troje & Bülthoff, 1996; among many others)? Are these representations holistic (e.g., view-based; Poggio & Edelman, 1990; Tarr & Pinker, 1991), or made of smaller components? (e.g., geons; Biederman, 1987; Biederman & Cooper, 1991)? Are internal representations complete (e.g., Cutzu & Edelman, 1996), or sparse (Archambault, O'Donnell, & Schyns, 1999; Rensink, O Regan, & Clark, 1997)? Two- or three-dimensional (Liu, Knill, & Kersten, 1995)? Colored or not (Oliva & Schyns, 2000; Tanaka & Presnell, 1999)? Are they hierarchically organized in memory (Brown, 1958; Rosch, Mervis, Gray, Johnson, & Boyes-Braem, 1976)? If so, is there a fixed entry point into the hierarchy (Gosselin & Schyns, 2001b; Jolicoeur, Gluck, & Kosslyn, 1984; Tanaka & Taylor, 1991)? What is the format of memory representations, and does it change uniformly across the levels of a hierarchy (Jolicoeur, 1990)? Does expertise modify memory representations (Tanaka & Gauthier, 1997; Schyns & Rodet, 1997) and the entry point to recognition (Tanaka & Taylor, 1991)?

To address these issues, researchers should embrace powerful methodologies that can assign the credit of behavioral performance (e.g., viewpoint-dependence, configural effects, color, speed of categorization, point of entry, expertise effects, and so forth) to properties of face, object, and scene representations in memory. However, the relationship between behavior and representations is tenuous, making representational issues the most difficult to approach experimentally.

In this chapter, we have taken an alternative approach that allows a rigorous understanding of the recognition process, without asking direct questions about unobservable memory representations. Our analysis builds on the *selective use of diagnostic information*, an important but neglected component of recognition. People who recognize faces, objects, and scenes do not use all the information available to them, but instead select the most useful (i.e., diagnostic) elements for the task at hand. The visual system knows what this information is and how it should be selectively extracted from the visual array to perform flexible categorizations of the same input.

To analyze the flexible use of information, we started from a set of plausible building blocks, the output of spatial filters in early vision (spatial scales), and examined how they were used during the recognition process. We explained that distinct visual cues for recognition often reside at different spatial scales, themselves processed by different frequency-specific channels in early vision. We showed that the use of this information for categorization tasks was not determined by early biases but could instead be flexibly adjusted to the requirements of the task at hand. Furthermore, in these circumstances, the perception of the stimulus could depend on the scale information selectively attended. Using Bubbles, a more powerful methodology, we pinpointed the scale information responsible for different categorizations of the same face. This is a rigorous depiction (see Schyns et al., 2002, for further formal developments) that opens up a number of new exciting research avenues to bridge the gap between high- and low-level vision.

Attention and Perception

The reviewed experiments with hybrids and Bubbles demonstrated that attention can exert a selective control on the scale information used for categorization. Further evidence of selective and task-dependent processing can be found in psychophysics. The detection of sinusoidal gratings worsens when spatial frequency varies across trials compared to the same gratings presented in blocks of constant spatial frequency (e.g., Davis & Graham, 1981), consistent with selective activation or monitoring of spatial frequency channels (Hübner, 1996).

The common underpinnings between the hybrid methodology, Bubbles, and the psychophysics of early vision provide one promising research avenue to specify the influence that the categorization task can exert on the perception of a face, object, or scene. For example, one could design a study combining hybrid categorization with psychophysical techniques to understand whether attention to a diagnostic spatial scale (or neglect of a scale) affects the filtering properties of the earliest stages of visual processing—such as contrast thresholds, frequency tuning, and orientation selectivity.

In a recent study, Sowden and Schyns (2000) have examined the visual implementation of selective, scale-specific extraction of visual cues. In a within-subjects design, observers were trained to detect near-threshold contrasts in low- and high-spatial frequency gratings cued with a distinct tone. They reported a decrement in grating detection when observers were miscued (e.g., when the LSF tone was followed by a HSF grating), supporting the occurrence of an expectancy effect. The categorization task could likewise cue people to scale-specific face, object, and scene features. The cueing in Sowden and Schyns (2000) suggests one possible implementation of the categorization-dependent perceptions reported in hybrids: modulations of contrast sensitivity could occur in spatial frequency channels as a function of task-related expectations, enhancing or lowering the availability of scale-specific information for subsequent processing. In this context, Bubbles delivers precious information (see figure 5.4). It predicts how scale information should be used in different parts of the visual field, for different categorizations of the same stimulus. It is in principle possible to examine how different parts of the visual field become sensitized to contrast and orientation as a function of categorization tasks. Evidence that categorization tasks can exert such early influence would have far-reaching implications for classical issues in cognitive science ranging from the depth of feedback loops in early vision, the early vs. late selection models of attention (Pashler, 1998), the bi-directionality of cognition (Schyns, 1998), the sparse vs. exhaustive perceptions of distal stimuli (Hochberg, 1982), to the cognitive penetrability of vision (Fodor, 1983; Pylyshyn, 1999).

A striking observation in studies with hybrid stimuli is that people who are induced to attend, and consequently perceive consciously, information depicted at only one scale appear to be unaware of some aspects of the cues at the other scale. This leads to the question of whether unattended scale information is nevertheless recognized covertly, and if so, at what level of specificity? For example, in a recent study (Morrison & Schyns, 2001), two groups of observers were initially sensitized to identify the faces of famous people at either low or high spatial frequencies (the other scale was noise). After a few trials, and without participants being told of a change, hybrids were presented that depicted the faces of two different celebrities, one at fine and the other at coarse scales. Both LSF and HSF groups performed similarly with respect to identifying the faces in hybrids: observers recognized the face at the sensitized scale accurately and claimed to be unaware of the identity of the face at the unattended scale. However, the groups differed as observers sensitized to HSFs detected the face at the unattended scale (for them, the coarse-scale face) more accurately than those in group sensitized to LSFs (in their case, the fine-scale face). This suggests that people can only perform a precise overt identification at the scale they attend, though cues at the other scale may permit other categorizations such as detection. Similar issues have been addressed in attention research (see Pashler, 1998). The added twist here is that different categorization tasks can be accomplished selectively with attended and unattended information.

Tasks, Spatial Content, and Size

There is an important relationship between spatial content and size. Images of different size may vary not only on the basis of specific metrics but also in terms of spatial content. This is because fine contours (fine-scale information) are better represented in large images compared to smaller versions (which constitute only the coarse-scale information of the larger image). For example, using faces again, certain judgments of expressions (e.g., happiness) are more resilient to changes in viewing distance than others (see Jenkins, Craven, Bruce, & Akamatsu, 1997). More generally, it will be interesting to examine how different categorization tasks of the same face, such as its gender, expression, age, identity, and so forth, specifically degrade with progressive increases in viewing distance. This will provide a better indication of the scale at which the information necessary to perform this categorization resides (particularly so if the degradation of performance is not linear with the decrease in stimulus size).

A similar reasoning applies to common object and scene categorizations. It is well known that people can apply categorizations at different levels of abstraction to the same stimulus (Rosch et al., 1976; for a review, see Gosselin & Schyns, 2001b). For example, the same animal can be called *Collie* at the subordinate level, *dog* at the basic level, and *animal* at the superordinate level. Of these three main levels, two (the basic and subordinate) are arguably closer to perception (see Schyns, 1998, for arguments). The categorization literature has often reported that people seem to be biased to the basic level. The nature of this bias remains a controversy. One possibility is to consider that in natural viewing conditions, we experience objects at many different distances. If, for example, basic-level categorizations were more resilient to changes of scale and viewing distances than subordinate categorizations, then the cues subtending the basic level would be present in most retinal projections of distal objects. This natural bias in the distribution of image cues could bias categorization processes to the basic level, suggesting an interaction between categorization tasks and the differential availability of their scale information.

Archambault, Gosselin, and Schyns (2000) confirmed this hypothesis. In a first experiment, subjects were asked whether two simultaneously presented objects (computer-synthesized 3D animals from eight different species, *bird, cow, dog, horse, frog, turtle, spider* and *whale*, rendered in 256 gray-levels with a Gouraud shading model) had the same basic-level (e.g., *whale*) or the same subordinate-level category (e.g., *Humpback whale*). Object pairs could appear in any one of five sizes, corresponding to 12, 6, 3, 1.5, .75, and .38° of visual angle on the screen. Note subjects could inspect the object pairs for as long as they wished, licensing the conclusion that the task was tapping into the absolute level of scale information required for the categorizations. In these conditions, the authors found that subordinate judgments were significantly more impaired by a reduction in stimulus size than basic judgments. Their second experiment confirmed the results in a straightforward naming task. Thus, constraints on the 2D proximal projection of 3D distal objects differentially modify the availability of scale-specific information for basic and subordinate categorizations.

In the flexible usage scenario, the requirements of information needed for different categorization tasks determine a bias to the scale where these cues are best represented. The experiments just reviewed suggest a natural bias for the finer scales in subordinate categorizations, whereas all scales are equally usable for basic categorizations. This suggests that basic categories are represented in memory either with shape cues that intersect all scales (e.g., a silhouette) or with different cues specific to each scale. In general, we believe that the interactions between the task demands of different categorizations and the structure of input information can selectively modulate the relative extraction of visual information at different spatial scales (coarse vs. fine) and spatial extents (global vs. local).

Concluding Remarks

Our main epistemological point is that one can acquire knowledge about the recognition process by carefully studying diagnostic information without asking questions (or even making assumptions) about memory representations (see also Schyns, 1998). This is a powerful approach because the information used encompasses all the visual features that mediate the recognition task at hand. These features, therefore, have a dual role. For high-level vision, they reflect the information required from memory to categorize the stimulus, and the job of low-level vision is to extract them from the visual array. Succinctly stated, the features involved in a recognition task bridge the gap between memory and the visual array. They set an agenda for research in high- and low-level vision.

Notes

The research described here was partially supported by ESRC grants R000237412 and R000223179 to Philippe G. Schyns.
   1. Because few bubbles were presented together at the coarsest and next to coarsest scales, co-occurrences of bubbles were rare and we restrict our analysis to the three finest scales.

References

Archambault, A., Gosselin, F., & Schyns, P. G. (2000). A natural bias for the basic-level? *Proceedings of the XXII Meeting of the Cognitive Science Society*, (pp. 60–65). Hillsdale, NJ: Erlbaum.
Archambault, A., O'Donnell, C., & Schyns, P. G. (1999). Blind to object changes: When learning one object at different levels of categorization modifies its perception. *Psychological Science, 10*, 249–255.
Bartlett J. C., & Searcy J. H. (1993). Inversion and configuration of faces. *Cognitive Psychology, 25*, 281–316.
Bayer, H. M., Schwartz, O., & Pelli, D. (1998). Recognizing facial expressions efficiently. *IOVS, 39*, S172.
Biederman, I. (1987). Recognition-by-components: A theory of human image understanding. *Psychological Review, 94*, 115–147.
Biederman, I., & Cooper, E. E. (1991). Priming contour-deleted images: Evidence for intermediate representations in visual object recognition. *Cognitive Psychology, 23*, 393–419.
Blakemore, C., & Campbell, F. W. (1969). On the existence of neurons in the

human visual system selectively sensitive to the orientation and size of retinal images. *Journal of Physiology (London), 203,* 237–260.

Breitmeyer, B. G. (1984). *Visual masking: An integrative approach.* New York: Oxford University Press.

Brown, R. (1958). How shall a thing be called? *Psychological Review, 65,* 14–21.

Bülthoff, H. H., & Edelman, S. (1992). Psychophysical support for a two-dimensional view theory of object recognition. *Proceedings of the National Academy of Science USA, 89,* 60–64.

Burt, D. M., & Perrett, D. I. (1997). Perceptual asymmetries in judgements of facial attractiveness, age, gender, speech and expression. *Neuropsychologia, 35,* 685–693.

Calder, A. J., Young, A. W., Keane, J., & Dean, M. (2000). Configural information in facial expression perception. *Journal of Experimental Psychology: Human Perception and Performance, 26,* 527–551.

Campbell, F. W., & Green, D. G. (1965). Optical and retinal factors affecting visual resolution. *Journal of Physiology, 181,* 576–593.

Campbell, F. W., & Robson, J. G. (1968). Application of the Fourier analysis to the visibility of gratings. *Journal of Physiology, 197,* 551–556.

Cutzu, F., & Edelman, S. (1996). Faithful representations of similarities among three-dimensional shapes in human vision. *Proceedings of the National Academy of Science, 93,* 12046–12050.

Davidson, M. L. (1968). Perturbation approach to spatial brightness interaction in human vision. *Journal of the Optical Society of America, 58,* 1300–1309.

DeValois, R. L., & DeValois, K. K. (1990). *Spatial vision.* New York: Oxford University Press.

Enroth-Cugel, C., & Robson, J. D. (1966). The contrast sensitivity of retinal ganglion cells of the cat. *Journal of Physiology (London), 187,* 517–522.

Farah M. J., Wilson K. D., Drain M., & Tanaka J. W. (1998). What is "special" about face perception? *Psychological Review, 105,* 482–498.

Findlay, J. M., Brogan, D., & Wenban-Smith, M. G. (1993). The spatial signal for sacadic eye-movements emphasizes visual boundaries. *Perception and Psychophysics, 53,* 633–641.

Fiorentini, A., Maffei, L., & Sandini, G. (1983). The role of high spatial frequencies in face perception. *Perception, 12,* 195–201.

Fodor J. (1983). *The modularity of mind.* Cambridge, MA: MIT Press.

Ginsburg, A. P. (1986). Spatial filtering and visual form perception. In K. R. Boff, L. Kaufman, and J. P. Thomas (Eds.), *Handbook of perception and human performance, II: Cognitive processes and performance.* New York: Wiley.

Gish, K., Shulman, G. L., Sheehy, J. B. & Leibowitz, H. W. (1986). Reaction times to different spatial frequencies as a function of detectability. *Vision Research, 26,* 745–747.

Gosselin, F., & Schyns, P. G. (2001a). Bubbles: A new technique to reveal the use of visual information in recognition tasks. *Vision Research, 41,* 2261–2271.

Gosselin, F., & Schyns, P. G. (2001b). Why do we SLIP to the basic-level? Computational constraints and their implementation. *Psychological Review, 108,* 735–758.

Gosselin, F., & Schyns, P. G. (2002). RAP: A new framework for visual categorization. *Trends in Cognitive Science. 6,* 70–77.

Graham, N. (1980). Spatial frequency channels in human vision: Detecting edges without edges detectors. In C. S. Harris (Ed.), *Visual coding and adaptability.* Hillsdale, NJ: Erlbaum.

Grice, G. R., Graham, L., & Boroughs, J. M. (1983). Forest before trees—It depends where you look. *Perceptions & Psychophysics, 33,* 121–128.

Henning, G. B., Hertz, B. G., & Broadbent, D. E. (1975). Some experiments bearing on the hypothesis that the visual system analyzes spatial patterns in independent bands of spatial frequency. *Vision Research, 15,* 887–897.

Hill, H., Schyns, P. G., & Akamatsu, S. (1997). Information and viewpoint dependence in face recognition. *Cognition. 62,* 201–222.

Hochberg, J. (1982). How big is a stimulus? In J. Beck (Ed.), *Organization and representation in perception* (pp. 191–217). Hillsdale, NJ: Erlbaum.

Hubel, D. H., & Wiesel, T. N. (1959). Receptive fields of single neurons in the cat's striate cortex. *Journal of Physiology, 148,* 574–591.

Hubel, D. H., & Wiesel, T. N. (1962). Receptive fields, binocular interaction, and functional architecture in the cat's visual cortex. *Journal of Physiology, 160,* 106–154.

Hübner, R. (1996). Specific effects of spatial-frequency uncertainty and different cue types on contrast detection: Data and models. *Vision Research, 36,* 3429–3439.

Jenkins, J., Craven, B., Bruce, V., & Akamatsu, S. (1997). Methods for detecting social signals from the face. *Technical Report of IECE, HIP96-39,* The Institute of Electronics, Information and Communication Engineers, Japan.

Jolicoeur, P. (1990). Identification of disoriented objects: A dual-systems theory. *Mind and Language, 5,* 387–410.

Jolicoeur, P., Gluck, M., & Kosslyn, S. M. (1984). Pictures and names: Making the connexion. *Cognitive Psychology, 19,* 31–53.

Kimchi, R. (1992). Primacy of wholistic processing and global/local paradigm: a critical review. *Psychological Bulletin, 112,* 24–38.

Leder H., & Bruce V. (1998). Local and relational effects of distinctiveness. *Quarterly Journal of Experimental Psychology, 51A,* 449–473.

Legge, G. E., & Gu, Y. (1989). Stereopsis and contrast. *Vision Research, 29,* 989–1004.

Liu, Z., Knill, D. C., & Kersten, D. (1995). Object classification for human and ideal observers. *Vision Research, 35,* 549–568.

Macho S., & Leder H. (1998) Your eyes only? A test of interactive influence in the processing of facial features. *Journal of Experimental Psychology: Human Perception and Performance, 24,* 1486–1500.

Marr, D., (1982). *Vision.* San Francisco: Freeman.

Marr, D., & Hildreth, E. (1980). Theory of edge detection. *Proceedings of the Royal Society of London, Series B, 207,* 187–217.

Marr, D., & Poggio, T. (1979). A computational theory of human stereo vision. *Proceedings of the Royal Society of London, Series B, 204,* 301–328.

Morgan, M. J. (1992). Spatial filtering precedes motion detection. *Nature, 355,* 344–346.

Morrisson, D., & Schyns, P. G. (1998). Exploring the interactions between face processing and attention. *Perception, 27,* 130.

Morrison, D. J., & Schyns, P. G. (1999). *Spatial scales in the Margaret Thatcher Illusion.* Unpublished manuscript.

Morrison, D. J., & Schyns, P. G. (2001). Usage of spatial scales for the categorization of faces, objects and scenes. *Psychological Bulletin and Review, 8,* 454–469.

Oliva, A., & Schyns, P. G. (1997). Coarse blobs or fine edges? Evidence that information diagnosticity changes the perception of complex visual stimuli. *Cognitive Psychology, 34,* 72–107.

Oliva, A., & Schyns, P. G. (2000). Diagnostic colors mediates scene recognition. *Cognitive Psychology, 41,* 176–210.

Pantle, A., & Sekuler, R. (1968). Size detecting mechanisms in human vision. *Science, 162,* 1146–1148.

Parker, D. M., & Costen, N. P. (1999). One extreme or the other or perhaps the golden mean? Issues of spatial resolution in face processing. *Current Psychology, 18,* 118–127.

Parker, D. M., & Dutch, S. (1987). Perceptual latency and spatial frequency. *Vision Research, 27,* 1279–1283.

Parker, D. M., Lishman, J. R., & Hughes, J. (1992). Temporal integration of spatially filtered visual images. *Perception, 21,* 147–160.

Parker, D. M., Lishman, J. R., & Hughes, J. (1997). Evidence for the view that temporospatial integration in vision is temporally anisotropic. *Perception, 26,* 1169–1180.

Perrett, D. I., Oram, M. W., & Ashbridge, E. (1998). Evidence accumulation in cell populations responsive to faces: An account of generalisation of recognition without mental transformation. *Cognition, 67,* 111–145.

Pashler, H. E. (1998). *The psychology of attention.* Cambridge, MA: MIT Press.

Poggio, T., & Edelman, S. (1990). A network that learns to recognize three-dimensional objects. *Nature, 343,* 263–266.

Pylyshyn, Z. (1999). Is vision continuous with cognition? The case for cognitive impenetrability of visual perception. *Behavioral and Brain Sciences, 22,* 341–423.

Rensink, R. A., O'Regan, J. K., & Clark, J. J. (1997). To see or not to see: The need for attention to perceive changes in scenes. *Psychological Science, 8,* 368–373.

Rosch, E., Mervis, C. B., Gray, W., Johnson, D., & Boyes-Braem, P. (1976). Basic objects in natural categories. *Cognitive Psychology, 8,* 382–439.

Schyns, P. G. (1998). Diagnostic recognition: Task constraints, object information and their interactions. *Cognition, 67,* 147–179.

Schyns, P. G., Bonnar, L., & Gosselin, F. (2002). Show me the features! Understanding recognition from the use of visual information. *Psychological Science, 13,* 402–409.

Schyns, P. G., Goldstone, R. L., & Thibaut, J. P. (1998). The development of features in object concepts. *Behavioral and Brain Sciences, 21,* 17–41.

Schyns, P. G., & Oliva, A. (1994). From blobs to boundary edges: Evidence for time- and spatial-scale-dependent scene recognition. *Psychological Science, 5,* 195–200.

Schyns, P. G., & Oliva, A. (1999). Dr. Angry and Mr. Smile: When categorization flexibly modifies the perception of faces in rapid visual presentations. *Cognition, 69,* 243–265.

Schyns, P. G., & Rodet, L. (1997). Categorization creates functional features. *Journal of Experimental Psychology: Learning, Memory & Cognition, 23,* 681–696.

Sergent, J. (1982). Theoretical and methodological consequences of variations in exposure duration in visual laterality studies. *Perception and Psychophysics, 31,* 451–461.

Sergent, J. (1986). Microgenesis of face perception. In H. D. Ellis, M. A. Jeeves, F. Newcombe, & A. M. Young (Eds.), *Aspects of face processing.* Dordrecht: Martinus Nijhoff.

Simons, D., & Wang, R. F. (1998). Perceiving real-world viewpoint changes. *Psychological Science. 9,* 315–320.

Snowden, R. J., & Hammett, S. T. (1992). Subtractive and divisive adaptation in the human visual system. *Nature, 355,* 248–250.

Sowden, P., & Schyns, P. G. (2000). Expectancy effects on spatial frequency processing: A psychophysical analogy to task-dependent processing of real-world objects and scenes. *Perception, 29,* 34.

Tanaka, J., & Gauthier, I. (1997). Expertise in object and face recognition. In R. L. Goldstone, D. L. Medin, & P. G. Schyns (Eds.), *Perceptual learning.* San Diego: Academic Press.

Tanaka, J. W., & Presnell, L. M. (1999). Color diagnosticity in object recognition. *Perception & Psychophysics, 61,* 1140–1153.

Tanaka, J., & Taylor, M. E. (1991). Object categories and expertise: Is the basic level in the eye of the beholder? *Cognitive Psychology, 15,* 121–149.

Tarr, M. J., & Pinker, S. (1989). Mental rotation and orientation-dependence in shape recognition. *Cognitive Psychology, 21,* 233–282.

Tarr, M. J., & Pinker, S. (1991). Orientation-dependent mechanisms in shape recognition: Further issues. *Psychological Science, 2,* 207–209.

Thomas, J. P. (1970). Model of the function of receptive fields in human vision. *Psychological Review, 77,* 121–134.

Troje, N., & Bülthoff, H. H. (1996) Face recognition under varying pose: The role of texture and shape. *Vision Research, 36,* 1761–1771.

Watt, R. J. (1987). Scanning from coarse to fine spatial scales in the human visual system after the onset of a stimulus. *Journal of the Optical Society of America A, 4,* 2006–2021.

Watt, R. J., & Morgan, M. J. (1985). A theory of the primitive spatial code in human vision. *Vision Research, 25,* 1661–1674.

Webster, M. A., & De Valois, R. L. (1985). Relationship between spatial frequencies and orientation tuning of striate-cortex cells. *Journal of the Optical Society of America, A, 2,* 1124–1132.

Wilson, H. R., & Bergen, J. R. (1979). A four mechanism model for spatial vision. *Vision Research, 19,* 1177–1190.

Witkin, A. P. (1987). Scale-space filtering. In M. A. Fischler and O. Firschein (Eds.), *Readings in computer vision: Issues, problems, principles and paradigms.* San Francisco: Morgan Kaufmann.

6

Image-Based Recognition of Biological Motion, Scenes, and Objects

ISABELLE BÜLTHOFF AND HEINRICH H. BÜLTHOFF

The task of understanding how objects and scenes are represented in the brain for the purpose of recognition is one of the hardest and most important questions in cognitive neuroscience. Our visual system is so swift and efficient at identifying our surroundings that we often do not appreciate the true complexity of the task. In figure 6.1 we illustrate a variety of problems that our visual system has to solve when recognizing objects.

When we are asked to point out all the chairs in the scene, we can do so easily despite variations in illumination, shape, or size of the chairs, although an unexpected location might slow down our completion of the task. If we are given the task of determining which chairs we could actually sit on, we would not include, for example, the chair on the desktop in this class, even though its image is the same size as that of the chair in the back room. We have included other "traps" in this scene that our visual system does not fall into when solving object recognition problems—can you find them all?

The images that our retina receives from any particular object can change dramatically with variations in orientation, illumination, distance, etc. Nevertheless, we can assign all these different images correctly to one and the same object or object category. Our recognition system is so good that we are always able to find our coffee mug in the morning, even if we are only half awake. This might fool us into thinking that any object can be recognized effortlessly from any and all viewpoints. However, several researchers have shown that not all views of an object are equally good in object-recognition tasks, even when the object is as familiar as a

FIGURE 6.1 This image of a complex scene illustrates some of the problems encountered in visual processing. See color insert.

coffee mug. For example, Palmer, Rosch, and Chase (1981) reported that certain canonical views are recognized more quickly than others. More recently, Blanz and colleagues (Blanz, Tarr & H. H. Bülthoff, 1999) investigated what makes a good or canonical view by using interactive computer graphics to allow unrestricted views and interactive exploration of objects. By investigating canonical views under ecological conditions they found that familiarity was a major factor in determining canonicality. This prompted them to suggest that participants relied more on their experience with particular views of an object than on object shape or function in the experiments. We will review the importance of familiarity for object recognition in a later part of this chapter.

The term "object recognition" can have different meanings: categorization (e.g., the furry animal across the street is a dog and not a cat), identification (e.g., the dog across the street is the one that belongs to the neighbor), or discrimination (the dog I see is a labrador and not a dachshund).

Researchers use a variety of implicit and explicit psychophysical tasks to investigate object recognition. In explicit tasks participants are asked to draw comparisons between two or more objects presented during the experiment. They are asked, for instance, if the object that they see in front of them had already been presented earlier in the experiment (old-new recognition) or whether two images presented simultaneously or consecutively in one trial depict the same object (same-different judgment). Or they might be required to recognize a previously viewed object each time it reappears among distractor objects (match-to-sample task). In all these tasks, certain aspects of the objects might be changed during testing: the viewpoints from which they are seen, for example, or their illumination. Thus, in explicit tasks participants are required to refer back to stored mental representations of objects explicitly learned to perform the task.

In implicit tasks, participants are not required to refer back to an object seen during the experiment. Instead, they must use stored mental representations accumulated over a lifetime, and match these mental representations to the presented object in order to categorize it or identify it correctly. For example participants in an object-naming task do not need to refer back to a particular exemplar of the category of dog to answer correctly "dog" when they are presented with the image of a dog that they have never seen before. They use previous visual experience with objects of that category in order to arrive at the correct classification. There are other implicit tasks in which participants have to make a judgment about certain properties of the objects that they see. For example, in object decision experiments (e.g., Schacter, Cooper, Delaney, Peterson, & Tharan, 1991; Williams & Tarr, 1997) participants were asked to decide whether each test image depicted an object that could exist in 3D space. Williams and Tarr (1997) showed in one of their experiments that when participants had studied objects before testing, they were faster in the subsequent decision task when studied objects were presented as compared to unstudied objects. In other words, participants were faster at processing the three-dimensional structures of primed objects than the structures of unstudied ones. Importantly, this priming occurred only when the test objects were possible. Williams and Tarr hypothesize that while some information about possible segments in possible and impossible objects could be stored in memory, this was not the case for impossible parts.

In this chapter we will review experiments using both explicit and implicit tasks to investigate object recognition using familiar objects (faces), unusual renderings of familiar objects (point-light walker), and novel scenes. While it is unlikely that participants would have already seen the particular renderings of familiar objects used in an experiment, they have definitely seen similar objects. For this reason, unfamiliar objects are used in many experiments to circumvent the problem of uncontrolled variations in prior exposure to objects. Another reason for using unfamiliar objects is that they allow us precise control over the types of features that are available for discrimination.

How our visual system represents familiar and unfamiliar three-dimensional (3D) objects for the purpose of recognition is a difficult and passionately discussed issue (e.g., Biederman & Gerhardstein, 1993; Tarr & H. H. Bülthoff, 1995). At the theoretical level a key question that any representational scheme has to address is how much the internal model depends on the viewing parameters. We will present two types of models regarding this issue and also address the question of whether the recognition process is more analytic (i.e., it is based on the decomposition of objects into parts and the specifications of the interrelations between these parts) or more holistic (i.e., it is based on matching directly whole images to imagelike views stored in memory).

One framework for object representation is largely viewpoint-independent and is based on a structural description of objects similar to 3D computer models (Biederman, 1987; Biederman & Gerhardstein, 1993; Marr, 1982; Marr & Nishihara 1978). In Marr's view vision is reconstruction, an analytical and hierarchical process that begins with local features and combines them into more and more complex structural descriptions of objects. Accordingly, the theories for object recognition described by the authors cited above are analytical.

The other group of recognition models is viewpoint-dependent and can be classified as a more holistic recognition scheme in that it does not treat various parts of the same object separately. Instead it suggests that objects are stored as a collection of views captured from specific viewpoints (H. H. Bülthoff & Edelman, 1992; H. H. Bülthoff, Edelman, & Tarr, 1995; Rock & DiVita, 1987; Tarr & H. H. Bülthoff, 1999; Ullman, 1979).

The advantage of a structural representation of objects and a more analytical recognition process is that it requires little memory. A single hierarchical and compact description is sufficient to allow recognition of an object from almost any viewpoint, since any particular view of an object can be generated during the recognition process by rotating the stored structural model in the appropriate manner. The hierarchical structural description of objects proposed by Marr is based on hierarchical arrangements of generalized cylinders (primitive-based theory). A cylinder corresponding to the main axis of an object forms the first level of the hierarchy. The locations and orientations of cylinders in the next level are specified relative to this cylinder. Each of the cylinders in this level serves as a reference point for cylinders at the next hierarchical level. Because the position of each part is defined relative to other parts of the object, the description of an object's shape will be the same regardless of the viewpoint from which it is seen (3D object-centered representation).

One major problem with this kind of object representation is that it is difficult to build 3D models from the information available in the two-dimensional (2D) images on our retina. Any 2D image is always consistent with infinitely many 3D interpretations. Furthermore, many experiments (see Blanz et al., 1999, and Palmer et al., 1981, cited earlier) suggest that familiar objects are not recognized equally well from all viewpoints.

Biederman's (1987) recognition-by-components (RBC) theory is motivated by the analytical and hierarchical recognition scheme developed by Marr. It represents objects with a set of 36 geometric shapes called geons. These geons differ from each other in certain nonaccidental features, meaning that specific features of each geon, like symmetry or co-linearity, are invariant over a wide range of transformations such as rotation, translation, or size. This makes them reliable diagnostic features for recognition. Unlike the 3D models of Marr and Nishihara's theory, the descriptions in Biederman's theory are not based on a 3D reconstruction of the object. Rather, the description simply specifies the geons that are visible in the image and the gross 2D spatial relationships among them. For example, geon A is above geon B, or geon A is to one side of geon B. This model predicts that recognition of an object will be viewpoint-independent as long as the same geons are visible at different viewpoints.

One problem with the RBC theory is that most natural objects such as flowers or trees are particularly difficult to represent with geons. In real life, people can quickly distinguish between different types of trees or flowers, even though making such visual distinctions would require using quite detailed object representations. Another problem is that a distinction between different objects is possible only at the basic level—that is, a geon-based structural description can differentiate between a chair and a table, but not necessarily between different types of chairs. Many fine structural variations between chairs would be lost because the basic features would be mapped into the same basic geons, resulting into a common geon structural description for various chairs.

Generally, recognition models based on structural representations can be expected to perform poorly only for those views in which the chosen perspective makes it difficult to recover the reference frame in which the object-centered description is to be formed. If an elongated object like a tree branch or a pen is shown from one end, for example, the major axis will be substantially foreshortened. The resulting difficulty in forming the characteristic description of the object in terms of its parts might result in reduced recognition performance. In all other cases, these theories predict similar recognition performance across different views.

There are two ways in which view-invariant recognition can be achieved; the first, which was described above, is to encode features that are easily recognized over a wide range of views. In the following we will describe a second possibility, in which multiple descriptions of an object are stored, each specific to a different viewpoint. Recognition is then based on matching the retinal image to stored views. Image-based mechanisms for object recognition require a large amount of memory, and ease and accuracy of recognition will depend significantly on viewpoint familiarity (e.g., Edelman & H. H. Bülthoff, 1992; Poggio & Edelman, 1990; Tarr & Pinker, 1990; Ullman & Basri, 1991; for a more detailed account of view-based models, see Tarr and H. H. Bülthoff, 1999). If we can compensate for changes of viewpoints with a normalization process, then we do not need to store all possible views of an object, only a few image-based representations will allow us to recognize an object from different viewpoints. In this way the amount of memory needed by the model is reduced. Similar processes could be devised for other variations such as changes in illumination. For viewpoint changes, a variety of different mechanisms have been proposed for generalizing from familiar to unfamiliar views, including mental rotation (Tarr & Pinker, 1990) and view interpolation (Poggio & Edelman, 1990).

In this chapter we will review several recognition experiments that, in our view, support the use of image-based mechanisms for object recognition. The research that we present here also pushes the boundaries of classic object recognition to incorporate new territory. We will review studies investigating the recognition of dynamic objects (biological motion), testing the recognition of scenes in virtual reality, and exploring the temporal aspect of object recognition.

Biological Motion

Dynamic objects can be recognized even in highly impoverished motion sequences in which no one frame alone has enough figural information to allow recognition (figure 6.2). Johansson's biological motion sequences (1973) showing point-light humans engaged in various dynamic activities are convincing demonstrations of this point. Most studies on biological motion perception have been concerned with bottom-up mechanisms of perception, investigating the extraction of low-level features and thus bypassing the need to deal with the nature of internal object models (Cutting, 1981; Cutting & Kozlowski, 1977; Hoffman & Flinchbaugh, 1982; Shibata, Sugihara, & Sugie, 1985; Webb & Aggarwal, 1982).

In our studies with Sinha on the recognition of biological motion pat-

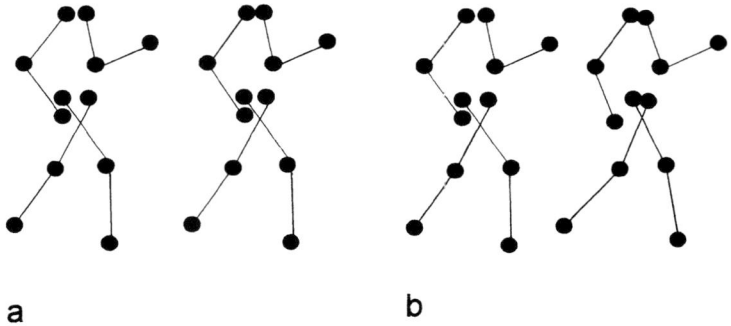

a   b

FIGURE 6.2. (*a*) Stereogram of a single frame of a film showing a walking person represented by dots only. (*b*) Stereogram of a depth-distorted walker. Crossfusers will notice that the 3D structure is severely distorted in *b* but not in *a*. Connecting lines between the dots of the walker are added for better visualization. The lines were not present in the experiments.

terns (Bülthoff, H. H. Bülthoff & Sinha, 1997, 1998), we were primarily interested in exploring which kind of internal representation (view-dependent or view-independent) the brain uses to recognize dynamic three-dimensional objects (point-light walkers). These studies will be reviewed here.

Any recognition theory of dynamic objects must make predictions about the extent to which internal motion models depend on viewing parameters. The possible strategies for recognizing dynamic objects are similar to those that have been discussed for the recognition of static objects. Viewpoint-independent models of recognition suggest that moving objects are stored as a collection of the 3D trajectories of a few feature points. If we assume that viewing transformations like rotation, translation, or scaling can be applied to this representation to match it against a motion sequence shown from a novel viewpoint, then that sequence should be equally recognizable from any viewpoint. In the image-based recognition framework, static objects are represented as a collection of 2D views. This framework can be extended to dynamic objects by storing 2D motion traces that are projections of the 3D trajectories of feature points onto the viewing plane. Dynamic 3D objects are then represented as a collection of several such 2D traces captured from various viewpoints.

In our study we used stimuli similar to Johansson's except that we employed 3D instead of 2D point trajectories to test whether or not the image-based recognition framework can account for recognition of 3D biological motion sequences.

There are two predictions that should be supported if a view-dependent mechanism mediates the recognition of dynamic objects. First, view familiarity should have a strong influence on recognition performance. That is, recognition should be easiest from viewing positions that are more common and from which participants are therefore more likely to have stored internal traces of dynamic objects than from unusual positions. The second prediction is that modifying the depth structure of 3D biological motion sequences should not have any effect on recognition performance as long as the 2D traces remain unchanged.

In what follows we will describe a *viewpoint-familiarity experiment* that we designed to test the first prediction. All the stimuli were based on one biological motion sequence of a human walking three steps in place (sequence duration approx. 2s). This biological motion sequence, presented on a computer monitor, tracked the 3D positions of 12 points located on the main joints of a male human recorded as he walked in place.[1] In all the experiments described below, only the points represented by small bright dots were visible, not the body itself (point-light walker, see example in figure 6.2). The stimuli always showed the same point-light walker sequence, but the viewpoint from which it was shown changed (figure 6.3).

The importance of view familiarity was investigated by measuring the recognition performance of participants viewing a point-light walker from various viewpoints. The participants first saw a sequence showing a view of the walker from above (polar view). The viewpoint changed incrementally from pole to equator for each of the following 13 sequence playbacks, either along the profile meridian ending with a profile equatorial view or

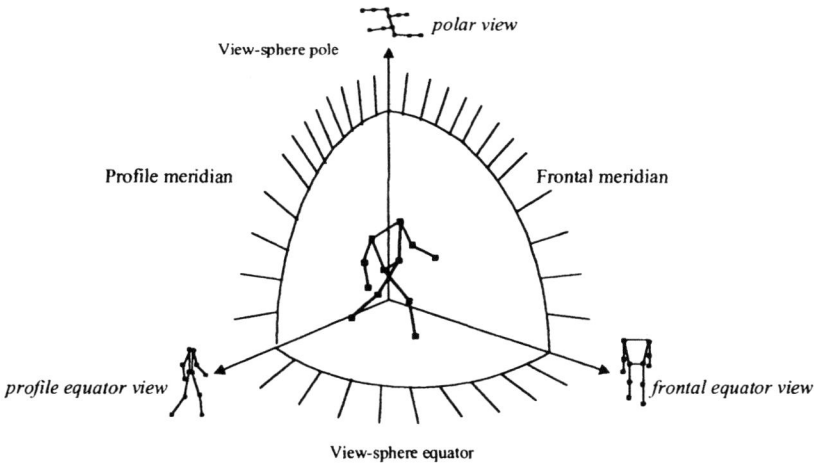

FIGURE 6.3. In the *view-familiarity experiment* the position of the viewpoint was moved systematically along the profile or the frontal meridian. In the *anomalous-depth structure experiment* the viewpoint was always situated on the equator at waist level. The bars along the meridians and equator indicate the viewing positions. The large walker is shown as viewed from an equatorial 3/4 view. Connecting lines were absent in all experiments.

along the frontal meridian to end with a frontal equatorial view (figure 6.3). The stimuli were presented either with or without binocular disparity (using LCD shutter glasses) to investigate whether information about the depth structure of the stimuli had any impact on recognition.

Each participant viewed the series of 14 sequence playbacks only once to minimize the influence of expectations on recognition performance. The participants did not know what kind of figure the moving points represented. They were asked to report after each sequence if they recognized a meaningful moving object or saw only random moving points. The viewing direction was recorded at which the participants first recognized a walking human. Polar views are less familiar to humans, so we would expect them to be less easily recognizable than viewpoints located along the equator.

Recognition performance along the different meridians is shown in figure 6.4. Recognition performance (percent correct recognition) averaged across all participants is plotted as a function of viewpoint along the frontal and the profile meridians. Viewing position in degrees is plotted along the abscissa. There are four curves corresponding to four testing conditions:

- *Frontal:* Recognition performance for sequences without depth information when viewed along the frontal meridian.
- *Profile*: Recognition performance for sequences without depth information when viewed along the profile meridian.
- *Frontal S* and *Profile S*: Recognition performance for sequences with depth information provided by stereoscopic presentation when viewed along the frontal and profile meridians.

Under all conditions the recognition curves indicated a strong viewpoint dependency. Recognition performance was poor for polar views where sequences were recognized less often than sequences viewed from the equator. Recognition performance was view-dependent even when the sequences were presented under stereoscopic viewing conditions.

The results of the viewpoint-familiarity experiment support the first prediction of the image-based recognition framework. If recognition performance were based on a viewpoint-invariant representation, then performance should not have been any worse from polar viewpoints than it was from equatorial viewpoints. In fact, the participants' performance was strongly tied to the familiarity of the viewpoint from which the sequence was observed. Furthermore, the results suggest that the participants' recognition performance was not based on the use of a viewpoint-invariant internal representation that could potentially have been constructed during a lifetime of experience in observing humans in motion.

Another hypothesis that seems capable of accounting for this pattern of results is based on the notion of the intrinsic information content of the stimuli. According to this idea, poor recognition performance for polar

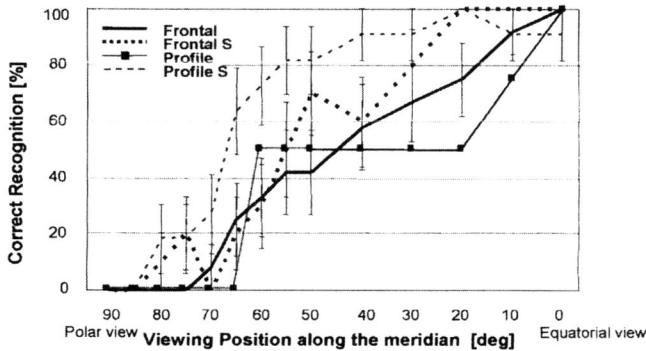

FIGURE 6.4. Results of the *familiarity experiment*. All results are shown with standard error bars. *Frontal:* Recognition performance along the frontal meridian. *Profile*: Recognition performance along the profile meridian. *Frontal S* and *Profile S*: Recognition performance for sequences with depth information.

sequences might be due not to the unfamiliarity of the viewpoint per se, but rather to the scanty information content of the sequences relative to the equatorial sequences. At the pole the elongated body of a human is seen strongly foreshortened. In Marr and Nishihara's (1978) model this would render recognition difficult if not impossible because the main axis of elongation is difficult to find in a foreshortened view.

Nevertheless, we should not forget that it is motion trajectories that are the basis for recognition here, not static point positions. The following two observations suggest that the evidence favors a viewpoint familiarity based explanation. First, if one focuses on the information inherent in motion trajectories, the polar sequence was no less informative than the equatorial sequence. The full extent of the motion trajectories was visible from both viewpoints because the point-light walkers were transparent and the dots were not occluded. Second, the results showed better recognition from viewpoints closer to the equator both for profile views and for frontal views. In terms of information content in the motion trajectories the frontal view at the equator is in fact less informative than the polar one because all the point trajectories are greatly foreshortened in a walker coming toward the observer. In this case the trajectories of the points on the swinging arms and legs lie mainly along the viewing axis and not on the image plane. Even so, these views of a human walker were much easier to recognize than polar views with much more pronounced point trajectories. The greater viewpoint familiarity was apparently able to compensate for the reduced information content.

Adding depth information to the stimuli did not facilitate recognition along the frontal meridian (there were too few participants under Profile S conditions for an evaluation of the depth parameter along the profile meridian). The main point of using stereoscopic viewing was to test if a viewpoint familiarity effect was present even when 3D stimuli were used. Unfamiliar views were hard to recognize even when the full structural information provided by binocular disparity was available and could theoretically be matched to a structural model after the appropriate transformation. This result suggests that the internal representation used to recognize biological motion is largely two-dimensional and that viewpoint familiarity is the primary determinant of the pattern of results that were observed in these experiments.

The second prediction of the image-based framework is that if the representation is largely 2D, then distorting the depth structure of the sequence should not impair recognition as long as the 2D traces are left unchanged. If depth information is an important part of the representation, then a depth-distorted sequence would not be perceived as a normal human in motion. We tested the importance of depth information in an *anomalous-depth experiment*, in which participants viewed distorted and undistorted walker sequences stereoscopically from different viewpoints.

Three kinds of sequences were presented: undistorted walkers, depth-distorted walkers, and various distractors (figure 6.5). Depth-distorted walkers and distractors were derived from the same original motion sequence of the undistorted walker.

To create depth-distorted walkers, each dot from the original figure was moved randomly along the depth (z) axis within the depth d of the bounding box. Thus, the depth structure of the original walker was manipulated while leaving its 2D projection unchanged. The small bars placed at each joint of the point-light walker in figure 6.5b indicate the possible displacement of each point. The 2D positions of the points of the depth-distorted walker are largely unchanged on the xy plane (see figure 6.5a and 6.5d). From other viewing positions (e.g., in the yz projection shown on the right in figure 6.5d), the original 2D pattern of a human figure is severely distorted (compare with the same view of the undistorted walker in figure 6.5c).

Distractors were generated by randomizing the positions of the dots along the x and z axes within the bounding box. The original motion trajectory of each point was preserved, but a constant offset in x and z direction was added to the point trajectories. The resulting distractors are perceived as random (nonhuman) patterns of points.

If the full 3D information is taken into account in the recognition process, we would expect participants to perceive our depth-distorted sequences as random objects from all viewpoints because the 3D structure of these depth-distorted walkers would be completely different from that of a human figure. The ratings assigned to these sequences would therefore be uniformly low for all viewing positions. Otherwise, if internal representation emphasized 2D congruence, then the rating might be expected to increase as we move from a viewing position perpendicular to the depth

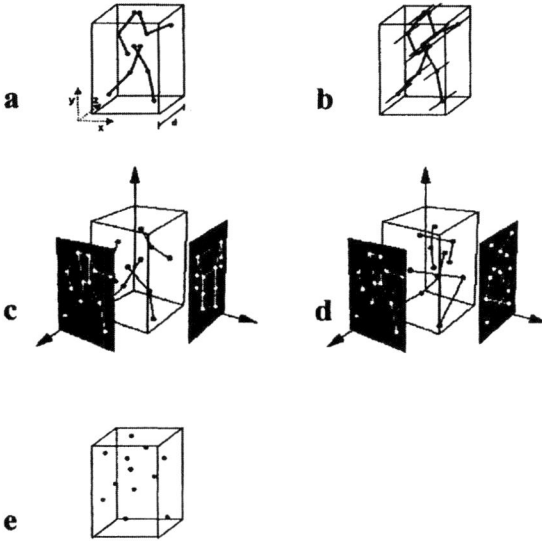

FIGURE 6.5. Three kinds of motion sequence were used in the *anomalous-depth structure experiment*. (a) Undistorted point-light walker shown within its bounding box. The three major axes are indicated. *d* is the depth of the bounding box. (b) Depth noise was added to the positions of the dots along the depth *z*-axis to create a depth-distorted walker. (c) Undistorted walker viewed from two viewpoints. (d) Depth-distorted walker from two viewpoints. (e) Example of a random point-light display.

axis (frontal view) to one parallel to it (profile view) and the 2D view grows more and more like the 2D projection of a human figure.

In the anomalous-depth experiment all sequences were presented from 11 different viewpoints along the equator. In other words, the walker was always viewed standing fully upright (figure 6.3). At 0° participants saw a profile equatorial view of the walker moving to the right, while at 90° they saw a frontal equatorial view of the figure walking toward the participant with its depth axis perpendicular to the viewing axis. The participants' task was to rate the 3D display on an ordinal scale of 1 to 5 in terms of its figural goodness as a human, where 1 corresponded to very random and 5 to very human. They saw all three types of sequences in random order repeatedly. Viewing position was also randomized. An equal number of each kind of stimulus (undistorted walker, depth-distorted walker, or distractor) was included in each experimental session. One session comprised a total of 165 presentations.

The results of this experiment are shown in figure 6.6. The ratings were averaged across all the participants and plotted as a function of viewing position in degrees. The main result was that those viewpoints preserving

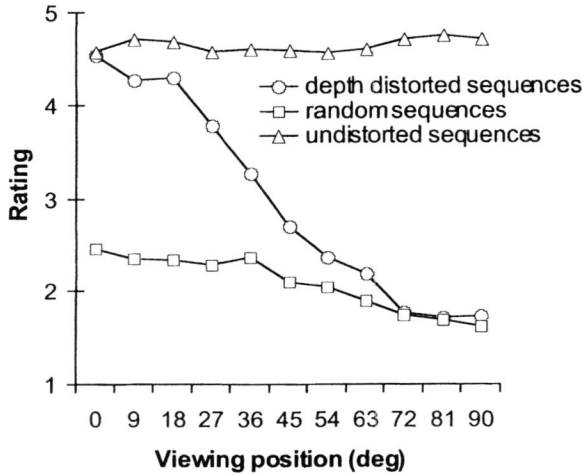

FIGURE 6.6. Results of the *anomalous-depth structure experiment.*

the normal 2D projections yielded percepts of a human walker (i.e., high ratings) even when the 3D structure diverged from the biological structure of a human. The depth-distorted sequence viewed from other positions yielded percepts of randomly moving dots (i.e., low ratings). Thus, ratings for the depth-distorted walker were strongly dependent on the viewing position. The drop in the ratings for the distorted walker corresponded to an increasing divergence between the 2D projections of the undistorted walker and those of the depth-distorted walker. The ratings for undistorted sequences were very high from all viewing positions; those for distractors remained consistently low regardless of the viewpoint.

The shape of all three curves in figure 6.6 can be understood best in the context of the image-based recognition framework, where the 2D projection contributes to recognition but the 3D structure does not. Participants appeared to use a metric for similarity that was heavily biased toward 2D traces. These findings indirectly suggest that internal representations themselves might be largely two-dimensional.

Since all three kinds of sequences were shown under stereoscopic viewing conditions, each particular view provided the same 3D information about the point-light structure but of course different 2D projections of the same moving object. Surprisingly, there was no indication that the participants were even aware of the depth scrambling; they rated the distorted walker as highly human as long as the 2D trace was undistorted. We investigated this lack of awareness of an anomalous depth structure in experiments that will not be discussed here (Bülthoff et al., 1998). Instead, we will now turn to a study of viewpoint effects in scene recognition.

Scene Recognition

Object recognition appeared to be strongly dependent on view familiarity in the last study. Is this also the case for the recognition of complex scenes? In the following we will review work by Christou and one of the authors (Christou & H. H. Bülthoff, 1997, 1998, 1999) that sheds some light on this question. In their study, Christou and H. H. Bülthoff investigated what kind of mental representation we form when exploring an unfamiliar virtual scene and how well we can generalize from familiar views of the scene to novel views that we have never seen before.

Until now, most scene-recognition experiments have been carried out in the real world or using photographs of real-world scenes (Hock & Schmelzkopf, 1980; Rowland, Franken, Bouchard, & Sookochoff, 1978; Shelton & McNamara, 1997). Generally, investigating human action and perception in complex environments places great demands on the experimental platform. First, for the results to be reproducible, precise control over the presented stimulus is required. Second, it must be easy to manipulate scene parameters if we are to carry out any kind of systematic research. Third, a holistic approach to the study of object representation via recognition performance requires a certain degree of interactivity between the participant and the environment and a closed action-perception loop. Finally, the ability to display complex, multisensory scenes is a prerequisite for providing a realistic setting. The natural environment as an experimental platform fails to fulfill the first two requirements. It was only with the advent of virtual environments that we were finally able to satisfy all the conditions listed above (Christou & H. H. Bülthoff, 2000).

More specifically, scene-recognition experiments carried out in real-world environments or with photographs entail uncontrolled variations in scene illumination (e.g., time of the day, clouds) and the presence of undesired features like landmarks (e.g., mountains), textures, or colors that might facilitate recognition without forcing the observer to make use of spatial knowledge (the main focus of interest). Thus, they falsely suggest generalized representation when testing recognition of familiar and novel views of the scenes. The use of photographs of a scene limits the number of available views of the scene and also lacks the dynamic and interactive components that might be important for spatial encoding.

Christou and H. H. Bülthoff provided the element of interactivity by letting participants use a special hand-held navigation device (SpaceBall, Spacetec IMC CO., Massachusetts,) to actively and dynamically navigate in a virtual scene. Furthermore, the visual cues in their virtual environment were carefully controlled. The participants' movements and viewing directions were limited to certain parts of the scene, thus addressing the problem of controlling the views experienced by the participants. The positions and viewing directions were recorded for later analysis and could be replayed to passive participants.

The purpose of the study reviewed here was to test whether participants

FIGURE 6.7. Interior view of the virtual attic of Wirtshaus Lichtenstein. From H. H. Bülthoff and H.A.H.C. van Veen, in M. Jenkin & L. Harris (Eds), *Vision and Action in Virtual Environments: Modern Psychophysics in Spatial Cognition Research, Vision and Attention*, p. 245 (Figure 12.5). New York: Springer. Reproduced with permission from Springer-Verlag. See color insert.

could recognize the virtual environment again when they viewed it from novel perspectives after first having been allowed to explore the environment from a limited set of directions. If the participants had truly formed a structural, view-independent representation of the scene, we would expect to see little difference between recognition performance for novel views and that for familiar views. Otherwise, if participants used an image-based representation of the environment, then generalization to views that had never been seen before should be much more difficult.

The stimulus was a virtual reconstruction of the intricately shaped attic of a real house (Wirtshaus Lichtenstein) located in the medieval town of Tübingen, Germany. An overall view of the reconstructed room is depicted in figure 6.7 and a floor plan is shown in figure 6.8. Distractor attics were built by using all the same building components (stairs, windows, doors) but altering their configuration. The scene was viewed on a computer monitor from a simulated viewpoint at a constant height from the attic floor.

Participants were allowed to familiarize themselves with the new environment by exploring it in three different fashions. We will describe each of them briefly, then describe the test procedure and finally review

Novel Direction (N)

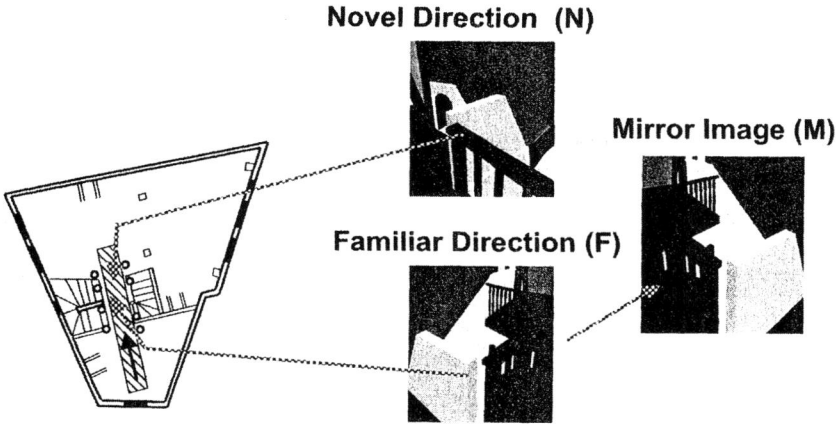

Mirror Image (M)

Familiar Direction (F)

FIGURE 6.8. The floor plan of the attic of Wirtshaus Lichtenstein is shown on the left. Double lines are walls, dark stripes on walls are windows, and squares are pillars or chimney ducts. Viewing direction (black arrow) is the opposite of that in figure 6.7. The patterned arrows indicate the rough direction from which the test pictures shown on the right were taken. Open circles indicate the positions of markers used in the experiments.

the purpose of each familiarization procedure. In the *active-familiarization procedure* the participants moved about the room by controlling their movements with a special motion-control device (SpaceBall). Participants learned to use the SpaceBall in a short training session before the active familiarization procedure. The use of the device is highly intuitive: the users grasp the SpaceBall around its equator and pull, twist, or push the ball in the direction that they wish to turn or move in the 3D scene that they are viewing. The rate of motion in the 3D scene is proportional to the force applied to the SpaceBall.

The hatched rectangle in the floor plan of figure 6.8 indicates the location of the walkway along which the participants were allowed to move virtually. Their viewing angle (the black arrow in figure 6.8) was always restricted to straight ahead and up to 60° to the left or right. This restriction meant that they could not fully rotate their view to look back at the environment from a new perspective. The participants received an auditory signal whenever they came into contact with objects or reached the limit of their allowed viewing range.

To motivate exploration of the scene, the participants were asked to find and acknowledge 14 markers (colored disks) placed in the room along the walkway. These are indicated by the open circles in figure 6.8. A two-digit code on each marker was visible only when the participants drew close enough. The participants had to enter the codes on the computer keyboard. This familiarization period generally lasted about 20 minutes, the time needed by the participants to locate all the markers. This exploration phase was recorded and could be replayed for passive participants.

In the *passive-familiarization procedure with static pictures*, the participants did not walk virtually through the room themselves, but instead were shown 50 pictures of the environment on the computer screen. The images were chosen to mimic as closely as possible the views experienced by the active participants, but the order in which the images were presented was scrambled to prevent the spatial-temporal sequence of images from giving the impression of moving through the room. In this procedure as well the participants were required to acknowledge the two-digit markers in the images to keep their attention focused on the images. Passive and active exploration time was similar.

In the *passive-familiarization procedure with film sequences*, the participants passively viewed the recorded exploration sequences of a control group. The control group took part in the active familiarization procedure described above. The major difference between the passive and control groups was the absence of volitional movements in the passive observers.

The tests administered after the training sessions were similar for all the familiarization procedures. The participants were shown pictures of 14 familiar views of the room (F) experienced at the moment they could read the two-digit code on the markers. They also saw 14 novel views of the room (N)—that is, views of the locations shown in the F images, but taken from another viewpoint not experienced during the training procedure. It was possible to present unfamiliar views from along the walkway because the participants had not been free to turn around while exploring. Intermingled among these were 14 mirror images of the 14 F images (M) obtained by swapping corresponding pixels on either side of the vertical medial bisector of the F images and 14 pictures of distractor rooms. Each participant was shown all of the test pictures. In a forced-choice task the participants had to determine if each picture corresponded to the familiar environment or to another room with the same components arranged differently. They were told that unfamiliar views of the room would be included, not just those they had experienced themselves.

Mirror images of the F viewing condition were not included in the test procedure after the passive-familiarization with film sequences, because the number of stimuli used in the test procedure was already so large (60 target images and 60 distractors). In every other respect the test procedure was the same as that used in all the other conditions.

The motivation of Christou and H. H. Bülthoff in designing the active-familiarization procedure was to investigate how well participants could generalize to novel views after active learning. The results were compared with those from the passive-familiarization procedure to assess the importance of interactive and dynamic exploration in scene recognition.

The third method, passive-familiarization procedure with film sequences, incorporated the dynamic components of active familiarization that were missing in the passive procedure, but omitted the volitional

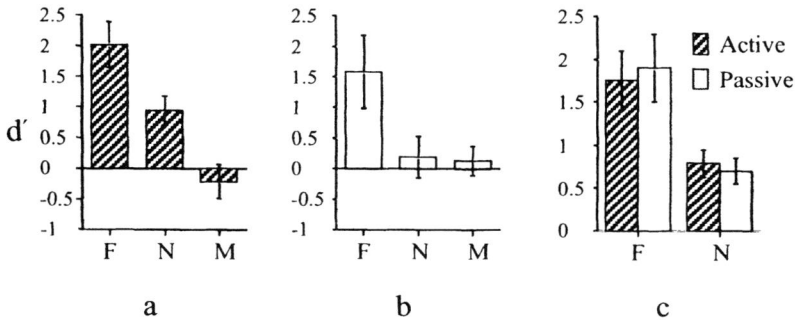

FIGURE 6.9. (a). Results averaged across all active participants. F familiar direction views; N novel direction views; M mirror images of familiar direction views. The error bars correspond to the 95% confidence limits of the mean. (b). Results averaged across all participants in the passive familiarization procedure with static pictures. (c). Results averaged across all active participants and their counterparts in the passive familiarization procedure with film sequences. Adapted from Christou & Bülthoff (1999) with permission of the Psychonomic Society, Inc.

aspect of navigation present in the active-familiarization procedure. This allowed Christou and H. H. Bülthoff to test the importance of volitional motion in scene recognition.

All the results are shown in figure 6.9. The mean of sensitivity measure d' was used to assess recognition performance for each test image type. For active participants (figure 6.9a), familiar views of the attic (F) were most easily recognized, but the d' score for novel views of the same environment (N) was still significantly greater than zero (as indicated by the 95% confidence interval). This means that subjects could identify N views as belonging to the target environment. The d' score for mirror (M) views was significantly worse than for the two other conditions. This suggests that mirror images were generally not mistaken for familiar or unfamiliar views of the attic.

When participants were familiarized with the environment by passively viewing static pictures (figure 9b), their recognition performance was best when they were shown familiar views, comparable to that of actively trained participants. Recognition performance for novel views was significantly lower than for familiar views and was also lower than for that of actively trained participants for the same task. Recognition performance for novel views was not significantly different from that for mirror images and not significantly different from 0.

After passive-familiarization with film sequences, the participants did not perform significantly worse than their active counterparts (figure 6.9c). Recognition performance for familiar views was similar in both groups; performance for novel views was also comparable in both groups and was significantly different from 0. Both active and passive participants were significantly better at recognition performance for familiar views than for novel views in this experiment; no mirror images were used.

In summary, recognition performance was best for familiar views of the attic, regardless of the training conditions. When participants had to recognize unfamiliar views of the attic, their performance was better than chance only when they had been trained actively or passively with film sequences, not when the training involved passive viewing of still shots. The assessment of the results given above is based on analyses of variance (ANOVA) of d' and post hoc analyses.

In general, the environment was successfully learned under all the conditions. Views nearest to the ones with which the participants were familiar were always recognized best. Better recognition for familiar views also suggests that all the participants had acquired a view-dependent mental representation of their surroundings.

Participants seldom categorized the mirror images as familiar, even though they were identical to the familiar views in terms of image features. This fact indicates that participants created an egocentric coding of the environment in which the visible environment was encoded within a body-centered reference frame as opposed to the creation of a list of components without spatial references.

In the context of scene recognition it is critical to study the importance of motion and interactive behavior because this is the way we usually learn about our environment. Participants trained with film sequences could generalize to novel views of the attic, although familiar views were always recognized much better. Thus, novel views were generally identified correctly. This indicates that although participants clearly appeared to have an egocentric (view-dependent) representation of the attic after training with film sequences, it was possible for them to generalize to novel views to some extent. Participants were able to do more than make 2D image interpolations, as the novel views could not have been generated in this way given the restricted exploration that was allowed. For example, new structural details appeared while others experienced during the training session disappeared in novel views.

When exploration was confined to the passive viewing of still pictures, participants were as good as the others at recognizing familiar views, but their ability to recognize novel views was significantly reduced. One could argue that better performance after the passive or active viewing of a film sequence could be due to the presence of depth cues that are provided by motion parallax or changes in interposition in the film sequence, but are missing in the static pictures. To test whether the difference in performance was due solely to the presence of such cues, Christou and H. H. Bülthoff designed a control experiment similar to the experiment using passive familiarization with static pictures except that they also included depth cues in the images by presenting them with binocular disparity (Christou & H. H. Bülthoff, Experiment 3, Technical Report No. 53, 1997). The results showed that adding depth information to the training with images did not improve recognition performance significantly. Thus, the decisive factor in achieving better recognition performance seemed to be the presence of motion, which temporally linked the images during training and thus provided more information about the spatial arrangement of the room's components.

A last goal in the study of Christou and H. H. Bülthoff was to assess the importance of volitional motion. The results reviewed so far have shown that motion per se was important, but that volitional motion did not lead to significantly better performance than passive motion. Nevertheless the active group had a nonsignificant advantage over the group that passively viewed film sequences in recognizing novel view (see figure 6.6c). Christou and H. H. Bülthoff (1998) repeated the passive-familiarization procedure with film sequences with passive and active groups of new participants. Both groups were tested immediately after training and again seven days later.

Active participants were significantly better than passive viewers at recognizing novel views of the attic after a seven-day delay, confirming the trend found immediately after the training. As in the previous experiments, the results showed no overall difference between the active and passive groups in their ability to recognize familiar views, indicating that both groups were equally attentive to the scene. Better recognition performance for novel views suggests that volitional motion allows the participants to build a more elaborate representation of their surrounding than their passive counterparts, hence facilitating enhanced recognition accuracy.

Similar findings were reported by Péruch and his co-authors (Péruch, Vercher, & Gauthier, 1995). They found a significant effect of training (active and passive) on recognition performance. After active movement participants were better able to locate spatially positioned objects in a 3D scene than after passive training. Wang and Simons (1999) also found that participants were better at compensating for view changes when given the task of detecting changes in a spatial array of real objects if these view changes were brought about by their own locomotion to a new viewpoint rather than by passive movement.

Temporal Continuity

In the previous section on scene recognition, we reviewed the benefits of temporal continuity in the presentation of stimuli (movies versus static images) for recognition performance. The last work we will review here follows up on this point. Wallis and H. H. Bülthoff (Wallis, 1998; Wallis & H. H. Bülthoff, 1997, 2001) investigated the importance of temporal contiguity in object recognition by asking the following question: How does our visual system link the different views of one object to create an object entity, especially when these views are very different from each other? In

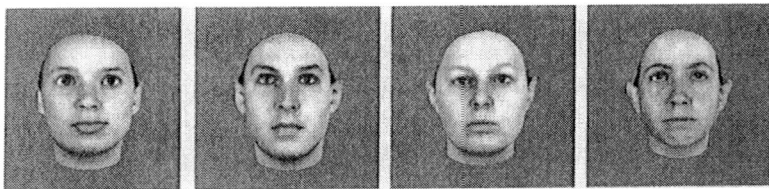

FIGURE 6.10. Set of 4 faces out of the 12 faces used to generate the stimuli used in the experiments reviewed in the temporal continuity section.

real life we seldom see only isolated snapshots of objects. Usually we explore novel objects by turning them around in our hands to explore them from all directions, or by walking around them. This way we can acquire a sequence of images gradually changing from the initial view of the object to a very different one within a short period of time (temporal contiguity). This general observation motivates the following question: Does our visual system use temporal contiguity to build mental representation of objects, thereby linking potentially very different views together?

While there is theoretical and neurophysiological evidence for the importance of temporal association of views in object recognition and visual memory (Edelman & Weinshall, 1991; Miyashita, 1988; Wallis & Baddeley, 1997), there are only a few psychophysical reports (e.g., Sinha & Poggio, 1996; Stone, 1998, 1999). Wallis and Bülthoff (2001) have proposed that our visual system uses temporal contiguity to associate images with one particular object. They tested this temporal association hypothesis by asking whether participants might be induced to confuse two different faces if these faces were associated in a coherent temporal sequence.

Twelve faces from 3D laser-scanned female heads were used as stimuli (figure 6.10). The faces were separated into three training sets of four faces each. Three-dimensional head models were generated by scanning the heads of volunteers with a laser scanner (Cyberware). The scanner sampled the texture and shape of each face. All nonfacial features such as hair were removed from the 3D head model. The processed heads were represented by approximately 70,000 vertices and the same number of color values.

Thomas Vetter and colleagues designed a method using optical flow and correspondence algorithms to automatically find corresponding vertices in 3D face models (Blanz & Vetter, 1999; Vetter and Poggio, 1997). With this method Wallis and H. H. Bülthoff (2001) were able to create artificial 3D morphs (average face) between all possible combinations of face pairs within each set. The texture and the 3D shape of both of the faces in each pair were manipulated in these morphs.

A sequence of five images was produced for each pair of faces A and B. A forward sequence began with a left profile view ($-90°$) of the original face A, a $-45°$ view of morph $\overline{AB}$ (average of face A and B), a

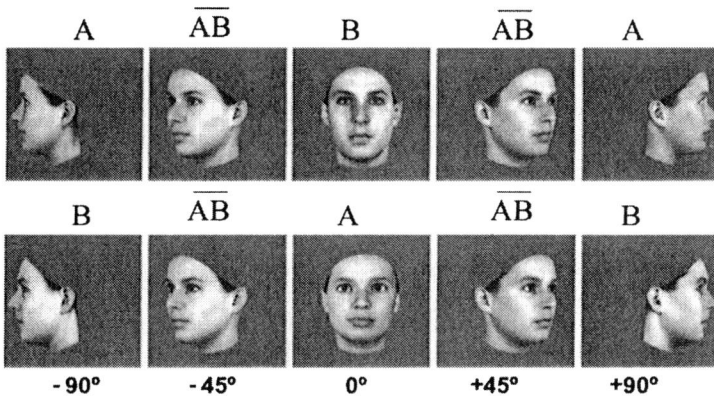

FIGURE 6.11. Example of forward sequences. Upper face row: Original head A was used to render left ($-90°$) and right ($+90°$) profile views of the face. Original face B is shown in a frontal view ($0°$). Morphs between original faces A and B were rendered in left and right $\pm 45°$ views. Lower row: Complementary sequence in which head A is shown in frontal view and head B is shown in profile. Morphs $\overline{AB}$ are identical in both sequences. Similar image sequences were calculated with all possible within-set pairs of faces.

frontal view ($0°$) of face B, a $+45°$ view of morph $\overline{AB}$, and finally a right profile ($+90°$) of face A (figure 6.11, upper row). A backward sequence showed the same images in reversed order. The training sequence consisted of the forward sequence followed by a backward sequence, followed by a forward sequence and a backward sequence again. Thus in one training sequence the participants saw a face turning from left to right and back again twice. The complementary training sequence was also created with face B in profile and face A in the frontal view (figure 6.11, lower row), resulting in a total of 12 training sequences per training set. To reduce the chance of artifacts stemming from a potential similarity between any two particular heads, the composition of the three training sets was varied for each participant. The participants were divided into two groups. Each group underwent a different kind of training with the stimuli before testing. We will first describe training and test procedures in a few words before explaining the purpose of the training procedures.

- *Training with sequential presentation.* Each participant in the first group saw all 36 stimulus sequences (12 sequences per training set, three training sets) presented in random order. Each image in the sequence was shown for 300 ms, followed immediately by the next to mimic a face rotating back and forth, as explained before.
- *Training with simultaneous presentation.* The familiarization procedure for the second group consisted of a simultaneous presen-

tation of images. All the faces and morphs from one forward sequence were shown together on the computer screen for 6000 ms,
which is equal to the total duration of the quadruple half-rotation
sequence used in the sequential presentation. The five images were
arranged on the computer screen around a fixation point.

After training, all the participants did a delayed match-to-sample task
in which, after a certain fixation period, one image was shown followed
by a mask and then a second image followed by a mask again (see figure
6.12). The participants had to decide whether the two images were different views of the same face or not. Half of the 384 trials presented
matches. In the other 192 trials, 96 of the test face pairs belonged to the
same training set (within set, WS) and 96 to different training sets (between set, BS). The test images were always a frontal followed by a profile
view or vice-versa; no morphed images were used during testing. All the
participants completed four blocks, two on the first day and two on the
following day. Each block consisted of a training phase followed by a
testing phase.

If views of objects are associated on the basis of their ordered appearance in time, then training with a sequential presentation should cause the
images grouped in one training sequence to be internally represented as
views of a single object. After such training, participants in the testing
phase would be expected to fail to differentiate between faces that were
linked together in a training sequence more often than between faces that
were not.

Wallis and H. H. Bülthoff (2001) used morphs in their training sequence. They were concerned that the morphs themselves, as intermediate

Trial:

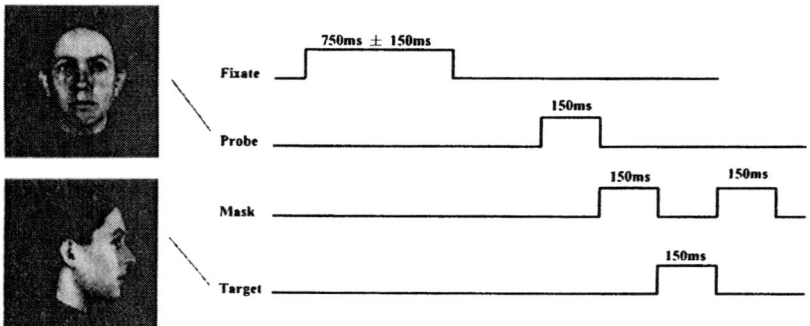

FIGURE 6.12. Delayed match-to-sample task. Two faces in different orientations
were displayed sequentially. Participants had to determine whether both images
originated from the same head or from two different heads.

views in the image sequence, might be an important factor in linking the faces together. Consequently the presence of morphs might affect the observers' performance more than the fact that the images were presented in sequential contiguity. Training with simultaneous presentation was included to test that possibility. The same images were shown in both training conditions, but temporal contiguity was a factor only in the sequential presentation. If the morphs were sufficient for the training effect, then it should appear after both training procedures.

In the testing phases the participants had to compare a profile to a frontal view, a difficult task (Troje & H. H. Bülthoff, 1996). The discrimination performance of the group trained with sequential presentation is shown in figure 6.13 across two training days. Performance was measured as the percent of correct answers in the mismatch trials—that is, correct rejections. The figure shows results for within set (WS) and between set (BS) comparisons. Participants were more likely to confuse those faces that had been associated temporally in a sequence (WS). An analysis of the results (ANOVA) indicated significantly poorer discrimination performance for faces learned in the WS condition than for faces learned in the BS condition.

Performance for BS faces appeared to increase slightly over the four blocks owing to increased familiarity with the stimuli (approximately 74% correct in the first block compared to 82% correct in the fourth block), but this was not the case for WS faces (approximately 70% correct in the first block compared to 71% in the fourth block). Thus, the difference in performance between BS and for WS comparisons was more pronounced on the second day (block 3 and 4).

When simultaneous presentation was used as a familiarization procedure, only a significant effect of block was present (data not shown). Performance improved slightly over the four blocks for both training sets. No effect of set (WS or BS) was observed in the discrimination performance of the two participant groups.

According to the temporal association hypothesis, if two heads had been viewed together in a coherent sequence during the sequential familiarization procedure (within set, WS), the participants should fail to differentiate between them more often than between faces that were also familiar but belonged to separate training sets—that is, that had not been presented together in one training sequence (between set, BS). The results after training with sequential presentation support the predictions of the temporal association hypothesis. Without any explicit training the participants learned to associate arbitrary views of different faces together. This means that not only is the degree of similarity between images important for object recognition but so too is the temporal proximity of the views.

The results from the second group of participants who had been trained with simultaneous presentations of the images indicated that the presence of morphs among the training images was not sufficient to cause the association of two different faces with each other. The results also demon-

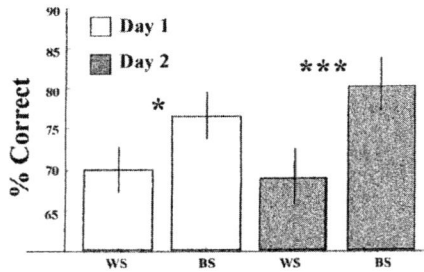

FIGURE 6.13. Discrimination performance of the group trained with sequential presentation across two training days. WS-within set and BS-between set comparisons. Significance of the difference between conditions WS and BS are indicated as follows: (P < 0.1)=*, (P < 0.001)=***.

strated that the simultaneous presentation of views of different faces was not sufficient to cause these faces to be associated with each other.

In another study with similar faces (Troje & H. H. Bülthoff, 1996), the performance of untrained subjects was poorer than the performance recorded here after training, suggesting that exposure to the morphs during the training sequences had not impaired overall performance in the task.

Another concern raised by the training procedures aside from possible interference from the presence of morphs was whether the participants had merely learned to associate together different views of different faces or whether the internal representation of the faces was altered.

A third experiment was conducted to test whether the various views had truly been linked to form the internal representation of a single face. A test group of participants completed the sequential presentation training as described above, while a control group was not trained. The subsequent testing phase was then altered to consist of image sequences for both groups. Half of the sequences were identical to those shown to the test group in the training phase. The others were no longer sequences using morphs as intermediate views between two different faces, but each sequence showed the actual appearance of a single rotating head. These sequences depicted faces of persons seen in the training phase, but this time they were not associated with another person's face. The participants of both groups had to report after viewing each sequence whether the head appeared to deform during rotation. Trained participants showed a significant tendency to rate the sequences that had been viewed during training as nondeforming, while the sequences showing different views of the same person were perceived as deforming. The answers from the untrained participants showed the opposite tendency. Apparently training caused the mental association of the frontal and profile views of those faces seen in the training sequence. The sequences seen during training seemed natural (nondeforming), while sequences depicting the true appearance of single rotating heads were judged as unnatural (deforming).

Faces are special objects (Kanwisher, McDermott, & Chun, 1997) for which we are experts. Thus we should be wary of lightly extrapolating the results reviewed here to other type of objects. The work done by Sinha and Poggio (1996), who investigated the role of learning in form perception using objects that were not faces, indicates that this concern is unfounded. They showed that participants built up different mental representations of the shape of ambiguous objects, depending on which views were temporally associated during the training phase. Thus, the temporal association effect found by Wallis and H. H. Bülthoff (2001) does not seem to be restricted to the special category of faces.

While we might find it surprising that we can be fooled into mistakenly assigning different faces to a single identity, we are just as bemused by a remark made by SB, a man who lost his sight at the age of 10 months and recovered vision 52 years later. While walking around a lamppost he noticed with great surprise that an object can "look different and yet be the same" (Gregory & Wallace, 1973). In Wallis and H. H. Bülthoff's experiments, the participants, who have experienced vision all their lives, expect their environment to be temporally stable because in real life objects do not suddenly metamorphose into other objects. Thus in contrast to SB, the participants of the experiments found it natural to assume that different images appearing in close succession belong to the same face, even when the images actually depicted different persons.

Summary and Conclusion

In this chapter we have reviewed experiments investigating the recognition of dynamic objects, scenes, and faces. The goal was to evaluate the holistic, view-based representation scheme and to assess its validity for the recognition of stimuli other than static objects.

The experiments that we reviewed in the first section showed that familiarity with specific viewpoints was an important factor in the recognition of biological motion sequences. Point-light walkers were more easily recognized in more familiar equatorial views than when they were viewed from above. A second set of experiments explored the importance of depth structure in the recognition of motion sequences. The results showed that irrespective of the 3D structure of the point-light walker, viewpoints preserving "normal" 2D point trajectories yielded high ratings for figural goodness as a human. The view-based model, which postulates the preeminence of 2D structure over 3D structure for recognition, can account for the results of both experiments. Thus, view-based representation schemes are valid models not only for the recognition of static objects but of dynamic objects as well.

In the second section, research on the exploration and recognition of virtual scenes was discussed. Participants explored a virtual attic by moving about the room via a virtual camera or a series of snapshots of the room. In the test phase, the recognition performance of the participants was always best for familiar views, reflecting a view-dependent encoding of the scene even after extensive self-initiated motion through the virtual attic. Generalization to novel views was observed only when participants had experienced dynamic motion through the scene during exploration. Spatio-temporal continuity in the training phase was necessary for the ability to generalize to novel views.

Temporal continuity as a tool for linking together disparate views of an object was the theme of the last section. If object recognition is based on multiple views, temporal continuity might link all these views to a single object. In the experiments by Wallis and H. H. Bülthoff, participants were trained by having them view film sequences in which the identity of a face changed as the head rotated. The participants failed to differentiate between face pairs that had been coupled in the film sequence more often than when the face pairs had not been viewed within the same sequence during training. These results are consistent with an object-recognition scheme in which multiple views are linked on the basis of their temporal contiguity.

In conclusion, all the psychophysical results reviewed in this paper present evidence that viewpoint-dependent representations and recognition processes play an important role in human object recognition.

Before closing this chapter, we would like to mention the fact that for centuries artists have been elegantly mastering visual puzzles that scientists are now laboring to solve. The sculptures of modern Swiss artist M. Raetz (1994) are a vivid demonstration of this point. In his exhibits we view sculptures that defy our everyday experience that walking around an object does not change its identity. His sculptures look like one thing from one side and like something completely different from another viewpoint (figure 6.14). It is a bewildering experience to walk around such sculptures and a beautiful artistic demonstration of the points discussed in the sections "Biological Motion" and "Temporal Continuity."

G. B. Piranesi (1720–1778; see Kupfer, 1992) and more recently M. C. Escher (1971) have produced beautiful pictorial depictions of impossible scenes much more fascinating than the trivially realistic views of Wirtshaus Lichtenstein used in the scene recognition experiments. It is a pleasure for the mind's eye to wander through the strange worlds that these artists have created. We cannot help but wonder whether virtual reality might not allow us to create replicas of these scenes that could be explored from within. Would it be possible for unsuspecting participants to learn to navigate in an impossible environment? Would they become aware of its incongruities? But let us not stray too far into the realm of imaginary experiments, we will keep on exploring the fantastic world of these artists in the classical way and enjoy their captivating pictorial world without ulterior psychophysical motives.

FIGURE 6.14. Sculpture by Markus Raetz (1994). Picture copyright © Pro Litteris, Zürich, Switzerland. Reproduced with permission of the artist. For an animated computer graphic visualization of a similar object see http://www.kyb.tuebingen.mpg.de/links/metamorphosis.html. See color insert.

Note

1. The data of the walking human used to create the point-light walker had been collected at the Gait Analysis Laboratory of the Spaulding Rehabilitation Hospital in Boston, Massachusetts.

References

Biederman, I. (1987). Recognition-by-components: A theory of human image understanding. *Psychological Review, 94*, 115–147.
Biederman, I., & Gerhardstein, P. C. (1993). Recognizing depth-rotated objects:

Evidence for 3D viewpoints invariance. *Journal of Experimental Psychology: Human perception and Performance. 19*, 1162–1182.

Blanz, V., & Vetter, T. (1999). A morphable model for the synthesis of 3D faces. *Proceedings of the 26th Annual Conference on Computer Graphics (Siggraph99*, pp. 187–194). Los Angeles: ACM Press.

Blanz, V., Tarr, M. J., Bülthoff, H. H. (1999). What object attributes determine canonical views? *Perception, 28*, 575–599.

Bülthoff, I., Bülthoff, H. H., & Sinha, P. (1997). *View-based representations for dynamic 3D object recognition.* (Technical Report No. 47, http://www.kyb. tuebingen.mpg.de/bu/techr/index.html). Tübingen, Germany: Max-Planck-Institut für biologische Kybernetik.

Bülthoff, I., Bülthoff, H. H., & Sinha, P. (1998). Top-down influences on stereoscopic depth-perception. *Nature Neuroscience 1*, 254–257.

Bülthoff, H. H., & Edelman, S. (1992). Psychophysical support for a 2-D view interpolation theory of object recognition *Proceedings of the National Academy of Science, 89*, 60–64.

Bülthoff, H. H., Edelman, S., & Tarr, M. J. (1995). How are three-dimensional objects represented in the brain? *Cerebral Cortex, 5*, 247–260.

Christou, C. G., & Bülthoff, H. H. (1997). *View-direction specificity in scene recognition after active and passive learning* (Technical Report No. 53, http:// www.kyb.tuebingen.mpg.de/bu/techr/). Tübingen, Germany: Max-Planck-Institut für biologische Kybernetik.

Christou, C. G., & Bülthoff, H. H. (1998). *Differences between active-explorers and passive-participants in virtual scene recognition* (Technical Report No. 62, http://www.kyb.tuebingen.mpg.de/bu/techr/). Tübingen, Germany: Max-Planck-Institut für biologische Kybernetik.

Christou, C. G., & Bülthoff, H. H. (1999). View dependence in scene recognition after active and passive learning. *Memory and Cognition, 27*, 996–1007.

Christou, C. G., & Bülthoff, H. H. (2000). Using realistic virtual environments in the study of spatial encoding. In Ch. Freksa et al. (Eds), *Spatial Cognition II*, (pp. 317–332). Berlin: Springer-Verlag.

Cutting, J. E. (1981). Coding theory adapted to gait perception. *Journal of Experimental Psychology: Human perception and performance, 7*, 71–87.

Cutting, J. E., & Kozlowski, L. T. (1977). Recognition of friends by their walk. *Bulletin of the Psychonomic Society, 9*, 353–356.

Edelman, S., & Bülthoff, H. H. (1992) Orientation dependence in the recognition of familiar and novel views of three-dimensional objects. *Vision Research, 32*, 2385–2400.

Edelman, S., & Weinshall, D. (1991). A self-organizing multiple-view representation of 3D objects. *Biological Cybernetics, 64*, 209–219.

Escher, M. C. (1971). *The Graphic Work of M. C. Escher.* New York: Ballantine Books.

Gregory, R. L., & Wallace, J. (1973). Recovery from early blindness: A case study. In *Experimental Psychology Society Monograph No. 2.* Cambridge, UK: W. Heffer & Sons.

Hock, H. S., & Schmelzkopf, K. F. (1980). The abstraction of schematic representations from photographs of real-world scenes. *Memory & Cognition, 8*, 543–554.

Hoffman, D. D., & Flinchbaugh, B. E. (1982). The interpretation of biological motion. *Biological Cybernetics, 42*, 195–204.

Johansson, G. (1973). Visual perception of biological motion and a model of its analysis. *Perception and Psychophysics, 14*, 201–211.

Kanwisher, N., McDermott, J., & Chun, M. M. (1997). The fusiform face area: A module in human extrastriate cortex specialized for face perception. *Journal of Neuroscience 17*, 4302–4311.

Kupfer, A. (1992). *Piranesis' Carceri'. Enge und Unendlichkeit in den Gefängnissen der Phantasie* (Tightness and limitlessness in fantasy's prisons). Stuttgart: Belser.

Marr, D. (1982). *Vision*. San Francisco: Freeman Publishers.

Marr, D., & Nishihara, H. K. (1978). Representation and recognition of the spatial organization of three-dimensional shapes. *Proceedings of the Royal Society of London, 200*, 269–294.

Miyashita, Y. (1988). Neural correlate of visual associative long-term memory in the primate temporal cortex. *Nature, 335*, 817–820.

Palmer, S., Rosch, E., & Chase, P. (1981). Canonical perspective and the perception of objects. In A. D. Baddley & J. Long (Eds.), *Attention and performance* (vol. 9, pp. 135–151). Hillsdale, NJ: Erlbaum.

Poggio, T., & Edelman, S. (1990). A neural network that learns to recognize three-dimensional objects. *Nature, 343*, 263–266.

Püruch, P., Vercher, J. L., & Gauthier, G. M. (1995). Acquisition of spatial knowledge through visual exploration of simulated environments. *Ecological Psychology, 7*, 1–20.

Raetz, M. (1994). *Polaroids 1978–1993*. Geneva: Musée Rath.

Rock, I., & DiVita, J. (1987). A case of viewer-centered object perception. *Cognitive Psychology, 19*, 280–293.

Rowland, G. L., Franken, R. E., Bouchard, L. M., & Sookochoff, M. B. (1978). Recognition of familiar scenes from new perspectives. *Perception and motor skill, 46*, 1287–1292.

Schacter, D. L., Cooper, L. A., Delaney, S. M., Peterson, M. A., & Tharan, M. (1991). Implicit memory for possible and impossible objects: Constraints on the construction of structural descriptions. *Journal of Experimental Psychology: Learning, Memory and Cognition, 17*, 3–19.

Shelton, A. L., & McNamara, T. P. (1997). Multiple views of spatial memory. *Psychonomic Bulletin & Review, 4*, 102–106.

Shibata, T., Sugihara, K., & Sugie, N. (1985). Recovering three-dimensional structure and motion of jointed objects from orthographically projected optical flow. *Transactions IECE 68-D*, 1689–1696.

Sinha, P., & Poggio, T. (1996). Role of learning in three-dimensional form perception. *Nature, 384*, 460–463.

Stone, J. V. (1998). Object recognition using spatio-temporal signatures. *Vision Research, 38*, 947–951.

Stone, J. V. (1999). Object recognition: View-specificity and motion-specificity. *Vision Research, 39*, 4032–4044.

Tarr, M. J., & Bülthoff, H. H. (1995). Is human object recognition better described by geon structural descriptions or by multiple views? Comments on Biederman and Gerhardstein (1993). *Journal of Experimental Psychology: Human Perception and Performance, 21*, 1494–1505.

Tarr, M. J., & Bülthoff, H. H. (1999). *Object recognition in man, monkey, and machine* (Cognition Special Issues). Cambridge, MA: MIT Press.

Tarr, M. J., & Pinker, S. (1990). When does human object recognition use a viewer-centered reference frame? *Psychological Science, 1,* 253–256.

Troje, N. F., & Bülthoff, H. H. (1996). Face recognition under varying pose: the role of texture and shape. *Vision Research, 36,* 1761–1771.

Ullman, S. (1979). *The interpretation of visual motion.* Cambridge, MA: MIT Press.

Ullman, S., & Basri, R. (1991). Recognition by linear combinations of models. *IEEE Transactions on Pattern Analysis & Machine Intelligence, 13,* 882–1005.

Vetter, T., & Poggio, T. (1997). Linear object classes and image synthesis from a single example image. *IEEE Transactions on Pattern Analysis and Machine Intelligence 19,* 733–742.

Wallis, G. M. (1998). Temporal order in human object recognition learning. *Journal of Biological Systems, 6,* 299–313.

Wallis, G. M., & Baddeley, R. (1997). Optimal unsupervised learning in invariant object recognition. *Neural computation, 9,* 883–894.

Wallis, G. M., & Bülthoff, H. H. (1997). Temporal correlations in presentation order during learning affects human object recognition. *Perception 26* (suppl.), 32.

Wallis, G. M., & Bülthoff, H. H. (2001). Effect of temporal association on recognition memory. *Proceedings of the National Academy of Sciences USA, 98,* 4800–4804.

Wang, R. F., & Simons, D. J. (1999). Active and passive scene recognition across views. *Cognition, 70,* 191–210.

Webb, J., & Aggarwal, J. (1982). Structure from motion of rigid and jointed objects. *Artificial Intelligence, 19,* 107–131.

Williams, P., & Tarr, M. J. (1997). Structural processing and implicit memory for possible and impossible figures. *Journal of Experimental Psychology: Learning, Memory, and Cognition, 23,* 1344–1361.

7

Visual Object Recognition

Can a Single Mechanism Suffice?

MICHAEL J. TARR

In actual, physical life I can turn as simply and swiftly as anyone. But mentally, with my eyes closed and my body immobile, I am unable to switch from one direction to the other. Some swivel cell in my brain does not work. I can cheat, of course, by setting aside the mental snapshot of one vista and leisurely selecting the opposite view for my walk back to my starting point. But if I do not cheat, some kind of atrocious obstacle, which would drive me mad if I persevered, prevents me from imagining the twist which transforms one direction into another, directly opposite. I am crushed, I am carrying the whole world on my back in the process of trying to visualize my turning around and making myself see in terms of "right" what I saw in terms of "left" and vice versa.

—Vladimir Nabokov

How do humans recognize 3D objects? This simple question leads to surprisingly complex answers. Indeed, object recognition is sufficiently difficult that state-of-the-art computer vision systems can only perform the most rudimentary visual tasks and, even then, only under highly constrained conditions. At the heart of what makes visual recognition difficult are two factors. First, we live in a world made up of 3D objects, yet only receive 2D stimulation on our retinae as sense input. Second, we live in a highly variable world in which images of objects change constantly owing to transformations in size, position, orientation, pose, color, lighting, and configuration. The challenge is to derive a consistent mapping from a potentially infinite set of images to a relatively small number of known objects and categories. It is a problem that the human visual system routinely and effortlessly solves.

How the mammalian brain solves the problem of visual recognition has been a topic of study since the early days of brain science. David Hubel and Torsten Wiesel (1959) received the Nobel Prize for their discovery that neurons in cat visual cortex that respond to boundaries between regions of light and dark are organized into columns according to their orientation preference. This critical result appeared to capture an important facet of visual processing—a visual system that is sensitive to *edges* positioned at different orientations in space. Once the particular orientations of edges are known, it seemed only a small step to "connect the dots"— joining edges into more complex descriptions of object shape. Edge-based representations appeared ideal for recognition: shape-defining edges often capture the critical features of objects and remain relatively invariant over many image transformations. Thus, most vision scientists came to believe that the goal of vision was to derive or reconstruct an edge-based description of object shape.

It was this belief that drove David Marr to develop two ideas that have dramatically influenced the study of visual object recognition. The first was a computational theory in which Marr and Ellen Hildreth (1980) proposed what they saw as the processing constraints needed to build a successful edge detector. They observed that an implemented version of their detector behaved much like some subclasses of visual neurons (so-called simple cells). Once Marr had a plausible algorithm for finding local edges in an image, he was able to argue that early visual processing derived increasingly complex representations of shape built from such local edges—at the endpoint of this progression was a 2D description of object shape referred to as the full primal sketch. To Marr, however, the full primal sketch was inadequate as a representation for visual recognition. Although the full primal sketch might be invariant over changes in the appearance of an object's surfaces owing to variations in lighting or small shifts in orientation, as a 2D representation described in a frame of reference based on the observer ("viewer-centered") the full primal sketch would still change dramatically with changes in object viewpoint. As such, recognition using only the full primal sketch seemed to require a potentially infinite number of 2D descriptions for each 3D object (one description for each unique view). Consequently, Marr believed that the representations underlying visual recognition should be insensitive to changes in viewpoint. This constraint led Marr to develop his second critical idea— 3D parts-based descriptions for object recognition.

Marr and Keith Nishihara (1978) proposed that the full primal sketch is used to derive a 3D representation by first adding information about the relative depths and orientations of surfaces and then by grouping such surfaces into 3D object parts. They argued that 3D volumes known as "generalized cylinders" formed an appropriate method for describing such parts. Critical to their theory was the fact that the visual frame of reference used in the generalized cylinder representation was based on the object itself ("object-centered"). As such, an object's description would not vary with changes in the viewpoint of the observer relative to the object. To Marr and Nishihara the use of an object-centered reference frame seemed a computationally elegant solution to the problem of how to derive a consistent mapping from variable images to a single object or class. Indeed, to a great many others studying the problem of vision, Marr and Nishihara's proposal seemed to offer the first tractable answer to the problem of visual recognition. This and related viewpoint-invariant parts-based models, most notably Biederman's (1987) Recognition-by-components theory (RBC), have had and continue to have enormous influence.

Pandora's Box

Much like Pandora's box, simple experiments can sometimes lead to unforeseen results. In 1984, most vision researchers took for granted some version of Marr and Nishihara's model of object recognition and, in particular, the idea that mental representations of objects are encoded using an object-centered reference frame. Only a handful of experimental psychologists, however, had attempted to test aspects of this model. Steven Pinker and I observed that the central question of whether objects were represented in a viewer-centered or an object-centered reference frame was unanswered. The few studies that had tried to address this issue had used familiar shapes (e.g., letters—see Corballis, Zbrodoff, Shetzer, & Butler, 1978) as stimuli and therefore could not distinguish between a true object-centered representation and a viewer-centered representation composed of many specific views of each shape at each familiar vantage point. Either approach would predict equivalent performance in terms of response speed and accuracy across familiar orientations—where they differed was in what happened at unfamiliar viewpoints. Unfortunately, because the stimuli used in most experiments were highly familiar, subjects had, in all likelihood, already encountered them in many orientations. Furthermore, many of the stimuli used in such studies were highly distinctive from one another—for example, the "tail" on a "Q" is not found in any other letter. Thus, apparent evidence for object-centered representations—for example, equivalent recognition performance for familiar objects across different viewpoints—may be misleading.

To address these concerns, Pinker and I designed a set of stimuli that fulfilled three criteria: (1) novelty; (2) no distinct local features; and (3) well-defined axes (to eliminate any need for viewpoint-dependent axis-finding procedures that might serve as a necessary precursor to recovering 3D parts). These simple 2D shapes (figure 7.1a) were used in a straight-

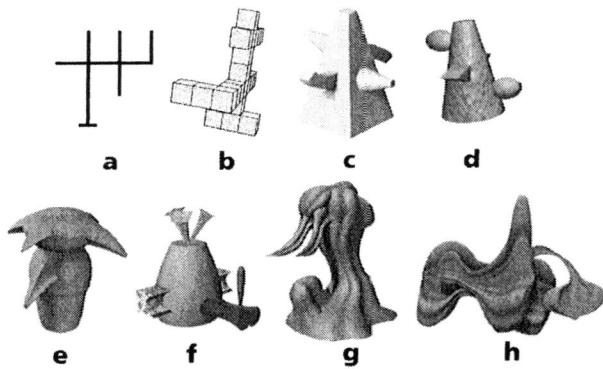

FIGURE 7.1. The evolution of the novel stimulus in our lab.

forward test of object- versus viewer-centered reference frames (Tarr &
Pinker, 1989). Subjects were trained to associate nonsense names (e.g.,
"KIP") with individual shapes shown at the upright and then practiced
naming the same shapes at selected orientations in the picture-plane. During this practice we observed that when subjects first encountered the
shapes in these new orientations, their naming performance varied as a
function of the distance between the unfamiliar orientations and the trained
upright orientation. Although this pattern of viewpoint dependence could
be taken as evidence for viewer-centered representations, we reasoned that
object-centered descriptions might take some time to develop. Indeed, as
subjects became more and more practiced at naming the objects, their
performance at all of the previously unfamiliar orientations became equivalent. Much as with familiar objects, this viewpoint invariance may be
attributed to two quite different underlying causes—subjects learning a
viewpoint-invariant object-centered representation for each shape or subjects learning multiple viewpoint-specific viewer-centered representations
for each shape.

To distinguish between these two possibilities, Pinker and I introduced
a condition in which subjects were shown the now-familiar shapes in new,
never-before-seen orientations. If subjects had learned the shapes in an
object-centered format, then their performance at the new orientations
should have been no different from their performance at the familiar orientations. Much to our surprise this is not what we found (we had been
expecting to confirm Marr's hypothesis!)—subjects' performance at the
new orientations varied systematically with the distance from the *nearest
familiar orientation*. This result is exactly what is predicted if subjects
were learning multiple orientation-specific shape representations at each
familiar orientation, a "multiple-views" description (figure 7.2). We also
observed that the magnitude of this viewpoint dependence was almost

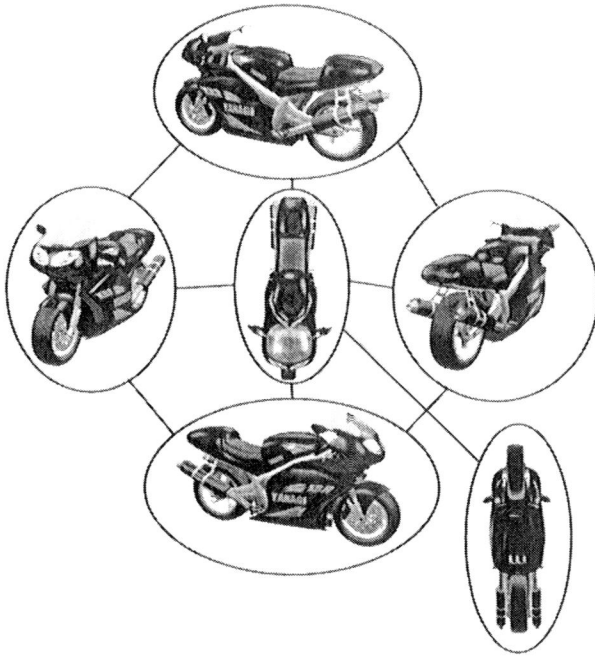

FIGURE 7.2. A possible multiple-views representation of a motorcycle—3D objects are represented as a set of viewpoint-specific models.

identical at the beginning of the experiment when subjects were familiar with the shapes in only the upright orientation and at the end of the experiment when subjects were familiar with the shapes in multiple orientations. Thus, a single shape recognition mechanism, based on learning objects in specific viewpoints and then mentally transforming unfamiliar viewpoints to the familiar views (sometimes referred to as "normalization"), appeared to be at work.

This apparently straightforward finding of viewpoint dependence in object recognition has become a critical result in motivating the research I have pursued in the years since. At the core of this research is the question of how humans recognize objects. At a more specific level, answering this question will require understanding the contributions of three aspects of recognition:

- The image geometry for objects and object classes and how it changes with changes in 3D orientation, illumination, etc.
- The level of categorization required for a given task, varying from coarse "basic-level" categorization to fine item-specific recognition.

• The differing degrees of perceptual expertise that observers have with specific object classes and how visual experience fine-tunes the recognition system to attain such expertise.

In the coming sections on three-dimensional object recognition, perceptual classification, and perceptual expertise, I take up each of these issues in turn, focusing on aspects of visual recognition for which these issues are central. The actual research reviewed in these sections explores these different aspects of recognition through a variety of converging techniques, including computer-graphics psychophysics, brain imaging using functional Magnetic Resonance Imaging (fMRI), and neuropsychology with brain-injured subjects.

Three-Dimensional Object Recognition

Given evidence for multiple-views across changes in picture-plane orientation, it was natural to wonder whether the result extended to the recognition of 3D objects rotated in depth. There are reasons to believe that rotations in depth might be treated differently from rotations in the picture-plane. The former produce geometric changes in the structure of the 2D image as 3D surfaces come in and out of view and change their orientation relative to the observer. In contrast, the latter have no impact on the 2D image structure, but do change the top-bottom and left-right relations between features relative to the observer. Thus, in the latter case viewpoint dependence may be a consequence of changes in the spatial relations within objects, rather than a fundamental organizing principle for visual representation.

Using what was (at the time!) state-of-the-art 3D software, I created a set of 3D stimuli that fulfilled the same criteria used in the original Tarr and Pinker study (figure 7.1b; although similar to the objects used in Shepard and Metzler's, 1971, classic study of mental rotation, my objects all contained a vertical axis clearly marked by a small "foot"). As in our earlier study, I trained subjects to name each object from the near-upright orientation and then had subjects practice recognizing the same objects in a selected set of viewpoints. Here, however, the practice viewpoints were generated by rotations in depth around either the vertical or the horizontal axis, as well as by rotations in the picture-plane. Following practice, new, never-before-seen viewpoints were generated by similar rotations interspersed among the now-familiar viewpoints. The results were astonishingly clean—for each axis of rotation there was a clear pattern of viewpoint dependence (Tarr, 1989, 1995). At the beginning of the experiment this pattern was systematically related to the distance from the single training view. Following practice and the introduction of new unfamiliar viewpoints, this pattern was systematically related to the distance from the nearest familiar view regardless of whether the view was generated by a

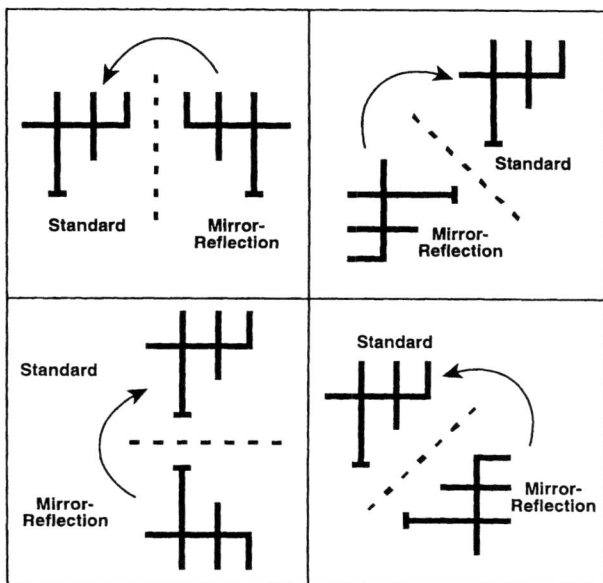

FIGURE 7.3. A 180° "flip-in-depth" is always the shortest path to align a mirror-reflected version of a 2D shape with its standard in a recognition task. Apparently the human visual system (unconsciously at least) knows this too. Adapted from Tarr and Pinker (1989).

rotation in depth or in the picture-plane. As before, the magnitude of this pattern was quite similar during both the initial recognition of new views and the recognition of additional new views following practice. Thus, together with my earlier findings, there seemed to be good evidence for generally applicable viewer-centered visual-recognition mechanisms.

Beyond the basic finding of viewpoint dependence, there was one other piece of evidence that strongly implicated viewpoint-dependent recognition processes in both the 2D and 3D versions of my experiments. In the 2D case we had run a variant in which subjects learned a "standard" version of each shape, but then following practice, were asked to apply the same name to mirror-reflected versions of the familiar shapes. We were puzzled to find that subjects showed the same relatively slow performance regardless of the picture-plane orientation of the unfamiliar mirror-reflected shape. Pinker and I came to the realization that this is exactly what is predicted by a recognition process that is normalizing unfamiliar mirror-reflected shapes at any orientation to a familiar view of the familiar standard version—for *any* orientation of a mirror-reflected shape, the shortest path to its standard is a 180° flip-in-depth (figure 7.3).

This result in itself does not provide definitive evidence for normalization between standard and mirror-reflected versions of shapes. One alternative is that when subjects encounter a mirror-reflected version of a familiar shape, they cannot deduce (consciously or unconsciously) a transformation that will align it with its standard and therefore resort to viewpoint-invariant object-centered features. In the 3D version of my experiment, however, I obtained results that ruled out this alternative: when subjects first encountered mirror-reflected versions of familiar 3D objects there was no rotation in 3D space that would bring the two into correspondence. Just as aligning mirror images of 2D shapes requires a third dimension, aligning mirror images of 3D objects requires a fourth dimension. Thus, subjects either needed to employ a *4D* mental transformation, turn the mirror-reflected object inside out (in the same way that an inside-out left-handed glove matches a right-handed glove), or use some other strategy. In the 3D case subjects did not show equivalent performance across different unfamiliar viewpoints of mirror-reflected objects; rather, they exhibited viewpoint dependence quite similar to that found for the recognition of standard versions of the objects in unfamiliar viewpoints. One possible alternative strategy in the face of a 4D transformation is to normalize the major vertical axis of the mirror-reflected objects into correspondence with the standard version and then observe whether the protruding parts were symmetrical between the pair. Regardless of the particular process used by subjects to compensate for changes in viewpoint (including "nontransformational" mechanisms such as those proposed by Perrett, Oram, and Ashbridge, 1998), the combination of findings from the 2D and 3D experiments provide compelling evidence for a multiple-views object representation that is matched to object images through viewpoint-dependent normalization procedures (figure 7.2).

Perceptual Classification Using
Viewpoint-Dependent Mechanisms

Object recognition, broadly defined, involves a wide range of tasks, including the recognition of specific individual objects and the classification of many different objects into a single category. The results from my 2D and 3D recognition experiments suggest that some aspects of recognition rely on viewpoint-dependent mechanisms, but do not address whether this is the only process available for recognition. Indeed, given that I intentionally made the stimuli highly confusable, my results may speak more to object-specific recognition, so-called subordinate-level tasks, rather than object categorization, so-called basic-level tasks. This hypothesis became known as the "dual systems" approach (e.g., Jolicoeur, 1990) and posited that while subordinate-level recognition might involve viewpoint-dependent processes, basic-level recognition, often thought to be the "default" level of access, was based on viewpoint-invariant processes.

Evidence for this dichotomy was rather slim, but gained some support from a study by Irving Biederman and Peter Gerhardstein (1993) in which viewpoint-invariant recognition performance was obtained for several sets of 3D objects containing distinctive features or parts—similar to basic-level categorization. Based on their results, Biederman and Gerhardstein argued that human object recognition typically occurs at the basic level where distinctive features are available to discriminate between object classes and therefore recognition is viewpoint invariant. In contrast, they argued that discrimination tasks on objects lacking distinctive features are the exception rather than the rule and therefore viewpoint-dependent recognition is rarely observed in the real world. My students, William Hayward, Isabel Gauthier, and Pepper Williams, and I wondered about this result. Although we had no strong belief that viewpoint-dependent processes extended to basic-level recognition, there were methodological issues in Biederman and Gerhardstein's study that led us to question their conclusions. In particular, in some experiments they used familiar common objects that were likely to have already been learned at multiple viewpoints, thereby masking any viewpoint-dependent recognition processes. In other experiments they used line drawings of novel objects containing highly distinctive features, but a task in which subjects were required to remember only one object at a time over a series of trials—such a task might have predisposed subjects to adopt a strategy in which they selectively relied on the local distinct features of the single object.

Are Basic-Level Recognition Tasks Viewpoint Dependent?

In order to assess the role of viewpoint-dependent recognition processes in discriminations that corresponded to the basic-level, we created several sets of novel 3D objects. Objects in each set were composed of combinations of parts based on the parts used by Biederman and Gerhardstein (1993). By using combinations of parts we were able to manipulate the similarity between objects within a given set. Specifically, in one set each object consisted of a single distinctive part and in several sets each object consisted of a central unique body-part with additional parts attached to it (examples of "multipart" objects are shown in figures 7.1c–d; the object in figure 7.1d is based directly on an object used by Biederman & Gerhardstein). Although these "additional parts" sometimes appeared in other objects in a given set, a particular part/position combination was never repeated. Thus, not only were objects in these latter sets unique in terms of their central parts but the order of all of the parts in a given object was also diagnostic for the identity of that object. That is, although the objects were never explicitly divided into categories, each object within a set was characterized by a unique set of 3D parts corresponding to a shape-defined basic-level class (Rosch, Mervis, Gray, Johnson, & Boyes-Braem, 1976). Employing each set separately, we ran an extensive series of experiments using a variety of recognition tasks, including object naming, pairwise matching, and the single object memory task used by Biederman and Gerhardstein. To our astonishment, the results were unequivocal in each and every case—viewpoint-dependent recognition performance was found regardless of the object set and the recognition task (Tarr, Williams, Hayward, & Gauthier, 1998; Hayward & Tarr, 1997). These effects, albeit smaller than those obtained for objects that did not contain distinctive features, were highly systematic across changes in 3D viewpoint and were unaffected by whether or not parts became visible or disappeared from view. We could reach only one conclusion: visual object recognition, regardless of the level of categorization, is mediated by viewpoint-dependent mechanisms.

This finding of viewpoint dependence was potentially problematic for extant viewpoint-dependent models of recognition that assumed template-like object representations, for instance, describing objects in terms of the X-Y coordinates of features in the 2D image (Poggio & Edelman, 1990) or the output of simple image filters similar to those seen in early vision (Edelman, 1993). Such representations did not seem suitable for supporting the visual recognition of object classes in that this task requires generalizing from known instances of a class to novel instances of the same class. Put another way, class-level recognition of objects requires a many-to-one mapping in which objects of varying shape are treated as equivalent. Undifferentiated two-dimensional template-like representations seemed ill-suited for this task in that no mechanisms had been offered for relating the similarity of visually different instances of each object class. Thus, two objects with only slightly different shapes might still be treated by the recognition system as completely unrelated. Within viewpoint-invariant part-based models, however, the class-level recognition is solved by using qualitative descriptions of object parts (Biederman, 1987). Consequently, visually similar instances of an object class are treated as related (or even identical) because they give rise to the same part-based representation, regardless of small variations in object shape. The challenge before us was to understand how viewpoint-dependent multiple-views object representations could support basic-level, as well as subordinate-level, recognition (see Tarr & Bülthoff, 1998).

Isabel Gauthier and I were intrigued by several computational models that used "multi-dimensional feature interpolation" to generalize from one instance of a class to new, never-before-seen instances of the same class (Beymer & Poggio, 1996; Moses, Ullman, & Edelman, 1996). This ability to generalize would allow a single model to account for the recognition of individual objects—that is, subordinate-level tasks—and for the recognition of object classes—that is, basic-level tasks. Such models assumed that viewpoint-dependent object representations were composed of large numbers of viewpoint-dependent local features, and that recognition of any object whether identical to a known object or unfamiliar involved measuring the local similarity between such features. Thus, as an alternative to globally attempting to compare input images to views of an objects, these models proposed local comparisons in which features of each object representation could "vote" for their presence in the image

(Perrett et al., 1998, provide neurophysiological evidence for similar "accumulation of evidence" mechanisms playing a role in viewpoint-dependent object recognition). The visual system could then simply tally up the votes for each object or class and decide on a winner (a particularly promising instantiation of this approach is presented in Riesenhuber & Poggio, 1999; the importance of this model for understanding visual recognition is discussed in Tarr, 1999).

Do Viewpoint-Dependent Mechanisms Support Within-Class Generalization?

Gauthier and I were interested in testing aspects of these models behaviorally. In particular, we asked whether viewpoint-dependent recognition processes could generalize between instances of a class. To this end we created a set of 2D shapes similar to the shape shown in figure 7.1a. We taught subjects individual names for the shapes and then had them repeatedly name each shape in several different orientations (a subordinate-level discrimination task among members of a basic-level class). Gauthier and I observed that when subjects named a shape in a given orientation and this trial was preceded by a trial in which the *same shape* had appeared in the *same orientation*, there was no effect of orientation—performance was equivalent regardless of the actual orientation of the shape (Gauthier & Tarr, 1997a). This result suggested that the visual recognition system had residual activation about the viewpoint-specific appearance of object shape from the previous trial that facilitated recognition on the subsequent trial. That is, there was visual generalization from a 2D shape to the identical 2D shape.

This result might not seem surprising. What is more important is that, as a set, the 2D shapes constituted a basic-level object class. Therefore, it was also possible to ask whether there was visual generalization from one instance of the basic-level shape class to a different instance of that same class. We designed a second experiment to test whether orientation information about one member of the class (a named shape) would transfer to another member of this class (a differently named shape). That is, although the task was subordinate-level naming, predictions were made about how the recognition of one member of a class would be affected by the prior recognition of another member of that same class. Thus, the experiment investigated the object representation common to two or more individuals—the basic-level for those particular exemplars. In this experiment we manipulated the degree of similarity between the preceding shape and the subsequent shape. We again found that repeating the same shape in the same orientation facilitated viewpoint-invariant recognition performance. Crucially, we also found that repeating a visually similar shape (same basic-level category), but not a visually dissimilar shape (different basic-level category), in the same orientation also facilitated performance that was independent of orientation (a similar orientation-dependent priming effect has been reported for the assignment of figure and ground; Gibson & Peterson, 1994). Thus, we obtained evidence for viewpoint-specific transfer from one instance of a class to a new member of that class. We concluded that recognition processes generalize across visually similar objects appearing in the same viewpoint even when the recognition task is to discriminate between these objects. Thus, based on evidence that viewpoint-dependent information about an individual object generalizes to other, visually similar objects—that is, other instances of the same basic-level object class, viewpoint-dependent mechanisms can mediate basic-level as well as subordinate-level recognition.

Gauthier and I also created a set of 3D objects (figure 7.1c) to investigate aspects of this question. The 3D set consisted of 6 pairs of differently named objects (cohorts) that within a pair shared the same distinct central part and the same attached parts, but with the attached parts in different arrangements so that the two members of each pair could be distinguished. Thus, each pair formed a distinct object class. We were interested in two specific predictions of a viewpoint-dependent class-general model of recognition. First, the processes we had observed for generalization across rotations in the picture-plane should also apply to rotations in depth. Second, in our earlier study subjects were always shown all of the objects in all of the test views—here we wondered whether a known view of one member of a class would facilitate the recognition of the other instance of the class that *had never been seen* in that view. Gauthier and I ran an experiment in which one member of each pair was shown to subjects in several viewpoints (different for each pair) and its cohort was shown to subjects only in one viewpoint. Following training, subjects named both members of each pair in a wide range of viewpoints, both familiar and unfamiliar. For the object actually seen at multiple viewpoints we observed a pattern of viewpoint dependence similar to that seen in my original 3D experiments—recognition performance was systematically related to the distance from the nearest familiar view. At the same time, we found that the cohort objects that had only been trained in one viewpoint showed a similar pattern of viewpoint dependence (Tarr & Gauthier, 1998). It was as if subjects had actually seen these objects from the viewpoints in which their cohorts had been seen and, therefore, were able to use such information to recognize these objects in what were completely unfamiliar viewpoints.

Before we could conclude that there was indeed viewpoint-specific transfer between visually similar cohorts we needed to run a critical control. An alternative account was that similar object geometry for both members of a cohort, in particular for new views generated by rotations in depth, produced the common performance patterns found for both members of each pair. We tested this possibility by running an experiment in which subjects were again trained to name both members of each pair, but where both members of a cohort pair were shown only in a single, common viewpoint during training (in the previous experiment one member of each pair was seen in several viewpoints during training). As before, we then tested their recognition performance across a wide range of viewpoints. The elegance of this control is that the cohort objects shown in only one viewpoint in the first experiment were shown in *exactly* the same viewpoints during training and test in this experiment—the only difference between experiments was the viewpoints in which the other member of each pair was shown. Compared to our first experiment we found different results; subjects' recognition performance for the cohort objects was highly viewpoint dependent, but now related to the distance from the single trained viewpoint. Most importantly, there was a dramatic difference between this experiment and the first experiment in terms of naming performance around the cohort views. In the first experiment the cohort objects showed facilitation as if they had actually been seen in these views; here there was no such facilitation. Taken together, our 2D and 3D studies indicate that viewpoint-dependent mechanisms are capable of class generalization and can support a range of recognition tasks spanning the continuum from basic-level categorization to item-specific recognition.

What Object Properties Mediate Viewpoint Dependence?

Although the results reviewed to this point provide evidence for the wide applicability of viewpoint-dependent mechanisms, they do not address the specifics of what constitutes a viewpoint-dependent representation. What is necessary is a format that is sufficiently flexible to adapt to tasks at many different categorical levels. My colleague Heinrich Bülthoff and I had observed that although the modal finding across many studies was viewpoint-dependent performance, the magnitude of this effect appeared to vary. We hypothesized that the mediating variable was the discriminability of the stimuli that were to be distinguished. We were interested in examining what kinds of representational features played a role in modulating these viewpoint-dependent processes.

To that end we (Tarr, Bülthoff, Zabinski, & Blanz, 1997) created four sets of novel 3D objects based on "paperclip" objects used in studies by Bülthoff and Edelman (1992): objects comprising five "tubes" connected end to end (figure 7.4a); objects comprising a distinctively shaped part in the central position and two tubes attached to each end of this part (figure 7.4b); objects comprising a distinct sequence of three different parts with one tube attached to each end (figure 7.4c); and objects comprising a distinct sequence of five different parts (figure 7.4d). For the objects with three and five distinctive parts, some parts appeared in more than one object, thereby making the local features, but not the part configurations, of a given object confusable with other objects in the set. The angles between tubes or parts were also varied for each object in each set so that along with differences in part shape, each object could be distinguished on the basis of the configuration of parts.

Using both a pairwise matching task and a naming task, we trained

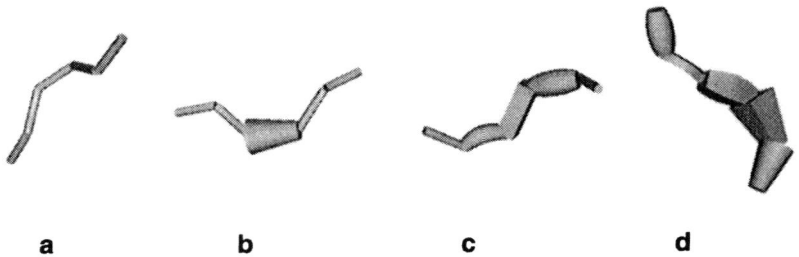

a   **b**   **c**   **d**

FIGURE 7.4. The novel 3D objects we created to assess the kinds of features used in viewpoint-dependent recognition. Objects are examples from the (a) five-tube set; (b) single distinctive part set; (c) three distinctive part set; and (d) five distinctive part set. Adapted from Tarr, Bülthoff, Zabinski, and Blanz (1997).

subjects to recognize objects in one viewpoint and then examined recognition performance across rotations in depth. Results for the five-tube and single distinctive part sets were consistent with our previous work; the magnitude of viewpoint dependence was quite large in the five-tube condition where no distinctive shape features were available, while the magnitude of viewpoint dependence was much smaller in the single distinctive part condition (Tarr et al., 1997). What is critical is the magnitude of this effect in the three distinctive part and five distinctive part conditions. Viewpoint-invariant part-based models (e.g., Biederman, 1987; Biederman & Gerhardstein, 1993) hypothesize that the building blocks of object representations are qualitatively defined *parts*—that is, 3D volumes that are recovered from the 2D image on the basis of viewpoint-invariant contrasts such as parallel/nonparallel and straight/curved. Critically, such parts are both individually and as a group recognized in a viewpoint-invariant manner (because individual parts are so recognized).[1] Therefore, these models appear to predict that adding distinct parts as in the three and five distinctive part conditions should, at a minimum, be no different than the single distinctive part condition and, at best, even less sensitive to changes in viewpoint given the additional distinguishing representational elements (for example, single distinctive part objects necessarily differ in only one part, but the three distinctive part objects always differed from one another by at least two parts). In contrast, Bülthoff and I (Tarr & Bülthoff, 1995) hypothesized that the building blocks of object representations are viewpoint-dependent features—for example, local surface patches that include texture and color. Critically, these features are both individually and as a group recognized in a viewpoint-dependent manner. At the same time, we pointed out that highly distinctive local features (although not configurations of such features) can circumvent this process by uniquely specifying the identity of an object—for instance, if each object in a set were painted with a differently colored spot (Tarr & Bülthoff, 1995). Therefore, we predicted that the most distinctive condition would be the single dis-

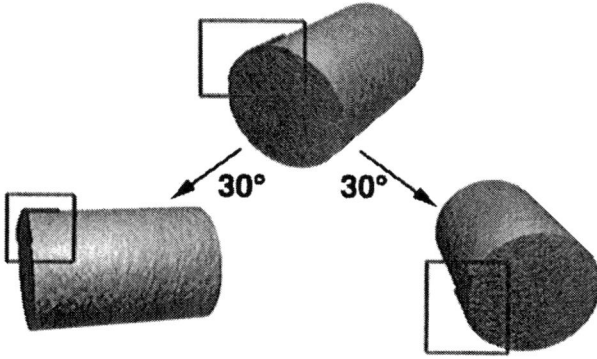

FIGURE 7.5. Equal-magnitude rotations for a single part that produce different local image features. The 30° rotation from center to left yields a qualitative shift from a cusp with a tangent line into an arrow vertex; the 30° rotation from center to right yields only a distortion of the cusp with a tangent line. Human observers are more sensitive to qualitative shifts in local features as compared to simple distortions in local features. Adapted from Hayward and Tarr (1997).

tinctive part case where the local features within each central part were distinctive from those in the other objects in the set. In contrast, in the three and five distinctive part conditions, the additional parts might be distinctive as elements of a configuration, but as local features they would add confusion across objects in that at least one other object in the set would contain the same features. Consequently we predicted that viewpoint dependence would increase in magnitude in the three distinctive part condition and would be even larger in the five distinctive part condition— possibly reaching the same level observed in the five-tube condition. This is precisely what we found in both the matching and naming tasks, indicating that object recognition involves viewpoint-dependent processes that are sensitive to the distinctiveness of local image features.

A similar conclusion can be reached from an experiment I ran with William Hayward (Hayward & Tarr, 1997). Here we had subjects simply recognize isolated parts across rotations in depth. For each part we generated two rotations of equal magnitude: one in which all of the local image features were distorted and one in which the local image features changed qualitatively (figure 7.5). Subjects learned a target view and then recognized one of the two rotated views in a sequential-matching task. Part-based models unquestionably predict that recognition should be equivalent across these two conditions in that the same part description should be derived in each instance.[2] In contrast, the image feature model predicts that changes in the local features should affect performance. In the experiment performance was consistent with a local feature account: subjects were faster to recognize the objects when the rotation produced only a distortion of the features present in the original image as compared to when the particular configuration of features present in the original image changed into a new configuration of features with the rotation. Although there is clearly a great deal of work to be done regarding the types of features that form viewpoint-dependent object representations, our results suggest that the geometry of objects is described in terms of configurations of local features; depending upon the distinctiveness of the features necessary to perform a given discrimination, recognition performance may appear more or less viewpoint dependent. Thus, we can hypothesize that a single visual recognition mechanism is sufficient to mediate the continuum of categorization tasks, from basic-level classification to item-specific recognition, with which we are presented.

Perceptual Expertise and the Fine-Tuning of Recognition Mechanisms

Up to this point I have focused on how object geometry and the specificity of the level of categorization can influence recognition performance. It is clear, however, that these two factors alone are insufficient to account for human recognition competence. A third factor, the degree of experience or expertise an observer has with a given object class, is equally important for understanding recognition behavior. Perhaps the most salient example of this factor of recognition is face recognition: humans are unquestionably more expert at recognizing human faces at the individual level then they are at recognizing members of any other stimulus class. There are many reasons for this high level of expertise. Two of the most critical are the social significance of faces and the fact that we are apparently predisposed to be interested in individual faces from the first moments of birth onward (Johnson & Morton, 1991). The fundamental question is whether humans are simply biologically predisposed to detect faces and then learn them using more generic visual recognition processes or whether humans have face-specific recognition mechanisms distinct from other recognition processes. Given the picture I have painted of human visual recognition as a flexible system capable of supporting a wide range of tasks, it has been my working hypothesis (in particular in collaboration with Isabel Gauthier) that while face recognition is certainly the most complex discrimination task most of us ever learn to perform, it is still part and parcel of general recognition mechanisms, albeit mechanisms that have been tuned to recognize specific faces through many years of experience with objects.

There have been several recent claims to the contrary. Researchers from both the behavioral and cognitive neuroscientific domains have garnered evidence that seems to suggest that faces are "special" and are processed by a recognition system distinct from that used for nonfaces (Kanwisher, 2000). Gauthier and I, however, observed that many of these studies, regardless of domain, had a common flaw: they tended to confound stimulus class, faces vs. objects, with the level of categorization, item-specific level vs. basic-level, and the level of expertise, expert vs. novice (Tarr & Gauthier, 2000). To better understand the relationship of face recognition to normal object recognition, we embarked on a series of experiments using behavioral psychophysics, fMRI, and brain-injured subjects. The underlying theme to all of these studies is careful control of the level of categorization and the level of expertise in addition to manipulation of the stimulus class.

Behavior

One of the most important pieces of evidence cited in favor of face-specific mechanisms is what is referred to as "configural sensitivity." Although this sometimes confusing term has been defined in many ways, the essential idea is that features within the representation are spatially located relative to one another with a great deal of specificity. For example, Tanaka and Sengco (1997) reported that subjects were faster to recognize a part of an individual's face—for example, Bob's nose—when it was shown in the context of the face as originally learned—Bob's nose in Bob's face—as compared to recognizing the same part when it was shown in the face with other parts in altered spatial positions—Bob's nose in Bob's face with the eyes moved farther apart. Crucially, they observed that the same effect could not be obtained for either inverted faces or for nonface objects—for instance, recognizing doors of houses with the windows either in the same position or relocated. Although this result might seem to provide some support for face-specific effects in part recognition, Gauthier and I felt that houses were an inadequate control for faces. In particular, few if any of Tanaka and Sengco's subjects were likely to be house experts, and even if they were, houses form a far more heterogeneous class as compared to faces.

To provide a better control set for faces, Gauthier and I supervised the creation of what became known as the "Greebles" (created by Scott Yu). Greebles were designed as a set of 60 objects that shared similar parts in similar spatial configurations (figure 7.1e). What made Greebles unique was that, as with faces, they were also organized hierarchically so that an individual Greeble could be recognized at multiple levels of categorical difficulty—a coarse level referred to a gender, an intermediate level referred to as family, and at the individual level (figure 7.6). Gauthier and I designed a test of configural sensitivity similar to that employed by Tanaka and Sengco. Subjects learned to name individual parts of each Greeble and were then tested on the recognition of such parts in either intact or altered configurations of the other parts. The critical manipulation in our study was not the use of Greebles per se, but how much experience subjects had at recognizing them. One group of subjects were tested as novices—that is, they had almost no practice at recognizing Greebles. A second group of subjects were tested as experts—that is, they had exten-

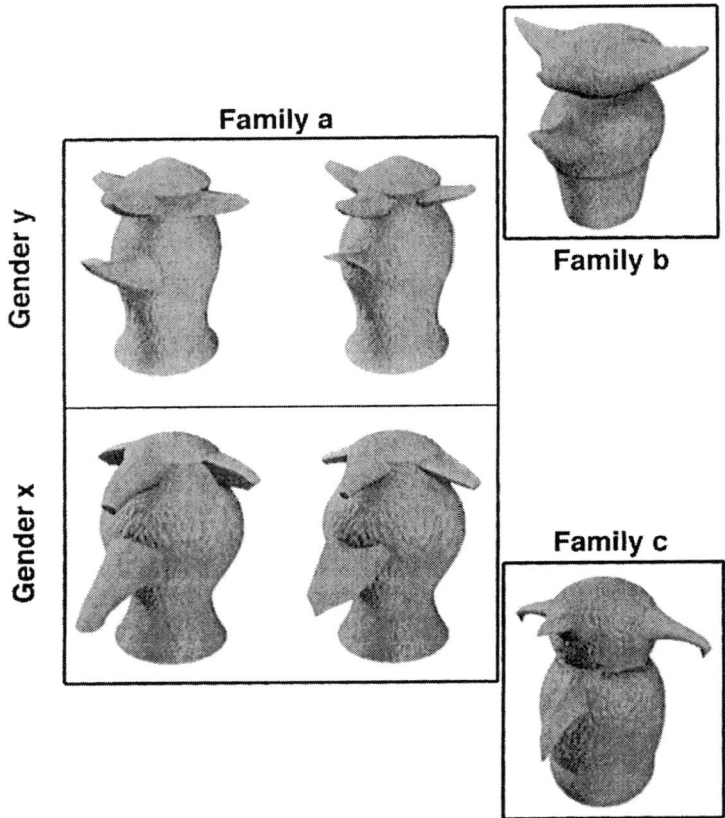

FIGURE 7.6. Examples of Greebles. Four Greebles from one family, two of each gender, are shown in the left-hand box. To the right, a Greeble from a different family is shown for each gender.

sive practice recognizing Greebles. To ensure that subjects were sufficiently expert, we used the rule that subjects had to practice recognizing Greebles until they were just as fast to name individual Greebles as they were to identify the Greeble gender or family—a fact of recognition behavior that is true for identifying faces (Tanaka. 2001; Tanaka & Gauthier, 1997), as well as other domains of expertise (Tanaka & Taylor, 1991). Our results supported the hypothesis that expertise, not faces per se, was responsible for the configural sensitivity observed in face recognition. Experts, but not novices, showed configural sensitivity in the recognition of Greeble parts, but only for Greebles in the trained upright orientation (Gauthier & Tarr, 1997b). That is, as with faces, we found that subjects were faster to recognize a part of an individual Greeble—for instance, the bottom protruding part of the top left Greeble shown in figure 7.6—

when it was shown in the context of the Greeble in which it was originally learned—for instance, the configuration of the top left Greeble as shown in figure 7.6—as compared to recognizing the same part when it was shown in the same Greeble with some of its parts in altered spatial positions—for instance, the top left Greeble in figure 7.6 with the left and right parts moved forward. In a subsequent study we have compared a wide range of putatively face-specific behavioral effects across Greeble novices and Greeble experts, and have consistently obtained facelike patterns of performance with experts, but not novices (Gauthier, Williams, Tarr, & Tanaka, 1998). For example, we found that practice recognizing picture-plane inverted Greebles had no impact on expert performance, but affected novice Greeble recognition. Although experts were faster overall at recognizing Greebles, practice with inverted Greebles did not diminish the advantage in recognition times for upright as compared to inverted Greebles. In contrast, the same amount of practice completely eradicated the difference in response times between upright and inverted Greebles for Greeble novices. Thus, we observe the same difficulty in encoding inverted Greebles for Greeble experts that is seen for inverted faces and for experts with other homogeneous object classes for their domain of expertise (Diamond & Carey, 1986).

Neuroimaging

A second source of evidence cited in favor of face-specific mechanisms comes from recent work in brain imaging, and, specifically fMRI. Several groups have been interested in the question of whether there is an identifiable neural module for face processing in the human brain (Kanwisher, McDermott, & Chun, 1997; Puce, Allison, Gore, & McCarthy, 1995; Sergent, Ohta, & MacDonald, 1992). A typical imaging study has involved having subjects either recognize or passively view familiar faces in one condition and common objects in the baseline condition. By subtracting the activation (as indicated by the degree of blood oxygenation in different areas of the brain) of the object condition from the face condition, one can localize the brain regions where additional processing occurs for faces relative to objects. Across multiple studies, researchers consistently found that one region of visual cortex, the fusiform gyrus, is especially active in face recognition.

Again, Gauthier and I wondered whether the best controls had been applied in these studies. Along with issues raised regarding the level of expertise, an obvious confound with stimulus class was the level of categorical access. Subjects in these experiments had to identify faces at the individual level ("Bob"), but objects only at the basic level ("bird"). In the studies using passive viewing a similar problem existed: the default level of access for faces is almost certainly the individual level, while for common objects it is typically the basic level. What we proposed was a face-recognition study without faces. We took a large collection of pictures of familiar common objects that could be readily named at both the basic and subordinate levels, verified that the default level of access for each was the basic level, and used the objects in an fMRI study. We compared brain activity in two conditions: one in which subjects matched a basic-level label to each picture (e.g., "bird" followed by a picture of a pelican) and one in which subjects matched a subordinate-level label to each picture (e.g., "pelican" followed by the same picture of a pelican). To control for possible differences in the semantic processing of basic- and subordinate-level labels we also ran a purely semantic task at both levels and subtracted the semantic activation from the picture-matching activation for both conditions. What we found bore out our hunch regarding earlier studies: as shown in figure 7.7, across 8 subjects we obtained a bilateral pattern of activation for the subordinate-level recognition of objects above and beyond the basic-level recognition of objects that was remarkably similar to that previously found for faces (Gauthier, Anderson, Tarr, Skudlarski, & Gore, 1997c).

Although our imaging results point toward a brain region that mediates subordinate-level recognition regardless of stimulus class, it is possible that by averaging across subjects we masked differences in the area mediating face processing and the area mediating object processing *within*

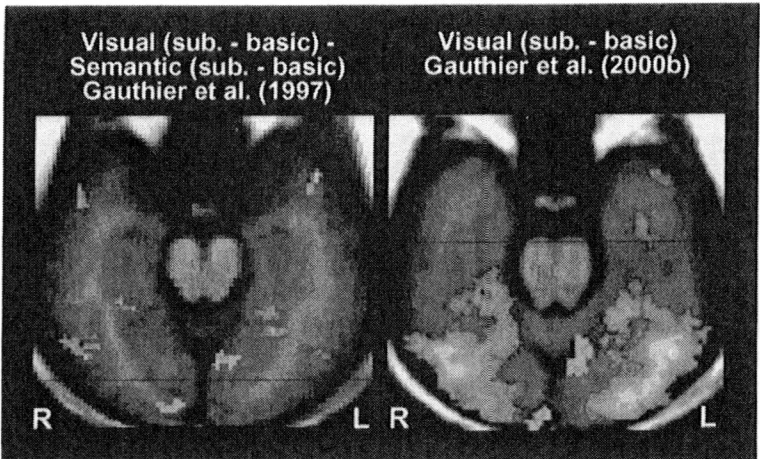

FIGURE 7.7. BOLD activation from fMRI that we obtained for the subordinate-level recognition of common objects over and above basic-level recognition. The "splotches" represent positive activation for this comparison overlaid on structural maps of the human brain. Progressively greater positive activation is depicted by progressively brighter areas within the splotches. See Gauthier et al. (2000b) for a discussion of how these activation maps correspond to the putatively face-selective regions of visual cortex and an interpretation of the additional regions of activation seen in the right panel. See color insert.

individual subjects. Thus, while the face and object areas may appear similar on average, individuals may have separable regions. Gauthier and I have recently addressed this concern by locating individual subjects' "face areas" using passive viewing of faces vs. objects. We then ran the same individuals in a basic-level versus subordinate-level recognition task with common objects. The individual results replicated our earlier group-averaged results even when the "face area" was defined precisely for each subject. Thus, we were able to observe the same pattern of brain activation for subordinate minus basic-level visual recognition in individual subjects (Gauthier, Tarr, et al., 2000b). This replication also included somewhat stronger methods (e.g., auditory presentation of object labels) and more stringent data analyses that established that the same voxels active in face recognition were active in subordinate-level recognition of nonface objects. Thus, within the resolution limits of fMRI, there appears to be no reason to posit brain regions specialized for the recognition of faces.

Gauthier and I were also interested in whether the specificity of the categorization judgment was the only factor driving activation in the fusiform gyrus. From our Greeble studies we knew that manipulating the level of expertise could produce a variety of different "face-specific" behavioral effects (including both configural sensitivity and inversion effects) with nonface objects (both novices and experts performed subordinate-level discriminations, so the level of access could not account for our earlier results). Thus, expertise level was a second factor confounded with the stimulus class in some imaging studies. The logical, but risky, study to run was one in which we created Greeble experts and used fMRI to monitor the reorganization of visual cortex over the acquisition of expertise. Such a design would allow us to study the role of expertise separately from any effects arising from the level of categorization.

As part of her Ph.D. dissertation, Gauthier (Gauthier, Tarr, et al., 1999) compared the brain regions active in the processing of faces and Greebles when subjects were novices and when subjects were experts. For both types of stimuli we used two methods to localize the areas of extrastriate cortex specifically associated with processing a given class of objects: passive viewing of faces or Greebles as compared to passive viewing of common objects; pairwise matching of upright faces or Greebles as compared to pairwise matching of inverted faces or Greebles. The activation patterns for novices were as predicted based on earlier imaging and behavioral studies of face recognition—a "face-specific" area in fusiform gyrus that was present for faces versus objects and for upright versus inverted faces, but not for Greebles versus objects or upright versus inverted Greebles. For Greeble experts a quite different and somewhat remarkable pattern was obtained. As shown in figure 7.8, experts exhibited much more focal activation in visual cortex and, in particular, activation in right fusiform gyrus in the precise location associated with face processing as measured in our two face-recognition tasks (Greebles minus

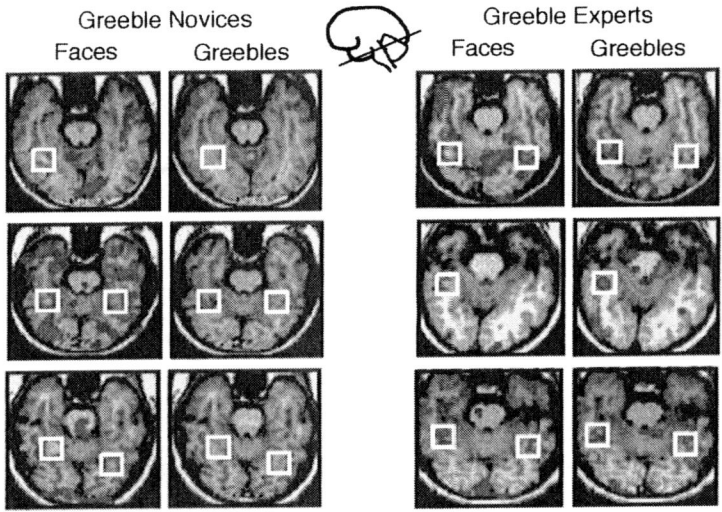

FIGURE 7.8. Brain activation in response to faces and Greebles for three Greeble novices and three Greeble experts. The left panels show the brain activation we obtained using fMRI for three novices when the passive viewing of common objects was subtracted from the passive viewing of faces or Greebles. The right panels show the activation for three experts in the same tasks. Only the voxels showing more activation for faces or Greebles than objects are shown (darker regions with higher activation depicted as brighter areas within these regions). The small squares denote the middle fusiform gyrus bilaterally (functionally defined) and the lateral occipital gyrus foci for one expert (bottom right). Adapted from Gauthier et al. (1999b). See color insert.

Objects and Upright Greebles minus Inverted Greebles). We also monitored changes in subjects' behavioral processing of Greebles during the acquisition of expertise and replicated our earlier results, demonstrating that Greeble experts show a range of "face-specific" effects when recognizing Greebles.

Gauthier followed up on our Greeble expertise study with an elegantly designed experiment in which she examined the brain mechanisms recruited by *extant* experts. She reasoned that if putatively "face-specific" extrastriate areas are recruited through experience, then perceptual expertise with almost any homogeneous category should produce a neural activation pattern similar to that obtained for faces and Greebles (in experts). Indeed, this is exactly what Gauthier, Skudlarski, Gore, and Anderson (2000a) found for both bird and car experts. Gauthier, Skudlarski, et al.'s results are particularly compelling in that they report activation in face-selective brain areas for bird experts when recognizing birds, but not cars, and for car experts when recognizing cars, but not birds—an interaction revealing that the preferred category depends directly on expertise. Reinforcing the connection between expertise in activation in face-selective brain regions is a correlational analysis between the bird and car experts' *behaviorally* assessed levels of expertise and their relative level of neural activation for birds and cars as measured in the right fusiform gyrus. Gauthier, Skudlarski, et al. (2000) found r's of 0.82 and 0.75 respectively for bird and car experts—astoundingly high correlations between a standard psychophysical test and the specific activation pattern obtained in a neuroimaging study.

Thus, behavioral and concurrent neural evidence is helping us to understand the mechanisms that lead to functional specialization in visual cortex. Rather than being organized along conceptual object categories, specific cortical areas are part of a highly plastic visual recognition system that can be tuned to perform efficient fine-level visual discriminations. Our manipulation of factors such as the level of categorization and the degree of expertise have revealed some of the elements of this complex system. Further understanding has been obtained by analyzing the responses of category-selective cortical regions other than fusiform gyrus. In particular, we have identified a region (bilaterally) in occipital lobe that is also selective for faces and other domains of expertise (Gauthier, Tarr, et al., 2000b). This functionally defined region is located relatively early in the visual pathway, indicating that the mechanisms responsible for expert recognition of objects from homogeneous classes are widely distributed.

Neuropsychology

A third and highly compelling source of evidence cited in favor of face-specific mechanisms comes from neuropsychology. Following brain injury due to stroke, head impact, or other insult some individuals appear to be dramatically impaired at visually recognizing objects even though their early perceptual mechanisms are intact. A particular version of this syndrome provides evidence for a specialized face-processing system—these brain-injured subjects, known as "prosopagnosics," show impaired face recognition, but are relatively good at nonface object recognition. Although researchers have pointed out that this deficit may apply more generally to the discrimination of visually similar members of any homogeneous category (Damasio, Damasio, & Van Hoesen, 1982), there has been a general consensus that prosopagnosic subjects provide one of the strongest pieces of evidence for face-specific recognition mechanisms.[3] In a test of whether prosopagnosia is a face-specific impairment rather than a consequence of the item-specific nature of face recognition, Martha Farah and her colleagues compared the recognition of faces and homogeneous classes of common objects, chairs or eyeglasses, for normal control subjects and one prosopagnosic subject. They found that in comparison to the controls the prosopagnosic subject's recognition performance was disproportionately worse for faces relative to objects. Their conclusion was that there exist face-specific neural mechanisms and that prosopagnosic impairment "cannot be accounted for as an impairment of within-category discrimination" (Farah, Levinson, & Klein, 1995, p. 673).

Farah et al.'s conclusion seemed at odds with the conclusions that Gauthier and I had reached on the basis of our behavioral and neuroimaging studies. Two open issues led us to question whether there might be more to prosopagnosic subjects' deficits than face-specific impairment. First, although discriminating between chairs or eyeglasses implicated subordinate-level recognition, there may have been local distinct features within both classes that allowed the prosopagnosic subject to perform better with common objects relative to faces. In contrast, control subjects with normal recognition processes would not need to rely on such local feature-based strategies and would show good recognition regardless of stimulus class. Second, we felt that it was important to consider prosopagnosic subjects' performance using measures other than percent correct—for example, response time or a bias-free measure such as sensitivity (which takes into account the ratio between the number of times that the subject responds correctly to a yes trial, called a "hit," and the number of times that the subject responds incorrectly to a no trial, called a "false alarm"). This latter point is critical in that prosopagnosic subjects may expend more effort attempting to identify objects as compared to faces. They also may believe that they are poorer at face recognition relative to common object recognition (e.g., a response bias that would change their accuracy for faces as opposed to other object categories, but would not affect their discrimination sensitivity for either faces or objects)—in our interactions with specific prosopagnosic subjects we had in fact noted that they do show stronger response biases than uninjured subjects, as well as speed-accuracy trade-offs.

In collaboration with Marlene Behrmann, we embarked on a series of experiments that systematically varied the level of categorization for common objects, Greebles, snowflakes (a highly homogeneous category), and faces (Gauthier, Behrmann, & Tarr, 1999). In each condition we ran identical experiments with uninjured controls and at least two prosopagnosic subjects and recorded both response times and sensitivity. Two results stand out. First, we found that the apparent disproportionate impairment for faces as compared to nonface objects could be replicated if we looked only at percent correct, but that response times showed a trade-off in that the prosopagnosic subjects took much longer to recognize the nonface objects relative to faces. Second, we observed that if we controlled the amount of time subjects could view stimuli from each class, the same prosopagnosic subjects revealed similar impairments, as measured by sensitivity, for recognizing both faces and nonface objects. Important to our hypothesis, when sensitivity for faces and nonface objects was equated, it became obvious that the prosopagnosic subjects' deficit became progressively more pronounced at the more specific levels of recognition regardless of the object category. To summarize our results, we have obtained evidence that independent of object category, our two prosopagnosic subjects are far more sensitive to the manipulation of the level of categorization as compared to our control subjects. Thus, apparent face-recognition deficits may be better explained as deficits in recognizing objects at more specific levels of discrimination.

Taken together, our behavioral, imaging, and neuropsychological work serves to implicate both the level of categorization and the level of perceptual expertise as important factors in visual recognition tasks. Indeed, it is our hypothesis that the interaction of these two factors is sufficient to explain the impressive specialization of face-recognition mechanisms in visual cortex. Future studies will continue to investigate this issue, for example, using far more sophisticated classes of novel objects (figures 7.1f, 7.1g, and 7.1h are examples of our newest creations: "Fribbles" "YUFOs," and "Pumpkins." These categories have properties that make them less "face-like"—for instance, YUFOs do not have the 2-1-1 part structure of faces and Pumpkins are asymmetric across all possible axes). If we also consider object geometry we have the foundations for forming a complete picture of recognition competence. Each of these aspects of recognition varies along a continuum that cannot be explained by simple dissociations between cognitive or neural systems. More likely is that we need to consider the interaction of all three factors and how a single recognition system can be flexible enough to adapt to the wide range of recognition contexts that we encounter every day. It is this problem that we turn to next.

Implications for Models of Recognition

My research to date has focused on elucidating the factors that are critical to understanding the cognitive and neurological bases of human object recognition. It is my contention that the results we have obtained over the past several years implicate a single highly plastic visual recognition system. The challenge over the coming years is to develop computational models that can account for these remarkable abilities. In a first attempt to simulate some of the complexity of human recognition competence, as part of his Ph.D. dissertation, Pepper Williams (1997) developed a neural-network model for shape recognition. His goal was to develop a model that could recognize a set of novel, complex multipart objects. Williams found that his relatively simple network, dubbed "WHOA" (now called "TEA"; see *http://www.tarrlab.org/tea*), was able to replicate a wide range of behavioral effects, including the generalization from known instances of an object category to new instances. Importantly, in addition to categorical knowledge, WHOA still showed item-specific sensitivity, thereby providing some evidence that a single system may be sufficient for seemingly disparate recognition tasks. Williams was also able to apply the WHOA, with no modifications, to the problem of learning Greebles. We found that the model did surprisingly well at simulating the onset of perceptual expertise and was again able to account for both generalization across category members and individuation within categories (Gauthier et al., 1998).

Although a single architecture may be sufficient for spanning a range of categorical levels, it is still likely that different elements of object representations may play different roles in recognition. A working hypothesis is that different spatial scales (analogous to blurry vs. sharp images; see figure 7.9) are differentially weighted at different levels of categorization. The essential idea is that complete images may provide too much information given that the problem of basic-level classification is to map many instances of a class onto a single category. There are reasons to believe that blurry, high-contrast images very similar to object silhouettes provide a description that is relatively stable over members of a perceptual class. Reasons include the fact that the WHOA model is one of several computational models (going back to Blum's classic 1967 paper) that have successfully used silhouettes to perform object classification, and the fact that there are known to be separable neural pathways for transmitting blurred high-contrast visual information and detailed lower contrast information.

FIGURE 7.9. Descriptions including surface detail, subtle changes in brightness, and fine shape differences may be necessary for making within-category discriminations. In contrast, descriptions including only high-contrast blurred information—similar to silhouettes—may support basic-level categorization. This figure illustrates the point that given complete images, instances of a given category are still quite different from one another, but given silhouette-like images, such instances become more similar. Interestingly, human infants receive visual input that is closer to the bottom row, suggesting that they may begin life by learning coarser visual categories and then move toward differentiating instances within these categories only during the later stages of development.

To investigate the role of silhouettes in recognition, we developed two lines of research: one in which we asked whether silhouettes contain enough information about objects to support visual recognition and one in which we examined whether there is sufficient information in object silhouettes to separate object categories. As part of his Ph.D. dissertation, William Hayward (1998) compared the recognition of common objects across rotations in depth in a sequential-matching tasks. After viewing an intact image of an object, the same object was presented again at either a 60° rotation that showed similar surfaces and parts to the original, but a quite different silhouette, or a 180° rotation that showed quite different surfaces and parts, but a silhouette that was a mirror-reflection of the original's silhouette. We found that subjects were actually faster and more accurate to recognize objects as being the same given the similar silhouettes as compared to similar surfaces or parts. This rather surprising result, as well as other data obtained using somewhat different recognition tasks (e.g., see Peterson, 1994), indicates that silhouettes appear able to mediate some aspects of visual recognition (although we have ample evidence that silhouettes are not the only type of information represented).

To get more directly at the question of what role silhouettes might play in recognition, Florin Cutzu and I developed several simple methods for measuring silhouette similarity. These ranged from computing point-by-point correspondences along the boundary of the silhouette to measuring the area of overlap between silhouettes. We conjectured that simply by clustering object instances based on silhouette similarity we would be able to separate most instances of one object class from instances of a second object class. To provide a strong test of our model we used silhouettes of cats and dogs—two highly similar categories. Importantly, exactly these stimuli had been used in a study in which it was demonstrated that human infants were capable of perceptually differentiating between these basic-level classes (Quinn & Eimas, 1994). Thus, we knew that babies were able to able to tell the cats from the dogs based purely on visual information—could our model do the same? Our results were quite clear: despite the high degree of similarity between cats and dogs (telling cars from chairs would not have been much of a challenge), we found that our relatively simple measure of silhouette similarity provided good separation between object classes (Cutzu & Tarr, 1997). Thus, we have some evidence that silhouette-like information is sufficient for basic-level categorization.

The possibility that silhouette-like information forms an important level of visual representation leads to an intriguing conjecture: limiting early visual input to silhouette-like information may be essential for forming stable perceptual categories. It is known that human infants are born somewhat myopic and prefer high-contrast images. Other than being an accident of development, is there any potential benefit to this state? If a developing visual system were to receive complete, fully detailed images, each object would appear quite distinct from all previously seen objects and a many-to-one mapping might not arise. In contrast, if the visual system initially receives only coarse information, then perceptual "bins" corresponding to categories may emerge (figure 7.9). As the visual system develops, increasingly finer information will become available, thereby allowing in-place coarse categories to be refined into subclasses and specific instances for within-category recognition tasks. Thus, while silhouette-like information may mediate the recognition of perceptual categories in adults, it may be even more important for acquiring such categories in the first place. In the study of language it has been suggested that "starting small" (Elman, 1993) in terms of memory span is essential for learning syntactic categories. Similarly, "starting blurry" may be essential for learning visual categories.

Some evidence for "starting blurry" has been gathered by Quinn, Eimas, and Tarr (2001). We found that 3- to 4-month-old infants could perceptually categorize cats and dogs given only their silhouettes. Interestingly, our experiments also revealed that infants were better at categorically separating the two species when using silhouette information from the heads as compared to the bodies of the animals. What is not yet known is whether this advantage is a consequence of intrinsically more information in the heads or a pre-wired preference to attend to heads and faces (see Johnson & Morton, 1991). Regardless, our results indicate that general shape or external contour information that is centered about the head is sufficient for young infants to form individuated perceptual categories of cats and dogs.

As already pointed out, silhouette-like information constitutes only one component of object representations. To support more specific levels of recognition, finer surface details and variations in shape must be considered (Tarr & Bülthoff, 1998). There are a number of recent models of recognition that have proposed object representations based on large collections of viewpoint-dependent local features. Indeed, there has been a remarkable trend toward the local view-dependent feature approach by several independent research groups (e.g., Edelman, 1995; Fukushima, 2000; Lowe, 2000; Riesenhuber & Poggio, 1999; Ullman & Sali, 2000). By allowing the repertoire of features to be quite broad, including local surface patches, local measures of color and brightness, oriented edges, and contour configurations, many of the details that are necessary for within-category recognition may be captured. At the same time the feature set may include more global regions that are sensitive only to high-contrast boundaries, thereby capturing the silhouette-like level of information. Thus, a single view of an object might include thousands of features at multiple spatial scales. Categorical recognition could be mediated by measuring similarity across the coarse levels of information—essentially adjusting the threshold for what counts as a match. For example, votes might be tallied across views of all known objects with similar silhouettes. More specific levels of categorization could be mediated by measuring similarity across finer and finer levels of information—increasing the threshold. As the information required for a given discrimination becomes more and more specific to a particular object, the number of features that will vote will become progressively more narrow, thereby implicating fewer and fewer known objects.

Representing objects as collections of viewpoint-dependent features leads to several fundamental questions. First, individual features are rarely distinctive enough to uniquely specify a single object or class—it is only the configuration of features that allows effective recognition. How then are local features within the representation related to one another? One straightforward answer is the object representation system is sensitive to the spatial co-occurrence of individual features. The more frequently any set of features are seen together at specific spatial positions, the more tightly they will be linked to one another (a form of what is known as Hebbian learning). Object representations will be composed of features whose spatial positions are more or less strongly related to one another— features that co-occur quite often in a given configuration will become strongly interdependent with the presence of a subset of the features ac- tivating the entire ensemble. For example, the surfaces found on a single part of an object will appear together quite frequently and will become strongly associated. In contrast, features that do not co-occur very often will be connected only weakly or not at all (Wallis & Rolls, 1997). For example, the surfaces found on different parts of an articulated object, will not appear together nearly as often as surfaces on the same part and, thus, will be only weakly associated. This simple statistical learning mechanism may provide an explanation for the configural sensitivity found in cases of perceptual expertise, including face recognition (Gauthier & Tarr, 1997b; Rhodes, Tan, Brake, & Taylor, 1989). The acquisition of expertise is marked by extensive practice differentiating similar instances from a single class, consequently many class-level features will co-occur in the same configuration with great frequency—for example, the eyes, nose, and mouth of human faces. Such oft-seen features will become tightly inter- dependent as the system is fined-tuned by experience. Thus, relocating the position of one such feature will impact the recognition of the other fea- tures, much as has been found for parts of human faces and for parts of Greebles when recognized by experts.

Second, if different views of objects are composed of different sets of features, how are different views within the representation related to one another? Interestingly a principle similar to that used to link features may be used to link different views of an object. The single most likely image to occur following a view of an object is another view of that same object. Therefore, a recognition system that is sensitive to the *temporal* co- occurrence of sets of features would learn, over experience, to link those views that arise from single objects, thereby forming a coherent, organized multiple-views representation (figure 7.2). Neurophysiological evidence suggests that neurons in visual cortex are indeed sensitive to co-occurrence over time; remarkably, even in those cases where there is no geometric similarity between the views that become associated (Miyashita, 1988; Wallis & Baddeley, 1997; see Bülthoff & Bülthoff, chapter 6 in this volume for additional discussion of this issue).

Conclusions

A relatively simple experiment exploring whether visual recognition is based on viewpoint-dependent or viewpoint-independent information has led to an extensive research program employing psychophysical and neuropsychological methods. At the core of this program has been the idea that there is a complex interaction among three aspects of recognition: the appearance of images of objects as they vary in the environment; the level of categorical specificity required for a given task; and the degree of experience the perceiver has with specific object classes. In my laboratory we have investigated each of these issues, asking whether a single visual-recognition system is sufficient to account for the continuum of behaviors seen in each case. Converging evidence provides a preliminary yes to this question. View-based, local-feature representations can account for the recognition performance observed across changes in viewpoint in subordinate-level recognition tasks. Similar viewpoint-dependent mechanisms appear capable of supporting basic-level recognition tasks and the recognition of new instances of familiar categories. Finally, the complete range of recognition tasks, including face recognition, can be accounted for by considering the degree of perceptual expertise. Thus, humans appear to have a single highly adaptable visual recognition system that can be fine-tuned by experience to support a spectrum of recognition behaviors (for a similar view see Schyns, 1998). Although there is, as always, much work to be done, we have begun to illuminate some of the properties of this remarkable system.

Notes

Many more details about this work can be obtained at *http://www.tarrlab.org* Much of the research presented in this chapter was supported by NSF Award SBR-9615819. Thanks to Isabel Gauthier, William Hayward, and Pepper Williams for not only collaborating on much of the research but also providing valuable feedback on several drafts. Thanks also to my other collaborators over the years: Marlene Behrmann, Heinrich Bülthoff, and Steven Pinker.

1. Biederman's (1987) part-based model does not predict *complete* viewpoint invariance. Rather, he hypothesizes that recognition is viewpoint-invariant only so long as the same part-based description may be recovered. Thus, self-occluding objects for which rotations in depth alter which parts are visible and occluded will require separate part descriptions for each unique configuration of parts and will be recognized in a viewpoint-invariant manner only when the same parts remain visible. The stimulus images used in both Tarr et al. (1997) and Hayward and Tarr

(1997) always showed the same configurations of parts and therefore Biederman's theory would predict complete viewpoint invariance for the conditions tested.

2. Note that parts-based models only make this prediction under viewing conditions in which the part description is equally recoverable from both views. The same is true for predictions of viewpoint invariance across views of more complex objects. In all of the studies reported here attempts were made to ensure that every view clearly showed the viewpoint-invariant features that are putatively used to recover 3D parts in Biederman's (1987) model. Thus, if this model were correct, all views should have been recognized equally well, which was not the case. That being said, it is difficult to definitively state that two views are equally "good" in terms of part recovery. However, if small gradations in pose across non-accidental views lead to differences in performance, then the recognition process is viewpoint dependent and inconsistent with extant viewpoint-invariant part-based models.

3. There is one published case in which brain injury produced the *opposite* deficit: intact face recognition with impaired object recognition (Moscovitch, Winocur, & Behrmann, 1997). Although such "double dissociations" are often held up as the strongest evidence in favor of separable systems, it is possible to obtain a double dissociation within a single system (Plaut, 1995). Moreover, our claims regarding the lack of face-specific processing should not be taken as an argument that brain areas preferential for faces do not exist. The reasons such areas exist are simply explainable by factors other than faces as a "special" object class. However, given the existence of such areas, we should be able to render them preferential for other domains of expertise—a result we have found in several studies (Gauthier Tarr, et al., 1999; Gauthier, Skudlarski, et al., 2000). Finally, it is also worth noting that the patient studied in Moscovitch et al. (1997) was unable to recognize Greebles—something he should be able to do if separable mechanisms for face (and other expert) recognition exist and are intact in his case (Gauthier, Behrmann, & Tarr, unpublished data).

References

Beymer, D., & Poggio, T. (1996). Image representations for visual learning. *Science, 272*, 1905–1909.

Biederman, I. (1987). Recognition-by-components: A theory of human image understanding. *Psychological Review, 94*, 115–147.

Biederman, I., & Gerhardstein, P. C. (1993). Recognizing depth-rotated objects: Evidence and conditions for three-dimensional viewpoint invariance. *Journal of Experimental Psychology: Human Perception and Performance, 19*, 1162–1182.

Blum, H. (1967). A transformation for extracting new descriptors of shape. In W. Wathen-Dunn (Ed.), *Models for the perception of speech and visual form* (pp. 362–380). Cambridge, MA: The MIT Press.

Bülthoff, H. H., & Edelman, S. (1992). Psychophysical support for a two-dimensional view interpolation theory of object recognition. *Proceedings of the National Academy of Sciences USA, 89*, 60–64.

Corballis, M. C., Zbrodoff, N. J., Shetzer, L. I., & Butler, P. B. (1978). Decisions about identity and orientation of rotated letters and digits. *Memory & Cognition, 6*, 98–107.

Cutzu, F., & Tarr, M. J. (1997). The representation of three-dimensional object similarity in human vision. In *SPIE Proceedings from electronic imaging: Human vision and electronic imaging II*, 3016 (pp. 460–471). San Jose, CA: SPIE.

Damasio, A. R., Damasio, H., & Van Hoesen, G. W. (1982). Prosopagnosia: Anatomical basis and behavioral mechanisms. *Neurology, 32,* 331–341.

Diamond, R., & Carey, S. (1986). Why faces are and are not special: An effect of expertise. *Journal of Experimental Psychology: General, 115*(2), 107–117.

Edelman, S. (1993). Representing three-dimensional objects by sets of activities of receptive fields. *Biological Cybernetics, 70,* 37–45.

Edelman, S. (1995). Representation, similarity, and the chorus of prototypes. *Minds and Machines, 5,* 45–68.

Elman, J. L. (1993). Learning and development in neural networks: The importance of starting small. *Cognition, 48,* 71–99.

Farah, M. J., Levinson, K. L., & Klein, K. L. (1995). Face perception and within-category discrimination in prosopagnosia. *Neuropsychologia, 33,* 661–674.

Fukushima, K. (2000). Active and adaptive vision: Neural network models. In S.-W. Lee, H. H. Bülthoff, & T. Poggio (Eds.), *Biologically motivated computer vision* (vol. 1811, pp. 623–634). Berlin: Springer-Verlag.

Gauthier, I., Anderson, A. W., Tarr, M. J., Skudlarski, P., & Gore, J. C. (1997). Levels of categorization in visual recognition studied with functional MRI. *Current Biology, 7,* 645–651.

Gauthier, I., Behrmann, M., & Tarr, M. J. (1999). Can face recognition really be dissociated from object recognition? *Journal of Cognitive Neuroscience, 11*(4), 349–370.

Gauthier, I., Behrmann, M., & Tarr, M. J. (2002). *Are Greebles like faces? Defining the domain in "domain-specific face processing."* Unpublished manuscript.

Gauthier, I., Skudlarski, P., Gore, J. C., & Anderson, A. W. (2000). Expertise for cars and birds recruits brain areas involved in face recognition. *Nature Neuroscience, 3*(2), 191–197.

Gauthier, I., & Tarr, M. J. (1997a). Orientation priming of novel shapes in the context of viewpoint-dependent recognition. *Perception, 26,* 51–73.

Gauthier, I., & Tarr, M. J. (1997b). Becoming a "Greeble" expert: Exploring the face recognition mechanism. *Vision Research, 37,* 1673–1682.

Gauthier, I., Tarr, M. J., Anderson, A. W., Skudlarski, P., & Gore, J. C. (1999). Activation of the middle fusiform "face area" increases with expertise in recognizing novel objects. *Nature Neuroscience, 2*(6), 568–573.

Gauthier, I., Tarr, M. J., Moylan, J., Anderson, A. W, Skudlarski, P., & Gore, J. C. (2000a). Does visual subordinate-level categorisation engage the functionally defined Fusiform Face Area? *Cognitive Neuropsychology, 17*(1/2/3), 143–163.

Gauthier, I., Tarr, M. J., Moylan, J., Anderson, A. W., Skudlarski, P., & Gore, J. C. (2000b). The fusiform "face area" is part of a network that processes faces at the individual level. *Journal of Cognitive Neuroscience, 12,* 495–504.

Gauthier, I., Williams, P., Tarr, M. J., & Tanaka, J. (1998). Training "Greeble" experts: A framework for studying expert object recognition processes. *Vision Research, 38*(15/16), 2401–2428.

Gibson, B. S., & Peterson, M. A. (1994). Does orientation-independent object recognition precede orientation-dependent recognition? Evidence from a cueing paradigm. *Journal of Experimental Psychology: Human Perception and Performance, 20,* 299–316.

Hayward, W. G. (1998). Effects of outline shape in object recognition. *Journal of*

Experimental Psychology: Human Perception and Performance, 24(2), 427–440.

Hayward, W. G., & Tarr, M. J. (1997). Testing conditions for viewpoint invariance in object recognition. *Journal of Experimental Psychology: Human Perception and Performance, 23*, 1511–1521.

Hubel, D. H., & Wiesel, T. N. (1959). Receptive fields of single neurons in the cat's striate cortex. *Journal of Physiology, 148*, 574–591.

Johnson, M. H., & Morton, J. (1991). *Biology and cognitive development: The case of face recognition.* Oxford, UK: Blackwell.

Jolicoeur, P. (1990). Identification of disoriented objects: A dual-systems theory. *Mind & Language, 5*, 387–410.

Kanwisher, N. (2000). Domain specificity in face perception. *Nature Neuroscience, 3*(8), 759–763.

Kanwisher, N., McDermott, J., & Chun, M. M. (1997). The fusiform face area: A module in human extrastriate cortex specialized for face perception. *Journal of Neuroscience, 17*, 4302–4311.

Lowe, D. G. (2000). Towards a computational model for object recognition in IT Cortex. In S.-W. Lee, H. H. Bülthoff, & T. Poggio (Eds.), *Biologically motivated computer vision* (vol. 1811, pp. 20–31). Berlin: Springer-Verlag.

Marr, D., & Hildreth, E. (1980). Theory of edge detection. *Proceedings of the Royal Society of London B, 207*, 187–217.

Marr, D., & Nishihara, H. K. (1978). Representation and recognition of the spatial organization of three-dimensional shapes. *Proceedings of the Royal Society of London B, 200*, 269–294.

Miyashita, Y. (1988). Neuronal correlate of visual associative long-term memory in the primate temporal cortex. *Nature, 335*, 817–820.

Moscovitch, M., Winocur, G., & Behrmann, M. (1997). What is special about face recognition? Nineteen experiments on a person with visual object agnosia and dyslexia but normal face recognition. *Journal of Cognitive Neuroscience, 9*(5), 555–604.

Moses, Y., Ullman, S., & Edelman, S. (1996). Generalization to novel images in upright and inverted faces. *Perception, 25*, 443–462.

Nabokov, V. (1990) Quotation from *Look at the harlequins!* Appears in *The new ambidextrous universe* by M. Gardner. (p. 307). New York: W. H. Freeman and Company.

Perrett, D. I., Oram, M. W., & Ashbridge, E. (1998). Evidence accumulation in cell populations responsive to faces: An account of generalisation of recognition without mental transformations. *Cognition, 67*(1,2), 111–145.

Peterson, M. A. (1994). Shape recognition can and does occur before figure-ground organization. *Current Directions in Psychological Science, 3*, 105–111.

Plaut, D. C. (1995). Double dissociation without modularity: Evidence from connectionist neuropsychology. *Journal of Clinical and Experimental Neuropsychology, 17*, 291–321.

Poggio, T., & Edelman, S. (1990). A network that learns to recognize three-dimensional objects. *Nature, 343*, 263–266.

Puce, A., Allison, T., Gore, J. C., & McCarthy, G. (1995). Face-sensitive regions in human extrastriate cortex studied by functional MRI. *Journal of Neurophysiology, 74*, 1192–1199.

Quinn, P. C., & Eimas, P. D. (1994). Studies on the formation of perceptually based basic-level categories in young infants. *Child Development, 65*, 903–917.

Quinn, P. C., Eimas, P. D., & Tarr, M. J. (2001). Perceptual categorization of cat and dog silhouettes by 3- to 4-month-old infants. *Journal of Experimental Child Psychology, 79*, 78–94.

Rhodes, G., Tan, S., Brake, S., & Taylor, K. (1989). Expertise and configural encoding in face recognition. *British Journal of Psychology, 80*, 313–331.

Riesenhuber, M., & Poggio, T. (1999). Hierarchical models of object recognition in cortex. *Nature Neuroscience, 2*(11), 1019–1025.

Rosch, E., Mervis, C. B., Gray, W. D., Johnson, D. M., & Boyes-Braem, P. (1976). Basic objects in natural categories. *Cognitive Psychology, 8*, 382–439.

Schyns, P. (1998). Diagnostic recognition: Task constraints, object information, and their interactions. *Cognition, 67*(1-2), 147–179.

Sergent, J., Ohta, S., & MacDonald, B. (1992). Functional neuroanatomy of face and object processing: A positron emission tomography study. *Brain, 115*, 15–36.

Shepard, R. N., & Metzler, J. (1971). Mental rotation of three-dimensional objects. *Science, 171*, 701–703.

Tanaka, J. W. (2001). The entry point of face recogntion: Evidence for face expertise. *Journal of Experimental Psychology: General, 130*, 534–543.

Tanaka, J. W., & Farah, M. J. (1993). Parts and wholes in face recognition. *Quarterly Journal of Experimental Psychology, 46A*, 225–245.

Tanaka, J. W., & Gauthier, I. (1997). Expertise in object and face recognition. In R. L. Goldstone, D. L. Medin, & P. G. Schyns (Eds.), *Mechanisms of perceptual learning* (vol. 36, pp. 83–125). San Diego, CA: Academic Press.

Tanaka, J. W., & Sengco, J. (1997). Features and their configuration in face recognition. *Memory and Cognition, 25*, 583–592.

Tanaka, J. W., & Taylor, M. (1991). Object categories and expertise: Is the basic level in the eye of the beholder? *Cognitive Psychology, 23*, 457–482.

Tarr, M. J. (1989) *Orientation dependence in three-dimensional object recognition.* Ph.D. Thesis, Department of Brain and Cognitive Sciences, Massachusetts Institute of Technology.

Tarr, M. J. (1995). Rotating objects to recognize them: A case study of the role of viewpoint dependency in the recognition of three-dimensional objects. *Psychonomic Bulletin and Review, 2*, 55–82.

Tarr, M. J. (1999). News on views: Pandemonium revisited. *Nature Neuroscience, 2*(11), 932–935.

Tarr, M. J., & Bülthoff, H. H. (1995). Is human object recognition better described by geon-structural-descriptions or by multiple-views? *Journal of Experimental Psychology: Human Perception and Performance, 21*, 1494–1505.

Tarr, M. J., & Bülthoff, H. H. (1998). Image-based object recognition in man, monkey, and machine. *Cognition, 67*(1-2), 1–20.

Tarr, M. J., Bülthoff, H. H., Zabinski, M., & Blanz, V. (1997). To what extent do unique parts influence recognition across changes in viewpoint? *Psychological Science, 8*, 282–289.

Tarr, M. J., & Gauthier, I. (1998). Do viewpoint-dependent mechanisms generalize across members of a class? *Cognition, 67*(1-2), 71–108.

Tarr, M. J., & Gauthier, I. (2000). FFA: A Flexible Fusiform Area for subordinate-level visual processing automatized by expertise. *Nature Neuroscience, 3*(8), 764–769.

Tarr, M. J., & Pinker, S. (1989). Mental rotation and orientation-dependence in shape recognition. *Cognitive Psychology, 21*, 233–282.

Tarr, M. J., Williams, P., Hayward, W. G., & Gauthier, I. (1998). Three-dimensional object recognition is viewpoint-dependent. *Nature Neuroscience, 1*(4), 275–277.

Ullman, S., & Sali, E. (2000). Object classification using a fragment-based representation. In S.-W. Lee, H. H. Bülthoff, & T. Poggio (Eds.), *Biologically motivated computer vision* (vol. 1811, pp. 73–87). Berlin: Springer-Verlag.

Wallis, G., & Baddeley, R. (1997). Optimal, unsupervised learning in invariant object recognition. *Neural Computation, 9*, 883–894.

Wallis, G., & Rolls, E. T. (1997). Invariant face and object recognition in the visual system. *Progress in Neurobiology, 51*, 176–194.

Williams, P. (1997). *Prototypes, exemplars, and object recognition*. Unpublished Ph.D. Dissertation, Department of Psychology, Yale University.

8

The Complementary Properties of Holistic and Analytic Representations of Shape

JOHN E. HUMMEL

The mental representation of object shape plays a central role in numerous activities, including object recognition (Biederman & Ju, 1988), categorization and category learning (Rosch & Mervis, 1975; Rosch, Mervis, Gray, Johnson, & Boyes-Braem, 1976; Saiki & Hummel, 1996, 1998a; Tversky & Hemenway, 1984), visual search (Enns, 1992), scene segmentation (Peterson & Gibson, 1994), and even visual reasoning and analogy (Goldstone, Medin & Gentner, 1991; Hummel, 2000; Hummel & Holyoak, 2001; Pedone, Hummel & Holyoak, 2001). What does it mean to represent an object's shape?

Representations of Shape

A representation of shape consists of four independent components (cf. Palmer, 1978). The first is a set of *primitives*—a vocabulary of basic elements that can be put together to describe a shape. Examples include pixels (as in the case of the raw retinal image), simple two-dimensional (2D) image features such as lines and vertices (Edelman, 1998; Poggio & Edelman, 1990; Riesenhuber & Poggio, 1999; Tarr & Bülthoff, 1995), more complex features such as volumetric (3D) parts (e.g., Marr & Nishihara, 1978), and approximations of volumetric parts (Biederman, 1987; Hummel & Biederman, 1992), among others.

The second component is a *reference frame*—a coordinate system that serves as the basis for specifying the arrangement of an object's features or parts. A reference frame is defined by three independent properties: an *origin*, which serves as a zero point, relative to which locations are defined; a *scale*, which maps distances (from the origin) onto numerical values (i.e., coordinates in the reference frame); and an *orientation*, which specifies the directions of extent of the coordinate system's axes (i.e., the direction in which each axis "points"). These properties are independent in the sense that any or all of them may be defined relative to the viewer, the object, or the environment. For example, it is possible to define a reference frame in which the origin and scale are defined relative to the object, but the orientation is defined relative to the viewer (see, e.g., Hummel & Stankiewicz, 1996a).

The third component of a representation of shape is a vocabulary of *relations* for specifying how an object's features or parts are arranged within the reference frame. The most direct approach is simply to represent the elements in terms of their coordinates in the reference frame: each coordinate expresses a numerical relation (namely, a distance along one axis) between an element and the origin of the reference frame. Coordinate-based coding is the dominant approach to representing relations among computational models of object recognition, and characterizes representations based on both 2D views (Edelman, 1998; Edelman & Poggio, 1991; Poggio & Edelman, 1990; Reisenhuber & Poggio, 1999; Tarr & Bülthoff, 1995) and 3D models (Lowe, 1985; Ullman, 1989, 1995; for reviews, see Hummel & Stankiewicz, 1996b, and Hummel, 2000). An alternative to direct coordinate-based coding is to represent an object's features or parts in terms of their relations, not to the origin of the reference frame, but to one another (e.g., Biederman, 1987; Clowes, 1967; Hummel & Biederman, 1992; Marr & Nishihara, 1978; Sutherland, 1968). The resulting representation is referred to as a "structural description." Representing relations explicitly affords tremendous flexibility in the vocabulary and form of the relations expressed. In addition to expressing relative location, elements can be represented in terms of their relative size, orientation, and so on, and these relations may be expressed categorically (e.g., "element A is above element B" or "A is larger than B"), metrically (e.g., "A is 4 units above B"; "A is 2.3 times larger than B"), or both (Hummel & Stankiewicz, 1998). By contrast, coordinate-based representations express only one type of relation (i.e., distance from the origin of the reference frame), and the coordinates are necessarily metrically precise.

The final aspect of a representation of shape concerns the *binding* of elements to one another and to their locations and/or relations (Hummel & Biederman, 1992). It is one thing to know that an image contains a square and a circle, and that one of these shapes is above the other; it is another to bind the shapes to their relations in order to specify that the circle is above the square rather than vice-versa. Likewise, knowing that an image contains features A, B, and C, and that locations d, e, and f are occupied is not the same as binding features to locations to specify which feature resides at which location. The issue of binding is closely related to (and easily confused with) the issue of relations, but they are importantly different: the latter refers to the *vocabulary* of relations used to express the configuration of an object's features or parts; the former refers to the manner in which elements or properties are conjoined with one another and with their locations and/or relations. There are two qualitatively different ways to represent these bindings: *statically* and *dynamically*.

A static binding is a conjunctive representation, in which collections of elements or properties in the world map onto individual elements of the representation. For example, each neuron in visual area V1 represents a conjunction (i.e., static binding) of a particular orientation to a particular spatial frequency, a particular location in the visual field, etc. Similarly, a neuron that responded only to, say, blue squares would represent a static binding of the color *blue* to the shape *square* (see figure 8.1a). Conjunctive bindings are static in the sense that the binding is fixed in the identity of the unit that represents it, with different units for different conjunctions (bindings) of the same properties.

The alternative to conjunctive coding is to represent separate properties with separate units, and bind them together *dynamically*, using some kind of "tag" that is external to the units themselves. For example, one set of units might represent colors and another shapes; a blue square and a red circle would be represented by "tagging" the unit for blue as bound to the unit for square and the unit for red as bound to the unit for circle (see figure 8.1b). In principle, many different binding tags are imaginable, but at present, the only neurally plausible tag is based on the use of time. The basic idea is that units that are bound together fire in synchrony with one another, and units that are not bound together fire out of synchrony (Gray & Singer, 1989; Hummel & Biederman, 1992; Strong & Whitehead, 1989; von der Malsburg, 1981/1994). A red circle and a blue square would be represented by unit(s) for red firing in synchrony with units for circle, while units for blue fire in synchrony with units for square (and out of synchrony with red and circle; figure 8.1c). A red square and a blue circle would be represented by the very same units, but the synchrony relations would be reversed (figure 8.1d). Numerous artificial neural networks use synchrony for binding, and there is a growing body of evidence for the role of synchrony for binding in biological nervous systems (see Singer & Gray, 1995, and Singer, 2000, for reviews).

The Complementary Properties of Static and Dynamic Binding

As summarized in table 8.1, static and dynamic binding have strikingly complementary properties, which as detailed in the next section, map di-

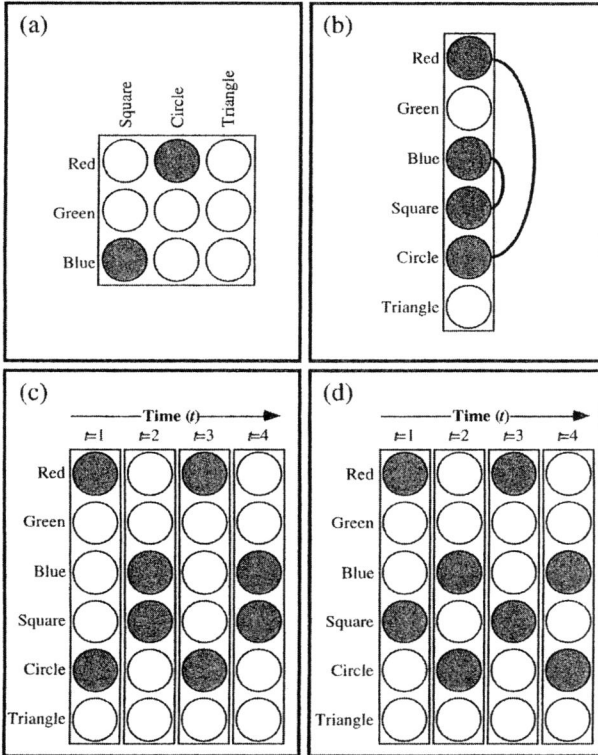

FIGURE 8.1. Illustration of static and dynamic binding. Gray circles represent active units, and white circles inactive units. (a) Representation of a red circle and a blue square using a static binding of color and shape. (b) Representation of a red circle and a blue square using a dynamic binding of color and shape, where arcs serve as binding tags. (c) Representation of a red circle and a blue square using synchrony of firing for dynamic binding. Successive panels of circles denote the same units at different points in time. (d) Representation of a red square and a blue circle using synchrony for binding.

rectly onto the properties of holistic and analytic representations, respectively. Perhaps the most obvious difference between them concerns how they pay the computational "cost" of binding. Static binding (i.e., conjunctive coding) pays the cost up front, at the level of representation: static binding designates a separate unit for every possible conjunction of properties. For example, representing image edges at eight different orientations, three spatial frequencies and five velocities at each of 100×100 locations, would require $8 \times 3 \times 5 \times 100 \times 100 = 1,200,000$ conjunctive units. The same eight orientations, three spatial frequencies, five velocities, and 10,000 locations, represented independently and bound together dy-

TABLE 8.1. Complementary properties of static and dynamic binding

	Static Binding (Holistic)	Dynamic Binding (Analytic)
Number of units required	Grows geometrically with the number of properties to be bound	Grows linearly with the number of properties to be bound
Capacity limits on processing	Few or none: permits substantial parallel processing	Potentially severe: permits little parallel processing
Role of attention	Largely automatic	Requires attention
Independence of bound properties	Bound properties are represented conjunctively	Bound properties are represented independently
Mapping onto Garner's (1974) terminology	Dimensions are integral	Dimensions are separable

namically, would require only $8 + 3 + 5 + 10{,}000 = 10{,}016$ units. And if the horizontal and vertical dimensions were represented independently of one another, then the number of units would drop to $8 + 3 + 5 + 100 + 100 = 216$.

Representing visual properties independently and binding them together dynamically thus requires geometrically fewer units than a static binding of the same properties. When the number of dimensions or properties becomes large, the number of units required to span the space of conjunctions can quickly become prohibitive. For example, the number of units required to statically bind elements to their interrelations grows exponentially with the number of relations (Saiki & Hummel, 1998a), making conjunctive coding completely impractical as an approach to representing the spatial relations among an object's features or parts. It is thus no coincidence that models of shape perception based exclusively on conjunctive coding (e.g., models in the view-based tradition) also represent objects in terms of their features' coordinates rather than their interrelations (for reviews, see Hummel, 2001, Hummel & Stankiewicz, 1996b).

In contrast to static binding, which pays the computational cost of binding in units, dynamic binding pays the cost in processing time. The reason is that dynamic binding is inherently capacity-limited and thus necessarily entails serial processing. For example, in the case of binding by synchrony, it is only possible to have a finite number of groups of neurons simultaneously active and firing *out* of synchrony with one another. There is no necessary limit on the number of neurons in any one synchronized group; the limit is on the number of groups. The size of this limit is proportional to the length of time between successive bursts of spikes from a given group of neurons divided by the temporal width of each burst (or, equivalently, on the temporal precision of a single neuron's spiking). A reasonable estimate of this limit is four to six separate groups (see Singer, 2000; Singer & Gray, 1995), a number that corresponds very closely to the observed capacity limits of visual attention and visual working memory (Bundesen, 1998; Luck & Beach, 1998; Luck & Vogel, 1997; see Hummel & Holyoak, in press).

The limited capacity of dynamic binding implies that some tasks must be performed sequentially. If a given task entails processing, say, 12 bindings, but the visual system can only represent four of those bindings at a time, then the task will require at least three processing steps (see Hummel & Holyoak, 1997). The capacity limit also makes dynamic binding dependent on attention to control which several potentially conflicting groups are bound at any given time (Hummel & Stankiewicz, 1996a; see also Logan, 1994; Stankiewicz, Hummel & Cooper, 1998; Treisman & Gelade, 1980). By contrast, although static binding requires a large number of units, the fact that separate conjunctions are represented by separate units makes it possible, at least in principle, to process many different conjunctions in parallel: 1,200,000 separate orientation-frequency-motion-location conjunction detectors may seem like a large number of units, but it may be a worthwhile investment if the alternative is to process 10,000 separate locations one at a time.

A second difference between dynamic and static binding—at least as important as their complementary costs—is that dynamic binding makes it possible to represent the bound properties independently of one another, whereas static binding does not. For example, a static binding of shapes to colors in which each unit codes for a specific color shape *conjunction* (e.g., *blue-and-square*, *blue-and-round*, *red-and-square*, *red-and-round*, etc.) does not represent color independently of shape. As a result it does not specify what a blue square has in common with a blue circle, or that a blue square has more in common with a blue circle than with a red circle: they are all simply different units (see figure 8.1a). Although this example is based on a strictly localist conjunctive code (i.e., with one unit per binding), Hummel and Stevens (2002; Holyoak & Hummel, 2000) demonstrate that this property is a mathematical inevitability of any conjunctive representation, including distributed conjunctive codes such as tensor products (Halford et al. 1994; Smolensky, 1990), circular convolutions (Metcalfe, 1990, 1991), holographic reduced representations (Plate, 1991) and recursive auto-associative memories (Pollack, 1990): conjunctive representations necessarily violate the independence of the bound properties. By contrast, dynamic binding makes it is possible to represent properties independently (i.e., assigning units to individual properties, such as *blue* and *square*, rather than conjunctions, such as *blue-and-square*) and still specify how properties go together. The resulting representation explicitly specifies what a blue square has in common with a red square and how they differ.

Whether preserving independence is desirable or not depends on the goals of the computation. The advantage of violating independence (as in the case of static binding) is that it makes it possible to make decisions: if category A is defined as *things that are both blue and square*, then a unit that binds blue to square statically can unambiguously discriminate A's from not-A's. An independent representation with color on one unit and shape on another would not discriminate them as cleanly. For example, a blue circle, which is not a member of A, would activate the "blue" part of the representation of A. The advantage of preserving independence is that it makes it possible for a representation to use (and reuse) the same elements in different combinations, and to appreciate what different bindings of the same elements have in common and how they differ. Effectively, the capacity for dynamic binding turns a representation into a symbol system (Hummel & Holyoak, 1997). The difference between symbolic and nonsymbolic representational systems is precisely that the former, but not the latter, can compose simple elements (symbols) into complex relational structures without losing the individual symbols in the process (Fodor & Pylyshyn, 1988; Newell, 1980; see also Hummel & Holyoak, 1997, in press; Hummel & Stevens, 2002).

The complementary properties of static and dynamic binding suggest a rule of thumb for the design of a visual system: conjunctions that can be exhaustively enumerated a priori, and those that need to be processed in parallel (such as the kinds of visual properties processed in visual area V1), should be bound together statically; by contrast, complex properties and properties that need to be represented explicitly—especially those that need to be represented in terms of a complex and potentially open-ended vocabulary of relations—should be represented independently and bound together dynamically. These rules of thumb are apparent in extant models of object recognition. View-based models, whose representations are based exclusively on simple features duplicated at each of many locations in the visual field, use static binding exclusively (i.e., with no use of dynamic binding). By contrast, structural description models, whose representations specify complex interrelations (including relative location, relative size, etc.) among complex features (e.g., the shape attributes of convex parts), must use a combination of both static binding (at the level of local image features) and dynamic binding (at the level of complex features and relations).

Binding and the Holistic/Analytic Distinction

The terms *holistic* and *analytic* may mean slightly different things to different people. I will use *holistic* to refer to representations that are generated and used "all of a piece"—representations that are difficult or impossible to evaluate in terms of their constituent dimensions or parts. An analytic representation is simply the opposite. It is a representation that affords analysis in terms of its constituent parts and their interrelations. The distinction between face recognition on the one hand and common object recognition on the other illustrates the difference between holistic and analytic representations. The visual representations that permit us to discriminate one person's face from another's are holistic, as evidenced by the fact that it is often easy to say who looks like whom, but barring obvious markings such as facial hair and scars, it is usually difficult to say why (Bartlett, Searcy & Abdi, chapter 1 this volume; Cooper & Wojan, 2000; Farah, 1990; Murray, Rhodes, & Schuchinsky, chapter 3 this volume; Palermo & Rhodes, in press; Tanaka & Farah, 1993). By contrast, the visual representations that allow us to recognize objects as members of a general class—including those that allow us discriminate faces from nonface objects (Cooper & Wojan, 2000)—are represented much more analytically, as evidenced by the ease with which we can say what objects have visually in common and how they differ (Hummel, 2000; Saiki & Hummel, 1998a; Thoma & Hummel, 2002).

Another example of holistic and analytic representations can be found in the relationship between color and shape. Color is defined by the physical dimensions of saturation, brightness, and hue. These dimensions are physically independent but they are psychologically *integral*, in that people have great difficulty making judgments about one without interference from the others (Garner, 1974; see also Cheng & Pachella, 1984): To the visual system, saturation, brightness, and hue are the single holistic dimension *color*. By contrast, it is possible to make judgments about an object's shape with little or no interference from its color, and vice versa: color and shape are psychologically *separable*.

As these examples illustrate, *holistic* (i.e., integral) and *analytic* (i.e., separable) are better described as relations among the dimensions defining a representation than as properties of a representation as a whole. The dimensions defining color are holistic (integral) with respect to one another, but they are analytic (separable) with respect to the dimensions defining shape. Similarly, some dimensions of the visual representation of shape are analytic with respect to one another, whereas others are holistic. Object parts are visually independent of (i.e., analytic with respect to) their spatial relations (Saiki & Hummel, 1998a), but the dimensions that permit us to discriminate one person's face from another's are holistic with respect to one another.

From a computational perspective, the distinction between holistic and analytic dimensions maps directly onto the distinction between static (conjunctive) and dynamic binding. In a given representation, two dimensions will be holistic with respect to one another to the extent that they are bound together statically (i.e., conjunctively) in that representation; they will be analytic to the extent that they are represented independently and bound together dynamically.[1] For example, if every unit in a given representation codes for a particular feature at a particular location (like the neurons in V1), then to that representation, feature identity is holistic with respect to location. Likewise, if every unit codes for some combination of brightness, saturation, and hue, then to that representation, brightness, saturation, and hue are holistic with respect to one another.

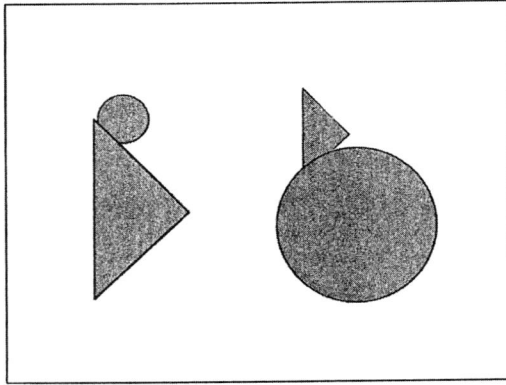

FIGURE 8.2 Two simple "objects." It is easy to appreciate that the circle on the left corresponds to the circle on the right in terms of its shape, but to the triangle on the right in terms of its spatial relations. Your ability to appreciate these alternative correspondences is a manifestation of your ability to perceive object parts independently of their spatial relations (Hummel, 2000).

The Strengths and Limitations of Holistic and Analytic Representations

As approaches to the representation of shape, holistic and analytic representations have complementary strengths and weaknesses that reflect their complementary solutions to the binding problem. In brief, analytic representations are flexible, expressive, and representationally efficient (i.e., many conjunctions can be represented with few units), but computationally "expensive" (i.e., limited in the number of conjunctions that can be processed in parallel). Holistic representations have limited flexibility and expressiveness, and they are representationally "expensive" (requiring a separate unit for each conjunction) but computationally "inexpensive" (permitting the processing of many conjunctions in parallel).

Consider first the case of analytic representations. The flexibility of an analytic representation derives from its ability to represent things independently of one another. An animal that can represent object shape independently of location in the visual field can respond to an object in the same way regardless of where its image projects to the retina. Similarly, representing an object's parts independently of their interrelations makes it possible to reason flexibly about those parts and relations. For example, consider the two simple "objects" in figure 8.2. Does the circle in the left-hand object correspond to the circle or the triangle in the right-hand object? In terms of shape, the circle on the left corresponds to the circle on the right; but in terms of relative size and location, the circle on the left corresponds to the triangle on the right. Your ability to appreciate these alternative correspondences stems directly from your ability to represent the shapes independently of their spatial relations, and vice-versa (Hummel, 2000).

There is substantial evidence for the role of analytic representations in human shape perception and object recognition. Using methods similar to those Garner (1974) used to demonstrate the perceptual separability of shape and color, Stankiewicz (in press) showed that our visual systems represent the dimensions defining an object's 3D shape (e.g., its aspect ratio and the curvature of its major axis) independently of the dimensions defining the angle from which it is viewed. This result suggests that our ability to recognize objects in novel viewpoints reflects, at least in part, our ability to perceptually separate the dimensions that define object shape from those that define viewpoint (see also Biederman, 1987; Biederman & Cooper, 1991a, 1992; Biederman & Gerhardstein, 1993, 1995; Hummel & Biederman, 1992). Similarly, Saiki and Hummel (1998a) showed that the human visual system represents an object's parts independently of their spatial relations (see also Logan, 1994), and Hummel and Stankiewicz (1996b) showed that, at least for attended stimuli, the visual representations that mediate object recognition, same-different judgments, and similarity judgments are based on explicit representations of the categorical relations among an object's parts (see also Saiki & Hummel, 1998b). By demonstrating that we perceive the attributes of object shape—including the spatial relations among an object's parts—both explicitly and independently of one another, these findings constitute direct evidence for the role of analytic representations in shape perception.

Indirect evidence for the role of analytic representations in shape perception comes from a variety of experiments supporting the behavioral predictions of specific structural description theories. These findings provide indirect support in the sense that they are not addressed to the analytic/holistic distinction per se, but rather to various other predictions (mostly concerning the role of viewpoint in object recognition) of specific models that postulate analytic representations. Specifically, as predicted by Biederman's (1987; Hummel & Biederman, 1992) structural description theory, our ability to recognize an object is insensitive to the location of its image in the visual field (Biederman & Cooper, 1991a), the size of the image (Biederman & Cooper, 1992), and left-right reflection (Biederman & Cooper, 1991a; Stankiewicz et al., 1998). Object recognition (Biederman, 1987) and visual priming for objects (Biederman & Cooper, 1991b) also appear to be mediated by an explicit representation of volumetric parts.

In summary, the strength of an analytic representation is that it provides tremendous flexibility and economy of representation, and serves as the foundation for complex symbolic representations and processes. Theories of shape perception based on analytic representations also provide a simple and strikingly complete account of many aspects of human shape perception, object recognition, and categorization. The limitation of analytic representations is that they depend on dynamic binding, and dynamic binding imposes a bottleneck on processing. As noted previously, dynamic binding is time-consuming and capacity-limited, and there is substantial evidence that it requires visual attention (Hummel & Stankiewicz, 1996a; Logan, 1994; Luck & Beach, 1998; Luck & Vogel, 1997; Treisman & Gelade, 1980).

The limitations of dynamic binding are problematic for theories based solely on analytic representations of shape (e.g., those of Biederman, 1987; Hummel & Biederman, 1992; and Marr & Nishihara, 1978). The process of generating an analytic representation cannot be any faster or more automatic than the process of dynamic binding, but object recognition apparently can be. Face recognition in the macaque can be accomplished to a high degree of certainty based on the *first* set of spikes to reach inferotemporal cortex (at least for over-learned faces; Oram & Perrett, 1992). Clearly, the macaque visual system recognizes faces without waiting around for several sets of desynchronized spikes. Although Oram and Perrett obtained their data using faces (which are known to be processed holistically) as stimuli, there is also behavioral evidence that people can recognize common (nonface) objects very rapidly. Intraub (1981) showed that people can recognize common objects presented at the rate of 10 per second (see also Potter, 1976). These findings suggest that object recognition is much too fast to depend exclusively on dynamic binding (Hummel & Stankiewicz, 1996a). Similarly, although dynamic binding—and therefore analytic representations—require visual attention, object recognition apparently does not, as shown by findings of both negative priming (e.g., Tipper, 1985; Treisman & DeSchepper, 1996) and positive priming (Stankiewicz et al., 1998; Stankiewicz & Hummel, in press) for unattended objects.

Holistic representations (based on static binding) are the complement of analytic representations (based on dynamic binding) in both their strengths and weakness. The strength of a holistic representation is that it carries bindings statically (i.e., conjunctively) in the units of representation, making dynamic binding unnecessary. Holistic representations can therefore be generated automatically and with minimal cost in terms of attention or working memory (Thoma & Hummel, 2002). The limitation of a holistic representation is that it lacks the flexibility and expressiveness of an analytic representation. For example, to a fully holistic representation of shape, the two objects in figure 8.2 are simply *different*. It does not even make sense to ask whether the circle on the left corresponds to the circle on the right: There is no "circle on the left," just the shape *as a whole*. A related limitation is that, because they bind elements to their relations conjunctively, holistic representations are sharply limited in the ways they can represent relations. As noted previously, the number of pairwise relations among an object's elements grows exponentially with the number of relations. As a result, holistic representations, although not logically constrained, are pragmatically constrained to represent features in terms of their coordinates, rather than their interrelations (see Hummel

& Stankiewicz, 1996b). In turn, the exclusive use of coordinates causes holistic representations to resemble metrically precise templates, which are less flexible and less expressive than explicit structural descriptions (Clowes, 1967; Sutherland, 1968).

It is worth noting in this context that the deep limitation of the view-based approach to object recognition (e.g., Edelman, 1998; Poggio & Edelman, 1990; Tarr & Bülthoff, 1995; see also Tarr, chapter 7 this volume, and the references therein) is that it relies exclusively on holistic representations of shape, making it fundamentally inconsistent with the structural aspects of shape perception reviewed earlier (Hummel, 1994, 2000, 2001; Hummel & Stankiewicz, 1996b). Although Tarr's critique of the structural description approach to recognition (which he identifies primarily with Marr & Nishihara, 1978, and Biederman, 1987) emphasizes the role of structural descriptions qua "3D view-invariant representations," the fundamental difference between the view- and structure-based accounts of object recognition concerns, not the role of viewer- versus object-centered representations, but the role of holistic versus structured (i.e., explicitly relational) representations of shape (Hummel, 1994; Hummel & Biederman, 1992; Hummel & Stankiewicz, 1996b; see Hummel, 2000, for a review). For example, the structural descriptions generated by the models of Hummel and Biederman (1992) and Hummel and Stankiewicz (1996a, 1998; Hummel, 2001) specify the spatial relations among object parts in *viewer-centered* coordinates. One reason is that, as detailed by Hummel (1994), representing spatial relations explicitly makes it possible to account for the view invariances and sensitivities that characterize human object recognition without having to postulate 3D object-centered representations, and without having to postulate complex "alignment," "normalization," or "transformation" operations to bring viewed images into correspondence with stored views.

Exploiting the Strengths of Holistic and Analytic Representations

This survey of the strengths and limitations of holistic and analytic representations suggests that any visual system that relied exclusively on one or the other as a basis for representing shape would have serious limitations. To a visual system that could only represent shape analytically, shape perception would be slow and laborious, always requiring visual attention and working memory. To a visual system that could only represent shape holistically, the visual world would be a mysterious place, full of objects that were either vaguely similar or vaguely dissimilar, but without any basis for saying *why* things seemed similar or not.[2]

In response to the complementary strengths and limitations of analytic and holistic accounts of shape perception, Hummel and Stankiewicz (1996a; Hummel, 2001) proposed a model of object recognition based on a hybrid analytic + holistic representation of shape. The basic idea starts with the observation that holistic representations based on static binding are not capacity-limited in the way that analytic representations are. The model uses dynamic binding to generate analytic representations whenever possible (e.g., when an object image is attended), but uses static binding to generate useful (if limited) holistic representations when dynamic binding fails (e.g., when an image in not attended). Importantly, the holistic (statically bound) and analytic (dynamically bound) components of the representation are not simply "joined at the hip." Rather, the holistic component represents the *substructure* of whatever subset of the analytic representation happens to be the focus of processing at a given instant. If the "subset" happens to be the entire object—that is, when the visual system fails to segment the object into independent parts, as when the image is not attended—then the "substructure" will be a holistic representation of the entire object. This holistic representation lacks the flexibility and view invariance of the analytic representation, but is capable of supporting recognition if the object is depicted in a familiar viewpoint. When the visual system succeeds in segmenting the object into parts, the holistic component represents the substructure (i.e., local features [Hummel & Stankiewicz, 1996a] or surface characteristics [Hummel, 2001]) of each part individually.

The analytic component of the model's representation consists of a collection of units that represent the shape attributes of an object's parts independently of one another, of their locations in the visual field, and of their interrelations. That is, each unit responds to one shape attribute or relation, and will respond to that attribute or relation regardless of the part's (or object's) other attributes and relations. As a result, the representation generated on these units is invariant with translation, scale, and left-right reflection (although, like human shape perception, it is sensitive to rotations about the line of sight and some rotations in depth). However, this same independence makes these units heavily dependent on dynamic binding: if more than one of an object's parts fires at a given instant, then the description generated on the independent units will be a meaningless jumble of unbound features (see Hummel & Stankiewicz, 1996a). The holistic component of the representation specifies the local features of each object part (or, when segmentation fails, the entire object) separately at each of several locations in a circular reference frame. That is, each unit responds to a specific feature *at a specific location* in the reference frame (i.e., a feature-location conjunction). The origin and scale of this reference frame are defined on whatever part (or object) it happens to be representing at the time, but its orientation is defined relative to the viewer. That is, although it is holistic, this representation is not completely viewer-centered: as a result, it is sensitive to rotation and left-right reflection but it is invariant with translation and scale.

The resulting model accounts for a large body of existing findings on human object recognition (including its view invariances and sensitivities, as well as the role of parts [Biederman & Cooper, 1991b] and explicit spatial relations [Hummel & Stankiewicz, 1996b] in shape perception) and generates several novel predictions. Most generally, it predicts that when the visual system succeeds in segmenting an object into its parts (i.e., when it succeeds in generating an analytic representation of the parts and their interrelations), shape perception will have the characteristics of a structural description: recognition will be largely invariant with variations in viewpoint, and part attributes will be represented independently of one another and their interrelations. When the visual system fails to segment an image into its parts, shape perception will have the characteristics of the holistic representation: recognition will be more sensitive to variations in viewpoint, and part attributes will not be represented independently of their locations.

These general predictions can be translated into the following more specific predictions about patterns of visual priming:

1. Attending to an object's image will visually prime (1a) that image, (1b) translated versions of that image (as when the image is moved from the left-hand side of the visual field to the right-hand side), (1c) scaled (larger or smaller) versions of that image, (1d) a left-right reflection of that image, and (1e) split versions of the image (as when the image is cut horizontally and the top half is placed below the bottom half, or cut vertically, and the left half placed to the right of the right half). Predictions 1a–1d correspond directly to the view invariances of the analytic representation: visual priming is expected to show the same invariances as the representations primed (see, e.g., Biederman & Cooper, 1991a). Prediction 1e follows from the fact that the units in the analytic representation are independent of their locations in the visual field and relations to one another. Imagine a split image of, say, a horse, with the left half of the image moved to the right, so that the horse is split in half, facing its own hind quarters. According to the model, attending to this image will prime the units representing the shape attributes of the horse's parts. Since these units are indifferent to the parts' locations, this priming will transfer to an intact version of the same image (in which the locations and interrelations are changed relative to their locations in the split image). Hence, for attended images, priming is predicted to transfer from a split image to its intact counterpart.

2. Viewing an image *without* attending to it will visually prime (2a) that image, (2b) a translated version of that image, and (2c) a scaled version of that image, but it will *not* prime (2d) a left-right reflection. Moreover, (2e) an unattended split image will not prime its intact counterpart. Predictions 2a–2d correspond to the view invariances and sensitivities of the holistic representation. (Recall that the origin and scale of the holistic representation are

defined relative to the object [or, more accurately, whatever subset of the object happens to be firing at a given instant], so the
representation generated there is invariant with translation and
scale.) Prediction 2e follows from the fact that each unit in the
holistic representation responds to a particular feature at a particular location. Thus, because splitting an image changes the
locations of its features, both in the image as a whole and relative
to one another, the theory predicts that priming an ignored split
image will not transfer to its intact counterpart. Hummel (2001)
reports simulation results corresponding to each of these predictions.

Brian Stankiewicz and his colleagues tested predictions 1a–1d and 2a–
2d, and the results were exactly as predicted. Attended images visually
primed themselves (Stankiewicz et al., 1998; Stankiewicz & Hummel, in
press), translated and scaled versions of themselves (Stankiewicz & Hummel, in press) and their left-right reflections (Stankiewicz et al., 1998).
Images viewed without attention visually primed themselves (Stankiewicz
et al., 1998; Stankiewicz & Hummel, in press) and translated and scaled
versions of themselves (Stankiewicz & Hummel, in press), but not left-
right reflection of themselves (Stankiewicz et al., 1998). Moreover, the
effects of viewpoint (same view vs. translated, scaled, or reflected) and
attention (attended vs. ignored) were strictly additive in all these cases:
the advantage in priming enjoyed by identical images over nonidentical
images was the same for both attended and ignored images (about 50 ms
in the case of left-right reflection and 0 ms in the case of translation and
scale changes). This additivity is consistent with the model's claim that
different representation mediate priming in the attended and ignored cases
(see Stankiewicz et al., 1998).

Thoma and Hummel (2002) tested predictions 1e and 2e and the results
were again exactly as predicted. Both intact and split attended images
primed intact versions of themselves, as did ignored intact images. However, ignored split images did not prime intact versions of themselves:
consistent with the hypothesis that ignored images are represented holistically, priming for ignored images did not transfer across deviations in
the (object-relative) locations of the objects' features. As in the case of
left right reflection, these effects were strictly additive, with identical images enjoying about 50 ms more priming than split primes in both the
attended and ignored conditions. These findings are particularly interesting
in the context of the distinction between analytic and holistic representations. The discussion in this chapter of the relation between analytic representations, dynamic binding, and visual attention predicts that attended
images should be represented analytically, and ignored images should be
represented holistically. The Thoma and Hummel findings directly support
this prediction.

A Hierarchy of Shape Representations

Up to this point, this chapter has focused on the differences between holistic and analytic representations of shape, and their relationship to the differences between static and dynamic solutions to the binding problem. One general way to summarize these differences is to say that analytic representations are structurally richer than holistic representations: Dynamic binding makes it possible to represent visual properties, features, parts, and relations independently of one another and still specify how they are bound together; in turn, this capacity makes it possible to represent arbitrarily complex relations (including hierarchical relations), and ultimately serves as the foundation for symbolic representations and processes. Holistic representations, lacking any basis for dynamic binding, lack this kind of flexibility and structural sophistication.

But this does not imply that holistic representations are devoid of relational information. Relational structures are present in holistic representations, but they are *implicit*; after all, the visual machinery that generates analytic representations of object shape must start with a holistic representation (such as the pattern of activation in V1) as input. Thus, although analytic representations are structurally "less sophisticated" than analytic representations, they are nonetheless more sophisticated than representations that are completely devoid of relational information (such as a simple list of features bound to neither relations nor locations).

Consistent with this observation, Palermo and Rhodes (2002) showed that attention plays an important role in generating the holistic representations that allow us to discriminate one face from another. Specifically, they showed that subjects were better able to recognize an isolated feature of a target face (either the eyes, nose, or mouth) when that feature was embedded in the context of the complete face (the context in which it was presented) than when it was presented in isolation, but that this beneficial effect of context obtained only when the target face was attended. The beneficial effect of the context (i.e., the complete face) in the attended condition is a replication of Tanaka and Farah (1993), and is evidence for holistic processing in that condition. Accordingly, the lack of any context effect in the unattended condition is evidence of a *lack* of holistic processing in that condition. These data suggest that attention is important for the holistic processing of faces, a finding that appears to at first blush be at odds with the findings of Thoma and Hummel and those of Stankiewicz and colleagues.

One potential explanation for the apparent discrepancy between the findings (and conclusions) of Palermo and Rhodes and those of Thoma, Stankiewicz, and colleagues concerns the differences between the task of discriminating faces and the task of recognizing objects. Faces are structurally very similar, so the (putatively) holistic representations we use to discriminate them must be metrically very precise. By contrast, the holistic representations postulated by the Hummel and Stankiewicz (1996a; Hummel, 2001) model are metrically very coarse, distinguishing only 17 different locations in a circular reference frame (the center, plus two distances from the center at each of eight orientations). It is entirely possible that the metric precision required for face discrimination requires visual attention (see La Berge & Brown, 1989, and Hummel & Stankiewicz, 1998, for discussions of the role of visual attention in generating metrically precise representations of shape).

Another potential explanation for the apparent discrepancy between the findings of Palermo and Rhodes and those of Thoma, Stankiewicz and colleagues—not mutually exclusive with the first—concerns the difference between holistic representations on the one hand and collections of "free-floating" features (i.e., features bound to neither locations or relations) on the other. As noted previously, holistic representations carry structural information, albeit implicitly. Free floating features do not. From an information theoretic perspective, holistic representations are therefore a great deal richer than collections of free-floating features, so from a sampling perspective, they should be proportionally more difficult to generate. It is conceivable that Palermo and Rhodes's subjects represented the target faces more holistically in the attended conditions, and more as free-floating features in the unattended conditions. But whatever the explanation for the apparent discrepancy between the Palermo and Rhodes findings and those of Thoma, Stankiewicz, and colleagues, it seems clear that, all other things being equal, analytic representations are more attention-demanding than holistic representations, and holistic representations may be more demanding than collections of free-floating features.

Other Factors Affecting Holistic and Analytic Representations of Shape

This chapter has focused on the role of attention in generating analytic representations of object shape. However, numerous other factors are likely to affect whether the visual system will generate an analytic representation of an object's shape, and some of these deserve mention. One is time. Representing an object's shape analytically entails segmenting the object's image into its constituent features or parts. The operations that perform this kind of segmentation depend on lateral communication between neurons representing local features (such as lines, vertices, etc.) in an object's image (Hummel & Biederman, 1992), and probably also exploit feedback from representations of known objects to representations of local image features (Peterson & Gibson, 1994). Such interactions take time and imply that analytic representations cannot be generated in any strictly feed-forward manner (Hummel & Stankiewicz, 1996a). Behaviorally, these considerations predict that recognition based on an analytic representation of shape should take longer than recognition based on a holistic representation (at least for the simple kinds of holistic representations postulated by Hummel & Stankiewicz, 1996a; holistic representations like those studied by Palmero & Rhodes, in press, may, like analytic representations, be time-consuming to generate). To my knowledge, this prediction remains to be tested.

A related factor that stands to affect whether the visual system will succeed in generating an analytic representation of an object's shape is whether the object's image presents the local cues (e.g., matched concavities; Hoffman & Richards, 1985) necessary for segmentation (Hummel & Biederman, 1992). Very "blobby" or irregular figures (such as lumps of clay) may afford few such cues, and may therefore be represented more holistically than figures that afford natural segmentation into features or parts. Finally, as suggested by the case of face recognition, there is reason to believe that discriminating one member of a class from other qualitatively similar instances may profit from metrically precise holistic coding (but see Hummel & Stankiewicz, 1998, for an alternative account of some kinds of subordinate-level recognition). But whether the goal is to permit recognition of unattended images, to permit rapid (potentially feedforward) recognition of objects in familiar views, to permit recognition of objects that do not afford part-based analysis, or to permit recognition of individuals based on fine metric differences, holistic coding affords numerous benefits as a complement to analytic coding.

Summary and Conclusion

A representation of object shape is analytic (i.e., structured) to the extent that it represents the attributes of that shape (e.g., features or part attributes) independently of one another and of their interrelations. A representation is holistic to the extent that it codes attributes and relations conjunctively, rather than independently. Analytic and holistic representations have strikingly complementary strengths and limitations as representations of object shape. Representing the attributes of shape independently of one another affords tremendous flexibility and expressiveness, but owing to the resulting need for dynamic binding, incurs a cost in terms of attention, working memory, and processing time. Binding the dimensions of a stimulus conjunctively, as in a holistic representation, does not incur the computational costs of an analytic representation, but neither does it afford the same flexibility or expressiveness. These considerations suggest that a "well designed" visual system would be configured to exploit the strengths of both analytic and holistic representations in order to minimize the deleterious effects of the weakness of either. The experimental findings reviewed here suggest that the human visual system is indeed configured to exploit the strengths of an analytic representation when it attends to a stimulus, and simultaneously enjoy the advantages of a holistic representation when it does not.

Notes

Preparation of this chapter was supported by NSF Grant SBR-9729023, and by grants from the UCLA Academic Senate and HRL Laboratories.
1. For the purposes of storage in long-term memory, even independent dimensions must at some point be bound together statically (see Hummel & Biederman, 1992). As such, it is perhaps more accurate to say that two dimensions will be psychologically holistic to the extent that the visual system *only* binds them statically (i.e., never represents them independently), and they will be analytic to the extent that it *ever* represents them independently.

2. There is some evidence that this is the visual world experienced by pigeons (Peissig, Young, Wasserman, & Biederman, 1999; Peissig, Young, Wasserman, & Biederman, in press; Sekuler, Lee, & Shuttleworth, 1996). It is not, however, the world experienced by people. In this context, it is interesting to speculate that analytic representations may be a late evolutionary development. Holistic representations are easy to learn: it is only necessary to learn conjunctions of more primitive elements. By contrast, analytic representations, which treat dimensions independently of one another, are very difficult to learn unless you start out with a representation that can already treat the relevant dimensions independently—that is, unless you start with a representation that is already analytic (Goldstone, 2001; Kellman, Burke, & Hummel, 1999).

References

Biederman, I. (1987). Recognition-by-components: A theory of human image understanding. *Psychological Review, 94,* 115–147.

Biederman, I., & Cooper, E. E. (1991a). Evidence for complete translational and reflectional invariance in visual object priming. *Perception, 20,* 585–593.

Biederman, I., & Cooper, E. E. (1991b). Priming contour deleted images: Evidence for intermediate representations in visual object recognition. *Cognitive Psychology, 23,* 393–419.

Biederman, I., & Cooper, E. E. (1992). Size invariance in visual object priming. *Journal of Experimental Psychology: Human Perception and Performance, 18,* 121–133.

Biederman, I., & Gerhardstein, P. C. (1993). Recognizing depth-rotated objects: Evidence and conditions for 3-dimensional viewpoint invariance. *Journal of Experimental Psychology: Human Perception and Performance, 19,* 1162–1182.

Biederman, I., & Gerhardstein, P. C. (1995). Viewpoint-dependent mechanisms in visual object recognition: A critical analysis. *Journal of Experimental Psychology: Human Perception and Performance, 21,* 1506–1514.

Biederman, I., & Ju, G. (1988). Surface versus edge-based determinants of visual recognition. *Cognitive Psychology, 20,* 38–64.

Bundesen, C. (1998). Visual selective attention: Outlines of a choice model, a race model and a computational theory. *Visual Cognition, 5,* 287–309.

Cheng, P. W., & Pachella, R. G. (1984). A psychophysical approach to dimensional separability. *Cognitive Psychology, 16,* 279–304.

Clowes, M. B. (1967). Perception, picture processing and computers. In N. L. Collins & D. Michie (Eds.), *Machine intelligence* (vol. 1, pp. 181–197). Edinburgh, Scotland: Oliver & Boyd.

Cooper, E. E., & Wojan, T. J. (2000). Differences in the coding of spatial relations in face identification and basic-level object recognition. *Journal of Experimental Psychology: Learning, Memory, & Cognition, 26,* 470–488.

Edelman, S. (1998). Representation is representation of similarities. *Behavioral & Brain Sciences, 21,* 449–498.

Edelman, S., & Poggio, T. (1991, April). Bringing the grandmother back into the picture: A memory-based view of object recognition. MIT A.I. Memo No. 1181.

Enns, J. T. (1992). Sensitivity of early human vision to 3-D orientation in line-drawings. *Canadian Journal of Psychology, 46,* 143–169.

Farah, M. (1990). *Visual agnosia: Disorders of object recognition and what they tell us about normal vision.* Cambridge, MA: MIT Press.

Fodor, J. A., & Pylyshyn, Z. (1988). Connectionism and cognitive architecture: A critical analysis. *Cognition, 28,* 3–71.

Garner, W. R. (1974). *The processing of information and structure.* Hillsdale, NJ: Erlbaum.

Goldstone, R. L. (2001). The sensitization and differentiation of dimensions during category learning. *Journal of Experimental Psychology: General, 130,* 116–139.

Goldstone, R. L., Medin, D. L., & Gentner, D. (1991). Relational similarity and the nonindependence of features in similarity judgments. *Cognitive Psychology, 23,* 222–262.

Gray, C. M., & Singer, W. (1989). Stimulus specific neuronal oscillations in orientation columns of cat visual cortex. *Proceedings of the National Academy of Sciences, USA 86,* 1698–1702.

Halford, G. S., Wilson, W. H., Guo, J., Gayler, R. W., Wiles, J., & Stewart, J. E. M. (1994). Connectionist implications for processing capacity limitations in analogies. In K. J. Holyoak & J. A. Barnden (Eds.), *Advances in connectionist and neural computation theory, Vol. 2: Analogical connections* (pp. 363–415). Norwood, NJ: Ablex.

Hoffman, D. D., & Richards, W. A. (1985). Parts of recognition. *Cognition, 18,* 65–96.

Holyoak, K. J., & Hummel, J. E. (2000). The proper treatment of symbols in a connectionist architecture. In E. Dietrich & A. Markman (Eds.), *Cognitive dynamics: Conceptual change in humans and machines* (pp. 229–264). Hillsdale, NJ: Erlbaum.

Hummel, J. E. (1994). Reference frames and relations in computational models of object recognition. *Current Directions in Psychological Science, 3,* 111–116.

Hummel, J. E. (2000). Where view-based theories break down: The role of structure in shape perception and object recognition. In E. Dietrich & A. Markman (Eds.), *Cognitive dynamics: Conceptual change in humans and machines* (pp. 157–185). Hillsdale, NJ: Erlbaum.

Hummel, J. E. (2001). Complementary solutions to the binding problem in vision: Implications for shape perception and object recognition. *Visual Cognition, 8,* 489–517.

Hummel, J. E., & Biederman, I. (1992). Dynamic binding in a neural network for shape recognition. *Psychological Review, 99,* 480–517.

Hummel, J. E., & Holyoak, K. J. (1997). Distributed representations of structure:

A theory of analogical access and mapping. *Psychological Review, 104,* 427–466.

Hummel, J. E., & Holyoak, K. J. (2001). A process model of human transitive inference. In M. L. Gattis (Ed.), *Spatial schemas in abstract thought* (pp. 279–305). Cambridge, MA: MIT Press.

Hummel, J. E., & Holyoak, K. J. (in press). A symbolic-connectionist theory of relational inference and generalization. *Psychological Review.*

Hummel, J. E., & Stankiewicz, B. J. (1996a). An architecture for rapid, hierarchical structural description. In T. Inui & J. McClelland (Eds.), *Attention and performance XVI: Information integration in perception and communication* (pp. 93–121). Cambridge, MA: MIT Press.

Hummel, J. E., & Stankiewicz, B. J. (1996b). Categorical relations in shape perception. *Spatial Vision, 10,* 201–236.

Hummel, J. E., & Stankiewicz, B. J. (1998). Two roles for attention in shape perception: A structural description model of visual scrutiny. *Visual Cognition, 5,* 49–79.

Hummel, J. E., & Stevens, G. (2002). *The proper treatment of symbols in a neural architecture.* Manuscript in preparation.

Intraub, H. (1981). Identification and processing of briefly glimpsed visual scenes. In D. Fisher, R. A. Monty, & J. W. Sender (Eds.), *Eye movements: Cognition and visual perception* (pp. 181–190). Hillside, NJ: Erlbaum.

Kellman, P. J., Burke, T., & Hummel, J. E. (1999). Modeling perceptual learning of abstract invariants. *Proceedings of the Twenty First Annual Conference of the Cognitive Science Society* (pp. 264–269). Mahwah, NJ: Erlbaum.

LaBerge, D., & Brown, V. (1989). Theory of attentional operations in shape identification. *Psychological Review, 96,* 101–124.

Logan, G. D. (1994). Spatial attention and the apprehension of spatial relations. *Journal of Experimental Psychology: Human Perception and Performance, 20* (5), 1015–1036.

Lowe, D. (1985). *Perceptual organization and visual recognition.* Boston: Kluwer Academic Publishers.

Luck, S. J., & Beach, N. J. (1998). Visual attention and the binding problem: A neurophysiological perspective. In R. D. Wright (Ed.), *Visual attention* (pp. 455–478). New York: Oxford University Press.

Luck, S. J., & Vogel, E. K. (1997). The capacity of visual working memory for features and conjunctions. *Nature, 390,* 279–281.

Marr, D., & Nishihara, H. K. (1978). Representation and recognition of three dimensional shapes. *Proceedings of the Royal Society of London,* Series B. 200, 269–294.

Metcalfe, J. (1990). Composite Holographic Associative Recall Model (CHARM) and blended memories in eyewitness testimony. *Journal of Experimental Psychology: General, 119,* 145–160.

Metcalfe, J. (1991). Recognition failure and the composite memory trace in CHARM. *Psychological Review, 98,* 529–553.

Newell, A. (1980). Physical symbol systems. *Cognitive Science, 4,* 135–183.

Oram, M. W., & Perrett, D. I. (1992). The time course of neural responses discriminating different views of the face and head. *Journal of Neurophysiology, 68,* 70–84.

Palermo, R., & Rhodes, G. (2002). The influence of divided attention on holistic face perception. *Cognition, 67,* 111–145.

Palmer, S. E. (1978). Fundamental aspects of cognitive representation. In E. Rosch & B. B. Lloyd (Eds.), *Cognition and categorization* (pp. 259–303). Hillsdale, NJ: Erlbaum.

Pedone, R., Hummel, J. E., & Holyoak, K. J. (2001). The use of diagrams in analogical problem solving. *Memory and Cognition, 29,* 214–221.

Peissig, J. J., Young, M. E., Wasserman, E. A., & Biederman, I. (1999). The pigeon's perception of depth-rotated shapes. *Cahiers de Psychologie Cognitive (Current Psychology of Cognition), 18,* 657–690.

Peissig, J. J., Young, M. E., Wasserman, E. A., & Biederman, I. (in press). Seeing things from a different angle: The pigeon's recognition of single geons rotated in depth. *Journal of Experimental Psychology: Animal Behavior Processes.*

Peterson, M. A., & Gibson, B. S. (1994). Must figure-ground organization precede object recognition? An assumption in peril. *Psychological Science, 5,* 253–259.

Plate, T. (1991). Holographic reduced representations: Convolution algebra for compositional distributed representations. In J. Mylopoulos and R. Reiter (Eds.), *Proceedings of the 12th International Joint Conference on Artificial Intelligence* (pp. 30–35). San Mateo, CA: Morgan Kaufmann.

Poggio, T., & Edelman, S. (1990). A neural network that learns to recognize three-dimensional objects. *Nature, 343,* 263–266.

Pollack, J. B. (1990). Recursive distributed representations. *Artificial Intelligence, 46,* 77–106.

Potter, M. C. (1976). Short-term conceptual memory for pictures. *Journal of Experimental Psychology: Human Learning and Memory, 2,* 509–522.

Riesenhuber, M., & Poggio, T. (1999). Hierarchical models of object recognition in cortex. *Nature Neuroscience, 11,* 1019–1025.

Rosch, E., & Mervis, C. B. (1975). Family resemblances: Studies in the internal structure of categories. *Cognitive Psychology, 7,* 573–605.

Rosch, E., Mervis, C. B., Gray, W. D., Johnson, D. M., & Boyes-Braem, P. (1976). Basic objects in natural categories. *Cognitive Psychology, 8,* 382–439.

Saiki, J., & Hummel, J. E. (1996). Attribute conjunctions and the part configuration advantage in object category learning. *Journal of Experimental Psychology: Learning, Memory, and Cognition, 22,* 1002–1019.

Saiki, J., & Hummel, J. E. (1998a). Connectedness and part-relation integration in shape category learning. *Memory and Cognition, 26,* 1138–1156.

Saiki, J., & Hummel, J. E. (1998b). Connectedness and the integration of parts with relations in shape perception. *Journal of Experimental Psychology: Human Perception and Performance, 24,* 227–251.

Sekuler, A. B., Lee, J. A. J., & Shettleworth, S. J. (1996). Pigeons do not complete party occluded figures. *Perception, 25,* 1109–1120.

Singer, W. (2000). Response synchronization, a universal coding strategy for the definition of relations. In M. S. Gazzaniga (Ed.), *The new cognitive neurosciences* (2nd ed.). Cambridge, MA: MIT Press.

Singer, W., & Gray, C. M. (1995). Visual feature integration and the temporal correlation hypothesis. *Annual Review of Neuroscience, 18,* 555–586.

Smolensky, P. (1990). Tensor product variable binding and the representation of symbolic structures in connectionist systems. *Artificial Intelligence, 46,* 159–216.

Stankiewicz, B. J. (in press). Evidence for separable dimensions in the perception of object shape. *Journal of Experimental Psychology: Human Perception and Performance.*

Stankiewicz, B. J., & Hummel, J. E. (in press). Automatic priming for translation- and scale-invariant representations of object shape. *Visual Cognition.*

Stankiewicz, B. J., Hummel, J. E., & Cooper, E. E. (1998). The role of attention in priming for left-right reflections of object images: Evidence for a dual representation of object shape. *Journal of Experimental Psychology: Human Perception and Performance, 24,* 732–744.

Strong, G. W., & Whitehead, B. A. (1989). A solution to the tag-assignment problem for neural networks. *Behavioral and Brain Sciences, 12,* 381–433.

Sutherland, N. S. (1968). Outlines of a theory of visual pattern recognition in animals and man. *Proceedings of the Royal Society of London* (Series B), *171,* 95–103.

Tanaka, J. W., & Farah, M. J. (1993). Parts and wholes in face recognition. *Quarterly Journal of Experimental Psychology: Human Experimental Psychology, 146A,* 225–245.

Tarr, M. J., & Bülthoff, H. H. (1995). Is human object recognition better described by geon structural descriptions or by multiple views? Comment on Biederman and Gerhardstein (1993). *Journal of Experimental Psychology: Human Perception and Performance, 21,* 1494–1505.

Thoma, V., & Hummel, J. E. (in press) *Direct evidence for holistic representations of object shape in the absence of visual attention.* Manuscript submitted for publication.

Tipper, S. P. (1985). The negative priming effect: Inhibitory effects of ignored primes. *Quarterly Journal of Experimental Psychology, 37A,* 571–590.

Treisman, A., & DeSchepper, B. (1996). Object tokens, attention, and visual memory. In T. Inui & J. McClelland (Eds.), *Attention and performance XVI: Information integration in perception and communication* (pp. 15–46). Cambridge, MA: MIT Press.

Treisman, A., & Gelade, G. (1980). A feature integration theory of attention. *Cognitive Psychology, 12,* 97–136.

Tversky, B., & Hemenway, K. (1984). Objects, parts, and categories. *Journal of Experimental Psychology: General, 113,* 169–193.

Ullman, S. (1989). Aligning pictorial descriptions: An approach to object recognition. *Cognition, 32,* 193–254.

Ullman, S. (1995). *High-level vision: Object recognition and visual cognition.* Cambridge, MA: MIT Press.

von der Malsburg, C. (1981/1994). The correlation theory of brain function (1994 reprint of a report originally published in 1981). In E. Domany, J. L. van Hemmen, & K. Schulten (Eds.), *Models of neural networks II* (pp. 95–119). Berlin: Springer.

9

Relative Dominance of Holistic and Component Properties in the Perceptual Organization of Visual Objects

RUTH KIMCHI

The perceptual relations between wholes and their component parts have been a controversial issue for psychologists and philosophers before them. The question is whether processing of the overall structure precedes and determines the processing of the component parts or properties, or whether the component properties are registered first and are then synthesized to form the objects of our awareness. There have been two opposite approaches to this issue: the early feature-analysis view and the holistic primacy view. According to the prevailing early feature-analysis view, perceptual processing begins with the analysis of simple features and elements that are later integrated into coherent objects. In this chapter, I present empirical findings that challenge this view, showing holistic primacy in different perceptual tasks and early in the course of perceptual processing.

There has been much confusion regarding the notion of holistic perception, owing in part to the looseness with which the term is used in the literature, often without a clear theoretical or operational definition. I use the term "holistic primacy" to refer to the view that holistic properties are primary in perception. A visual object, viewed as a whole, has both holistic properties and component properties or parts. Holistic properties are properties that depend on the interrelations between the component parts. In this context the terms "holistic," "global," and "configural processing" are often used interchangeably to express the hypothesis that holistic properties, rather than component properties, dominate perceptual processing.

I begin with a very brief review of the early feature-analysis view and empirical evidence that supports it. Next, I present the holistic primacy view. I then review and discuss in detail behavioral findings that demonstrate the relative dominance of holistic versus component properties in the discrimination, identification, and classification of visual objects. The following section focuses on recent experiments that have studied the microgenesis of the perceptual organization of visual objects. This microgenetic analysis is particularly revealing because it provides information about the relative dominance of holistic and component properties during the evolution of the percept. I then discuss the implications of all these findings for the longstanding dichotomy between analytic versus holistic perception, arguing that recent developments in the psychological and physiological research on visual perception weaken this dichotomy. The research on visual perception provides increasing evidence for a highly interactive perceptual system in which both simple properties and holistic properties play a role in the early organization of visual objects.

Early Feature Analysis

The early feature-analysis viewpoint, which has its roots in the Structuralist school of thought (e.g., Titchener, 1909), holds that objects are initially decomposed into simple features and components. Perceptual wholes are constructed by integrating these features and components. A modern representative of this viewpoint is the computational approach to vision by Marr (1982) that claims that the visual primitives are local geometric properties of simple form components such as sloped line segments. Similarly, the feature-integration theory (e.g., Treisman, 1986; Treisman & Gormican, 1988) assumes that simple features and components are analyzed at early stages of perceptual processing. Focused attention is then needed to establish spatial relations between components and to integrate them into coherent objects.

The early feature-analysis approach has been supported by many experimental findings, both physiological and psychological, and has dominated cognitive psychology for several decades. I review very briefly some of the evidence for early feature analysis. An extensive review can be found in Treisman (1986).

Physiological Evidence

Physiological studies using single-cell recording and autoradiographic techniques have shown that the cortical areas most directly connected to visual input (V1 and V2) contain cells that are sensitive to distinct visual properties such as orientation, luminance, color, motion, and spatial frequency (Hubel & Wiesel, 1962, 1977; Schiller, 1986; Zeki, 1978, 1993). The outputs of these cells often form retinotopic maps that preserve retinal topography. These findings have suggested that the visual system analyzes visual objects into separate simple properties, each of which is organized by position.

Psychological Evidence

A major source of support for the early feature-analysis view comes from psychophysical studies that have focused on the determinants of effortless texture segmentation and visual search (e.g., Beck, 1982; Julesz, 1984; Treisman, 1988).

In visual search the task is to detect as quickly and as accurately as possible the presence or absence of a target among other items (distractors) in the display. The number of distractors varies. Correct reaction times (RTs) to the target are examined as a function of the total number of items (target and distractors) in the display, and the slope of the RT function over number of items indicates search rate. If the time to detect the target is independent, or nearly independent, of the number of items in the display and the target seems to pop out (as for example, a diagonal line among vertical ones, see figure 9.1), then target search is considered fast and efficient, and target detection occurs under widely spread attention. If the time to detect a target increases as the number of other items in the display increases, then search is considered difficult and inefficient, and target detection requires focused attention (e.g., Duncan & Humphreys, 1989; Enns & Kingstone, 1995; Treisman & Gormican, 1988). Note that a continuum of search rates exists with search efficiency increasing the more discriminable from each other are the target and distractors.

In a typical texture discrimination task an array composed of two groups of elements (either side by side or one embedded into the other) is presented very briefly (for less than 150 ms). Texture segregation is considered effortless if it can be done without scrutiny, namely, if it occurs under these very brief exposure durations (e.g., Julesz, 1981).

Given the widespread view that early perceptual processes are rapid,

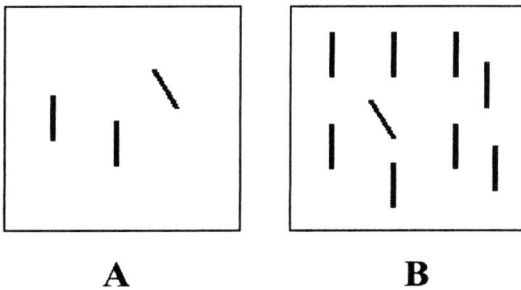

FIGURE 9.1 A pop-out of a diagonal line among vertical lines: the diagonal line is detected as easily in a nine-item display as in a three-item display.

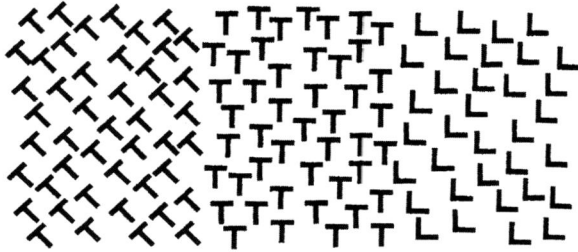

FIGURE 9.2. A group of tilted Ts is easily segregated from a group of upright Ts (disparity of line orientation), whereas a group of upright Ls (disparity of line arrangement) is not. After Beck (1982).

spatially parallel, and effortless whereas later processes are more effortful, time-consuming, and attention demanding (e.g., Neisser, 1967; Treisman, 1982), visual pop-out and effortless texture segmentation for a given feature have been interpreted as evidence that it is extracted by early perceptual processes and is included in the set of visual primitives (e.g., Julesz, 1984; Treisman, 1982; Treisman & Gelade, 1980).

Visual pop-out was found for targets that differ from distractors in simple properties such as orientation, color, size, and curvature. An example of pop-out owing to orientation disparity is presented in figure 9.1. These simple properties were also found to mediate effortless texture segregation (e.g., Julesz, 1981, 1984; Treisman, 1982). For example, as illustrated in figure 9.2, disparity of line orientation (as between an upright T and a tilted T) enables easy segregation between groups of elements, whereas differences in the spatial relationships between features (as between an upright T and an upright L) do not (e.g., Beck, 1966, 1967). Likewise, a single tilted T pops out among upright Ts, but a single L does not (e.g., Ambler, Keel, & Phelps, 1978). These and similar findings of efficient and effortless detection for simple properties have been taken as evidence for the early feature-analysis view.

The Primacy of Holistic Properties

In contrast to the atomistic view of the Structuralist school of thought, the Gestaltists (e.g., Koffka, 1935; Kohler, 1947; Wertheimer, 1955) argued for the primacy of whole units and organization in the percept. A basic tenet of the Gestalt view is that a whole is qualitatively different from the complex that one might predict by considering only its parts. The Gestaltists' notion of perceptual organization implies that wholes are organized prior to perceptual analysis of their properties and components.

Despite the prevalence of the early feature-analysis approach, students of perception have continued to grapple with the problem of perceptual organization originally recognized by Gestalt psychology (e.g., Kubovy & Pomerantz, 1981; Palmer & Rock, 1994; Pomerantz & Kubovy, 1986). A modern version of the Gestalt approach is the view that holistic properties are primary in perception (e.g., Chen, 1982; Kimchi, 1992; Navon, 1977; Uttal, 1988). The Gestaltists' claim that the whole is different from the sum of its parts can perhaps be captured by holistic properties such as closure, symmetry, and certain other spatial relations between the component parts. Such properties do not inhere in the component parts, and cannot be predicted by considering only the component parts (e.g., Garner, 1978; Kimchi, 1994; Navon, 1977; Rock, 1986). In the last two decades or so, work on issues such as perceptual grouping, part-whole relationships, perception of global and local aspects of visual patterns, and context effects in object perception have yielded findings that challenge the early feature-analysis view.

In the next two sections I review in detail studies that demonstrate perceptual dominance of holistic/configural properties. The first section focuses on the role of holistic properties in the identification, discrimination, and classification of visual objects. The second section focuses on the relative dominance of holistic properties during the evolution of the percept.

Dominance of Holistic Properties in Identification and Discrimination of Visual Objects

The Global Advantage Effect

In the spirit of the Gestalt psychology, Navon (1977) proposed that perceptual processing proceeds from global structuring toward more fine-grained analysis. This *global precedence hypothesis* has been tested by studying the perception of hierarchical patterns in which larger figures are constructed by suitable arrangement of smaller figures. An example is a set of large letters constructed from the same set of smaller letters having either the same identity as the larger letter or a different identity (see figure 9.3). The larger letter is considered a higher level unit relative to the smaller letters, which are, in turn, lower level units. Properties of the higher level unit are considered to be more global than properties of the lower level units by virtue of their position in the hierarchical structure. In a typical experiment, observers are presented with such stimuli and are required to identify the larger (global) or the smaller (local) letter in separate blocks of trials. All else being equal, *global advantage* is observed: the global letter is identified faster than the local letter, and conflicting information between the global and the local levels exerts asymmetrical global-to-local interference (e.g., Navon, 1977).

Several studies have demonstrated important boundary conditions of global advantage, pointing out certain variables that can modulate the ef-

LOCAL LEVEL

		S	H
GLOBAL LEVEL	S	sSSSSs SsSSSSs S SsSSSSs **Consistent**	HHHHHHH HHHHHHH H HHHHHHH **Conflicting**
	H	S S S S S S SSSSS S S S S S S S **Conflicting**	H H H H H H HHHHHH H H H H H H **Consistent**

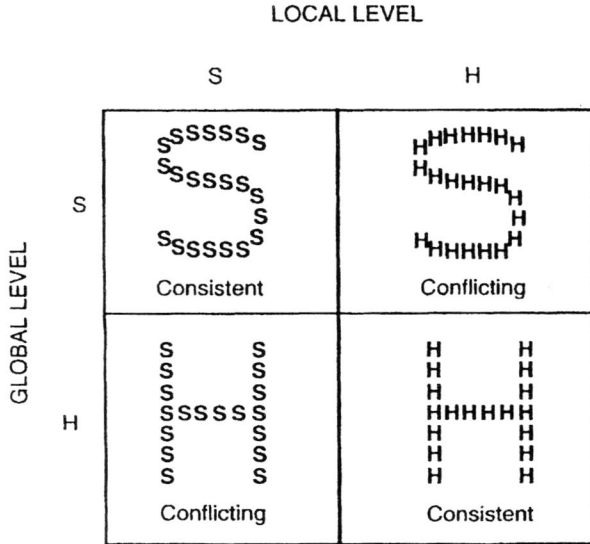

FIGURE 9.3. An example of Navon's type hierarchical stimuli: large Hs and Ss are composed of small Hs and Ss. After Navon (1977).

fect. Global advantage is less likely to occur when the overall visual angle of the hierarchical stimulus exceeds 7°–10° (e.g., Kinchla & Wolfe, 1979), with foveal than peripheral presentation (e.g., Pomerantz, 1983), with spatial certainty than spatial uncertainty (e.g., Lamb & Robertson, 1988), with sparse than dense elements (e.g., Martin, 1979), with few relatively large elements than many relatively small elements (e.g., Kimchi, 1988; Yovel, Yovel, & Levy, 2001), with long than short exposure duration (e.g., Luna, 1993; Paquet & Merikle, 1984), and when the goodness of the local forms is superior to that of the global form (e.g., LaGasse, 1994; Sebrechts & Fragala, 1985).

The mechanisms underlying the global advantage effect or its locus are still disputed. Several investigators interpreted global advantage as reflecting the priority of global properties at early perceptual processing (e.g., Broadbent, 1977; Han, Fan, Chen, & Zhuo, 1997; Navon, 1977, 1991; Paquet & Merikle, 1988), possibly as a result of early perceptual-organizational processes (Behrmann & Kimchi, in press). Other investigators suggested that global advantage arises in some postperceptual process (e.g., Boer & Keuss, 1982; Miller, 1981a, 1981b; Ward, 1982). It has also been claimed that global advantage is mediated by low-spatial frequency channels (e.g., Ivry & Robertson, 1998; Shulman & Wilson, 1987).

Notwithstanding the lack of consensus regarding the mechanisms underlying the effect, global advantage is normally observed with the typical stimuli used in the global/local paradigm (i.e., larger figures made up of many, relatively small figures), to the limits of visibility and visual acuity (see Kimchi, 1992, for an extensive review).

Kimchi (1992) has raised several concerns about the interpretation of global advantage as evidence for the primacy of holistic properties. The primacy of holistic properties implies that a property that is defined as a function of the interrelations among components would dominate the component properties. This is what was intended to be tested in the global/local paradigm with the hierarchical stimuli: whatever the components are, spatial relationships between the components would have perceptual priority. The nature of the components and their perceptual status in relation to the global configuration was actually ignored. However, as I have argued elsewhere (Kimchi, 1992, 1994), the local elements of the hierarchical letters (see figure 9.3) are not the component properties of the larger letter. The local properties of the letter H, for example, are, among others, vertical and horizontal lines. Furthermore, the nature of the components and their perceptual status in relation to the global configuration may have consequences for the interpretation of experimental findings obtained in the global/local task. For example, Kimchi and Palmer (1982, 1985) have shown that many-element patterns, like those typically used in the global/local paradigm, are perceived as global form associated with texture, and the form and texture are perceptually separable. Patterns composed of few, relatively large elements, on the other hand, are perceived as a global form and figural parts. A similar distinction between patterns in which only the position of the elements matters for the global form, and patterns in which both the position and the nature of the elements matter, was proposed independently by Pomerantz (1981, 1983). If the local elements of many-element patterns serve to define texture or are mere placeholders, then they may not be represented as individual figural units at all. Therefore, it is not clear whether a faster identification of the global configuration should be accounted for by its level of globality, thus suggesting global precedence, or rather, by a qualitative difference between identification of a figural unit versus a textural molecule.

Another issue is that the difference between global and local properties, as operationally defined in the global/local paradigm, may be captured in terms of relative size, and relative size alone rather than level of globality, may provide a reasonable account for obtained global advantage with hierarchical patterns (Navon & Norman, 1983). Yet the difference between holistic and component properties is not necessarily their relative size. To distinguish, for example, the closedness of a square (a holistic/configural property) from its component vertical and horizontal lines on the basis of their relative sizes would seem to miss the point. Rather, as noted earlier, the essential characteristic of holistic properties is that they do not inhere in the components, but depend instead on the interrelations among them. Lasaga (1989) and Kimchi (1994; Kimchi & Bloch, 1998) attempted to compare directly between component properties and properties that are defined on the spatial relationships between the components. It has even been demonstrated that configural properties need not be necessarily global. These studies are discussed later.

Pop-out Search and Effortless Texture Segregation for Higher Level Properties

Although earlier visual search studies showed visual pop-out for simple features, more recent studies have shown fast and efficient search also for certain higher level properties such as three-dimensional orientation, lighting direction, and surface slant (Enns & Rensink, 1990, 1991; Kleffner & Ramachandran, 1992), for part-whole information (Wolfe, Friedman-Hill, & Bilsky, 1994), and for global configuration (Kimchi, 1998; Rensink & Enns, 1995; Saarinen, 1995).

For example, Enns and Rensink (1990) found pop-out among items defined by the spatial relations between lines when the items correspond to three-dimensional objects that differ in spatial orientation (figure 9.4A); however, search was slow and inefficient for similar items that appear two-dimensional (figure 9.4B). These findings suggest sensitivity to three-dimensional structure in early perceptual processing.

Configural effects in visual search were demonstrated by Rensink and Enns (1995). Targets and distractors were Mueller-Lyer configurations differing in wing arrangements (wings-in versus wings-out; see figure 9.5). Two critical conditions were the different-overall condition (figure 9.5A) in which the target central line is the same as the distractor central lines, but the overall length of the target and distractor configurations is different, and the different-segment condition (figure 9.5B) in which the target item differs from the distractor items only in the physical length of the central

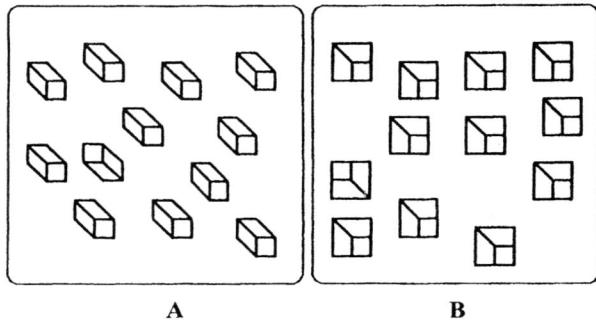

A   B

FIGURE 9.4. (A) Visual pop-out among items that correspond to three-dimensional objects that differ in spatial orientation. (B) No pop-out is observed for similar items that appear two-dimensional. Reprinted from Enns, J. T., & Rensink, R. A., A model for the rapid interpretation of line drawings in early vision, *Vision Search 2*, (Gale, Carr & Brogan, Eds.), (Fig. 4.2, p. 76). Copyright 1992, with permission from Taylor & Francis Group, UK.

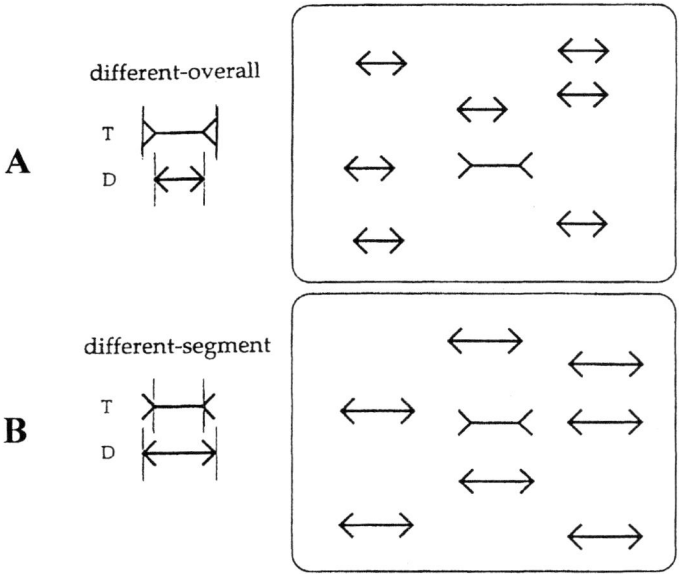

FIGURE 9.5. An example of the stimuli in Rensink and Enns (1995) visual search experiment. (A) Target (T) that has the same central line as the distractors (D) but differs from the distractors in overall length pops out. (B) Search for target that differs from the distractors in the length of the central line but has a similar overall length is difficult. Adapted from Rensink & Enns (1995), with permission.

line. Line length is known to support visual pop-out for isolated line segments (e.g., Treisman & Gormican, 1988). The question is whether visual search is governed by the segment length or by the overall length. If search were based on the component segments, then search would be faster in the different-segment condition than in the different-overall condition. The results, however, showed high-speed pop-out search for the latter but not for the former condition, indicating that visual search was based on complete configurations rather than on the component line segments.

Studying visual search for global configuration and local elements of hierarchically constructed patterns, Kimchi (1998) showed visual pop-out for the global configuration of many-element stimuli. In separate blocks, participants were required to detect the presence or absence of a global target or a local target. In the global search, the target differed from the distractors only in the global shape (figure 9.6A and C); in the local search, the target differed from the distractors only in the local elements (figure 9.6B and D). When target and distractors were many-element patterns, the results showed high-speed pop-out search for the global targets, whereas

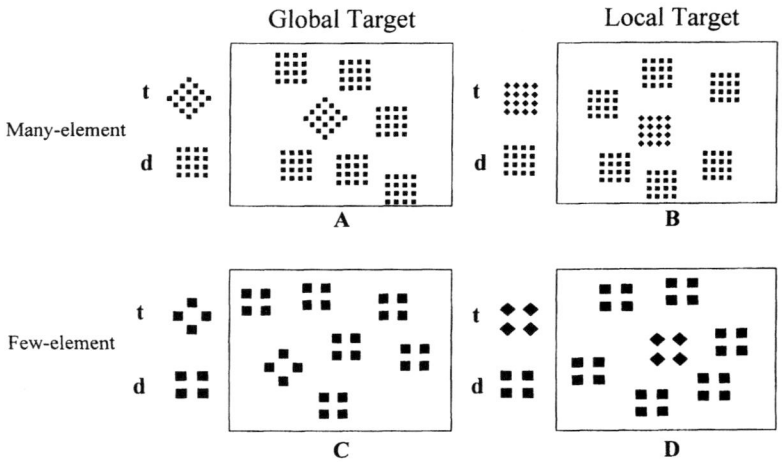

FIGURE 9.6. The targets (t) and distractors (d) in Kimchi's (1998) visual search experiment. Global diamond configuration of many-element pattern pops out among global square configurations even though target and distractors have the same local elements (A), and local diamonds of few-element stimuli pop-out among local squares even though target and distractors have the same global configurations (D). Search for local diamond elements in a display of many-element patterns composed of squares (B), and search for global diamond configuration in a display of few-element square configurations (C) are more difficult.

search for the local targets was slow and inefficient. For the few-element patterns, on the other hand, search for local targets was faster than search for global targets (see also Enns & Kingstone, 1995), demonstrating the effect of number and relative size of elements on global superiority. I will return to this point later. The slow search rate for the local targets in the many-element condition cannot be accounted for by discrimination difficulty owing to their small size because previous results with similar patterns, in different and similar paradigms, suggest that the relevant factor is the relative rather than the absolute size of the elements (e.g., Kimchi & Palmer, 1982; Kimchi & Peled, 1999).

Texture-segregation experiments have shown that a group of triangles pops out in a field of arrows, and a group of pluses is effortlessly detectable in a field of Ls (e.g., Williams, 1992). These easy, effortless texture segregations are presumably mediated by closure and intersection, respectively. Interestingly, the effectiveness of line orientation for texture segregation is reduced when the elements in the array have similar properties such as intersection and closure (e.g., a group of Xs is not as easily detectable in a field of pluses as is a group of diagonal lines in a field of vertical lines, Beck, 1982). It seems that similarity in configural properties overrides differences in simple properties (even differences that produce better segregation in single-line element array), but not vice versa (e.g., pluses and Ls).

These findings indicate that features that are much more complex than simple geometric features can be extracted very rapidly from a visual array, and therefore are presumably available in early perceptual processing.

Perceptual Context Effects: Object and Configural Superiority

OBJECT SUPERIORITY EFFECT

Other investigations of the holistic primacy issue have examined performance with lines presented in a context. For example, Weisstein and Harris (1974) required participants to determine which of four possible diagonals is present in a briefly flashed visual array. The diagonal lines were presented either alone or in the context of vertical and horizontal lines that carried no task-relevant information in terms of task requirements. The context lines were either configured to suggest three-dimensional objects or arranged to appear two-dimensional, lacking figural unity. Examples of the stimuli used by Weisstein and Harris are presented in figure 9.7. This and other studies have shown that a barely visible, briefly flashed line segment can be identified more accurately when it is part of a pattern that

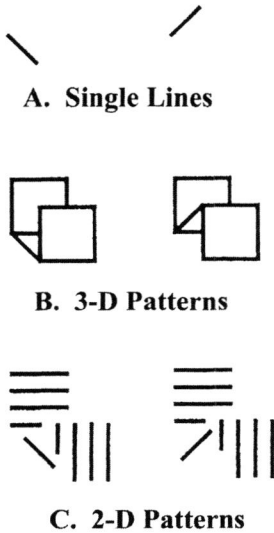

A. Single Lines

B. 3-D Patterns

C. 2-D Patterns

FIGURE 9.7. The object superiority effect: the discrimination between the two oriented lines (A) is easier when the lines are embedded in a three-dimensional context (B) than in a flatter context (C). After Weisstein & Harris (1974).

looks unified and three dimensional than when it is part of a flatter pattern (e.g., Enns & Prinzmetal, 1984; Weisstein & Harris, 1974) or when presented alone (e.g., McClelland, 1978; Williams & Weisstein, 1978). The former facilitatory effect (three-dimensional vs. flat context) has been called the *object superiority effect*, and the latter (three-dimensional context vs. no context) the *object line effect*. Hereafter, I use the term "object superiority" to refer to these two effects because the results have been attributed to properties of the object level.

Research concerned with object superiority focused on stimulus properties that can account for the effect. In addition to three-dimensionality (e.g., Lanze, Weisstein, & Harris, 1982), these include connectedness (e.g., Chen, 1982) and structural relevance (e.g., McClelland & Miller, 1979; Weisstein, Williams, & Harris, 1982). Line masking (e.g., Klein, 1978), and the amount of line detail located on and about the fixation (e.g., Earhard, 1980; Earhard & Armitage, 1980) impair context effectiveness.

CONFIGURAL SUPERIORITY EFFECT

Further experiments have shown that identification or discrimination of line segments and other simple stimuli can be improved by the addition of a context that creates a configuration that is clearly only two dimensional in appearance (e.g., Pomerantz, Sager, & Stoever, 1977; Williams & Weisstein, 1978). Pomerantz et al. (1977) presented participants with four stimuli arranged in a square, three of which were identical to one another, whereas the fourth was always different. Participants were required to locate the odd stimulus, which was randomly located at one of the four corners of the square. In one condition, the stimuli were single diagonal lines (figure 9.8A). In another condition, the same context (a right

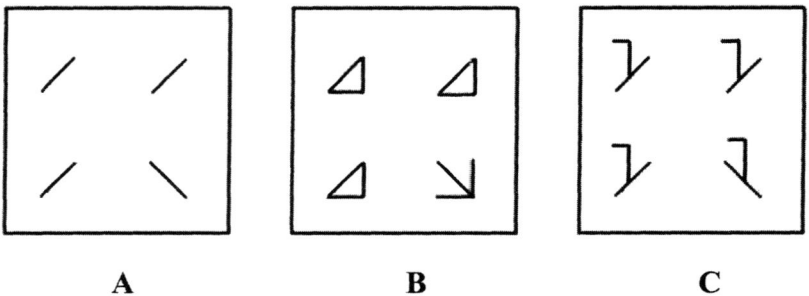

A   B   C

FIGURE 9.8. The configural superiority effect: the discrimination between diagonal lines (A) is improved when a context of a right angle is added to each diagonal line that converts the stimuli into triangles and arrows (B). Discrimination becomes more difficult when context converts the diagonal lines into the configurations in (C). After Pomerantz (1981).

angle) was added to each diagonal line that converted the stimuli into triangles and arrows (figure 9.8B). Reaction times to locate the odd stimulus were much faster for the configurations than for the lines. This and similar findings of improvement have been called *configural superiority effect* (e.g., Pomerantz, 1981; Pomerantz et al., 1977). It has been suggested that configural superiority is due to emergent properties that are possessed by perceptual wholes and do not inhere in their component parts, and are salient to the human perceptual system (e.g., Pomerantz, 1981; Pomerantz & Pristach, 1989).

It is important to note that context can also impede performance (e.g., Pomerantz, 1981). For example, adding a context to the diagonal lines presented in figure 9.8A that converts them into the configurations in (B) improves discrimination, but adding a context that converts them into the configurations in (C) actually impedes discrimination. These findings clearly indicate that performance with configurations cannot be predicted from performance with their components in isolation (as in the whole is different from the sum of its parts), but they also raise several issues regarding the interpretation of the configural superiority effect.

One potential problem is relative discriminability. It may be argued that configural superiority reflects an advantage that would be observed with any two stimuli that differed in discriminability, rather than an indication that performance is dominated by configural properties. For example, open versus closed figures may be more discriminable than right versus left diagonal lines, and it is this difference in discriminability that accounts for the faster performance with the triangles and arrow than with the diagonal lines. Attempts to circumvent this issue (Kimchi, 1994; Kimchi & Bloch, 1998; Lasaga, 1989) are discussed in the next section.

Another issue is that configural properties may not surface if they are not correlated with response categories. Pomerantz and Pristach (1989) attempted to provide diagnostic criteria for configural properties using attentional measures. They constructed visual configurations by the orthogonal combination of line segments, and reasoned that if the line segments have been grouped into configurations, spreading attention among them should be easy, and selective attention to the individual segments should be difficult. They found, however, that their selective and divided attention tasks may fail to diagnose configural interaction among the line segments because configural properties can go undetected if they are not correlated with response categories in a useful way.

Relative Dominance of Configural Versus Component Properties

Lasaga (1989) and Kimchi (1994; Kimchi & Bloch, 1998) used a different approach to evaluate the relative dominance of component and configural properties that circumvents the issues discussed above. They obtained in-

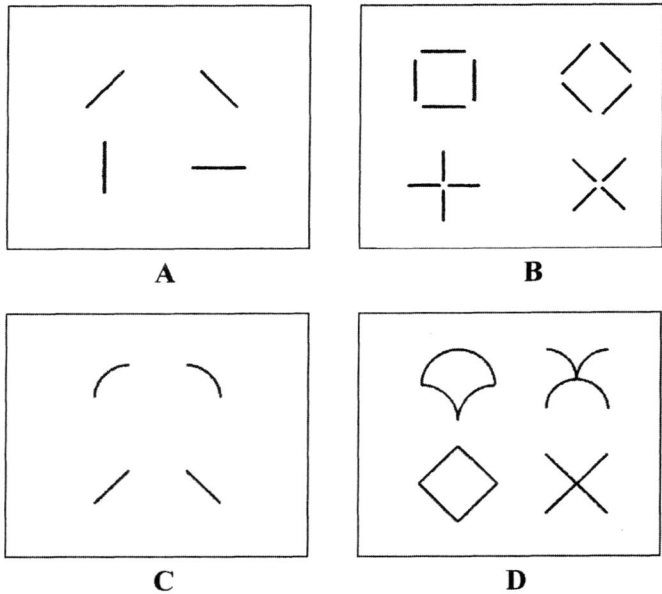

FIGURE 9.9. Examples of the stimulus sets in Kimchi's (1994) and Kimchi and Bloch's (1998) discrimination and classification experiments. Four simple lines that vary in orientation (A) are configured into the stimuli in (B). Four simple lines that vary in curvature (C) are configured into the stimuli in (D). Note that for the stimuli in (D), configurations that share configural properties are not, unlike those in (B), simple rotation of one another. Figures A and B are reprinted from Kimchi (1994), with permission from Pion Ltd., London. Figures C and D are reprinted from Kimchi (1998), with permission from Psychonomic Society Publications.

formation about the relative discriminability of the components and then examined whether discriminability of the components had an effect on performance with the configurations. They reasoned that if the discrimination between stimuli that have dissimilar configural properties is always easier than discrimination between stimuli that have similar configural properties, irrespective of the discriminability of their component properties, and if classification according to configural properties is the easiest one, then perceptual dominance of the configural properties can be inferred.

To follow the logic underlying this approach, consider the stimulus sets presented in figure 9.9. Discrimination and classification performance with the four simple lines that vary in orientation (A) showed that discrimination between the two diagonal lines is more difficult than between any other pair of lines, and the classification that involves grouping of the horizontal and vertical lines together and the two diagonal lines together is significantly faster and more accurate than the two other possible groupings (Kimchi, 1994; Lasaga & Garner, 1983). These simple stimuli were then grouped to form a new set of four stimuli (B). The relevant groupings were those that produced stimuli that differed in highly discriminable component properties (e.g., diagonal vs. vertical lines), but shared a configural property (e.g., closure), and those producing stimuli that shared a component property (e.g., diagonal lines), but differed in configural property (closed vs. open).

The pattern of performance with the simple lines predicts that a discrimination between a stimulus consisting of vertical and horizontal lines and a stimulus consisting of diagonal lines (e.g., a square vs. a diamond) would be easier than a discrimination between a pair of stimuli that have similar component lines (e.g., a diamond vs. an X), and that the easiest classification would be the one that involves grouping of the square and plus together and the diamond and X together. Contrary to this prediction, the two most difficult discriminations were square versus diamond, and plus versus X—that is, between stimuli that had dissimilar component properties but similar configural properties (closure in the first pair and intersection in the second). Therefore, the difficulty in the discrimination may be attributed solely to the similarity of the configural property in each of these pairs. Moreover, the discrimination between a pair of stimuli that differs in a configural property was equally easy, whether or not they differed in component properties. For example, the discrimination between square and plus was as easy as the discrimination between square and X, despite the fact that the first pair shares component properties and the second pair does not. The easiest classification performance was the one that was presumably based on configural properties, and the next easiest classification was the one that was presumably based on component properties (Kimchi, 1994).

Similar results were also observed for other connected and disconnected configurations (Kimchi & Bloch, 1998; Lasaga, 1989). Furthermore, similar results were also observed with stimulus sets in which stimuli that shared a configural property, were not, unlike those in (B), a simple rotation of each other (Kimchi & Bloch, 1998). An example is four lines that varied in curvature (C) and were configured into the new stimuli presented in (D).

These findings show clearly that when both configural and component properties are present in the stimuli and can be used for the task at hand, performance is dominated by configural properties, regardless of the discriminability of the component properties. When configural properties are not effective for the task at hand, discrimination and classification can be based on component properties, but there is a significant cost of time relative to performance based on configural properties.

Global Versus Configural Properties

Although the terms "global" and "configural" are often used interchangeably, recent research indicates that configural properties need not be global. As noted earlier, the difference between global and local properties (as operationally defined in the global/local paradigm) may be captured in terms of relative size. Yet, the critical difference between holistic/configural and component properties is not their relative size.

Kimchi (1994) reasoned that in order to examine whether the distinction between global and configural has a psychological reality, it is necessary to orthogonally manipulate level of globality (global vs. local) and type of property (configural vs. simple), and to study the processing consequences of this manipulation. With hierarchical stimuli, it is possible to construct stimuli in which different types of properties are present at the global and the local levels of the stimulus. Accordingly, Kimchi employed hierarchical stimuli that varied in configural (closure) and simple (line orientation) properties at the global or the local levels. The orthogonal combination of type of property and level of structure produced four sets of four stimuli each, presented in figure 9.10. The two congruent sets (A and D) consisted of stimuli in which the same type of property (closure in A and line orientation in D) was present at the global and the local levels. The two incongruent sets (B and C) consisted of stimuli in which a different type of property was present at the global and at the local level (closure on the global level and orientation at the local level in C, and orientation at the global level and closure at local level in B). Participants were required to classify a set of four stimuli on the basis of either the variability present at the global level (the global classification task) or the variability present at the local level of the stimuli (the local classification task).

The results showed that global classification based on closure was as fast as local classification based on closure, whereas global classification based on line orientation was faster than local classification based on line orientation. Performance with the different stimulus sets showed that global and local classifications were equally fast for stimulus set A and for stimulus set B, both of which had closure at the local level. Global classification was faster than local classification for stimulus set C and for stimulus set D, both of which had line orientation at the local level. These results indicate that global advantage depended on the type of property involved in local discrimination. Global advantage was observed when local discrimination involved a simple property (line orientation), but not when it involved a configural property (closure).

Han, Humphreys, and Chen (1999) used different stimuli (arrows and triangles) and the typical global/local task. One set of stimuli consisted of larger arrows made of smaller arrows that varied in the orientation of the arrows (down left or down right). The orientation of the local arrows was

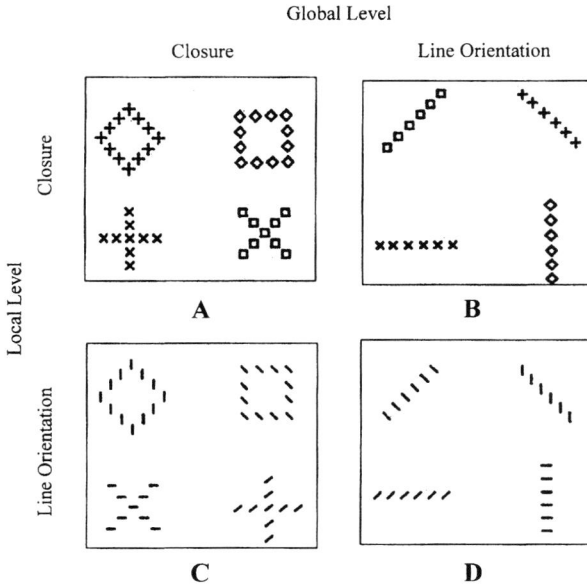

FIGURE 9.10. The stimulus sets in Kimchi's (1994, Experiment 5) global/local classification experiment. The stimuli are produced by orthogonal combination of type of property (closure—closed/open, line orientation) and hierarchical level (global, local). Reprinted from Kimchi (1994), with permission from Pion Ltd., London.

either consistent or inconsistent with that of the global arrow. Another set of stimuli consisted of larger arrows or triangles made up of arrows or triangles. The shapes at the global and the local levels were consistent or inconsistent. Han et al. found a global advantage (i.e., faster reaction times for global than for local identification and global-to-local interference) for both orientation discrimination and closure discrimination, but the global advantage was much weaker for the closure discrimination task than for the orientation discrimination task. Under divided-attention conditions, there was a global advantage for orientation but not for closure discrimination tasks. Interestingly, when participants responded to the orientation of line segments in closed shapes, global advantage was observed as in the case of orientation discrimination in open shapes, suggesting that it is the relevance of the property to task rather than its mere presence that matters.

Thus, both Kimchi's (1994) and Han et al.'s (1999) results indicate that relative global or local advantage for many-element patterns depends on whether discrimination at each level involves configural or simple properties. When local discrimination involves a configural property like closure, the global advantage markedly decreases or even disappears relative to the case in which discrimination at that level involves a simple property like orientation.

These findings converge with the findings reviewed earlier that show a relative perceptual dominance of configural properties. They also suggest that configural properties are not necessarily global or larger. Leeuwenberg and van der Helm (1991) also claim that holistic properties that dominate classification and discrimination of visual forms are not always global. According to the descriptive minimum principle approach proposed by Leeuwenberg and van der Helm, the specification of dominant properties can be derived from the simplest pattern representations, and it is the highest hierarchical level in the simplest pattern representation, the "superstructure," that dominates classification and discrimination of visual forms. The "superstructure" is not necessarily global or larger.

Dominance of Holistic Properties During the Microgenesis of the Percept

The findings discussed so far indicate that certain holistic/configural properties dominate discrimination and classification performance, and are accessible to rapid search. These findings, however, do not necessarily imply that holistic properties are available in early perceptual processing. This is especially the case with discrimination and classification performance because it can be based on later rather than earlier representations.

A different, perhaps more direct way to examine the availability of holistic properties in early perception is to study the time course of the development of the percept, namely the microgenesis of the percept. This microgenetic analysis would reveal information about the relative dominance of holistic and component properties during the evolution of the percept.

Kimchi (1998, 2000) used primed matching to study the microgenesis of the perceptual organization of hierarchical stimuli and line configurations. The basic procedure (Beller, 1971) is as follows. Participants view a priming stimulus followed immediately by a pair of test figures, and they must judge, as rapidly as possible, whether the two test figures are the same as each other or different from one another. The speed of *same* responses to the test figures depends on the representational similarity between the prime and the test figures: responses are faster when the test figures are similar to the prime than when they are dissimilar to it. Thus, primed matching enables us to assess implicitly the participant's perceptual representations. By varying the duration of the prime, we can tap earlier and later representations (Kimchi, 1998, 2000; Sekuler & Palmer, 1992). The logic underlying these experiments is as follows. At a short prime duration only the early representation of the priming stimulus is available and can act as a prime. Therefore, responses to test figures that are similar to the early representation of the priming stimulus should be facilitated.

Later representations are available only at longer prime durations, facilitating positive responses to test figures that are similar to these representations. Thus, if we construct test figures that are similar to the prime in configural or in component properties, then responses to such test pairs at different prime durations should reveal which properties are available in earlier and later representations of the priming stimulus.

Microgenesis of the Perceptual Organization of Hierarchical Stimuli

Kimchi (1998) studied the microgenesis of the perceptual organization of hierarchical stimuli that vary in number and relative size of their elements. The priming stimuli were few- and many-element patterns presented for various durations (from 40 ms to 690 ms). The test stimuli consisted of two hierarchical patterns each. There were two types of same-response test pairs defined by the similarity relation between the test figures and the prime. In the element-similarity test pair, the figures were similar to the prime in their elements but differed in their configurations. In the configuration-similarity test pair, the test figures were similar to the prime in their global configurations but differed in their elements. In addition, an X was presented as a neutral prime, and served as a baseline condition for the two types of test pairs. An example of priming stimuli and their respective same- and different-response test pairs is presented in figure 9.11A.

If the local elements are initially represented and the global configuration is constructed only later, then at short prime durations correct "same" responses to the element—similarity test figures are expected to be faster than responses to the configuration-similarity test figures. The opposite pattern of results is expected if the global configuration is initially represented. In that case, at short prime durations correct "same" responses to the configuration-similarity test figures are expected to be faster than responses to the test figures having the same elements as the prime. Given that prime-test similarity in elements entails dissimilarity in configuration, and vice versa (see figure 9.11A), two possible effects may contribute to differences between configuration-similarity and element-similarity test pairs: a facilitation owing to prime-test similarity, and an interference due to prime-test dissimilarity. Facilitation and inhibition are assessed in comparison to the neutral condition. At longer prime durations, the differences between the two types of test pairs are expected to disappear because presumably both the global configuration and the elements are represented by then.

The results for the few-element stimuli, presented in figure 9.11B, showed an early representation of the local elements: prime-test similarity in elements produced faster responses than similarity in configuration at the shorter prime durations (40, 90, and 190 ms). This difference was mainly due to interference produced by dissimilarity in elements. The ab-

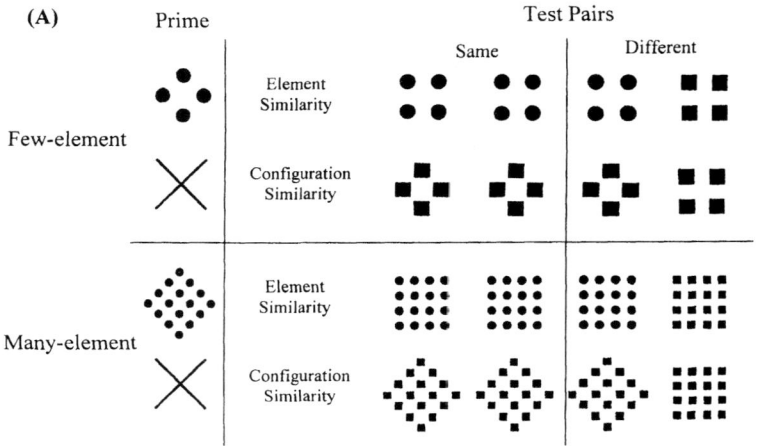

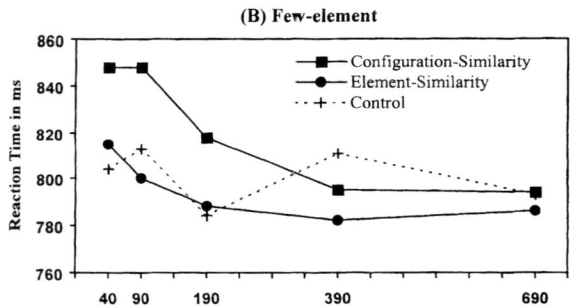

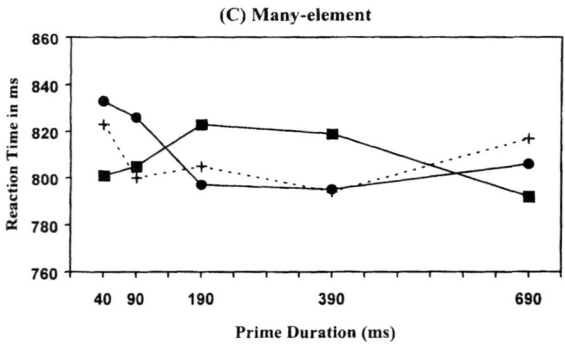

FIGURE 9.11. (A) Examples of the priming stimuli and the same- and different-response test pairs for few-element and many-element patterns in Kimchi's (1998) primed-matching experiment with hierarchical stimuli. (B) Mean correct same RTs for each prime-test similarity (element-similarity, configuration-similarity, and neutral) as a function of prime duration, for the few-element primes, and (C) for the many-element primes. Adapted with permission from Kimchi 1998.

sence of facilitation for the element-similarity condition suggests an early representation of the configuration, albeit a weak one. No significant differences between element and configuration similarity, and no significant facilitation or inhibition, were observed at the longer prime durations of 390 and 690 ms, suggesting that by then elements and configuration were equally available for priming.

The results for the many-element stimuli (figure 9.11C) showed an early representation of the configuration: prime-test similarity in configuration produced faster responses than similarity in elements at the shorter prime durations (40 and 90 ms). Both facilitation owing to configuration similarity and inhibition owing to configuration dissimilarity contributed to this difference. The pattern of reaction time seemed to reverse at the longer prime duration of 190 and 390 ms: element similarity actually produced significantly faster responses than similarity in configuration. No priming effects were observed at the 690 ms prime duration.

Taken together, these results indicate that the relative dominance of global configuration and elements in the course of the organization of hierarchical stimuli depends on the number and relative size of the elements. A pattern composed of a few, relatively large elements is represented initially in terms of both its individual elements and its global configuration, but the representation of the global configuration is weaker than that of the elements. The global configuration consolidates with time and becomes equally available for priming as the elements at around 400 ms. On the other hand, the initial representation of a pattern composed of many, relatively small elements is its global configuration, without individuation of the elements. The individuation of the elements occurs later in time: the elements are available for priming at about 200 ms, and for a while they seem to be somewhat more readily available for priming than the global configuration. By 700 ms, the global configuration and the elements of the many-element patterns seem to be equally available for priming.

The finding of early representation of the global configuration of many-element stimuli is compatible with the global advantage effects under short exposure durations (e.g., Navon, 1977; Paquet & Merikle, 1984), and the availability of the global configuration to rapid search (Kimchi, 1998), observed for similar many-element stimuli. Furthermore, the findings from visual search discussed earlier indicate that the individuation of the local elements of many-element patterns not only consumes time but also demands focused attention. These results also suggest that the consolidation of the global configuration of few-element patterns demands attention.

Microgenesis of the Perceptual Organization of Line Configurations

Configural dominance in discrimination and classification tasks was observed both for connected line configurations (e.g., Kimchi & Bloch, 1998;

Lasaga, 1989) and for disconnected ones (e.g., Kimchi, 1994). Kimchi (2000) studied the relative dominance of the configurations and the component lines during the microgenesis of such stimuli, again using primed matching. In one experiment (Kimchi, 2000, Experiment 1), the priming stimuli were a diamond and a cross that varied in the connectedness between their line components (no gap, small gap, and large gap), and were presented at various durations (from 40 to 390 ms). The figures in the configuration-similarity test pair were similar to the prime in both configuration and line components, whereas the figures in the component-similarity test pair were similar to the prime in lines but dissimilar in configuration. A random array of dots was used as a neutral prime and served as a control condition for the assessment of facilitation and inhibition effects. The priming stimuli and the same- and different-response test pairs are presented in figure 9.12. For this set of stimuli, priming effects of the configuration would manifest in facilitation for the configuration-similarity condition, and possibly interference for the component-similarity condition (owing to dissimilarity in configuration). Priming effects of the line components would manifest in facilitation for both similarity conditions (because both types of test pairs are similar to the prime in components).

The results (see figure 9.13) showed early availability of the configuration, manifested in facilitation for the configuration-similarity test pairs and inhibition for the component-similarity test pairs observed under the shortest exposure duration of 40 ms. These effects were more pronounced for the no-gap (A) and the small-gap (B) conditions than for the large-gap condition (C), suggesting that proximity between the line segments has an effect on the early availability of global configuration and components.

In a second experiment, with the stimuli presented in figure 9.14A, no effect of proximity was found (Kimchi, 2000, Experiment 2). In this experiment, the primes were square configurations that varied in proximity between the components (small gap, large gap). The figures in the configuration-similarity test pair were similar to the prime in configuration but dissimilar in components, whereas the figures in the component-similarity test pair were similar to the prime in components but dissimilar in configuration. For this set of stimuli, priming effects of the configuration would manifest in facilitation for the configuration similarity condition and possibly interference for the component similarity condition (owing to dissimilarity in configuration). Priming effects of the line components would manifest in facilitation for component similarity conditions and possibly interference for the configuration similarity condition (owing to dissimilarity in components).

The results, presented in figure 9.14B and C, showed priming effects of the configuration (i.e., facilitation for configuration-similarity and inhibition for component-similarity) that were equally strong and equally

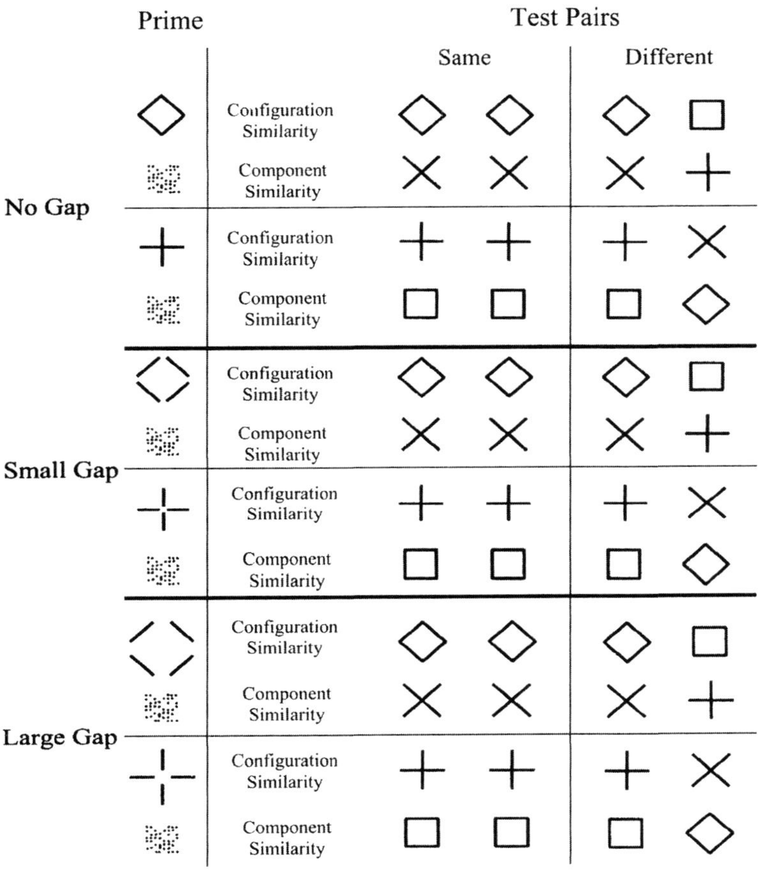

FIGURE 9.12. The priming stimuli and the same- and different-response test pairs for the no gap, small gap, and large gap conditions, in Kimchi's (2000, Experiment 1) primed-matching experiment with line configurations. Adapted with permission from Kimchi (2000).

early (observed under 40 ms prime duration) for strong proximity/small gap (B) and weak proximity/large gap (C). The results of these two experiments suggest that proximity between components seems to have a larger effect on the relative dominance of the global configuration when only closure (as in the diamond prime) or only collinearity (as in the cross prime) is present in the stimulus than when closure and collinearity are combined (as in the latter square primes).

A recent study by Kimchi and Hadad (2002) showed early priming

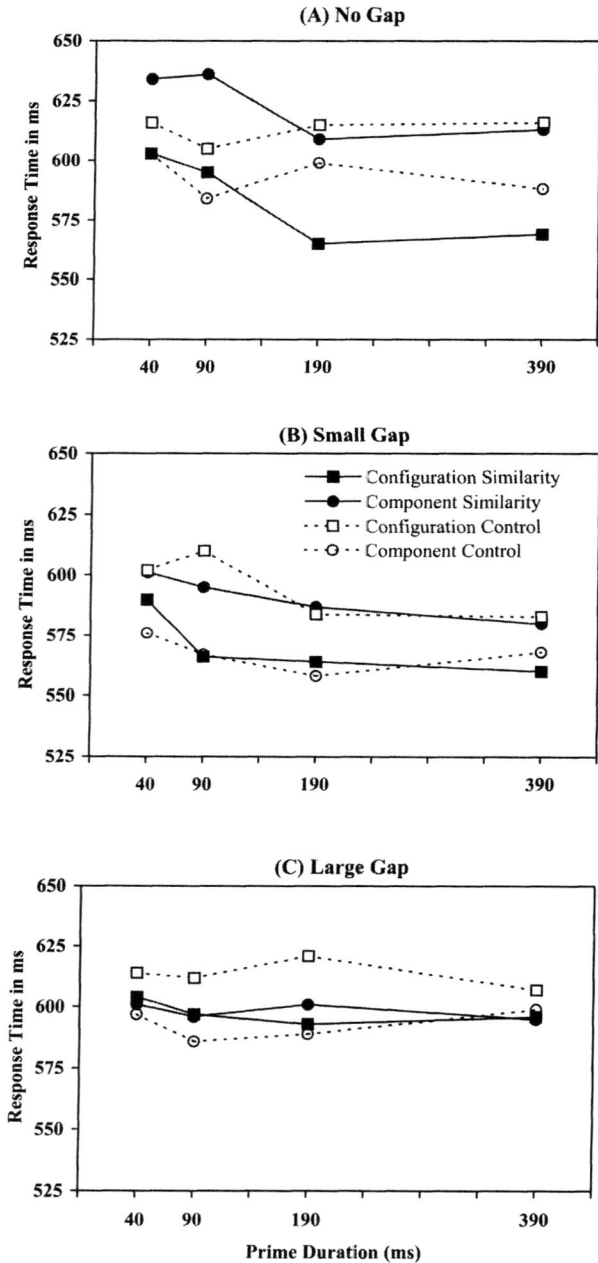

FIGURE 9.13. Mean correct same RTs for each prime-test similarity as a function of prime duration (collapsed across prime type) for each gap condition in the primed-matching experiment with line configurations. Reprinted from Kimchi (2000) with permission from Elsevier Science.

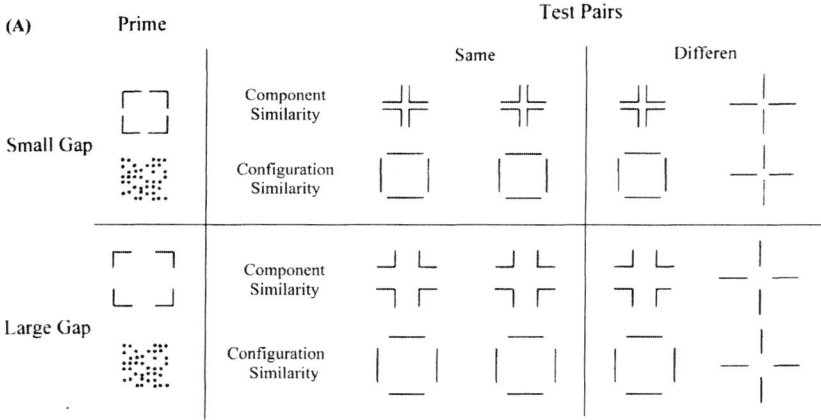

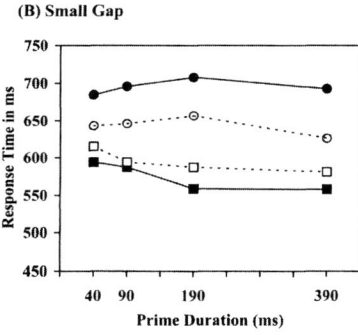

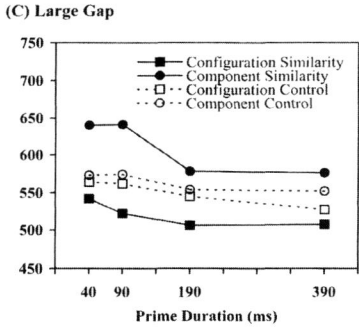

FIGURE 9.14. (A) The priming stimuli and the same- and different-response test pairs for the small gap and large gap conditions in Kimchi's (2000, Experiment 2) primed-matching experiment with square configurations. (B) Mean correct "same" RTs for each prime-test similarity as a function of prime duration for small gap, and (C) for large gap. Reprinted from Kimchi (2000) with permission from Elsevier Science.

effects of the configuration even in the absence of collinearity or closure when the disconnected primes were familiar (upright letters). The configuration of similar disconnected unfamiliar primes (inverted letters) was available only later in time.

Taken together, the microgenetic analysis revealed relative dominance of global configuration or elements at different times along the progressive development of the percept, depending on the number of elements and their relative size (for hierarchical stimuli), and an early configural organization of line segments, the strength of which depends on proximity, collinearity, closure, and familiarity.

Analytic Versus Holistic Perception Revisited

The conventional early feature-analysis view holds that early perceptual processing is characterized by rapid processes that extract simple features in parallel over space and register them in independent spatiotopic maps. Whole objects are constructed by integration of these simple features via serial and time-consuming processes (e.g., Treisman, 1986, 1991).

The findings reviewed in this chapter clearly challenge this view. Holistic properties, namely properties that are defined as a function of interrelations among components, have been found to dominate discrimination and classification performance (e.g., Kimchi, 1994), to be accessible to rapid search (e.g., Rensink & Enns, 1995), and to be available for priming even under very short exposure durations (Kimchi, 1998, 2000). These findings provide converging evidence for early representation of holistic properties. In light of this evidence, a view that holds that only simple features are available in early perceptual processing and that these features are integrated later to produce perceptual wholes is hardly tenable. However, several findings suggest that positing holistic primacy as a rigid perceptual law is hardly tenable, either. Early relative dominance of either global structure or of components has been found, depending on certain stimulus factors (Kimchi, 1998, 2000). Configural dominance has been found with certain configurations but not with others (e.g., Pomerantz, 1981), and the relative dominance of configural properties versus component properties has been found to depend on its relevance to the task at hand (e.g., Han et al., 1999; Pomerantz & Pristach, 1989).

It is possible, then, that the resolution of the controversy between early feature-analysis and holistic primacy will not rest on one or the other side of the analytic versus holistic dichotomy. The results of the microgenetic analysis (Kimchi, 1998, 2000) are particularly instructive because they show that the relative dominance of configural and component properties varies during the evolution of the percept. The most important implication of the microgenetic results is that early perceptual processing involves organization, presumably grouping and segregation processes as proposed by Gestalt psychology. These processes rely on a host of cues, such as proximity, connectedness, collinearity, closure, and symmetry. Recent research has shown that input from higher level object representations also contributes to rapid grouping and segmentation (e.g., Kimchi & Hadad, 2002; Peterson, 1994, chapter 10 this volume; Peterson & Gibson, 1994; Vecera & Farah, 1997).

This view of early organizational processes implies that early perceptual processing involves interactions among components, and in this sense it can be considered holistic or global. However, organizational processes do not necessarily render the dominance of the global or the configural aspects. Grouping can produce weak or strong configurations, a mere aggregation of elements, or configurations that preempt the components. Furthermore, it is suggested that organization is flexible to a degree; it may change during the microgenesis of the percept, and may even be somewhat modulated by task requirements. An important empirical issue is to determine the conditions and the cues that support strong versus weak grouping. For example, recent findings indicate that closure is a powerful grouping cue (Han et al., 1999; Kimchi, 1994; Kovacs & Julesz, 1994). Further research is required to address this issue.

The popularity of the early feature-analysis view has been in part due to the logical relations between components and configurations: components can exist without a global configuration, but a global configuration cannot exist without components, therefore components need to be prior to the configuration. Similarly, if holistic/configural properties do not inhere in the component properties but rather emerge from the interrelations among components, then logic dictates the priority of the components. However, the logical structure of the stimulus does not necessarily predict processing consequences (see Garner, 1983; Kimchi, 1992; Kimchi & Palmer, 1985). Consider, for example, hierarchical patterns like the ones presented in figures 9.3 and 9.11. Such patterns provide a clear case of asymmetry in the logical structure of the stimuli, and this asymmetry holds both for few- and many-element patterns. Yet, few- and many-element patterns differ from one another in their perceived organization (Kimchi & Palmer, 1982), in the perceptual relations between elements and configuration (Kimchi & Palmer, 1985; Klein & Barresi, 1985), and in the microgenesis of their organization (Kimchi, 1998). These findings demonstrate that processing assumptions cannot be made on the basis of logical relations in the stimulus domain alone.

In the same vein, the description of holistic or configural properties as "emergent" is only supported as a description of the stimulus. There is no actual necessity for emergent properties to be perceptually derived. Configural properties might be computed from relevant component properties, but it is also possible that they are directly detected by the perceptual system (i.e., without the component properties having a psychological reality of their own). Thus, both component and holistic properties (whether "emergent" or not) must be treated as stimulus aspects. Whether holistic properties dominate component properties at a certain level of processing or whether they are extracted earlier than component properties are empirical questions.

Another major contributor to the popularity of the early feature-analysis view has been influence from physiology. Earlier work on the physiology of vision, most notably the work of Hubel and Wiesel (e.g., 1959, 1968), has fostered the idea of specific feature detectors that extract simple stimulus features, and the feed-forward view. The flow of neural information from the retina to the higher level cortical areas has been characterized as proceeding from responses to simple features in small receptive fields to responses to more complex stimulus configurations in larger receptive fields, in a strictly feed-forward way.

Serious concerns have been raised, however, about using physiological evidence to draw conclusions about perceptual experience (e.g., Uttal, 1997), as the relations between neural events and perceptual experience are not straightforward. But even within a physiological framework, recent findings, in the cortex, of horizontal interactions and massive back projections from higher to lower centers of the visual system (see Spillmann, 1999, for a review) challenge the classical feed-forward view and suggest a highly interactive system. For example, responses of neurons in the primary visual cortex (V1) to stimuli inside the classical receptive fields can be modulated by contextual stimuli outside the receptive field, (e.g., Lamme, Super, & Spekreijse, 1998; Zipser, Lamme, & Schiller, 1996), suggesting that even the earliest stage of visual cortical processing is involved in complex visual perception. These and similar findings suggest that certain holistic perceptual phenomena such as configural superiority are not unfeasible from a physiological point of view, as has been widely assumed.

Concluding Remarks

Both psychological and physiological evidence suggest that early perceptual processing provides more sophisticated structures than has been assumed by the early feature-analysis view. Psychological studies have provided converging evidence (much of which has been reviewed in this chapter) for perceptual primacy of certain holistic properties, suggesting that perceptual wholes are not perceived by independent processing of components. Physiological studies indicate that organization (i.e., grouping and segregation) takes place as early as the primary visual cortex (e.g., Westheimer, 1999). These recent developments in psychological and physiological research on visual perception make the controversy between analytic and holistic perception seem too simplistic. Given that the goal of the perceptual system is identification and recognition of objects, scenes, and events in the environment, it is possible that the human perceptual system is more sensitive to configural properties because they are environmentally relevant. But no sequential model, either a model in which component properties are extracted first, followed by the extraction of configural properties, or one in which configural properties precede component properties, is compatible with recent findings. There is now increasing evidence that suggests a highly interactive perceptual system in which both simple properties and holistic/configural properties are represented in the early organization of a visual object.

References

Ambler, B. A., Keel, R., & Phelps, E. (1978). A foveal discriminability difference for one vs. four letters. *Bulletin of the Psychonomic Society, 11*(5), 317–320.

Beck, J. (1966). Perceptual grouping produced by changes in orientation and shape. *Science, 154,* 538–540.

Beck, J. (1967). Perceptual grouping produced by line figures. *Perception and Psychophysics, 2*(11), 491–495.

Beck, J. (1982). Textural segmentation. In J. Beck (Ed.), *Organization and representation in perception* (pp. 285–317). Hillsdale, NJ: Erlbaum.

Behrmann, M., & Kimchi, R. (in press). Visual perceptual organization: Lessons from lesions. In R. Kimchi, M. Behrmann, & C. Olson (Eds.), *Perceptual organization in vision: Behavioral and neurological perspectives.* Hillsdale, NJ: Erlbaum.

Beller, H. K. (1971). Priming: Effects of advance information on matching. *Journal of Experimental Psychology, 87,* 176–182.

Boer, L. C., & Keuss, P. J. G. (1982). Global precedence as a postperceptual effect: An analysis of speed-accuracy tradeoff functions. *Perception & Psychophysics, 13,* 358–366.

Broadbent, D. E. (1977). The hidden preattentive process. *American Psychologist,* 109–118.

Chen, L. (1982). Topological structure in visual perception. *Science, 218*(4573), 699–700.

Duncan, J., & Humphreys, G. W. (1989). Visual search and stimulus similarity. *Psychological Review, 96*(3), 433–458.

Earhard, B. (1980). The line-in-object superiority effect in perception: It depends on where you fix your eyes and what is located at the point of fixation. *Perception and Psychophysics, 28*(1), 9–18.

Earhard, B., & Armitage, R. (1980). From an object-superiority effect to an object-inferiority effect with movement of the fixation point. *Perception and Psychophysics, 28*(4), 369–376.

Enns, J. T., & Kingstone, A. (1995). Access to global and local properties in visual search for compound stimuli. *Psychological Science, 6*(5), 283–291.

Enns, J. T., & Prinzmetal, W. (1984). The role of redundancy in the object-line effect. *Perception and Psychophysics, 35*(1), 22–32.

Enns, J. T., & Rensink, R. A. (1990). Influence of scene-based properties on visual search. *Science, 24,* 721–723.

Enns, J. T., & Rensink, R. A. (1991). Pre-attentive recovery of three-dimensional orientation from line drawings. *Psychological Review, 98*(3), 335–351.

Garner, W. E. (1978). Aspects of a stimulus: Features, dimensions, and configurations. In E. Rosch & B. B. Lloyd (Eds.), *Cognition and categorization* (pp. 99–133): Hillsdale, NJ: Erlbaum.

Garner, W. R. (1983). Asymmetric interactions of stimulus dimensions in perceptual information processing. In T. J. Tighe & B. E. Shepp (Eds.), *Perception, cognition, and development: Interactional analysis.* Hillsdale, NJ: Erlbaum.

Han, S., Fan, S., Chen, L., & Zhuo, Y. (1997). On the different processing of wholes and parts: A psychophyiological analysis. *Journal of Cognitive Neuroscience, 9,* 687–698.

Han, S., Humphreys, G. W., & Chen, L. (1999). Parallel and competitive processes in hierarchical analysis: Perceptual grouping and encoding of closure. *Journal of Experimental Psychology: Human Perception and Performance, 25*(5), 1411–1432.

Hubel, D. H., & Wiesel, T. N. (1959). Receptive fields of single neurones in the cat's striate cortex. *Journal of Physiology, 148,* 574–591.

Hubel, D. H., & Wiesel, T. N. (1962). Receptive fields, binocular interaction and functional architecture in the cat's visual cortex. *Journal of Physiology London, 160*(1), 106–154.

Hubel, D. H., & Wiesel, T. N. (1968). Receptive fields and functional architecture of monkey striate cortex. *Journal of Physiology, 195,* 215–243.

Hubel, D. H., & Wiesel, T. N. (1977). Functional architecture of macaque monkey visual cortex. *Proceedings of the Royal Society of London, B, 198,* 1–59.

Ivry, R., & Robertson, L. C. (1998). *The two sides of perception.* Cambridge, MA: MIT Press.

Julesz, B. (1981). Figure and ground perception in briefly presented isodipole textures. In M. Kubovy & J. R. Pomerantz (Eds.), *Perceptual organization* (pp. 27–54). Hillsdale, NJ: Erlbaum.

Julesz, B. (1984). Textons, the elements of texture perception, and their interactions. *Nature, 290,* 91–97.

Kimchi, R. (1988). Selective attention to global and local levels in the comparison of hierarchical patterns. *Perception and Psychophysics, 43,* 189–198.

Kimchi, R. (1992). Primacy of wholistic processing and global/local paradigm: A critical review. *Psychological Bulletin, 112*(1), 24–38.

Kimchi, R. (1994). The role of wholistic/configural properties versus global properties in visual form perception. *Perception, 23,* 489–504.

Kimchi, R. (1998). Uniform connectedness and grouping in the perceptual organization of hierarchical patterns. *Journal of Experimental Psychology: Human Perception and Performance, 24*(2), 1105–1118.

Kimchi, R. (2000). The perceptual organization of visual objects: A microgenetic analysis. *Vision Research, 40,* 1333–1347.

Kimchi, R., & Bloch, B. (1998). Dominance of configural properties in visual form perception. *Psychonomic Bulletin and Review, 5*(1), 135–139.

Kimchi, R., & Hadad, B. (2002). Influence of past experience on perceptual grouping. *Psychological Science, 13,* 41–47.

Kimchi, R., & Palmer, S. E. (1982). Form and texture in hierarchically constructed patterns. *Journal of Experimental Psychology: Human Perception and Performance, 8*(4), 521–535.

Kimchi, R., & Palmer, S. E. (1985). Separability and integrality of global and local levels of hierarchical patterns. *Journal of Experimental Psychology: Human Perception and Performance, 11*(6), 673–688.

Kimchi, R., & Peled, A. (1999). *The role of element size in the early organization of hierarchical stimuli.* Unpublished manuscript.

Kinchla, R. A., & Wolfe, J. M. (1979). The order of visual processing: "Top-down," "bottom-up," or "middle-out." *Perception and Psychophysics, 25*(3), 225–231.

Kleffner, D. A., & Ramachandran, V. S. (1992). On the perception of shape from shading. *Perception & Psychophysics, 52,* 18–36.

Klein, R. (1978). Visual detection of line segments: Two exceptions to the object superiority effect. *Perception and Psychophysics, 24*(3), 237–242.

Klein, R. M., & Barresi, J. (1985). Perceptual salience of form versus material as a function of variations in spacing and number of elements. *Perception & Psychophysics, 73*, 440–446.

Koffka, K. (1935). *Principles of Gestalt psychology.* New York: Harcourt Brace Jovanovich.

Kohler, W. (1929/1947). *Gestalt psychology.* New York: Liveright.

Kovacs, I., & Julesz, B. (1994). Perceptual sensitivity maps within globally defined visual shapes. *Nature, 370*(6491), 644–646.

Kubovy, M., & Pomerantz, J. (Eds.). (1981). *Perceptual organization.* Hillsdale, NJ: Erlbaum.

LaGasse, L. L. (1994). Effects of good form and spatial frequency on global precedence. *Perception & Psychophysics, 53*, 89–105.

Lamb, M. R., & Robertson, L. (1988). The processing of hierarchical stimuli: Effects of retinal locus, location uncertainty, and stimulus identity. *Perception and Psychophysics, 44*, 172–181.

Lamme, V. A., Super, H., & Spekreijse, H. (1998). Feedforward, horizontal, and feedback processing in the visual cortex. *Current Opinions in Neurobiology, 8*, 529–535.

Lanze, M., Weisstein, N., & Harris, J. R. (1982). Perceived depth vs. structural relevance in the object-superiority effect. *Perception and Psychophysics, 31*(4) 376–382.

Lasaga, M. I. (1989). Gestalts and their components: Nature of information-precedence. In B. Shepp & S. Ballesteros (Eds.), *Object perception: Structure and process* (pp. 165–202). Hillsdale, NJ: Erlbaum.

Lasaga, M. I., & Garner, W. R. (1983). Effect of line orientation on various information-processing tasks. *Journal of Experimental Psychology: Human Perception and Performance, 9*(2), 215–225.

Leeuwenberg, E., & van der Helm, P. (1991). Unity and variety in visual form. *Perception, 20*(5), 595–622.

Luna, D. (1993). Effects of exposure duration and eccentricity of global and local information on processing dominance. *European Journal of Cognitive Psychology, 5*(2), 183–200.

Marr, D. (1982). *Vision.* San Francisco: W. H. Freeman.

Martin, M. (1979). Local and global processing: the role of sparsity. *Memory and Cognition, 7*, 476–484.

McClelland, J. L. (1978). Perception and masking of wholes and parts. *Journal of Experimental Psychology: Human Perception and Performance, 4*(2), 210–223.

McClelland, J. L., & Miller, J. (1979). Structural factors in figure perception. *Perception and Psychophysics, 26*(3), 221–229.

Miller, J. (1981a). Global precedence in attention and decision. *Journal of Experimental Psychology: Human Perception and Performance, 7*, 1161–1174.

Miller, J. (1981b). Global precedence: Information availability or use Reply to Navon. *Journal of Experimental Psychology: Human Perception and Performance, 7*, 1183–1185.

Navon, D. (1977). Forest before trees: The precedence of global features in visual perception. *Cognitive Psychology, 9*, 353–383.

Navon, D. (1991). Testing a queue hypothesis for the processing of global and local information. *Journal of Experimental Psychology: General, 120,* 173–189.

Navon, D., & Norman, J. (1983). Does global precedence really depend on visual angle? *Journal of Experimental Psychology: Human Perception and Performance, 9,* 955–965.

Neisser, U. (1967). *Cognitive psychology.* New York: Appleton-Century-Crofts.

Palmer, S. E., & Rock, I. (1994). Rethinking perceptual organization: The role of uniform connectedness. *Psychonomic Bulletin and Review, 1*(1), 29–55.

Paquet, L., & Merikle, P. M. (1984). Global precedence: The effect of exposure duration. *Canadian Journal of Psychology, 38,* 45–53.

Paquet, L., & Merikle, P. M. (1988). Global precedence in attended and nonattended objects. *Journal of Experimental Psychology: Human Perception and Performance, 14*(1), 89–100.

Peterson, M. A. (1994). Object recognition processes can and do operate before figure-ground organization. *Current Directions in Psychological Science, 3,* 105–111.

Peterson, M. A., & Gibson, B. S. (1994). Must shape recognition follow figure-ground organization? An assumption in peril. *Psychological Science, 9,* 253–259.

Pomerantz, J. R. (1981). Perceptual organization in information processing. In J. R. Pomerantz & M. Kubovy (Eds.), *Perceptual organization* (pp. 141–180). Hillsdale, NJ: Erlbaum.

Pomerantz, J. R. (1983). Global and local precedence: Selective attention in form and motion perception. *Journal of Experimental Psychology: General, 112*(4), 516–540.

Pomerantz, J. R., & Kubovy, M. (1986). Theoretical approaches to perceptual organization: Simplicity and likelihood principles. In K. R. Boff, L. Kaufman, & J. P. Thomas (Eds.), *Handbook of perception and human performance* (vol. 2, pp. 36.31–36.46). New York: Wiley.

Pomerantz, J. R., & Pristach, E. A. (1989). Emergent features, attention, and perceptual glue in visual form perception. *Journal of Experimental Psychology: Human Perception and Performance, 15,* 635–649.

Pomerantz, J. R., Sager, L. C., & Stoever, R. J. (1997). Perception of wholes and their component parts: Some configural superiority effects. *Journal of Experimental Psychology: Human Perception and Performance, 3*(3), 422–435.

Rensink, R. A., & Enns, J. T. (1995). Preemption effects in visual search: evidence for low-level grouping. *Psychological Review, 102,* 101–130.

Rock, I. (1986). The description and analysis of object and event perception. In K. R. Boff, L. Kaufman, & J. P. Thomas (Eds.), *Handbook of perception and human performance* (vol. 33, pp. 1–71). New York: Wiley.

Saarinen, J. (1995). Visual search for global and local stimuus features. *Perception & Psychophysics, 23,* 237–243.

Schiller, P. H. (1986). The central visual system. *Vision Research, 26*(9), 1351–1386.

Sebrechts, M. M., & Fragala, J. J. (1985). Variation on parts and wholes: Information precedence vs. global precedence., *Proceedings of the Seventh Annual Conference of the Cognitive Science Society,* 11–18.

Sekuler, A. B., & palmer, S. E. (1992). Perception of partly occluded objects: A microgenetic analysis. *Journal of Experimental Psychology: General, 121*(1), 95–111.

Shulman, G. L., & Wilson, J. (1987). Spatial frequency and selective attention to local and global information. *Neuropsychologia, 18,* 89–101.

Spillmann, L. (1999). From elements to perception: Local and global processing in visual neurons *Perception, 28,* 1461–1492.

Titchener, E. (1909). *Experimental psychology of the thought process.* New York: Macmillan.

Treisman, A. (1982). Perceptual grouping and attention in visual search for features and for objects. *Journal of Experimental Psychology: Human Perception and Performance, 8,* 194–214.

Treisman, A. (1986). Properties, parts and objects. In K. R. Boff, L. Kaufman, & J. P. Thomas (Eds.), *Handbook of perception and human performance* (vol. 35, pp. 1–70). New York: Wiley.

Treisman, A. (1988). Features and objects: The Fourteenth Bartlett Memorial Lecture. *Quarterly Journal of Experimental Psychology, 40A*(2), 201–237.

Treisman, A. (1991). Search, similarity, and integration of features between and within dimensions. *Journal of Experimental Psychology: Human Perception and Performance, 17*(3), 652–676.

Treisman, A., & Gelade, G. (1980). A feature-integration theory of attention. *Cognitive Psychology, 12,* 97–136.

Treisman, A., & Gormican, S. (1988). Feature analysis in early vision: Evidence from search asymmetries. *Psychological Review, 95*(1), 15–48.

Uttal, D. H. (1997). Do theoretical bridges exist between perceptual experience and neurophysiology? *Perspectives in Biology and Medicine, 40,* 280–302.

Uttal, W. R. (1988). *On seeing forms.* Hillsdale, NJ: Erlbaum.

Vecera, S. P., & Farah, M. J. (1997). Is visual image segmentation a bottom-up or an interactive process? *Perception and Psychophysics, 59,* 1280–1296.

Ward, L. M. (1982). Determinants of attention to local and global features of visual forms. *Journal of Experimental Psychology: Human Perception and Performance, 8,* 562–581.

Weisstein, N., & Harris, C. S. (1974). Visual detection of line segments: An object-superiority effect. *Science, 186*(4165), 752–755.

Weisstein, N., Williams, M. C., & Harris, C. S. (1982). Depth, connectedness, and structural relevance in the object-superiority effect. Line segments are harder to see in flatter patterns. *Perception, 11*(1), 5–17.

Wertheimer, M. (1923/1955). Gestalt theory. In W. D. Ellis (Ed.), *A source book of Gestalt psychology* (pp. 1–16). London: Routledge & Kegan Paul.

Westheimer, G. (1999). Gestalt theory reconfigured: Max Wertheimer's anticipation of recent developments in visual neuroscience. *Perception, 18,* 5–15.

Williams, A., & Weisstein, N. (1978). Line segments are perceived better in a coherent context than alone: An object-line effect in visual perception. *Memory and Cognition, 6*(2), 85–90.

Williams, D. (1992). Cooperative parallel processing in depth, motion, and texture perception. In J. Brannan (Ed.), *Applications of parallel processing in vision* (pp. 167–225). Amsterdam: North Holland.

Wolfe, J. M., Friedman-Hill, S., & Bilsky, A. R. (1994). Parallel processing of part-whole information in visual search tasks. *Perception and Psychophysics, 55*(5), 537–550.

Yovel, G., Yovel, I., & Levy, J. (2001). Hemispheric asymmetries for global and local visual perception: Effects of stimulus and task factors. *Journal of Experimental Psychology: Human Perception and Performance, 27,* 1369–1385.

Zeki, S. (1978). Functional specialization in the visual cortex of the rhesus monkey. *Nature, 274,* 423.

Zeki, S. (1993). *A vision of the brain.* Cambridge, MA: Blackwell Scientific Publications.

Zipser, K., Lamme, V. A., & Schiller, P. H. (1996). Contextual modulation in primary visual cortex. *Journal of Neuroscience, 16,* 7376–7389.

10

Overlapping Partial Configurations in Object Memory

An Alternative Solution to Classic Problems in Perception and Recognition

MARY A. PETERSON

The assumption that depth and figure-ground assignment are established before object memories are accessed—the "depth-and-figure-first assumption"—provided a foundation for much visual perception and visual cognition research in the 20th century. Its foundational status arose in part because it was a critical component of the Gestalt psychologists' critique overturning the Structuralist view. The Structuralists held that the visual field was organized primarily by the operation of past experience. In contrast, the Gestalt psychologists proposed that some initial aspects of organization—grouping and figure-ground segregation in particular—must be accomplished before past experience can affect perception. To support their view with respect to figure-ground segregation, the Gestaltists showed that a border shared by two novel regions was more likely be seen as the bounding edge of the region that was relatively smaller in area, more convex, enclosed, and/or symmetric. The novel region to which the bounding edge was assigned was seen as the shaped *figure*. The region lying on the opposite side of the border typically appeared to be shapeless (at least near the shared border) and to continue behind the figure, forming a back*ground* for the figure.

The Gestalt psychologists demonstrated that factors like symmetry, convexity, relative area, and enclosure affected figure assignment with novel displays—displays for which past experience putatively could not affect perception. They assumed that these factors were innate and did not depend upon past experience. The Gestalt psychologists called these factors "configural cues" because they affected the likelihood that a region would appear to be shaped (i.e., to be seen as a *configuration*). In order to avoid using the term "configural" differently in this chapter from the way it is used in many of the other chapters in this volume, I will refer to the Gestalt "configural cues" as the Gestalt "shaping cues." As in the other chapters in this book, the terms "configural" and "configuration" will refer to information concerning parts (features)[1] and their spatial interrelationships.

Another reason for the foundational status of the depth-and-figure-first assumption is that it provides a solution to an object-recognition problem arising on another commonly held assumption, the "holistic-substrate assumption." In the holistic-substrate assumption, whole, bounded regions of uniform color, luminance, texture, and so on form the substrate for object recognition. Before object memories are accessed, whole regions might be subdivided into parts (or features), but all parts (features) detected for a given region would be matched to object memories. This holistic-substrate assumption raises a problem, called the "intrinsic contour problem" by Nakayama, Shimojo, and Silverman (1989). The intrinsic contour problem will be defined by reference to figure 10.1a, which depicts multiple objects located at different distances from the viewer. For

a.

b.

FIGURE 10.1. A schematic representation of three objects located at different distances from a viewer (a). The white regions outlined in black portray a cat and a pine tree. The black region is clearly seen to portray a woman. In (b), the black region has been extracted from the scene in (a) so that its bounding contours can be seen. It is clear that the contours on the bottom and right side are not intrinsic to a woman.

such three-dimensional scenes it is likely that, from any given vantage point, the projections of at least some of the objects will overlap. With overlap, the bounding edges of regions in the visual field do not necessarily correspond to the bounding edges of objects. The black region in figure 10.1a provides a good example. The viewer can readily identify the black region as a silhouette of a woman (who is standing behind and to the left of a white tree, with a white cat sitting in front of her). In figure 10.1b, the black region has been extracted from the scene above. Here it can clearly be seen that a substantial amount of the bounding contour of the black region—the portion along the bottom and the right side—is unlikely to be the boundary of a woman. These portions of the bounding contour are "extrinsic" to the object portrayed by the black region, whereas the remaining portions are "intrinsic" to that object. It has been argued that recognition processes conducted over whole regions would surely fail unless there were some way to first eliminate extrinsic portions of the bounding contours so that only intrinsic contours are matched to object memories (Nakayama et al., 1989).

Nakayama et al. (1989) used the depth-and-figure-first assumption to solve the intrinsic contour problem. They proposed that, following depth segregation, those edges lying on roughly the same depth plane (or surface) are deemed intrinsic edges for purposes of object recognition, whereas edges lying on different depth planes are deemed extrinsic and, hence, irrelevant for recognition processes. Thus, although Nakayama et al. (1989) dropped the assumption that recognition operates over entire bounded regions, the application of the depth-and-figure-first assumption allowed them to retain a version of the holistic-substrate assumption in which object recognition operates over whole *surfaces* rather than over whole regions.

The depth-and-figure-first assumption has played an important role in our understanding of visual perception and cognition. Evidence obtained in my laboratory shows that it is a false and unnecessary assumption, however. In this chapter, I begin by briefly reviewing evidence indicating that, contrary to the depth-and-figure-first assumption, memories of object structure are accessed before, and exert an influence on, figure assignment. I then show that the intrinsic contour problem can be solved without appealing to the depth-and-figure-first assumption, if one also drops the holistic-substrate assumption. The intrinsic contour problem does not arise if one assumes that those object memories that affect figure assignment are (1) *partial*, in that they are smaller than an entire region or surface, and (2) *configurational*, in that they specify a configuration of parts or features rather than a single part or feature. Next, I report empirical evidence consistent with the operation of partial configurational object memories. Finally, historical antecedents for the notion of partial configurations will be discussed (e.g., Mozer, 1991; Wickelgren, 1969) and integrated with both recent physiological evidence (e.g., K. Tanaka, 1996) and recent computational investigations (e.g., Ullman, 2001).

Evidence of Object-Memory Effects on Figure Assignment

Despite the almost universal acceptance of the depth-and-figure-first assumption, evidence supporting it is surprisingly scant; it arises from two lines of research. First, the Gestalt psychologists demonstrated that perceptual organization *could* occur without any contribution from past experience. These demonstrations were taken to indicate that perceptual organization *always* occurred without any contribution from past experience. Reaching the latter conclusion is clearly an instance of faulty logic, however (Peterson, 1999). Second, Warrington and James (1988) showed that a visual agnosic, whose ability to identify objects was impaired, could, nevertheless, perform figure-ground tasks normally. On the assumption that a lesion interferes with higher level processes but leaves lower level processes intact, this pattern of behavior was interpreted as evidence that figure-ground segregation precedes access to object memories (e.g., Marr, 1982). This conclusion, too, is faulty. It is simply not the case that all patterns of intact versus spared processes indicate that the processes are hierarchically ordered. Indeed, Peterson, de Gelder, Rapcsak, Gerhardstein, & Bachoud-Lévi (2000) tested another visual agnosic, AD, on a task assessing influences on figure assignment from memories of object structure. The type of task we used will be described below. For now, suffice it to say that AD showed normal influences from object memories on figure assignment, even though she was severely impaired at identifying objects. Thus, it seems that identification responses cannot serve as an adequate index of whether or not object memories are accessed before figure-ground relationships are determined.

Until my students and I began investigating whether or not object memories could be accessed prior to figure assignment, there were no direct tests of this question (see Peterson, 1999). Figure 10.2 shows samples of the displays we used to investigate whether or not past experience with particular objects could affect figure assignment. In each display, two adjacent regions shared at least one border. The shared border sketched a known object along one side; this side of the border was called the *high-denotative side* because a large percentage of pilot observers agreed on which object was portrayed there. (Therefore, on that side, the border was taken to *explicitly refer to*, or *to denote*, that known object.) The pilot observers did not tend to agree on a single known object that could be seen along the opposite side of the border. In fact, very few reported that any known object was portrayed there. Therefore, the side of the border opposite to the high-denotative side was called the *low-denotative side*. We assumed that the high- and low-denotative sides of the border differed in the degree to which they provided a good match to object memories, with the high-denotative side providing a good match and the low-denotative side providing a poor match (Peterson, Harvey, & Weidenbacher, 1991).

We showed these displays to observers in either an upright orientation

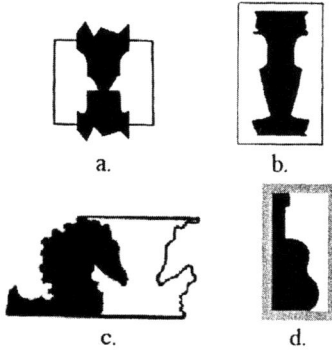

FIGURE 10.2. Sample displays used in research in my laboratory. The displays in (a) and (b) are biased toward the interpretation that the black region is the figure. In (a), the T-junctions where the frame of the white region meets the border of the black region are cues that the black region is in front. In (b), the black region is symmetric and enclosed. The white regions are high in denotivity, however. Hook-nosed face profiles are sketched along the white side of the vertical portions of the black-white border in (a); standing women are sketched along the white side in (b). These displays were originally published in Peterson et al. (1991). © 1991 by the American Psychological Association. Reprinted with permission. In (c), the black region is high in denotivity (it portrays a portion of a seahorse when it is seen as figure) and the white region is symmetric around a vertical axis. Peterson and Gibson (1994) used displays like these to investigate the relative strength of the object memory cue and the Gestalt configural cue of symmetry. (The displays used by Peterson and Gibson (1994) were presented on gray backgrounds; the white regions were not outlined in black as shown here.) This figure is adapted from Peterson and Gibson (1994) with permission from Blackwell Publishing Co. The display in (d) is an example of displays in which denotivity was the only known cue distinguishing the two regions; they were equal in area and local convexity. A portion of a guitar is sketched along the black side of the black-white border.

(i.e., the orientation in which the known object was portrayed in its upright orientation, as in figure 10.2) or an inverted orientation (the orientation is which the known object was rotated from its typical upright orientation by 180°, as can be seen by viewing figure 10.2 with the book turned upside down). Under these two conditions, we asked observers to report where the figure appeared to lie with respect to the border shared by the two adjacent regions.

The orientation manipulation was designed to reveal whether or not object memories affected figure assignment, according to the following reasoning. Changing the display orientation from upright to inverted should not affect the strength of any Gestalt shaping cues that were present. The properties of area, convexity, symmetry, and/or enclosure are unchanged when a stimulus is inverted. Likewise, any depth cues that were present were unchanged by inverting the stimulus. For instance, the black region in figure 10.2a overlaps the white region (note the T-junctions where they meet); the T-junctions are unchanged when the stimulus is viewed upside down. Therefore, if figure assignment is determined solely by Gestalt shaping cues and/or by depth cues (such as T-junctions), inverting the stimulus should not change it.

In contrast, objects that have a canonical orientation are less familiar when they are rotated 180° from their canonical orientation (i.e., when they are inverted). Consistent with this claim, both behavioral and physiological evidence indicates that object memories code an object's canonical orientation (Jolicœur, 1985; Perrett, Oram, & Ashbridge, 1998; Tarr & Pinker, 1989). For instance, Jolicœur (1985) found that the latency to correctly identify objects is longer when the objects are inverted rather than upright. Perrett, Oram, and Ashbridge (1998) found that it takes longer for activity to accumulate in a population of temporal cortical cells when their preferred object is inverted.[2] Therefore, we reasoned that the orientation manipulation provided a means to assess whether or not past experience in the form of memories of object structure contribute to figure assignment. We hypothesized that any increased likelihood of seeing high-denotative regions[3] as figures in upright compared to inverted displays would reflect contributions to figure assignment from object memories coding the typical orientation of the object.[4]

In a number of experiments, my colleagues and I found that observers were more likely to perceive high-denotative regions as figures in upright rather than inverted displays.[5] (For reviews, see Peterson, 1994a, 2003.) In some experiments, observers viewed figure-ground displays for long durations and reported on alternations in which region appeared to be figure at the shared border (Peterson et al., 1991; Peterson & Gibson, 1993, 1994b; Hochberg & Peterson, 1993). In other experiments, observers viewed briefly exposed, masked displays and reported which of two adjacent regions first appeared to be the figure at their common border (Gibson & Peterson, 1994; Peterson & Gibson, 1994a). In some experiments, we assessed whether or not object memories affected figure assignment when they competed with depth cues and/or Gestalt shaping cues (Peterson et al., 1991; Peterson & Gibson, 1993, 1994a; Peterson & Kim, 2001). In other experiments, we assessed the effects of object memories on figure assignment when no other known depth or Gestalt shaping cues were present (Gibson & Peterson, 1994; Peterson & Gibson, 1993, 1994b; Peterson et al., 2000; Peterson, Gerhardstein, Mennemeier, & Rapcsak, 1998).

Across these different experiments, object memory effects on figure assignment were observed both when object memory cues were the only cues distinguishing one region from another and when object memory cues competed with other cues. This is not to say that object memory cues necessarily dominated the other cues relevant to figure assignment when placed in competition with them. Object memory cues neither consistently dominated depth and Gestalt shaping cues, nor were they consistently dominated by them (Peterson et al., 1991; Peterson & Gibson, 1993, 1994a). Instead, in the situations we have tested, it seemed that the object memory cue was given approximately the same weight in figure assignment as the other shaping cues; when they competed, each determined figure assignment approximately half the time. Thus, the object memory cue is not the only organizing factor, nor is it necessarily the dominant factor. Instead, it appears to be one more cue among an ensemble of cues that affect figure assignment (Peterson, 1994b). Consequently, our results cannot be taken to support a return to Structuralism (Peterson, 1999). In contrast to both Structuralism and the view that prevailed following the Gestalt revolution, we proposed that soon after an edge is detected in the visual input, object memories are accessed along both sides of the edge in parallel. In our view, object memories are accessed at the same time as the depth cues and the Gestalt shaping cues are being analyzed (Peterson, 1994a; Peterson & Gibson, 1993, 1994a, 1994b); the available output of all of these processes is combined to determine figure assignment. In this view, all edges are initially ambiguous. The more strongly cued side of the edge is perceived to be the shaped figure (where "cues" include memories of object structure as well as Gestalt shaping cues). (See Peterson, 2003; Peterson et al., 2000, for an explicit statement of a recent model, and Peterson & Kim, 2001, for empirical tests of the model.)

Recall that one reason for the almost universal acceptance of the depth-and-figure-first assumption was that it buttressed the holistic-substrate assumption by offering a solution to the intrinsic contour problem. Once we had obtained evidence indicating that object memories can be accessed prior to figure assignment, it was important to examine whether problems such as the intrinsic contour problem could be solved without appealing to the depth-and-figure-first assumption. In the next section, I will show that the intrinsic contour problem does not arise if one drops the holistic-substrate assumption and assumes instead that portions of regions, surfaces, and contours can access object memories.

Solving the Intrinsic Contour Problem Using
Overlapping Partial Configurations

Suppose that object recognition is not necessarily conducted over whole surfaces or whole regions. Suppose instead that partial configurations in the input can be matched to partial configurations in object memory; that within the ventral cortical pathway, most likely in posterior regions, known objects are represented by a number of "overlapping partial configurations" (Peterson, 1995, 1998; Peterson & Hector, 1996). In what follows, I elaborate on this proposal, first by explaining the reasons for proposing that the representations are "overlapping," "partial," and "configurational" in nature and then by explaining how they can be used to solve the intrinsic contour problem.

Overlapping Partial Configurations

Two reasons underlie the claim that the object memories affecting figure assignment are configurational in nature. First, the orientation dependency of the object-memory effects on figure assignment indicates that the relevant object memories code an object's structure with respect to its typical upright orientation. Second, object-memory effects on figure assignment are not observed when the features or parts are present but spatially reconfigured (Gibson & Peterson, 1994; Peterson et al., 1991, 1998, 2000). This is true even when observers are well aware of how the reconfigured (i.e., rearranged) objects were created and of the correspondence between the features of the original and reconfigured objects (Peterson et al., 1991). Thus, knowledge of what object would be seen were the features ordered properly in space is not sufficient for object-memory effects on figure assignment. The proper structure, or configuration, must be present in the stimulus. Therefore, the object memories that affect figure assignment must code both the parts (features) and their spatial relationships with respect to upright. In other words, the relevant object memories must code configurations.[6]

The relevant configurations are further considered "partial" in that they constitute less than a whole object, surface, region, or contour.[7] It is likely that these partial configurations reside in posterior regions of the cortex, such as V4 or TEO (posterior inferotemporal cortex), for four reasons. First, cells in posterior regions have small receptive fields (RFs); the average RF size is 4.8° in V4 and 5.4° in TEO, whereas the average RF size in anterior inferotemporal cortex is 16.5° (Kobatake & Tanaka, 1994). Therefore, it is likely that the RFs of cells in posterior ventral cortical regions would encompass portions of an object, whereas the RFs of cells in anterior ventral cortical regions would encompass the whole object. Second, it is likely that representations stored in posterior cortical regions could be accessed quickly enough to affect figure assignment, which is known to occur early in processing (e.g., Zipser, Lamme, & Schiller 1996), whereas there might not be enough time to access representations in more anterior regions. Third, posterior regions of the cortex are retinotopically mapped. Retinotopy would be useful for coding the spatial relationships between the features within a partial configuration. (Generalization to new instances would be possible even with retinotopic coding if the features were sufficiently abstract and if a number of similar but different instances were stored.) Fourth, retinotopic coding and small RFs would be useful for localizing object memory effects along portions of regions, surfaces, or contours.

Future research will have to determine which brain regions form the substrate for the partial configurations that affect figure assignment per se.

(Relevant research by Tanaka, 1996, identifying the critical features of cells in various portions of the ventral cortical pathway is discussed later in the chapter.) Future research will also be needed to determine how small the partial configurations can be. For those object memories contributing to figure assignment, I assume that a partial configuration codes the ordered features constituting at least two parts delimited by successive minima of curvature (Hoffman & Richards, 1985), although I do not assume that parts are explicitly represented.

Finally, it is assumed that the partial configurations coding known objects are "overlapping" in that a given feature, or part, is likely to be represented in more than one partial configuration. Overlapping partial configurations can be used to distinguish between two objects constructed of the same parts in different spatial arrangements. Thus, the overlapping property is a powerful property for partial configurations to have. (I return to this point later when I discuss the antecedents for this proposal.) Furthermore, if a single feature is represented in more than one partial configuration, its location can be specified relative to a number of different features, not just those coded in a single partial configuration. If we assume that the partial configurations are established on the basis of prior experience with objects in the three-dimensional world, it follows that a given feature is not likely to be visible every time an object is encountered; it might be invisible from a given vantage point. Therefore, different partial configurations may be formed in different experiences with a single object. Yet the different partial configurations will overlap because they will share some of the same parts or features.

Reassessing the Intrinsic Contour Problem

The intrinsic contour problem does not arise if one assumes that object-memory contributions to figure assignment arise from overlapping partial configurations and are specified for portions of contours rather than for whole continuous contours, whole regions, or whole surfaces (Peterson, 1995). Consider the outcome of spatially partial access to object memories for figure 10.1a. As illustrated in figure 10.3, partial memories of configured features of a woman would be accessed along the top and the left side of the black region in figure 10.1a, but not along the bottom and the right side. Indeed, along the bottom and the right side, no particular partial configurations would be activated above the threshold by the black region. Consequently, object-memory cues favoring assigning figural status to the black region might be strong along the region's top and left side and weak along its bottom and right side. In contrast, object-memory cues favoring assigning figural status to the white regions where they share a border with the black region would be strong along the bottom and right side and weak along the top and left side. Partial memories of the configured features of a cat would be accessed for the white region adjacent to the bottom of the black region, and partial memories of the configured features

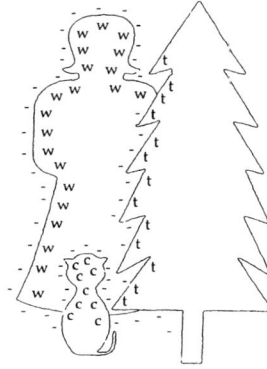

FIGURE 10.3. Figure 10.1a with proposed partial matches to object memories indicated. Portions of the contours that provide a good match to a woman are indicated by a "w"; those that provide a good match to a cat, by a "c"; and those that provide a good match to a tree, by a "t." The dashes indicate portions of contour that don't provide a good match to an object memory.

of a pine tree would be accessed for the white region to the right of the black region. No particular configural matches would be signaled for the white region adjacent to the top and left side of the black region.

It is clear that object-memory cues alone do not determine figure and depth assignment in figures 10.1a and 10.3. The T-junctions located where the borders of the cat and the tree intersect the border of the woman are local depth cues specifying that the white regions lie in front of the black region there. Furthermore, the white region portraying the pine tree is symmetric, whereas the black region is asymmetric; and the white region portraying the cat is smaller in area than the black region. Both symmetry and smallness of relative area are Gestalt shaping cues that should operate to increase the likelihood that those white regions are seen as figures at the borders they share with the black region. Thus, figure 10.3 provides no evidence that partial configurational object memories affect figure assignment. What is needed is research investigating whether or not different contributions to figure assignment from object memories can arise along different portions of a continuous contour (i.e., a contour for which no other depth cues serve as segmentation cues). In the next section, I describe an experiment using displays satisfying this requirement.

Empirical Evidence for Partial Object-Memory
Effects on Figure Assignment

Joanne Hector and I (Peterson & Hector, 1996) used displays like those in figure 10.4 to investigate the proposal that object-memory effects on

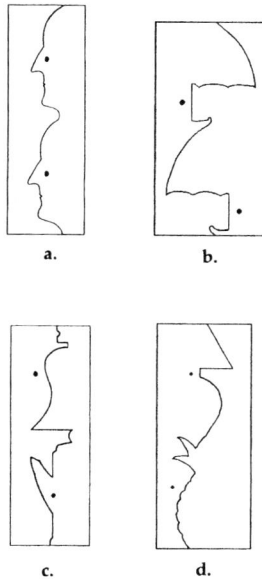

FIGURE 10.4. Sample stimuli used by Peterson and Hector (1996). Same-side stimuli are shown in (a) and (c); different-side stimuli in (b) and (d). Same object versions of each type of stimuli are shown in the top row; different object versions are shown in the bottom row. In (a) and (c) the high denotative region lies on the right side of the central contour. In (a) two profile faces are portrayed one above the other on the right side of the central contour; in (c), a bell is portrayed above a coffeepot on the right side of the contour. In (b), two umbrellas are portrayed one above the other. The top umbrella lies on the left side of the central contour; the bottom umbrella lies on the right side of the central contour. In (d), a table lamp is sketched along the left side of the central contour above a pineapple, sketched along the right side of the central contour. All four possible right-left combinations of dot locations are shown in these panels. For each display observers indicated whether the top and bottom dots were located "on" or "off" the region that appeared to be figure locally. Responses consistent with object memories would be, for the top and bottom dots, respectively, "on" and "on" for figures 10.4a and 10.4b; "off" and "on" for figure 10.4c, and "on" and "off" for figure 10.4d.

figure assignment can differ for different portions of a continuous contour, as predicted if the relevant object memories are partial configurations (or if matches are detected locally). In each display, a rectangle was divided into two halves by a central articulated contour containing no T-junctions or other cues delimiting different objects. The central contour depicted portions of two objects, one above the other (in half of the displays the two objects were identical; in the other half of the displays, the two objects were different).[8]

The two objects could lie on either the same side of the central contour (as in figures 10.4a and 10.4c), or on different sides (as in figures 10.4b and 10.4d). The side of the contour on which the two known objects were portrayed in same-side stimuli was high in denotivity; the opposite side was low in denotivity. In different-side stimuli, the two regions on either side of the central contour were equal in region-wide denotivity because each region was high in denotivity along half of the central contour and low in denotivity along the other half of the central contour. Hence, when considered as wholes, the two regions of different-side stimuli were medium in denotivity. The two regions of different-side stimuli differed in their local denotivity, however. One region was high in denotivity in the top portion of the display, but not in the bottom portion, whereas the other region was high in denotivity in the bottom portion of the display, but not in the top portion. The right and left sides of the displays were equated for other cues known to affect figure assignment. In particular, they were equated for total area and for summed local convexity, using a procedure derived from Stevens and Brook's (1988) scheme of classifying local convexities. These displays were designed to allow us to investigate whether object-memory effects on figure assignment are holistic or local under conditions where competition from other factors was removed (to the extent possible, see below).

Predictions

In the holistic-substrate assumption, each of the right and left sides of the display, as whole bounded regions, would serve as substrates for access to object memories. Object-memory effects on figure assignment would therefore necessarily be specified for whole regions, and observers would be expected to perceive whole regions as figures. In this view, observers might nevertheless be more likely to see the high denotative region of same-side stimuli as the figure than either of the two medium-denotivity regions of different-side stimuli. This would follow because there is different cross-contour competition in these two types of stimuli, with more cross-contour competition in the different-side displays than in the same-side displays. In both cases, however, object-memory influences on figure assignment should favor the perception of whole regions as figures. Because there are no depth cues along the central contour to separate portions of the regions into different surfaces, the same prediction holds if recognition is surface based, as proposed by Nakayama et al. (1989). Implicit in the holistic access view is the associated assumption that object-memory contributions to figure assignment are specified for the entire region, rather than being localized along those portions of continuous contours that match partial configurations in memory.[9]

In contrast, on the overlapping partial configuration hypothesis, object-memory effects on figure assignment can be specified locally for those for portions of the continuous central contour matching partial configurations in memory. As a consequence, object-memory contributions to figure assignment can differ for different portions of a continuous contour. In the different-side stimuli shown in figure 10.4, partial configuration memories would signal good matches along the top left and the bottom right side of the central contour and poor matches locally along the opposite sides of those portions of the contour. Therefore, object-memory cues to figure assignment should favor the perception of the left side as the figure along the top portion of the central contour, and the right side as figure along the bottom portion of the contour. For different-side stimuli, no other cues (such as T-junctions) signal a subdivision of the contour and no other known cues operate to favor a crossover interpretation. Consequently, if observers perceive figure assignment *crossing over* from one side to the other along the central contour more often in different-side displays than in same-side displays, that will be taken as evidence that object memories can exert a local influence on figure assignment. It will be important to show that these differences between same-side and different-side displays are obtained for upright but not inverted stimuli to rule out uncontrolled stimulus differences between the two types of displays.

Uniform Connected Regions

Palmer and Rock (1994) have shown that there exists a tendency to perceive uniform connected regions as part of the same shape. In both the same-side and the different-side stimuli used by Peterson and Hector (1996), the two regions on either side of the central contour were necessarily bounded regions of uniform luminance; this design feature was necessary to permit a contrast between holistic and partial access to object memories. Consequently, in addition to object-memory contributions to figure assignment, a tendency for uniform connected regions to cohere might be contributing to the perceived organization of these displays. Even if object-memory contributions to figure assignment arise from overlapping partial configurations, perceptions of crossover interpretations may not be the dominant percept for different-side displays because of competition from the cue of uniform connectedness. Nevertheless, if object-memory influences on figure assignment can be localized along portions of a contour, crossover reports should be more likely for upright different-side stimuli than for inverted different-side stimuli or for either upright or inverted same side stimuli.

Method

Outline drawings of 20 different stimuli were used, 10 same-side stimuli (as in figures 10.4a & 10.4c) and 10 different-side stimuli (as in figures 10.4b & 10.4d). The high denotative side was balanced across stimuli. Half of the stimuli were shown in an upright orientation; the other half were shown in an inverted orientation. Each observer saw each stimulus once only, in either an upright or an inverted orientation on a white screen. The stimuli subtended 3.4° to 6.4° in height and 0.9° to 1.7° in width. (Observers participated in groups as large as 8. Different observers sat at different distances from the projection screen.)

We assessed observers' perceptions of figure assignment indirectly via their reports regarding two blue probe dots placed on the displays. One dot was presented in the top half of the display; the other dot was presented on the bottom half of the display. The two dots were presented on either the same region or on different regions. Sample dot locations are shown in figures 10.4a–10.4d. We used four combinations of right (R) and left (L) top and bottom cue locations (RR, LL, RL, and LR, for the top and bottom cues, respectively).

Displays were presented for one second. Immediately after the displays disappeared, observers ($N = 24$) indicated by circling their answer on a response box (divided into two halves vertically) whether each of the two dots appeared to be located on or off the perceived figure. This procedure was adapted from research by Stevens and Brooks (1988), who used reports regarding a single dot in an experiment demonstrating that convexity exerted strong local effects on figure assignment. When the right/left cue location was crossed with the same-side/different-side stimuli, there were an equal number of trials on which the top and bottom probe dots lay on the same side or different sides of the central contour. The dots were equally divided across the other conditions of the experiment.

Observers' "on" and "off" responses regarding the probe dots were translated into figure responses, as follows. "On" responses were taken to indicate that the region the dot was placed on was perceived as the figure, at least locally, and that the region lying on the opposite side of the central contour was perceived as ground, at least locally. "Off" responses were taken to indicate that the region the dot was placed on was perceived as the ground, at least locally, and that the region lying on the opposite side of the central contour was perceived as the figure, at least locally. If responses to both dots shown in a single trial indicated that the same region was seen as figure in both the top and the bottom of the display, a "whole-region" interpretation was recorded for that trial. If responses to the two dots shown on a single trial indicated that a different region was seen as figure at the top and the bottom of the display, a "crossover" interpretation was recorded for that trial. For both whole-region and crossover interpretations, reports were scored as consistent or inconsistent with the object memory cues carried by the central contour.

Examples of responses that would be coded as whole-region interpretations would be responses for the top and bottom dots in figure 10.4a of "on" and "on," respectively, or responses to the top and bottom dots in figure 10.4c of "on" and "off," respectively. The whole-region interpretation inferred from those responses to figure 10.4a would be scored as *consistent* with the object-memory cues, whereas the whole-region interpretation inferred from those responses to figure 10.4c would be scored as *inconsistent* with the object-memory cues. Examples of responses that would be coded as crossover interpretations would be responses to the top and bottom dots in figure 10.4b of "on" and "on," respectively, or responses to the top and bottom dots in figure 10.4d of "off" and "on," respectively. The crossover interpretation reported for figure 10.4b would be scored as *consistent* with the object-memory cues, whereas the crossover interpretation reported for figure 10.4d would be scored as *inconsistent* with the object-memory cues. As is evident from the examples described above, whole-region interpretations were not necessarily inferred from identical responses to the two probe dots, nor were crossover interpretations necessarily inferred from different responses to the two probe dots.

Results

The percentages of crossover reports obtained in all conditions are shown in figure 10.5. As predicted on an overlapping partial configuration account, more crossover figure assignments were obtained for upright different-side stimuli (37.5%) than for inverted different-side stimuli (20.8%) or for either upright or inverted same-side stimuli (16.7% and 20%, respectively). A within-subjects ANOVA with two factors showed this interaction between stimulus type and orientation to be significant, $F(1, 23) = 10.44$, $p < .005$. Post hoc tests indicated that observers saw a significantly larger percentage of crossover interpretations when they were viewing upright different-side stimuli than when they were viewing stimuli in any of the other conditions.

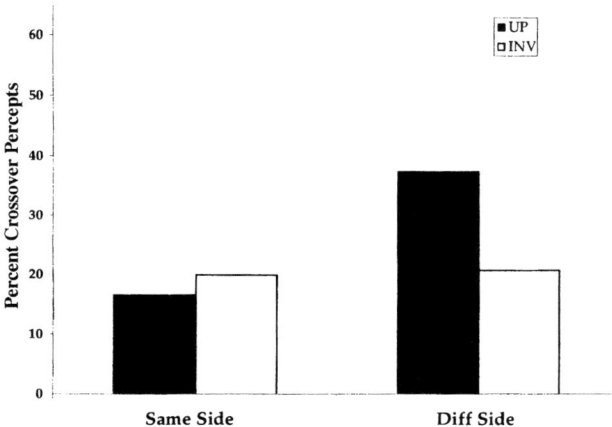

FIGURE 10.5. Percent crossover percepts seen as a function of orientation (upright versus inverted) and stimulus type (i.e., whether the upper and lower high denotative portions of the contour were on the *same side* or *different sides*. Whole region reports = (1 − crossover reports).

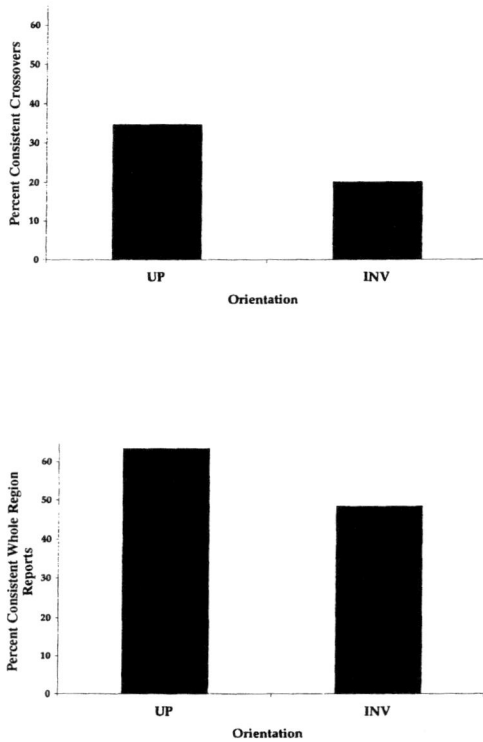

FIGURE 10.6. Top panel: Crossover interpretations that were consistent with the object memory cue in different-side stimuli (stimuli in which the upper and lower high denotative portions of the contour were on *different sides*). Bottom panel: Whole-region interpretations that were consistent with the object memory cue in same-side stimuli (stimuli in which the upper and lower high denotative portions of the contour were on the *same side*).

Restricting attention only to different-side stimuli and to those cross-over interpretations that were consistent with object-memory cues, we again observed a significantly larger percentage of crossover reports for upright (34.7%) than for inverted (20.1%) different-side stimuli, t(23) = 2.96, p < .01 (see top panel of figure 10.6).[10] The fact that more crossover interpretations consistent with object-memory effects were obtained for upright than for inverted different-side stimuli supports the idea that orientation-dependent object memories exert spatially local influences on figure assignment. These results are just what would be expected if the object memory effects on figure assignment arise from partial configurations in memory.

More than half the responses were whole-region interpretations (76.3%). Thus, this experiment also shows that there exists a tendency for uniform connected regions to cohere as a single figure, although this tendency was weaker for upright different-side stimuli than for stimuli in the other conditions. (The percentage of whole-region interpretations [1-% crossover interpretations] for each condition can be deduced from figure 10.5.) Not all of the whole-region interpretations were consistent with object-memory cues. Of those that were, significantly more were obtained for upright (63.3%) than for inverted (48.3%) same-side stimuli, $t(23) =$ 3.09, $p < .01$ (see the bottom panel of figure 10.6).[11]

Discussion

This experiment replicates our previous research showing that high denotative regions are more likely to be seen as figures in upright displays than in inverted displays. In addition, these results extend our previous research by showing that object-memory effects on figure assignment can be expressed for portions of a continuous contour; they need not be expressed for an entire continuous contour, region, or surface. Thus, these results falsify the holistic-substrate assumption. Furthermore, these results show that the depth-and-figure-first assumption is not necessary to solve the intrinsic contour problem. The intrinsic contour problem can be solved by conceiving of object-memory cues as mediated by memories of partial configurations of known objects rather than by memories of whole objects. (Although the results of the present experiment provide evidence for the operation of partial configurations, they cannot speak to the question of whether or not the partial configurations in memory are *overlapping*.)

We are currently extending the Peterson and Hector (1996) experiment using shorter stimulus exposures and measuring figure assignment via different methods. It is expected that these experiments will provide converging evidence for the proposal that object-memory effects on figure assignment arise from memories of partial configurations.

In the next section, I summarize the historical antecedents for, and recent computational and physiological evidence supporting a role for, partial configurations in perception.

Antecedents and Recent Consistent Evidence and Models

The proposal regarding overlapping partial configurations was inspired by Wickelgren's (1969) proposal that spoken words are coded as overlapping collections of context-sensitive allophones rather than as context-independent phonemes, and by elaborations of that idea by Rumelhart and McClelland (1986) and Mozer (1991). More recently, K. J. Tanaka and colleagues have identified neurons in the ventral cortical stream that respond selectively to features that are intermediate in complexity between simple features and whole objects. In addition, computational modeling efforts by Ullman and colleagues have pointed to the utility of overlapping fragmentary memories of faces and objects. A brief review of the antecedents and the recent consistent physiological and computational evidence follows.

Speech and Word Perception

Wickelgren (1969) proposed that each sound in a word is represented in the context of the sound produced immediately before and immediately afterwards (that is, within a three-place representation) rather than as a context-independent phoneme. For sounds at the beginning or the end of a word, a place marker indicating a word ending (#) is part of the context. These context-sensitive codes, labeled "Wickelphones" by Rumelhart and McClelland (1986), provide a solution to the problem of how we distinguish between different words comprising the same phonemes in different relative positions. Wickelgren considers words such as "crust" and "struck" comprising the same unordered phonemes: /k/, /r/, /u /, s/, /t/. The context-sensitive representations of these two words are very different. "Crust" would be represented by the context sensitive codes $_{\#}c_r$, $_cr_u$, $_ru_s$, $_us_t$, and $_st_{\#}$; whereas "struck" would be represented by the context sensitive codes $_{\#}s_t$, $_st_r$, $_tr_u$, $_ru_k$, and $_uk_{\#}$. An important property of Wickelphones is that they can distinguish two words comprising the same phonemes in different orders without appealing to a separate representation of order. The overlap between Wickelphones represents order implicitly rather than explicitly.

Wickelphones were rejected when they were first proposed on the grounds that they were not parsimonious. To account for speech perception, one needed to postulate many more Wickelphones than phonemes (e.g., approximately 10^6 Wickelphones versus 40–50 phonemes). Addressing the issue of parsimony, Wickelgren argued that the brain had more than enough capacity to represent the required number of context-sensitive codes. Many other theorists considered the required number of Wickelphones too large, however, in part because of the computational cost related to the number of connections between Wickelphones. Rumelhart and McClelland (1986) cleverly reduced the number of Wickelphones that were required to represent all English words to the more manageable number of 460 by using a feature representation of the individual phonemes and then creating a reduced set of nonredundant Wickelphone detectors. Although it is not yet clear how (or whether) context-sensitive codes are used for spoken word recognition, it is clear that a parsimony argument isn't a strong argument against them.

In his computational model of written word recognition, Mozer (1991) expanded Wickelgren's three-place representation to a four-place representation called a letter cluster unit. This expansion was necessary to avoid problems posed by Pinker and Prince (1988) concerning the repetition of mid-word elements (e.g., there are two "ana" units in the Wickelphone representation of banana, but there is no provision for repetition of Wickelphones). In Mozer's model, different words were represented by different patterns of activity across letter cluster units. Mozer (1991) estimated that 6000 letter cluster units would be required to represent all the written words known to an individual English speaker.

As Mozer (1991) pointed out, the property that the clusters represent three letters is not critical. Therefore, the estimated number of required letter cluster units is not critical, either. What is important are the ideas that (1) cluster units represent more than one letter and less than the entire word, and (2) overlapping letter cluster units provide an implicit code of the ordering of the word components. Although the number of letter cluster units might be large relative to the number of letters, the letter cluster units could prove to be more parsimonious than a letter representation scheme because there is no need to represent the order of the units separately. Both the Wickelphones and Mozer's (1991) letter cluster units are clearly antecedents to the proposal regarding overlapping partial configurations in object memory.

Object Recognition

In object recognition, as well as in spoken and written word recognition, it has often been assumed that a relatively small number of features (or parts) represents a large number of different entities. For instance, Biederman (1987, 1995) proposed that a small number (< 36) of volumetric components served as the components of object representation. With a small number of representational components, a list of features (or parts) will be insufficient to distinguish one object from another, just as a list of phonemes or letters is insufficient to distinguish one word from another; the relationships between the components must be specified as well. Hummel and Biederman (1992) faced this problem directly and presented a computational model of how the visual system might separately and explicitly code the components of an object and their spatial interrelationships. Their model used phase synchrony in neural responses to dynamically bind parts together into particular spatial relationships. As discussed by Hummel (chapter 8 this volume), dynamic binding requires some time to operate. However, the literature on spoken and written word recognition clearly raises the alternative possibility that overlapping partial configurations could implicitly represent spatial ordering for objects as well as for words. In what follows, I discuss recent computational models that test the feasibility of representing objects by overlapping partial codes and recent physiological evidence suggesting that the brain uses similar representations.

COMPUTATIONAL MODELING

Ullman and Sali (2000; Ullman, Vidal-Naquet, & Sali, 2002) recently described a fragment-based computer vision system for classifying objects at the basic level (e.g., as cars or as faces rather than as particular cars or particular faces).[12] Classification has been difficult for computer vision systems, although human observers accomplish it with ease. In Ullman and Sali's (2000) model, an algorithm first extracted overlapping image fragments from a training set of gray-scale images of objects in the category of interest (cars or faces). The fragments were selected to maximize the information about a class of objects rather than a specific object. A modest number of fragments of intermediate complexity and size met this criterion, as did some larger fragments of reduced resolution. Fragment types for faces included hairline regions, eye regions, mouth regions, and regions including the mouth and the chin or the nose and the corners of the eyes. Fragment types for cars included wheel well regions, regions including portions of the hood and the windshield, or portions of the bumper and the lights, or portions of a tire and the chassis. Note that many of the fragments constituted portions of nameable parts of the object rather than the whole nameable part or the whole object. The fragment types including more than one feature constituted "binding fragments"; these fragments had a large amount of overlap with other fragments, both those coding single features and those coding whole objects in low resolution. The binding fragments constitute a form of context-sensitive code.

Ullman and colleagues tested the algorithm's ability to use these fragments to classify novel faces and cars. In addition, they compared performance with intermediate complexity fragments versus whole object views. Classification performance was much better when intermediate complexity image fragments (including binding fragments) were used rather than fragments coding a whole view. Moreover, the addition of explicit relative location information did not improve the algorithm's performance. Thus, Ullman and his colleagues demonstrated that a computer vision system could attain excellent object classification using redundant, overlapping fragments as building blocks; explicit relative location information was unnecessary. Together with the results reported by Rumelhart and Mc-Clelland (1986) and Mozer (1991), these computational results suggest that context-sensitive fragmentary codes can account for a wide variety of behaviors (e.g., object classification and spoken and written word recognition).

Ullman (2001) demonstrated further that overlapping fragments of the types used by Ullman and Sali (2000) for classification could also operate to segment an object from a crowded background. This is important because previous computational attempts to perform segmentation under such realistic conditions without employing object memories as segmentation cues have consistently failed (Ullman, 2001).[13] Ullman's computational research attesting to the computational necessity of using object memories to aid the segmentation process reinforces our interpretation of our empirical results. His results also show that the proposal that overlapping partial configurations can affect figure assignment is computationally feasible.

Ullman's overlapping fragments differ from the overlapping partial configurations discussed earlier in this chapter in that they constitute both internal features and features that can be identified along a contour or an edge. In our empirical research investigating object memory effects on figure assignment, my colleagues and I have used silhouettes—stimuli lacking internal details. It would be interesting to investigate whether, even in a detailed image, fragments of bounding edges are more important for figure assignment than fragments including internal details. (Results obtained for figure-ground segregation might contrast with those obtained for classification.) Conversely, it would be interesting to investigate whether object-memory effects on figure assignment are altered by the presence of consistent or inconsistent surface details.

PHYSIOLOGICAL EVIDENCE

Recent physiological research has identified cells that respond to features of intermediate complexity (i.e., between simple features and full object representations) both in retinotopically coded regions V2, V4, and TEO (the posterior inferotemporal lobe) and in TE (the anterior inferotemporal lobe) (Kobatake & K. J. Tanaka, 1994; Tanaka, 1996). Perrett and Oram (1998) review both their own related work and K. J. Tanaka's, indicating that as one proceeds along the ventral cortical stream stimulus features of increasing complexity are required to elicit cell responses. Neurons that respond to feature conjunctions are sensitive to the presence and relative position of more than one simple feature. Perrett and Oram (1998) conclude that when several such cells are active simultaneously, they can jointly specify the relative locations of many simple features, thereby solving the binding problem. Thus, there is physiological evidence that neurons in the ventral cortical stream are specialized for conjunctive coding— the general type of coding required for Wickelphones, letter cluster units, and overlapping partial configurations. More work must be done to identify the particular types of conjunctive codes that are established for a class of objects. Furthermore, more research is needed to determine whether or not the conjunctive codes that have been identified in various ventral cortical structures can underlie the effects attributed to the operation of overlapping partial configurations in this chapter.

An assumption, derived from the physiological literature and adopted in this chapter, is that knowledge of objects is stored in different forms in different parts of the visual system and used for different processing purposes. Although some memories of object structure may be holistic, they are not all holistic. Partial configurations, and even smaller features, are coded as well. These partial configurational memories, constituting less than the whole object, are likely to be stored in relatively posterior brain regions.

Summary

The intrinsic contour problem (and other considerations) led many theorists to suppose that object memories can be accessed only following figure assignment. Nevertheless, there is now a significant amount of evidence indicating that some form of object memories affect figure assignment. Some of that evidence was reviewed in this chapter. Next, it was shown that the intrinsic contour problem arises only on the assumption that whole regions, surfaces, or continuous contours are matched to holistic object memories. It does not arise if one assumes that (1) the object-memory effects on figure assignment arise from overlapping partial configurations in memory, and (2) matches can be made over portions of regions rather than whole regions. An experiment demonstrating that object-memory effects on figure assignment can be localized along portions of continuous contours was reported. The results were consistent with the proposal that these effects originate from object memories coded as partial configurations (although they cannot speak to whether or not overlapping partial configurations are stored in memory). Next, the historical precedents for the proposed overlapping partial configurations were reviewed and recent computational approaches using partial configurations for image classification and scene segmentation were discussed. Finally, recent physiological evidence indicating that some of the object representations in the posterior ventral cortical stream have the characteristics required of partial overlapping configurations was reviewed. Thus, converging evidence from theoretical, empirical, computational, and physiological domains supports the idea that overlapping partial configurations play an important role in object perception.

Notes

This chapter was written while the author was supported in part by a grant from the National Science Foundation (BCS 9906063). Thanks to Michael Corballis, Mike Mozer, and Gillian Rhodes for helpful comments on a previous draft.
    1. The terms "part" and "feature" are used interchangeably in this chapter in order to avoid commitment to any particular theoretical approach to part or feature types.
    2. The preferred object of the cells investigated by Perrett et al. (1998) was a particular kind of object, a face. Nevertheless, given behavioral evidence indicating orientation dependency in object recognition as well as in face recognition, I believe that Perrett et al.'s interpretation of their evidence can easily be extended to objects other than faces.
    3. The predictions regarding object-memory effects on figure assignment refer to the portion of the contour where a familiar object is sketched. However, for the sake of simplicity, I will use the term "high-denotative region" rather than the more cumbersome phrase "the high denotative side of the contour." As will become clear later in the chapter, the question of whether or not object-memory

contributions to figure assignment are necessarily region wide is open to empirical test.

4. We did not assume that these memories of object structure necessarily coded the whole object. This issue is addressed explicitly in the present chapter.

5. This is the pattern shown by the visual agnosic patient AD, who was tested with displays like those in figure 10.2d.

6. Note that in using the term "configurations" here, I mean only to imply that the spatial relationships between the features are coded, not the manner in which they are coded (i.e., precisely versus categorically).

7. Authors such as Ivry and Robertson (1998) and Sergent (1982) prefer to use the term "local" for "high-spatial frequency information." However, that is not my intention here.

8. We did not have a large enough set of stimuli for a sensitive analysis of whether the identity of the two objects was important. Consequently, this manipulation will not be mentioned again.

9. Vecera & O'Reilly's (1998, 2000) computational model of object-memory effects on figure assignment makes this whole-region assumption.

10. This analysis can be done only for different-side stimuli. No crossover interpretation would be consistent with object memory cues for same-side stimuli.

11. This analysis could not be done for different-side stimuli because whole-region reports for either side could be considered consistent with (holistic) object-memory cues. Similarly, we could not test the orientation-dependency of whole-region interpretations for different-side stimuli because there were no clear predictions regarding which whole-region interpretation might be seen.

12. Note that in a classification task, faces constitute just another basic-level category object. The features types used to classify faces versus cars, then, would not be expected to differ substantially.

13. Mozer, Zemel, Behrmann, and Williams (1992) presented a computation model that, when shown pre-segmented geometric shapes, could extract features that could later be used to segment two overlapping shapes (that did not share any contours) from one another. Inasmuch as the learned features in the model of Mozer et al. reflect prior experience, they can be said to be memories, as well. Note that the features extracted in this model, like the effective features in Ullman's model, were not as large as the whole object.

References

Biederman, I. (1987). Recognition by components: A theory of human image understanding. *Psychological Review, 94*, 115–147.

Biederman, I. (1995). Visual object recognition. In S. F. Kosslyn and D. N. Oshershon (Eds.), *An invitation to cognitive science*, 2nd ed. (pp. 121–165). Cambridge, MA: MIT Press.

Gibson, B. S., & Peterson, M. A. (1994). Does orientation-independent object recognition precede orientation-dependent recognition? Evidence from a cueing paradigm. *Journal of Experimental Psychology: Human Perception and Performance, 20*, 299–316.

Hochberg, J., & Peterson, M. A. (1993). Mental representations of occluded objects: Sequential disclosure and intentional construal. *Giornale Italiano di Psicologia, 20*, 805–820.

Hoffman, D. D., & Richards, W. A. (1984). Parts of recognition. *Cognition, 18,* 65–96.

Hummel, J., & Biederman, I. (1992). Dynamic binding in a neural network for shape recognition. *Psychological Review, 99,* 480–517.

Ivry, R. B., & Robertson, L. C. (1998). *The two sides of perception.* Cambridge, MA: MIT Press.

Jolicœur, P. (1985). The time to name disoriented objects. *Memory & Cognition, 13,* 289–303.

Kellman, P. J., & Shipley, T. F. (1991). A theory of visual interpolation in object perception. *Cognitive Psychology, 23,* 141–221.

Kobatake, E., & Tanaka, K. (1994). Neuronal selectivities to complex object features in the ventral visual pathway of the macaque cerebral cortex. *Journal of Neurophysiology, 71,* 856–867.

Marr, D. (1982). *Vision.* New York: W. H. Freeman.

Mozer, M. C. (1991). *The perception of multiple objects.* Cambridge, MA: MIT Press.

Mozer, M. C., Zemel, R. S., Behrmann, M., & Williams, C. K. I. (1992). Learning to segment images using dynamic feature binding. *Neural Computation, 4,* 650–665.

Nakayama, K., Shimojo, S., & Silverman, G. H. (1989). Stereoscopic depth: Its relation to image segmentation, grouping, and the recognition of occluded objects. *Perception, 18,* 55–68.

Palmer, S., & Rock, I. (1994). Rethinking perceptual organization: The role of uniform connectedness. *Psychonomic Bulletin & Review, 1,* 29–55.

Perrett, D. I., & Oram, M. W. (1998). Visual recognition based on temporal cortex cells; Viewer-centered processing of pattern configuration. *Zeitschrift für naturforschung, 53,* 518–541.

Perrett, D. I., Oram, M. W., & Ashbridge, E. (1998). Evidence accumulation in cell populations responsive to faces: An account of generalization of recognition without mental transformations. *Cognition, 67,* 111–145.

Peterson, M. A. (1994a). Shape recognition can and does occur before figure-ground organization. *Current Directions in Psychological Science, 3,* 105–111.

Peterson, M. A. (1994b). The proper placement of uniform connectedness. *Psychonomic Bulletin and Review, 1,* 509–514.

Peterson, M. A. (1995). *The relationship between depth segregation and object recognition: Old assumptions, new findings, and a new approach to object recognition.* Unpublished manuscript.

Peterson, M. A. (1998). Figure-ground illuminates object recognition. Talk given in the Object and Face Recognition Symposium at *the International Neuropsychological Symposium,* Jerusalem, Israel.

Peterson, M. A. (1999). On the role of meaning in organization. *Intellectica, 28,* 37–51.

Peterson, M. A. (2003). On figure, grounds, and varieties of amodal surface completion. In R. Kimchi, M. Behrmann, & C. Olson (Eds). *Perceptual organization in vision: Behavioral and neural perspectives.* Hillsdale, NJ: Erlbaum.

Peterson, M. A., de Gelder, B., Rapcsak, S. Z., Gerhardstein, P. C., & Bachoud-Lévi, A.-C. (2000). Object memory effects on figure assignment: Conscious object recognition is not necessary or sufficient. *Vision Research, 40,* 1549–1567.

Peterson, M. A., Gerhardstein, P. C., Mennemeier, M., & Rapcsak, S. Z. (1998). Object-centered attentional biases and object recognition contributions to scene segmentation in right hemisphere- and left hemisphere-damaged patients. *Psychobiology*, *26*, 557–570.

Peterson, M. A., & Gibson, B. S. (1993). Shape recognition contributions to figure-ground organization in three-dimensional display. *Cognitive Psychology*, *25*, 383–429.

Peterson, M. A., & Gibson, B. S. (1994a). Must shape recognition follow figure-ground organization? An assumption in peril. *Psychological Science*, *5*, 253–259.

Peterson, M. A., & Gibson, B. S. (1994b). Object recognition contributions to figure-ground organization: Operations on outlines and subjective contours. *Perception & Psychophysics*, *56*, 551–564.

Peterson, M. A., Harvey, E. H., & Weidenbacher, H. L. (1991). Shape recognition inputs to figure-ground organization: Which route counts? *Journal of Experimental Psychology: Human Perception and Performance*, *17*, 1075–1089.

Peterson, M. A., & Hector, J. E. (1996, November). *Evidence for the piecemeal nature of pre-depth object recognition processes.* Paper presented at the annual meeting of the Psychonomic Society, Chicago, IL.

Peterson, M. A., & Kim, J. H. (2001) On what is bound in figures and grounds. *Visual Cognition. Special Issue: "Neural Binding of Space and Time," 8*, 329–348.

Pinker, S., & Prince, A. (1988). On language and connnectionism: Analysis of a parallel distributed processing model of language acquisition. *Cognition*, *28*, 73–193.

Rumelhart, D. E., & McClelland, J. L. (1986). On learning the past tense of English verbs. In J. L. McClelland & D. E. Rumelhart (Eds.), *Parallel distributed processing: Explorations in the microstructure of cognition. Volume II: Psychological and biological models* (pp. 216–271). Cambridge. MA: MIT Press/ Bradford Books.

Sergent, J. (1982). The cerebral balance of power: Confrontation or cooperation. *Journal of Experimental Psychology: Human Perception and Performance, 11*, 846–861.

Stevens, K. A., & Brooks, A. (1988). The concave cusp as determiner of figure-ground. *Perception, 17*, 35–42.

Tanaka, K. (1996). Inferotemporal cortex and object vision. *Annual Review of Neuroscience, 19*, 109–139.

Tarr, M. J., & Pinker, S. (1989). Mental rotation and orientation-dependence in shape recognition. *Cognitive Psychology, 21*, 233–282.

Ullman, S. (2001, March). Top-down processes in recognition and segmentation. Talk given at the Annual Meeting of the Cognitive Neuroscience Society, New York.

Ullman, S., & Sali, E. (2000). Object classification using fragment-based representation. In S.-W. Lee, H. H. Bülthoff, & T. Poggio (Eds.), *Biologically motivated computer vision, 1811* (pp. 73–87). Berlin: Springer-Verlag.

Ullman, S., Vidal-Naquet, M., & Sali, E. (2002). Visual features of intermediate complexity and their use on classification. *Nature Neuroscience, 5*, 682–687.

Vecera, S. P., & Farah, M. J. (1997). Is visual image segmentation a bottom-up or an interactive process? *Perception & Psychophysics, 59*, 1280–1296.

Vecera, S. P., & O'Reilly, R. C. (1998). Figure-ground organization and object recognition processes: An interactive account. *Journal of Experimental Psychology: Human Perception and Performance, 24,* 441–462.

Vecera, S. P., & O'Reilly, R. C. (2000). A reply to Peterson. *Journal of Experimental Psychology: Human Perception and Performance.*

Warrington, E, K. & James, M. (1988). Visual apperceptive agnosia: A clinico-anatomical study of three cases. *Cortex, 24,* 13–32.

Wickelgren, W. A. (1969). Context-sensitive coding, associative memory, and serial order in (speech) behavior. *Psychological Review, 76,* 1–15.

Zipser, K., Lamme, V. A., & Schiller, P. H. (1996). Contextual modulation in primary visual cortex. *Journal of Neuroscience, 15,* 7376–7389.

11

Neuropsychological Approaches to Perceptual Organization

Evidence from Visual Agnosia

MARLENE BEHRMANN

The visual world consciously perceived is very different from the raw visual information or retinal mosaic of intensities and colors that arises from external objects. From the overwhelming influx of different colors and shapes that stimulate the individual retinal receptors, an object is seen as detached and separable from the adjacent objects and surfaces. This organization occurs despite the fact that parts of a single object may be spatially or temporally discontinuous, may have different colors, or may even transect several different depth planes. Additionally, because most surfaces are opaque, portions of objects are routinely hidden from view and, as we move around, surfaces continually undergo occlusion and fragmentation. As is apparent from this description, the objects of phenomenal perception are not given in any direct way in the retinal image. Some internal processes of organization must clearly be responsible, then, for producing a single, coherent percept. The goal of this chapter is to explore how the multitude of visual inputs contained in an image are integrated such that coherent entities are ultimately derived.

The processes "by which bits and pieces of visual information that are available in the retinal image are structured into the larger units of perceived objects and their interpretations" (Palmer, 1999) are generally classified under the umbrella term "perceptual organization." The study of these visual processes has a relatively short history; roughly 100 years

295

ago, the Gestalt psychologists began to recognize and articulate the complexity of perceptual organization, and much of the real progress made today can trace its roots to the insights of these psychologists (Kellman, 2000). Although the Gestalt work on perceptual organization has been widely accepted as identifying crucial phenomena of perception, there has been, until the last decade or so, relatively little theoretical and empirical emphasis on perceptual organization. And, to the extent that progress has been made, there still remain many open questions. This paucity of understanding is well captured by the comment by Palmer (2003) that "We have not got the answers (to perceptual organization) yet; indeed, it is not entirely clear what the questions are!" (p. 1). As is evident from this, there is considerable work to be done in order to understand the behavioral mechanisms underlying perceptual organization.

In addition to trying to understand the functional processes involved in perceptual organization, there is much to be done to understand how these principles are neurally instantiated and what brain mechanisms might be involved. Recent neurophysiological advances have revealed much about the specificities of neuronal responses such as orientation selectivity, ocular dominance, and wavelength and directional selectivity. However, it is not clear how the fragments represented by these local analyzers are assembled to provide a unified percept.

One possible approach to understanding both the psychological and the neural mechanisms involved in perceptual organization is to study the performance of individuals whose visual behavior is impaired following brain damage. In particular, the patients described in this chapter have problems with processes involved in structuring pieces into larger units—the very definition of perceptual organization—and, therefore, their performance can shed light on issues related to perceptual organization. This approach, together with the emerging and converging evidence from other research domains such as cognitive psychology, functional neuroimaging, and neurophysiology, potentially offers important insights into the perceptual system.

The first section of this chapter will outline three main empirical issues falling under the domain of perceptual organization: figure-ground organization, visual interpolation, and grouping. The second section will contain a description of the patients with whom we are concerned, followed in the third section by an examination of the nature of the impairment in perceptual organization, in relation to figure-ground organization, visual interpolation, and grouping. We then provide some summary observations and comments about both the psychological and the neural aspects of agnosia and perceptual organization.

Processes of Perceptual Organization

Central questions that are being investigated in studies of perceptual organization concern the nature, ordering, and interactivity of the different processes of perceptual organization. It is in the context of these questions that we examine the neuropsychological data. There has been growing awareness that perceptual organization is not a monolithic entity, but, rather, comprises a multiplicity of processes. Because the neuropsychological work mainly revolves around three of these processes—figure-ground segregation, visual interpolation, and grouping—we focus on them specifically. As will be evident shortly, however, the exact ordering of these processes is controversial and there is far more interaction between them than independence.

The crucial goal of *figure-ground* segregation is to assign contours in the image as belonging to the figural regions, thereby giving them shape, while the ground region extends behind them shapelessly. The figure appears closer to the observer and has the shape imparted by the dividing contour whereas the ground appears farther away and extends behind the contour. Figure-ground segregation also relies on depth information, particularly pictorial cues from occlusion, and, hence, processes such as visual completion and interpolation may play a role here, too. Just as the Gestalt psychologists proposed principles that govern grouping of elements in a display, so there are principles that govern figure-ground segregation. These include relative size of regions, repetition of regions, orientation, contrast, symmetry, parallelism and even conscious intent (Rubin, 1921). Contemporary psychologists have added others, including familiar shape, convexity/concavity contrast, surroundedness, and lower region (see Palmer, 2000, 2002; Peterson, 2003, for review).

Visual interpolation is the term applied to a variety of processes by which partially present information appears to be extended and continued. Partially occluded surfaces and objects are perceived as being complete in a rather effortless and automatic fashion, and this perception appears to include their shape, texture, and color. The process by which this completion occurs is often referred to as amodal completion to indicate that the completed portion is not supported by local stimulation or sensory information. Exactly what underlies amodal completion is under much discussion; while some argue that past experience with a square, for example, drives one to complete an occluded square, others suggest that the simplicity or Pragnanz of the display determines the completion. Yet others, such as Kellman and Shipley (1991), argue that the Gestalt principle of good continuation applies here. The relatability theory (Kellman, 2003; Kellman & Shipley, 1991; Kellman & Shipley 1992) that formalizes the Gestalt principle of good continuation suggests that the visual system connects two noncontiguous edges that are relatable (collinear). The likelihood of "seeing" a completed figure increases systematically with the size of the angle that must be interpolated, with the 50% threshold of completion occurring at around 90° and increasing probability of seeing it as complete as the angle approaches 90°. According to this view, relatability is a general principle of unit formation and applies not only to amodal completion but also to illusory or subjective contours in which contours that do not actually exist in the image are perceived.

It has been proposed that contour interpolation that supports relatability occurs early in the visual system (Kovács, 2000). Physiological evidence suggests that neurons in early visual areas (such as V2) respond to the presence of illusory contours, with about 40% of neurons in this area becoming active when presented with stimuli that induce illusory contours in human perception (Heitger, von der Heydt, Peterhans, Rosenthaler, & Kubler, 1998; Peterhans & von der Heydt, 1991; von der Heydt, Peterhans, & Baumgartner, 1984). Neurons in V1 also respond to illusory contours, although their response is both weaker and slower than that observed in V2; the temporal sequence of these data is consistent with the claim that the V1 response is a consequence of feedback from later areas (Lamme & Roelfsema, 2000; Lee & Nguyen, 2001). Other neuropsychological data from patients with hemispatial neglect are consistent with this; several studies have shown that collinear contours may be completed pre-attentively and may influence the extent to which contralesional information, which is usually extinguished, may be preserved and reported (Gilchrist, Humphreys, & Riddoch, 1996; Humphreys, 2002; Mattingley, Davis, & Driver, 1997). Recent neuroimaging data have also shown that occipital regions and posterior temporal regions play a role in the integration of contours into a whole image (Gerlach et al., 2002).

The organizational processes concerned with *grouping* were a central focus of the work of the Gestalt psychologists, particularly that of Max Wertheimer, and his observations and principles are still referred to today. The well-known Gestalt laws of grouping include grouping by proximity, similarity, common fate, good continuation, and closure. A number of other principles have been added to the list more recently (Palmer, 1999, 2003, 2002; Sekuler & Bennett, 2001). These include synchrony (visual events that occur at the same time will be perceived as going together), common region (elements located in the same visual space will be grouped together), and element connectedness (elements that are connected by other elements tend to be grouped together). Once elements that belong together are determined, they can be grouped to form a superordinate, wholistic object or, alternatively, can be decomposed into their constituent parts.

Although we have laid out these processes in a sequential order, it is worth noting at this stage that there is much debate concerning the strictly serial and feedforward model of stages of processing. The debate essentially involves the relative independence and ordering of the different stages of processing. One might think, for example, of figure-ground segregation not as a separate process entirely but rather as an instance of perceptual grouping given that the contour is not only assigned to the figure but is also bound to or grouped with it (Palmer, 2003; Palmer & Brooks, 2000). Additionally, figure-ground segregation might not even be a separate process but rather the outcome of an interaction between configural cues and depth cues (Peterson, 2002) and may involve top-down feedback from object representations (Vecera & O'Reilly, 1998). Amodal completion may also be thought of as an instance of perceptual grouping: both visible and invisible contours might be computed from local, oriented operators that are grouped by good continuation, as in relatability theory (Kellman & Shipley, 1992), and then the output of these operators contributes to the global shape.

The temporal staging of these various processes has been the subject of a number of other empirical studies and is undergoing much heated debate. The perceptual processes underlying classical grouping phenomena have traditionally been assumed to work in parallel on an early, 2D representation and to create an initial set of discrete elements on which later perceptual operations are performed. On some accounts, these processes operate pre-attentively to represent units to which attention is deployed (Moore & Egeth, 1997). Whether this is indeed so is debatable. Some researchers have argued that grouping does not occur as early as has been widely assumed. Instead, they have suggested that it operates after depth information has been extracted (Rock & Brosgole, 1964), and after lightness constancy (Rock, Nijhawan, Palmer, & Tudor, 1992) and perceptual completion (Agostini & Galmonte, 2002; Palmer, Neff, & Beck, 1996; Palmer, 2003) have been achieved.

Other findings have supported the arguments in favor of early grouping but have proposed that the representations derived by these early principles are much more complex and detailed than has been considered previously. For example, early levels of processing are sensitive to complex, scene-based properties (Enns & Rensink, 1990; He & Nakayama, 1992), to complete configurations rather than to components (Rensink & Enns, 1995) and to configural and to part-whole information (Kimchi, 1998). Finally, there are also recent data that show that some high-level cues, which have always been assumed to operate in a later, top-down fashion and to reflect access to memories of the structure of known objects, can influence perceptual processing very early on. For example, much recent work by Peterson and colleagues has shown that object knowledge can come into play early on, at pre-figural levels potentially, to influence figure-ground segregation (Peterson, 2003 Peterson & Gibson, 1994) and perceptual grouping (Kimchi & Hadad, 2002). Palmer and Rock (1994b), in their influential view of perceptual organization, did not order the stages strictly so that processing at one stage must necessarily be complete before the next stage is initiated; instead, they suggested that the various operations can occur in cascaded fashion. However, they also claimed that there is an architectural ordering of the stages that is required by the logical constraints of the task, which supports some of the seriality of the system (Palmer, 2003). Taken together, these findings rule out a pure "early" view of grouping and suggest that organizational factors likely do not operate solely at the level of the two-dimensional retinal image but may also play a role once some organization and interpretation have occurred.

The above debate suggests that the early operation of grouping principles is more complex than originally thought and may be a result both of the feedforward pass and the recurrent sweep of the connectivity of the visual system. It is well known that there are considerable feedback connections in the visual system (Felleman & Van Essen, 1991; Lamme & Roelfsema, 2000) and neurophysiological (Bullier, Schall, & Morel, 1996; Lee & Nguyen, 2001) and electrophysiological data support the role of recursive feedback mechanisms in perceptual organization (Doniger et al., 2000), involving even very early visual areas (Hopfinger, Buonocore, & Mangun, 2000). As is apparent from this discussion, there is a general lack of consensus regarding the functional properties of the perceptual organization system as well as its temporal characteristics. A full review of the evidence is beyond the scope of this chapter, but we do raise these challenges to alert the reader to the complexity of the problem. Two recent books deal with these issues directly and may be consulted for further information: one is on segmentation and grouping by Shipley and Kellman (2001) and the other is on the psychological and neural bases of visual perceptual organization by Kimchi, Behrmann, and Olson (2003).

The focus of the present work is restricted to the neuropsychological data and it is to those data that we now turn to examine the evidence.

Visual Agnosia

"Visual agnosia" refers to the failure to identify or recognize even common objects presented in the visual modality. This recognition deficit is not secondary to a generalized intellectual dysfunction nor to a fundamental sensory problem (such as an hemianopia). That patients fail to name objects also cannot be attributed to a deficit in their knowledge of objects nor to a failure in producing the name for the object; when the patients are blindfolded and the same objects are presented for haptic recognition, for example, object recognition is normal. Additionally, the patients are able to provide definitions of the objects, given the auditory label. Agnosia reflects a modality-specific deficit in gaining access to long-term representations from vision and is not attributable to a conceptual failure of some sort. Importantly, when an agnosic patient fails to recognize an object, there is no evidence for the availability of information about the object through another response modality; for example, the patient is unable to gesture the use of the object correctly. This pattern distinguishes patients with agnosia from those with optic aphasia who are able to gesture the response correctly despite the failure to name the object (Lhermitte & Beauvois, 1973).

At one end of the spectrum, the term "visual agnosia" includes a fairly low-level visual deficit manifest as the inability to extract featural elements from a display despite intact sensation of the basic properties of the stimulus (for example, brightness perception). Many patients with this form of deficit have suffered carbon monoxide poisoning, resulting in small, disseminated lesions in the cortex, or mercury or lead poisoning or a closed head injury, all of which have diffuse effects in the brain. At the other end of the spectrum, agnosia includes a rather higher level deficit reflecting the failure to assign meaning to an object despite the derivation of an intact percept (Farah, 1990; Humphreys & Riddoch, 2001), although the extent to which perception is truly normal is debatable. It is this latter form of agnosia that has been referred to as "perception stripped of meaning" (Teuber, 1968). These two ends anchor the dichotomy between apperceptive and associative agnosia originally proposed by Lissauer (1890). While the apperceptive agnosic patients appear to be impaired at deriving the form of the object, associative agnosic patients supposedly can derive percepts well but have difficulty matching form information with stored memories (see Farah, 1990; Humphreys & Riddoch, 1987).

Although the dichotomy between apperceptive and associative agnosia is useful, recent studies have attested to its inadequacy and have attempted to elaborate the spectrum of impairments (Humphreys, 1999; Warrington & Taylor, 1978). By the classic definition of these two types of agnosia, the apperceptive patients are those who cannot copy or match visual forms, whereas the associative patients can copy and match forms but cannot associate them with knowledge that would allow them to name or categorize them. One clear challenge to this dichotomy comes from a third type of patient labeled "integrative agnosia" (IA), and it is this type of agnosia with we are primarily concerned here.

Patient CK is a good example of an individual who suffers from integrative visual agnosia. CK was only able to recognize 16 out of 23 (70%) three-dimensional common objects presented to him for an unlimited period of time (normal subjects score 23/23); (Behrmann, Moscovitch, & Winocur, 1994; Behrmann, Winocur, & Moscovitch, 1992; Moscovitch, Winocur, & Behrmann, 1997). His errors include calling a smoking pipe "a straw," a card of matches "a card with writing," a padlock "an earring," a saw "a knife," pliers "clothes peg." He was, however, able to identify all 23 of the same objects with tactile presentation. He also defined in detail all the objects correctly when presented with the name auditorily. For example, he defined a duck as "an animal, marine life, with webbed feet and a bill"; a card of matches as "a cardboard container, the container flipped open, the log sticks are struck against the cordite strip"; and a pipe as "a short, hollow object, larger on one end, 120° angle, for leisurely smoking using tobacco." The detailed and descriptive definitions, which he was able to provide in response to the auditory label of the very objects he failed to recognize from visual input, reflect the preservation of his knowledge of objects.

Patient CK produces a reasonably good rendition of targets consisting of black and white geometric figures, as shown in figure 11.1. However, he does so in an unusual way: the numbers assigned to the different strokes indicate the order in which the lines were drawn. Instead of deriving the

Target   CK's copy

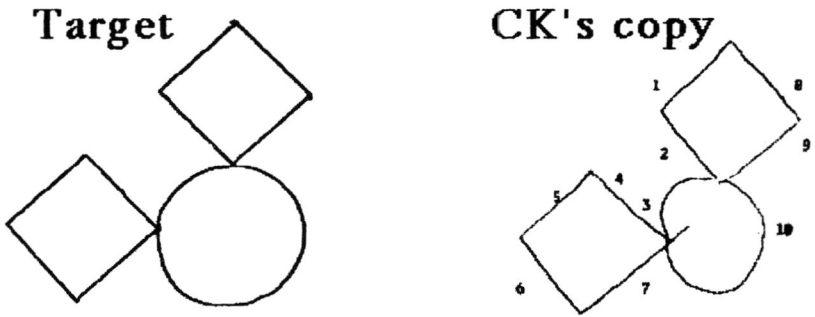

FIGURE 11.1. Copy of target (left) by CK with the numbers indicating the order of the strokes (from Behrmann et al., 1992).

holistic percept of two diamonds and a circle as unimpaired subjects might do, CK copies the individual lines slavishly and segmentally, without appearing to appreciate the identities. A similar pattern is noted when he copies text; CK copies the text in the same font as the target and does not appreciate the identity of the letters. This pattern poses a quandary for the classical agnosia dichotomy: CK can clearly copy figures or text and should, thus, be classified as an associative agnosic but the manner in which the copying is done is piecemeal and segmental and is clearly not normal. This slavish bit-by-bit copying is considered one of the hallmark features of integrative agnosia in which the impairment appears to affect mid- or intermediate level vision.

The label "integrative agnosia" was coined by Riddoch and Humphreys (1987) on the basis of their studies with patient HJA (Humphreys, 1999; Humphreys & Riddoch, 1987; Humphreys et al., 1994; Humphreys, Riddoch, Quinlan, Price, & Donnelly, 1992). The term was originally used to refer to the patient's inability to integrate disparate elements of a display, which are themselves available, into a coherent form. For example, they reported that HJA was impaired at search tasks that require the binding of visual elements in a spatially parallel manner across a field containing multiple stimuli; he was disproportionately slowed, relative to control subjects, in detecting the presence of an inverted T among upright Ts. In contrast, his search was efficient and rapid for targets that did not require a combination of elements such as a target "/" among multiple "|"s (Humphreys, 1999; Humphreys & Riddoch, 1987; Humphreys et al., 1994, 1992). Note that when the demands for integration are low, HJA and other integrative agnosic patients perform significantly above chance levels: they can make same/different judgments accurately on two stimuli, which share area and brightness but not shape (aspect ratio changes from square to rectangle; Efron, 1968; see figure 11.2).

Two problems emerge in trying to refine the definition of integrative agnosia. The first is that there are very few studies of such individuals

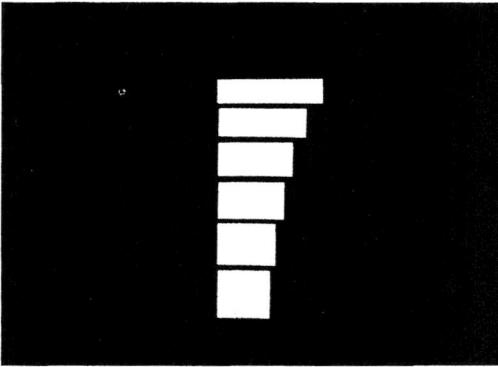

FIGURE 11.2. Efron shapes equated for area and brightness: two stimuli are placed before the patient for same/different judgments. Integrative agnosic patients usually perform reasonably well on this test of geometric form discrimination.

and so there is much to be done in delineating the key features of the disorder (see Humphreys, 2000, for a useful review). The second, related point is that, of those studies that have been done, the patients are not always fully characterized, and the focus of the work is usually rather circumscribed with a particular emphasis on one aspect of the problem. As such, we are left with uncertainty about the definition of the problem and about which patients can be classified by this term. The apparent failure to consider all parts of the stimulus in deriving a unitary representation of the input is probably key to IA. It is this inability to integrate the elements into a well-formed shape, the failure to group features into a larger, meaningful whole, and the overzealous parsing of the display that make these patients ideal for further investigations of perceptual organization. The purpose of this chapter is to elucidate the central features of IA and to discuss them in relation to the three processes of perceptual organization alluded to above. In doing so, we will first outline some exclusion criteria for IA and then describe the inclusion criteria.

What Is Not IA

Among the exclusion criteria for IA is a severe perceptual deficit: patients whose perceptual deficit is so extensive that it affects the extraction of simple features from a display are not classifiable as having IA. For example, patients who perform at chance on the Efron test (see figure 11.2) are considered to have a more marked deficit in encoding basic properties of form (more in line with apperceptive agnosia). These patients will not be considered further (see Benson & Greenberg, 1969; Campion & Latto, 1985; Davidoff & Warrington, 1993; Goodale & Milner, 1992; Mapelli & Behrmann, 1997; McMullen, Fisk, Phillips, & Maloney, 2000; Vecera & Behrmann, 1997; Warrington & Davidoff, 2000). Additionally, patients who show normal performance on simple geometric form matching but who appear to be limited in the amount of perceptual information they can process are also excluded. These patients' performance deteriorates when the perceptual characteristics of the target itself are made more complex and when resource demands are increased even if the perceptual judgment required is simple (Grossman, Galetta, & D'Esposito, 1997). Such difficulties have occasionally been attributed to an attentional or working memory limitation (Coslett, Stark, Rajaram, & Saffran, 1996; Thaiss & de Bleser, 1992) and, although these patients fit the definition of integrative agnosia in some respects, they have additional problems and will not be considered further.

At the other extreme are patients whose perceptual performance is too good even if their object recognition is not. Such patients fit the standard classification of associative agnosia, although, again, as mentioned above, this is a rather coarse description for what is likely to be a host of different disorders. One example that fits this definition is an individual who was able to match nonsense figures well and who matched the size and position of stimuli well but showed significant problems in face, letter, and object recognition (Kertesz, 1979). That the matching task was done well suggests that the stimuli are probably reasonably well perceived, distinguishing him from patients with integrative agnosia.

A second type of associative agnosic patient to be excluded is an individual whose deficit in recognizing objects extends beyond perception. Though the patient's perceptual performance resembles integrative agnosia, the patients have an accompanying recognition deficit in another input modality or a problem in the long-term representation of objects. De Renzi and Lucchelli (1993), for example, report that their patient, Annalisa, has relatively good performance on the Efron test, along with reasonably good copying and poor performance on overlapping objects (see below for more on this). These patterns fit the definition of IA. However, Annalisa clearly had additional problems extending beyond a visual perceptual deficit. For example, she was impaired at recalling perceptual details of items from long-term memory. Also, when given the auditory labels of two objects, she was unable to describe the perceptual difference between them and she was in the intermediate range of severity on tactile recognition (see also patient of Davidoff & Wilson, 1985). The patient of Grailet, Seron, Bruyer, Coyette, & Frederix (1990) also showed many of the diagnostic features of integrative agnosia. However, he too appeared to have a deficit that extended beyond visual perceptual processing in that he was impaired at tactile object recognition and drew poorly from memory. These additional deficits call into question the competence of his long-term knowledge. We will not consider these patients as suffering from IA per se and will restrict our discussion to patients whose long-term representations are intact. It is worth noting, however, that longstanding IA may have adverse effects on long-term representations; visual memories might begin to deteriorate if not refreshed or updated by intact perceptual descriptions and, unfortunately, this may be the case for patient HJA (Riddoch, Humphreys, Gannon, Blott, & Jones, 1999).

What Is IA?

A rough criterion for inclusion in this category is that the patients should have the features from the display available to them but be unable to utilize them further. Additionally, they should be able to make discriminations between forms that place minimal demand on integration. Thus, individuals with IA have relatively well preserved low-level visual processes including discrimination of line length, spatial localization of dots, color and motion processing. They can also make line orientation and size judgments at normal levels (Davidoff & Warrington, 1993; Gauthier, Behrmann, & Tarr, 1999; Humphreys, 1999).

As mentioned above, one way in which the IA deficit manifests is in copying performance. RN and SM1 (to be differentiated when SM2 is introduced below) are two other IA patients, who, like HJA and CK, are able to copy well, as evident in their copies of complex figures such as the Rey-Osterreith figure (see figure 11.3) and a copy of a beach scene

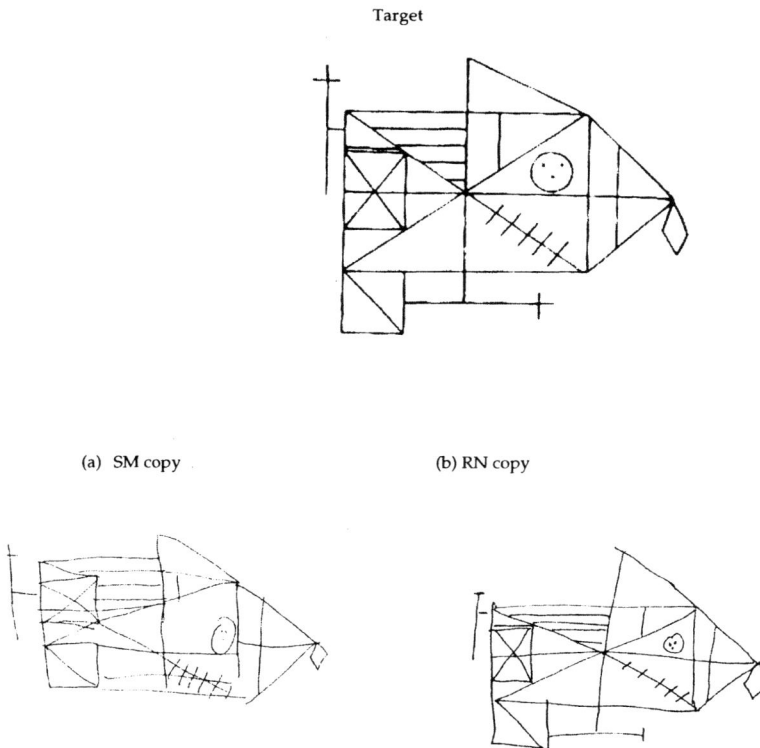

FIGURE 11.3. Copies of Rey-Osterrieth figure by patients RN and SM1.

Target

(a) SM copy   (b) RN copy

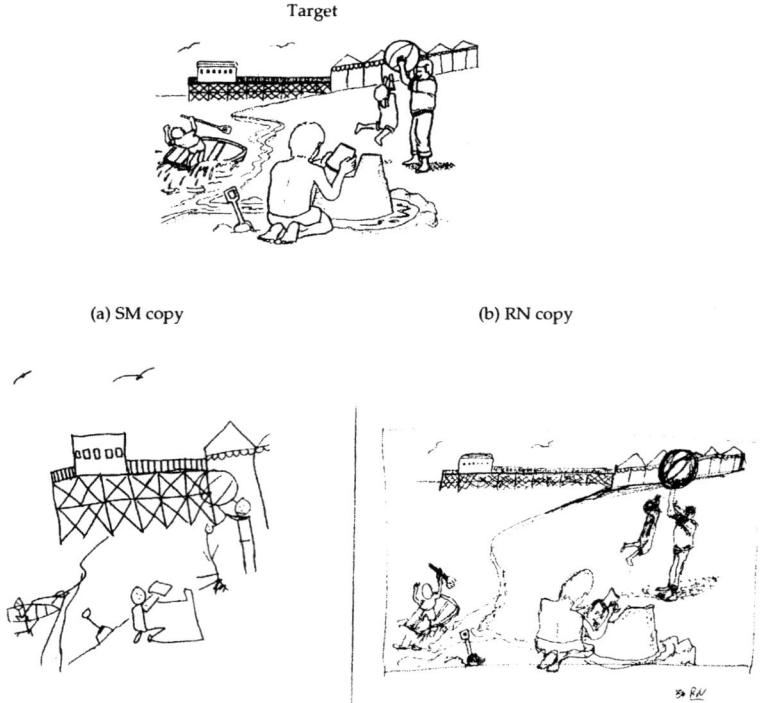

FIGURE 11.4. Copy of beach scene by SM1 and RN.

(see figure 11.4). Both, however, are noticeably slow and segmental in their copying with laborious slavish efforts.

Another way in which the IA deficit manifests is in the patients' performance on segregating items, which are presented in an overlapping display. For example, in the stimulus displayed in figure 11.5, patient CK performed extremely poorly. He was, on occasion, able to match the features that protrude from the overlapping display, like the edge of the stick of the flag, but was unable to decide which objects were present. This was true even when he was not required to identify the objects per se but merely to match them to an array of choices placed below the overlapping display. The impairment in segmentation was also seen when he was given the set of overlapping figures, as shown at the top of figure 11.5, and asked simply to trace the outline of each different object with a different colored crayon. He first outlined in different colors the components of the object that did not overlap in the central region and that did not require segmentation. Once this was done and he now had to segment the overlapped region, he picked up a crayon, placed it at the intersection of two contours, and held it there for a long time without proceeding. He then had a strong emotional reaction and refused to complete the task, arguing

FIGURE 11.5. Display of overlap and choices for matching. Overlapping section at top also used for coloring contours.

that he had no idea in which direction to continue, as he did not know which lines belonged to which objects. HJA shows a very similar pattern and his outlining of overlapped objects is demonstrated in Humphreys & Riddoch (2001).

The fragmented nature of the patients' perception also comes through clearly in their object-recognition errors. Their responses to black-and-white line drawings (see figure 11.6) are consistent with the claim that they can extract some, but not all the relevant information from the display. Patient RN, for example, identified the harmonica as a "stereo or computer," presumably picking up on the little "keys" (air holes). He also called an octopus a "bug" and a pretzel a "snake." We see a similar pattern in patient SM1 who called an octopus a "spider" and a harmonica a "cash register." The piecemeal description of objects is characteristic of other IA patients. HJA, for example, tends to oversegment objects so that even when presented with a single item such as a paintbrush, he is convinced that two separate objects are present in the display. In his response to a picture of a pepperpot, he responded "a stand containing three separate pans; the top has a design on its lid, the second has a slightly smaller diameter than the top pan; the bottom pan has a wider diameter than the

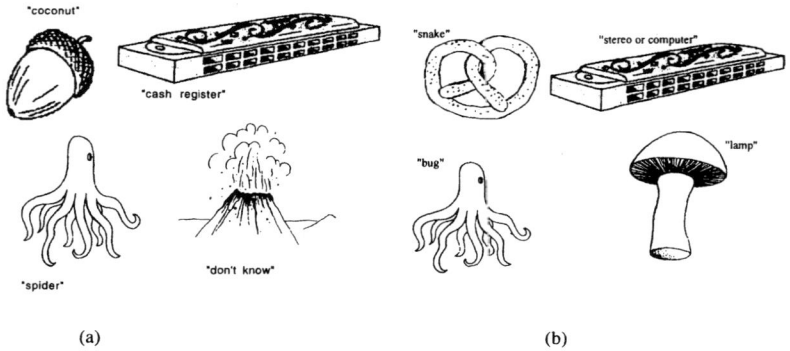

FIGURE 11.6. (a) RN's and (b) SM1's naming errors on Boston Naming Test.

second pan and is longer in length" (p. 399, Humphreys & Riddoch, 1984). This oversegmentation is also seen in SM2 (Butter & Trobe, 1994) who, when presented with a display of a few items, stated that several objects were present as he identified parts as separate items. Shown a cup and asked to identify it, he stated that it was "a large oval item together with a smaller oval item (pointing to the handle)." This oversegmentation can also apply to individual letters; patient FGP (Kartsounis & Warrington, 1991) selected subparts of individual letters, reporting R as D and Q as O.

Almost all of the IA patients are impaired at face recognition, with the exception of CK, as well as object recognition, and are also alexic, although this is not true of every patient. Their alexia usually manifests in very slow reading (Mycroft, Behrmann, & Kay, 2003); for example, SM1 is able to read accurately (98% correct) but requires roughly 104 ms to process each letter in a word. Accuracy is also high for HJA, but he requires a significant amount of time (355 ms per letter) for letter processing (Oßwald, Humphreys, & Olson, 2002). RN also requires a substantial increase in time (178 ms) for each additional letter, although his accuracy is also affected, as he reads only 80% of words correctly. The patterns reported here are all in contrast with the minimal increase required by normal subjects for words up to 6 or 7 letters in length (Frederiksen & Kroll, 1976).

A final common characteristic of the performance of these patients is that they typically benefit from the addition of surface information. Color, motion, or other surface cues seem to help the integration of form elements into a coherent perceptual whole. Thus, HJA identifies real objects correctly about 60% of the time in contrast with photographs (40%) and line drawings (30%). The same is true of patient CK, who also benefits from color and other surface cues, which lead to roughly 25% improvement in his object identification (Behrmann et al., 1992). Through the addition of surface information such as luminance and texture, contrasting parts may be observed and used especially in cases where edge-based segmentation is impaired. In addition, depth information, conveyed both by binocular disparity cues as well as head movements, assists with the segmentation of parts of an object and allows partially occluded surfaces to be recovered (Chainay & Humphreys, 2000).

In sum, at the present time, we take as the defining features of IA the disproportionate impairment in perceptual processing when there are multiple elements to be encoded and integrated and when exposure duration or stimulus quality is affected. This manifests in overlapping displays, in copying and in object and word identification (although the deficit may also be evident under many other conditions). When sufficient time is available and encoding can be done serially, or when cues to the segmentation are present (for example, color or other surface properties), performance is somewhat better.

We should also note one other dramatic finding observed in some, but not all IA patients; because this pattern is not evident in all patients, we have not included it as a core characteristic of the deficit. The pattern under discussion concerns the fact that the patients' perception of silhouettes may be better than of line drawings. Interestingly and counterintuitively, in some cases, the presence of local information may even reduce the efficiency of visual recognition. For example, both patients HJA (Lawson & Humphreys, 1999; Riddoch & Humphreys, 1987) and SM2 (Butter & Trobe, 1994) were better at identifying pictures presented as silhouettes rather than line drawings as the internal details apparently led to incorrect segmentation. HJA scored 72% for silhouettes and 64% for line drawings when tested in 1997 (reported by Riddoch et al., 1999). The difference between stimulus types was even more dramatic in patient SM2, who identified 23% of black-and-white line drawings and 48% silhouettes. Note that, in both cases, performance on silhouettes is still far from normal (control subjects for SM2 scored 92.5%). Nevertheless, the advantage for silhouettes over line drawings is in direct contrast to the behavior of non-neurological subjects who benefit significantly from the presence of additional contours. Not all patients do better on silhouettes, as neither CK, SM1, nor RN show this advantage and FGP identified only 3 out of 12 silhouette drawings of common objects.

Neuropsychological Evidence

In the following section, the evidence from patients with agnosia concerning perceptual organization is reviewed for each of the three processes outlined above. Again, although there may be other patients in the literature who fit the IA definition, we have selected only those patients ($n = 7$) for whom sufficient information is provided in the reports. In an attempt to coordinate the findings across the different studies, in table 11.1 we have summarized the neurological status of the different patients and their performance on the three processes.

TABLE 11.1: Biographical data and summary of performance of 7 patients with integrative agnosia across a range of perceptual organization measures

Patient	Biographical Details	Lesion Details	Figure Ground	Overlapping	Amodal Completion	Illusory Contours	Grouping
HJA (Humphreys, 1999; Humphreys & Riddoch, 1987; Humphreys et al., 1994; Humphreys, Riddoch, Quinlan, Price, & Donnelly, 1992; Riddoch & Humphreys, 1987; Riddoch, Humphreys, Gannon, Blott, & Jones, 1999)	61-year-old male; right-handed; detailed testing at many ages, currently 80 years old	Stroke at age 61; bilateral lesions of occipital cortices extending forward to temporal lobes; Bilateral superior altitudinal defect	Poor	Poor	Poor	?	Poor
CK (Behrmann, Moscovitch, & Winocur, 1994; Behrmann, Winocur, & Moscovitch, 1992; Moscovitch, Winocur, & Behrmann, 1997)	41-year-old male; right-handed	Car accident; bilateral thinning of occipital cortices and hypoperfusion on SPECT; Left hemianopia largely resolved	Poor as noise increases	Poor	Poor	Poor	?
SM1 (Behrmann & Kimchi, 2002; Behrmann & Kimchi, 2003a; Gauthier, Behrmann, & Tarr, 1999; Marotta, McKeeff, & Behrmann, 2002)	26-year-old male; right-handed	Car accident; contusion in the right anterior and posterior cerebral regions accompanied by deep shearing injury in the corpus callosum and left basal ganglia; no field defect	Good	Poor	Poor	Good	?
CR (Gauthier et al., 1999)	22-year-old male	Metabolic encephalopathy affecting right temporal lobe	Good	Poor	Poor	?	Good (?)
RN (Behrmann & Kimchi, 2002; Behrmann & Kimchi, 2003a; Marotta et al., 2002)	43-year-old male	Stroke following myocardial infarction; negative MRI scan; no field defect	Good	Poor	Good	Good	Poor
SM2 (Butter & Trobe, 1994)	43-year-old male; right-handed	Right hemianopia; MRI—high-intensity signal abnormalities, consistent with progressive multifocal leukoencephalopathy	?	Poor on complex displays	?	Poor	Poor
FGP (Kartsounis & Warrington, 1991)	71-year-old female; handedness?	Left hemianopia; Mild cerebral atrophy	Poor	Poor	Poor	Poor	Poor

FIGURE 11.7. Figure-ground segregation task modified from VOSP, Warrington and James (1991).

Figure-Ground Segregation

One way used to assess figure-ground processing in the patients is to present a display in which a figure is embedded in a noisy background and then to require the subject to detect the presence or absence of the figure. Such a task is incorporated into the Visual Object and Space Perception battery (VOSP; Warrington & James, 1991) and an example of a stimulus from this task is shown in figure 11.7. Patient FGP (Kartsounis & Warrington, 1991) failed consistently (13/20, 8/20, and 12/20) on this task, whereas CK performed reasonably well on this standard version of the task. When the task was adapted, however, so that the level of noise became progressively greater, CK became more impaired at detecting the presence of the X although normal subjects still continue to do well (see figure 11.7, left panel, for example of the display with increasing complexity of the background; Behrmann et al., 1994). Both SM1 and RN scored 20/20 on the original version and CR scored 18/20, failing to detect the X twice when it was present. Of course, we do not know whether the performance of these three patients would be adversely affected when the degree of background noise is increased and so the data remain somewhat equivocal in this regard.

We should note that the failure to derive the figure is not obviously attributable to a problem in processing the spatial frequency information. One may notice that in displays such as this, the background (noise) is carried by the high spatial frequency components and the figure is carried by the low spatial frequency components. To the extent that this is known, the patients do not have a specific problem in processing either high or low spatial frequency information (see Behrmann and Kimchi, 2003a) and therefore, this does not explain the failure to segregate figure from ground. Additionally, this spatial frequency explanation cannot account for the patients' problems in segregating overlapping line drawings so this explanation is unlikely to hold.

As noted above, the impaired performance on overlapping displays relative to displays containing the same stimuli presented in isolation may also be attributable to poor figure-ground segregation. Patient FGP, for example, performed poorly at identifying a whole range of displays in which the shapes overlapped. This included displays where the contour of the shapes overlapped, where the contours were nonoverlapping but the items were totally superimposed (for example, a circle drawn entirely within the boundaries of a square), and where the overlapping shapes were solid rather than transparent. She was also impaired at identifying how many objects are present in three-dimensional displays. HJA also performs more poorly on overlapping than nonoverlapping displays (Riddoch & Humphreys, 1987). In the recent follow-up study with him, it took him only 0.6 s to name an individual letter when it was nonoverlapping but 1.5 s when it overlapped. This contrasts with the normal subjects who required a mean of 0.4 s in both conditions.

Performance on overlapping versus nonoverlapping displays is also worse for CR, SM1, and RN on visually embedded Poppelreuter figures (similar to figure 11.5) where multiple figural overlaps require complex contour analysis. Interestingly, SM2 was impaired on overlapping displays depending on the extent of the overlap. Asked to identify objects presented overlapping, he scored 94% correct when the borders of the objects did not overlap extensively but only roughly 66% when the overlap was increased (in contrast with the 99% correct by the control subjects). This is also true of HJA (see following discussion of Giersch, Humphreys, Boucart, & Kovacs, 2000). The ability to make use of features that do not overlap also exemplified the performance of patient CK, as described above, and when he was forced to segment the image by the contours that overlapped, he was completely unable to do so. We have chosen to ascribe the problems in overlapping figures to the more general problem of figure-ground segregation, but this may not be absolutely correct. Patients may be impaired on overlapping shapes for a variety of reasons; for example, they may fail tasks with such shapes because of the susceptibility of contour completion processes to noise (intersecting lines; see below) or they may be laboriously tracing out the contours as they would do if they were copying. This ambiguity highlights the fact that perceptual organization processes are not well understood and much remains to be explained. For the current purpose, however, we would just point out that the patients perform poorly on overlapping shapes and that such displays clearly tap into the need for deriving coherence from complex images.

Visual Interpolation

Many real-world conditions require visual interpolation processes, including conditions of occlusion where amodal completion is engaged and where illusory contours are perceived. Indeed, as stated above, according to some accounts, these different conditions may entail the same mechanisms (Kellman, Yin, & Shipley, 1998; Shipley & Cunningham, 2001). We will consider the perception of amodal completion and illusory con-

(a)   (b)

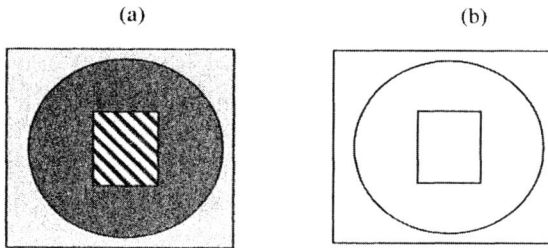

FIGURE 11.8. (a) Overlapping geometric shapes in different, solid colors and (b) the same displays but rendered as line drawings with the different contours in different colors.

tours separately, however, in order to determine whether there are any dissociations evident between them in the patient performance.

AMODAL COMPLETION

Several studies have examined amodal completion in IA patients, although the methods (and results) vary quite widely. For example, patient FGP was asked to identify simple geometric shapes, which were solid in color and displayed one superimposed on top of the other—in one display, a small solid red triangle might appear on top of and in the center of a larger green square which, in turn, was placed on top of and in the center of a larger blue circle (for example, see figure 11.8a). FGP succeeded in identifying all three shapes on only 4 out of 15 trials even with prolonged stimulus duration. Interestingly, she was able to identify all the shapes placed in the center, and fewer of those in the intermediate and outer positions, which require completion. A similar problem was noted for colored line drawings of concentric geometric shapes (figure 11.8b). Although we do not know this definitively, we assume that report of the shapes was better when the shapes were presented in isolation. The failure to derive the shapes when overlapping suggests a problem in interpolation and completion when only a partial image is evident. Similar data from patient FGP are presented in the previous section on figure-ground segregation, reflecting the close relationship between figure-ground segregation and amodal completion.

My colleagues and I have also been interested in the extent to which the patients can complete occluded images, and we have had occasion to test some IA patients on an experiment that uses displays that require completion. The experiment was originally designed to examine whether normal subjects can attend to features of an occluded object as well as they can attend to features of a single object—that is, whether they exhibit object-based attention to occluded objects. To explore this, we used a

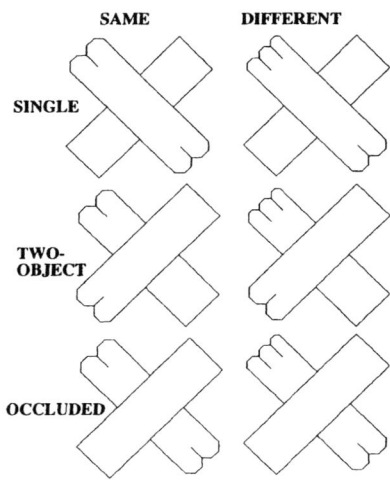

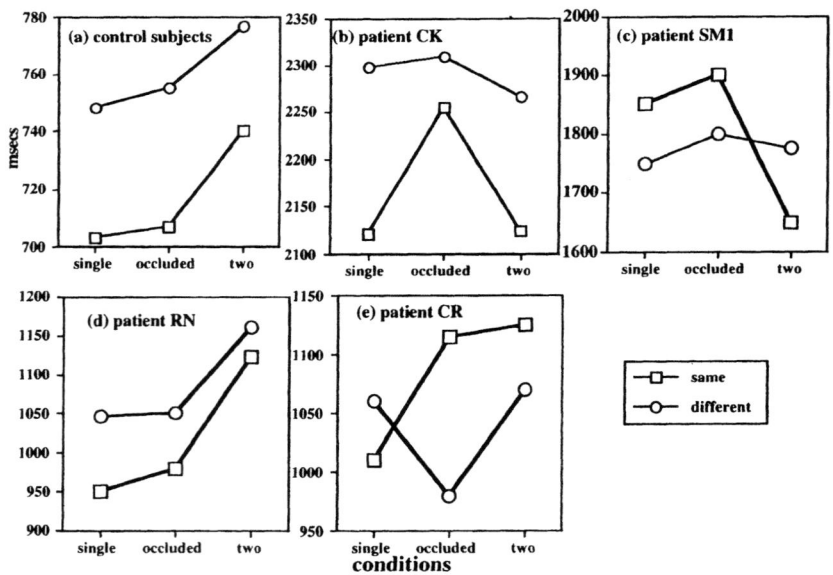

FIGURE 11.9. (Upper panel) Examples of display from Behrmann et al. (1998); (Lower panel) Performance of (a) normal subjects and four patients with integrative agnosia, with each display (b-e) reflecting the data of a single patient.

paradigm in which subjects were required to decide, as quickly as possible, whether the number of bumps appearing at two of the four possible ends of overlapping rectangle were the same or not (Behrmann, Zemel, & Mozer, 1998, 2000). As shown in figure 11.9 (upper panel), there are three conditions in this task, reflected in the rows, all of which are crossed with same/different judgments, as reflected in the columns. In the single-object condition, the bumps appear at the ends of a single, unoccluded object. In the two-object condition, the bumps appear at the end of two different objects, and, in the occlusion condition, the bumps appear at the ends of a single, occluded object.

The main result using this task was that normal subjects make the bumps decision equally quickly on the single and occluded objects, and both of these conditions are faster than the two-object condition (see figure 11.9 leftmost upper panel), consistent with notions of object-based attention. Note that object-based attention here likely emerges from the ability to complete the display amodally, as we have argued previously (Behrmann, et al., 2000).

Importantly, the advantage for the single and occluded object over the two-object condition was not obtained for three of the four agnosic patients we tested (see remaining panels in figure 11.9). Only patient RN performs similarly to the control subjects, although his intercept is considerably raised (note, however, that he is somewhat older than the control subjects reported here and so this may account for the overall slowing in base reaction time). The other patients are all slower than the control subjects, despite the fact that they are all fairly close in age. Of interest is that, although some of these patients do show an advantage for the single-object condition relative to the two-object condition, as in the case of CR, none really shows the pattern whereby single and occluded conditions are equivalent and both differ from the two-object condition. Note that the distance between the ends of the objects in the single and occluded cases is larger than the distance between the ends in the two-object condition; this may explain why SM1 performed better in the two-object case than in the other two conditions.

Patient HJA's ability to complete images has also been tested fairly extensively. For example, in a recent study, Giersch, et al. (2000) tested him on a task containing three stimuli that were either separated, transparently superimposed, in silhouette, or occluded (see examples in figure 11.10, Experiment 2). HJA and the control subjects were required to match the reference stimulus to one of two choices where the alternative choice contained the same three stimuli but in a different spatial arrangement. There was a 500 ms delay between the target and choice displays. HJA was significantly slowed at making decisions on occluded displays relative to all other displays. Interestingly, his performance with silhouettes was good, as has been reported previously (Riddoch & Humphreys, 1987) and no different from that on separated or superimposed displays. The good

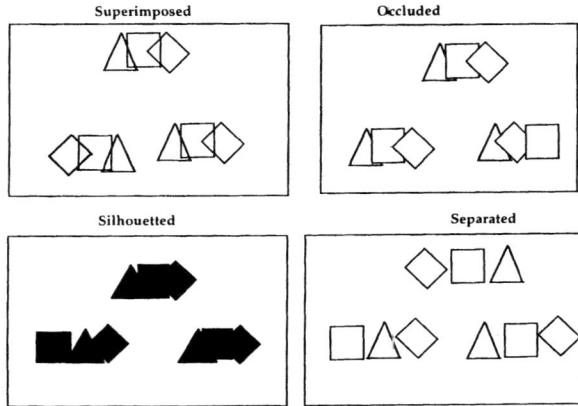

FIGURE 11.10. Superimposed, occluded, silhouetted, and separated displays from Giersch et al. (2000).

performance on silhouettes is consistent with data reported below, showing that he is disadvantaged by the presence of local details.

Despite the ability to compute collinear line segments, HJA's performance on occluded displays is not normal and reveals that the local contours are poorly bound into more global representations of shape even though they themselves might be correctly computed. In a different experiment containing three occluded or superimposed stimuli from which HJA had to select a single stimulus, which matched the central shape, he chose the completed shape as often as he chose the mosaic or partial, incomplete shape. This is in contrast to the control subjects, who chose the mosaic most often (consistent with the 2D representation). Whereas the control subjects could ignore the completion, HJA could not. That HJA could complete occluded contours but not always use this information correctly is most obviously evident in a copying task on which he drew in the occluded contour as if the real contour were present. For example, when a shape interrupted the collinear line of a square so that it was no longer visible, HJA drew in the missing collinear segment on 26 out of 47 trials. He did not include additional contours in displays where there was no occlusion. These findings all suggest that he can interpolate occlusion correctly, although he appears not to be able to exploit it for the purpose of figure-ground differentiation.

Based on the apparent ability to compute the occluded shape but the failure to match this shape when it appears in the presence of other shapes, Giersch et al. (2000) argue that contour interpolation is an early visual process, that occurs prior to the assignment of the contours to more global shapes. They attribute HJA's preserved ability to the more elementary operation of binding form elements into contours, which, they show, is indeed normal (for further discussion, see Humphreys, 2002). Using a set of cards containing displays of a smoothly aligned, closed path of Gabor elements embedded in a random array of Gabor elements of the same spatial frequency and contrast (Pennefather, Chandna, Kovacs, Polat, & Norcia, 1999), they required HJA to trace the Gabor contour on each card. They then used a staircase procedure to establish a threshold. This procedure has been used successfully with various pathological populations (Kovács, Polat, Pennefather, Chandna, & Norcia, 2000) and examples of the cards are shown in figure 11.11. Threshold is reflected in terms of parameter Δ, which is the ratio of average background spacing over contour spacing, and it ranges between 1.2 to 0.5 in steps of 0.05. This parameter expresses "relative noise density" and reflects signal-to-noise ratio; the smaller the Δ value, the better performance (Kovács et al., 2000). HJA obtained a Δ of 0.65, well within the normal range of performance, which is around 0.69 (SD 0.09). The preserved ability on this test is thought to reflect the intact pattern and spatial extent of long-range interaction among orientation-tuned neurons in primary visual cortex.

That contour interpolation can be intact and underlie amodal completion but still not suffice for figure-ground segregation may also explain the performance of SM1 who, on the identical contour-integration task described above, obtained a threshold of 0.6, clearly within normal limits. Of interest is that he still performed poorly on the amodal completion task (see figure 11.9c). On this latter task, he did not obtain an advantage in processing features from a single object, either occluded or complete, compared with two objects. The findings indicate that intact contour interpolation may not suffice for object-based attention just as it may not suffice for figure-ground segregation. Instead, both object-based attention and

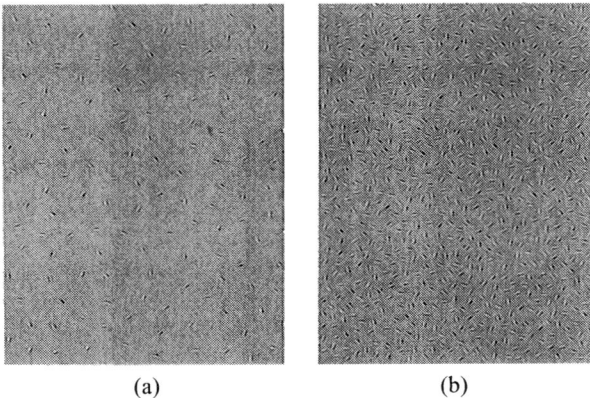

(a)   (b)

FIGURE 11.11. Examples of displays from Kovacs et al., (2000) of contours made of local Gabor units. (a) easy and (b) difficult. The target is a line made of the Gabor units and the target is located toward the bottom left in (a) and upper right in (b).

figure-ground segregation require that form elements be bound into coherent object descriptions.

ILLUSORY FIGURES

Illusory figures are perceived where inducing elements are positioned so
that their contours align to form the edges of a closed figure. Under the
correct circumstances, observers then perceive an opaque figure of about
the same reflectance as the background surface in front of and partly occluding the black elements, which are then amodally completed behind
the illusory figure.

Patient FGP was dramatically impaired on any task requiring the perception of subjective contours. For example, shown Kanisza-type figures
of circles, triangles, and squares, not only did she comment that she only
perceived little curves and no real shape, but she was even unable to
discriminate the geometric shape given the choices. Additionally, she was
impaired at deciding which of two outline shapes would make up a triangle
(see figure 11.12). She stated that she only saw "three little L's," suggesting
a fundamental impairment in deriving the completed contours. Using a
two-choice procedure, she scored 13/20 on the easy and 10/20 on the
difficult discriminations; of course, one might easily also attribute this to
a problem in good continuation and, indeed, as noted below, she performs
poorly on tasks of continuation and closure. When she was shown displays
in which a contour was created by aligned line terminators to give the
impression of one shape superimposed on another, she failed to detect the
illusory contour.

The findings from the various patients indicate that IA individuals are
mostly impaired at various forms of visual interpolation, including amodal
completion and illusory contours, although this is not perfectly consistent
across all patients. We examine the implications of the variability in the
final section.

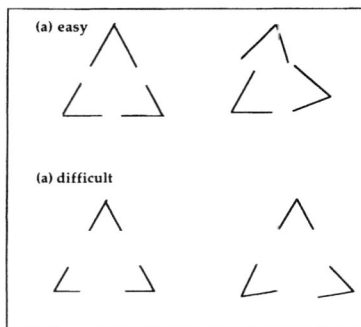

FIGURE 11.12. (a) easy and (b) difficult discriminations of illusory shapes from
Kartsounis and Warrington (1991).

Perceptual Grouping

The final organization process we discuss is perceptual grouping, and of all the different processes of perceptual organization, this has been the one most extensively explored in IA. Of course, there are many ways in which elements can be grouped and some, but not all these ways have been explored in patients.

HJA is apparently unable to exploit the Gestalt principle of collinearity. For example, in one study he was required to make perceptual matches with fragmented line drawings (Boucart & Humphreys, 1992). The fragments in the line drawings could be aligned and collinear, or they could be misaligned so they were no longer collinear but the overall shape had the same spatial frequency as before. In contrast to normal subjects who showed an advantage for the collinear displays, this was not the case for HJA. This is somewhat surprising given his intact contour detection discussed above and his ability to compute occlusion (even though this may not aid in his depth assignment for figure-ground segregation). One might have expected that the ability to link contour elements into elongated contours would assist in the computation of collinearity. Interestingly, HJA did show a sensitivity to the global form; his performance was better when he was required to discriminate between items that had different global orientation than between those with the same orientation. HJA's failure to deal with collinear fragmented forms is suggestive of a problem in integrating local, intact contours into more global, multicontour shape representations and is also compatible with his failure to use the local information for object recognition. This impairment may explain his preference for silhouettes and, as we shall see below, it may be compatible with his performance on hierarchical stimuli.

The ability to use collinearity may also be important for successful performance on other tests of fragmented objects (although undoubtedly many other perceptual skills are also required). Patient SM2 performed poorly on the Hooper Visual Recognition test in which fragments of a contour are shown and subjects assemble these to determine the item (items are not that different from figure 11.12). For example, when displays containing fragmented parts of objects rotated from their normal position were shown to SM2, he was unable to recognize any (normal controls 89%). Two other paradigms have been used extensively to investigate grouping and they are the visual search task and the global/local task. These are discussed in turn.

The ability to group is also useful under some conditions in visual search tasks. In normal subjects, when the distractors are homogeneous and can be grouped together, target detection is efficient and rapid whereas search is slowed and inefficient when the distractors are heterogeneous and require serial encoding. When searching for a T among inverted Ts in a field, HJA showed a similar serial pattern to the control subjects when the distractors were heterogeneous. Of interest is that he could not exploit

CONSISTENT

```
S S S S          H     H
S                H     H
S S S S          H H H H
      S          H     H
S S S S          H     H
```

INCONSISTENT

```
H H H H          S     S
H                S     S
H H H H          S S S S
      H          S     S
H H H H          S     S
```

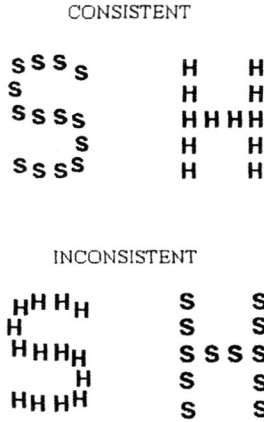

FIGURE 11.13. Stimuli used in local/global tasks in which the local and global stimuli are consistent (above) or not (below).

the similarities and potential for grouping among the homogeneous distractors, with the result that he made many errors and his search function was slow and affected by the number of distractors present (Humphreys et al., 1994, 1992). A similar pattern was seen when HJA searched for abstract forms rather than letters. In contrast, HJA manifested normal search functions when the target was of a different orientation from the distractors. Taken together, these findings reflect the fact that the impairment in integrative agnosia is reflected in tasks that require the binding of visual elements in a spatially parallel manner across a field (Humphreys & Riddoch, 2001; Humphreys et al., 1994).

The final domain we discuss is that of processes involved in deriving hierarchical configurations from discrete elements. These processes are engaged frequently in the real world; bicycles have wheels, which, in turn, have spokes and this requires that parts of objects must be bound into global wholes. The paradigm most often exploited to study the ability to deal with elements and wholes is modelled after that of Navon (1977) in which hierarchical stimuli are used and in which the local elements may or may not be consistent with the global item. For example, stimuli may consist of a global letter H made up of small letter Hs or small letter S. Whereas the former are consistent, the latter are not (see figure 11.13). Such stimuli are useful in order to examine whether global identity can be derived and whether local information interferes with this derivation or vice versa. It is generally thought that the local elements are grouped to form the global shape and grouping of the elements may be based, for example, on proximity, similarity of luminance or shape, or good continuity (Han & Humphreys, 2002).

In one block of trials, subjects report the identity of the global letter and in a second, they report the identity of the local letters. Typically, normal observers exhibit a global advantage such that the global item is identified more rapidly than the local items (the so-called forest-before-the-trees effect; Navon, 1977; Yovel, Yovel & Levy, 2001). Additionally, global interference is observed such that in cases where the local and global information are inconsistent, there is interference from the global identity onto naming the local item but not vice versa. Much recent research has been concerned with identifying the neural substrate that mediates the processing of the local and global elements. One result from this research is that the right hemisphere appears to be biased for global processing whereas the left hemisphere appears to be biased for local processing (Fink et al., 1996), although these hemispheric asymmetries may be relative rather than absolute (Polster & Rapcsak, 1994).

Given the compositional nature of the stimuli and the tendency of patients to oversegment, one would predict that the integrative agnosic patients would be easily captured by local elements or parts and would then have difficulty deriving unified wholes from the input. This is precisely the case for patients RN (Behrmann & Kimchi, 2003a, 2003b) and CR Behrmann and Kimchi, 2003c). Figure 11.14 below shows the data from the control subjects as well as from three patients (we return to a discussion of SM1 shortly). As is evident from this figure, the normal control subjects show the expected global advantage and a trend toward global-to-local interference (under foveal presentation with unlimited exposure durations, one does not always obtain a strong interference effect). Of particular interest are the data from RN and CR, which contrast with the normal subjects and in which there is local dominance; performance is faster for local than global shapes and there is interference from local to global in the inconsistent case. These findings strongly support the claim that the patients' processing is directed toward the elements rather than the configuration per se.

But this pattern of local capture is not seen in all integrative agnosic patients. This pattern was not observed in HJA nor in patient SM1. Let us consider HJA first: he responded more quickly to global than to local stimuli (roughly 300 ms difference). His responses to global letters were relatively normal and it was his response to local letters that was slowed, although he showed no impairment when the local elements were presented in isolation (Riddoch & Humphreys, 1987). However, unlike normal subjects, he showed no interference from global to local identification (although, as we see above, even the normal subjects do not always show this and it is paradigm-dependent). The explanation offered for HJA's pattern is that there is separate and independent processing of global and local forms (Humphreys, 1999) and this is supported by the presence of a global advantage without global-to-local interference. The idea is that global shape can be derived by HJA but is not embellished with more

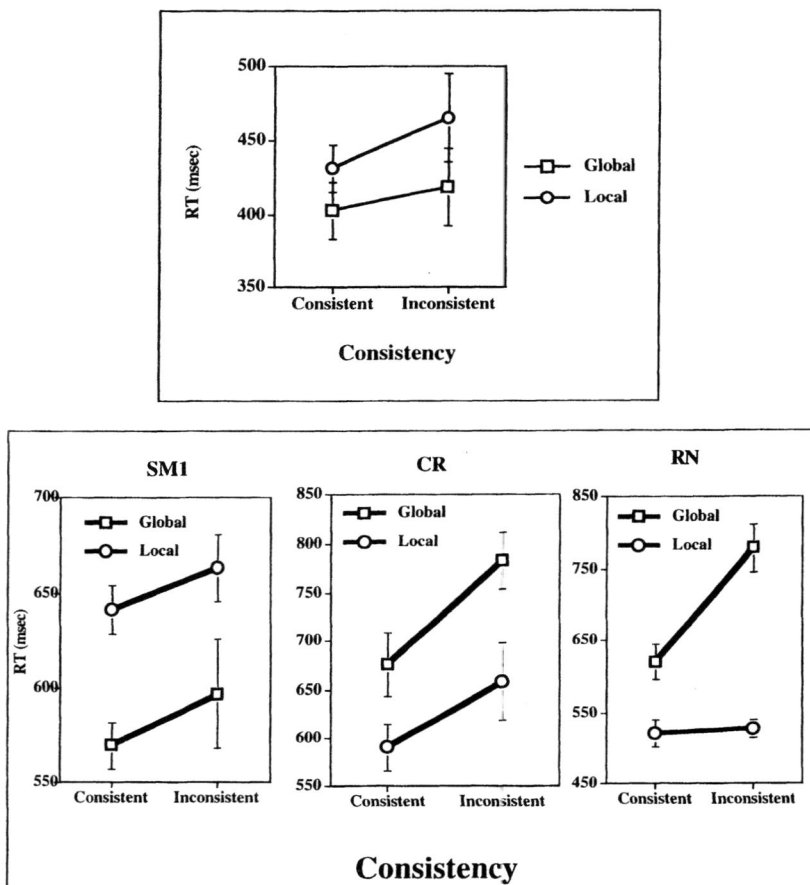

FIGURE 11.14. RT performance of control subjects (above) and three patients with integrative agnosia in a global/local letter identification task.

detailed local information and so the two forms are not synthesized. To derive sufficient local information for object identification, HJA may then have to process the parts serially, and this may lead to the segmental, piecemeal performance. This explanation is consistent with the data from Boucart and Humphreys (1992) mentioned above revealing his sensitivity to global shape despite the inability to exploit the collinearity of the fragmented elements. It also meshes well with his ability to derive form from the global outline of the silhouette in the absence of the internal features.

But not all the data seem compatible with this explanation. For example, HJA's ability to match and identify objects appears not to be greatly influenced by the global properties of objects under some conditions. For example, when an object is foreshortened and the global shape altered, his performance is not greatly affected. Also surprising is that his performance appears to be more reliant on local distinctive features of an object; when a primary distinctive feature is no longer salient in an image, performance is adversely affected (Humphreys & Riddoch, 1984). But HJA is not the only IA patient exhibiting global precedence and no interference; this is the pattern shown by SM1 too (see figure 11.14). SM1's ability to derive the global configuration is particularly puzzling as he has a clear unilateral right-hemisphere lesion and in terms of hypotheses about right-hemisphere tuning for global properties of stimuli, he should be dramatically impaired.

We have previously offered an explanation for SM1's apparent success with these Navon figures. We have shown, for example, that when a hierarchical stimulus is presented for a brief exposure duration (unlike the unlimited duration used for presenting the Navon figures), SM1 no longer performs as well as normal controls in deriving the global configuration (Behrmann & Kimchi, 2003a). Additionally, under more challenging conditions, such as when there are few, rather than many, local elements that need to be grouped, SM1 does not derive the global form from the elements. These findings suggest that SM1 is indeed impaired at grouping, although his impairment might not be as severe as that of the other patients. Under the appropriate testing conditions, however, the deficit is easily revealed. This explanation might also apply to HJA but whether it does is not known at present.

Recent findings from the study of normal perceptual organization suggests that the impairment in deriving the global configuration may be a direct consequence of weakened grouping. For example, Han, Humphreys, & Chen, (1999) have proposed that there is an interaction between perceptual organization based on Gestalt laws and that based on hierarchical processing (see also Han & Humphreys, 1999). In their experiments, they required subjects to discriminate stimuli at the local or global level and manipulated the strength of grouping by including background distractors. When the grouping between local elements was weakened, the perception of global structure was impeded (Han & Humphreys, 1999), manifest as a reduction in the global advantage. These findings are relevant for IA and suggest that a reduction in grouping ability, as in CR and RN, directly results in the local advantage.

One other issue that may help us resolve and understand the relationship between hierarchical processing and grouping, as well as other forms of perceptual organization, is that of the microgenesis or detailed time course of these different processes. Recent studies by Kimchi (Kimchi, 1998, 2000) with normal subjects have revealed a change in the representation derived from the stimulus as a function of time. Whereas early on in the course of processing, subjects appear to represent the elements, later on at longer durations, the configuration is represented and this is the source of the global advantage. We have begun exploiting this method for more detailed analysis of the patients' performance in an attempt to uncover the mechanisms mediating the derivation of global configuration (Behrmann & Kimchi, 2003b). One possible explanation for the apparent differences observed across patients is that all integrative agnosic patients are impaired at deriving global configuration—however, with enough time, some of them (such as SM1 and HJA) may eventually succeed. Only a detailed analysis of the time course of processing in the patients can resolve this.

Taken together, the findings clearly indicate some pattern of impairment in grouping processes in almost all patients, although the vagaries of the studies and patients do not allow us to make good comparisons between the patients. This domain clearly requires further exploration.

Caveats and Qualifications

The focus of this chapter has been on a select subgroup of individuals with visual perceptual deficits acquired in adulthood. These patients exhibit integrative agnosia, a deficit in which they appear to have the building blocks of perception available to them but are unable to use them to configure shapes. We have deliberately excluded other types of patients (apperceptive agnosic, associative agnosic, attentional deficits) as well as integrative agnosic patients who meet our criteria but for whom insufficient detail is available. Before concluding, however, there is one other group of patients whom we have not discussed but deserves to be contrasted with IA patients and these are individuals with simultanagnosia. In some ways, IA and simultanagnosia are very similar and so comparing them is important.

Simultanagnosia is the term applied to those patients who, following lesions to the junction of parietal and occipital regions bilaterally, may be able to detect or identify individual visual objects or their features but may be unable to process multiple objects simultaneously. These patients may also exhibit a host of other impairments including spatial disorientation, abnormal eye movements, and inaccurate visually guided reaching (Balint, 1909), but our focus here is on the apparent problem in perceptual organization and its relationship to integrative agnosia. The simultanagnosic deficit has been labeled "dorsal simultanagnosia" to differentiate it from the impairment in interpreting visual arrays that occurs with letter-by-letter reading (Farah, 1990). This latter impairment occurs following lesions to more ventral areas, typically in the left hemisphere. Of relevance to us here, however, is that there are aspects of the performance of dorsal simultanagnosic patients that resemble the patterns described above in relation to visual agnosia. The striking feature of dorsal simultanagnosia is that the patient's visual experience becomes captured by a local detail or individual object, to the exclusion of all other aspects of the scene (Coslett & Saffran, 1991; Rafal & Robertson, 1995).

Some recent case reports highlight the perceptual difficulties of these patients. For example, patient KB (Karnath, Ferber, Rorden, & Driver, 2000) could recognize a square or circle drawn on paper but when they overlapped, she was unable to identify both. She was able to identify only individual objects in a visual scene and was unable to recognize the general theme of the picture. The pathological visual capture of local elements was so striking that she was virtually unable to identify a global shape using Navon hierarchical stimuli even when the stimulus exposure duration was unlimited. Although she identified the local letter correctly on 91% of the trials, she managed to name the global letter on only 5 out of 96 trials and, on the incorrect trial, she gave the local letter as a response on 77 of the incorrect trials. This local capture resembles the pattern reported for the integrative agnosic patient, RN, reported above. It is interesting to note that KB was slowed in reporting the local letter when it was inconsistent with the global letter, revealing evidence for some processing of the global letter albeit insufficient for it to reach threshold for overt identification. One possible explanation is that local capture is not diagnostic of a particular perceptual problem. Indeed, similar, albeit milder impairments in selectively identifying the global hierarchical letter has been reported in patients with unilateral right-hemisphere lesions around the temporo-parietal junction (Doricchi & Incoccia, 1998; Robertson, Lamb, & Knight, 1988) and for patients with degenerative disorders and diffuse cortical atrophy (Coslett, Stark, Rajaram, & Saffran, 1995; Stark, Grafman, & Fertig, 1997).

Although there is some similarity between simultanaganosic and integrative agnosic patients, there are also major differences. Integrative agnosic patients do not show spatial disorientation, do not bump into objects, and do not exhibit optic ataxia. Moreover, they do not appear to be limited in their ability to report the presence of multiple objects even if they cannot identify them all correctly. Humphreys (1999) suggests that the distinction between the two phenomena is best characterized as a difference between spatial representation between parts of a single object (integrative agnosia) versus spatial representation between objects (simultanagnosia).

Conclusion

This chapter has been concerned with a specific subpopulation of patients who are unable to bind contours into wholistic shapes despite the apparent availability of the contours (as is known for some cases) and other low-level features of the image. Because these patients appear to have the building blocks for perception but cannot derive the final shape, they may provide some insight into normal mechanisms of perceptual organization. We examined the performance of these patients in relation to three main processes of perceptual organization: figure-ground segregation, visual interpolation, and grouping. The study of these patients offers much potential for understanding perceptual organization.

A review of the findings from 7 patients all of whom have been tested relatively extensively leads to a few general conclusions. As a group, the patients appear to be impaired in the three processes we have dealt with. It is the case, however, that detailed examination of the individual patients does not reveal uniformity across the patients. Three of the patients are clearly impaired at figure-ground organization, while three patients are reasonably good and there are no persuasive data from the final patient. Five patients are impaired at amodal completion and one is reasonably good. There is similar discrepancy on some of the other dimensions. It is the case, however, that all patients are impaired on at least one of the organizational processes.

A critical question is where does the variability come from and is it informative? At this stage it is difficult to answer either question. The variability might emerge from the fact that patients may differ in severity. For example, whereas patients HJA and CK appear to be impaired on all processes, RN is impaired on only a subset. Degree of deficit may provide an explanation but it is not clear how to validate this claim. Additional testing with some means of external validation for these processes is clearly needed. A second explanation for the variability might be the lesion site and qualitative, not quantitative, differences between the patients. Again, this is notoriously difficult to nail down in a neuropsychological population because of the extent of the lesion site and so we cannot reach any definitive conclusions about lesion site and overt behavioral deficit. What is clear from all this is that much remains to be done to develop a further understanding of the relationship between neural mechanisms and perceptual organization but also to understand how the different perceptual processes are related to each other and to other forms of visual processing such as object discrimination and identification.

At this stage, suffice it to say that the available data are rich and interesting and provide clear suggestions for future research and clarification. We expect that these ongoing neuropsychological investigations, in conjunction with the emerging data from other methods such as single neuron recordings, functional imaging, and detailed behavioral studies with normal subjects, will help clarify the mechanisms, both psychological and neural, that mediate the organization of the chaotic input to the visual system.

Notes

This chapter was largely written while the author was on sabbatical at the Weizmann Institute of Science, Israel. The work was supported by grants from The Weston Visiting Professorship at the Weizmann Institute of Science, Israel; the

James McKeen Cattell Sabbatical award; a Binational Science Foundation grant to MB and Rutie Kimchi; and NIMH grant MH54766. I thank Rutie Kimchi, Mary Peterson, Gill Rhodes, Christan Gerlach, and Anjan Chatterjee for their valuable comments on this chapter.

References

Adler, A. (1944). Disintegration and restoration of optic recognition in visual agnosia. *Archives of Neurology and Psychiatry, 51*, 243–259.

Agostini, T., & Galmonte, A. (2002). Perceptual organization overcomes the effects of local surround in determining simultaneous lightness contrast. *Psychological Science, 13*(1), 89–93.

Arguin, M., Bub, D. N., & Dudek, G. (1996). Shape integration for visual object recognition and its implication in category specific visual agnosia. *Visual Cognition, 3*(3), 221–275.

Balint, R. (1909). Seelenlahmung des 'Schauens', optische Ataxiem raumliche Storung der Aufmerksamkeit. (Paralysis of "looking," optic ataxia, and the spatial disturbance of attention). *Monatsschrift fur Psychiatrie und Neurologie* (25), 51–81.

Bartolomeo, P., Bachoud-Lèvi, A., De Gelder, B., Dalla Barba, G., Brugieres, P., & Degos, J. D. (1998). Multiple-domain dissociation between impaired visual perception and preserved mental imagery in a patient with bilateral extrastriate lesions. *Neuropsychologia, 36*(3), 239–249.

Bartolomeo, P., Bachoud-Lèvi, A. C., Degos, J. D., & Boller, F. (1998). Disruption of residual reading capacity in a pure alexic patient after a mirror-image right hemispheric lesion. *Neurology, 50*(1), 286–288.

Behrmann, M., & Kimchi, R. (2003a). What does visual agnosia tell us about perceptual organization and its relationship to object recognition? *Journal of Experimental Psychology: Human Perception and Performance.*

Behrmann, M., & Kimchi, R. (2003b). Perceptual organization in visual agnosia. In R. Kimchi, M. Behrmann, & C. Olson (Eds.), *Perceptual organization in vision: Behavioral and neural perspectives.* Hillsdale, NJ: Erlbaum.

Behrmann, M. and Kimchi, R. (2003c). Studies with agnosic patient, CR. Unpublished observations.

Behrmann, M., Moscovitch, M., & Winocur, G. (1994). Intact visual imagery and impaired visual perception in a patient with visual agnosia. *Journal of Experimental Psychology: Human Perception and Performance, 20*(5), 1068–1087.

Behrmann, M., Winocur, G., & Moscovitch, M. (1992). Dissociations between mental imagery and object recognition in a brain-damaged patient. *Nature, 359*, 636–637.

Behrmann, M., Zemel, R., & Mozer, M. C. (1998). Object-based attention and occlusion: Evidence from normal subjects and a computational model. *Journal of Experimental Psychology: Human Perception and Performance, 24*(4), 1011–1036.

Behrmann, M., Zemel, R., & Mozer, M. C. (2000). Occlusion, symmetry, and object-based attention: Reply to Saiki (2000). *Journal of Experimental Psychology: Human Perception and Performance, 26*(4), 1497–1505.

Benson, D. F., & Greenberg, J. P. (1969). Visual form agnosia. *Annual Review of Neuroscience, 20*, 82–89.

Boucart, M., & Humphreys, G. W. (1992). The computation of perceptual structure from collinearity and closure: Normality and pathology. *Neuropsychologia, 30*(6), 527–546.

Bullier, J., Schall, J. D., & Morel, A. (1996). Functional streams in occipito-frontal connections in the monkey. *Behavioural Brain Research, 76,* 89–97.

Butter, C. M., & Trobe, J. D. (1994). Integrative agnosia following progressive multifocal leukoencephalopathy. *Cortex, 30,* 145–158.

Campion, J., & Latto, R. (1985) Apperceptive agnosia due to carbon monoxide poisoning, an interpretation based on critical band masking from disseminated lesions. *Behavioral and Brain Sciences, 15,* 227–240.

Chainay, H., & Humphreys, G. W. (2000). The real object advantage in agnosia: Evidence for a role of shading and depth in object recognition. *Cognitive Neuropsychology, 12,* 175–191.

Coslett, H. B., & Saffran, E. M. (1991). Simultanaganosia: To see but not two see. *Brain, 114,* 1523–2545.

Coslett, H. B., Stark, M., Rajaram, S., & Saffran, E. M. (1995). Narrowing the spotlight: A visual attentional disorder in Alzheimer's disease. *Neurocase, 1,* 305–318.

Davidoff, J., & Warrington, E. K. (1993). A dissociation of shape discrimination and figure-ground perception in a patient with normal acuity. *Neuropsychologia, 31*(1), 83–93.

Davidoff, J., & Wilson, B. (1985). A case of visual agnosia showing a disorder of presemantic visual classification. *Cortex, 21*(2), 121–134.

de Gelder, B., Bachoud-Lèvi, A. C., & Degos, J. D. (1998). Inversion superiority in visual agnosia may be common to a variety of orientation polarised objects besides faces. *Vision Research, 38*(18), 2855–2861.

De Renzi, E., & Lucchelli, F. (1993). The fuzzy boundaries of apperceptive agnosia. *Cortex, 29,* 187–215.

Delis, D. C., Robertson, L. C., & Efron, R. (1986). Hemispheric specialization of memory for visual hierarchical stimuli. *Neuropsychologia, 24,* 205–214.

Doniger, G., Foxe, J. J., Murray, M. M., Higgins, B. A., Snodgrass, J. G., Schroeder, C. E., & Javitt, D. C. (2000). Activation timecourse of ventral visual stream object-recognition areas: High density electrical mapping of perceptual closure processes. *Journal of Cognitive Neuroscience, 12*(4), 615–621.

Doricchi, F., & Incoccia, C. (1998). Seeing only the right half of the forest but cutting down all the trees. *Nature, 394,* 75–78.

Duncan, J., & Humphreys, G. W. (1989). Visual search and stimulus similarity. *Psychological Review, 96*(3), 433–458.

Efron, R. (1968). What is perception? *Boston Studies in Philosophy of Science, 4,* 137–173.

Enns, J. T., & Rensink, R. A. (1990). Influence of scene-based properties on visual search. *Science, 24,* 721–723.

Etcoff, N., Freeman, R., & Cave, K. R. (1991). Can we lose memories of faces? Content specificity and awareness in a prosopagnosic. *Journal of Cognitive Neuroscience, 3*(1), 25–41.

Farah, M. J. (1990). *Visual agnosia: Disorders of object recognition and what they tell us about normal vision.* Cambridge, MA: MIT Press.

Felleman, D. J., & Van Essen, D. C. (1991). Distributed hierarchical processing in the primate cerebral cortex. *Cerebral Cortex, 1,* 1–47.

Fink, G. R., Halligan, P. W., Marshall, J. C., Frith, C. D., Frackowiak, R. S. J., & Dolan, R. J. (1996). Where in the brain does visual attention select the forest and the trees? *Nature, 382,* 626–628.

Fink, G. R., Halligan, P. W., Marshall, J. C., Frith, C. D., Frackowiak, R. S. J., & Dolan, R. J. (1997). Neural mechanisms involved in the processing of global and local aspects of hierarchically organized visual stimuli. *Brain, 120,* 1779–1791.

Frederiksen, J. R., & Kroll, J. F. (1976). Spelling and sound: Approaches to the internal lexicon. *Journal of Experimental Psychology: Human Perception and Performance, 2*(3), 361–379.

Gauthier, I., Behrmann, M., & Tarr, M. J. (1999). Can face recognition really be dissociated from object recognition? *Journal of Cognitive Neuroscience, 11*(4), 349–370.

Gerlach, C., Aaside, C. T., Humphreys, G. W., Gade, A., Paulson, O. B., & Law, I. (2002). Brain activity related to integrative processes in visual object recognition; Bottom-up integration and the modulatory influence of stored knowledge. *Neuropsychologia, 40,* 1254–1267.

Giersch, A., Humphreys, G., Boucart, M., & Kovacs, I. (2000). The computation of occluded contours in visual agnosia: Evidence for early computation prior to shape binding and figure-ground coding. *Cognitive Neuropsychology, 17,* 8, 731–759.

Gilchrist, I. D., Humphreys, G. W., & Riddoch, M. J. (1996). Grouping and extinction: Evidence for low-level modulation of visual selection. *Cognitive Neuropsychology, 13*(8), 1223–1249.

Goodale, M. A., & Milner, A. D. (1992). Separate visual pathways for perception and action. *Trends in Neurosciences, 15*(1), 20–24.

Goodglass, H., Kaplan, E., & Weintraub, S. (1983). *Boston Naming Test.* New York: Lea and Febiger.

Grailet, J. M., Seron, X., Bruyer, R., Coyette, F., & Frederix, M. (1990). Case report of a visual integrative agnosia. *Cognitive Neuropsychology, 7*(4), 275–309.

Grossberg, S. (1997). Cortical dynamics of three-dimensional figure-ground perception of two-dimensional pictures. *Psychological Review, 104*(3), 618–658.

Grossberg, S., & Mingolla, E. (1985). Neural dynamics of form perception: Boundary completion, illusory figures and neon color spreading. *Psychological Review, 92*(2), 173–211.

Grossman, M., Galetta, S., & D'Esposito, M. (1997). Object recognition difficulty in visual apperceptive agnosia. *Brain and Cognition, 33,* 306–342.

Han, S., & Humphreys, G. W. (1999). Interactions between perceptual organization based on Gestalt laws and those based on hierarchical processing. *Perception and Psychophysics, 6*(7), 1287–1298.

Han, S., & Humphreys, G. W. (2002). Segmentation and selection contribute to local processing in hierarchical analysis. *Quarterly Journal of Experimental Psychology, 55A*(1), 5–21.

Han, S., Humphreys, G. W., & Chen, L. (1999). Parallel and competitive processes in hierarchical analysis: Perceptual grouping and encoding of closure. *Journal of Experimental Psychology: Human Perception and Performance, 25* (5), 1411–1432.

He, Z. J., & Nakayama, K. (1992). Surfaces versus features in visual search. *Nature, 359,* 231–233.

Heitger, F., von der Heydt, R., Peterhans, E., Rosenthaler, L., & Kubler, O. (1998). Simulation of neural contour mechanisms: representing anomalous contours. *Image and Vision Computing, 16,* 407–422.

Hirsch, J., DeLaPaz, R. L., Relkins, N. R., Victor, J., Kim, K., Li, T., Borden, P., Rubin, N., & Shapley, R. (1995). Illusory contours activate specific regions in human visual cortex: Evidence from functional magnetic resonance imaging. *Proceedings of the National Academy of Sciences, 92,* 6469–6473.

Hochberg, J. (1981). Levels of perceptual organization. In M. Kubovy and J. R. Pomerantz (Ed.), *Perceptual organization* (pp. 255–278). Hillsdale, NJ: Erlbaum.

Hopfinger, J. B. Buonocore, M. H., & Mangun, G. R. (2000). The neural mechanisms of top-down attentional control. *Nature Neuroscience, 3*(3), 284–291.

Humphreys, G. W. (1999). Integrative agnosia. In G. W. Humphreys (Ed.), *Case studies in vision* (pp. 41–58). London: Psychology Press.

Humphreys, G. W. (2003). Binding in vision as a multi-stage process. In R. Kimchi, M. Behrmann, & C. Olson (Eds.), *Perceptual organization: Behavioral and neural perspectives.* Hillsdale, NJ: Erlbaum.

Humphreys, G. W., & Riddoch, M. J. (1984). Routes to object constancy: Implications from neurological impairments of object constancy. *Quarterly Journal of Experimental Psychology, 36A,* 385–415.

Humphreys, G. W., & Riddoch, M. J. (1987). *To see but not to see: A case-study of visual agnosia.* Hillsdale, NJ: Erlbaum.

Humphreys, G. W., & Riddoch, M. J. (2001). Neuropsychological disorders of visual object recognition and naming. In F. Boller & J. Grafman (Eds.), *Handbook of neuropsychology* (Vol. 4). Amsterdam: Elsevier Science.

Humphreys, G. W., & Riddoch, M. J., Donnelly, N., Freeman, T., Boucart, M., & Muller, H. M. (1994). Intermediate visual processing and visual agnosia. In M. J. Farah & G. Ratcliff (Eds.), *The neuropsychology of high-level vision* (pp. 63–101). Hillsdale, NJ: Erlbaum.

Humphreys, G. W., & Riddoch, M. J., Quinlan, P. T., Price, C. J., & Donnelly, N. (1992). Parallel pattern processing and visual agnosia. *Canadian Journal of Psychology, 46*(3), 377–416.

Karnath, H. O., Ferber, S., Rorden, C., & Driver, J. (200). The fate of global information in dorsal simultanagnosia. *Neurocase, 6,* 295–306.

Kartsounis, L., & Warrington, E. K. (1991). Failure of object recognition due to a breakdown in figure-ground discrimination in a patient with normal acuity. *Neuropsychologia, 29,* 969–980.

Kellman, P. J. (2000). An update on Gestalt psychology. In B. Landau, J. Sabini, E. Newport, & J. Jonides (Eds.), *Essays in honor of Henry and Lila Gleitman.* Cambridge, MA: MIT Press.

Kellman, P. J. (2003). Visual perception of objects and boundaries: A four-dimensional approach. In R. Kimchi, M. Behrmann & C. Olson (Eds.), *Perceptual organization in vision: Behavioral and neural perspectives.* Mahwah, NJ: Erlbaum.

Kellman, P. J., & Shipley, T. F. (1991). A theory of visual interpolation in object perception. *Cognitive Psychology, 23,* 141–221.

Kellman, P. J., & Shipley, T. F. (1992). Perceiving objects across gaps in space and time. *Current Directions in Psychological Science, 1*(6), 193–199.

Kellman, P. J., Yin, C., & Shipley, T. F. (1998). A common mechanism for illusory and occluded object completion. *Journal of Experimental Psychology: Human Perception and Performance, 24*(3), 859–869.

Kertesz, A. (1979). Visual agnosia: The dual deficit of perception and recognition. *Cortex, 15,* 403–419.

Kimchi, R. (1998). Uniform connectedness and grouping in the perceptual organization of hierarchical patterns. *Journal of Experimental Psychology: Human Perception and Performance, 24*(2), 1105–1118.

Kimchi, R. (2000). The perceptual organization of visual objects: a microgenetic analysis. *Vision Research, 40,* 1333–1347.

Kimchi, R., Behrmann, M. and Olson, C. (2003). *Visual perceptual organization: Behavioral and neural perspectives.* Hillsdale, NJ: Erlbaum.

Kimchi, R., & Hadad, R. (2002). Influence of past experience on perceptual grouping. *Psychological Science, 13,* 41–47.

Kohler, W. (1920/1950). Physical gestalten. In W. D. Ellis (Ed.), *A sourcebook of Gestalt psychology* (pp. 17–54). New York: Humanities Press.

Kovács, I. (2000). Human development of perceptual organization. *Vision Research, 40,* 1301–1310.

Kovács, I., Polat, U., Pennefather, P. M., Chandna, A., & Norcia, A. M. (2000). A new test of contour integration deficits in patients with a history of disrupted binocular experience during visual development. *Vision Research, 40,* 1775–1783.

Lamb, M. R., Robertson, L. C., & Knight, R. T. (1989). Attention and interference in the processing of global and local information: Effects of unilateral temporal-parietal junction lesions. *Neuropsychologia, 27*(4), 471–483.

Lamb, M. R., Robertson, L. C., & Knight, R. T. (1990). Component mechanisms underlying the processing of hierarchically organized patterns—inferences from patients with unilateral cortical lesions. *Journal of Experimental Psychology: Learning, Memory and Cognition, 16,* 471–483.

Lamme, V. A. F., & Roelfsema, P. R. (2000). The distinct modes of vision offered by feedforward and recurrent processing. *Trends in Neuroscience, 23*(11), 571–579.

Lawson, R., & Humphreys, G. W. (1999). The effects of view in depth on the identification of line drawings and silhouettes of familiar objects. *Visual Cognition, 6*(2), 165–195.

Lee, T. S., & Nguyen, M. (2001). Dynamics of subjective contour formation in the early visual cortex. *Proceedings of the National Academy of Sciences, 98*(4), 1907–1911.

Lhermitte, F., & Beauvois, M. F. (1973). A visual-speech disconnexion syndrome: Report of a case with optic aphasia, agnosic alexia and colour agnosia. *Brain, 96,* 695–714.

Lissauer, H. (1890). Ein fall von seelenblindheit nebst einem beitrage zur theorie derselben. (A case of visual agnosia with a contribution to theory). *Archiv Fur Psychiatrie und Nervenkranheiten, 21,* 222–270.

Liu, Z., Jacobs, D., & Basri, R. (1999). The role of convexity in perceptual completion: beyond good continuation. *Vision Research, 39,* 4244–4257.

Mapelli, D., & Behrmann, M. (1997). The role of color in object recognition: Evidence from visual agnosia. *Neurocase, 3,* 237–247.

Marotta, J. J., McKeeff, T., & Behrmann, M. (2002). The effects of inversion and rotation on face processing in prosopagnosia. *Cognitive Neuropsychology, 19*(1), 31–47.

Mattingley, J. B., David, G., & Driver, J. (1997). Pre-attentive filling in of visual surfaces in parietal extinction. *Science, 275,* 671–674.

McMullen, P. A., Fisk, J. D., Phillips, S. J., & Maloney, W. J. (2000). Apperceptive agnosia and face recognition. *Neurocase, 6,* 403–414.

Mendola, J., Dale, A. M., Fischl, B., Liu, A. K., & Tootell, R. B. H. (1999). The representation of real and illusory contours in human cortical visual areas revealed by functional magnetic resonance imaging. *Journal of Neuroscience, 19,* 8560–8572.

Moore, C., & Egeth, H. (1997). Perception without attention: Evidence of grouping under conditions of inattention. *Journal of Experimental Psychology: Human Perception and Performance, 23*(2), 339–352.

Moscovitch, M., Winocur, G., & Behrmann, M. (1997). What is special about face recognition? Nineteen experiments on a person with visual object agnosia and dyslexia but normal face recognition. *Journal of Cognitive Neuroscience, 9*(5), 555–604.

Mycroft, R., Behrmann, M., & Kay, J. (2003). *Letter-by-letter reading in visual agnosia.* Manuscript in preparation.

Navon, D. (1977). Forest before trees: The precedence of global features in visual perception. *Cognitive Psychology, 9,* 353–383.

Oßwald, K., Humphreys, G. W., & Olson, A. (2002). Words are more than the sum of their parts: Evidence from letter-by-letter reading in normal and alexic readers. *Cognitive Neuropsychology, 19*(8), 675–695.

Palmer, S. E. (1999). *Vision science: From photons to phenomenology.* Cambridge, MA: MIT Press.

Palmer, S. E. (2003). Understanding perceptual organization and grouping. In R. Kimchi, M. Behrmann, & C. Olson (Eds.), *Perceptual organization: Behavioral and neural processes.* Hillsdale, NJ: Erlbaum.

Palmer, S. E., & Brooks, J. L. (2000). *Common fate as a determinant of figure-ground organization.* Manuscript submitted for publication.

Palmer, S., Neff, J., & Beck, D. (1996). Late influences on perceptual grouping: Amodal completion. *Psychonomic Bulletin and Review, 3(1),* 75–80.

Palmer, S. E., & Rock, I. (1994a). On the nature and order of organizational processing: A reply to Peterson. *Psychonomic Bulletin and Review, 1,* 515–519.

Palmer, S. E., & Rock, I. (1994b). Rethinking perceptual organization: The role of uniform connectedness. *Psychonomic Bulletin and Review, 1*(1), 29–55.

Pennefather, P. M., Chandna, A., Kovács, I., Polat, U., & Norcia, A. M. (1999). Contour detection threshold: repeatability and learning with "contour cards." *Spatial Vision, 2*(3), 257–266.

Peterhans, E., & von der Heydt, R. (1991). Subjective contours—Bridging the gap between psychophysics and physiology. *Trends in Neuroscience, 14*(3), 112–119.

Peterson, M. A. (2003). On figures, grounds and varieties of surface completion. In R. Kimchi, M. Behrmann, & C. Olson (Eds.), *Perceptual organization in vision: Behavioral and neural perspectives.* Mahwah, NJ: Erlbaum.

Peterson, M. A., & Gibson, B. S. (1994). Must shape recognition follow figure-ground organization: An assumption in peril. *Psychological Science, 9,* 253–259.

Peterson, M. A., de Gelder, B., Rapcsak, S. Z., Gerhardstein, P. C., & Bachoud-Lévi, A. C. (2000). Object memory effects on figure assignment: Conscious object recognition is not necessary or sufficient. *Vision Research, 40,* 1549–1567.

Polster, M. R., & Rapcsak, S. Z. (1994). Hierarchical stimuli and hemispheric specialization: Two case studies. *Cortex, 30,* 487–497.

Rafal, R., & Robertson, L. (1995). The neurology of visual attention. In M. Gazzaniga (Ed.), *The cognitive neurosciences* (pp. 625–648). Cambridge, MA: MIT Press.

Rensink, R., & Enns, J. T. (1995). Preemption effects in visual search: Evidence for low-level grouping. *Psychological Review, 102,* 101–130.

Ricci, R., Vaishnavi, S., & Chatterjee, A. (1999). A deficit of intermediate vision: Experimental observations and theoretical implications. *Neurocase, 5,* 1–2.

Riddoch, M. J., & Humphreys, G. W. (1987). A case of integrative visual agnosia. *Brain, 110,* 1431–1462.

Riddoch, M. J., Humphreys, G. W., Gannon, T., Blott, W., & Jones, V. (1999). Memories are made of this: The effects of time on stored visual knowledge in a case of visual agnosia. *Brain, 122,* 537–559.

Robertson, L. C., Lamb, M. R., & Knight, R. T. (1988). Effects of lesions of temporal-parietal junction on perceptual and attentional processing in humans. *Journal of Neuroscience, 8*(10), 3757–3769.

Rock, I., Nijhawan, R., Palmer, S. E., & Tudor, L. (1992). Grouping based on phenomenal similarity of achromatic color. *Perception, 21,* 779–789.

Rubin, E. (1921). *Visuell Wahrgenommene Figuren.* Copenhagen: Glydenalske boghandel.

Sekuler, A., & Bennett, P. (2001). Generalized common fate: Grouping by common luminance changes. *Psychological Science, 12(6),* 437–444.

Shipley, T. F., & Cunningham, D. W. (2001). Perception of occluding and occluded objects over time: Spatiotemporal segmentation and unit formation. In T. F. Shipley & P. J. Kellman (Eds.), *From fragments to objects* (pp. 557–586). Amsterdam: Elsevier.

Shipley, T. F., & Kellman, P. J. (2001) *From fragments to objects.* Amsterdam: Elsevier.

Sparr, S. A., Jay, M., Drislane, F. W., & Venna, N. (1991). A historic case of visual agnosia revisited after 40 years. *Brain, 114,* 789–800.

Stark, M. E., Grafman, J., & Fertig, E. (1997). A restricted "spotlight" of attention in visual object recognition. *Neuropsychologia, 35*(9), 1233–1249.

Tarr, M. J., & Pinker, S. (1990). When does human object recognition use a viewer-centered reference frame? *Psychological Science, 1*(4), 253–256.

Teuber, H.-L. (1968). Alteration of perception and memory in man. In L. Weiskrantz (Ed.), *Analysis of behavioral change.* New York: Harper and Row.

Thaiss, L., & Bleser, R. D. (1992). Visual agnosia: A case of reduced attentional "spotlight"? *Cortex, 28,* 601–621.

Vaishnavi, S., Greenberg, A., & Chatterjee, A. (1999). A preattentive visual deficit without visual agnosia. *Journal of the International Neuropsychological Society, 5,* 107.

Vecera, S. P., & Behrmann, M. (1997). Spatial attention does not require preattentive grouping. *Neuropsychology, 11,* 30–43.

Vecera, S. P., & O'Reilly, R. (1998). Figure-ground organization and object recognition processes: An interactive account. *Journal of Experimental Psychology: Human Perception and Performance, 24*(2), 441–462.

von der Heydt, R., & Peterhans, E. (1989). Mechanisms of contour perception in monkey visual cortex. *Journal of Neuroscience, 9*(5), 1731–1748.

von der Heydt, R., Peterhans, E., & Baumgartner, G. (1984). Illusory contours and cortical neuron responses. *Sciences, 224*(4654), 1260–1262.

Warrington, E. K., & Davidoff, J. (2000). Failure at object identification improves mirror image matching. *Neuropsychologia, 38*(9), 1229–1234.

Warrington, E. K., & James, M. (1991). *The Visual Objects and Space Perception Battery.* Suffolk, UK: Thames Valley Test Company.

Warrington, E. K., & Taylor, A. M. (1978). Two categorical stages of object recognition. *Perception, 7,* 695–705.

Yovel, G., Yovel, I., & Levy, J. (2001). Hemispheric asymmetries for global and local visual perception: Effects of stimulus and task factors. *Journal of Experimental Psychology: Human Perception and Performance, 27*(6), 1369–1385.

12

Scene Perception

What We Can Learn from Visual Integration and Change Detection

DANIEL J. SIMONS, STEPHEN R. MITROFF,
AND STEVEN L. FRANCONERI

As we view our world, each eye movement causes a dramatic shift in the retinal position of every object in a scene, every blink interrupts visual sensation, and moving objects occlude other objects. Somehow our perceptual system makes sense of this varying information and we experience a stable visual world. How do we sense stability in the face of such disruptions? What sorts of representations underlie this experience?

Scenes can be described in terms of the quantity and quality of the information available for representation. To adequately describe the nature of the representations underlying our experience, we must ascertain both how many items in a scene are retained and how much detail about each item is retained. Although these dimensions are not necessarily independent, after all, both are forms of visual information. The distinction will prove useful in characterizing the possible inferences we can draw from studies of visual representations. Almost all models of visual stability concur that some information from a scene is preserved from one view to the next, but such models vary dramatically in their proposals for both the *completeness* and the *precision* of these representations. That is, the proposed representations vary in how many items they include and how much detail about those items is retained. A complete representation is one that includes all the items in a scene. Note, though, that a complete representation could be as vague as a brief verbal description of the items or as detailed as a photographic representation of infinite precision. Maximally precise representations preserve all of the information about encoded items, although not all items in the scene would necessarily be encoded. Representations can be complete, but imprecise as well as precise, but incomplete.

Many early explanations for our experience of visual stability assumed the need for representations that are both complete and precise replicas of the world. Ancient Greek models assumed that any demonstration of contact between the self (or soul) and objects in the external world was sufficient evidence for such a representation of the world. For example, Democritus was satisfied that accurate perception was possible because he noted the complete reflection of the world on the pupil (Lindberg, 1976). Such models simply assumed that representations were inherently accurate and largely ignored discrepancies between the visual world and its retinal projection. Given this assumption, they also did not consider the need to adjust representations in the face of eye movements. In contrast, medieval explanations (e.g., those of Al-Kindi, Kepler), which also accepted the importance of storing a complete and precise representation of the world, noted the existence of disparities between the retinal image and the world. These theorists searched for mechanisms that could correct for such discrepancies (Lindberg, 1976). More recently, Descartes proposed the need for a correction to produce an accurate representation of the world in the motions of the pineal gland (see Gibson, 1966; Van Hoorn, 1972) and Helmholtz argued that unconscious inference (or cerebration) allows accurate representations of the three-dimensional world from the roughly two-dimensional retinal image (Helmholtz, 1866/1924).

In contrast to these beliefs in a complete and precise internal representation, other theorists argue that our internal representations minimize the information preserved from one glance at a scene to the next (e.g., Irwin, 1991; Rensink, 2000a). These models argue that our experience of a stable, continuous visual world derives, not from a complete internalization of the world, but instead from the *absence* of such a representation. If our visual system simply assumes that the world is stable and unchanging, then there is no need to represent it internally in order to experience it as stable; the world itself can serve as a memory for most visual details (O'Regan, 1992). Only those items that are needed for action from one view to the next (Hayhoe, 2000) or that are the current focus of attention (Horowitz & Wolfe, 1998; Rensink, 2000a) need to be preserved across views. These models vary in the degree of precision in the representations of this small set of items, some positing relatively precise representations of many features (Luck & Vogel, 1997) and others arguing for more abstract representations (Irwin, 1991).

To distinguish between all of these contrasting models of the completeness and precision of our representations, we must determine our capacity to store and integrate visual details from one view to the next. The clearest empirical evidence suggesting the existence of complete and precise representations comes from work on visual pattern masking. Pattern masking occurs when normal processing of one stimulus is disrupted by the presentation of a second stimulus. Without a masking stimulus, briefly presented visual stimuli persist with great precision in an iconic memory for up to 300 msec after the stimulus has been removed (Sperling, 1960). However, if a mask appears shortly after the stimulus and prior to the report, the stimulus and the mask are integrated and further independent processing of either the stimulus or the mask is impaired (Breitmeyer, 1984; Kahneman, 1968). Optimal masking occurs when the mask shares features in common with the target stimulus such that when the two stimuli are superimposed, observers cannot easily separate them. The fact that the mask is most effective when it has the same features as the target suggests that relatively detailed information about those features is preserved, at least for a brief period.

A more stringent test of the completeness and precision of the representation requires observers to visually integrate two displays and then to report the emergent result. In a classic visual integration task, observers viewed two successive, complementary 12-dot patterns drawn from a 5 × 5 array. When these 12-dot arrays were integrated into a single 24-dot array, only one location in the 5 × 5 array never contained a dot. When presented sequentially, success in locating the empty location depends on integrating the two patterns over time. Consistent with the integration occurring during pattern masking, observers can readily perform this task when the two images appear successively at the same location in space and are projected to the same retinal position (i.e., when observers are fixating; Di Lollo, 1980).

The existence of such precise and complete representations raises the possibility that our experience of visual stability arises from the merging of consecutive views of a scene into a single representation. However, the perceptual demands of a masking experiment are quite different from those of the real world. As we view scenes in the real world, we move our eyes (saccade) 3–4 times each second and visual information is processed primarily when the eyes are stable during a fixation—relatively little new visual information is processed during saccades (e.g., Campbell & Wurtz, 1978). As the eyes move, the projection of each object in the world shifts to a new part of the retina, in contrast to the relatively stable retinal projections in visual masking experiments. Consequently, even if our visual system does store a complete and precise representation in an iconic memory, visual integration with subsequent fixations would require an adjustment for such eye movements so that the two representations would be aligned. That is, the visual system would need to create a single representation of the world based on many different images on the retina; an object occupying a single location in space, but projected to different locations on the retina, needs to be perceived as the same object.

The primary purpose of this chapter is to consider the nature of the

First display   **Second display**

Integration:
What results
when the two
pictures are
combined?

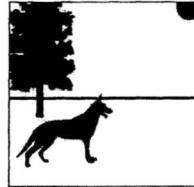

Preview Priming:
What kind of
animal is in the
second picture?

Change Detection:
Has a change
been made to the
second picture?

FIGURE 12.1. A cartoon illustration of three methods used to study the nature of the information preserved across views.

information retained from one view to the next. Does the visual system retain a precise and complete representation and integrate it across a saccade? Or, does our experience of stability derive from the absence of such representations? We address these questions by exploring evidence from two distinct, but related lines of research: (1) studies of visual integration and facilitation across eye movements and (2) studies of change detection. Most studies of visual integration focus entirely on the consciously accessible products of visual integration. Given that measures dependent on explicit awareness might well underestimate the amount of information preserved across views, we also examine evidence from more sensitive implicit measures of integration such as cross-saccade priming. Priming studies infer the nature of the information preserved across views by measuring the influence of information presented on one view on processing of the subsequent view (see figure 12.1 for a schematic illustration of these methods of studying the representations preserved from one view to the next).

Following our discussion of visual integration, we provide a more thorough discussion of evidence from studies of change detection. If observers can detect a change from one view of a scene to the next, then they must have represented some information from the first view and compared it to the subsequent view. As in studies of visual integration, most studies of change detection rely on reports of the consciously accessible product of the comparison process as a dependent measure. Given that explicit reports might well underestimate the precision and completeness of the preserved information, we also evaluate the possibility that more sensitive, implicit measures might reveal evidence for change detection in the absence of awareness. In the final section, we speculate about the sorts of information that might be expected to be preserved across views, and we argue that in the absence of awareness, representations likely are limited to those aspects of our visual world that are needed from one instant to the next.

Visual Integration Across Saccades

In order for visual integration of complete and precise representations to underlie our experience of visual stability, observers must be able to combine information from one fixation to the next, and the visual system must somehow account for the corresponding change to the retinal projection. In one intuitive visual integration model (McConkie & Rayner, 1976), information from one fixation enters a visually integrative buffer, much like an iconic store. Then, after a saccade, visual information from the next fixation also enters this buffer. Rather than displacing the current contents, the second fixation is integrated with the previous fixation, much as two overhead transparencies can be combined when overlaid. To accomplish this integration, each fixation would first be adjusted to match an internal model of the locations of objects in the world. All subsequent fixations could then be compared to this internal model. This precise and complete model would thereby allow visual stability because each fixation could be mapped to a single representation (see also Trehub, 1991, 1994).

If this sort of visual integration underlies our experience of stability, observers should be able to integrate two patterns that appear successively in the same spatial position, even if the patterns are projected to different retinal positions on each fixation. A number of studies have used the missing-dot task (Di Lollo, 1980) described above to explore this possibility (Bridgeman & Mayer, 1983; Irwin, Yantis, & Jonides, 1983; Jonides, Irwin, & Yantis, 1982, 1983; Rayner & Pollatsek, 1983). As in the studies of visual integration of patterns within a fixation, observers are asked to integrate two 12-dot patterns, thereby determining the location of the one dot missing from the 5×5 array. Recall that when the two dot patterns are presented to the same retinal location within a single fixation, observers can integrate the patterns. To study integration across saccades, the two complementary 12-dot patterns are presented to different retinal locations across an eye movement. One pattern is presented parafoveally and observers move their eyes to fixate it. During the saccade, the original pattern is replaced by its complementary 12-dot pattern. Once the saccade is complete, observers try to identify the location of the missing dot.

Initial evidence using this task supported the claim that observers maintain a precise and complete representation and that they can integrate it with subsequent patterns following an eye movement (Jonides et al., 1982). However, these initial findings resulted from a display artifact in which the original pattern persisted on the monitor, allowing integration of patterns projected to the same retinal location. (Bridgeman & Mayer, 1983; Irwin et al., 1983; Jonides et al., 1983; Rayner & Pollatsek, 1983). Despite repeated attempts over the next 10 years, no subsequent studies have provided convincing evidence that observers can integrate such complex patterns across an eye movement (e.g., Irwin, 1991; Irwin, Brown, & Sun, 1988; Irwin, Zacks, & Brown, 1990). Even though the two patterns occupy the same location in space, observers cannot combine them to form a single, coherent representation.

However, these results do not support the conclusion that we lack any representation of the pre-saccade pattern. Even if observers do not have an internal representation that is sufficiently precise and complete to perform the dot-integration task, they might still preserve some information from one view to the next. In fact, one recent study provides some support for a more limited form of visual integration (Hayhoe, Lachter, & Feldman, 1991). In this study, observers attempted to perceive a shape that was visible only if they were able to combine information across several fixations. Three consecutive views each presented a single dot that defined a corner of a triangle, and observers were asked to judge whether the top angle formed by integrating the patterns was acute or obtuse. Observers succeeded in judging the angle, suggesting that they retained enough information from one fixation to the next to determine the spatial relationships among the dots. This study provides evidence that some information can be preserved across views. However, it provides relatively little support for the idea that integration of complete and precise representations of entire scenes underlies our experience of stability in the real world— the task required only that a minimal amount of information be preserved.

Taken together, these studies suggest that some information might be preserved across saccades, but that information might not be precise or complete enough to support the visual integration model of visual stability. The typical inference from these findings is that we do not maintain a precise and complete visual representation across an eye movement. Note, however, that this inference is not logically supported by these experiments. Although successful visual integration requires a precise and complete representation, the failure to integrate two patterns does not imply the absence of a representation. All of these studies of visual integration depend on explicit reports of the features of the combined percept. Observers might well have a precise and complete representation but simply fail to perform the comparison (Angelone, Levin, & Simons, 2001; Levin,

Simons, Angelone, & Chabris, in press; Simons, 2000). Or, more importantly, the results of the comparison might simply be unavailable to awareness. In other words, evidence from these studies could only confirm the existence of preserved information if that information were accessible to conscious report. Such explicit reports of preserved information could underestimate the amount of information that actually is preserved and integrated from a glance at a scene, thus more sensitive measures are needed to adequately test for the presence of preserved information.

Implicit Measures of Visual Integration: Priming from a Prior View

Priming is one potentially more sensitive approach to exploring the nature of the information preserved across views. Priming occurs when the prior presentation of one stimulus leads to more rapid or accurate processing of a subsequent stimulus. Note that priming measures do not require visual merging of the details of the two stimuli. Rather, facilitation provides evidence that some information extracted on one fixation influences the perception of an object on the next fixation.

In a typical priming study, observers respond only to the second stimulus, and the effects of the first stimulus result in changes in the response latency or error rate. Observers initially fixate the center of a screen and a preview picture is presented away from fixation. They then initiate an eye movement from fixation to this preview, and during the saccade, the original picture is replaced with a target picture that observers are asked to name (see Rayner, McConkie, & Ehrlich, 1978; Rayner, McConkie, & Zola, 1980).

In such priming studies, naming of the target picture is faster if the preview is identical to the target than if it is just a location marker such as an asterisk (Henderson, 1992; Henderson, Pollatsek, & Rayner, 1987, 1989; Pollatsek, Rayner, & Collins, 1984; Pollatsek, Rayner, & Henderson, 1990). This finding alone demonstrates that some information about the preview object is represented across views. Furthermore, the preview benefit does not seem to require explicit awareness of the relationship between the preview and the target. Through systematic variation of the similarity of the preview to the target we can determine how complete and precise a representation is preserved across the saccade. If the preview and target must be identical in order to produce facilitation, then if priming occurs, the representation of the preview must be complete and precise. Such a representation is more likely to be based on something akin to a visual image than on an abstract, nonvisual encoding of a few features of the object; if all of the details must be preserved with absolute precision in order to produce priming, then it seems implausible that an observer could rapidly abstract (e.g., verbally label) all of those details into a nonvisual representation. In contrast, if the preview produces priming when the preview and target are visually distinct exemplars of a category (e.g., a collie and a doberman, when observers are required to name the object at the basic level, dog), then the representation need not incorporate visual details of the preview. Instead, an abstract conceptual or verbal code would suffice.

The preview benefit does not appear to require a precise visual representation. Although naming latency is 100–130 ms faster when the preview is identical to the target than when it is just an asterisk, naming is equally fast when the preview picture is 10% larger or smaller than the target (Pollatsek et al., 1984). Thus, at a minimum, the preserved representation does not maintain precise scale information. Furthermore, naming is speeded by approximately 90 ms when the preview and target are different examples of the same category (e.g., two different pictures of horses; see also Pollatsek et al., 1990). Similarly, previews with the same name but different appearances (i.e., homonym pairs such as "bat") speed naming by approximately 50 ms. Apparently, relatively abstract, nonvisual representations (e.g., verbal, phonological, and semantic information) underlie much if not all of the preview benefit, suggesting that representations need not be precise.

Summary

Although some information clearly is preserved across saccades and used to facilitate processing on subsequent fixations, evidence from visual integration studies, both explicit pattern merging and implicit naming facilitation, provide little or no support for the preservation of complete and precise visual information across saccades. The convergence of the results from these tasks provides some support for the notion that we lack detailed internal representations altogether. However, this conclusion depends on confirming a null result, so the logical inference that we lack such representations is unsupported. Successful integration and facilitation require a representation, but failed integration and facilitation do not eliminate the possibility that observers do represent all of the information from a scene with perfect precision. The preview effects suggest that some information is preserved, even when observers are unaware of the nature of the preview or its relationship to the target. Thus, the more sensitive measures did reveal a greater degree of integration than did the explicit measures. This finding raises the possibility that even more sensitive measures might reveal the existence of more complete and precise representations. One such measure might be the ability to detect changes from one view to the next.

Using Change Detection to Explore
Preserved Representations

In a visual integration task, observers must retain all of the details from one view and merge them with a subsequent view. If the representation is incomplete, they will be unable to perform the task. In contrast, detecting a change from one view to the next requires only that observers retain and compare the information that changed, even if that information was only a small subset of the potentially changing information. Successful change detection requires a representation of the pre-change object and a comparison to the post-change object, but observers need not maintain a complete and precise representation of the entire scene. Thus, change detection provides a less stringent and possibly more sensitive measure of whether any precise information is retained from one view to the next.

In other respects, most change detection studies rely on methods similar to those used in studies of visual integration. Observers view the original and changed display and then report whether or not they consciously detected a difference between the displays. Consistent with the failure to integrate displays and with the notion that observers do not maintain a complete and precise representation of each fixation, observers often fail to detect large changes to scenes from one view to the next.

Inferring the Precision of Representations

As in studies of integration and preview effects, most early studies of change detection focused on the ability to compare information from sequential fixations by making a change during a saccade (saccade-contingent changes). In one of the more dramatic early examples, observers read lines of text that AlTeRnAtEd CaSe with each letter (McConkie & Zola, 1979). Periodically, during a saccade, every letter changed case. Observers did not notice changes that coincided with an eye movement, even though the changes were impossible to ignore if they occurred during a fixation. Similarly, observers often miss large, saccade-contingent changes made to photographs of natural scenes (Grimes, 1996; Henderson & Hollingworth, 1999; McConkie & Currie, 1996).

More recent studies have extended these findings of "change blindness" to forms of visual disruption other than saccades (for recent overviews, see Rensink, 2000a; Simons, 2000; Simons & Levin, 1997). For example, change blindness occurs when a change occurs during a blink (O'Regan, Deubel, Clark, & Rensink, 2000), a flashed blank screen (Pashler, 1988; Rensink, O'Regan, & Clark, 1997; Simons, 1996), and during a cut or pan in a motion picture (Hochberg, 1986; Levin & Simons, 1997; Simons, 1996). Change blindness occurs for simple, artificial displays (e.g., Pashler, 1988; Rensink, 2000b; Simons, 1996) as well as for photographs of natural scenes (e.g., Rensink et al., 1997), and it can even occur during a real-world interaction (Simons & Levin, 1998).

Interestingly, change blindness can sometimes occur even in the absence of visual masking of the change location by a disruption. For example, change blindness occurs when distracting elements are briefly flashed over the display without covering the change location (O'Regan, Rensink, & Clark, 1999; Rensink, O'Regan, & Clark, 2000). The additional elements apparently draw attention away from the signal caused by the change. Furthermore, change blindness can occur in the absence of any visual disruption whatsoever. When an original photograph of a scene gradual fades into a modified one, observers often fail to notice the change (Simons, Franconeri, & Reimer, 2000); the change signal is visible when attention is focused on the change location, but the change occurs too slowly to attract attention.

The recent introduction of the flicker paradigm (Rensink et al., 1997) has allowed a more systematic exploration of the completeness and precision of the information retained from one view to the next. In the flicker paradigm, an original and modified display alternate repeatedly, separated by a blank screen (thereby giving the display its flickering appearance). The blank screen serves as a visual disruption, and successful change detection often requires many cycles of alternation. As in other change detection studies, in the absence of a transient signal, change detection requires observers to represent and compare the original and modified feature. Measuring the latency of change detection also allows an assessment of the completeness of the representation. If observers could represent all of the information in a display and compare it all to the modified display, change detection should happen rapidly, typically within a cycle or two. However, if representations are less complete, observers will need more cycles to detect the change because they will be able to compare less information on each cycle.

One recent series of studies explored the completeness of representations by varying the number of items in the display (Rensink, 2000b). If the number of items in the display exceeds the holding capacity of visual short-term memory, observers should need additional cycles to detect the change. This methodology allows an estimate of the number of items observers can retain and compare across views. These studies found that observers could retain and compare approximately four to six items with each exposure to the display (Rensink, 2000b), suggesting that the representation of each view is limited to the amount of information that can be encoded with focused attention (note that this number was somewhat larger for some change types, perhaps owing to grouping strategies). These studies further suggest that representations are relatively incomplete, limited to a small subset of the potentially changing items in the scene. However, representations of these items might be relatively precise. In a change detection task using simple shapes (Luck & Vogel, 1997), subjects were unable to remember more than four objects across a disruption. However, they could remember many features of each object (e.g. size, color), suggesting that their representations of those objects were reasonably precise.

Given that successful change detection requires some preserved information from the initial view, failed change detection has been taken to suggest the absence of such representations. However, as for explicit measures of visual integration, this inference rests on faulty logic (see Simons, 2000). Change blindness does not imply the absence of a representation;

rather, it shows only that observers do not have *explicit* access to the relevant contents of the previous view. Furthermore, change blindness could also result from a failed comparison process (Angelone et al.; 2001; Simons, 2000). As for studies of integration, one way to explore the possibility that explicit reports underestimate the completeness and precision of our representations is to adopt more sensitive measures of change detection. Given that successful detection requires a representation, if more sensitive measures reveal detection, then they also reveal the existence of a representation. Recently, a number of studies have explored whether more information is preserved than findings of change blindness initially suggested.

Changed Detection Without Awareness

Most forms of visual disruption serve to mask or eliminate the change signal that would otherwise direct attention to the change automatically (Simons & Levin, 1997). In the absence of such a signal, how is attention eventually focused on the change location? The two major accounts for successful change detection each lead to different implications for how the visual system represents and processes changes. First, change detection might be based entirely on explicitly available representations and comparisons. In the flicker task, observers shift attention from one item to the next until they happen to encode and compare the feature that is changing (Mitroff & Simons, in press). According to this hypothesis, explicit measures of change detection are appropriate estimates of the amount of information retained and compared across views, and changes will not be detected without awareness. That is, implicit measures of change detection will provide no additional evidence for the existence of complete and precise representations. Alternatively, change detection might occur without awareness, thereby revealing the existence of more complete and precise representations (Rensink, 2000a).

Evidence for implicit change detection falls into three categories: *identification*, *localization*, and *registration*. Implicit identification requires that observers represent information about the identity of the changed item even if they lack awareness of the change itself (Thornton & Fernandez-Duque, 2000). Such a representation requires some precision in the representation of the features of the original and/or changed object. Implicit localization requires that observers be drawn to or gain access to the change location even if they do not consciously detect the change (Fernandez-Duque & Thornton, 2000; Smilek, Eastwood, & Merikle, 2000). However, such representations need not include much precision about the object's properties or features. Implicit registration is the weakest claim: the change need only influence performance in some way in the absence of awareness of the change. Evidence for registration requires minimal completeness and precision and does not specify any functional role for implicit detection in the eventual explicit detection of the change

(Hayhoe, Bensinger, & Ballard, 1998; Rensink, 1998; Williams & Simons, 2000). Here we briefly discuss the existing evidence for each of these claims and then argue that, in fact, none of the evidence supports the claim that changes are implicitly detected (see Mitroff & Simons, in press; Mitroff, Simons, & Franconeri, 2001, for details).

IMPLICIT IDENTIFICATION

Only one published study has claimed support for implicit identification in the absence of awareness (Thornton & Fernandez-Duque, 2000). In these studies, observers were faster to judge the orientation of a cued item when a changed item in the display had the same orientation as the cued item, even if observers reported being unaware of the change. Although this finding suggests that observers processed the identity of the changed item without awareness, the study did not control for the spatial relationship between the cued and the changed items. On the critical trials in this experiment, the changed item was always diametrically opposite the target item. Thus, the relative positions of the changed item and the target item were predictable, and observers could become aware of the spatial contingency. When we replicated this finding but eliminated the consistent and predictable spatial relationship between the changed item and the cued item, the effect of the changed item on the orientation judgment was eliminated (Mitroff et al., 2001). That is, when the predictable spatial relationship between the cued target and the changed item was random, the presence of an unreported change no longer influenced judgments about the target. If the change were implicitly detected in the original experiment, then the predictability of the spatial relationship should have been irrelevant. Furthermore, given that observers might have been aware of this spatial relationship, it seems reasonable to suggest that the performance benefit from undetected changes can be attributed to an explicit strategy of attending to the diametrically opposite item rather than to implicit change detection. It is possible, of course, that future studies will reveal the existence of implicit identification, but our evidence suggests that such representations might not surface with more sensitive measures.

IMPLICIT LOCALIZATION

As for implicit identification, claims of implicit localization can also be explained by taking explicit strategies into account. The primary study supporting the existence of implicit localization found better-than-expected guessing of the change location when observers did not detect the change; given a two-alternative choice, observers showed better than 50% selection of the changed item when they were unaware of the change (Fernandez-Duque & Thornton, 2000). Yet, the study did not control for the possibility that observers could improve their performance by explicitly adopting a strategy of eliminating items known not to have changed. If observers determined that one of the two alternative items had not changed, then they would "guess" the correct item. This explicit strategy of eliminating one item predicts the levels of guessing found in the original study. Furthermore, the number of items observers are able to eliminate accurately predicts guessing performance across repeated cycles of the change (Mitroff et al., 2001). Other recent findings suggesting implicit localization (Smilek et al., 2000) can also be explained entirely by explicit mechanisms, with no need for implicit detection (Mitroff et al., 2001). Consequently, studies of implicit localization provide no evidence that scene representations are any more complete or precise than would be expected based on explicit measures of detection.

IMPLICIT REGISTRATION

As for implicit identification and localization, most findings supporting claims of implicit registration can be attributed to explicit mechanisms. For example, no-change responses are sometimes slowed by the presence of an unnoticed change (Williams & Simons, 2000). Yet, such effects could be attributed to variations in the confidence of these responses. When observers are more confident they tend to respond more rapidly, and observers might have generally been more confident when they correctly responded no-change. In fact, after taking into account the contributions of confidence, the presence or absence of a change accounted for only 2.5% of the remaining response time variance (Mitroff et al., 2001). Although confidence might just be another measure of implicit detection, it could also reflect explicit detection. Consequently, the finding that response-time differences can be attributed to confidence raises the possibility that such effects do not require implicit detection.

A similar line of research has found that fixation duration is affected by the presence of an undetected change (e.g., Hollingworth, Williams, & Henderson, in press): observers fixate longer on a changed object, relative to trials with no change, even when they did not detect the change. This finding could be consistent with implicit registration of a change, but it does not provide strong evidence for detection without awareness. Fixation duration in this case might simply be a more sensitive measure of explicit change detection in that observers might have been somewhat aware of the change. Likewise, the finding could result from confidence differences or from other explicit strategies. The concern that a purported implicit measure is just a more sensitive measure of explicit detection applies to other evidence of detection as well. A convincing demonstration of implicit detection would need to dissociate performance from sensitive measures of explicit detection (Reingold & Merikle, 1988), ideally showing that the result could not be attributed to awareness of the change. Given this ambiguity, both lines of research are consistent with the claim that implicit registration does not exist, and performance is no different than would be expected based on explicit mechanisms alone.

Summary

Apparently, change detection may not occur in the absence of awareness, and explicit measures of change detection might not necessarily underestimate the completeness and precision of our representations. Our claim that change detection, at least in the absence of a change signal, depends only on an explicit comparison process (Mitroff & Simons, in press; Mitroff et al., 2001) is consistent with the idea that observers are generally unaware of much of their environment. If observers were able to access and compare all of the items in a scene from one view to the next, then they would readily detect changes when looking for them. However, the failure to detect such changes does not imply the absence of a representation (Simons, 2000). Change blindness could well result from a failure to compare an existing, complete, and precise representation of one view to the subsequent view. In fact, more sensitive measures might well reveal the presence of such representations even in the face of change blindness. For example, observers typically failed to report the removal of a striped basketball, even when they were asked repeatedly whether anything had changed. However, when asked specifically if a ball had been present before, they discovered that they did have a representation of the ball and even reported some details correctly (e.g., see Simons, Chabris, Schnur, & Levin, in press). They failed to detect the change, even though they represented some details from the pre-change scene. If such detailed representations exist, then change blindness does provide evidence that detailed and complete representations are not always compared from one view to the next. Combined with evidence against implicit change detection, these studies suggest the existence of a limited capacity comparison process (see also Scott-Brown, Baker, & Orbach, 2000; Scott-Brown & Orbach, in press).

Much of visual perception occurs without awareness, and although we may not need to store the results of such percepts internally, there are almost certainly some cases in which performance would be enhanced by representing, however transiently, some of the contents of a scene. In the concluding section we consider what aspects of scene perception tend to occur without awareness and whether these effects imply complete or precise representations.

Representations, Actions, and the Experience of Stability

Findings from studies of visual integration and change detection provide relatively little evidence that we achieve an experience of visual stability by forming and combining complete and precise representations. However, the tasks used to study integration and change detection measure aspects of perception that might not require precise representations. Most judgments about objects do not require rapid and accurate detection of changes.

One area that does appear to require relatively precise information is action. In order to act on our world, we must represent the shapes and positions of objects with sufficient precision to avoid colliding with them or to successfully grasp them. Such actions certainly require precise percepts, and they might well require precise representations and comparisons from one view to the next. Consequently, visually guided action might be an appropriate domain to explore the possibility that representations are both complete and precise and that they can be integrated across views.

More importantly, visually guided action can be measured without explicit verbal reports and often is more precise than such reports. For example, observers better estimate the slope of a hill when they respond by manually adjusting a board than when they provide a verbal estimate (Proffitt, Bhalla, Gossweiler, & Midgett, 1995). People also adjust their actions in response to visual feedback without explicit awareness of the corrections. For example, expert table tennis players make small paddle adjustments during their stroke that correct the trajectory of the swing (Bootsma & van Wieringen, 1990), but they are not ordinarily aware of these fine adjustments. Similarly, initial saccades to a target are often inaccurate, but they are quickly followed by corrective saccades that bring the projection of the target into the fovea (e.g., Deubel, Wolf, & Hauske, 1982; Shebilske, 1976). Again, observers typically are unaware of both the error and the correction (Becker & Fuchs, 1969; Deubel et al., 1982). Such implicit corrections occur even when the target of a saccade is slightly displaced just after the beginning of the eye movement (Bridgeman, Hendry, & Stark, 1975). In fact, observers are often unaware of their eye movements altogether (e.g., Bridgeman, 1992).

These implicit corrections are useful in that they allow the eye movement targeting system to operate more efficiently. However, it is not clear that they require a complete or precise representation; they could be driven solely from the perceptual information currently at hand, and not from the representation of information across the saccade. In a test of this possibility, observers made an eye movement to a target and then tried to report the direction that the target shifted during the eye movement (Deubel, Schneider, & Bridgeman, 1996). If they could successfully report the direction, then they must have retained information about the first saccade target position. They could only judge the direction of the object's movement if they had stored the initial saccade target position and then compared that representation to the new position. Consistent with previous work, when the target object was present at the conclusion of the saccade, observers failed to notice the displacement. Critically, in this experiment, the reappearance of the target object was sometimes delayed until after the end of the first saccade. This temporal "gap" in which no object was visible helped observers to report the direction of the second displacement. Thus, observers can become aware of their corrective saccades even for displacements that typically are not detected. This finding suggests that the initial position of the target is represented with relatively good precision even after a second saccade and even if observers are unaware of having made the corrective saccade. Thus, some information about the positions of objects in the display is preserved from one fixation to the next, and this position information has sufficient precision to drive subsequent actions.

Given the importance of spatial information in constraining action, it seems reasonable that the visual system might store relatively precise and complete representations of the spatial relations between objects and the observer. Such representations need not be long-lasting, perhaps surviving only for a few fixations, because most actions do not require comparisons over long intervals. These representations might reduce the complexity of navigating and aid in our understanding of the visual world. Although the world may largely serve as its own memory (O'Regan, 1992) with relatively little need to internalize visual details, in order to act in the world we might need to retain some details about spatial layout.

Even if some information were preserved, explicit awareness of every fixation correction would make some simple tasks unbearably complex (e.g., finding a friend at the airport). If our visual system can accomplish the task of preserving just enough information to allow appropriate action, then we would have little need for complete representations of every aspect of our visual world (Hayhoe, 2000). Most of the representations we would need from one instant to the next involve just those properties of the world that can guide actions (such as corrective eye movements and motor adjustments). For example, our motor system can automatically update our own position relative to objects in the world, taking into account the relevant changes (Simons & Wang, 1998). This updating mechanism contributes to the experience of a stable world by integrating just enough information to allow for immediate actions. Furthermore, we rarely need to be aware of the representations underlying our actions. Anecdotally, too much awareness might actually impair performance. For example, thinking too much about a tennis swing can cause a volley to go into the net.

In contrast to positional information needed for motor control, we do not need to maintain a complete and precise internal representation of the features of objects. For the most part, objects and their features do not change from one moment to the next, and we rarely need to integrate textures across a saccade. Provided that the target of an eye movement is roughly in the right place following a saccade and that we can identify it with a minimally precise and somewhat abstract representation, our visual system can simply assume that everything else in the world remains unchanged. This assumption of stability provides an experience of a continuous, unchanging world, thereby explaining change blindness and the failure to integrate patterns across eye movements. Only when the change is particularly significant (i.e., a large displacement or a change to the meaning of the scene) will it affect our immediate actions. Under those conditions, it is more likely to draw attention and be noticed. Thus, important events might well be represented, but for the most part, our representations of the world could be relatively incomplete and only marginally precise without disrupting our experience of a stable visual world.

Conclusion

Much of perception does not require that information be preserved from one view to the next. Our review of the visual-integration and change-detection literatures suggests that precise and complete visual representations may be unnecessary for our experience of a stable, continuous visual world. Instead, our experience of stability is driven by precise representations of the information needed to guide action, accompanied by an assumption that the properties of objects in the world are unlikely to change across views. Of course, more sensitive measures might reveal the existence of complete, precise representations of all aspects of the visual world, but such detailed representations are not needed to explain our experience of an unchanging world from one view to the next.

Notes

Daniel Simons was supported by NSF Grant #BCS-9905578 and by an Alfred P. Sloan research fellowship. Stephen Mitroff was supported by an NSF graduate fellowship. Steven Franconeri was partially supported by a Department of Defense Graduate Fellowship. Please address all correspondence to Daniel Simons (*dsimons@wjh.harvard.edu*).

References

Angelone, B. L., Levin, D. T., & Simons, D. J. (2001). *Representation and comparison failures in change blindness.* Manuscript submitted for publication.

Becker, W., & Fuchs, A. F. (1969). Further properties of the human saccadic system: Eye movements and corrective saccades with and without visual fixation points. *Vision Research, 2,* 1247–1258.

Bootsma, R. J., & van Wieringen, P. C. W. (1990). Timing an attacking forehand drive in table tennis. *Journal of Experimental Psychology: Human Perception and Performance, 16*(1), 21–29.

Breitmeyer, B. G. (1984). *Visual masking: An integrative approach.* New York: Oxford University Press.

Bridgeman, B. (1992). Conscious vs. unconscious processes: The case of vision. *Theory and Psychology, 2*(1), 73–88.

Bridgeman, B., Hendry, D., & Stark, L. (1975). Failure to detect displacement of the visual world during saccadic eye movements. *Vision Research, 15*(6), 719–722.

Bridgeman, B., & Mayer, M. (1983). Failure to integrate visual information from successive fixations. *Bulletin of the Psychonomic Society, 21*(4), 285–286.

Campbell, F. W., & Wurtz, R. H. (1978). Saccadic omission: Why we do not see a grey-out during a saccadic eye movement. *Vision Research, 18,* 1297–1303.

Deubel, H., Schneider, W. X., & Bridgeman, B. (1996). Postsaccadic target blanking prevents saccadic suppression of image displacement. *Vision Research, 36*(7), 985–996.

Deubel, H., Wolf, W., & Hauske, G. (1982). Corrective saccades: Effect of shifting the saccade goal. *Vision Research, 22*(3), 353–364.

Di Lollo, V. (1980). Temporal integration in visual memory. *Journal of Experimental Psychology: General, 109*(1), 75–97.

Fernandez-Duque, D., & Thornton, I. M. (2000). Change detection without awareness: Do explicit reports underestimate the representation of change in the visual system? *Visual Cognition, 7*(1/2/3), 323–344.

Franconeri, S. L., & Simons, D. J. (2000). The role of abstract representations and motion signals in change detection. *Investigative Ophthalmology & Visual Science, 41*(4), S420.

Gibson, J. J. (1966). *The senses considered as perceptual systems.* Boston: Houghton Mifflin.

Grimes, J. (1996). On the failure to detect changes in scenes across saccades. In K. Akins (Ed.), *Perception (Vancouver Studies in Cognitive Science)* (vol. 2, pp. 89–110). New York: Oxford University Press.

Hayhoe, M. (2000). Vision using routines: A functional account of vision. *Visual Cognition, 7,* 43–64.

Hayhoe, M. M., Bensinger, D. G., & Ballard, D. (1998). Task constraints in visual working memory. *Vision Research, 38*(1), 125–137.

Hayhoe, M., Lachter, J., & Feldman, J. (1991). Integration of form across saccadic eye movements. *Perception, 20,* 393–402.

Helmholtz, H. V. (1866/1924). *Treatise on physiological optics* (J. P. C. Southall, Trans.). (Vol. 3). Rochester, NY: The Optical Society of America.

Henderson, J. M. (1992). Object identification in context: The visual processing of natural scenes, *46*(3), 319–341.

Henderson, J. M., & Hollingworth, A. (1999). The role of fixation position in detecting scene changes across saccades. *Psychological Science, 10*(5), 438–443.

Henderson, J. M., Pollatsek, A., & Rayner, K. (1987). Effects of foveal priming and extrafoveal preview on object identification, *Journal of Experimental Psychology: Human Perception and Performance 13*(3), 449–463.

Henderson, J. M., Pollatsek, A., & Rayner, K. (1989). Covert visual attention and extrafoveal information use during object identification. *Perception and Psychophysics, 45*(3), 196–208.

Hochberg, J. (1986). Representation of motion and space in video and cinematic displays. In K. R. Boff, L. Kaufman, & J. P. Thomas (Eds.), *Handbook of perception and human performance* (Vol. 1: Sensory Processes and Perception, pp. 22.21–22.64). New York: Wiley.

Hollingworth, A., Williams, C. C., & Henderson, J. M. (in press). To see and remember: Visually specific information is retained in memory from previously attended objects in natural scenes. *Psychonomic Bulletin & Review.*

Horowitz, T. S., & Wolfe, J. M. (1998). Visual search has no memory. *Nature, 394*(6693), 575–577.

Irwin, D. E. (1991). Information integration across saccadic eye movements. *Cognitive Psychology, 23,* 420–456.

Irwin, D. E., Brown, J. S., & Sun, J.-S. (1988). Visual masking and visual integration across saccadic eye movements. *Journal of Experimental Psychology: General, 117*(3), 276–287.

Irwin, D. E., Yantis, S., & Jonides, J. (1983). Evidence against visual integration across saccadic eye movements. *Perception and Psychophysics, 34*(1), 49–57.

Irwin, D. E., Zacks, J. L., & Brown, J. S. (1990). Visual memory and the perception of a stable visual environment. *Perception and Psychophysics, 47*(1), 35–46.

Jonides, J., Irwin, D. E., & Yantis, S. (1982). Integrating visual information from successive fixations. *Science, 215,* 192–194.

Jonides, J., Irwin, D. E., & Yantis, S. (1983). Failure to integrate information from successive fixations. *Science, 222*(4620), 188.

Kahneman, D. (1968). Method, findings, and theory in studies of visual masking. *Psychological Bulletin, 70,* 404–425.

Levin, D. T., Simons, D. J., Angelone, B. L., & Chabris, C. F. (in press). Memory for centrally attended changing objects in an incidental real-world change detection paradigm. *British Journal of Psychology.*

Levin, D. T., & Simons, D. J. (1997). Failure to detect changes to attended objects in motion pictures. *Psychonomic Bulletin and Review, 4*(4), 501–506.

Lindberg, D. C. (1976). *Theories of vision from Al-Kindi to Kepler.* Chicago: University of Chicago.

Luck, S. J., & Vogel, E. K. (1997). The capacity of visual working memory for features and conjunctions. *Nature, 390*(6657), 279–281.

McConkie, G. W., & Currie, C. B. (1996). Visual stability across saccades while viewing complex pictures. *Journal of Experimental Psychology: Human Perception and Performance, 22,* 563–581.

McConkie, G. W., & Rayner, K. (1976). Identifying the span of the effective stimulus in reading: Literature review and theories of reading. In H. Singer & R. B. Ruddell (Eds.), *Theoretical models and processes of reading* (2nd ed., pp. 137–162). Newark, DE: International Reading Association.

McConkie, G. W., & Zola, D. (1979). Is visual information integrated across successive fixations in reading? *Perception and Psychophysics, 25*(3), 221–224.

Mitroff, S. R., & Simons, D. J. (in press). Changes are not localized before they are explicitly detected. *Visual Cognition.*

Mitroff, S. R., Simons, D. J., & Franconeri, S. L. (2001). *The siren song of implicit change detection.* Manuscript in revision.

O'Regan, J. K. (1992). Solving the 'real' mysteries of visual perception: The world as an outside memory. *Canadian Journal of Psychology, 46*(3), 461–488.

O'Regan, J. K., Deubel, H., Clark, J. J., & Rensink, R. A. (2000). Picture changes during blinks: Looking without seeing and seeing without looking. *Visual Cognition, 7,* 191–212.

O'Regan, J. K., Rensink, R. A., & Clark, J. J. (1999). Change-blindness as a result of "mudsplashes." *Nature, 398*(6722), 34.

Pashler, H. (1988). Familiarity and visual change detection. *Perception and Psychophysics, 44*(4), 369–378.

Pollatsek, A., Rayner, K., & Collins, W. E. (1984). Integrating pictorial information across eye movements. *Journal of Experimental Psychology: General, 113*(3), 426–442.

Pollatsek, A., Rayner, K., & Henderson, J. M. (1990). Role of spatial location in integration of pictorial information across saccades. *Journal of Experimental Psychology: Human Perception and Performance, 16*(1), 199–210.

Proffitt, D. R., Bhalla, M., Gossweiler, R., & Midgett, J. (1995). Perceiving geographical slant. *Psychonomic Bulletin and Review, 2*(4), 409–428.

Rayner, K., McConkie, G. W., & Ehrlich, S. F. (1978). Eye movements and integrating information across fixations. *Journal of Experimental Psychology: Human Perception and Performance, 4,* 529–544.

Rayner, K., McConkie, G. W., & Zola, D. (1980). Integrating information across eye movements. *Cognitive Psychology, 12,* 206–226.

Rayner, K., & Pollatsek, A. (1983). Is visual information integrated across saccades? *Perception and Psychophysics, 34*(1), 39–48.

Reingold, E. M., & Merikle, P. M. (1988). Using direct and indirect measures to study perception without awareness. *Perception & Psychophysics, 44,* 563–575.

Rensink, R. A. (1998). Mindsight: Visual sensing without seeing. *Investigative Opthalmology and Visual Science, 39,* 631.

Rensink, R. A. (2000a). The dynamic representation of scenes. *Visual Cognition, 7,* 17–42.

Rensink, R. A. (2000b). Visual search for change: A probe into the nature of attentional processing. *Visual Cognition, 7,* 345–376.

Rensink, R. A., O'Regan, J. K., & Clark, J. J. (1997). To see or not to see: The need for attention to perceive changes in scenes. *Psychological Science, 8*(5), 368–373.

Rensink, R. A., O'Regan, J. K., & Clark, J. J. (2000). On the failure to detect changes in scenes across brief interruptions. *Visual Cognition, 7,* 127–146.

Scott-Brown, K. C., Baker, M. R., & Orbach, H. S. (2000). Comparison blindness. *Visual Cognition, 7,* 253–267.

Scott-Brown, K. C., & Orbach, H. S. (in press). Contrast discrimination, nonuniform patterns and change blindness. *Proceedings of the Royal Society, B.*

Shebilske, W. L. (1976). Extraretinal information in corrective saccades and inflow vs. outflow theories of visual direction constancy. *Vision Research, 16*(6), 621–628.

Simons, D. J. (1996). In sight, out of mind: When object representations fail. *Psychological Science, 7*(5), 301–305.

Simons, D. J. (2000). Current approaches to change blindness. *Visual Cognition, 7,* 1–15.

Simons, D. J., Chabris, C. F., Schnur, T., & Levin. D. T. (in press). Preserved representations in change blindness. *Consciousness and Cognition.*

Simons, D. J., Franconeri, S. L., & Reimer, R. L. (2000). Change blindness in the absence of a visual disruption. *Perception, 29,* 1143–1154.

Simons, D. J., & Levin, D. T. (1997). Change blindness. *Trends in Cognitive Sciences, 1*(7), 261–267.

Simons, D. J., & Levin, D. T. (1998). Failure to detect changes to people in a real-world interaction. *Psychonomic Bulletin and Review, 5*(4), 644–649.

Simons, D. J., & Wang, R. F. (1998). Perceiving real-world viewpoint changes. *Psychological Science, 9*(4), 315–320.

Smilek, D., Eastwood, J. D., & Merikle, P. M. (2000). Does unattended information facilitate change detection? *Journal of Experimental Psychology: Human Perception and Performance, 26*(2), 480–487.

Sperling, G. (1960). The information available in brief visual presentations. *Psychological Monographs: General and Applied, 74*(11), 1–29.

Thornton, I. M., & Fernandez-Duque, D. (2000). An implicit measure of undetected change. *Spatial Vision, 14*(1), 21–44.

Trehub, A. (1991). *The cognitive brain.* Cambridge, MA: MIT Press.

Trehub, A. (1994). What does calibration solve? *Behavioral and Brain Sciences, 17,* 279–280.

Van Hoorn, W. (1972). *As images unwind: Ancient and modern theories of visual perception.* Amsterdam: University Press Amsterdam.

Williams, P., & Simons, D. J. (2000). Detecting changes in novel, complex three-dimensional objects. *Visual Cognition, 7,* 297–322.

13

Eye Movements, Visual Memory, and Scene Representation

JOHN M. HENDERSON AND
ANDREW HOLLINGWORTH

The main objective of this chapter is to develop a framework for understanding the nature of scene representations generated during extended, dynamic visual perception. The chapter is structured as follows. First, we outline six critical phenomena that present an interesting puzzle for theories of scene representation. Second, we describe and contrast two general theoretical approaches to scene representation—a localist-minimalist approach, and a visual memory approach. In this review, we highlight important differences in the assumptions these approaches make about the level of detail included in scene representations and the role that visual memory plays in perception. Finally, we review recent evidence bearing on these two approaches, and we argue that the weight of the evidence, as well as the ability to accommodate the six critical phenomena, favors the visual memory approach.

Scene Representation: Six Critical Phenomena

Saccadic Eye Movements Are an Important Component of Scene Perception

Because of the optical structure of the eyes, the gradient of cone density in the retina, and the preferential mapping of foveal photoreceptors onto visual cortical tissue, acuity and color sensitivity are best at the point of fixation and drop off precipitously and continuously with increasing visual eccentricity (Anstis, 1974; Mullen, 1990; Riggs, 1965). The highest quality visual information is acquired from the region of the scene that projects to the fovea, an area of each retina corresponding to about the central 2° of the viewed scene. The fact that high-acuity vision is restricted to a relatively small central region of the entire visual field places an important constraint on human perception. The visual system overcomes this constraint by rapidly and efficiently maneuvering the fixation point around a visual scene via high-velocity eye movements called saccades (Buswell, 1935; Henderson & Hollingworth, 1998, 1999b; Rayner, 1998; Yarbus, 1967). An example fixation sequence (scan pattern) is shown in the top panel of figure 13.1. During a saccade, the point of regard sweeps rapidly across the scene (shown by the lines in figure 13.1). During a fixation, the point of regard is relatively (though not perfectly) still for about 330 ms on average (shown by the dots in figure 13.1). Pattern information is acquired during the fixations; information useful for perceptual analysis of the scene typically cannot be acquired during a saccade due to saccadic suppression (Matin, 1974; Volkmann, 1986).

We Have the Undeniable Perceptual Experience of a Complete and Detailed Visual World

Interestingly, despite the fact that the eyes saccade about three times each second and vision is suppressed during saccades, we do not experience the tens of milliseconds that transpire during these movements as blank periods or "holes" in our visual experience, nor do we experience the world as the series of discrete snapshots that result from each fixation. Instead, when we look around our visual environment, we have the perceptual experience of a complete, full-color, highly detailed, and stable visual world. That is, our perceptual experience suggests to us that the visual system in some sense creates a high-resolution internal copy of the external world. Indeed, visual phenomenology has traditionally motivated much of the theoretical work in human and computer vision, and the experience of a complete and detailed visual world has been a major consideration in recent theoretical treatments of scene representation, visual memory, and the nature of consciousness (e.g., Dennett, 1991; O'Regan, 1992; Rensink, 2000a; Wolfe, 1999).

Precise, Pre-Categorical, Metrical Sensory Information Is Not Carried Across Saccades

Given the strong constraints on visual acuity and color sensitivity across the retina, the generation of the sort of detailed internal visual representation that might underlie perceptual experience would seem to require the storage of a high-resolution sensory image across each saccade, with im-

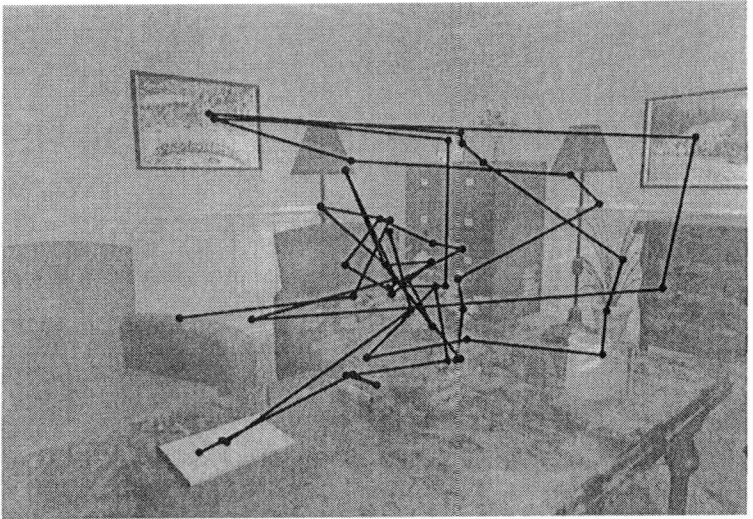

FIGURE 13.1. The top panel shows a typical scan pattern for a viewer attempting to commit a scene to memory. The dots in the scan pattern represent fixations, and the lines represent saccades. The contrast of the scene has been reduced in the figure to better show the scan pattern. The bottom panel shows a gray-scale version of a scene used in the experiments described in this chapter. In the experiments, the scenes were presented in full color. The bottom panel also shows two critical scene regions defined for the experiments. Region A surrounds the target object that changes in an experiment. In some experiments, entrance into or exit from Region A triggers a change to the target object (Toward and Away Conditions). Region B surrounds an alternative change-triggering region: In some experiments, a display change to the target object in Region A is generated only when the eyes enter Region B (Other Object Condition). The regions are software-defined and are invisible to the viewers in the experiments.

ages from consecutive fixations overlapped or spatially aligned to form a composite image. Indeed, there is a long and venerable history of this sort of proposal in vision science (for reviews see Bridgeman, Van der Hejiden, & Velichkovsky, 1994; McConkie & Currie, 1996). We will refer to this general proposal as the *composite sensory image hypothesis*. Traditionally, the composite sensory image hypothesis has been instantiated by models in which a sensory image (i.e., a precise, highly detailed, metrically organized, pre-categorical image) is generated during each fixation and stored in a temporary buffer, with sensory images from consecutive fixations spatially aligned and fused in a system that maps a retinal reference frame onto a spatiotopic frame (Breitmeyer, Kropfl, & Julesz, 1982; Davidson, Fox, & Dick, 1973; Duhamel, Colby, & Goldberg, 1992; Feldman, 1985; Jonides, Irwin, & Yantis, 1982; McConkie & Rayner, 1976; O'Regan & Levy-Schoen, 1983; Pouget, Fisher, & Sejnowski, 1993; Trehub, 1977). In such models, the composite image formed during consecutive fixations might be aligned by tracking the extent of the saccade (via afferent or efferent pathways) or by comparing the similarity of the individual images themselves.

Although many different instantiations of the composite sensory image hypothesis have been proposed, psychophysical and behavioral data from the vision and cognition literatures have overwhelmingly provided evidence against it. This work has been extensively reviewed elsewhere (see, e.g., Irwin, 1992a, Irwin & Andrews, 1996; Pollatsek & Rayner, 1992; Rayner, 1998), so we will not devote much time to it here. However, it is worthwhile gaining an appreciation for the general nature of the evidence.

Perhaps the most convincing evidence against the composite sensory image hypothesis arises from direct demonstrations that viewers are unable to fuse simple visual patterns across saccades. In these paradigms, viewers are required to integrate a pre-saccade and post-saccade pattern in order to successfully accomplish the task. The logic of these experiments is that if visual patterns can be fused in a spatiotopically based sensory memory system, then performance should be similar in a transsaccadic condition in which the environmental spatial position of the patterns is maintained but retinal position is displaced owing to a saccade, and a condition in which position in both retinal and environmental spatial reference frames is maintained within a fixation.

For example, when two dot patterns forming a matrix of dots are presented in rapid succession at the same retinal and spatial position within an eye fixation, a single fused pattern is perceived and performance (e.g., identification of a missing dot from the matrix) can be based upon this percept (Di Lollo, 1980; Eriksen & Collins, 1967; Irwin, 1991). However, when the two patterns are viewed with similar timing parameters at the same external spatial position but different retinal positions across a saccade, no such fused percept is experienced and performance is dramatically reduced (Bridgeman & Mayer, 1983; Irwin, 1991; Irwin, Brown, & Sun, 1988; Irwin, Yantis, & Jonides, 1983; Irwin, Zacks, & Brown, 1990;

Jonides, Irwin, & Yantis, 1983; O'Regan & Levy-Shoen, 1983; Rayner & Pollatsek, 1983). In the latter case, overall performance is limited to and constrained by the capacity of short-term memory (Irwin et al., 1988). Other effects that might be expected based on the formation of a composite image via sensory fusion, such as spatiotopically based visual masking, are also not observed (Irwin et al., 1988; Irwin et al., 1990).

Changes to Scenes Are Often Very Difficult to Consciously Detect Across Saccades and Other Visual Disruptions, a Phenomenon Known as "Change Blindness"

Viewers are apparently insensitive to visual changes in an image across a saccade or other visual disruption, a phenomenon that has recently come to be called "change blindness" (Rensink, O'Regan, & Clark, 1997; Simons, 2000; Simons & Levin, 1998; see also Simons, Mitroff, & Franconeri, chapter 12 this volume). Change blindness has been taken as a second source of evidence against the composite sensory image hypothesis; if sensory images are fused across saccades, one might expect that mismatches in those images would be noticed. Though coming into more prominence recently, the relative insensitivity of viewers to changes across saccades has been known in the visual stability and transsaccadic integration literatures at least since the mid-1970s, when advances in eyetracking and visual display technology first provided investigators the opportunity to change a display contingent on the detection of the onset of a saccade. Some of the earliest reports of this phenomenon involved scene changes (Bridgeman, Hendry, & Stark, 1975) and text changes in reading (Rayner, 1975, 1978).

One example of change blindness is observed when an image is spatially displaced during a saccade. Such displacements should be quite detectable if pre- and post-saccade sensory images are aligned and integrated via subtraction of the spatial extent of the saccade. In an early study, Bridgeman et al. (1975) demonstrated that a scene could be spatially displaced during a saccade with no conscious experience that the stimulus had shifted position, and with little or no disruption to the performance of a visual task. This insensitivity to spatial displacement across saccades has subsequently been replicated many times (e.g., Currie, McConkie, Carlson-Radvansky, & Irwin, 2000; Bridgeman & Stark, 1979; Henderson, 1997; Irwin, 1991; Mack, 1970; McConkie & Currie, 1996; McConkie, Zola, & Wolverton, 1980; O'Regan, 1981; Verfaillie, De Troy, & Van Rensbergen, 1994; Whipple & Wallach, 1978). An interesting exception to these findings has been reported by Deubel, Schneider, & Bridgeman (1996); participants were found to be sensitive to spatial displacement of a target during a saccade when a blank interval was inserted following the saccade and prior to the reappearance of the spatially shifted target. Although this is an intriguing suggestive finding regarding the representation of spatial position across saccades, an alternative explanation is that viewers became aware of their corrective eye movements when the fixation prior to the corrective movement was increased in duration (fixate-wait-correct) compared to when the corrective movement was made immediately (fixate-correct).

Changes to other visual properties are similarly difficult to detect across a saccade. For example, McConkie and Zola (1979) demonstrated that readers are insensitive to changes in the visual properties of text from fixation to fixation. In these experiments, participants read text made up of characters of alternating case (e.g., ThIs iS iN aLtErNaTiNg CaSe). During a given saccade, the case of all characters was swapped (e.g., tHiS Is In AlTeRnAtInG cAsE). These case changes were not noticed by readers and had very little if any effect on reading rate or comprehension.

Similar insensitivity to changes in visual features of an image across a saccade has been shown with pictures of objects and scenes. For example, Henderson (1997) showed that it is very difficult to detect a change to the specific contours of an object from fixation to fixation. Participants were asked to fixate a point on a computer screen. A line drawing of an object was then presented to the right of fixation. About half of the contours of the object were presented; the other contours were occluded by black stripes (as an object might appear when viewed through a picket fence). The participant executed a saccade to the object as soon as it appeared. During the saccade, the object remained exactly the same, changed to reveal the complementary set of contours, shifted one stripe width in position, or changed to a different object. The participant was asked to indicate if any change occurred. Participants failed to detect the majority of contour changes or position shifts. In a control condition in which the changes took place at the same retinal and spatial position (and at the same visual eccentricity as the preview had appeared) within a fixation, change detection was quite good. This latter result ensures that the contours and positions could be discriminated at the visual eccentricity used in the across-saccade experiment.

Insensitivity to visual change across a saccade has also been demonstrated during natural scene viewing where available semantic constraints might be expected to support encoding of visual information. For example, in a striking demonstration of the insensitivity of a viewer to scene changes, McConkie and Grimes (McConkie, 1990, 1991; first published as Grimes, 1996) reported a study in which viewers studied full-color pictures of scenes over extended viewing times. The participants were instructed to view the scenes in preparation for a relatively difficult memory test. They were further told that something in a scene would occasionally change and that they should press a button if and when that happened. Participants' eye movements were monitored during viewing with a fast and accurate eyetracker, and one region of a scene was changed during the nth saccade, where n was predetermined prior to the experiment. The striking result was that viewers often failed to detect what would seem to be very obvious perceptual (and conceptual) changes in the scene. For example, none of the participants detected that the hats on two central men in a scene switched heads (Grimes, 1996). If visual information were accumulating across saccades in a spatiotopically organized representational system, then these sorts of visual changes should be easily detectable. These results have been taken to call into question the idea that any kind of detailed visual scene representation is retained and integrated across saccades (e.g., O'Regan, 1992; Rensink, 2000a, 2000b; Wolfe, 1999).

Other visual stimulus changes such as enlargements and reductions of object size often go unnoticed when they take place during a saccade (Henderson, 1997; Henderson, Pollatsek, & Rayner, 1987; Pollatsek, Rayner, & Collins, 1984). Visual changes to complete scenes and scene elements across a saccade can be imperceptible, including changes to spatial orientation, color, and even object presence (Grimes, 1996; Henderson & Hollingworth, 1999a; McConkie, 1991; McConkie & Currie, 1996). Change blindness can also be observed in other paradigms, such as when a blank field is inserted between two scene images to simulate a saccade (Rensink et al., 1997), when multiple gray patches (similar to mud splattering on a windshield) are presented on a scene simultaneously with the scene change (O'Regan, Rensink, & Clark, 1999), during blinks (O'Regan, Deubel, Clark, & Rensink, 2000), across film splices (Levin & Simons, 1997), and even in the real world when an object is interposed between the observer and a changing object during the change (Simons & Levin, 1998; see Simons & Levin, 1997, Simons, 2000, for review). In general, when local transient motion signals that usually accompany a change are removed from the input, or when multiple motion signals are present, detection of what would otherwise be a highly visible change becomes extraordinarily difficult.

Importantly, change blindness appears to be mediated by attention: once a change has been detected, it is then very easy to see. In the transsaccadic change-detection paradigm, changes are much more easily detected when they occur during a saccade toward the changing object (Currie et al., 2000; Hayhoe, Bensinger, & Ballard, 1998; Henderson & Hollingworth, 1999a) than during a saccade away from that object (Henderson & Hollingworth, 1999a). Similarly, transsaccadic integration is heavily weighted toward the saccade target (Henderson, 1994; Henderson & Anes, 1994; Irwin & Andrews, 1996), at least partly due to the fact that attention is mandatorily allocated to the saccade target prior to a saccade (Deubel & Schneider, 1996; Henderson, 1993, 1996; Henderson, Pollatsek, & Rayner, 1989; Hoffman & Subramanian, 1995; Irwin & Gordon, 1998; Kowler, Anderson, Dosher, & Blaser, 1995; Rayner, McConkie, & Ehrlich, 1978; Shepherd, Findlay, & Hockey, 1986). In the change-blindness literature, detection of changes is better in the flicker paradigm for scene regions rated to be of higher interest (Rensink et al., 1997), for semantically unexpected objects (Hollingworth & Henderson, 2000a), at locations to which attention has been explicitly directed (Scholl, 2000), and at locations near fixation (Hollingworth, Schrock, & Henderson, 2001). Intuitively, once a change has been detected, attention dwells on that region, making the change thereafter quite obvious to the viewer.

Some Relatively Detailed Representations Coding Visual Properties Do Survive a Saccade, Leading to Transsaccadic Preview Benefits

Irwin and colleagues have demonstrated in a transsaccadic partial report task that the perceptual properties of up to four visual patterns can be retained across saccades in visual short-term memory (Irwin & Andrews, 1996). Carlson-Radvansky (Carlson-Radvansky & Irwin, 1995; Carlson-Radvansky, 1999) has shown that structural descriptions of simple visual patterns can be retained across saccades. In transsaccadic object identification studies, participants are faster to identify an object when a preview of that object is available prior to the saccade than when no preview is available (e.g., Henderson, 1992, 1994, 1997; Henderson & Siefert, 1999, 2001; Henderson et al., 1987, 1989; Pollatsek et al., 1984; Pollatsek, Rayner, & Henderson, 1990). Furthermore, preview benefits for objects can be affected by visual changes such as replacement of one visual token with another token of the same conceptual type (Henderson & Siefert, 2001) and mirror reflections (Henderson & Siefert, 1999, 2001). The influence of visual change on preview benefit is more pronounced when the spatial location of the target object remains constant compared with when the location changes (Henderson, 1994; Henderson & Anes, 1994). These results strongly suggest that some visual properties are preserved in the representation that is retained across saccades, and furthermore that such representations are tied to spatial position.

Scene Memory for Large Numbers of Scenes over Extended Time Periods Is Exceptionally Good

Despite the fact that viewers are relatively insensitive to changes in scenes, other research has shown very good long-term memory for scenes. For example, Nickerson (1965) had participants view 200 black and white photographs for 5 each; on an old-new recognition test, participants correctly recognized 92% of the pictures (controlling for false alarm rate). Shepard (1967) similarly demonstrated 97% correct recognition for 612 color pictures when tested immediately and 99.7% when tested two hours later. Standing, Conezio and Haber (1970) showed participants 2560 pictures for 10 sec each over several days. Memory for the entire set of pictures was well over 90% correct. Furthermore, memory for a subset of 280 thematically similar scenes, which required remembering more details about the pictures than general category or gist, was 90% correct. Standing et al. (1970) also manipulated the left-right orientation of the scene at study and test, and showed that participants could recognize the studied picture orientation 86% of the time after a 30 sec retention interval and 72% of the time after 24 hours. Good memory for objects in scenes has also been shown in paradigms investigating eye movements and scene encoding (Friedman, 1979; Parker, 1978).

Summary

The six critical findings reviewed above present an interesting puzzle for theories of scene representation: visual acuity is limited and eye movements provide for sampling of the visual field; we experience the world as stable, complete, and detailed despite eye movements; composite sensory images are not combined across saccades; scene changes are often very difficult to detect; some information survives saccades and leads to preview benefits; and visual memory for scenes can be exceptionally good. On the one hand, the inability to fuse images across saccades and change blindness suggest that visual scene representations are impoverished at best and nonexistent at worst. On the other hand, transsaccadic preview benefits and exceptional scene memory, as well as visual phenomenology, suggest that a more complete and detailed visual representation of a viewed scene is created. How can these findings be reconciled? In the next section, we outline two theoretical approaches to scene memory and scene representation that attempt to account for the six critical findings.

Theoretical Accounts of Scene Representation and Visual Memory

Localist-Minimalist Approaches

Placing primary emphasis on the change-blindness phenomenon, several recent theories have rejected the notion that a global detailed scene representation is ever generated. In these *localist-minimalist* theories, scene memory phenomena are downplayed as the result of retention of scene gist, and the perceptual experience of a complete visual world is taken to be an illusion. For example, O'Regan (1992) proposed that because the world is its own memory, the visual system does not need to store visual information from fixation to fixation. On this view, visual stability and coherence are illusions brought about by the fact that visual information can be sampled from the world when needed via shifts of attention and fixation (O'Regan, 1992; O'Reagan et al., 1999; Rensink et al., 1997). Indeed, based on demonstrations that visual search does not become more efficient with high levels of practice, Wolfe (1999) has argued that there are no perceptual consequences of having attended and perceived specific objects in the environment. According to Wolfe, "when attention is deployed away from some previously attended object or locus, no trace of the effects of attention remain in the visual representation" (1999, p. 75).

Thus, on this view, once the eyes have moved on, there should be no coherent visual representation to integrate across fixations. Examples of this general approach include the proposals of O'Regan (1992), Simons and Levin (1997), Wolfe (1999), Irwin (1992a; Irwin & Andrews, 1996), and Rensink (2000a, 2000b). Perhaps the most complete and explicit localist-minimalist theories are the Object File Theory of Transsaccadic Integration (Irwin, 1992a, 1992b; Irwin & Andrews, 1996), which builds on the original Object File Theory (Kahneman & Triesman, 1984; Kahneman, Triesman, & Gibbs, 1992), and Coherence Theory (Rensink, 2000a, 2000b). As a class, localist-minimalist theories assume that scene representation consists of sensory coding of the current retinal image (typically with acknowledgment of image degradation as a function of retinal eccentricity), a coherent visual representation of the currently attended scene region or object (and perhaps a few other objects actively attended in visual short-term memory), and a sketchy semantic representation of the gist of the scene along with the identities of previously attended objects, and a course representation of the spatial layout of the scene.

We term this general theoretical position "localist-minimalist" because of its commitment to the assumption that at any given moment coherent visual representations are generated only for a limited scene region, typically the region currently attended or at most the last three or four attended regions (*localism*), and to the assumption that visual representations are retained for no more than a few seconds and so are not available to be integrated into a composite scene representation (*minimalism*). Though the details differ in a number of ways, we can also find a commitment to representational localism and minimalism in recent theorizing in computer vision (e.g., Ballard, 1991, 1996; Ballard, Hayhoe, Pook, & Rao, 1997; Brooks 1991) and in philosophy (e.g., Dennett, 1991; Churchland, Ramachandran, & Sejnowski, 1994).

A Visual Memory Theory of Scene Representation

Based on data we have recently collected that is incompatible with the localist-minimalist view (reviewed below), we propose an alternative theory of scene representation that rejects the notions of localism and minimalism. The theory instead posits that a relatively detailed scene representation is built up in long-term memory over time and across successive fixations (Hollingworth & Henderson, 2002). The theory states that visual detail is retained both over the short term in a visual short-term memory buffer similar to that envisioned in Irwin's (1992a; Irwin & Andrews, 1996) Object File Theory (though the specifics of exactly what is retained in our views differ somewhat), and over the longer term, in long-term scene memory of the sort described in the extended scene memory literature (Standing et al., 1970; see also Friedman, 1979). At the same time, the theory acknowledges that these visual representations are not sensory in nature (Hollingworth & Henderson, 2002).

In Visual Memory Theory, the allocation of attention to a scene region gates sensory processing of that region, which (1) leads to the generation of visual token representations that are abstracted away from the sensory properties in the image, but that code the visual properties of that object or region, including object shape and position, and (2) leads to the activation of semantic representations and identities of attended objects (Henderson, 1994; Henderson & Anes, 1994; Henderson & Siefert, 1999, 2001). Object shape is abstractly coded in a representational system such as a view-based structural description (Carlson-Radvansky & Irwin, 1995; Carlson-Radvansky, 1999; see also Bulthoff, Edelman, & Tarr, 1995), and position is abstractly coded in multiple spatial reference frames including an allocentric (i.e., scene-based) reference frame (Henderson, 1994; Henderson & Anes, 1994). Similarly, other visual properties such as color can be coded, albeit in an abstract rather than sensory form (see below). It is proposed that these abstracted representations are actively maintained in a short-term memory store as long as attention is directed at them. This short-term memory store has many of the properties typically associated with classic conceptions of short-term memory, including limited capacity and abstract format (Irwin & Andrews, 1996). We further postulate that short-term scene memory has a property of the conceptual short-term memory system proposed by Potter and colleagues (Potter, 1999): processing in STM leads both to consolidation of the information as part of the overall scene representation and to transfer of the information into a more stable long-term memory representation. However, in our view, both visual and semantic representations can be consolidated and transferred to LTM.

In addition to encoding information at fixation, transsaccadic memory is particularly likely to contain information about the saccade target (Currie et al., 2000; Henderson & Hollingworth, 1999a; Irwin & Andrews, 1996) because attention is obligatorily allocated to the target of an impending saccade (e.g., Hoffman & Subramanian, 1995; Kowler et al., 1995; Sheperd et al., 1986). Once the eyes begin to move (or the scene is otherwise removed from view), sensory representations established during the prior fixation quickly decay (Sperling, 1960), leaving only the abstracted representations that are currently held in STM, along with the information that has been transferred to long-term memory. When the eyes land and a new fixation begins, the visual information stored in STM will be compared to information encoded in the current fixation. If the information is similar enough, it will be integrated; otherwise an error signal will be generated and the change will be detected. Because information from the saccade target prior to a saccade and from the fixation point following the saccade are the regions of the scene most likely to be attended before and after the saccade, changes to these regions are most likely to be noticed (Henderson & Hollingworth, 1999a; Henderson & Hollingworth, 2003; Hollingworth & Henderson, in press), and similarities in these regions are most likely to be integrated in a transsaccadic integration paradigm (Henderson, 1994; Henderson et al., 1989).

Importantly, in Visual Memory Theory, when the information needed to detect a change (or to support an integrated scene representation) is not currently held in STM, that information can be retrieved from long-term memory if it was successfully encoded and stored during a previous fixation (Hollingworth & Henderson, 2002; Hollingworth, Williams, & Henderson, 2001). Attention to the relevant scene region greatly increases the probability that the information will be retrieved from LTM because local information in the scene provides a strong retrieval cue for long-term memory. Because of the tight link between attention and fixation, returning the eyes to a scene region increases the chances of detecting a change to that region. Even if the object has been deleted from the region, the spatial position of fixation and the coding of nearby scene information provide a retrieval context for that object (Henderson & Hollingworth, 1999a). These basic assumptions (the coupling of attention and fixation, and enabling retrieval via attention and fixation), account for the strong tendency for late detections in the change detection paradigm to take place only when the changed object is refixated (Henderson & Hollingworth, 1999a; Hollingworth & Henderson, 2002; Hollingworth et al., 2001).

In the context of Visual Memory Theory, it is important to draw a distinction between sensory representations and abstract visual representations. Specifically, representation of detailed visual information does not imply the preservation of a sensory image. In our view, the representations that are retained and integrated across saccades are visually specific, but abstract. We take "sensory representation" to refer to a complete, precise, pre-categorical, maskable, and metrically organized image of the visual scene (Irwin 1992b; Neisser, 1967; Sperling, 1960). In contrast, an "abstract visual representation" is an imprecise, postcategorical, nonmaskable, and noniconic visual description encoded in the vocabulary of visual computation. This same point has been made by Irwin and colleagues in their study of transsaccadic integration, and the distinction maps well onto the distinction in the "iconic memory" literature between visual and informational persistence on the one hand, and visual short-term memory on the other (Irwin, 1992b; see also Coltheart, 1980). Importantly, abstract visual representations can still be considered visual in that they represent visual properties such as object shape, albeit in a nonsensory format. A good candidate for the abstract representation of shape is a structural description; recent evidence suggests that shape may be encoded and retained across saccades in this representational format (Carlson-Radvansky & Irwin, 1995; Carlson-Radvansky, 1999). Note that abstract visual representations are not to be taken as equivalent to conceptual representations, which code semantic properties of the viewed scene, nor are they meant to be linguistic descriptions of scene properties. Examples of ab-

stracted visual representations are structural descriptions (e.g., Biederman, 1987; Marr, 1982; Palmer, 1977) and hierarchical feature representations (e.g., Riesenhuber & Poggio, 1999), which are neither conceptual
nor linguistic.

In summary, in Visual Memory Theory, transsaccadic change detection
is a function of (1) initial attention to and encoding of information from
a scene region as an abstract visual representation, (2) retention of that
representation either in an active state in short-term memory and/or in an
inactive state in long-term memory, (3) generation of a new representation
to compare to the stored representation, (4) retrieval of the stored representation back from LTM into STM if it is not already currently active,
and (5) comparison of the original representation with the new representation. A strength of the theory is that it draws on independently motivated
principles that have been established in the memory literature; Visual
Memory Theory places a great deal of the explanatory machinery for
change detection and for transsaccadic integration firmly on the shoulders
of visual memory, both short and long term. Although the theory assumes
that nowhere in the system are precise sensory images retained across
saccades, it nevertheless posits that a relatively detailed scene representation can be generated and stored over time. This scene representation
comes about via the storage of abstract visual representations of local
objects and scene elements in long-term memory (what we have called
"long-term object files;" Hollingworth & Henderson, 2002), tied together
with a spatial representation of object locations. Cognitive representations
including object and scene identity and meaning are also generated during
fixations, and these can also be stored both in short-term and long-term
memory along with more specific visual representations coded by the long-
term object files.

It is important that we be clear about the domain and scope of the
Visual Memory Theory. The theory is meant to capture the nature of the
scene representations that are generated, retained, and available for comparison and integration across extended viewing time and multiple eye
fixations. Thus, the nature of the representations that support conscious
experience of change, or indeed the conscious experience of anything, is
beyond the scope of the theory. The theory is agnostic about whether
conscious perceptual experience derives from the initial sensory representations (i.e., iconic, precategorical representations), the more abstract perceptual representations that ultimately result from sensory processing, the
visual memory representations that we are focusing on in this chapter, or
something else.

Specification of the degree to which a theory of scene representation
is meant to apply to conscious experience is important because there has
been some confusion in the literature about what theories of "change blindness" or, less assumption-bound, change detection failure, are trying to
account for. For example, the Coherence Theory proposed by Rensink

(2000b) appears to be an account of the nature of conscious experience, and the role of attention in generating that experience. Similarly, Wolfe (1999; Wolfe, Klempen, & Dahlen, 2000) has proposed a theory of the relationship between attentional deployment and perceptual processing that appears to be an attempt to explain conscious perception rather than visual representation, though the theory does clearly include assumptions that speak to the latter issue. Such an emphasis on phenomenology is consistent with historical approaches to perception, in which the purpose of perceptual theory is to explain perceptual experience. For example, as Milner and Goodale put it, "From this perspective, the task of visual science boils down to the problem of understanding how the spatiotopic mosaic of light striking the retina is parsed into the array of discrete objects and events that comprise one's perceptual experience." (1995, p. 5). Visual Memory Theory is aimed at explaining the nature of the representations that are generated from a scene, whether or not those representations support conscious experience. This restriction of scope is not meant to downplay the importance of perceptual experience, but rather to highlight the fact that much interesting perceptual (and cognitive) machinery neither gives rise to, nor is available to, such experience.

Recent Evidence Bearing on Visual Memory and Scene Representation

In a series of studies, we have sought to determine whether the visual representation of natural scenes is better accounted for by localist-minimalist theories or by Visual Memory Theory. We have used two general methods to explore this question. First, we have tested participants' ability to detect changes to objects that were attended within a scene but are not within the current focus of attention at the time of the change (Henderson & Hollingworth, 1999a; Hollingworth & Henderson, 2002; Hollingworth et al., 2001). Second, we have tested participants' memory for the visual form of a previously attended object by asking them to discriminate an original target object from a similar distractor (Hollingworth & Henderson, 2002). Localist-minimalist theories hold that coherent object representations disintegrate when attention is withdrawn and thus predict that change detection and forced-choice discrimination for previously (but not currently) attended objects should be at chance. Consistent with the Visual Memory Theory, however, both change-detection and forced-choice discrimination performance has revealed that quite detailed visual object representations are retained in memory from previously attended objects. Participants detect visual changes to previously attended objects on a significant percentage of trials and demonstrate accurate forced-choice discrimination performance on object memory tests.

Change Detection Experiments

In one set of experiments, we have employed a change-detection paradigm in which a target object in a natural scene was changed during a saccadic eye movement within the scene (Henderson & Hollingworth, 1999a, 2001; Hollingworth & Henderson, 2002; Hollingworth et al., 2001). Participants were asked to view pictures of common environments to prepare for a difficult memory test, and in addition were asked to monitor the scenes for changes. In a critical set of conditions, a target object was changed during a saccade away from that object after it had been fixated the first time (away condition) or during a saccade to a different object in the scene (other object condition). In the away condition, the change was triggered when the participant's gaze shifted from the target object (after it had first been fixated) to any other region of the scene. In the other object condition, the change was triggered when the participant's gaze moved into a pre-specified nontarget region from anywhere else in the scene. This paradigm is illustrated in the bottom panel of figure 13.1. In several experiments, the other object region was only activated after the target object had received at least one fixation (e.g., Hollingworth & Henderson, 2002; Hollingworth et al., 2001). Thus, in these away and other object conditions, the target object was attended at some point prior to the change but was no longer within the current focus of attention when the change occurred. The assumption that visual attention had been withdrawn from the target object prior to the change depends on evidence from numerous studies demonstrating that visual attention must be allocated to the target of the next saccadic eye movement prior to its execution. For example, Hoffman & Subramanian (1995) provided evidence that participants could not attend to one object in the visual field when preparing a saccade to another object, even when such a strategy would have led to better performance (see also Henderson, 1996; Kowler et al., 1995; Sheperd et al., 1986). Therefore, in both the away and other object conditions of our experiments, visual attention is directed away from the target object and to a different object in the visual field prior to the saccade that triggers the change. Participants' ability to detect such changes therefore provides evidence about whether visual object representations disintegrate upon the withdrawal of attention or whether visual object representations are preserved after the withdrawal of attention and accumulate during extended visual exploration of a scene.

CHANGE DETECTION RESULTS

We have tested four change manipulations: *Deletion* of the target object from the scene (Henderson & Hollingworth, 1999a; 2003); *type changes* in which the target object is replaced with another object from a different basic-level category (Henderson & Hollingworth, 2003; Hollingworth & Henderson, 2002); *token changes* in which the target object is replaced with another object from the same basic-level category (Henderson & Hollingworth, 2001; Hollingworth & Henderson, 2002; Hollingworth et al., 2001), and *rotations* in which the target object is rotated 90° around its vertical axis (Henderson & Hollingworth, 1999a; Hollingworth & Henderson, 2002). In each of these conditions, change-detection performance for previously attended objects is significantly above the false alarm rate (which is typically under 10%, and often as low as 1–2%). Deletions are detected best (~75% correct), followed by type changes (~40% correct). Token changes and rotations are more difficult to detect but are still noticed on a significant percentage of trials (~30% correct for each). These results are not consistent with localist-minimalist theories. Moreover, localist-minimalist theories have particular difficulty accounting for the detection of token changes and rotations. It is possible that a deletion or type change might alter the gist of the scene if a representation of gist is detailed enough to code the identities of individual objects. In addition, if participants retained abstract identity codes from previously recognized objects, such information could likewise support the detection of a change to the presence or basic-level identity of the target. Both possibilities would be broadly consistent with the localist-minimalist viewpoint because these theories allow for the representation of the identities of previously attended objects, and for a representation of the gist of the scene. However, token changes and rotations should not alter the gist of the scene nor should such changes be detectable based on the retention of a basic-level identity code from the target. Instead, participants' ability to detect token changes and rotations suggests that a visual representation of the target object was retained after attention had been withdrawn from that object. These results also demonstrate that sustained visual attention to a changing object is not a necessary condition for the detection of a visual change, a result that is inconsistent with localist-minimalist theories (e.g., O'Regan et al., 2000; Rensink et al., 1997; Rensink, 2000a; Wolfe, 1999) but consistent with Visual Memory Theory

In addition to the primary detection results, converging evidence in support of Visual Memory Theory comes from three other results obtained in these studies: delayed detection until after refixation, semantic consistency effects, and implicit effects of change on fixation duration. These results are discussed next.

DELAYED DETECTION

In the studies described above, object changes were often missed when they first occurred, only to be detected later during viewing when the target object happened to be refixated. In other words, the probability of detecting a change increased if the target object was refixated after it had changed. This phenomenon of delayed change detection suggests (1) that visual object representations were retained in memory after attention was withdrawn, and (2) that refixating the changed object provided a cue to retrieve and compare the stored visual object representation to current perceptual information. In addition, participants often fixated many intervening scene regions over the course of a number of seconds (approximately 5 see on average) between the target change and the first refixation of the (now changed) target. Given the strong capacity constraints on VSTM, it is therefore likely that the retention of target object information occurred in long-term memory rather than in VSTM.

SEMANTIC CONSISTENCY EFFECTS

A second strand of converging evidence comes from a manipulation of the semantic consistency of the target object in the scene (Hollingworth et al., 2001). In this study, participants viewed line drawings of scenes in which the target object was either semantically consistent with the scene (e.g., a microscope in a laboratory) or semantically inconsistent (e.g., a teddy bear in a laboratory). The target object was replaced by another token of the same basic-level category during a saccade away from that object. Scene memory research has demonstrated that the memory representation of semantically inconsistent objects is more detailed and/or complete compared to semantically consistent objects (e.g., Friedman, 1979). If visual object representations can accumulate in long-term memory during the online perceptual processing of a scene, then changes to semantically inconsistent objects should be detected more accurately than changes to consistent objects. We found that inconsistent objects were fixated for more time than were inconsistent object (see also Friedman, 1979; Henderson, Weeks, & Hollingworth, 1999), and that changes to those objects, including visual changes, were detected better. Note that localist-minimalist theories cannot account for the effect of semantic consistency on these types of change detections because they predict that change detection for previously attended objects should be at floor regardless of semantic consistency, and regardless of the amount of encoding time spent on the object. According to these theories, once attention is withdrawn, visual representations are not preserved.

IMPLICIT EFFECTS OF CHANGE ON FIXATION DURATION

It is important to consider what can and cannot be concluded about visual representation from the results of explicit change detection experiments. The logic of change blindness experiments has been the following: if visual representations can be retained across disruptions such as a saccade, then mismatches between the retained representation and current input should be obvious and detectable. The problem with this logic is that it requires additional assumptions about the relationship between conscious experience and the underlying representations. In particular, it assumes that the experience of change directly reflects the nature of the representations generated during visual perception. This sort of assumption is deeply rooted in the traditional study of perception, where an explanation of perceptual experience is taken to be the *prima facie* goal of the scientific enterprise of vision science. Undermining this assumption of the transparency of mechanism through experience, though, is the fact that much of our perceptual machinery operates below the level of conscious awareness. For example, we are not aware that vision is suppressed during saccades. Indeed, most people are not aware that they are making saccadic eye movements at all: in our experiments, participants are often astonished when, during the debriefing session, we inform them about the nature of the eye movements we have just recorded from them.

In our third, and perhaps most important line of evidence bearing on the nature of scene representation, we have observed that explicit change detection significantly underestimates the extent to which visual information is retained in memory from previously attended objects. To look for implicit effects in our scene experiments, on trials in which a change occurred but was not explicitly detected (i.e., participants did not push the response button to indicate detection of a change), we examined gaze duration on that object for the first entry of the eyes into the object region after the change. Gaze duration is the sum of the durations of all fixations from the entry of the eyes into an object region to the exit of the eyes from that region. Gaze duration for "miss" trials was compared to the equivalent entry in the condition when no change occurred. Across multiple studies, we have observed a large and robust elevation of gaze duration for miss trials compared to the no-change control trials (Henderson & Hollingworth, 2003; Hollingworth & Henderson, 2002; Hollingworth et al., 2001). For example, in Hollingworth et al. (2001), we found that when a token change was not explicitly detected, mean gaze duration on that object after the change was 749 ms. For the equivalent entry when no change occurred, mean gaze duration was 499 ms. Such implicit effects were observed despite many intervening fixations on other objects between the change and the first refixation of the target. In Hollingworth et al. (2001), participants made an average of 13.5 fixations between the (never detected) change and the next fixation on that object, and increased gaze durations were observed despite this passage of time. Like the phenomenon of delayed explicit detection, the finding that gaze durations on changed targets increased following many intervening fixations suggests that visual object representations were retained in long-term memory after the withdrawal of attention and so were available to influence subsequent fixation time on that object. It seems that despite participants' failure to report the changes, detection was nevertheless taking place within the visual system. Thus, the failure to overtly report a change does not provide evidence that the information needed to detect that change has not been stored. In general, large and robust implicit effects of change raise doubts about the validity of change detection as a measure of visual representation. Implicit effects of scene and object changes have also recently been reported by Hayhoe et al. (1998), Fernandez-Duque and Thornton (2000), and Williams and Simons (2000).

We should note that the presence of implicit detection does not imply that the detection process is itself implicit. As we have noted elsewhere (Hollingworth & Henderson, 2002), implicit effects may be due to cases in which participants do not have enough evidence, or are not confident enough, to press the response button indicating that they noticed a change, but nonetheless have an explicit feeling that a change may have taken place (see Mitroff, Simons, & Franconeri, 2002; Simons et al., chapter 12 this volume). We have recently called these effects covert detections rather than implicit detections to make clear that we are not making any theoretical commitments to separate implicit memory or detection systems (Henderson & Hollingworth, 2003).

In summary, the frequent failure of participants to explicitly report a change in a visual display was initially taken by many investigators as evidence for the absence of visual representation. Our findings demonstrate instead that when more indirect or implicit measures of change detection, such as fixation duration, are used to assess visual representation, robust evidence of visual representation is obtained. It is interesting to note that this situation is not unprecedented within visual cognition. Early studies in what came to be known as the negative priming literature used an explicit report paradigm to investigate the visual representation of ignored stimuli (Rock & Gutman, 1981). Finding little evidence of explicit memory, Rock and Gutman reasoned that ignored stimuli received little or no perceptual processing and produced no memory trace. Subsequent studies using more indirect and implicit measures, however, demonstrated substantial perceptual processing of (Tipper, 1985) and remarkably stable memory traces for (DeSchepper & Treisman, 1996) ignored stimuli. Thus, converging sources of evidence suggest that explicit report is not a reliable measure of visual representation.

Forced-Choice Discrimination Experiments

Given the potential interpretative difficulties of change detection studies, we have also conducted experiments in which we directly tested participants' memory for previously attended objects using a forced-choice paradigm (Hollingworth & Henderson, 2002). Memory for a target object was tested during the online perceptual exploration of a scene (an *online memory test*) and after the scene had been removed for a number of minutes (a *long-term memory test*). In the former, participants viewed 3D-rendered, color scenes of common environments while their eye movements were monitored. After the initiation of each trial, the computer waited until the target object had been fixated at least once, assuring that it had been focally attended prior to the test. Then, during a saccade to another object on the other side of the scene, the target object was obscured by a salient pattern mask that extended just beyond its boundaries. Because the appearance of the mask coincided with a saccade to a different object in the scene, the target object was not currently attended when the mask appeared. The appearance of the mask initiated a forced-choice memory test in which two object alternatives were displayed sequentially within the scene: the original target and a distractor object. The distractor was either a different token from the same basic-level category (token discrimination) or identical to the target object except rotated 90 degrees in depth around the vertical axis (orientation discrimination). Because the localist-minimalist view holds that coherent visual representations disintegrate once attention is withdrawn from an object, that view predicts that discrimination performance should be at chance for previously attended objects. In contrast, the Visual Memory Theory predicts that discrimination should be significantly above chance because it posits that visual representations can be retained in memory after the withdrawal of attention. Consistent with the prediction of Visual Memory Theory, we found that both token and orientation discrimination were quite accurate (86.9% and 81.9% correct, respectively). In addition, on many trials, participants fixated multiple other objects in the scene between the last fixation on the target object prior to the onset of the mask and the initiation of the forced-choice test. Such longer term retention would appear to be beyond the capabilities of VSTM, again suggesting that long-term memory played a significant role in the online construction of a scene representation.

To test long-term memory for objects in scenes directly, we also conducted a forced-choice discrimination test after the scene had been removed for a number of minutes (between 5 and 30 min). Similarly to the online test, for each studied scene, participants viewed two versions of that scene in the test session: one that was identical to the studied scene and a distractor scene that differed only in the target object. The distractor object was either a different type, different token, or the same object rotated in depth. This longer retention interval did not cause much of a decrement in discrimination performance compared to online discrimination. Mean type-discrimination performance was 93.1% correct, mean token-discrimination performance was 80.6% correct, and mean orientation-discrimination performance was 81.9% correct. The similarity between discrimination performance on the online and long-term tests suggests that visual object representations are stable after attention is removed, at least over the retention intervals we tested. Our long-term memory results are consistent with evidence from the picture memory literature suggesting very good memory for the visual form of whole scenes (Standing et al., 1970) and for the visual form of individual objects within scenes (Friedman, 1979; Parker, 1978).

These data, along with the change detection results reviewed above, provide unequivocal evidence that visual object representations accumulate in memory from previously attended objects, forming a relatively detailed scene representation. Contrary to proposals based on change blindness, abstract visual representations do not necessarily decay upon the withdrawal of attention.

Other Evidence for Visual Representation

In addition to the evidence that we presented above concerning the nature of scene representation, there are other sources of evidence that converge on the conclusion that a relatively detailed visual representation must be generated and stored at some level by the visual system. These include the evidence on perceptual learning and perceptual priming. We do not have space to review these literatures here, but we do want to note that it would be difficult to account for such important perceptual and cognitive phenomena without positing that relatively detailed visual representations of some sort can be generated and stored in long-term memory.

Conclusion

We began this chapter by outlining six critical phenomena that must be accounted for by a complete theory of scene perception and scene representation. We then suggested that recent theorizing based on a localist-minimalist view of scene representation cannot adequately accommodate this array of phenomena. In contrast to localist-minimalist theories, we proposed a Visual Memory Theory in which known memory processes are used to provide an integrated framework for understanding scene perception and representation. The theory posits that abstract but visually rich scene representations are encoded and retained in short- and long-term visual memory. The theory explicitly acknowledges the role of eye movements in the encoding and retrieval of scene representations, and places the weight of an explanation for scene representation firmly on the shoulders of established memory processes.

Notes

Preparation of this chapter was supported by the National Science Foundation (SBR 9617274 and ECS 9873531) and the Army Research Office (DAAD-19-00-1-0519). The contents of this chapter are the opinions of the authors and should not be construed as an official Department of the Army position, policy, or decision. We thank the Eye Movements and Visual Cognition group at Michigan State University for their helpful comments on an earlier draft of this chapter. Please address correspondence to John M. Henderson, Department of Psychology and Cognitive Science Program, 221 Psychology Research Building, Michigan State University, East Lansing, MI, 48824-1117. Email may be addressed to john@eyelab.msu.edu.

References

Anstis S. M. (1974). A chart demonstrating variations in acuity with retinal position. *Vision Research, 14*, 589–592.

Ballard, D. H. (1991). Animate vision. *Artificial Intelligence, 48*, 57–86.

Ballard, D. H. (1996). On the function of visual representation. In K. Akins (Ed.), *Perception: Vancouver studies in cognitive science* (pp. 111–131). New York: Oxford University Press.

Ballard, D. H., Hayhoe, M. M., Pook, P. K., & Rao, R. P. (1997). Deictic codes for the embodiment of cognition. *Behavioral & Brain Sciences, 20*, 723–767.

Biederman, I. (1987). Recognition-by-components: A theory of human image understanding. *Psychological Review 94*, 115–147.

Breitmeyer, B. G., Kropfl, W., & Julesz B. (1982). The existence and role of retinotopic and spatiotopic forms of visual persistence. *Acta Psychologica, 52*, 175–196.

Bridgeman, B., Hendry, D., & Stark, L. (1975). Failure to detect displacements of the visual world during saccadic eye movements. *Vision Research, 15*, 719–722.

Bridgeman, B., & Mayer, M. (1983). Failure to integrate visual information from successive fixations. *Bulletin of the Psychonomic Society, 21*, 285–286.

Bridgeman, B., & Stark, L. (1979). Omnidirectional increase in threshold for image shifts during saccadic eye movements. *Perception & Psychophysics, 25*, 241–243.

Bridgeman, B., Van der Heijden, A. H. C., & Velichkovsky, B. M. (1994). A theory of visual stability across saccadic eye movements. *Behavioral and Brain Sciences, 17*, 247–292.

Brooks, R. A. (1991). New approaches to robotics. *Science, 253*, 1227–1232.

Bülthoff, H. H., Edelman, S. Y., & Tarr, M. J. (1995). How are three-dimensional objects represented in the brain? *Cerebral Cortex, 5*, 247–260.

Buswell, G. T. (1935). *How people look at pictures.* Chicago: University of Chicago Press.

Carlson-Radvansky, L. A. (1999). Memory for relational information across eye movements. *Perception & Psychophysics, 61*, 919–934.

Carlson-Radvansky, L. A., & Irwin, D. E. (1995). Memory for structural information across eye movements. *Journal of Experimental Psychology: Learning, Memory and Cognition, 21*, 1441–1458.

Churchland, P. S., Ramachandran, V. S., & Sejnowski, T. J. (1994). A critique of pure vision. In C. Koch & S. Davis (Eds.), *Large scale neuronal theories of the brain.* (pp. 23–60). Cambridge, MA: MIT Press.

Coltheart, M. (1980). Iconic memory and visible persistence. *Perception & Psychophysics, 27*, 183–228.

Currie, C., McConkie, G., Carlson-Radvansky, L. A., & Irwin, D. E. (2000). The role of the saccade target object in the perception of a visually stable world. *Perception & Psychophysics, 62*, 673–683.

Davidson, M. L., Fox, M. J., & Dick, A. O. (1973). Effect of eye movements on backward masking and perceived location. *Perception & Psychophysics, 14*, 110–116.

Dennett, D. C. (1991). *Consciousness explained.* Boston: Little, Brown.

DeSchepper, B., & Treisman, A. (1996). Visual memory for novel shapes: Implicit coding without attention. *Journal of Experimental Psychology: Learning, Memory, and Cognition, 22*, 27–47.

Deubel, H., & Schneider, W. X. (1996). Saccade target selection and object recognition: Evidence for a common attentional mechanism. *Vision Research, 36*, 1827–1837.

Deubel, H., Schneider, W. X., & Bridgeman B. (1996). Postsaccadic target blanking prevents saccadic suppression of image displacement. *Vision Research, 36*, 985–996.

Di Lollo, V. (1980). Temporal integration in visual memory. *Journal of Experimental Psychology: General, 109*, 75–97.

Duhamel, J. R., Colby, C. L., & Goldberg, M. E. (1992). The updating of the representation of visual space in parietal cortex by intended eye movements. *Science, 255*, 90–92.

Eriksen, C. W., & Collins, J. F. (1967). Some temporal characteristics of visual pattern recognition. *Journal of Experimental Psychology, 74*, 476–484.

Feldman, J. A. (1985). Four frames suffice: a provisional model of vision and space. *Behavioral and Brain Sciences, 8*, 265–289.

Fernandez-Duque, D., & Thornton, I. M. (2000). Change detection without awareness: Do explicit reports underestimate the representation of change in the visual system? *Visual Cognition, 7*, 324–344.

Friedman, A. (1979). Framing pictures: The role of knowledge in automatized encoding and memory for gist. *Journal of Experimental Psychology: General, 108*, 316–355.

Grimes, J. (1996). On the failure to detect changes in scenes across saccades. In K. Akins (Ed.), *Perception: Vancouver studies in cognitive science* (vol. 5., pp. 89–110). New York: Oxford University Press.

Hayhoe, M. M., Bensinger, D. G., & Ballard, D. H. (1998). Task constraints in visual working memory. *Vision Research, 38*, 125–137.

Henderson, J. M. (1992). Identifying objects across eye fixations: Effects of extrafoveal preview and flanker object context. *Journal of Experimental Psychology: Learning, Memory, and Cognition, 18*, 521–530.

Henderson, J. M. (1993). Visual attention and saccadic eye movements. In G. d'Ydewalle & J. Van Rensbergen (Eds.), *Perception and cognition: Advances in eye movement research* (pp. 37–50). Amsterdam: North Holland.

Henderson, J. M. (1994). Two representational systems in dynamic visual identification. *Journal of Experimental Psychology: General, 123*, 410–426.

Henderson, J. M. (1996). Visual attention and the attention-action interface. In K. Aikens (Ed.), *Perception: Vancuover studies in cognitive science (Vol V)* pp. 290–316). Oxford: Oxford University Press.

Henderson, J. M. (1997). Transsaccadic memory and integration during real-world object perception. *Psychological Science, 8*, 51–55.

Henderson, J. M., & Anes, M. D. (1994). Effects of object-file review and type priming on visual identification within and across eye fixations. *Journal of Experimental Psychology: Human Perception and Performance, 20*, 826–839.

Henderson, J. M., & Hollingworth, A. (1998). Eye movements during scene viewing: An overview. In G. Underwood (Ed.), *Eye guidance in reading and scene perception* (pp. 269–283). Oxford: Elsevier.

Henderson, J. M., & Hollingworth, A. (1999a). The role of fixation position in detecting scene changes across saccades. *Psychological Science, 10*, 438–443.

Henderson, J. M., & Hollingworth, A. (1999b). High-level scene perception. *Annual Review of Psychology, 50*, 243–271.

Henderson, J. M., & Hollingworth, A. (2003). Eye movements and visual memory: Detecting changes to saccade targets in scenes. *Perception & Psychophysics, 65*, 58–71.

Henderson, J. M., Pollatsek, A., & Rayner, K. (1987). The effects of foveal priming and extrafoveal preview on object identification. *Journal of Experimental Psychology: Human Perception and Performance, 13*, 449–463.

Henderson, J. M., Pollatsek, A., & Rayner, K. (1989). Covert visual attention and extrafoveal information use during object identification. *Perception & Psychophysics, 45*, 196–208.

Henderson, J. M., & Siefert, A. B. (1999). The influence of enantiomorphic transformation on transsaccadic object integration. *Journal of Experimental Psychology: Human Perception and Performance, 25*, 243–255.

Henderson, J. M., & Siefert, A. B. C. (2001). Types and tokens in transsaccadic object integration. *Psychonomic Bulletin & Review, 8*, 753–760.

Henderson, J. M., Weeks, P. A. Jr., & Hollingworth, A. (1999). Effects of semantic consistency on eye movements during scene viewing. *Journal of Experimental Psychology: Human Perception and Performance, 25*, 210–228.

Hoffman, J. E., & Subramaniam, B. (1995). The role of visual attention in saccadic eye movements. *Perception and Psychophysics, 57*, 787–795.

Hollingworth, A., & Henderson, J. M. (2000). Semantic informativeness mediates the detection of changes in natural scenes. *Visual Cognition, 7*, 213–235.

Hollingworth, A., & Henderson, J. M. (2002). Accurate visual memory for previously attended objects in natural scenes. *Journal of Experimental Psychology: Human Perception and Performance, 28*, 113–136.

Hollingworth, A., Schrock, G., & Henderson, J. M. (2001). Change detection in the flicker paradigm: The role of fixation position within the scene. *Memory & Cognition, 29*, 296–304.

Hollingworth, A., Williams, C. C., & Henderson, J. M. (2001). To see and remember: Visually specific information is retained in memory from previously attended objects in natural scenes. *Psychonomic Bulletin & Review, 8*, 761–768.

Irwin, D. E. (1991). Information integration across saccadic eye movements. *Cognitive Psychology, 23*, 420–456.

Irwin, D. E. (1992a). Visual memory within and across fixations. In K. Rayner (Ed.), *Eye movements and visual cognition: Scene perception and reading* (pp. 146–165). New York: Springer-Verlag.

Irwin, D. E. (1992b). Memory for position and identity across eye movements. *Journal of Experimental Psychology: Learning, Memory, and Cognition, 18*, 307–317.

Irwin, D. E., & Andrews, R. (1996). Integration and accumulation of information across saccadic eye movements. In T. Inui and J. L. McClelland (Eds.), *Attention and performance XVI: Information integration in perception and communication* (pp. 125–155). Cambridge, MA: MIT Press.

Irwin, D. E., & Gordon, R. D. (1998). Eye movements, attention and transaccadic memory. *Visual Cognition, 1–2*, 127–155.

Irwin, D. E., Brown, J. S., & Sun, J-S. (1988). Visual masking and visual integration across saccadic eye movements. *Journal of Experimental Psychology: General, 117*, 276–287.

Irwin, D. E., Yantis, S., Jonides, J. (1983). Evidence against visual integration across saccadic eye movements. *Perception & Psychophysics, 34*, 35–46.

Irwin, D. E., Zacks, J. L., & Brown, J. S. (1990). Visual memory and the perception of a stable environment. *Perception & Psychophysics, 47*, 35–46.

Jonides, J., Irwin, D. E. & Yantis, S. (1982). Integrating visual information from successive fixations. *Science, 215*, 192–194.

Jonides, J., Irwin, D. E., & Yantis, S. (1983). Failure to integrate information from successive fixations. *Science, 222*, 188.

Kahneman, D., & Treisman, A. (1984). Changing views of attention and automaticity. In R. Parasuraman and D. Davies (Eds.), *Varieties of attention* (pp. 29–61). New York: Academic Press.

Kahneman, D., Treisman, A., & Gibbs, B. J. (1992). The reviewing of object files: Object-specific integration of information. *Cognitive Psychology, 24*, 175–219.

Kowler, E., Anderson, E., Dosher, B., & Blaser, E. (1995). The role of attention in the programming of saccades. *Vision Research, 35*, 1897–1916.

Levin, D. T., & Simons, D. J. (1997). Failure to detect changes to attended objects in motion pictures. *Psychonomic Bulletin & Review, 4*, 501–506.

Mack, A. (1970). An investigation of the relationship between eye and retinal image movement in the perception of movement. *Perception & Psychophysics, 8*, 291–298.

Marr, D. (1982). *Vision.* San Francisco: W. H. Freeman.

Matin, E. (1974). Saccadic suppression: A review and an analysis. *Psychological Bulletin, 81*, 899–917.

McConkie, G. W. (1990). *Where vision and cognition meet.* Paper presented at the Human Frontier Science Program Workshop on Object and Scene Perception, Leuven, Belgium.

McConkie, G. W. (1991). Perceiving a stable visual world. In J. Van Resnbergen, M. Devijver, & G. d'Ydewalle (Eds.), *Proceedings of the sixth European conference on eye movements* (pp. 5–7). Leuven, Belgium: Laboratory of Experimental Psychology.

McConkie, G. W. & Rayner, K. (1976). Identifying the span of the effective stimulus in reading: Literature review and theories of reading. In H. Singer & R. B Ruddell (Eds.), *Theoretical models and processes in reading* (pp.137–162). Newark, DE: International Reading Association.

McConkie, G. W., & Currie, C. B. (1996). Visual stability while viewing complex pictures. *Journal of Experimental Psychology: Human Perception and Performance, 22*, 563–581.

McConkie, G. W., & Rayner, K. (1976). Identifying the span of the effective stimulus in reading: Literature review and theories of reading. In H. Singer & R. B Ruddell (Eds.), *Theoretical models and processes in reading* (pp. 137–162). Newark, DE: International Reading Association.

McConkie, G. W., & Zola, D. (1979). Is visual information integrated across successive fixations in reading? *Perception & Psychophysics, 25*, 221–224.

McConkie, G. W., Zola, D., & Wolverton, G. S. (1980). *How precise is eye guidance?* Paper presented at the annual meeting of the American Educational Research Association, Boston, MA.

Milner, D. A., & Goodale, M. A. (1995). *The visual brain in action.* Oxford: Oxford University Press.

Mitroff, S. R., Simons, D. J., & Franconeri, S. L. (2002). The siren song of implicit change detection. *Journal of Experimental Psychology: Human Perception and Performance, 28*, 798–815.

Mullen, K. T. (1990). The chromatic coding of space. In C. Blakemore (Ed.), *Vision: Coding and efficiency* (pp. 150–158). Cambridge: Cambridge University Press.

Neisser, U. (1967). *Cognitive psychology*. Englewood Cliffs, NJ: Prentice-Hall.

Nickerson, R. S. (1965). Short-term memory for complex meaningful visual configurations: A demonstration of capacity. *Canadian Journal of Psychology, 19*, 155–160.

O'Regan, J. K. (1981). The convenient viewing location hypothesis. In D. F. Fisher, R. A. Monty, and J. W. Senders (Eds.), *Eye movements: Cognition and visual perception.* (pp. 289–298) Hillsdale, NJ: Erlbaum.

O'Regan, J. K. (1992). Solving the "real" mysteries of visual perception: The world as an outside memory. *Canadian Journal of Psychology, 46*, 461–488.

O'Regan, J. K., Deubel, H., Clark, J. J., & Rensink, R. A. (2000). Picture changes during blinks: Looking without seeing and seeing without looking. *Visual Cognition, 7*, 191–212.

O'Regan, J. K., & Levy-Schoen, A. (1983). Integrating visual information from successive fixations: Does trans-saccadic fusion exist? *Vision Research, 23*, 765–768.

O'Regan, J. K., Rensink, R. A., & Clark, J. J. (1999). Change blindness as a result of "mudsplashes." *Nature, 398*, 34.

Palmer, S. E. (1977). Hierarchical structure in perceptual representation. *Cognitive Psychology, 9*, 441–474.

Parker, R. E. (1978). Picture processing during recognition. *Journal of Experimental Psychology: Human Perception and Performance, 4*, 284–293.

Phillips, W. A. (1974). On the distinction between sensory storage and short-term visual memory. *Perception & Psychophysics, 16*, 283–290.

Pollatsek, A., & Rayner, K. (1992). What is integrated across fixations? In K. Rayner (Ed.), *Eye movements and visual cognition: Scene perception and reading* (pp. 166–191). New York: Springer-Verlag.

Pollatsek, A., Rayner, K., & Collins, W. E. (1984). Integrating pictorial information across eye movements. *Journal of Experimental Psychology: General, 113*, 426–442.

Pollatsek, A., Rayner, K., & Henderson, J. M. (1990). Role of spatial location in integration of pictorial information across saccades. *Journal of Experimental Psychology: Human Perception & Performance, 16*, 199–210.

Potter, M. C. (1999). Understanding sentences and scenes: The role of conceptual short-term memory. In V. Coltheart (Ed.), *Fleeting memories* (pp. 13–46). Cambridge, MA: MIT Press.

Pouget, A., Fisher, S. A., & Sejnowski, T. J. (1993). Egocentric spatial representation in early vision. *Journal of Cognitive Neuroscience, 5*, 150–161.

Rayner, K. (1975). The perceptual span and peripheral cues in reading. *Cognitive Psychology, 7*, 65–81.

Rayner, K. (1978). Eye movements in reading and information processing. *Psychological Bulletin, 85*, 618–660.

Rayner, K. (1998). Eye movements in reading and information processing: 20 years of research. *Psychological Bulletin, 124*, 372–422.

Rayner, K., McConkie, G. W., & Ehrlich, S. (1978). Eye movements and integrating information across fixations. *Journal of Experimental Psychology: Human Perception and Performance, 4,* 529–544.

Rayner, K., & Pollatsek, A. (1983). Is visual information integrated across saccades? *Perception & Psychophysics, 34,* 39–48.

Rensink, R. A. (2000a). The dynamic representation of scenes. *Visual Cognition, 7,* 17–42.

Rensink, R. A. (2000b). Seeing, sensing, and scrutinizing. *Vision Research, 40,* 1469–1487.

Rensink, R. A., O'Regan, J. K., & Clark, J. J. (1997). To see or not to see: The need for attention to perceive changes in scenes. *Psychological Science, 8,* 368–373.

Riesenhuber, M., & Poggio, T. (1999). Hierarchical models of object recognition in cortex. *Nature Neuroscience, 2,* 1019–1025.

Riggs, L. A. (1965). Visual acuity. In C. H. Graham (Ed.), *Vision and visual perception* (pp. 321–49). New York: Wiley.

Rock, I., & Gutman, D. (1981). *Journal of Experimental Psychology: Human Perception & Performance, 7,* 275–285.

Scholl, B. J. (2000). Attenuated change blindness for exogenously attended items in a flicker paradigm. *Visual Cognition, 7,* 377–396.

Shepard, R. N. (1967). Recognition memory for words, sentences, and pictures. *Journal of Verbal Learning and Verbal Behavior, 6,* 156–163.

Shepherd, M., Findlay, J. M., & Hockey, R. J. (1986). The relationship between eye movements and spatial attention. *Quarterly Journal of Experimental Psychology, 38A,* 475–491.

Simons, D. J. (1996). In sight, out of mind: When object representations fail. *Psychological Science, 7,* 301–305.

Simons, D. J. (2000). Current approaches to change blindness. *Visual Cognition, 7,* 1–16.

Simons, D. J., & Levin, D. T. (1997). Change blindness. *Trends in Cognitive Sciences, 1,* 261–267.

Simons, D. J., & Levin, D. T. (1998). Failure to detect changes to people during a real-world interaction. *Psychonomic Bulletin and Review, 5,* 644–649.

Sperling, G. (1960). The information available in brief visual presentations. *Psychological Monographs, 74* (11, Whole No. 498).

Standing, L. (1973). Learning 10,000 pictures. *Quarterly Journal of Experimental Psychology, 25,* 207–222.

Standing, L., Conezio, J., & Haber, R. N. (1970). Perception and memory for pictures: Single-trial learning of 2500 visual stimuli. *Psychonomic Science, 19,* 73–74.

Tipper, S. P. (1985). The negative priming effect: Inhibitory priming by ignored objects. *Quarterly Journal of Experimental Psychology: Human Experimental Psychology, 37,* 571–590.

Trehub, A. (1977). Neuronal models for cognitive processes: Networks for learning, perceptin, and imagination. *Journal of Theoretical Biology, 65,* 141–169.

Verfaillie, K., De Troy, A., & Van Rensbergen, J. (1994). Transsaccadic integration of biological motion. *Journal of Experimental Psychology: Human Perception and Performance, 20,* 649–670.

Volkmann, F. C. (1986). Human visual suppression. *Vision Research, 26,* 1401–1416.

Whipple, W. R., & Wallach, H. (1978). Direction-specific motion thresholds for abnormal image shifts during saccadic eye movements. *Perception & Psychophysics, 24*, 349–355.

Williams, P., & Simons, D. J. (2000). Detecting changes in novel, complex three-dimensional objects. *Visual Cognition, 7*, 297–322.

Wolfe, J. M. (1999). Inattentional Amnesia. In V. Coltheart (Ed.), *Fleeting memories* (pp. 71–94). Cambridge: MIT Press.

Wolfe, J. M., Klempen, N., & Dahlen, K. (2000). Postattentive vision. *Journal of Experimental Psychology: Human Perception & Performance, 26*, 693–716.

Yarbus, A. L. (1967). *Eye movements and vision.* New York: Plenum Press.

Index

Abdi, Hervé, 4, 7, 21–48
abstract visual representations, 367
action, 349
adjacent dependencies, 9
agnosia, 272, 300–326
See also integrative agnosia
amodal completion, 297, 313–18
analytic processing, of objects, 10–15
analytic representations
of shape, 212–30
strengths of, 223–29
Anderson, A.W., 198
anomalous depth structure experiment,
153, 156–58
apperceptive agnosia, 301
Archambault, A., 140
artificial language learning, 9–10
associative agnosia, 301, 304
attention, 138–39, 212–29
autoassociative models, 38–42

Bartlett, James C., 4, 7, 21–48, 78
basic-level recognition, 184–206
Beale, J.M., 101
Behrmann, Marlene, 14, 200, 295–327
Benton Face Recognition Test (BFRT),
33–35
BFRT. *See* Benton Face Recognition
Test

Biederman, Irving, 56, 150, 179, 184–
85, 206–7nn.1–2
binding, dynamic, 214–18, 221, 224,
229
binding fragments, 288
binding problem, 213
binding, static, 214–218, 222–24, 229
biological motion, 151–58
Blanz, V., 148
blurriness, 204
Bonnar, L., 130
Boston Naming Test, 308
Bradshaw, J., 55
brain
and holistic representations, 69–70
imaging, 193–95
injury, 207n.3, 296
and three-dimensional objects, 152
Brake, S., 83
Brent, H.P., 66
Bruce, V., 24, 25, 27–28, 77, 83–84,
108
Bubbles method, 8, 9, 130–36, 138
Bülthoff, Heinrich H., 11, 146–73,
189, 190
Bülthoff, Isabelle, 11, 146–73

Campbell, F.W., 124
canonical views, 148, 274
Carey, S., 62–63, 64–65

385